Techniques for monitoring the comparability of examination standards

Edited by: Paul Newton, Jo-Anne Baird,
Harvey Goldstein, Helen Patrick and Peter Tymms

QCA wishes to make its publications widely accessible.
Please contact us if you have any specific accessibility requirements.

First published in 2007

ISBN 1-85838-977-1

Printed in Malta.

The Qualifications and Curriculum Authority is an exempt charity under Schedule 2 of the Charities Act 1993.

Qualifications and Curriculum Authority
83 Piccadilly
London
W1J 8QA
www.qca.org.uk

Acknowledgements

Many people have been involved with the production of this book, all of whose contributions I would like to acknowledge with gratitude.

The plan for the book originated during discussions of the Standards and Comparability Working Group, whose external members included Elizabeth Gray, Jeremy Pritchard, Tom Bramley, Alastair Pollitt, Robert Adams, Raymond Tongue, Jo-Anne Baird and Anne Marie Duffy. The project began within the Quality Assurance division of the QCA – under the auspices of Dennis Opposs and Angus Alton – subsequently transferring to the Regulation and Standards division.

The plan for the book became reality with the support of many colleagues from across QCA. Alison Wood deserves special mention for keeping the project on track so efficiently. Alison and I were assisted by Petra Travers, Amy Glassborow, Dominic Devine, John Tallis, Raoul Dutta, Claire Thomson, Amie Tilford, John Barwick, Heidi Gilchrist, Jennifer Adset, Graeme Curry, Siobhan Dawson, Andrew Ryan, Joe Kaler, Fatima Lampreia Carvalho, Nehanda Wright and Tamsin Barton.

The book would not have been possible were it not for the support and encouragement of the British examining boards: especially AQA, Edexcel and OCR (based in England); but also WJEC (Wales), CCEA (Northern Ireland) and SQA (Scotland). In addition to those already mentioned, we were generously supported by Sylvia Green, Martin Taylor, Simon Eason, Jackie Greatorex, Liz Phillips, Rob van Krieken (and by our regulatory colleagues) Linda Badham, Denver Davies and Roger McCune.

Thanks to Geoffrey Clarke and Martin Owen for their support in quality assuring the statistical content, and to Dennis Opposs for quality assuring the book as a whole. A special thank you to Bruce Nicholson, for unwavering commitment to a successful publication process.

A number of organisations kindly gave their permission to reproduce artwork. Thanks to Dr Barbara Malak-Minkiewicz (IEA secretariat) and to Emma Parker (AQA Copyright Officer).

I am especially indebted to my fellow members of the editorial board – Jo-Anne Baird, Helen Patrick, Harvey Goldstein and Peter Tymms – who brought a wealth of experience to the table as well as a range of different perspectives. The book benefited as much from our differences of opinion as from our consensus. The book also benefited from full and frank discussion of chapter drafts at the author workshop. Thanks to the participants (mentioned in the appendix to the editorial introduction) and to the workshop organiser, Margaret Atkins.

Finally, to all of the contributors, thank you for putting up with what may at times have seemed like a never-ending quality assurance process – from the author workshop to the numerous rounds of editorial review. I do hope you agree that the end result is a success story worthy of our considerable efforts.

Paul Newton, Lead Editor.

Foreword

Our examination system is unique. Students have a wide choice of subjects at both GCSE and A level. For most of these subjects there is a choice of which examination board to select. The students' achievements are then reported using a grading scale. That means that almost all students end up with a unique set of certificated results. Yet the same students will use these sets of results to compete against each other for places in educational institutions or in the jobs market. That competition is only fair if there is confidence about the comparability of standards across these examination results. Comparability of examination standards is therefore of prime concern to QCA.

This situation perhaps explains why there has been so much work about comparability in England in the last few decades. However, there has been no attempt to bring it all together in one place. That is what we have now done.

In publishing this book QCA is hoping to help advance and stimulate thinking about comparability as well as to make widely available expert commentaries on the techniques used to monitor it. We have attempted to make the book as readable as possible so that it is suitable for a wider audience than this subject normally attracts.

In September 2007, Ed Balls, Secretary of State for Children, Schools and Families, announced the Government's intention to legislate to create a new independent regulator of qualifications and tests, taking over the role of QCA as regulator, and reporting directly to Parliament rather than to Ministers. An interim regulatory organisation will be in place, within QCA, in the spring of 2008, to prepare for those changes. We intend to use this book as a focus for the interim regulator to hold the ring for expert debate about the comparability of standards in qualifications.

QCA is very grateful to all the experts who have contributed to this book. We hope that assessment organisations, academics and others in this country and beyond will find it an invaluable reference and a source to inspire further thinking and practice.

Isabel Nisbet
Director, Regulation and Standards, QCA

Contents

EDITORIAL INTRODUCTION

Paul Newton, Jo-Anne Baird, Harvey Goldstein, Helen Patrick and Peter Tymms

England operates a qualifications market in which a limited number of providers are accredited to offer curriculum-embedded examinations in many subject areas at a range of levels. The most significant of these qualifications are:

- the major 16+ school-leaving examination, the General Certificate of Secondary Education (GCSE)

- the principal 18+ university selection examination, the General Certificate of Education, Advanced level (A level).

Although some examinations are offered by only a single examining board, the majority are offered by more than one. And, although each examination syllabus must conform to general qualifications criteria, and generally also to a common core of subject content, the syllabuses may differ between boards in other respects. A crucial question, therefore, is whether it is easier to pass a particular examination with one board rather than another. In fact, this is just one of many similarly challenging questions that need to be addressed.

In recent years, central government has increasingly ensured the regulation of public services and, since 1997, the Qualifications and Curriculum Authority (QCA) has been empowered to exercise regulatory authority over the qualifications market in England. One of the ways in which this has been exercised is through commissioning and conducting investigations into comparability, to identify whether a common standard has been applied across different examinations. For both GCSE and A level, examination standards are expected to be comparable when:

- different versions of the same examination are provided, by a single examining board, within the same year (within-board comparability)

- different versions of the same examination are provided, by different examining boards, within the same year (between-board comparability)

- different versions of the same examination are provided, by a single examining board, from one year to the next (comparability over time)

- different examinations are provided, both within and between boards, across subject areas (between-subject comparability).

1

The rationale for the book

For many decades now, the comparability of examination standards has been monitored using a variety of techniques. Most of these were originally developed, used and refined by researchers working within examining boards. Over that time, the boards have published a large number of investigations into comparability. Many of these were described in two major reviews, covering the periods 1964–1977 and 1978–1984 respectively, Bardell *et al.* (1978) and Forrest and Shoesmith (1985). These reviews focused exclusively upon studies of between-board comparability: the form of comparability that many considered to be the most important.

Given that nothing similar had been prepared since 1985, despite many studies having been undertaken during the intervening period, it seemed that a third review was long overdue. Indeed, something more than this seemed to be called for. During the decades since 1985, responsibility for commissioning and undertaking comparability monitoring studies had fallen increasingly to the regulator. In addition, the early emphasis upon between-board comparability had broadened to highlight other forms, especially comparability over time. Most significantly, though, developments in comparability theory and practice had begun to raise important questions concerning the range of monitoring techniques available.

Although methods which rely upon the judgement of subject matter experts have been present from the outset of comparability monitoring, they have changed significantly over time; as have methods which rely upon the statistical analysis of examinations data. And, whereas an early enthusiasm for statistical methods (based upon the use of common tests or common examinees) waned during the 1980s and 1990s, it has recently been reinvigorated (with the advent of multilevel modelling).

Given this evolutionary course, the first decade of the third millennium seemed to be an appropriate point at which to take stock of issues such as the following:

- to what extent have the trends in different techniques reflected real methodological progress?

- to what extent are the techniques ultimately based upon the same problematic assumptions?

- are certain techniques to be preferred over others?

- to what extent can each of the methods be improved and is there scope for developing entirely new approaches?

Instead of compiling a descriptive summary of monitoring studies, QCA decided to sponsor a more analytical investigation into the techniques upon which such studies are based; hence, *Techniques for monitoring the comparability of examination standards*.

The process of producing this book

This book was commissioned by QCA on the basis of recommendations from its Standards and Comparability Working Group (a research orientated group with representation from the examining boards and regulators). To appoint, guide and quality-assure the work of chapter authors, QCA appointed an editorial board of five members, together representing a range of perspectives – both academic and professional – and reflecting many decades of expertise in comparability monitoring. Following a competitive tendering process, the editorial board subsequently appointed a panel of authors who represented a similar range of perspectives and wealth of experience.

The main aim of the exercise was to produce a state-of-the-art account of techniques used to monitor the comparability of examination standards in England. Authors were appointed to cover specific techniques, with a number of additional introductory chapters to contextualise the exercise. Each author of methodological chapters was challenged with providing a clear discussion of the technique in question; including its logic, history of use, approach, evolution, technical characteristics, strengths, limitations and potential for improvement.

The quality assurance process was extensive, with considerable exchange between editors and authors. This included a two-day workshop, which provided an opportunity for a wider group of assessment experts to engage with the production of the book. The main activity of the workshop involved sessions in which first drafts of the chapters were reviewed. This was partly to provide additional editorial support, given the wealth of expertise of the participants, but also partly to help the authors and editors identify the main themes and issues that were arising, both chapter-specific and more general. Participants in the workshop are listed in Appendix 1. Our thanks are extended to this group, for providing so many valuable insights.

At the workshop, we offered interested participants the opportunity to write a commentary, should they wish to develop further thoughts on any of the chapters. We envisaged that this would facilitate debate over potentially controversial issues, or provide space for adding particularly salient insights concerning the theory or practice of the technique. The commentaries were quality-assured by the editorial board in a similar manner to the chapters.

Finally, although the authors of each chapter were commissioned to a specific remit, and although influenced by a strong editorial process, they were also encouraged to express their own views. As such, they do not necessarily write with a single voice; nor with a similar perspective on the relative strengths and weaknesses of the techniques discussed; nor even with the same perspective on comparability itself, come to that.

The purpose of this book was at least as much to pose new questions as to answer old ones. And we recognised from the outset that any answers we did provide would not be conclusive. This is not an enterprise characterised by straightforward solutions to problems. Even agreeing the precise meaning of questions can prove problematic, let alone providing rational answers; and providing workable solutions presents yet another level of complexity. We have certainly not reached the end of our journey, but we hope that we have successfully extended the good start made by others. This book helps to tell the story so far.

The audience

As work progressed, it became increasingly clear that we needed to sharpen our remit. Instead of producing a manual which explained everything there is to know about each technique, we decided to produce a handbook that would capture essences: foregrounding underlying conceptual issues and providing references for further reading. By way of illustration, we hope that the book might be useful to:

- enable new assessment researchers to understand the techniques in sufficient depth to be confident in engaging in studies based upon them

- direct any assessment researcher, with responsibility for running comparability monitoring studies, to additional sources which provide full technical details

- provide any educational researcher with sufficient understanding to evaluate studies based upon the techniques.

Although part of the rationale in publishing the book was to promote openness and transparency concerning comparability monitoring, it was written primarily by assessment researchers for assessment researchers. Our aim was to prepare a state-of-the-art review of theory and practice – from a uniquely English perspective – to support practitioners and theorists of the future; both in England and further afield.

The chapters

Following these introductory words the book begins with a general introduction to comparability monitoring in England, written by **Paul Newton**, which sets the scene for the chapters that follow. Newton provides a brief introduction to the qualifications system in England, describing the delivery of the principal school-leaving and university selection examinations. He follows this with a basic explanation of comparability theory. He then highlights the way in which comparability, including comparability monitoring, has increasingly become a central feature of the regulation of qualifications in England.

Kathleen Tattersall subsequently takes us through a historical tour of comparability in England. She traces the roots of England's modern educational and examinations systems back into the 19th century, and to the selection systems of the major universities and the civil service. Tattersall's chapter illustrates how comparability concerns have been a feature of public debate in England for over 150 years. She highlights three significant stages in the history of comparability in England: the nationalisation of qualifications, i.e. the creation of a single system; the expansion of the system and growth in the number of boards and syllabuses; and, finally, an increasingly formal and powerful regulation of the system.

Colin Robinson introduces comparability from a technical perspective. He focuses on methods for maintaining the comparability of examination standards (rather than methods for monitoring the maintenance of comparability, which are the focus of this book). In addition to explaining present-day practice, he also discusses how we arrived here; highlighting, in particular, debates which have occurred over 'norm-referencing' and 'criterion-referencing'.

The chapter by **Jo-Anne Baird** is the last of the introductory scene-setting ones. Baird teases out what different stakeholders might mean by comparability and considers how these lay views relate to more technical ones. Having identified certain meanings as unsatisfactory – such as those based on pass rates alone – she guides us through a range of more credible definitions: from the technical to the social; from the judgemental to the statistical. Baird finishes by addressing the very thorny question of how to choose between competing definitions.

We then turn to the main substance of the book, with the first of two sets of chapters on techniques for monitoring comparability. These concern techniques that involve applying human judgement to examination papers and performances. **Alastair Pollitt, Ayesha Ahmed and Victoria Crisp** begin this section with a discussion of demands analysis. They explain why the simple question 'is this examination paper more demanding than another?' conceals a very complicated debate on the nature of demand. Fortunately, they do an excellent job of unpicking it, making crucial distinctions between terms such as 'difficulty', 'demands' and 'overall demand'. Having discussed a range of methods for exploring demands, they consider how better to describe, compare and compensate for them.

Robert Adams provides the first of a two-part discussion of what have become known generically as cross-moderation methods. These techniques require subject matter experts, typically senior examiners, to compare examination performances between two or more examinations. Adams focuses particularly upon identification and ratification studies, the most common of the early manifestations. He provides some particularly useful practical insights into how to run this kind of study. He highlights some of the weaknesses of early cross-moderation methods, by way of introduction to the following chapter.

A revolution in cross-moderation methodology occurred with the introduction of the paired comparison technique. **Tom Bramley** introduces this one, tracing its roots to the psychologist Thurstone. The main difference between earlier approaches and paired comparison is that the latter requires judges to make a straightforward overall decision – better or worse – between pairs of scripts from different examinations. These decisions can then be compared to identify a trait of perceived quality, and the average perceived quality of scripts from the different examinations provides some insight into comparability. This method is especially attractive since it provides a way to control for the severity or lenience of individual judges.

Next, we turn to the second of the two main sets of chapters, exploring techniques which involve the control of background factors and the statistical modelling of results. **Roger Murphy** begins this section with a discussion of methods based upon common tests. Using this methodology, performance on a 'reference' test, exam or element is taken as a proxy measure of the construct in question. Comparing performance in different examinations against performance in the reference test can provide some insight into comparability. Murphy outlines the strengths and weaknesses of techniques based on this principle, but ends on a fairly pessimistic note.

Robert Coe is more optimistic about the use of methods based upon common examinees. Using this technique, common candidate groups are taken to be their own control, such that (on average) the same students might be expected to perform similarly across different examinations. These methods have been used especially to compare standards across different subjects. Despite the substantial technical and theoretical assumptions which need to be made, Coe sees some promise here. He considers these methods to be particularly fit for certain uses of results, particularly when result profiles from various subject areas (e.g. A level physics, mathematics and religious studies) are used to predict performance in distantly related ones (e.g. degree-level psychology).

Taking this section to its logical conclusion, **Ian Schagen and Dougal Hutchison** discuss the use of multilevel modelling. This technique takes statistical control as far as practical measurement will allow. It provides some insight into comparability by investigating the mean grade differences between examinations that remain once a range of significant background variables have been controlled for. Multilevel modelling is a relatively new weapon in the comparability monitoring armoury, and the authors are very positive about its potential.

Finally, the book ends with a conclusion. We consider what we have learned from over half a century of comparability monitoring work, as well as what we are still unsure of. We compare the relative strengths and weaknesses of the various methods, and provide recommendations for future research and practice.

References

Bardell, G.S., Forrest, G.M., & Shoesmith, D.J. (1978). *Comparability in GCE: A review of the boards' studies, 1964-1977*. Manchester: Joint Matriculation Board on behalf of the GCE Examining Boards.

Forrest, G.M., & Shoesmith, D.J. (1985). *A second review of GCE comparability studies*. Manchester: Joint Matriculation Board on behalf of the GCE Examining Boards.

Appendix 1 List of workshop participants

Martin	Adams	Research Machines
Robert	Adams	Assessment and Qualifications Alliance
Angus	Alton	Qualifications and Curriculum Authority
Jo-Anne	Baird	University of Bristol (AQA at the time of the workshop)
Andrew	Boyle	Qualifications and Curriculum Authority
Tom	Bramley	Cambridge Assessment
Robert	Coe	University of Durham
Simon	Eason	Assessment and Qualifications Alliance
Gill	Elliott	Cambridge Assessment
Mike	Forster	Oxford Cambridge and RSA Examinations
Dee	Fowles	Assessment and Qualifications Alliance
Amy	Glassborow	Qualifications and Curriculum Authority
Harvey	Goldstein	University of Bristol
Jeffrey	Goodwin	Edexcel
Elizabeth	Gray	Oxford Cambridge and RSA Examinations
John	Gray	University of Cambridge
Jackie	Greatorex	Cambridge Assessment
Malcolm	Hayes	Edexcel
Sandra	Johnson	Assessment Europe
Mike	Kingdon	Assessment Consultant
Iasonas	Lamprianou	University of Manchester
Alison	Matthews	Qualifications and Curriculum Authority
Michelle	Meadows	Assessment and Qualifications Alliance
Roger	Murphy	University of Nottingham
Paul	Newton	Qualifications and Curriculum Authority
Bruce	Nicholson	Publications Consultant
Isabel	Nisbet	Qualifications and Curriculum Authority
Tim	Oates	Cambridge Assessment
Dennis	Opposs	Qualifications and Curriculum Authority
Helen	Patrick	Assessment Consultant
Liz	Phillips	Welsh Joint Education Committee
Anne	Pinot de Moira	Assessment and Qualifications Alliance
Alastair	Pollitt	Assessment Consultant
Mick	Quinlan	National Assessment Agency
Jonathan	Robbins	The Talent Centre Ltd
Colin	Robinson	Assessment Consultant (QCA at the time of the workshop)
Ian	Schagen	National Foundation for Educational Research
Gordon	Stobart	Institute of Education, University of London
Steve	Strand	University of Warwick
Neil	Stringer	Assessment and Qualifications Alliance
Kathleen	Tattersall	Institute of Educational Assessors
Raymond	Tongue	Welsh Joint Education Committee
Peter	Tymms	University of Durham

Rob	van Krieken	Scottish Qualifications Authority
Colin	Watson	National Assessment Agency
Chris	Wheadon	Assessment and Qualifications Alliance
Chris	Whetton	National Foundation for Educational Research
Alison	Wood	National Assessment Agency (QCA at the time of the workshop)

1

CONTEXTUALISING THE COMPARABILITY OF EXAMINATION STANDARDS

Paul E. Newton

Abstract

The purpose of this introductory chapter is to set the scene for the chapters that follow. This will involve providing:

1. a sense of the social and political climate in which debates over comparability are conducted in England (Part 1)

2. a description of the unique organisational, structural and procedural components of examining in England (Part 2)

3. an introduction to what comparability might actually mean in this context (Part 3)

4. an indication of steps taken, through regulatory mechanisms, to facilitate the comparability of examination standards (Part 4).

1   The public face of comparability

This book is concerned with comparability: the application of the same standard across different examinations. In England, webs of comparability link a multitude of examinations: between examining boards; over time; across subjects; and so on. In fact, the number and variety of such links imply comparability challenges on a scale that is probably unparalleled in the rest of the world. Comparability dominates debate over the quality of large-scale educational assessments in England, often to the exclusion of other technical concerns. Furthermore, the extent to which comparability has been achieved is frequently a matter for high-profile national debate, often drawing in senior politicians and spokespeople from a variety of stakeholder groups. Desmond Nuttall once described comparability as 'the English disease' (Murphy & Broadfoot, 1995, p. 54). It is certainly an enduring fixation of educational discourse here.

The roots of this fixation can be traced back to the roots of examining in England. Yet, despite the controversies of comparability having been very well rehearsed, debate is as alive today as it ever has been. A glance at any of the major national newspapers during mid-August of any year, when public examination results are officially announced, clearly illustrates this.

We begin with an illustration of the significance of comparability in England, by considering how it tends to be represented through news media, such as national newspapers. Consider the following quotation, for example:

> Pressure is today mounting on the government's exams watchdog to take action over "easier" A levels.
>
> [...] a leading exam expert and designer of the original modular A level, this morning blamed the qualifications and curriculum authority (QCA) for failing to ensure that all A levels are comparable in difficulty.
>
> Calling the results "depressing reading", [he] claimed that a 5.3% fail rate in English compared with nearly 20% in mathematics proved that there were different standards for different subjects.
>
> Echoing allegations already levied by headteachers, [he] said: "Students are choosing easier A levels. If people are switching from mathematics and science to the easier subjects it will mean that we will lose our ability to compete in the 21st century economy – we will lose our technological, manufacturing and engineering base."
>
> He went on to blame the QCA for failing to address the problems: "The QCA have once again failed to ensure comparability between subjects – it is their job to do so. They need to find a way of getting people examining different subjects together to discuss how they will examine to the same standards.
>
> He admitted that such a task was "not easy to do", but claimed that the QCA hadn't even begun to look into the question. He added that he thought that to make results comparable, mathematics needed to be made a little easier, and the arts subjects brought into line with the harder sciences and languages.
>
> Curtis (2003)

The quotation was taken from one of England's major national newspapers, the *Guardian*, during 2003. In different years, different comparability concerns arise. The default criticism tends to be that standards in our major national examinations have been allowed to slip over time, an inference that is drawn from evidence of continually increasing pass rates (Warmington & Murphy, 2004; Newton, 2005a). In 2003, though, the major story was an apparent lack of comparability between A level standards in different subjects, as inferred from evidence of differential pass rates.

The quotation is useful for highlighting a range of points that need to be appreciated in order to understand the necessity of monitoring the comparability of examination standards in England and, consequently, the need for this book. These points include the following:

- comparability is a major topic of national debate, filling many newspaper column-inches each year; it is therefore of major political significance

- comparability has genuine real-world importance, since it has a direct impact on students – from their subject choices to their life chances – with implications for the structure of society itself

- even those notionally 'within' the system, including senior examiners, are not averse to criticising it

- criticisms can often be fairly naïve, tending to be based on evidence from pass rates alone

- calls for action can also be fairly naïve, assuming that there must be a straightforward solution to any identified comparability challenge.

In short, comparability is a concern of major social and political significance in England. However, at the same time, many commentators fail to grasp quite how complicated the underlying issues are. To some extent, this is understandable, since comparability is a very complex and enigmatic concept indeed.

Unfortunately, the chapters that follow will not solve the complex enigma of comparability. Instead, what they will do is to help trace its roots, to help unpack its meanings, and to present a state-of-the-art account of the techniques that have been used to investigate it. They explore these issues from a peculiarly English perspective, in a context which is characterised, in particular, by the operation of multiple examining boards, providing parallel examinations, and competing with each other for market share.

2   England's qualifications system

The particular challenges of comparability in England can only be appreciated in relation to the unique organisational, structural and procedural characteristics of its qualifications system. These will be introduced below.

2.1 England

In writing this book, we debated whether it should be centrally concerned with comparability in the four 'home nations' of the United Kingdom (England, Scotland, Wales and Northern Ireland), or about comparability in England, Wales and Northern Ireland, or simply about comparability in England. This wasn't a straightforward debate, for a range of reasons.

On the one hand, England, Wales and Northern Ireland share a common public examination system. This is based primarily around the Advanced level (A level) and the General Certificate of Secondary Education (GCSE), in the context of which most recent comparability monitoring work has been undertaken. Moreover, UK comparability monitoring studies usually include qualifications offered in both Wales and Northern Ireland.

On the other hand, the impetus for comparability monitoring work has tended to come mainly from England, where GCSEs and A levels are offered by a number of different boards. In both Wales and Northern Ireland, there is only one examining board, and comparability has been less of an enduring fixation there than in England.

The system in Scotland offers different qualification titles from those offered in England, Wales and Northern Ireland – including Standard Grade, Highers and Advanced Highers – although the assessment approaches employed and the overall qualifications structure are similar. On occasion, qualifications from Scotland have featured in UK comparability monitoring studies; some of the technical development has also stemmed from Scotland (for example, Kelly, 1976).

On balance, it was decided that the situation in England – including the operation of multiple examining boards, providing parallel examinations, and competing with each other for market share – was sufficiently distinct and salient to justify focusing the book on this country alone. Having said this, the following pages will make reference to the context in Wales and Northern Ireland where relevant.

2.2 England's comparability contexts

To understand the nature of comparability in England, the characteristics of England's principal assessment systems need to be understood: our tests, examinations and qualifications. Although often used quite loosely, the conventional application of these terms is as follows:

- tests – non-certificated National Curriculum tests, particularly at ages 11 and 14

- examinations – the major 16+ (school-leaving) and 18+ (university entry) certificated examinations

- qualifications – the full range of certificated educational assessments on offer, from school-leaving examinations to licensing tests and degrees.

These national assessments, and the extent to which they have been the subject of comparability monitoring exercises, are explained below.

Comparability of National Curriculum test standards

A National Curriculum was introduced in England during 1988. For the first time ever, it set out programmes of study in a range of subject areas as a statutory entitlement for all students in state-maintained schools. It also specified standards of attainment according to which all students would be assessed.

Prefaced by a pre-compulsory Foundation Stage, the National Curriculum is delivered in four compulsory Key Stages, through which students progress by age:

- Key Stage 1 (Years 1 and 2) ending at age 7

- Key Stage 2 (Years 3 to 6) ending at age 11

- Key Stage 3 (Years 7 to 9) ending at age 14

- Key Stage 4 (Years 10 and 11) ending at age 16.

During each of the four key stages, there is a statutory requirement upon schools to deliver five programmes of study – for English, mathematics, science, information and communication technology and physical education. For a range of other subjects – including design and technology, history, geography, modern foreign languages, art and design, music and citizenship – programmes of study are available, but their delivery is only statutory at certain key stages.

From its origins in proposals from the Task Group on Assessment and Testing (DES/WO, 1988), assessment of the National Curriculum was intended to be based primarily upon teacher judgement. Even now, National Curriculum tests are only administered at the end of Key Stages 1–3, and only for certain subjects, which means that most National Curriculum assessment (in Years 1 to 9) is still based upon teacher judgement. The introduction of the National Curriculum and, in particular, its assessment have been discussed at some length by both Daugherty (1995) and Shorrocks-Taylor (1999).

With a growing emphasis upon target setting and school accountability during the 1990s, tests of the National Curriculum grew in prominence. Since 1995, particular importance has been placed upon results from National Curriculum tests in English, mathematics and science, which are administered at the end of Key Stages 2 and 3, and are attempted by almost all students in England (since the tests are statutory). A single national test is administered for each subject, in each key stage, each year (unlike the situation that exists for public examinations).

To enable the comparison of schools, student-level results are aggregated to school level. These figures are published nationally and locally, and have been the subject of an extensive debate about their legitimacy (for example, Goldstein, 2001; Statistics Commission, 2005). Schools are compared in terms of whether their results are better or worse from one year to the next and in terms of whether their results are better or worse than those in other schools. Schools establish performance targets for their students to aspire to, and schools are set performance targets to which they must aspire.

Results are not only aggregated to school level, but also to local authority level and to national level. The figures are used as an index of the overall quality of education in England, and the Government has its own set of performance targets, expressed in terms of the percentage of students who attain specified levels of attainment in each of the National Curriculum tests at each key stage.

Clearly, the high stakes associated with test results – particularly for schools and politicians – necessitate a high degree of comparability of standards between test versions, since a new version of each test is produced each year. Each test undergoes a rigorous development process, and a variety of experimental and judgemental techniques is used to help ensure the maintenance of test standards over time.

Although national testing has operated for over a decade now, there has only been one formal comparability monitoring exercise, which explored comparability between tests administered in 1996 and versions administered in 1999, 2000 and 2001 (Massey *et al.*, 2003). The lack of monitoring work in this area explains why the title of this book specifies techniques for monitoring the comparability of examination standards, rather than also extending to test standards.

Comparability of GCSE examination standards

GCSE examinations (which are not statutory) were introduced in 1988. GCSEs – rather than National Curriculum tests – are the principal means by which 16-year-olds are assessed at the end of Key Stage 4, the end of compulsory education in England. GCSEs tend to involve students studying a subject-specific syllabus over a period of two years, and a typical student might study eight to ten GCSEs.

By present-day standards, the GCSE was a long time in the making. It was announced, many years before it was finally delivered, as 'a common system of examining at 16+', which would supersede both the existing General Certificate of Education Ordinary level (GCE O level) and the Certificate of Secondary Education (CSE).

The O level had been in existence since 1951 and was awarded on a subject basis. However, it was a relatively exclusive examination, targeted primarily at the most able 20% of students nationally. In 1965, the CSE was introduced to cater for students of somewhat lower levels of attainment, notionally the next 40%. The aim of the GCSE was to cater for all students, resulting in the widespread adoption of a form of differentiated assessment based upon 'tiers' of entry.

Nearly all students in state-maintained and independent schools study for GCSE examinations. They are available in a wide range of subjects, from astronomy to manufacturing to Welsh as a second language; although not all students will have access to all courses because schools and colleges can only offer a limited range. Students have an element of choice over which subjects to study although, for the majority of GCSE students in schools, a core of subjects is compulsory. Almost all GCSE examinations are offered by several examining boards, which operate in competition with each other; this represents a particular driver for comparability monitoring work.

As for National Curriculum test results, GCSE results are aggregated from student level to school level, to local authority level and to national level, and are used for student, school and national target setting and for accountability purposes. Moreover, as a school-leaving examination, the stakes associated with GCSEs are high for students as well. Again, then, the demands for comparability of standards are high.

A considerable amount of the early comparability monitoring work focused on O level and CSE examinations, and a considerable amount of the more recent work has focused on GCSE.

Comparability of A level examination standards

According to figures from the Department for Education and Skills (DfES, 2006), 77% of 16-year-olds remained in full-time education in England during 2004–5. Of the same cohort of 16-year-olds, 42% were studying at least one general A level or AS level (as their highest qualification), with an additional 3% studying at least one vocational A level (as their highest qualification). Equivalent figures for the corresponding cohort of 17-year-olds were: 63% (full-time education); 35% (general A/AS); 5% (vocational A level).

Since the 1950s, the A level has functioned as England's principal pre-university examination, catering primarily for students on two-year programmes. Although other pre-university examinations are available, including the International Baccalaureate and more vocationally related qualifications, the A level has remained the most popular. Having said this, while the substantial majority of young entrants to undergraduate study do so with traditional A levels (84% in 2001), the majority of entrants aged 21 or older now do so without traditional A levels (71% in 2001). In fact, mature students now comprise the majority of the undergraduate population (see Admissions to Higher Education Steering Group, 2004, p. 16).

A levels are offered by the same examining boards that offer GCSEs, again on a competitive basis. Students have complete freedom of choice over which subjects to study at A level, constrained only by the range that is delivered in their school or college. Their subject choices are likely to be influenced by career aspirations and (for those who plan sufficiently in advance) by the entry requirements of the higher education institutions to which they intend subsequently to apply.

The A level was originally targeted at only a fraction of the small percentage of the nation that studied for O levels. Partly due to its longevity, but perhaps mainly due to its exclusivity, it became known as the Gold Standard. In recent years, the A level has been offered to many more students, and is now taken by over a third of the national cohort. Students generally study for A level examinations in the two years immediately following GCSE, and many then progress directly to university, contingent on having attained a satisfactory profile of A level grades.

Assessment at A level changed quite radically with the reforms of Curriculum 2000, which constituted a response to concerns expressed in a major review of 16–19 qualifications conducted during the mid-1990s (see Dearing, 1996). From the early 1990s onwards, there had been a growing trend for syllabuses to be converted from 'linear' to 'modular', the main difference being the staging of the assessment: linear courses culminate in a suite of 'terminal' examination papers; modular courses offer assessments throughout the two-year programme. With the Curriculum 2000 reforms, all A level courses were 'modularised'. Generally speaking, this meant that the new A levels consisted of three units which corresponded to the work of the first year, and three units which corresponded to the work of the second year.

The modularisation of A levels has meant that students can now be examined in smaller chunks, at two examination sessions each year, shortly after having studied the relevant content of each chunk. More significantly, once students have been examined on all three units of the first year, they are eligible to 'cash in' their units for the award of an AS level. The AS level is both a free-standing qualification and the first half of an A level. Students who wish to complete the full A level study their second three (A2) units and then cash them in (alongside their AS units) at the end of the second year. Students typically study four AS subjects in their first year, then continue with three of them in year two, to convert them into full A levels.

The A level is a high-stakes qualification for students, being the principal tool for university selection in England. Higher education (HE) departments use A level results in different ways. Some offer places to students contingent on their attaining a fairly specific profile of grades (for example, grade A in a mathematical subject and at least grade C in two other A level subjects, with a preference for quantitative ones). Others offer places contingent on a less specific profile (for example, at least grade C in at least three A level subjects). The Universities and Colleges Admissions Service has established a points system (the UCAS Tariff) to report achievement for entry to HE in a numerical format. In particular, it enables comparisons between applicants with different types and volumes of achievement. So, for example, a grade A at A level is worth 120 points, the same as a straight pass on a BTEC National Diploma. Similarly, a grade D at A level is worth 60 points, the same as a grade A at AS level. Some HE departments will make an offer simply in terms of the UCAS Tariff; for example, a score of at least 240 points, which equates to two grade As at A level, or four grade Ds.

As with the earlier tests and examinations, results are aggregated to school, local authority and national level, with associated stakes for individuals and institutions at each level. The effective operation of the system is a similarly high-stakes concern for those high-ranking civil servants and ministers who have ultimate responsibility for it. Reflecting the high profile of these uses and consequences, a considerable amount of comparability monitoring work in England has focused upon A level standards.

Comparability of other qualification standards

In addition to A level, which is known as a 'general' qualification, many other qualifications are available to students in post-compulsory education, typically of a more 'vocational' nature.

In a recent report (QCA, 2005a), the regulators for England, Wales and Northern Ireland identified three distinct types of vocational qualification:

1. National Vocational Qualifications (NVQs) are work-related, competence-based qualifications. They reflect the specific skills and knowledge needed to do a job effectively, and show that a candidate is competent in a particular area of work.

2. Vocationally Related Qualifications (VRQs) are also work-related, but tend to be less job-specific. They reflect the general skills and knowledge needed in the workplace.

3. Other General [vocational] Qualifications (OGs) are practical, but may not be particularly work related. They reflect skills like dance, music and drama, and tend to include graded examinations as part of their assessment.

NVQs constitute the largest proportion of vocational qualifications. Unlike GCSEs and A levels, they tend not to be assessed through large-scale examinations. Instead, NVQ assessment is individualised and relies upon each candidate being able to demonstrate to an assessor that s/he has acquired the competencies required of the job, as specified in the National Occupational Standards for each NVQ.

In the context of tests and examinations, comparability tends to relate to the test or examination itself, that is, whether it results in the award of a given level or grade to the right group of students. In the context of qualifications such as NVQs, where assessors award passes, levels or grades directly, comparability does not have the same meaning, and it can not be investigated in the same way. For this reason, the comparability of standards between vocational qualifications has not been monitored using the kind of techniques discussed in the following chapters.

2.3 England's examinations

As indicated above, most of the comparability work in England has focused on the major 16+ and 18+ public examinations: O levels, CSEs, GCSEs and A levels. The major examinations currently available – GCSE and A level – are offered, in England, by three examining boards:

1. Assessment and Qualifications Alliance (AQA)

2. Edexcel

3. Oxford, Cambridge and RSA examinations (OCR).

They are also offered by boards in Northern Ireland and Wales:

4. Northern Ireland Council for the Curriculum, Examinations and Assessment (CCEA)

5. Welsh Joint Education Committee (WJEC).

The examining boards are nowadays known by the more general term 'awarding bodies', the latter extending also to organisations that award qualifications other than public examinations. Throughout this chapter, and throughout the book, they will generally be referred to as examining boards, with the more general term reserved for reference to all organisations that award qualifications.

GCSE and A level examinations

Each GCSE and A level is classified within a subject group, as illustrated in Tables 1 and 2. Within each of these subject groups may fall a range of subject titles; and examinations for each subject title are often offered by more than one examining board. So, for example, the category Other Modern Languages includes Italian (as

Table 1 Number of (full course) GCSEs sat in the UK during summer 2006
(aggregated across boards)

Subject category	Male	%	Female	%	Male and female	Cumulative % A* to C (M & F)
Mathematics	371,875	50	378,695	50	750,570	54
English	362,007	50	359,755	50	721,762	62
English Literature	275,845	48	296,316	52	572,161	68
Science: double award	238,097	50	241,692	50	479,789	58
Design and Technology	203,118	55	168,554	45	371,672	59
French	104,825	44	131,364	56	236,189	65
History	118,082	51	113,575	49	231,657	67
Geography	118,849	56	94,620	44	213,469	66
Art	86,035	41	126,322	59	212,357	72
Religious Studies	69,184	43	90,497	57	159,681	71
Physical Education	99,614	65	53,212	35	152,826	61
Information and Communication Technology	60,888	56	48,713	44	109,601	62
Drama	37,369	37	63,439	63	100,808	71
Science: single award	47,884	50	48,490	50	96,374	25
German	42,567	47	47,744	53	90,311	69
Business Studies	51,452	58	37,905	42	89,357	60
Statistics	35,751	52	32,580	48	68,331	71
Spanish	25,287	41	36,856	59	62,143	69
Music	31,048	51	29,620	49	60,668	73
Science: Biology	33,717	56	26,365	44	60,082	88
Media/Film/TV Studies	28,718	50	28,803	50	57,521	61
Science: Chemistry	32,800	58	23,964	42	56,764	90
Science: Physics	33,031	59	23,004	41	56,035	91
Home Economics	3,042	7	43,486	93	46,528	54
Business and Communication Systems	21,106	51	20,534	49	41,640	57
All other subjects	8,359	24	25,859	76	34,218	54
Other Modern Languages	12,932	44	16,256	56	29,188	82
Other social sciences	8,009	29	19,994	71	28,003	57
Classical subjects	8,507	52	7,798	48	16,305	88
Humanities	7,779	48	8,345	52	16,124	47
Expressive arts	3,492	35	6,574	65	10,066	55
Other sciences	4,816	49	5,003	51	9,819	53
Welsh: second language	4,183	44	5,388	56	9,571	69
Welsh: first language	2,525	48	2,687	52	5,212	70
Welsh Literature	1,896	46	2,271	54	4,167	70
Mathematics (additional)	1,709	52	1,573	48	3,282	91
Economics	2,293	72	878	28	3,171	73
Irish	1,130	44	1,430	56	2,560	83
Social Science	443	35	820	65	1,263	49
Other technology subjects	1,002	90	116	10	1,118	37
All subjects	**2,467,488**	**49**	**2,534,094**	**51**	**5,001,582**	**62**

Data provided by Simon Eason, AQA

Table 2 Number of GCE A levels sat in the UK during summer 2006 (aggregated across boards)

Subject category	Male	%	Female	%	Male and female	% grade A (M & F)
English	26,821	31	59,819	69	86,640	22
General Studies	27,450	47	31,517	53	58,967	12
Mathematics	34,093	61	21,889	39	55,982	44
Biology	22,597	41	32,293	59	54,890	24
Psychology	13,485	26	39,136	74	52,621	18
History	23,634	50	23,310	50	46,944	25
Art and Design subjects	13,195	31	28,794	69	41,989	30
Chemistry	20,393	51	19,671	49	40,064	31
Geography	17,694	54	14,828	46	32,522	26
Media/Film/TV Studies	14,116	46	16,848	54	30,964	14
Business Studies	18,080	59	12,568	41	30,648	17
Physics	21,408	78	5,960	22	27,368	29
Sociology	6,488	24	20,833	76	27,321	21
Sport/PE studies	13,640	62	8,194	38	21,834	14
Technology subjects	11,086	59	7,598	41	18,684	17
Expressive Arts/Drama	5,360	29	13,312	71	18,672	18
Religious Studies	5,619	31	12,586	69	18,205	27
Economics	11,714	67	5,741	33	17,455	32
Law	6,029	40	9,212	60	15,241	20
French	4,624	32	10,026	68	14,650	35
ICT	9,052	64	5,156	36	14,208	9
Political Studies	6,722	59	4,623	41	11,345	29
Music	5,648	54	4,759	46	10,407	18
All other subjects	4,649	47	5,314	53	9,963	17
Mathematics (further)	5,106	70	2,164	30	7,270	57
Other modern languages	3,039	43	3,970	57	7,009	44
Spanish	2,133	33	4,387	67	6,520	37
Computing	5,629	90	604	10	6,233	15
German	2,369	38	3,835	62	6,204	38
Classical subjects	2,690	43	3,496	57	6,186	37
Science subjects	3,068	73	1,141	27	4,209	23
Communication studies	665	31	1,449	69	2,114	22
Home Economics	83	8	1,004	92	1,087	18
Welsh	182	19	771	81	953	20
Irish	109	33	220	67	329	49
All subjects	**368,670**	**46**	**437,028**	**5**	**805,698**	**24**

Data provided by Simon Eason, AQA

well as Arabic, Japanese, Russian, Urdu and so on), and GCSE Italian is offered by both AQA and Edexcel.

The scale of examining

Public examinations are administered on a large scale. Almost all students in England will take at least one GCSE examination during their final year of compulsory education. To appreciate this scale, the numbers of students in a typical UK age cohort are illustrated by the figures in Table 3.

Table 3 The mid-2004 projection, from the Government Actuary Office, of the number of 18-year-olds in the UK during 2007

Country	Projection
England	665,240
Scotland	64,923
Wales	40,872
Northern Ireland	26,097
E, W, NI	**732,209**
UK	**797,132**

From Table 1, it can be seen that the number of GCSE mathematics and English examinations sat each year is of the same order as an annual student cohort for England, Wales and Northern Ireland combined. (Here, 'sat' means the number of students awarded either a passing grade, A* to G, or a fail, U, in each subject.) The very small proportion of the final year cohort that does not take English and mathematics is compensated for by a similarly small number who sit the examination either as 'early entry students', or later as 're-sit students' or as 'returning adults'. On the other hand, GCSEs in certain subject areas are awarded to a small number of students, of the order of only a few thousand for subject groups such as Economics and Irish.

During the final years of compulsory education, students are allowed to exercise (a limited amount of) choice over which subjects to study for GCSE. This means that the groups of students studying each subject are not necessarily equally representative of the student cohort. For example, although for most of the major subject areas the gender balance is fairly evenly split, this is not universally true. And, for certain subject groups, gender-biased subject preferences are quite extreme. Using an arbitrary criterion of a gender imbalance greater than 40:60, subject preferences appear to be gender-biased for 9 of the 40 subject groups in Table 1. The most extreme trends are evident for subjects in the Home Economics and Other Technology groups, which are heavily biased towards female and male students respectively (see Stobart *et al.*, 1992, for an interesting discussion of gender-biased subject choice at GCSE).

At A level, since students tend to study only three or four subjects, and since the A level cohort is around a third of the size of the national cohort, the total number of A levels sat is considerably smaller. (Here, 'sat' means the number of students awarded either a passing grade, A to E, or a fail, U, in each subject.) The subject groups with the highest number of awards at A level include English, General Studies, Biology, Mathematics and Psychology, all with over 50,000 awards made during summer 2006 (see Table 2). At the other extreme, only just over 300 awards were made for A level Irish.

At A level, the evidence of gender-biased subject preference is even clearer, with 22 of the 35 subject groups exceeding the gender imbalance criterion of 40:60. Certain subject groups are clearly male dominated, such as Computing, Physics and Further Mathematics; others are clearly female dominated, such as Home Economics, Psychology and Sociology.

In all, around 6.5 million GCSE and A level awards are made each year. Since each award represents performance across a number of examination components, the number of individual examination papers, projects, practicals, pieces of coursework and so on that are taken, marked and graded is much higher.

Finally, returning to the point noted at the beginning of this chapter, Tables 1 and 2 indicate quite clearly the apparent differences in attainment between students in different subject areas. For example, 91% of the GCSE physics cohort was awarded grade C or above in 2005, in contrast with only 47% of the GCSE humanities cohort. Similarly, 57% of the A level further mathematics cohort was awarded grade A, in contrast with only 9% of the A level information and communication technology (ICT) cohort. For further useful analyses of examination statistics, see Vidal Rodeiro (2005) and Claessen (2005).

Setting examinations

Both GCSEs and A levels require students to be assessed through a series of examination components, typically comprising some combination of written papers, practical tasks and coursework projects. Written papers are designed, marked and graded by examining boards. This process is known as 'external' assessment. Practical tasks (for example, physics investigations, or music performances) tend to be designed by examining boards, and might be marked by students' teachers or by visiting examiners from the board. Coursework projects are often designed by teachers, or by students in collaboration with teachers, within tightly defined parameters laid down by examining boards. Coursework is usually marked by students' teachers, and marks awarded to coursework are moderated by examiners appointed by the board. This process is known as 'internal' assessment. Even when marks are awarded internally, the grading process is ultimately external. (Moderation and grading processes will be explained shortly.) The nature and role of coursework in public qualifications has recently received considerable scrutiny, following a review of coursework at GCSE (QCA, 2005b). Concerns over fitness for purpose, backwash effects upon teaching and potential for cheating have led to the exclusion of coursework from mathematics and to a refocusing and tightening of arrangements in many others.

Examinations are structured differently at GCSE and A level. A level examinations are modularised, and examinations are available at set points throughout both years, normally in January and June. GCSE examinations tend still to be terminal, with examinations available only at the end of the course in June of the second year, though some have elements of modularisation with examinations available at other times.

GCSEs, unlike A levels, tend to offer differentiated written papers and tasks, that is, alternative 'tiers' of entry. The idea of tiering is to provide all students with a suitably challenging assessment experience. In subjects where differentiation occurs primarily by outcome (i.e. where a single assessment is accessible to all students) tiers are not used; for example in, history, music, humanities and so on.

Nowadays, the typical GCSE will have two tiers of entry: a higher tier targeted at the higher grades (A* to D); and a foundation tier targeted at the lower grades (C to G). This differentiated system allows for students on the higher tier to attain one of the lower grades, should they happen to perform slightly lower than anticipated (E). However, students who fail to achieve grade E on the higher tier fail the examination entirely (Ungraded); and students can only achieve at best a grade C, no matter how well they actually perform.

Examination papers and their associated mark schemes begin development some two years prior to their being administered. They are prepared by Principal Examiners, who work for examining boards on a freelance basis. Principal Examiners are usually appointed from the ranks of experienced examiners, and will generally have undergone an informal apprenticeship with a board over a period of years, as well as more formal training.

Written papers at both GCSE and A level involve a range of assessment formats, which might include selected-response questions (for example, multiple choice) and short- or long-answer constructed-response questions (which might be either structured or unstructured); questions may sometimes require the use of maps, diagrams, tables, graphs, photos and so on. Typically, written papers comprise some balance of mainly short- and long-answer questions, with relatively few selected-response questions. In the past, it was not uncommon for candidates to be allowed to choose between optional questions; this practice is far less usual nowadays.

In summary, the tradition of examining in England has emphasised the importance of validity by assessing:

- a reasonably wide range of knowledge, skill and understanding

- knowledge and understanding through written expression

- skill through performance

- depth of knowledge, skill and understanding in specific areas.

As a consequence, though, the tradition has sacrificed an element of reliability, given the problems inherent in assessments designed to more 'authentic' specifications, problems such as sampling error and marking error. Incidentally, despite the prevalence of comparability monitoring over the years, there has been no tradition of reliability monitoring in England. There is a small body of published work containing evidence of marking reliability (for example Murphy, 1978; 1982; Newton, 1996), but virtually none containing evidence of the overall reliability of examination results (Black & Wiliam, 2006; cf. Please, 1971; Willmott & Nuttall, 1975).

Marking examinations

The number of examiners required to mark all GCSE and A level examinations each year is somewhere in the region of 60,000; the majority are employed to mark GCSE written papers. Examiners are employed by examining boards under temporary contracts, during examination periods. They are often practising or recently retired teachers, and they are required to have a substantial professional understanding of the subject area for which they are marking.

Examiners score student performance according to mark schemes developed alongside the examination paper or task, and refined once the first responses are seen. Students' examination performances are referred to as 'scripts' where this can mean either a student's response to a single written paper, or to the full corpus of work completed by a student for an examination (across all components).

Examiners, for each syllabus within each examining board, are structured hierarchically. At the top is the Chief Examiner, with responsibility for the entire examination. Beyond the examination for which s/he has responsibility, the Chief Examiner will report to a Chair of Examiners, who oversees standards across different syllabuses within a single subject area, or group of related subjects. Each Chair of Examiners reports to the awarding body Accountable Officer.

At the next level down from the Chief Examiner, with responsibility for individual components – including the preparation of assessment tasks and mark schemes – are Principal Examiners. Each Principal Examiner may be supported by Team Leaders, each of whom will train, and manage the marking of, a number of Assistant Examiners. This hierarchy is represented in Figure 1.

Before any marking takes place, all examiners undergo training and standardisation in the application of the mark scheme. Again, this is hierarchically managed, as more senior markers train and standardise less senior members of their team. The aim is to ensure that the Principal Examiner's application of the mark scheme is applied by all examiners. During the marking period, samples of work are collected from examiners and the marking is checked by their supervisor. The supervisor will give feedback to modify inappropriate application of the mark scheme and, ultimately, may decide that an examiner's marking is too discrepant to allow her/him to continue.

Figure 1 The marking hierarchy

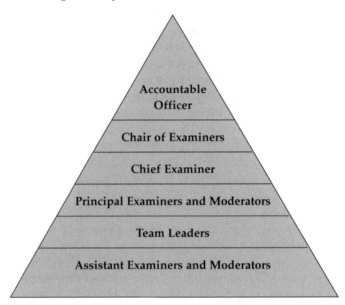

Examination scripts, primarily written documents, are normally sent directly from schools and colleges to examiners, who mark the scripts at home. After the marking process is completed, examiners return the marked scripts to examining boards, alongside mark-sheets that contain a record of the marks awarded. These marks are either input manually or, as is more common nowadays, input automatically using optical mark-reading technology. Scripts are not returned to schools or students unless a request is formally made.

Where components are internally assessed, samples of teacher-marked work are checked by examining board moderators – who are trained to apply the agreed standard – and a teacher's marks may be brought in line with those of the moderator if they are sufficiently discrepant. Where teacher-assessment marks are consistently harsh or lenient, they are brought into line through statistical methods. Where they are inconsistently discrepant, the full corpus of work from a school may need to be moderated. A similar training, standardisation and management hierarchy exists for internally assessed components as for externally assessed components with Principal Moderators, Team Leaders and Assistant Moderators.

This approach to marking was once described by the chief executive of the regulatory authority for England as a 'cottage industry' (HoC/ESC, 2003, Ev 57). It is certainly a cumbersome and expensive process, and is vulnerable not simply to marking inaccuracy, for example in the manual addition of marks (threatening product quality), but also to other types of threat, such as postal strikes, theft of delivery vans, depot fires and the like (threatening product delivery). For reasons such as these, there has been a drive to modernise the system – and the marking process in particular – through the development of electronic technologies. Script scanning and web-based marking are now being successfully introduced.

Grading examinations

Grading is the process by which mark scales are divided into mark bands, such that marks within each band represent a particular grade. The minimum mark required for the award of each grade is known as the 'grade boundary' mark. Grading, therefore, involves the identification of grade boundary marks.

This process is important because even ostensibly parallel versions of the same subject examination can differ, from one year to the next, in terms of how easy or hard it is to achieve marks. If (near the top of the mark range) the year 2 examination is five marks easier than the year 1 examination then, to apply the year 1 standard to the year 2 exam, the (grade A) grade boundary will need to be raised by five marks. The process of adjusting grade boundaries is what allows examining boards to claim comparability.

In contrast to many international high-stakes tests and examinations, the vast majority of GCSE and A level examinations are not pre-tested. As such, the identification of grade boundary marks is largely post hoc, as described in Chapter 3. Specially designed linking studies are not undertaken for a range of reasons. A principal reason is feasibility, given the huge numbers of examinations involved. The risk to confidentiality of the materials is another driver, as is the fact that materials are publicly available once administered live. Equally, though, since GCSEs and A levels employ complex assessment procedures, and since their content, process and statistical frameworks tend to be revised on a fairly regular basis, pre-test linking studies might often return quite contestable grade boundary recommendations anyhow.

Reporting examination results

Each year, students entered for the summer examination session complete their final examinations by the end of June. By mid-August, following an intense period of marking and grade awarding, the results are ready to be returned to students. Schools are sent notification of grades achieved by individual students, to whom this information is then forwarded (some boards send results directly to students). A level results are also sent directly to the Universities and Colleges Admissions Service, where the data are used to identify whether students have satisfied entry criteria set by the departments to which they applied. Certificates are produced somewhat later.

Where a school is of the opinion that a student has not been awarded the correct grade, it is at liberty to challenge the award. These challenges, known as Enquiries About Results, may lead to a student's grade either remaining the same, being raised or (less frequently) being lowered. If a school disagrees with the outcome of the enquiry, it is at liberty to lodge an Appeal. Appeals are directed, in the first instance, to the relevant examining board. If a school is unhappy with the outcome of its Appeal, the school may escalate it to an independent body, the Examinations Appeals Board.

2.4 England's organisational and qualifications structure

Both the organisational structure and the qualifications structure influence the nature of comparability challenges in England.

Figure 2 Five degrees of separation

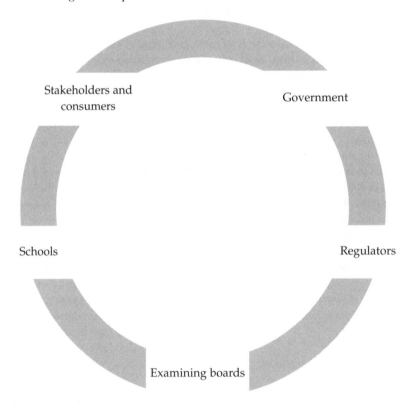

Organisational structure

It is possible to identify at least five degrees of separation between the general public as stakeholders in England's qualifications system and the general public as consumers of its products (see Figure 2). At the highest level, stakeholders exert power over central government, influencing qualifications policy and practice through national elections, voting on the basis of the declared political intentions of the major parties. Once in power, central government is able to influence qualifications policy and practice directly through the DfES. It also exerts power indirectly, since only qualifications and their associated courses that the DfES approves may be funded from public money.

The regulators influence policy and practice at the next level down. They are instituted and funded by central government and their purpose is essentially to ensure that the system operates in the best interests of the stakeholders and consumers. In England, responsibility for regulation of the GCSE and A level system lies with the Qualifications and Curriculum Authority (QCA); a similar role is undertaken in Wales and Northern Ireland, respectively, by the Department for Education, Lifelong Learning and Skills (DELLS) and the Council for the Curriculum, Examinations and Assessment (CCEA). These organisations also have a role in advising government on qualifications policy, and in helping government and examining boards to put qualifications policy into practice.

Associated with the QCA is an organisation called the National Assessment Agency (NAA). It is technically part of the QCA, and is located in the same building, although it operates 'at arm's length'. The NAA is charged with the task of coordinating the modernisation of the examination system, as well as with the development of National Curriculum tests (which are regulated by the QCA, hence the need to operate 'at arm's length').

The examining boards function at the next level down, with direct operational responsibility for processing GCSE and A level examinations. As noted earlier, they include:

- Assessment and Qualifications Alliance (AQA)

- Edexcel

- Oxford, Cambridge and RSA examinations (OCR)

- Northern Ireland Council for the Curriculum Examinations and Assessment (CCEA)

- Welsh Joint Education Committee (WJEC).

In addition to running GCSE and A level examinations, these five examining boards also offer a range of other, typically more vocational, qualifications. To reflect this broad base they are now known as awarding bodies, or more specifically as the Unitary Awarding Bodies.

The five examining boards operate in competition with each other. In the past, this competition focused particularly upon the content and structure of the syllabuses that they offered. Nowadays, with much tighter restrictions upon syllabus content and structure, competition focuses more upon the quality of service provided, including the quality of support provided to teachers. Whereas students have an element of choice concerning which subjects to study (complete choice at A level and some choice at GCSE), the choice of which syllabus will be delivered, and hence which examining board is chosen, is typically exercised by the subject departments of schools and colleges.

The examining boards collectively run the Joint Council for Qualifications (JCQ), in collaboration with two other boards: the Scottish Qualifications Authority (SQA) and City and Guilds. JCQ has responsibility for coordinating shared: guidance to schools; understanding of good practice in examining; research; public statements; and statistical releases.

Although only five examining boards offer GCSE and A level examinations, the regulators for England, Wales and Northern Ireland recognise over 100 awarding bodies. Many of these are small, typically offering vocational or occupational qualifications in a narrow field. In addition to the recognised (i.e. regulated) awarding bodies, it has been estimated that 900 or so unrecognised (i.e. unregulated) organisations also award qualifications in the UK (PricewaterhouseCoopers, 2005).

Examining boards deal directly with schools and colleges ('centres'), which manage the processes of registration and administration on behalf of primary consumers, the students ('candidates').

Qualifications structure

In recent years, considerable work has been done to rationalise England's qualifications system. This has involved, in particular, the creation of a National Qualifications Framework (NQF). The NQF provides a formal structure for those qualifications that are offered by recognised awarding bodies and that have been formally accredited by the regulators (more follows on the accreditation process). It is intended to help learners make informed decisions about the qualifications they want to pursue, by comparing the levels of different qualifications and by identifying different progression routes.

The NQF has nine levels, and each accredited qualification is located at one of these. Examples of qualifications located at each level include:

Level 8	Specialist awards (PhD degree level)
Level 7	Level 7 Diploma in Translation (Masters degree level)
Level 6	Level 6 National Diploma in Professional Production Skills (Honours degree level)
Level 5	Level 5 BTEC Higher National Diploma in 3D Design
Level 4	Level 4 Certificate in Early Years
Level 3	A level, Level 3 Certificate in Small Animal Care
Level 2	GCSE Grades A* to C, Level 2 NVQ in Agricultural Crop Production
Level 1	GCSE Grades D to G, Level 1 NVQ in Bakery
Entry level	Entry Level Certificate in Adult Literacy

A database of qualifications accredited to the NQF – the National Database of Accredited Qualifications – can be found from the QCA website (www.accreditedqualifications.org.uk). It does not include qualifications offered by universities and colleges of higher education, since regulation of the higher education sector is the responsibility of the Quality Assurance Agency (QAA).

3   The very idea of comparability

This chapter opened by characterising comparability – the application of the same standard across different examinations – as an enduring fixation of educational discourse in England. That shouldn't be taken to imply that comparability is a uniquely English concern; far from it – the challenges of comparability are truly international. However, they are not necessarily understood, manifested, or responded to in similar ways, and they do not always assume the same social or political significance elsewhere (for example, Wolf, 2000).

The idea of applying the same standard across different examinations is a deceptively complex one: deceptively complex because it seems so simple.

3.1 The 'straightforward' situation: parallel versions

It is easiest to understand comparability when the same standard has to be applied across two examinations that differ only in terms of the specific questions posed. In this situation, the two versions of an examination will have been constructed according to identical criteria, in order to represent the same content or process framework of assessment objectives and to satisfy the same statistical blueprint for results. Expressed less technically, this means that they will have been designed to assess exactly the same thing (for example, attainment in A level physics), using exactly the same number, kind and quality of questions. With this level of control, so the story goes, the only factor that might still vary somewhat is the overall difficulty of each examination, that is, how many marks a random sample of students from the same population would tend to achieve on average.

Figure 3 is intended to illustrate this situation, given two versions of the same imaginary A level physics examination, from 2006 and 2007, each marked from a total of 80. For each version, it represents both the mark scale (from 0 to 80) and the grade scale (from U to A). In England, examination standards are associated with grades rather than with raw marks. To decide which students are awarded which grades, the raw mark scale is divided into a series of bands. So, any student who scored between 0 and 18 marks on the 2006 version would have received a U for the component, whereas any student who scored 19 or more would have received at least grade E. The lowest raw mark for the award of each grade is known as the grade boundary mark; thus, in 2006, the E/U grade boundary mark was 19.

Figure 3 A representation of the process of maintaining standards

2006 Raw mark scale

Grade	Mark
A	80
:	:
E	25
E	24
E	23
E	22
E	21
E	20
E	19
U	18
U	17
U	16
U	15
:	:
U	0

2007 Raw mark scale

Mark	Grade
80	A
:	:
25	E
24	E
23	E
22	E
21	E
20	U
19	U
18	U
17	U
16	U
15	U
:	:
0	U

The implication from Figure 3 is that lower attaining candidates tended to find the examination easier in 2007 than in 2006. Putting this more formally, students of a certain level of attainment would, on average, have scored around two marks more on the 2007 version of the examination than on the 2006 version. Given this fact, had the E/U grade boundary on the 2006 version (19 marks) simply been carried over to the 2007 version, then it would have been easier to get a grade E in 2007 than in 2006. To ensure comparability of standards between versions, the E/U grade boundary needed to be raised by two marks, to adjust for the fact that the 2007 examination tended to be two marks easier for low attaining students.

The English are certainly not the only ones who go to great lengths to attempt to achieve comparability of standards across parallel versions of tests and examinations. Psychometricians in many countries are engaged in this kind of enterprise, albeit from slightly different perspectives on occasion. In the United States, for example, this kind of enterprise would tend to be known as equating. (See Kolen & Brennan, 2004, for a state-of-the-art discussion of techniques for equating, written largely from a North American perspective.) Instead of identifying different grade boundary marks for different versions, marks on subsequent versions would be scaled to the standard of the first. In effect, using Figure 3 as an example, a raw mark of 21 on the 2007 version would be scaled to an adjusted score of 19; that is, students who achieved a raw mark of 21 would be awarded an adjusted score of 19. When equating, the entire raw mark range is scaled in this way. The idea here is that scores should carry the standard, such that any particular score should have the same meaning across all versions. For English examinations, only grade boundary marks require adjustment.

3.2 A complex situation: non-parallel versions

The idea of applying the same standard across different examinations becomes much harder to understand when the versions in question differ in more respects than simply the specific questions posed and, hence, overall difficulty. In the North American literature, this situation would tend to be described as 'scaling to achieve comparability' or, more generally still, as 'linking'. In fact, the term 'linking' is used in both a general and a more specific sense. Kolen & Brennan (2004), for example, describe linking as an entire continuum that has 'equating' as an ideal extreme; for two tests to be equated, they must (at least) have been built to identical content and statistical frameworks. However, they also note the tendency to apply the term more specifically, to that part of the continuum to which 'equating' does not apply: particularly, when tests have been built to different content and statistical frameworks.

Imagine that between 2006 and 2007 the A level physics syllabus had changed substantially, for example around one-third of the old content had been dropped and replaced with new content (and, perhaps, less of it). In addition, while still being marked from a total of 80, the kinds of questions asked had also changed substantially, for example, many of the old multiple-choice questions had been replaced with a single essay question. Although, notionally, the same construct is assessed by both versions – attainment in A level physics – in reality, the assessed constructs may be substantially different.

In situations like this, it is generally accepted that the two versions cannot be equated, in any strict sense. Why not? Primarily, because students who studied the earlier syllabus will have attained somewhat different kinds of knowledge, skill and understanding from those who studied the later syllabus. That is, marks on the 2006 version will reflect a certain level of 'old physics', while marks on the 2007 version will reflect a certain level of 'new physics'. As such, no adjusted score – or grade boundary – could ever carry exactly the same meaning across versions.

To a purist, it might simply seem impossible to apply exactly the same standard across different versions of an examination, when those versions differ more than in terms of difficulty. Purist logic, though, can be challenged by a more pragmatic 'common sense'. This common sense would argue that there must be some way in which something like the same standard could be applied, even across substantially different versions of an A level physics examination.

The most fundamental challenge of comparability, then, is to identify the sense in which something like the same standard can be applied across versions of examinations that differ more than in terms of difficulty. Unfortunately, comparability theory is not at all well developed, although theoretical work has begun in both the United States and in England (for example, Christie & Forrest,

1981; Mislevy, 1992; Linn, 1993; Cresswell, 1996; Wiliam, 1996; Fitz-Gibbon & Vincent, 1997; Baird *et al.*, 2000; Goldstein, 2000; Newton, 2005b).

As noted above, in the United States, where much of the theoretical and empirical work has been undertaken, the idea of linking – rather than equating – is often used to convey the essence of comparability: it is somehow like equating, but not quite as good, or as strong, or as statistically robust, or something like that. That might seem too casual a definition for an academic text; unfortunately, though, there is no clear academic consensus over what comparability/linking actually means, and explanations offered do tend to be quite woolly.

Regardless of how the theory of linking or comparability might differ from that of equating, the practice is essentially the same. It either involves adjusting grade boundary marks on version 2 to reflect the standard of version 1, or it involves adjusting all marks on version 2 to reflect the standard of version 1.

So far, in this section, we have considered the case of two versions of an A level physics examination, based upon substantially different syllabuses and examined in substantially different ways. In this situation, it might seem reasonable to assume that there must be some way in which something like the same standard can be applied. But what about a more extreme case, for example, the application of the same standard across different subject examinations?

At least in England, it still seems commonsensical to many stakeholders that there must be some way in which something like the same standard can be applied across (let's say) A level physics and A level psychology. After all, they have the same qualification title (A level), which implies that they somehow represent attainment at the same educational level. More importantly, their grades are often treated equivalently by university selectors when making admissions decisions: particularly, for subjects like law or psychology, which select from students who have made very different A level subject choices.

There would certainly seem to be a social imperative, in the English context, to apply the same standard across examinations in different subjects. Exactly what this might mean, though, is very far from obvious. Similar comparability challenges are faced around the world. The states of Australia, for example, have grappled with this challenge for many years, and have adopted essentially pragmatic solutions, based upon complex statistical adjustments. What those states tend not to be clear on, though, is the precise logic of the adjustments nor exactly what the adjusted scores mean (see Nuyen, 1986; Partis, 1997; McGaw *et al.*, 2004).

3.3 A highly complex situation: multiple non-parallel versions

The English qualifications system is probably unique in the complexity of the comparability challenges that it faces or, put another way, in the number and diversity of examinations whose standards are at least notionally linked. The case of GCSE usefully illustrates the point.

At the time of writing this chapter, the examining board OCR had three distinct syllabuses for mathematics at GCSE. Syllabus A was the standard option, with two externally examined written papers (40% weighting each) and an internally assessed coursework component (20% weighting). Both of the written papers were offered at three levels – foundation tier, intermediate tier and higher tier – with overlapping grade ranges. Syllabus B was the 'Maths in Education and Industry' option, supported by an independent curriculum body. It too had two externally examined written papers and an internally assessed coursework option, but with a different weighting between the written papers (30% and 50%). The qualification had a quasi-modular structure, meaning that the first paper could be taken early. Syllabus C was billed as the 'tried and tested' modular approach. Students sat at least two module tests from a suite of ten (15% weighting each) – the best two of which counted – plus a tiered terminal unit examination (50% weighting) and an internally assessed coursework component (20% weighting).

So, for GCSE mathematics alone, OCR had to ensure comparability of examination standards at equivalent grade boundaries:

- from one year to the next for Syllabus A (B and C, respectively)

- across the tiers of Syllabus A (B and C, respectively)

- between Syllabuses A, B and C.

Of course, OCR wasn't the only examining board to offer GCSE mathematics. In fact, at the time of writing, all five of the GCSE examining boards offered at least one mathematics syllabus. Not including pilot examinations, AQA offered three (including a statistics option); CCEA offered one; Edexcel offered three (including a statistics option); and WJEC offered two.

Each of the GCSE examining boards had to ensure comparability of examination standards for GCSE mathematics in exactly the same way as OCR. Moreover, all five of the examining boards needed to apply the same standard in the same way.

If this wasn't complex enough, within each GCSE subject area, each examining board is expected to ensure comparability of standards across subject areas. In short, a grade C in mathematics is supposed to be of the same standard as a grade C in astronomy, manufacturing, Welsh as a second language, and so on.

And if this wasn't complex enough, not only is it required that comparability of standards be ensured from one year to the next across all subject areas, but there is also a supposition that – if by extension alone – comparability of standards should be ensured from one decade to the next. Indeed, the widespread use of aggregated GCSE results for monitoring trends in educational standards explicitly requires this. This is not only despite substantial changes that are made to individual syllabuses on a fairly regular basis, but also despite substantial changes that occur less frequently in assessment formats and curriculum organisation.

Beyond GCSE, there is a further expectation of comparability of standards between qualifications at the same level of the National Qualifications Framework (NQF). This is less precisely formulated. However, it is still explicitly stated that, for example, a Level 2 NVQ represents the same standard as a GCSE awarded at grades A* to C; while a Level 1 NVQ represents the same standard as a GCSE awarded at grades D to G.

4 Facilitating the comparability of standards

Over the years, a major driver behind the move towards increased regulation has been concern over the comparability of examination standards: not simply the conspiracy theory that standards might deliberately be manipulated to improve market share, but also the belief that increased regulation could help prevent standards from losing alignment 'accidentally'. Consequently, much of the work of the regulators has focused on the comparability of examination standards.

There are three main dimensions to regulation, as it pertains to comparability:

1. specifying system regulations

2. ensuring adherence to system regulations

3. monitoring the technical quality of examinations and results.

4.1 Specifying system regulations

System regulations are specified at a range of levels, in a number of documents prepared jointly by the regulators (of England, Wales and Northern Ireland), of which the following are central:

1. *The regulatory authorities' accreditation handbook* (2003)

2. *The statutory regulation of external qualifications* (2004)

3. *GCSE, GCE, VCE, GNVQ and AEA code of practice* (2006/7).

The first two of these specify the procedures and criteria by which awarding bodies may gain recognised status, allowing them to offer qualifications within the NQF, and by which individual qualifications may be accredited to the NQF. The third specifies procedures to be followed at all major stages involved in processing the named qualifications. All of these documents can be found on the QCA website (www.qca.org.uk).

Before an awarding body is given recognised status, the regulator will conduct a review of its systems and procedures. This focuses primarily on governance, experience, expertise, financial stability and quality assurance arrangements for developing and delivering qualifications. The review is designed to ensure that the awarding body is capable of offering qualifications within the framework to the required quality standards.

Once an awarding body is recognised it may submit qualifications for accreditation. Qualifications need to satisfy the common criteria (specified within *The statutory regulation of external qualifications*) and, normally, also additional subject criteria (specified separately for examinations in each subject for each qualification type).

The common criteria specify generic regulations for the development of qualifications covering the following areas, as well as additional criteria specific to different qualification types:

- function of qualifications

- content of qualifications

- assessment in qualifications

- determination and reporting of results.

Subject criteria relate to features that are required to be common across all syllabuses developed for the same award (for example, GCSE economics), including:

- aims

- content

- opportunities for developing key skills

- assessment objectives and their weighting

- schemes of assessment

- attainment standards (i.e. grade descriptions for key grade boundaries).

Subject criteria are located on the QCA website, while the individual qualification syllabuses, developed by awarding bodies to the satisfaction of the subject criteria, are located on their own websites.

Finally, the code of practice specifies a range of regulations according to which qualifications must be processed, covering the following areas:

- the responsibilities of awarding bodies and awarding body personnel

- the relationship between awarding bodies and centres

- preparing question papers, tasks and mark schemes

- standardising marking: external assessment

- standardising marking and moderation: internal assessment

- awarding, marking review, maintaining an archive and issuing results

- candidates with particular requirements

- malpractice

- enquiries about results and appeals

- access to marked examination scripts.

Clearly, across all of these documents, there is a heavy emphasis upon commonality. And this emphasis is driven, in large part, by our enduring fixation with comparability.

4.2 Monitoring adherence to system regulations

Examining boards are monitored by the regulators against the requirements of the accreditation criteria. Not all qualifications or boards are monitored with equal frequency. The nature and frequency of monitoring is determined taking into account the level of risk posed to the public interest (using criteria such as examination entry size).

Examining boards are monitored by checking published information and by carrying out interviews, questionnaires and surveys. Visits are also made to boards and centres to observe and test their systems, and to evaluate their self-assessment activities. Procedural monitoring is undertaken to ensure compliance with the code of practice, including attending question paper evaluation meetings, standardisation meetings and grade awarding meetings.

If an examining board is identified as not complying fully with the accreditation criteria, it will be required to rectify the non-compliance within a specified period. Where necessary, a regulator has the power to apply sanctions, which might extend to withdrawing accreditation.

4.3 Monitoring the technical quality of examinations and results

The technical quality of examination grades – the principal system output – is defined primarily in terms of the accuracy of inferences that can be drawn from them regarding student attainment (for example, Messick, 1989). Evidence concerning the accuracy of inferences from grades can be categorised under one of three main headings:

- Validity – the extent to which results reflect attainment across the full range of knowledge, skill and understanding that is intended to be assessed by the examination, and nothing more than this.

- Reliability – the likelihood that a different version of the same examination would award students the same results.

- Comparability – the extent to which the same standard is applied across different examinations, or across different versions of the same examination.

The criteria and (particularly) codes of practice, described earlier, help to ensure the validity, reliability and comparability of grades by specifying structures and (particularly) procedures that are associated with high-quality outputs. They require, for instance, that marking consistency be monitored as the marking proceeds, and that feedback be given to examiners once inconsistency is detected (improving reliability). Similarly, they require that Question Paper Evaluation Committees are convened to identify changes needed to bring draft versions of question papers and mark schemes up to scratch (improving validity), and they indicate the range of information that must be considered when establishing grade boundaries (improving comparability).

There is a range of other mechanisms for monitoring the technical quality of examinations and results, including Script Review meetings. During these meetings, which target examinations identified as under scrutiny during a particular year, the question papers and work produced in response to them are evaluated in detail by independent expert subject consultants. During the autumn of 2006, for example, Script Reviews in England involved 70 consultants, 100 question papers and 1000 candidate scripts.

Controls are also put in place to monitor just how technically accurate the examination results turned out to be. As such, these tend to require post hoc investigations, designed to monitor aspects of validity, reliability and comparability. Techniques for monitoring the comparability of examination standards are, of course, the topic of this book. Comparability monitoring has, for many decades, represented a dominant concern of examination researchers in England, with only a very limited amount of research into other key concerns, such as:

- the consistency with which different markers would award grades to the same scripts (reliability evidence)

- the consistency with which different versions of the same examination would result in equivalent grades for the same students (reliability evidence)

- the accuracy of examination results as predictors of future performance (validity evidence)

- the extent to which examination results are affected by factors that ought not to affect them (validity evidence).

Early efforts to monitor comparability were, in the main, undertaken collaboratively by the examining boards (for example, Bardell et al., 1978; Forrest & Shoesmith, 1985), although sometimes also by bodies with more of a regulatory overview (for example, SCAA/Ofsted, 1996). More recently, though, the regulators have funded monitoring exercises on a regular basis, far more systematically than had any of their predecessor agencies.

Since it was set up in 1997, the QCA has undertaken, or commissioned, investigations into a range of comparability contexts, comparing standards over time, across boards, across subjects and even between qualification types (for example, QCA, 2001; QCA, 2003; QCA, 2006a). In particular, the QCA, in collaboration with DELLS and CCEA, runs a programme known as the Standards Review. This programme was established to monitor standards in five-yearly cycles in each major GCSE and A level subject area (originally comparing standards across examinations separated by a five-year period, although the reviews no longer operate on a strict five-yearly basis in all subjects). A description of the review programme can be found in QCA (2006b). The QCA also occasionally initiates Special Investigations, which investigate specific subjects for which there is some reason (such as an unusual pattern of results) to suspect a comparability problem. Although conclusions from these studies are often somewhat tentative, where they have been persuasive they have been used to guide awarding decisions in subsequent years, to bring into alignment standards that appeared awry.

Finally, the QCA has occasionally invited international experts to evaluate whether key quality assurance systems, such as those described earlier, have functioned adequately. For example, in 2001, an independent panel of advisers was invited by the QCA to review the adequacy of the system designed to maintain GCE A level standards. The invitation was extended in the context of a year-on-year improvement in examination results that had raised questions in some minds about whether rising performance standards reflected declining demands in the examinations. The panel was fairly positive concerning the adequacy of the system, despite being quite explicit concerning the problem they saw in conducting such a review. As they stated in the first sentence of their first conclusion: 'There is no scientific way to determine in retrospect whether standards have been maintained' (Baker *et al.*, 2002). This would seem to be a useful starting point for the remainder of this book.

5 Conclusion

The comparability of examination standards is, and has been for many decades, a topic for hot debate in England, both within academic and professional circles and within society more generally. This enduring fixation with comparability is perhaps not surprising given the multiple high-stakes uses to which examination results are put – particularly in relation to selection and accountability – and the fact that nearly all students' life chances are affected by them. The significance of the debate is heightened by the fact that there exist multiple examining boards, offering essentially parallel qualifications within a regulated marketplace. It is given further energy by the particular features of the system that make comparability so hard to investigate, for example: the relative 'authenticity' of examinations, including the combination of different forms of assessment; the use of multiple tiers of entry for GCSE; the relatively small numbers of subjects studied for A level; subject choice, leading to examination populations with vastly differing characteristics, and to some examinations having only small numbers of entries; the almost complete absence of pre-testing; and so on. It is in this highly charged and highly confusing context that the following chapters have been written. As explained earlier, they don't claim to solve the complex enigma of comparability, but they do aim to present a state-of-the-art account of the many techniques that have been used to investigate it over the years.

References

Admissions to Higher Education Steering Group. (2004). *Fair admissions to higher education: Recommendations for good practice*. Nottingham: Department for Education and Skills.

Baird, J., Cresswell, M.J., & Newton, P. (2000). Would the *real* gold standard please step forward? *Research Papers in Education, 15*, 213–229.

Baker, E., Sutherland, S., & McGaw, B. (2002). *Maintaining GCE A level standards: The findings of an independent panel of experts*. London: Qualifications and Curriculum Authority.

Bardell, G.S., Forrest, G.M., & Shoesmith, D.J. (1978). *Comparability in GCE: A review of the boards' studies, 1964–1977*. Manchester: Joint Matriculation Board on behalf of the GCE Examining Boards.

Black, P., & Wiliam, D. (2006). The reliability of assessments. In J. Gardner (Ed.), *Assessment and learning* (pp. 119-131). London: Sage Publications.

Christie, T., & Forrest, G.M. (1981). *Defining public examination standards*. Schools Council Research Studies. London: Macmillan Education.

Claessen, M.J.A. (2005). *Provision of GCE A level subjects*. Statistics report series No. 2. Cambridge: Cambridge Assessment.

Cresswell, M.J. (1996). Defining, setting and maintaining standards in curriculum-embedded examinations: Judgemental and statistical approaches. In H. Goldstein & T. Lewis (Eds.), *Assessment: Problems, developments and statistical issues* (pp. 57-84). Chichester: John Wiley and Sons.

Curtis, P. (2003, August 14). QCA comes under fire over 'easier' A levels. *The Guardian*.

Daugherty, R. (1995). *National curriculum assessment: A review of policy 1987–1994*. London: The Falmer Press.

Dearing, R. (1996). *Review of qualifications for 16–19 year olds*. London: School Curriculum and Assessment Authority.

Department for Education and Skills. (2006). *Participation in education, training and employment by 16–18 year olds in England: 2004 and 2005*. SFR21/2006. London: Department for Education and Skills.

Department of Education and Science/Welsh Office. (1988). *National curriculum task group on assessment and testing: A report*. London: Department of Education and Science and the Welsh Office.

Fitz-Gibbon, C.T., & Vincent, L. (1997). Difficulties regarding subject difficulties: Developing reasonable explanations for observable data. *Oxford Review of Education, 23*, 291–298.

Forrest, G.M., & Shoesmith, D.J. (1985). *A second review of GCE comparability studies.* Manchester: Joint Matriculation Board on behalf of the GCE Examining Boards.

Goldstein, H. (2000). Discussion (of the measurement of standards, by David Bartholomew). In H. Goldstein & A. Heath (Eds.), *Educational standards* (pp. 138-149). Oxford: Oxford University Press for The British Academy.

Goldstein, H. (2001). Using pupil performance data for judging schools and teachers: Scope and limitations. *British Educational Research Journal, 27*, 433–442.

House of Commons, Education and Skills Committee. (2003). *A level standards.* Third report of session 2002–03. HC 153. London: The Stationery Office Limited.

Kelly, A. (1976). *The comparability of examining standards in Scottish Certificate of Education Ordinary and Higher grade examinations.* Dalkeith: Scottish Certificate of Education Examination Board.

Kolen, M.J., & Brennan, R.L. (2004). *Test equating, scaling, and linking: Methods and practices* (2nd ed.). New York: Springer Verlag.

Linn, R.L. (1993). Linking results of distinct assessments. *Applied Measurement in Education, 6*(1), 83–102.

Massey, A., Green, S., Dexter, T., & Hamnett, L. (2003). *Comparability of national tests over time: Key stage test standards between 1996 and 2001.* London: Qualifications and Curriculum Authority.

McGaw, B., Gipps, C., & Godber, R. (2004). *Examination standards: Report of the independent committee to QCA.* London: Qualifications and Curriculum Authority.

Messick, S. (1989). Validity. In R.L. Linn (Ed.), *Educational measurement* (3rd ed., pp. 13-103). New York: American Council on Education and Macmillan Publishing Company.

Mislevy, R.J. (1992). *Linking educational assessments: Concepts, issues, methods, prospects.* Princeton: Educational Testing Service.

Murphy, R.J.L. (1978). Reliability of marking in eight GCE examinations. *British Journal of Educational Psychology, 48*, 196–200.

Murphy, R.J.L. (1982). A further report of investigations into the reliability of marking of GCE examinations. *British Journal of Educational Psychology, 52*, 58–63.

Murphy, R.J.L., & Broadfoot, P. (Eds.). (1995). *Effective assessment and the improvement of education: A tribute to Desmond Nuttall.* London: Falmer Press.

Newton, P.E. (1996). The reliability of marking of General Certificate of Secondary Education scripts: Mathematics and English. *British Educational Research Journal, 22,* 405–20.

Newton, P.E. (2005a). Threats to the professional understanding of assessment error. *Journal of Education Policy, 20,* 457–483.

Newton, P.E. (2005b). Examination standards and the limits of linking. *Assessment in Education, 12,* 105–123.

Nuyen, N.A. (1986). Equating achievement across subjects: Is it possible? The Queensland experience. *Studies in Educational Evaluation, 12,* 245–250.

Partis, M.T. (1997). *Scaling of tertiary entrance marks in Western Australia.* Osbourne Park, Western Australia: Western Australia Curriculum Council.

Please, N.W. (1971). Estimation of the proportion of examination candidates who are wrongly graded. *British Journal of Mathematical and Statistical Psychology, 24,* 230–238.

Pricewaterhousecoopers. (2005). *The market for qualifications in the UK.* London: Qualifications and Curriculum Authority.

Qualifications and Curriculum Authority. (2001). *Five year review of standards: A level psychology.* London: Qualifications and Curriculum Authority.

Qualifications and Curriculum Authority. (2003). *Report on comparability between GCE and International Baccalaureate examinations.* London: Qualifications and Curriculum Authority.

Qualifications and Curriculum Authority. (2005a). *Monitoring of vocational qualifications (2004).* London: Qualifications and Curriculum Authority.

Qualifications and Curriculum Authority. (2005b). *A review of GCE and GCSE coursework arrangements.* London: Qualifications and Curriculum Authority.

Qualifications and Curriculum Authority. (2006a). *Review of standards in A level computing and ICT: 1998–2004.* London: Qualifications and Curriculum Authority.

Qualifications and Curriculum Authority. (2006b). *QCA's review of standards: Description of the programme.* London: Qualifications and Curriculum Authority.

School Curriculum and Assessment Authority/Office for Standards in Education. (1996). *Standards in public examinations 1975 to 1995: A report on English, mathematics and chemistry examinations over time*. London: School Curriculum and Assessment Authority.

Shorrocks-Taylor, D. (1999). *National testing: Past, present and future*. Leicester: The British Psychological Society.

Statistics Commission. (2005). *Measuring standards in English primary schools: Report by the Statistics Commission on an article by Peter Tymms*. London: Statistics Commission.

Stobart, G., Elwood, J., & Quinlan, M. (1992). Gender bias in examinations: How equal are the opportunities? *British Educational Research Journal, 18,* 261–276.

Vidal Rodeiro, C.L. (2005). *Provision of GCE A level subjects*. Statistics report series No. 1. Cambridge: Cambridge Assessment.

Warmington, P., & Murphy, R. (2004). Could do better? Media depictions of UK assessment results. *Journal of Education Policy, 19,* 285–300.

Wiliam, D. (1996). Standards in examinations: A matter of trust? *The Curriculum Journal, 7,* 293–307.

Willmott, A.S., & Nuttall, D.L. (1975). *The reliability of examinations at 16+*. Schools Council Publications. Basingstoke: Macmillan Education.

Wolf, A. (2000). A comparative perspective on educational standards. In H. Goldstein & A. Heath (Eds.), *Educational standards* (pp. 9-30). Oxford: Oxford University Press for The British Academy.

2

A BRIEF HISTORY OF POLICIES, PRACTICES AND ISSUES RELATING TO COMPARABILITY

Kathleen Tattersall

Abstract

This chapter which describes developments in education and assessment in England from the mid 19th century to the present day is in three parts:

1. the emergence of a 'national system' (the 1850s to the end of the Second World War)

2. the development and expansion of the system (1945 to the 1990s)

3. the emergence of a regulated system from the 1990s onwards.

The role of comparability at each stage of these developments is highlighted.

1   An emerging national system of education and examinations

1.1 Overview

Comparability is a fundamental requirement of England's assessment system: between providers of the same product, qualifications, subjects, the demands of tests and tasks, between assessor judgements of students' work and across time. Comparability is also an essential element of England's accountability methodology and is expected to guarantee to governments, the general public, students and selectors that assessment is fair, equitable and reliable. Without assurances of equivalence between different instruments and outcomes that are used to make selections for jobs or a university place or to aid future learning, the basis of decision-making is flawed. The more intense the competition for work, places on courses or financial reward, the more intense is the pressure on the assessment system to demonstrate the steps taken to assure comparability.

From the outset, comparability was a major driver in the English examination system, emerging as an issue in the mid 19th century, growing in importance as new examining boards came into being and the examination system emerged in the early 20th century; it continues to shape educational and assessment policies in the 21st century.

England's modern educational and examination systems are rooted in the 19th century. Competitive examinations for university entrance were a consequence of the establishment in 1836 of the University of London, which enabled two existing colleges, University and King's, to award degrees, the first outside Oxford and Cambridge (linked in the public mind as 'Oxbridge') universities' awards. In 1838 the University of London set a matriculation examination to facilitate objective selection for entry to the two colleges in order to avoid the privilege inherent in the Oxbridge systems. An entrance examination for the civil service came into being in the 1860s. Other landmark developments, including the 1870 'Foster' Education Act, the 1902 'Balfour' Education Act and the foundation of new 'red-brick', civic universities in cities such as Manchester, Leeds and Liverpool, opened education to a wider group of learners. Improved administration by a Board of Education (1899) and Local Education Authorities (LEAs, a consequence of the 1902 Balfour Act) facilitated the growth of the education system. These developments marked the end of education geared almost exclusively to privilege, social class and males, and the beginning of today's national system of education and examinations.

As the 19th century progressed, grant-aided and public schools began to look to universities for guidance on standards in order that they could better prepare their students for university or a profession. London's 1838 matriculation examination and, later (1851), its intermediate examination provided such guidance on the range of subjects across the arts, classics and mathematics with which the university would expect well-educated prospective entrants to be familiar. Oxford (1857), Cambridge, London and Durham (1858) also responded to the demands of schools by providing syllabuses and examinations that candidates could take locally in their own schools. The requirements were specific to the needs of particular universities and were part of the hotchpotch of examinations which characterised the period; a far cry from today's national, closely regulated examination system, which measures individual and institutional achievement and is central to national accountability.

1.2 The emergence of comparability as an issue

The existence of several providers of examinations – London and Oxford and Cambridge – raised the issue of comparability of demand. As early as 1849 London granted admission to students who had satisfied the matriculation requirements of Oxford or Cambridge, thus implicitly accepting equivalence across the requirements. However, no reciprocal recognition seems to have been forthcoming from the two ancient universities. In later years, following the introduction of the School and Higher School Certificates in 1917, London would take a more active and questioning stance of the demands of other boards' examinations.

From the outset, it was important to Oxford and Cambridge that they should act together on important issues. Thus, in 1857, the Cambridge Syndics, debating what title to confer on those who succeeded in their new 'Local' examinations, considered:

> ...that it is of great importance to the success of the proposed system of Examinations that the Universities of Oxford and Cambridge should act together harmoniously on this matter.[1]

However, disagreements emerged in 1859 when the two universities could not agree a common timetable as requested by 52 prominent headmasters. This opened the way in due course to questions regarding the respective standards of their examinations: in May 1872, a headmaster wrote in the following terms to *The Times:*

> Oxford pitches her standard, if not too high, higher than her Sister University. No junior can pass at Oxford without satisfying the Examiners, in addition to the preliminary subjects, as to his knowledge in a foreign language, mathematics or chemistry; while at Cambridge the subjects of an English education only may suffice. And again, in the case of seniors, Oxford sets no special books to be read in Latin, Greek, French, or German; whereas Cambridge does. As the public value of the Oxford and Cambridge certificates is much the same, masters, parents, and pupils naturally prefer entering for Cambridge.[2]

The Times correspondence about standards took on a personal flavour when an individual who had been failed by Oxford but passed by Cambridge claimed that his experience was evidence of the universities' disparate standards. The Secretary to the Syndicate, George Forest Browne, entered into protracted correspondence in *The Times.* Mr Browne's final letter, citing maturation as a possible reason for the different outcomes of the student's experience, was not sent as by then the correspondence had grown stale:

> RB's experience as a Candidate, when fully stated, does not... prove his point. He failed in the summer at Oxford, and after that salutary lesson and the experience which one examination gives he passed with considerable credit with Cambridge six months later, a most important six months at his time of life. That the latter was a correct estimate of his ability is shown by the fact which slips out inadvertently – that Oxford afterwards gave him the very high honour of a First Class in the Senior Examination.[3]

Public scrutiny of question papers and observations on their standards put the spotlight on comparability within a university's own school examinations, across time and across providers. In 1893, the standard of arithmetic in the Junior paper of Cambridge was considered by one critic of the Syndicate to be as difficult as that of its Senior paper of 1883.

> 'Is it supposed', the critic asked, 'that boys' brains are better than they were ten years ago, or are we to work longer hours?'[4]

The examinations of the University of London were also drawn into the debate in a letter to the *Journal of Education* dated 1 September 1893:

> Sir, You would much oblige by telling me what is the comparative value of the London Matriculation certificate with that of the Cambridge Higher Local. I was astonished to hear a lady the other day state that the two examinations are of similar value. So far as my experience goes, the Matriculation certificate is not equal to that of the Cambridge Senior Local, and to compare it with the Higher Local approaches the absurd... The late Secretary to the University of Cambridge... considered a pass in the Cambridge Higher Local equal to a B.A. pass of Cambridge University, and a Cambridge Higher Local Honours certificate equal to a B.A. in Honours.[5]

The letter provoked a response from a headmistress who appreciated the complexities and different demands of syllabuses and examinations and realised how misleading superficial comparisons could be, a view echoed a century later by those charged with considering the vexed question of standards over time:

> It is difficult to compare the two examinations, as they are so different in their natures. To matriculate, a candidate must pass in all seven subjects at the same time, and has little choice of subjects; while to obtain a Higher Local certificate, except that she must take mathematics or languages, she can choose what subjects she likes, and take them when she likes. As a pupil of mine, who knew no mathematics, learnt enough in a year to pass the Higher Local, besides working at other subjects, I think the difference in the standard of the two examinations cannot be so very great.[6]

Concern was also voiced that having several examining boards would result in unhealthy competition, which would lower standards. A letter to the *Pall Mall Gazette* in December 1894, under the sub-heading 'Downward Competition of Examining Boards', did not mince its words:

> It must not be imagined for a moment that its (College of Preceptors) examinations – or the Locals – are really independent exterior tests of a school's efficiency. These boards are competing boards; they exist upon the recognition afforded them by schoolmasters and schoolmistresses... Examiners are 'satisfied' by a rudimentary knowledge of arithmetic, reading aloud, and the answering of papers in religious knowledge and English. Such complacency would find in a glass of water and a crust, nectar and ambrosia. Even at that the 'Local' examiners reject a quarter of the candidates, and their customers the teachers grumble. As a result a process of downward competition seems to be setting in.[7]

A century later similar allegations would be made by a television programme, *Dispatches*, which, unlike the *Pall Mall Gazette*, reached millions of homes (this is discussed later).

The examination scene was complicated further by the arrival of the new civic universities, most notably those in the north. The Northern Universities' Joint Matriculation Board (NUJMB) was established in 1903 by the Universities of Manchester, Leeds and Liverpool (formerly the single federated Victoria University) on receiving their separate charters. In its later years, reflecting its 1978 decision to operate nationally rather than in the self-determined region of the north and the midlands, the board described itself simply as the Joint Matriculation Board (JMB), dropping the northern reference.

The board's prime purpose was to ensure comparable entry requirements across the three founding universities, which were joined by Sheffield in 1905, with Birmingham completing the board's membership in 1916. Schools in the north and the midlands increasingly looked to the JMB for guidance on subject content and standards as they prepared students for university entrance.

1.3 The codification of school examination provision

By the early years of the 20th century, about one hundred separate examinations existed, with each major profession, as well as the universities, setting its own specific conditions of entry, 'without,' according to the President of the Board of

Education in 1917, 'there being much regard to the general educational convenience of the country'. Many considered this unregulated plethora of examinations to be detrimental to the education of able students who wanted to keep open their options of a professional career or university entrance. The Board of Education's Consultative Committee observed in 1911:

> More than four-fifths of those who left grant-aided secondary schools after reaching the age of 14 did so without sitting for a public examination; on the other hand, of the twenty-nine candidates who entered for Bedford College scholarships in 1909, eight had already taken three public examinations, eight had taken four, three had taken five, two had taken six and one had taken seven examinations.
>
> Petch (1953, p. 65)

Worries about the effect of multiple examinations on their students, scepticism about their comparability and the limited currency of certificates, led headteachers to call for a codification of examinations. The JMB received a resolution in February 1904 to this effect from the Incorporated Association of Headmasters (Petch, 1953, p. 53). They argued for an examination *system* in which the certificates of any approved examining board would have widespread acceptance. For such a system to operate, authoritative assurances would be needed that the certificates were broadly equivalent in respect of the range of subjects tested, their standard and format. In 1903, the Board of Education's Consultative Committee had circulated plans for a scheme of school-leaving certificates but the proposals had been shelved. In 1909, the Committee returned to the issue, but it was not until 1911 that a system of school examinations at two levels was formally proposed. The Committee's recommendations for a School (leaving) Certificate (SC) for 16-year-olds and a Higher School Certificate (HSC) designed to allow entry into any university finally came into being in 1917.

The Consultative Committee proposed that certificates would record attainment across an agreed range of subjects, some 'main' others 'subsidiary', with Pass and Credit standards, providing some consistency in the subjects studied and the standard reached. The subjects were arranged in Groups and, in order to achieve a certificate, students had to demonstrate their attainment across subjects in different Groups. The eight university-based boards (see Table 1) became 'approved' boards and were invited to set, mark and certificate the examinations under the jurisdiction and authority of a central coordinating authority, the Board of Education. As the certificates would follow the same format and encompass the same Groups of subjects, it was intended that attainment at agreed standards would obviate the need for specific university matriculation examinations; in the event the HSC was accepted as the basic standard for matriculation but universities continued to specify their own additional entry requirements, a practice that continues today. Most professions too were willing to accept that the certificates were equivalent and sufficient for their entry purposes provided that specific subject requirements were met. The NUJMB's 1926 Syllabuses and Regulations typically contained several pages listing the different entry and matriculation conditions of universities and leading professional organisations.

The Secondary Schools Examinations Council (SSEC) minutes of 14 February 1931 record approval of the JMB's proposal to offer, as optional subjects for study beyond the basic requirements for a certificate, vocational subjects such as navigation, spinning and weaving, and mechanical engineering. This meant that these subjects came to be examined by the university examining boards. There was, however, no attempt made to bring within the system any of the vocational examinations (e.g. those of City and Guilds) that had proliferated in the 19th century especially in the years after the Great Exhibition of 1851. This exclusion was entirely in keeping with the prevailing views that 'trade' was not relevant to education. However, the exclusion of vocational examinations from the national system at this early stage would have a detrimental effect on generations of learners and result in vocational examinations being accorded a lower status than their academic counterparts. Attempts to address this issue and demonstrate comparability would drive national assessment policy and shape examining board structures in the last decades of the 20th century.

The Board of Education exercised its coordinating responsibilities for the School Certificate system through an advisory committee, the SSEC, on which all eight examining boards were represented until the Committee's reconstitution in 1946 when, as a result of their opposition to the teacher assessment recommendations of the 1943 Norwood Report, they were dropped from the Committee. The SSEC remained in existence until 1964 when it was replaced by the Schools Council.

1.4 The School and Higher School Certificates

The SSEC's remit in relation to comparability was to secure reasonable equivalence in the demands of the Group requirements and the examination standards of the examining boards. 'Reasonable' was not defined, nor did the SSEC have powers to enforce an interpretation or regulate the activities of the examining boards, which remained under the control of the autonomous universities. The Committee suggested improvements to the examining boards and made recommendations to the Board of Education. It had no powers to approve either syllabus content or the range of subjects that a university could demand in the Higher Certificate for its specific matriculation requirements, which undermined the comparability of the system. The modest expectations of the SSEC of the examining boards were expressed in a later report:

> The independence of the Examining Boards (is) subject only to the condition that certificates should be reasonably equivalent and should be awarded in accordance with an agreed scheme of requirements... It is all to the good that they should have their own characteristics and their own ways of doing things; yet it remains true that they are engaged on common work. They possess indeed unrivalled opportunities for studying the techniques of examining and for trying out experiments in regard to the type of examination papers which are most suitable in School and Higher Certificate Examinations. It is the more necessary that knowledge gained should be brought into the common stock, and that all possible steps should be taken to promote a frank interchange of ideas and experiences.
>
> SSEC (1932, paragraph 20, p. 20)

If not satisfied with the standards of an examining board, the Board of Education could withdraw its approval but this sanction was never applied; had it been, no state-funded secondary school would have been permitted to enter the examinations of the board in question – not unlike the situation after the 1988 Education Act when state-funded schools were not allowed to offer courses that did not appear on the statutory list of approved qualifications. Given the ramifications, particularly where an offending examining board served a large number of schools – as did the JMB, London and the Oxford Delegacy – it was in the interests of all parties to agree a way forward.

In the absence of formal structures, it was not easy for the examining boards to work together on assessment issues or speak with a single voice on policy matters. The minutes of the Cambridge Syndicate are revealing. The minutes of its Joint Committee for Examinations (which included Syndics and representatives of the leading teacher associations) refer to a long-running difference of opinion with London, which, perhaps understandably, was unwilling to passively accept the standards of other providers, as it had been in the mid 19th century, without clear evidence of equivalence. London demanded 'a higher standard' for matriculation but did not make clear to either Cambridge or the SSEC exactly what its requirements were. The minutes of the Syndicate's General Purposes Committee meeting of 15 March 1918 record:

> It appears that pressure will be brought to bear on London by the Board of Education, HMIs etc. Meanwhile, what ought we to do? Not to raise our own standard to try to fit a standard which we cannot gauge. We have not the necessary information before us.[8]

The lack of agreement on what constituted the required standard of attainment was a worry to teachers. In October the Joint Committee for Examinations urged the Syndicate to:

> ... put before the London Matriculation Board the difficulty experienced by candidates in attaining 'good' in each of the three English papers and in each of the Mathematics papers and to urge the acceptance of one aggregate 'good' standard in each of these two subjects.[9]

The row rumbled on well into the 1920s and resurfaced in a more serious form in 1931 when the SSEC conducted one of its intermittent investigations into the School Certificate, which was also investigated in 1918 and 1924. Similar investigations were made of the Higher School Certificate in 1920, 1936 and 1937.

Unusually, the 1931 findings were published, 'in view of the growing importance of the examination... and of the criticisms of the examination, some of them useful but not all of them well informed, which have appeared in the press and elsewhere' (SSEC, 1932, p. 5). The investigators' report referred to London's refusal to accept the central tenet of the School Certificate: that the syllabuses, examinations and marking of each examining board were of the same standard and made equal demands on candidates. This dissent was a clear challenge to the authority of the Board of

Education over the universities and, therefore, over the examinations they ran. London demanded the right to satisfy itself first hand of the quality of the students' work in the examinations of the smaller examining boards, Durham and Bristol, by checking the standard of their syllabuses, questions and marking of scripts. This was unacceptable to Durham, Bristol and the investigators who commented in the 1931 report:

> This [subjects] the Examining Boards to a kind of dual control, the control of the SSEC... and the control of a powerful University... It is of vital importance to [the Examining Boards] that their certificates should be accepted for matriculation purposes by the University of London... When the School Examinations were reorganised ... it was assumed that the Universities would one and all be willing to leave this question of standards to the SSEC and that no University would seek to interfere with the immediate responsibility of an Examining Body for the conduct of its own School Certificate Examination.
>
> SSEC (1932, p. 51)

Differences of view between examining boards meant that the SSEC was not in a position to give a ringing endorsement to the comparability of the standards and procedures of the examining boards. Its limited remit – not extending to syllabus approval – also meant that it could not express confidence that there was comparability between different syllabuses in the same subject and across subjects, even though equality of standards was an implicit requirement of a Group award. In reality, there was considerable variation between the syllabuses of different examining boards and between alternative syllabuses of individual examining boards – it would be another half century before syllabuses would have to conform to Subject Cores or National Criteria. Frequent alterations to Group requirements, changes of subject content across years and differences between the demands of subjects within Groups further obfuscated comparability between subjects and from year to year.

1.5 Reliability of markers

As more students entered for examinations, the unreliability of markers' judgements emerged as a further concern. This problem had been exposed many years before the introduction of the School Certificate system by Professor F.Y. Edgeworth of Oxford University in his statistical analysis of university and civil service examinations (Edgeworth, 1888). In the case of the civil service examinations, Edgeworth had observed that one-third of scripts marked by different examiners received a different mark and, further, that in a re-examination of scripts by the same examiner one-seventh received a different mark (Roach, 1971, p. 284). Similar findings would be observed in cross-moderation studies conducted by the GCE examining boards in the 1950s and 1960s (Bardell *et al.*, 1978).

Placing candidates accurately in grades (several, or pass/fail) was, therefore, fraught with difficulties. This unreliability would be offset, Edgeworth suggested, by multiple marking and designing examinations with a number of components: the more individuals marked a piece of work, the more likely it was that a 'true value' would emerge; the more components were aggregated, the more likely that individual marker errors would cancel out. Edgeworth's conclusions and his suggested remedies continue to influence examining practices in the 21st century.

How to improve markers' reliability was a hot topic at an international conference on examinations in Eastbourne in May 1931, leading to considerable research in Europe and the United States (Montgomery, 1965, p. 260). In 1936, Hartog, Rhodes and Burt summarised the context of the research:

> Professor F.Y. Edgeworth, many years ago, found that the marks allotted independently by twenty-eight different examiners to a single piece of Latin prose varied from 45 to 100 per cent, and made a number of other investigations on variability in marking. In the United States, Messrs. Starch and Elliot, and in France, M. Laugier and Mlle. Weinberg, have found similar results, but no systematic comparison has hitherto been published of the marks allotted by a number of different examiners and by different boards of examiners, all experienced and qualified for their task, to sets of scripts actually written at public examinations. Both the English and French Committees have attacked this subject... The results are similar in the two countries and equally disquieting.
>
> Hartog et al. (1936, Preface, paragraph vi)

The research confirmed Edgeworth's findings of half a century earlier: in England the marks given by 14 examiners to 15 School Certificate history scripts varied considerably. The same individuals marking the same scripts some 12–19 months later produced an even greater level of variation with 92 cases out of 210 receiving different pass, fail or distinction classifications. How to address the problem? A sole marker was thought to be the ideal solution (though this assumed intra-marker consistency) – but proved unrealistic as entries for the examinations increased. Double marking was a possibility – provided that there was an adequate supply of reliable examiners; this practice was adopted for English examinations by some boards until burgeoning entries for the subject in the early 1980s made it impossible to recruit sufficient examiners.

Another possible solution was more detailed marking schemes to provide tighter parameters for examiners' judgements. However, the SSEC's investigators were not enthusiastic: their comments on the JMB's Higher School Certificate history examination in the 1937 investigation pre-date a later debate about the relative merits of holistic or atomised marking:

> The application of a detailed marking scheme to each answer might possibly be defended on certain grounds... [But] it is apt in time to become merely mechanical... The Investigators have seen nothing in the system as applied here to suggest that this examination has received any benefit from it, or that it is in any way superior to the practice of assessing the value of each individual answer as a whole. At times the Investigators were at a loss to understand on what principle the marks were being awarded... and the indication of errors in the scripts was definitely inconsistent.
>
> SSEC (1939, p. 16)

Marker reliability was not the only problem; other factors were known to affect the reliability of examinations:

> There is also the element of chance due to the variability of conditions for individual candidates, arising from illness or accident, which it is difficult to estimate statistically. It may be reduced, in a rough and ready way, when examining boards take into account school-records in border-line cases. Then there is the element of chance due to variability in the difficulty of the papers set. Some examining boards dealing with large numbers of candidates attempt to reduce marker variability by correcting the marks assigned by the examiners to candidates, so as to make them conform [in accordance with a suggestion of Edgeworth] to a curve regarded from experience as being suitable for the particular examination. This last expedient helps to avoid violent fluctuations in the proportion of those who pass or fail, or are awarded marks of credit and distinction...
>
> Hartog *et al.* (1936, Preface, paragraph ix)

School records, attempts to ensure consistency in the demands of papers within and across years, adjustments to distributions and individual examiners' marks were all part of the armoury that the School Certificate examining boards used to underpin comparability. Little has changed, although researchers now have the benefit of sophisticated computing and technological tools to analyse the variables that have a bearing on assessment outcomes.

1.6 Standards

It was one thing for all markers to be reliable, another for questions and the expected responses to be set at the appropriate standard. Chief Examiners were key to the process – they set the papers and their marking, assumed to be 'correct', was the absolute standard against which individual markers were measured. These assumptions remain at the heart of the examining process. As an early publication of the JMB put it:

> We have, in fact, imposed the standard of the chief examiner on the whole panel, but what guarantee have we that this standard is the correct one? What units have the chief examiners to measure by? Actually none whatever. They are very experienced examiners, but we have only their opinion to go upon... What can the chief examiner do to maintain the same standard as at an examination held twelve months before? It has been claimed that it cannot be done... Experienced and conscientious examiners vary one from another, they cannot all have got the correct and absolute standard – one or more may [by accident] have found it, but which? There is no means of telling.
>
> Crofts & Caradog Jones (1928, p. 44)

The problem, therefore, was not the marking as such but the determination of the credit standard of a certificate made up of attainment in several subjects:

> Taking the subjects all round, one may say that good examiners can and do place the candidates in their correct order of merit. The difficulty is the fixing of the absolute standard; having obtained the order of merit of the candidates, should they all pass, or should they all fail, or where ought the line to be drawn?
>
> Crofts & Caradog Jones (1928, p. 47)

It was particularly important to the JMB and other examining boards with large entries for School and Higher School Certificate to maintain consistency from year to year: the award of scholarships and other financial rewards as well as entry to university courses were determined by success in the examinations. There were, however, no joint arrangements in the first instance for the examining boards to agree a common interpretation of the Pass standard; the JMB's solution to the problem was a statistical one:

> Where large numbers of candidates are being dealt with, the variation of standard among them in the mass from year to year is small, or, at any rate, small compared with the variations we know take place in the standard of examiners. The candidates are not like a fruit crop, which may suffer blight and produce poor results in any one year; in normal times variations in standard are small, and we should err very little if we kept the percentage of passes in the important subjects fairly constant from year to year.

> The Chief Examiners should therefore be asked… whether their percentage of passes differs much from previous years, and if so to state what in their opinion is the cause of the difference, and whether there is any reason why the figures should not be altered so that the final figure might be brought into line with the previous one.
>
> Crofts & Caradog Jones (1928, pp. 45–46)

The use of statistics to moderate outcomes and provide year-on-year comparability, which continues to operate in the English examining system, had been adopted by the JMB as early as 1918 when its governing body resolved:

> That the attention of the examiners for the Higher School Certificate should be drawn to the disparity between the different subjects in the results of the examination in Higher Alternative papers, and to the irregularities from year to year in the same subjects in that examination, and that the Board should suggest that a percentage of from 10 to 15 candidates obtaining 260 marks out of 400 should be roughly the norm to follow.
>
> Quoted in Petch (1953, p. 137)

It is not clear whether this imperfect solution was adopted universally but by 1931 the SSEC investigators could refer with some confidence to the 'two recognised standards' in each subject, the 'norm-referenced' – and, therefore, 'clearly understood' – Credit standard and the 'less clearly defined Pass standard':

> The Examining Boards have been reasonably successful in maintaining a steady credit standard in each main subject. In any given examination the credit mark may vary from subject to subject and it is not necessarily the same for a given subject from year to year. The credit standard in a subject in an examination is… best described not in terms of the credit mark but broadly speaking as the standard which a given percentage of the candidates offering the subject in question in that examination will reach… Generally speaking credit is obtained by about half the candidates, but it would be quite untrue, even as a general statement, to say that the credit standard is mechanically fixed to give this result. There is a fairly definite relationship between the credit and the pass marks in a subject; thus in one large examination the pass mark is 4/5ths and in another 7/9ths of the credit mark: and of late the Examining Boards have been endeavouring to keep the pass standard reasonably uniform from year to year.
>
> SSEC (1932, paragraph 30, p. 31)

Some 75 years after the publication of the 1931 report, the investigators' pithy acknowledgement of the difficulty of setting standards in any given year and maintaining comparable standards across years resonates powerfully:

> The practice of keeping the percentage of credits and passes nearly constant from year to year is reasonable, if the general performance of candidates is from year to year practically the same; but if there is a real and continuous improvement in the general quality of work in a subject and the percentages of passes shows no corresponding rise, it follows that the standard of the examination is unintentionally being raised. Alternatively, an influx of pupils from weak forms might result in candidates being passed who in former years would have failed. All that can be said on this matter is that these possibilities should be kept in mind, the situation watched, and alterations made when these seem justified. If for example it was found that in a given subject and on comparable papers the performance of candidates on the papers set in 1930 and 1931 was distinctly better than that of their predecessors, say five years earlier, there would be good grounds for increasing the percentage of passes and credits.
>
> SSEC (1932, paragraph 35, p. 41)

The reference to comparable standards across years made an impression on at least one examining board Secretary, Mr Crofts of the JMB; his personal copy of the report, to which the author had access, underlines the words 'five years earlier' and a handwritten note reads, 'Would there? Why not 50 or 100 years earlier?'

Norm-referencing may have helped examining boards with large entries to maintain some consistency across their subjects and years, but was less helpful to those whose entries were very low. Entries were distributed unevenly across the eight providers and little reliance could be placed on statistical comparisons of the awards of different boards. In 1930, London (20.4%) and the NUJMB (28.0%) accounted for almost half of all the 63,117 School Certificate entries while at the other end of the spectrum Bristol (0.8%) and Durham (1.9%) accommodated less than 3%. Table 1 shows the changed pattern of entries (expressed as a percentage) between 1918 (the first year of the examination) and 1930.

Table 1 Percentage distribution of candidates among the several examinations

	1918	1930
Oxford and CJB	8.8	11.9
Oxford Local	33.4	16.9
Cambridge Local	17.9	11.0
NUJMB	14.8	28.0
London	12.4	20.4
Durham	1.9	1.9
Bristol	0.3	0.8
Wales	10.5	9.1
Total no. of candidates	22,873	63,117

The full table can be found in SSEC, 1932, paragraph 19, p. 19.

All of the issues of comparability, which emerged during the period of the School Certificate, remain relevant in the 21st century. The first examining boards were conscious of their responsibility to demonstrate comparability within the marking of particular subjects, to set consistent standards for their subjects and certificates, and to ensure that there was widespread public acceptance of, and confidence in, their work. They developed new techniques of assessment, sought more reliable ways to ask questions and improve marking, credit answers and standardise the increasing number of examiners they employed. Individually they inched their way to solutions, which today are commonplace, but in the 1920s and 1930s were quite revolutionary. The JMB, for example, introduced new-style papers in geography – 'answer books with the questions displayed in such a way, and with such detail, as to indicate not only precisely what the examiners were asking about but also approximately how much length they were asking for' (Petch, 1953, p. 94) – in an attempt to achieve better reliability in the marking. The inevitable charges of lowering standards accompanied such changes.

2   Development and expansion of a national system of education and assessment

By the end of the 1930s a national examination system, loosely coordinated by the Board of Education, was well established. The School and Higher School Certificates provided schools with a reasonably stable benchmark and students with worthwhile targets. Along with matriculation requirements, the examinations largely determined the curricula of public and state-funded secondary schools. Judged by 21st century levels, examination entries remained low. In 1947, 107,356 candidates took the School Certificate examination and 26,322 were entered for the Higher School Certificate (Gosden, 1983, p. 75). The first GCE O level examinations in 1951 were taken by around 134,000 candidates, while A level attracted about 37,000 candidates (Bardell et al., 1978, p. 13).

2.1 GCE O and A level examinations

Wartime provided the impetus to re-examine social policies which the 1945–1951 government enacted. Education underwent major changes. The 1944 Butler Act opened opportunities to a wider social group by raising the school-leaving age from 14 to 15 and establishing the principle of free secondary education within a tripartite system of secondary schools. A year earlier, the Norwood enquiry into the curriculum and examinations had proposed that future examinations should be single-subject based in order to unshackle schools from the diktat of the examining boards and encourage more students to take examinations (Board of Education, 1943). By being free to drop their weak subjects, students would be better able to demonstrate their achievements. This approach was not welcomed universally. Some, such as the headmaster of Liverpool Collegiate School, Mr A.L. Kneed, argued that there would continue to be a demand for attainment across a range of subjects. Writing in the *Liverpool Echo* in January 1952, he claimed that a certificate would only have currency if it contained five or six subjects, including English, mathematics and a foreign language (see endnote 10) – not so different in range from the former School Certificate and similar to later proposals for a baccalaureate-type Diploma. A system of teacher assessment at 16 with external examinations at 18, primarily for university selection, was also proposed. However, both this recommendation and rearguard attempts to retain broader requirements for certification were unsuccessful.

The new General Certificate of Education examination at Ordinary, Advanced and Scholarship levels came into being in 1951, but selection at 11 for grammar, technical and modern secondary schools and a school-leaving age of 15 (16 from 1974) continued to limit the number of students taking GCE O level. Candidates for O level had to be at least 16 years of age on the 1 December preceding the examination, a requirement that provoked bitter opposition from the examining boards and schools. This minimum age requirement was relaxed for the 1953 series of examinations when headteachers had to certify that it was educationally desirable for younger students to take the examination and that they were likely to pass in the subjects they had studied.

The main concern about the new GCE O level was the linking of its pass standard from 1952 onwards (1951 was a transitional year) to the credit standard of the School Certificate which, it was considered by many headteachers, would deprive students, who would have met the former pass standard, of a certificate. The headteachers were also unhappy that the new examination would be pass/fail with no distinguishing credit or distinction 'grades'. Schools were encouraged to report to students their marks but it was not until 1975 that formal grades were recorded on O level certificates (although some boards provided unofficial grades).

In his same 1952 *Liverpool Echo* article, the outspoken Mr Kneed of Liverpool Collegiate School was blunt about what was perceived to be an unhelpful raising of the bar:

> This raising of the standard can mean only one thing – not, I fear, that by a stroke of the pen the children in our schools get cleverer the more work is done, but that a much larger number of children will go out into life without any certificate at all, though they have completed five years at grammar school and not done too badly…

> The idea of parity has gone so far as to remove incentives from the good worker and the able child because now no difference is made between the bare pass and the really high mark. The child who gets 51% and the child who gets 90% are both awarded just a pass – no credit, no distinction for the really good performer, no evidence as to what is a child's strongest suit, or promising line.[10]

A new comparability concern materialised with the first results: the different levels of attainment of boys and girls. Mr E.R. Wood of the High School for Boys, Hereford, wrote to the *Times Educational Supplement (TES)* on 30 November 1951:

> The Cambridge Local Examinations Syndicate has recently issued a table of percentage results for the General Certificate in the summer of 1951. The results at ordinary level show the performances of boys and girls separately, and a comparison of them is startling. In English literature, for instance, 75.6% of the girls passed, but only 54.7% of the boys. The superiority of girls' results is marked in nearly every subject, including such science

papers as physics and general science, and if we divide the total number of passes by the total number of scripts in each sex, we find 62.6% of girls successful, as contrasted with only 54.4% of boys. The Syndicate's figures for passes at advanced level are not given according to sex, so that we have no evidence as to whether girls are also superior to boys in advanced work.

It would be interesting to know of teachers in mixed schools whether the apparent superiority of girls as examination candidates accords with their experience. If it is generally true, what is the explanation? Superior intelligence? Greater conscientiousness? Better teaching? And does it last?[11]

In the years that followed, Mr Wood's questions would continue to provoke debate and research into gender (Elwood & Comber, 1996) and other equity issues that could have a bearing on attainment (Gipps & Murphy, 1994).

The new O level was intended to be used by grammar schools and not by technical and modern schools, which were discouraged by government from entering whole classes for the examination. Many schools ignored government advice:

One of the problems which is arising in connection with the new examination concerns its use by increasing numbers of pupils presented by technical colleges and modern secondary schools, whose needs are not identical with those of the grammar schools.[12]

Attempts to restrict the GCE examination to grammar school students resulted in a proliferation of local leaving certificates for technical and modern school students provided by LEAs and others. Such certificates had no national currency.

In 1953 a new board, the Associated Examining Board (AEB), was approved as the ninth (excluding Northern Ireland, but including Wales) GCE examining board, sponsored by City and Guilds, mainly to provide examinations for the growing numbers of students interested in technical and vocationally related subjects. (The number was reduced to eight in 1964 with the demise of Durham and then to seven in 1990 when the SUJB merged with Cambridge.) Appendix 1 represents the boards' histories. However, it was not until the 1960s and the advent of the Certificate of Secondary Education (CSE) which brought into public examinations a large new population and new comparability challenges, that the need for local certificates disappeared. Until then, the majority of students left school with no formal qualifications. In 1958 a mere 13% of school leavers left education with five or more O levels. In 1960, 18.8% of leavers attained one or more A levels and fewer than 5% went on to university. As late as 1972, 43% of students left school without even attempting a qualification.

2.2 Collaboration to achieve comparability across different providers' examinations

The increased demand for university places, which gradually followed the introduction of the GCE, made it important to demonstrate comparability across examination providers so that results could be used with confidence. The same was true in respect of employers, many of whom set basic entry requirements of a pass standard in English and mathematics. As entries for O level and A level grew, more assistant examiners were required, increasing the pressures on comparability. More detailed mark schemes were required to ensure a consistent understanding by the examiners of what could be credited – the report of the chemistry cross-moderation study undertaken by the GCE boards in 1953 refers to London's:

> ...very detailed marking scheme, which was necessitated by the large number of examiners (13 on each paper).[13]

More systematic standardising arrangements were put in place by individual examining boards to ensure reliable marking.

The Secretaries to the GCE examining boards were conscious that they needed a formal structure to demonstrate that their examinations led to reliable and comparable outcomes for students. From the outset, therefore, they met regularly,

> with a view to checking the co-ordination of pass standards at ordinary and advanced levels.[14]

These meetings became the backbone of inter-board co-operation and collaboration on standard setting, certification and administration. In March 1952 the Secretaries agreed to the JMB's suggestion to:

> Arrange experimental enquiries regarding standards, beginning with Chemistry A level, a subject which might be less likely than others to raise controversial problems.[15]

The first enquiry (in March 1953 using the 1952 papers) established a format for cross-moderation studies, which the examining boards conducted each year in an agreed range of subjects at both O and A level: a conference of senior examiners who studied syllabuses, papers, mark schemes and scripts to determine whether the standard of the board under scrutiny was the same as that which they applied in their own board. The report of the 1953 cross-moderation GCE chemistry study refers to different interpretations of subjects and different lengths and design of papers but dismisses these as having 'no bearing upon the aim of the enquiry... differences could be ignored'; the examiners 'could detect no difference of standard as between the... examining boards'. The report went on:

> It appeared therefore that the differing statistics of entries and percentage passes are not primarily due to differences in the general standards of the examinations, and that in view of the perennial difficulty of establishing a hard and fast line as between pass and fail there is general agreement... as to what represents the bare Advanced pass level in their subject. The differences in the statistics may be due to differences in the fields from which the boards draw their entries.[16]

The issues identified in this and subsequent cross-moderation studies led to research becoming part and parcel of the GCE examining boards' work. Research departments with high-profile directors were established: its former Secretary, Dr Petch, headed that of the JMB, created in 1964. A further indication of the value the GCE examining boards attached to research came in 1970 when a Standing Committee of GCE Research Officers was founded to:

> ... deal with matters of common interest, including the comparability of standards.[17]

Prior to the establishment of a common timetable, it was possible for candidates to be entered for the same subject with different examining boards. These dual entries were a fruitful source of the boards' own research into comparability. Two studies in 1958 (when 1,311 O level and 41 A level candidates had taken, in the same series, the examinations of two different boards) and in 1966 (11,674 O level and 1,524 A level dual entries) were undertaken. The report of the 1966 study (UK GCE Examination boards, 1971) concluded that, as 70% of candidates at both levels were awarded the same grade (replicating the findings of the 1958 study and Edgeworth's 1888 work), there was no major difference in standard between the examining boards. Variations in awards to the remaining 30% were attributed to factors such as the preparation of candidates, their familiarity with one syllabus and not another, their choice of questions, 'which on one day can be disastrously ill-judged (but) can on another day be sensible and related to (the candidate's) capacity', motivation and chance. In later years a national system of assessment and accountability would be less tolerant of such variations.

The examining boards reported their individual and collaborative research in their annual reports and occasional publications, such as those of the JMB. The latter addressed specific issues, including comparative performance across subjects (subject pairs analyses), the topic of a 1982 publication (Forrest & Vickerman, 1982). The JMB's motive for publicising the work was simple:

> For the public in general and for teachers, pupils, parents, employers and most users of examination results the question of comparability of standards in public examinations is probably seen as a simple matter: they expect a given grade to indicate the same standard of performance irrespective of the examining board which awarded it, the subject in which it was achieved and the year in which it was gained. It can certainly be argued very strongly that all users of public examination results are entitled to assume that the examining boards ensure that comparability of standards does exist, especially in examinations which claim to have national currency.
>
> Forrest & Vickerman (1982)

The report concluded that:

> Subject pairs analyses have... thrown new light on comparative standards in examinations in the same subject provided by different boards, both where inter board projects in the GCE are concerned and also in the case of the joint 16+ examinations provided by the consortia in which CSE boards work with the JMB. The general picture which emerges is that, as far as the performances of the JMB candidates offering these particular examinations are concerned, the examining boards, both GCE and CSE, are much more successful in achieving comparability between the different examinations they provide in the same subjects than is usually acknowledged by outside commentators on public examinations.
>
> Forrest & Vickerman (1982)

Whether that conclusion was shared outside the examining community is a matter for speculation as the report was couched in dense and technical language, impenetrable for the general reader. How to explain specialised issues effectively to different audiences continues to challenge researchers and examining boards.

Increasingly, the government expressed its interest in all aspects of comparability. It was as concerned to have value for public money (from which most examination fees were paid) as to be assured that a national standard existed across the examining boards. The House of Commons Expenditure Committee considered the issue in 1976 (House of Commons Expenditure Committee, 1977).

This prompted the examining boards collectively to publicise their comparability research more widely. Two publications in 1978 (Bardell et al., 1978) and 1985 (Forrest & Shoesmith, 1985) described the numerous studies that had been conducted between 1964 and 1985. The preface of the 1978 publication explained why the Secretaries were trying to reach a wider public:

> In a climate of growing public interest in public examinations comparability of grading standards is a popular focus of attention; and of the various aspects of comparability – between subjects, between standards in a subject in different years, between modes of examining and between boards – the last usually generates the most earnest and heated debate.
>
> Bardell et al. (1978)

Ironically, while the examining boards were working together increasingly to demonstrate comparable standards, matriculation requirements – a major driver for the 1917 School Certificate system – continued to diverge, as the JMB's 1956 annual report makes clear:

> There are divergences of opinion between the Board and the other matriculating boards as to what university entrance requirements should be. In consequence automatic 'interavailability' comes to an end with the introduction of revised requirements on 1 November 1956. The achievement of interavailability for the period, 1951–1956, was an advance in educational procedure in this country, even though Oxford and Cambridge Universities have both stood apart from the agreement.[18]

While GCE A level was regarded as the basic general entry requirement, some universities refused to accept for entry purposes new subjects, including the AEB's sociology and the JMB's general studies. Use of English, on whose design the JMB, Cambridge and Oxford collaborated and which was designed to improve the standard of communication of entrants to higher education, also met with opposition, in spite of evidence that some undergraduates had a poor command of written English:

> Among freshmen in general the level of ability to write English is disappointingly low. The suitability of the present GCE Examination in English Language at the Ordinary level is not here being criticised so far as it concerns the 16-year old candidate for whom it was designed, although opinion about this aspect of the examination is not wholly favourable.

It seems to be generally agreed however that the degree of ability to express oneself which might be accepted from the 16-year old candidate is not sufficient at university entry, that too often apparently such facility as may be present at 16 is not encouraged to develop *pari passu* with the development which goes on in the other aspects of the Sixth form curriculum. It may well be that if all the students were sufficiently 'literate' at entry, some of them might lapse into comparative 'illiteracy' while at the university unless care were taken to ensure that further development is actively encouraged and fostered within the university itself. That is a matter for the university authorities themselves; the duty of the Board is to ensure that at entry those who have been examined by the Board as potential university students have gone further than what is now accepted as O-level English Language.[19]

In the event, 'use of English' never became a universal requirement, being regarded by some universities as an additional obstacle to recruitment, and the examination disappeared in due course, demonstrating the importance of higher education's buy-in to new initiatives. This would be an important factor in the Curriculum 2000 reform of A level and the acceptance of vocational examinations as an alternative entry route.

2.3 The Schools Council and the CSE examination

In 1964 the Schools Council replaced the SSEC as the national overseeing body with a remit to co-ordinate the examining system. The Council worked in partnership with the education community and the examining bodies. Local Education Authorities (LEAs), teacher unions, subject associations and the examining boards were among the several organisations represented on its large, unwieldy governing council. The arrangement was in keeping with the freethinking of the 1960s, a far cry from later national overseeing bodies, which, with every new manifestation, accrued ever-greater powers of control over, and regulation of, the examining system. As its numerous publications demonstrate, the partnership was productive: the Council encouraged innovative approaches to teaching, learning and assessment, and sponsored individual and collaborative research projects by examining boards and university education departments (for example, Christie & Forrest, 1980, 1981). Bodies such as the National Foundation for Educational Research (NFER) carried out research into assessment techniques (Willmott, 1977), methods of moderation and comparability (for example, Skurnik, 1974). In an era when it was possible to make public statements that awards could err by +/- one grade without causing a general furore or destroying confidence in the integrity of the system, Willmott's study, based on 1973 data, was able to conclude that standards of the GCE examining boards were 'roughly' comparable (Willmott, 1977).

A new examination, the Certificate of Secondary Education (CSE), came into being in the 1960s to accommodate the ability range immediately below that taking the GCE:

Assuming that up to 20% of the total 16-year old age group may be expected to attempt GCE O-level in four or more subjects, we think the examination we propose might be taken in four or more subjects by candidates in the next 20% below these, and should be so designed that a substantial majority of pupils within this group would obtain passes in this range of subjects. We think that up to a further 20% of the age group might attempt individual subjects.

Ministry of Education (1960)

Fourteen new examining boards were established in England and Wales (a fifteenth, in Northern Ireland, came into being later) to administer the new examination on a regional basis. Appendix 2 shows the geographical distribution of the new CSE boards. With the addition of these new examining boards, the total number of CSE/GCE boards rose to 22, thus exacerbating the problem of comparability across providers. With the exception of the Associated Examining Board, brought into being in 1953 under the sponsorship of City and Guilds to provide a broader range of syllabuses and examinations, many of them vocational, and targeted at the growing further education population, the GCE examining boards were under university governance. By contrast, LEAs played a prominent role in the CSE boards' creation and their chief executive officers, rather than vice-chancellors, chaired their governing councils. Although teachers had always been involved in the policy and subject development committees of the GCE examining boards, they were the majority interest on the corresponding CSE committees. Teachers were also active as examiners and as moderators for coursework assessments, a feature of all CSE examinations.

3 Comparability issues relating to the CSE examination

3.1 Links with GCE O level

In order to benchmark the new examination against an established standard, the CSE's highest grade was linked with the GCE O level pass standard with the minimum point of CSE grade 1 (the highest of the examination's five grades) defined as equivalent to the minimum point of the O level pass standard. No formal mechanisms existed across the CSE boards to effect equivalence between awards made on different syllabuses and question papers, designed for different ability ranges and administered by separate organisations with their own decision-making processes. There were, however, several Schools Council-sponsored GCE/CSE cross-comparability exercises (such as Willmott, 1977) which, among other findings, highlighted the difficulties of comparing grades across regions of the CSE boards as well as between CSE and GCE O level. Not only were the sizes of the regions different but the nature of the schools within them also varied. Some comprised LEAs that had abolished selection and changed to comprehensive educational provision; in other LEAs selection continued to characterise secondary education. As Willmott observed:

School differences are in some cases enough to confuse the application of the chosen analytical method.

Willmott (1977)

The link with the GCE O level standard was a mixed blessing. On the one hand equivalence between CSE grade 1 and the GCE O level pass standard was essential to the public's acceptance of the examination. On the other, the newcomer, catering for a different range of ability, was inevitably seen as the poor relation of the established examination. A generation later, GNVQ and other vocational examinations would run into the same problem. The CSE's difficulties were compounded when formal and certificated grades of A–E, with D and E below the old pass standard, were introduced into GCE O level in 1975; a lower O level grade proved more attractive than a CSE certificate to many students and their parents. The GCE examining boards took steps to ensure a common interpretation of the new grades: the University of Cambridge Local Examinations Syndicate's (UCLES) Annual Report for 1976 records that:

> ...to ensure comparability of standards between the GCE Boards at grades D and E, a series of inter-board agreement trials in each of eight widely taken subjects was held in the early part of the year.[20]

3.2 Question choice

Both GCE and CSE external examinations provided candidates with a choice of questions, a further complication for comparability within and between examinations and across the two systems. In Willmott & Nuttall's research into the reliability of 16+ examinations (Willmott & Nuttall, 1975), a GCE paper in their sample provided a choice of five out of ten questions while a CSE mathematics paper allowed a choice of five out of twenty-four questions. The possible combinations across the entry for the latter examination in particular were huge, raising questions about the internal consistency of the examinations. Research of this kind, together with more clearly defined objectives and content which would be examined, led in due course to a drastic reduction in the choice of questions within examination papers. In turn, more focused examining would result in a narrowing of what was taught and learned – assessment would increasingly come to drive the curriculum.

3.3 Curriculum freedom

Choice of questions within examination papers reflected the mood of the times. The CSE examination was intended to follow and support the curriculum; the 'curriculum comes first' was the mantra of the 1960s. The blossoming curriculum development movement of the period looked to the examining system to legitimise new projects, new subjects, new approaches to learning, with the support and encouragement of the Schools Council (Schools Council History, for example). Both CSE and GCE examining boards were keen to cooperate with projects instigated by foundations such as Nuffield, with new innovative alternatives offered to schools as alternatives to more traditional approaches. The practice of the GCE boards was for one of them on behalf of the others to provide the examination as long as it was in project form. All of the GCE examining boards reserved the right to provide separate examinations once the period of the project had ceased.

The Schools Council encouraged diversity, and the structure of the CSE examination was a vehicle for that. The examination embraced three approaches to assessment:

Mode 1 syllabuses and examinations were set and marked externally by the boards; in Mode 2 the board set and marked examinations on a school's own syllabus; Mode 3 provided for the school to determine its syllabus, set its examination and carry out the marking subject to approval and moderation by the board. Although Mode 3 was possible in the GCE system, it flourished in the CSE, with a huge growth in the number of schemes following the introduction of the examination.

The growth of Mode 3 schemes and the absence of criteria for subjects and awarding compounded the complexities of setting and applying a national standard consistently across examinations within and across CSE examining boards. Approval and moderation procedures for Mode 3 were varied. The Associated Lancashire Schools Examining Board (ALSEB), the smallest of the CSE boards whose first Secretary had been recruited from the JMB whose stringent procedures it adopted, exercised tight control over syllabuses and examinations through its subject panels. The panels were responsible for both Mode 1 and Mode 3 syllabus approval and awards, in order to apply common judgements to subject requirements and standards of award.

At the other extreme the West Yorkshire and Lindsey Regional Examination Board (TWYLREB) implemented the concept of curricula designed to meet local needs to a greater extent than any other of the CSE boards; its provision was almost entirely Mode 3 with only a handful of Mode 1 examinations. It handled Mode 3 quite separately from Mode 1 on the basis that imposing its view of what a subject should be would stifle innovation. Schools in TWYLREB's region were therefore afforded greater freedom to pursue their own ideas; it was said that at its height there were 10,000 Mode 3 schemes in Yorkshire alone. Whatever the benefits to teaching and learning, this liberal approach to subject content and the standards of awards left the examining board open to the criticism that standards within and across modes were not comparable.

This criticism was somewhat unfair as all the boards, including TWYLREB, opened their doors to research into their standards, particularly into the equivalence of grades awarded in Modes 1 and 3. This research, while detecting some tendency towards leniency in Mode 3, showed no startling differences (Nuttall, 1973). The leniency was considered to relate to the greater motivation of candidates and teachers alike on schemes that had been designed by teachers for specific groups of students:

> It could be argued that apparently high performance in Mode 3 is only to be expected when a teacher decides not only what to teach, but what to assess and how and when it should be assessed.
>
> Matthews (1985)

Mode 3 courses in all CSE examining boards increased in number and diversity after the raising of the school leaving age to 16, with innovative schemes designed to meet the needs of this new cohort coming on stream in 1974. Many of these – for example, 'preparation for living' – were criticised for their standard and for diluting the curriculum entitlement of students, some of whom dropped basic subjects like mathematics and science at age 14 – a practice which the introduction in 1988 of the National Curriculum with its required range of subjects, including English, mathematics and science, brought to an end. These new courses added to concerns about the value of Mode 3 schemes and their comparability with externally provided syllabuses and assessments. The 1977 Annual Report of UCLES, the Cambridge board, expressed a commonly held view:

> The Syndicate questions whether the use of many thousands of Mode 3 examinations, each set and marked by individual schools or small groups of schools, is consistent with the notion of a national standard and national qualifications.[21]

3.4 Coursework

The assessment of work that students undertook during the course of study was central to CSE examinations and also featured in some GCE schemes. The JMB, for example, had introduced an English O level in 1967 based entirely on coursework, which proved to be extremely popular and was the forerunner of the Northern Examinations and Assessment Board's (NEAB) joint 16+ (later GCSE) syllabus. The examination continued until 1994 when the rules governing coursework were tightened and 100% course-assessed examinations were proscribed. The increased use of coursework added to the difficulties of applying comparable standards across schools, regions and nationally.

While the assessment of work undertaken during the course of study widened the scope of what could be assessed and offset the limitations of end-of-course examinations, there was no agreement on what coursework constituted: was it normal, day-to-day class work (continuous assessment), or specific pieces of work designed to assess particular objectives – for example, a field study in geography or an historical enquiry? How to standardise teachers' assessments to achieve comparability between individual assessors and across schools was a major challenge – in essence the same problem as standardising examiners but on a greater scale and more geographically dispersed.

Methods of moderation included sampling work on site or by postal exchange, and moderation by consensus (that is, teachers meeting to assess work, discuss and agree standards). The efficacy of the system depended on the quality of the assessments of both teachers and moderators, which raised questions about the training they had undertaken in order to make valid and reliable assessments. The consensus approach was later to be favoured as educationally beneficial and effective in the report commissioned by the government, prior to the introduction of the National Curriculum, from the Task Group on Assessment and Testing (DES/WO, 1988a), but its recommendations were judged too costly to implement.

The provision of equal opportunities to all students to demonstrate their attainment through work that was sufficiently challenging was a further factor. Parental pressure on teachers, the potential for cheating and the possible influence of social class on attainment were also concerns that exercised researchers and sociologists (Broadfoot, 1979). The debate about these and other issues is as lively in the 21st century as it was in the 1960s, with new factors such as access to the Internet adding to concerns about the reliability of coursework. The QCA's response in 2006 to those concerns was to restrict coursework to the classroom in order to prevent work being plagiarised from the Internet.

Regional provision, school-based examinations and coursework assessments militated against a national standard despite the best efforts of the CSE Secretaries who, like their GCE counterparts, worked together in the pursuit of comparable standards. Strong links were forged between the CSE examining boards and researchers working for other educational organisations such as the NFER. The appointment in 1976 of Desmond Nuttall, a prominent researcher, to the post of Secretary to the Middlesex Regional Examining Board further illustrated the value afforded to the contribution of research to examination development.

With the encouragement and support of the Schools Council, the CSE boards collaborated on cross-moderation exercises, developed methods of moderation, worked with teachers to raise awareness of standards, using marked examination scripts and other materials. However, regardless of these efforts, the complex structure of the examination meant that comparability was an elusive concept. Despite this weakness, however, the CSE examination provided long-overdue recognition to the achievements of a growing number of school leavers who otherwise would have had no formal externally validated record of their educational success. Entries grew rapidly in the first years of the examination from 230,977 in 1965 to 982,721 in 1969 (Gillan, 2003).

3.5 A single system of examining at 16+?

It seems to be the fate of all examinations, in England at least, to be criticised as soon as they have come into being as being irrelevant to prevailing educational opinion: it was true of the GCE in the 1950s, of the CSE in the 1960s, of the GCSE after 1988 and of the revised A levels in 2002. Such criticisms highlight the time taken to implement new concepts in systems where new courses, generally lasting for two years, need to have been approved at least 18 months prior to implementation. Turning educational and assessment systems around takes time and careful planning – and during that process other developments and changes can make 'new' thinking seem outmoded.

In the 1960s the two end-on systems of CSE and GCE O level theoretically catering for 40–60% of the school population (in practice a wider group) co-existed uneasily in an expanding system of comprehensive education. Comparability between the standards of the two examinations was open to question; employers and the general public were confused by two grading systems; two administrative structures duplicated costs, time and effort without adding value to students. In 1971, the Schools Council determined to investigate the feasibility of combining the GCE O level and CSE examinations and invited the examining boards to set up consortia to develop joint 16+ courses for pilot examinations involving a limited number of students (Schools Council, 1971); these feasibility studies came to fruition in 1974. Many of the GCE and CSE partnerships that were formed at that time stayed in existence and continued to offer examinations leading to the award of both O level and CSE certificates. The JMB provided the GCE element for three consortia – Associated Lancashire Schools Examining Board (ALSEB)/North West Regional Examinations Board (NWREB); The West Yorkshire and Lindsey Regional Examining Board (TWYLREB); The West Midlands Examination Board (TWMEB) – which were responsible for 15 of the 42 feasibility studies carried out nationally. The JMB and the four northern CSE boards (ALSEB, North Regional Examinations Board (NREB), NWREB, Yorkshire Regional Examinations Board (YREB)) under the umbrella of the Northern Examining Association (NEA) continued to offer the subjects of the original feasibility studies and additional subjects were developed as joint 16+ examinations.

The 16+ debate coincided with the government's growing interest in education and its relevance to the modern world. Prime Minister Jim Callaghan's speech in October 1976 at Ruskin College, Oxford, questioned whether education equipped school leavers with the tools required by industry and with the basic skills of literacy and numeracy, recurring themes over the next 30 years. The speech opened the way to more central control of what was taught and assessed in schools and, therefore, of examination syllabuses and their standards. Vocational provision, so long on the fringe of the national examining system, became a priority, with the launch of government-funded initiatives such as the Technical and Vocational Education Initiative (TVEI), intended to bridge the academic and vocational divide.

Against this background the debate about a single system of examining at 16+ was played out over several years. The government set up a committee, chaired by Sir James Waddell, which in 1978 recommended a single system, subject to the development of general and subject-specific national criteria in the main subjects (20 in all) with aims, objectives, content and skills and more specifically targeted examinations (DES, 1978). Their purpose was to provide a firmer basis for comparability across subjects and providers by tighter control of syllabuses, examinations and administration. The CSE and GCE examining boards established a Joint Council for the GCSE to develop these criteria and in 1984 the government agreed to the introduction of the General Certificate of Secondary Education (GCSE) for first examination in 1988. Four geographically based Groups in England (plus one in Wales and a sixth in Northern Ireland), each comprising at least one GCE and one CSE board, were approved to develop and administer the new examination in England and Wales. They were charged with carrying forward the O level/CSE standards with GCSE grades at C and above to be determined by awarders drawn from the GCE tradition and the lower grades to be determined by those drawn from the CSE tradition. In spite of these strictures, most awarding committees worked as one to determine the grades. The new Groups were voluntary partnerships; however, mergers followed and by the mid-1990s four merged examining boards offered the GCSE examination in England. Fewer syllabuses followed the reduction in providers, giving a better basis to achieve comparability across subjects.

Other changes to the examination system supported the tighter control of syllabus provision. The Waddell report had recommended that:

> Arrangements for the central coordination of 16+ examinations should be strengthened and a central body should be responsible for securing agreement on criteria... and for coordinating further preparations.
>
> Department of Education and Science (1978, paragraph 127 (iv))

Accordingly, the Secondary Examinations Council (SEC), which replaced the Schools Council in 1984, was given a stronger remit than any of its predecessors to approve syllabuses and co-ordinate examination provision. Responsibility for the school curriculum was given to a separate body, the School Curriculum Development Committee (SCDC). The examining groups saw the need for even closer collaboration to provide self-regulation and to agree and apply comparable standards. The mechanism for this collaborative work was the Joint Council for the GCSE, supported by a forum of GCSE Secretaries. The current co-ordinating body, continuing the role of the original Joint Council, is the Joint Council for Qualifications (JCQ), established in 2004.

None of these arrangements for the co-ordination of the GCSE affected the governance of GCE A level, which remained the responsibility of the independent GCE examining boards. Their Secretaries continued to meet to discuss A level issues until the emergence of new boards such as London Examinations and the NEAB whose responsibilities embraced both 16+ and post-16 examinations.

4   The GCSE examination

4.1 Tiered examinations

Before giving approval to the introduction of the GCSE examination the Secretary of State had to be satisfied that a single *system* was able to assess the full range of ability. Would GCSE be an umbrella system with different syllabuses or sub-sets and/or papers targeted at different ranges of ability? Or would it be a single *examination* with a single syllabus and assessment tasks for the whole ability range? From the outset, UCLES took the view that in an examination spanning the ability range accommodated by GCE O level and CSE:

> The only way to prevent a substantial fall in standards is to create a tiered examination with different but related syllabuses and question papers for different ability groups, and with regulations which will ensure that the abler students take tests which will extend them to their full capacity.[22]

In the debate that followed, the Schools Council commissioned further research into examining across the ability range (Tattersall, 1983) and a view emerged eventually that, while all GCSE examinations had to differentiate effectively across the ability range, the nature of subjects should be the main determinant of how this would be achieved. In broad terms subjects fell into two categories – those which set common tasks with a range of responses, that is, differentiation by outcome; and those which set papers designed for sub-sets of the ability range with a restricted number of grades available on the papers, that is, differentiation by task using tiered examinations. As time went by the rules for differentiation changed and tiered papers became the norm from which few exceptions were permitted. Tiered content also characterised some GCSE subjects, requiring early choice of courses, not unlike the choice of CSE or O level course, which many had thought the single system would make unnecessary.

Overlapping grades on tiered papers were new challenges to comparability and fairness and prompted a raft of research (Good & Cresswell, 1988), which addressed questions such as: is a grade C, which is achieved on the higher tier – where the grade is the lowest available – of the same standard as a grade C attained on a lower tier where it is the highest available grade? Are the demands of different papers and questions, which target some or all of the same grades, comparable? Is it right to limit the aspirations of students to papers with a cap on the grades that can be awarded? Is it right to give no recognition to the attainments of students who fail to achieve the lowest grade on the higher tier? Do awarders apply consistent grading standards across differentiated papers? How to explain to the public the intricacies of a system that rewarded candidates highly for a seemingly limited performance, as exemplified by low marks for grade C on the higher tier?

4.2 Grade-related criteria

The system was spared the difficulties that would certainly have arisen had explicit criteria, as requested in 1984 by the then Secretary of State, Sir Keith Joseph, been adopted for the award of grades. His speech to the North of England Conference in January 1984 touched on clearer definitions of the objectives of examinations:

> First, I can offer an account of what the minimum level to be attained at 16 by 80–90% of pupils would entail in a few areas of the curriculum, taken by way of example, and I repeat that I am talking about a minimum level. In English pupils would need to demonstrate that they are attentive listeners and confident speakers... that they can read straightforward written information and pass it on without loss of meaning, and that they can say clearly what their own views are....
>
> Joseph (1984)

He went on to say:

> It is clear that one cannot compare what pupils now achieve in the largely norm referenced 16+ examinations with the objective [of raising standards]... because that objective can be fulfilled only if the examinations become more criterion referenced... The more the examinations can measure in absolute terms... the easier it will be to motivate pupils to attain higher absolute standards by a proper acknowledgement of what they can do.
>
> Joseph (1984)

Sir Keith's expectations were that 'grade-related criteria which will specify the knowledge, understanding and skills expected for the award of particular grades' would be developed to ensure a clearer meaning for pupils and clearer goals for teachers (DES, 1987). The SEC's Grade Criteria Working Parties' approach fell short of the Secretary of State's expectations but was complex, unwieldy and unlikely to achieve consistency within and across subjects, or be comprehensible to a wider audience:

... numerous and complex criteria – in the case of history, for example, ten sub elements across three domains, and criteria for four levels of performance within each sub-element, resulting in forty statements of performance for teachers and examiners to use in the assessment of candidates and for those interested in the performance of candidates to interpret.

Department of Education and Science (1987)

The initiative died a death, other than taking the much weaker form of grade descriptions, but the search for absolute criteria to define grades and levels of achievement resurfaced with the National Curriculum and its ill-fated numerous Statements of Attainment. The comments of an AEB research publication are pertinent to both failed initiatives:

It is linguistically naïve to believe that criteria... can ever be made sufficiently precise for their use not to involve subjective judgements of the type which they are intended to avoid... It is technically naïve to expect the use of complex aggregation rules to enable detailed descriptions of candidates' attainments to be inferred from summary measures like grades or that such rules, because they are explicit, necessarily operate in a way which is consistent with natural notions of fairness... It is philosophically naïve to assume that fair judgements can only be made if every candidate's script is judged by precisely the same set of criteria... It is psychologically naïve to assume... that performance is not profoundly affected by the context of the task being carried out.

Cresswell (2000)

4.3 Tighter curriculum controls

GCSE National Criteria carried the government into the secret garden of the curriculum, transforming its undergrowth into an orderly public park. Government recognised the potential of assessment for bringing about changes to the curriculum, influencing teaching and learning and monitoring educational standards. The 1988 Education Act brought about the National Curriculum and new central overseeing bodies, the School Examinations and Assessment Council (SEAC) and its sister organisation, the National Curriculum Council (NCC). They were given statutory powers over the National Curriculum and its assessment at four key stages (at ages 7, 11, 14 and 16), including GCSE syllabuses and examinations, a seismic shift from coordination to regulation of the system. The existing GCSE National Criteria were changed to accommodate the National Curriculum and tightened to enforce more explicit comparability across syllabuses in the same subject. New constraints on the numbers of syllabuses each examining board could develop were introduced, which led to a further cull of syllabuses, particularly Mode 3.

With every change of the rules, new syllabuses were required – more frequently than had ever previously been the case. This had compounded the difficulties of maintaining consistent standards from year to year, with no stable benchmark against which to measure curriculum requirements and examination standards.

Only those 16+ syllabuses on a list approved by the Secretary of State could be used in state-funded schools – reminiscent of the School Certificate. A narrow definition of 'General' excluded from the GCSE vocational-type subjects such as woodwork and metalwork, even though these had been assessed by both GCE and CSE examinations. However, broader subjects such as business studies; craft, design and technology (CDT); electronics; and travel and tourism continued to provide a vocational route in GCSE whose standards were deemed by Ofsted in 1996 to be 'broadly in line with those in other GCSE courses' (Ofsted, 1996a). In later years the policy of excluding vocational subjects from GCSE would be reversed through the development of Vocational GCSEs.

From an early stage, the GCSE was thought by some to be an 'anachronism' (Nuttall, 1993), having been in gestation for 18 years and its introduction coinciding with the development of a statutory National Curriculum. A national system of assessment opened the possibility of abolishing the seven grades of GCSE and replacing them, in the National Curriculum subjects at least, with the ten-level scale, which reported attainment at the end of key stages. Some believed that the scale would provide a more positive report of attainment at age 16, that it would raise aspirations, open horizons and provide better differentiation. A single scale across the four key stages would also facilitate the tracking of students' progress from primary to the end of secondary education. Whatever its educational merits, the proposal for a single scale raised questions about the relationship of ten National Curriculum levels to seven GCSE grades and there were doubts as to whether a change to a single scale would maintain consistent standards:

> [There are difficulties with a proposed] move from the lettered grades A–G, designating GCSE performance, to the 10-level numbered scale in which 10 and 9 differentiate within the present A grade, but 7 and 6 do not match the present C and D, and 4 will be the lowest grade to be reported by the GCSE. Here there are not only problems of achieving comparability between the two scales, but also of providing the more searching test looked for at the top end within an examination to be taken by the great majority of the age group.[23]

Had the proposal been adopted solely in the ten subjects of the National Curriculum, a ten-point numbered scale would have run side by side with a seven-point lettered scale. That prospect was not attractive and neither was the option of changing to a numbered scale for all GCSE subjects. The proposal was quietly dropped.

5   An accountable and regulated national assessment system

Four interlocking themes dominated the post-1988 era, converging in the last years of the century to create an accountable and regulated national assessment system: regulation, accountability, standards over time, and post-16 education and assessment. These developments were both driven by and raised the stakes for comparability. Comparability was a key factor too in the drama that developed as the new system came on stream.

5.1 Regulation

The 1988 Education Act, together with GCSE National Criteria, marked the end of a long tradition of a largely decentralised and unregulated approach to teaching, learning and assessment. Thereafter, the curriculum and assessment came under tighter central control; the remit of the central overseeing body (see Appendix 3 for an overview of the English advisory and regulatory boards governing examinations) was strengthened from one of loose coordination to tight regulation. Devolution in the late 20th and early 21st centuries to Wales and Northern Ireland of responsibility for education required separate regulatory organisations in each country and co-ordination across all three of them to ensure consistency in qualifications that crossed national boundaries.

Initially, the statutory regulatory powers over public examination syllabuses and assessments governed only the period of compulsory education to age 16; the control of post-16 examination provision did not come on stream until relatively late in the day. Control of syllabuses and assessment procedures became more stringent with every new manifestation of the central overseeing body: the SEAC (from 1988) exercised powers over the assessment of the statutory curriculum that the GCSE examined at Key Stage 4. The regulator oversaw revisions to National Curriculum assessments and to GCSE arising from the plethora of legislation, reports and enquiries which appeared in the 1990s. Arrangements for the GCSE were tightened to ensure better comparability; coursework, for example, was capped in favour of seemingly more reliable external, end-of-course examinations. A code of practice (initially for GCSE but extended later to other examinations) was developed with the aim of minimising differences in procedures that might have a bearing on comparability; awarding procedures, for example, were codified. Scrutinies and probes into examinations were carried out on a more frequent basis to expose and rectify any perceived weaknesses. The force of regulation waxed and waned over the years: self-regulation came and went in the mid-1980s; the heavy handedness that followed gave way briefly to a light touch in the early 1990s.

A not insignificant driver behind the pressure for increased regulation was a nagging fear that the examining boards might not simply be competing in terms of the quality of their syllabuses and support to teachers, but they might also be competing in terms of (lower) attainment standards (making it easier to get a grade with one examining board rather than another). There was nothing new about such fears, as the 1894 correspondence in the *Pall Mall Gazette*, quoted earlier in this chapter, demonstrates.

However, the medium of television was able to plant the notion of nefarious examining and awarding practices in the minds of a far larger audience than a newspaper could ever hope to influence: the introduction to the 1995 Channel 4 television programme *Dispatches* claimed:

> On *Dispatches* tonight, an investigation that goes right to the heart of British education, casting the gravest doubt on any claim that standards are rising. Sarah Marris penetrates the closed world of the examination system. A story of papers deliberately made easier and grades deliberately made better; all in the name of competition and market forces. It's an exam system where money talks.[24]

A complaint of unfair and unjust treatment, brought by a member of the AEB's staff who had featured in the programme, was upheld by the Broadcasting Standards Commission who ruled (June 1997) that 'the theme of the programme – deliberate and secretive grade-rigging by the examining boards – was at best an exaggeration and, accordingly, unfair'. This ruling offered a vindication of the integrity of those involved in the examining process. However, although the ruling made clear that there was no persuasive evidence that examining boards manipulated their standards to attract more candidates (merely speculation, typically based upon a naive understanding of the system and of the significance of differential pass rates), such allegations were damaging and helped to pave the way towards greater regulation of the examinations system.

As statutory powers over qualifications related initially only to the period of compulsory education, they did not extend to GCE A levels, which were taken, in the main, by post-16 students and were still governed largely by university-dominated councils. However, the GCE examining boards were under increasing pressure to conform to tighter controls: A level principles and subject cores were introduced to improve comparability and rationalise the number of syllabuses on offer. The cores were developed with the somewhat unwilling cooperation of the GCE boards, which were conscious of the restrictions on the freedom of the GCSE examining boards (that the National Criteria had brought) to develop the curriculum as they wished. Although the cores were a far cry from National Criteria, allowing considerable flexible interpretation, they nevertheless defined an agreed body of knowledge and skills, which enhanced, to some extent, consistency across A level syllabuses. In 1994, following a 1993 HMI inspection of the quality and standards of A/AS level examinations, a voluntary code of practice was drawn up for GCE, which was merged with the GCSE Code (mandatory from 1994) in 1997. The code laid down strict procedures for all stages of the examining process, from syllabus design to awarding, its intention being 'to promote quality and consistency across all examination boards and thereby minimise differences which hindered… (the achievement of) common and unchanging standards' (NEAB, 1996, p. 1). The 1994 GCE Code restricted the role of coursework (an upper limit of 20% in the majority of subjects) in A level. Conditions were also laid down by the regulator for the development of modular schemes, reflecting the concerns that Ofsted had expressed in the 1993 report about the comparability of standards of A level linear and modular schemes.

The universities' 'ownership' of the GCE examining boards protected them from undue interference from SSEC (the Secondary Schools Examination Council) and its successor organisations. However, the universities' stake in the system was weakened by the administrative separation of the GCSE and the GCE in 1988. The mergers of examining boards, which followed that change led most of the universities to withdraw from the governance of examining boards. By the mid-1990s, only Cambridge and the northern universities remained an integral part of the examining boards they had created in the 19th century. Durham had long disappeared from the scene; JMB's formal ties with its five founding members were loosened when it became part of the NEAB and then dismantled when the AQA was created, although the new organisation sought higher education representation from Universities UK; Oxford sold its interests to UCLES and the AEB; London took a back seat when its examining arm merged with BTEC, bowing out entirely when Pearson acquired the business in 2002.

The dilution of university influence on the school examination system facilitated the greater involvement of the post-1988 statutory regulators in the examining boards' GCE operations; the autonomy which they had enjoyed for so long disappeared. Under SCAA (from 1993) and later QCA (from 1997), regulation of syllabuses (or 'specifications' of what was to be examined, as they came to be called) and assessment was extended to all examinations, including A level and those vocational examinations that claimed equivalence to either GCSE or A level – GNVQ and, later VCE. National Vocational Qualifications (NVQs) came into the framework too, but it proved more difficult to regulate vocational boards, which regarded such attempts as threats to their commercial existence. Some of the smaller boards were willing to take their chances in the marketplace with unregulated products.

By the end of the 20th century, the concept of accreditation had been introduced in England. This brought all aspects of examining board governance and procedures under the scrutiny of the QCA in its regulatory role. In particular, the examining boards had to demonstrate that their quality assurance procedures were sound and that they conformed in full to the QCA's requirements, including the code of practice. While these steps minimised the opportunities for different procedures which would impact on comparability of standards later, events would reveal the difficulty of controlling the interpretations and actions of human beings.

5.2 Accountability

Accountability became a central requirement of public service organisations in the last decades of the 20th century. In education, the comparability of assessment outcomes was thrown into sharp focus when performance tables were introduced in the mid-1990s to monitor the system. These tables, colloquially known as 'league tables', ranked schools according to the performance of their candidates in the GCSE and GCE A level examinations without, in the first instance at least, taking into account social and other factors that could influence examination performance. Schools and colleges were, therefore, held to account for the grades their students attained.

In most countries the assessment of individuals and the monitoring of the system are different functions, and they had been in England when the Assessment of Performance Unit (APU) operated from the mid-1970s until the advent of the National Curriculum. In reality, the examining system's disparate administration and complexities were ill-suited to a role wider than its prime function of assessing and reporting the attainment of individuals. The gradual inclusion in the performance tables of vocational as well as academic assessments compounded the difficulties of guaranteeing comparability across the data. By means of the tables, teachers, schools, LEAs and examining boards were held to account for the attainment of their students and, in due course, for the value they added to their educational progress. Powers of inspection of education were strengthened. National Targets were set to raise the standards of education. A consequence of these developments was changes in the pattern of entries for individual examining boards as schools sought courses that would deliver the best outcomes for their students, fuelling claims, not unlike those made in the 1890s and by the *Dispatches* television programme, that awards were affected by market considerations and that the examining boards' standards were, therefore, inconsistent.

As greater precision and reliability were demanded of the examining system by individual candidates and their parents, and by schools anxious to demonstrate that their place in the 'league tables' was accurate, questions were raised not only about the accuracy of marking but about standards across the examining boards. The examining boards' reputation for fairness, integrity and probity came under increased scrutiny, leading to further demands for greater controls over the system. A single examining board was seen by many as the solution to comparability. However, the fundamental characteristics of the examining system – loose criteria, qualitative questions and marking – which made comparability a difficult issue to address, would continue to manifest themselves, regardless of whether there was a single or multiple providers.

A further consequence of the pressures on the system to deliver greater reliability was an increase in requests to the examining boards for special arrangements (extra time, for example, for students with special assessment needs) and consideration (where particular circumstances such as bereavement might have impaired an individual's performance). Challenges to published grades and National Curriculum levels also increased, a reflection of the concerns of schools that their published data were inaccurate. Greater degrees of accuracy, reliability, consistency and precision were sought from the system than examinations based on qualitative rather than quantitative judgements could deliver. Concerns about consistency across providers, between subjects and across years gathered pace and motivated successive regulators to control more tightly the activities of the examining boards.

5.3 Standards over time

The use of public examinations data for reporting attainment relied on there being a constant, unchanging standard, maintained over time, within and across subjects and providers. In reality this was not a straightforward matter, as acknowledged by SCAA/Ofsted (1996). Syllabus and examination changes, different styles of questions, new knowledge and society's expectations all combined to obscure comparability across time. Earlier reports on the issue (Backhouse, 1978) had arrived at similar conclusions in a period of much less change in syllabuses and examinations. Even though it was impossible to *prove* that standards had remained roughly comparable in a rapidly changing world, the examining boards' own researchers expended efforts to expose the issues and reassure the regulator and the public that all possible steps were being taken to underpin consistent standards (Massey, 1994; Newbould, 1994).

Concerns that standards had fallen were particularly acute at GCE A level, which had remained remarkably stable until the 1980s when both curricular and grading changes were made. On the curriculum front, subject cores led to a flurry of new syllabuses, which, while being more relevant to students and providing a greater degree of comparability across examining boards, unsettled what had been a largely unchanged examination. In terms of grading, the original 'Pass' and 'Distinction' categories had been replaced in 1963 by a new A–E grading system accompanied by SSEC guidelines for the proportions of candidates within each grade band: 10% A, 15% B, 10% C, 15% D and 20% E. Although the GCE boards themselves were critical of the grading scheme and did not follow the guidelines uniformly (Whittaker & Forrest, 1983), they remained the official guidelines for awarding until 1987.

In that year the examining boards were asked by SEC (still in the full flush of its search for absolute grade criteria) to award A level grades on the basis of examiners' judgement of the quality of work at three key boundaries, grades A, B and E, the remaining grades being arithmetically determined according to an agreed formula. The shift of emphasis from norm-referencing tempered by qualitative judgements to a weak form of criterion-referencing tempered by statistical data opened the way for a steady annual increase in the percentages of candidates succeeding in A level which, in turn, led to a greater demand for places in higher education. By 1995, 72% of students in England stayed in education beyond age 16, compared with 13% in 1955, while the proportion of 18-19-year-olds who advanced to higher education increased from 4% in 1955 to 31% in 1995.

Charges that the examining boards were lowering their standards, and complaints from universities that the examination provided them with insufficient differentiation to select their intake resulted in the 1996 SCAA/Ofsted investigation into standards over time. Although the investigation acknowledged that statistical shifts over time did not provide evidence of a change in standard, recommendations were made to monitor standards more frequently. A national library of scripts and a system for retention of scripts to assist future studies were established. Worryingly for the examining boards, many of which had already merged voluntarily, thus reducing the number of providers, the study urged the government to act on Sir Ron Dearing's recommendation for a further rationalisation in the number of examining boards to facilitate tighter control of the system.

5.4 Post-16 education and assessment

Successive governments had found it difficult to get a handle on the 16–19 phase of education. A levels were considered too specialised (a long-standing criticism) and, as more students entered further education, inappropriate in respect of both curriculum and standard for the new cohort. A variety of failed initiatives – proposals to extend the grading scale, an Advanced Ordinary level examination and a Certificate of Extended Education with a standard between O level grades A–C/CSE grade 1 and A level grade E – which were intended to address the narrowing effect of A level on students' education peppered the late 1970s and 1980s. In 1988 the Higginson Committee recommended five 'leaner' but 'tougher' A level syllabuses of a slightly lower standard to broaden sixth-form studies, which would also have accommodated some learners for whom the A level standard was beyond reach (DES/WO, 1988b). The government rejected the recommendations and chose instead to retain the A level with an Advanced Supplementary examination, half the content but assessed at the A level standard which the Government guarded.

Far from broadening the appeal of A level, the new structure raised issues of comparability between the grades of a half or a full A level course, as did full and short course GCSEs in the 1990s. An Audit Commission report was critical of the 30% fall-out rate from A level courses: about one third of students who embarked on A level did not complete the course, and about one third of those who did complete were ungraded (Audit Commission/Ofsted, 1993). The report questioned whether an examination that failed to meet the needs of the majority of candidates represented value for public money.

The development of modular schemes of assessment in the 1990s was one answer to the problem, encouraging more students to continue their A level courses and attain grades that may have seemed beyond their reach had they not had the benefit of periodic feedback on their progress. By 1997 modular schemes accounted for 30% of all entries. Increases in the percentages of students attaining the 'pass' standard led to concerns that a modular approach provided an easier route to grades. Ofsted's 1996 enquiry was, however, confident that standards were comparable across modular and linear A level schemes:

> There was no evidence in the 1996 examinations of any significant differences in the standards being set at the grade boundaries, between the modular and linear syllabuses inspected.
>
> Ofsted (1996b)

Alongside the continuing focus on the quality and standard of A level, the Government began to feel its way increasingly to a vocational solution to a broader-based post-16 curriculum. Developments in the 1980s such as the Certificate of Pre-Vocational Education (CPVE) ran up against a similar problem to that which had dogged the CSE – how to ensure a link with an established standard (A level) while encouraging diversity and experimentation. Other attempts (TVEI, for example) to increase the take-up and status of vocational examinations administered in the main by separate vocational awarding boards also came to grief on the altar of comparability.

A different solution emerged (DES/DoE/WO 1991): the establishment of distinct learning routes for post-16 education: A levels (overseen by SEAC), General National Vocational Qualifications (GNVQ) and NVQ under the control of the National Council for Vocational Qualifications (NCVQ).

School and vocational examining boards were urged to work together to administer GNVQ alongside GCSE and A level provision. However, continuing references to the A level 'gold standard' made it nigh on impossible to establish vocational education as worthwhile in its own right. As Sir Geoffrey Holland, former Permanent Secretary at the Department of Employment, observed in 1995:

> A levels, far from being the gold standard that ministers and a lot of other people think they are, are in fact an altar on which have been sacrificed the enthusiasm and the hopes and, indeed, many of the capabilities of about half of our young people.[25]

5.5 Convergence and resolution

The search for a solution to the problem of linking the various strands of post-16 education in such a way as to ensure comparability and parity of esteem continued, with two major reviews in 1995/1996: Gordon Beaumont's *Review of 100 NVQs and SVQs* (Beaumont, 1996) and Ron Dearing's *Review of qualifications for 16–19 year olds* (Dearing, 1996). Dearing was charged with the responsibility to make more coherent the fragmented post-16 education system. His report's numerous recommendations included creating a single national framework of academic and vocational qualifications; reducing the number of examining boards (from four to three, in line with the three vocational boards offering GNVQ: RSA, BTEC and CGLI) and giving them responsibility for all general qualifications, vocational and academic, thus reflecting the span of responsibilities of the newly merged Department for Education and Employment; introducing an entry-level standard for those students working at a level below GCSE; introducing an Advanced Subsidiary standard (that is, lower than A level); unitising the post-16 curriculum to facilitate broader courses and credit accumulation. New A/AS-level syllabuses would be needed to deliver these particular recommendations.

The government's 1997 response to the review, *Guaranteeing standards* (DfEE, 1997), set the scene for a fundamental overhaul of post-16 qualifications which brought A levels firmly into the National Qualifications Framework, controlled and regulated by the new QCA, which replaced SEAC and NCVQ in 1997. The new body was given powers to regulate qualifications, whatever their genesis. *Guaranteeing standards* envisaged the bringing together of academic and vocational qualifications into a single administrative structure through the creation of unitary examining boards. The clear intention was to address through such structural changes comparability across providers and parity of esteem between academic and vocational examinations. The education and employment communities generally welcomed the proposals.

Guaranteeing standards also pursued the question of how many examining boards a national system of assessment could sustain. A single board was dismissed on grounds of scale and three emerged as the favoured number. A new government in 1997 made clear at an early stage its support for three unitary awarding boards in a press release in June 1997:

> We believe that there should be three awarding boards – each offering GCE A levels, GCSE and GNVQs. These boards will be best placed to take forward our commitment to support broader A levels and upgraded vocational qualifications – both underpinned by rigorous standards and key skills.

We also want a reduction in the number of GCE syllabuses... a single point of accountability and a single trading name.

... The new Qualifications and Curriculum Authority (QCA) [will] work with the awarding boards and the Department to develop a rigorous regulatory regime, building on self-regulation where that works best.

We... will expect to see far greater comparability in standards between similar examination syllabuses to avoid some papers being seen as 'easy'.[26]

The reduction from four to three examining boards could only be achieved through a coming together or merger of two of the existing boards: in the event the AEB and NEAB joined forces to create the Assessment and Qualifications Alliance (AQA), at first a joint venture, but very quickly becoming a fully merged organisation in 2000. The City and Guilds of London Institute, which had been party to the initial discussions to create this new unitary awarding board, chose to remain an independent organisation.

5.6 The Curriculum 2000 A level system in operation

As the new millennium opened, the examination scene was very different from that which had existed throughout the late 19th and 20th centuries. Structural changes in government departments and the examining boards had been brought about by the demand for greater comparability across qualifications. A national framework of qualifications had been created comprising both academic and vocational qualifications. National Curriculum assessments at defined key stages together with the qualifications system provided the data to monitor and evaluate the education system. The newly found stability would be disrupted by the introduction of new A levels for first teaching in 2000, unitised, and with a new mid-way Advanced Subsidiary standard. Curriculum 2000 sparked a controversy which opened the way for further consideration of the 14–19 curriculum and assessment framework.

A new unitised AS/A2 system was fraught with comparability challenges, not least the requirement that the new A level awards in 2002 would be comparable with those of the old A level awards. To deflect criticism that modular, or 'unitised', assessment would be somehow easier than terminal assessment, all Curriculum 2000 A levels were required to include an element of 'synopticity' in the assessment of A2 units (often operationalised as a single synoptic unit). The idea of synoptic assessment was that it should require a student to draw upon ideas from across the entire syllabus, to demonstrate a depth of understanding and to identify links between core concepts.

The system comprised two qualifications, one of which was embedded in the other. Designing papers for an as yet unexemplified standard – the new AS – was far from easy. How to combine three units at AS standard, representing 50% of the total A level – but also leading to an AS award – with three units at the A2 standard (50%) – all six leading to the full A level award – presented a huge challenge to awarders. The robust technical and statistical information, which examining boards relied on to monitor their standards in more settled times, was not available, although, as ever, the interpretation of statistics would be an issue: would an increase in the percentage of candidates who succeeded in A level represent a lower, the same or an improved standard? The very nature of a unitised structure, even with strict limitation on retaking units, suggested that students would be more likely to reach higher levels of attainment than in a single end-of-course examination – or to drop out before completion, if early module results were disappointing. Prior certificated attainment at AS raised a major question: should the A2 awards be used to keep steady the percentage pass rate? Would students be rewarded on the basis of their performance, or would statistical considerations moderate – or determine – the outcome?

As the first round of the new examinations unfolded it became clear that the statistical outcomes of the new system would look very different from those of the old. The new Advanced Subsidiary qualification had given students and their teachers quality feedback on progress and a prognosis of their likely overall A level award. For students who were on track to attain a good A level grade, the feedback encouraged them to stay the course; for others whose AS performance was more modest, there was the opportunity to drop out with an AS certificate as proof of their attainment. The likelihood was that there would be an enhanced pattern of A level awards, which would bear little comparison with the awards of previous years. There would be no way of knowing, other than reliance on examiners' expertise, whether the A level standard had been carried forward.

None of the issues raised by the introduction of a new qualification was new, much was at stake in 2002 and several reputations were on the line: of the government which had involved itself in the detail of the system; of the regulators, anxious to ensure consistent interpretation of their code of practice and bring the new examination safely home; of the awarding boards, anxious to ensure that the awards were fair and consistent, based on evidence, and would stand up to public scrutiny. All parties were conscious of their responsibility to guarantee fair and equitable treatment of all candidates and to enhance the standing of the new examination. The outcome has been well documented: charges of foul play by the examining boards; allegations of inconsistent practices and different interpretations of the code of practice by Accountable Officers who over-rode awarders' qualitative decisions in the interests of statistical comparability; claims of interference and unwarranted pressure on the examining boards to maintain levels of awards consistent with previous years by the regulator; assertions of a lack of control by the government. High profile resignations followed the publication of the 2002 results. Public trust in the system fell to a low level. An enquiry, conducted by the former Chief Inspector, Mike Tomlinson, was set up but resulted in very few changes of grades, suggesting that examiners and Accountable Officers had, in general, exercised sound judgements. The House of Commons Education and Skills Committee conducted an investigation (2003). Comparability in its many guises had come home to roost.

The A level 'crisis' and the consequent weakening of the examination in the eyes of the public opened the way for a more fundamental appraisal of the system. Mike Tomlinson was asked, in 2003, to undertake a review of the curriculum and qualifications across the 14–19 phase of education. Many believed that the curriculum remained narrow and insufficiently focused on the needs of industry and that it failed to meet the needs of a large number of students who either disappeared from education or left compulsory education with a low level of basic skills and few other skills. The review, published in 2004, recommended a Diploma system, more akin to the baccalaureate system favoured by many European countries and reminiscent of the School Certificate with its Group requirements – and its accompanying comparability issues.

It also recommended (as had the Norwood report of 1943) that at 16 assessments should be largely in the hands of teachers, with appropriate moderation and their standards informed by benchmark tests and materials provided by the Regulator and the awarding boards. Greater use of the Internet and online marking was envisaged to standardise and make more reliable teacher assessments. Like previous attempts to place greater reliance on the judgements of teachers on work undertaken by students during the course of study, this particular recommendation was not accepted by the government. The reluctance to introduce this fundamental change to the system demonstrated how much remained to be done to raise the standard and status of assessment carried out by teachers. Regardless of the demonstrable inherent unreliability of all forms of assessment, public confidence in the reliability of externally provided assessment remained high, as did the belief that assessments carried out by teachers could not be relied on.

Tomlinson's central recommendation – the replacement of the existing qualifications system by the Diploma – was also not accepted, with politicians from the Prime Minister down giving their support to GCE A levels which had been so highly criticised a mere two years earlier. However, a more selective Diploma system – Specialised Diplomas in defined applied areas of learning – was agreed, to come on stream in 2008. Existing qualifications will contribute to those Diplomas, as will teachers' assessment of students' work carried out during the course. An overall grade for the Diploma will be determined.

Whether the grading system will command the confidence of universities, employers and the wider public will make or break the Diplomas. The acceptability of the Diplomas will depend on comparability across components, across providers and across time. Nothing changes; comparability is *the* pre-requisite of public trust and confidence in examinations and qualifications.

6 Concluding remarks

As this historical survey shows, comparability has been ever-present in the English examination system. From the outset there were multiple providers, which were expected by schools and their students to provide syllabuses and examinations of a comparable standard that would open doors to higher education and the professions. The early examination bodies, all university based, explored ways of ensuring that standards remained constant from year to year, across providers and within individual subject areas. Marker reliability in particular was the focus of research in the 19th century and the findings remain relevant to the 21st century. As the examinations became more competitive with ever increasing numbers of students, demands for consistency and comparability resulted in the codification of the system through School and Higher School Certificates; all examining boards continued to take seriously the need for comparability, creating research departments, undertaking joint studies and commissioning research from outside bodies. The government's increasing involvement in, and control over, the curriculum and assessment added new dimensions to the need for reliability and comparability: a National Curriculum and assessment system; the use of examinations as a means of evaluating the efficacy of the system as a whole and of individual schools and colleges; a belief that fewer examining boards would facilitate comparability; a loosely coordinated system gradually giving way to one of regulation underpinned by legislation. Although for most of the 20th century the emphasis was on reliable and comparable school-based examinations, as the century drew to a close, parity and comparability between academic and vocational examinations became an urgent issue, central to the raising of standards of learning and attainment and the development of skills appropriate to the 21st century. The modernisation of the examining system to meet these challenges and make use of new technologies is underway. All the indications are that as new approaches to assessment of the knowledge, skills and qualities required for the future are developed, comparability will continue to be a key and fundamental requirement of the English examination system.

Endnotes

1   Grace of 19 November 1857, in Graces Book 1857–1887, Cambridge Assessment Archive, EX/UC.

2   Letter to *The Times* by an unnamed headmaster, annotated by G.F. Browne as May 1872, in Graces Book 1857–1887, Cambridge Assessment Archive, EX/UC 1.

3   Manuscript letter to *The Times* by G.F. Browne (Secretary of the University of Cambridge Local Examinations Syndicate) (undated, but around 1872) which was not sent, 'correspondence having ceased', in Graces Book 1857–1887, Cambridge Assessment Archive, EX/UC 1.

4   Manuscript quote from a correspondent to the University of Cambridge Local Examinations Syndicate, December 1893, in Notes on Examination Papers, p. 5, Cambridge Assessment Archive, PP/JNK 2/1.

5   Letter from 'Brenda' to the editor of the *Journal of Education*, 1 September 1893, in Newspaper Cuttings file, Cambridge Assessment Archive, PP/JNK 2/2.

6   Letter from J. Chaplin, BA, dated 4 September 1893 to the editor of the *Journal of Education*, in Newspaper Cuttings file, Cambridge Assessment Archive, PP/JNK 2/2.

7   Article entitled 'The Sins of the Secondary Schoolmaster – II' in the *Pall Mall Gazette*, 8 December 1894, in Newspaper Cuttings file, Cambridge Assessment Archive, PP/JNK 2/2.

8   Minutes of meeting of University of Cambridge Local Examinations Syndicate's General Purposes Committee, 15 March 1918, in Assistant Secretary's Minutes Book, Cambridge Assessment Archive, C/CB 1/2.

9   Minutes of meeting of University of Cambridge Local Examinations Syndicate's Joint Committee for Examinations, 28 October 1918, Cambridge Assessment Archive, C/JCE 2/1.

10 *School Examinations*, article by Mr A.L. Kneed, Headmaster, Liverpool Collegiate School, *Liverpool Echo*, 17 January 1952, JMB Cuttings Scrapbook, AQA Archive, Manchester.

11 Letter from Mr E.R. Wood, High School for Boys, Hereford to the *Times Educational Supplement*, 30 November 1951, JMB Cuttings Scrapbook, AQA Archive, Manchester.

12 Ninety-third Annual Report to the University (1951), University of Cambridge Local Examinations Syndicate, Cambridge Assessment Archive.

13 One hundred and thirteenth Annual Report to the University (1971), University of Cambridge Local Examinations Syndicate, Cambridge Assessment Archive.

14 Comparison of the Standards of Different Examining Boards, Preliminary Report on the 1953 GCE Chemistry study, JMB, Cambridge Assessment Archive, PP/TSW 3/6.

15 Minutes of a meeting held in Bristol, March 17th and 18th 1952. Unpublished minutes, in *Secretaries of examining boards 1948–1960*. Cambridge Assessment Archive: PP/TSW 3/5.

16 Comparisons of the Standards of Different Examining Boards, Preliminary Report on the 1953 GCE chemistry study, JMB, Cambridge Assessment Archive, PP/TSW 3/6.

17 One hundred and thirteenth Annual Report to the University (1971), University of Cambridge Local Examinations Syndicate, Cambridge Assessment Archive.

18 Fifty-third Annual Report to the Universities constituting the Joint Matriculation Board (1956), being the report for the year ended 30 September 1956, published by the JMB, AQA Archive, Manchester.

19 Fifty-seventh Annual Report to the Universities constituting the Joint Matriculation Board (1960), being the report for the year ended 30 September 1960, published by the JMB, AQA Archive, Manchester.

20 One hundred and eighteenth Annual Report to the University (1976), University of Cambridge Local Examinations Syndicate, Cambridge Assessment Archive.

21 One hundred and nineteenth Annual Report to the University (1977), University of Cambridge Local Examinations Syndicate, Cambridge Assessment Archive.

22 One hundred and nineteenth Annual Report to the University (1977), University of Cambridge Local Examinations Syndicate, Cambridge Assessment Archive.

23 Annual Report of the Schools Examination Syndicate for the year ending 30 September 1991 (1991), Cambridge University Reporter, Annual Reports – Lent Term 1992, Special No. 15.

24 'Making the Grade', *Dispatches*, Channel 4, 11 October 1995.

25 Sir Geoffrey Holland Permanent Secretary at the Department for Education and Employment from January 1993 to January 1994 quoted in the *Times Educational Supplement*, 17 March 1995.

26 Blackstone announces new structure of awarding bodies, press release 150/97, 19 June 1997, Department for Education and Employment.

References

Audit Commission/Office for Standards in Education. (1993). *Unfinished business: Full-time educational courses for 16–19 year olds*. London: Her Majesty's Stationery Office.

Backhouse, J.K. (1978). *Comparability of grading standards in science subjects at GCE A level*. Schools Council Examinations Bulletin 39. London: Evans/Methuen.

Bardell, G.S., Forrest, G.M., & Shoesmith, D.J. (1978). *Comparability in GCE: A review of the boards' studies, 1964–1977*. Manchester: Joint Matriculation Board on behalf of the GCE Examining Boards.

Beaumont, G. (1996). *Review of 100 NVQs and SVQs: A report submitted to the Department for Education and Employment*. London: National Council for Vocational Qualifications.

Board of Education. (1943). *Curriculum and examinations in secondary schools (Norwood Report)*. London: His Majesty's Stationery Office.

Broadfoot, P. (1979). *Assessment, schools and society*. London: Methuen.

Christie, T., & Forrest, G.M. (1980). *Standards at GCE A-level: 1963 and 1973*. Schools Council Research Studies. London: Macmillan Education.

Christie, T., & Forrest, G.M. (1981). *Defining public examination standards*. Schools Council Research Studies. London: Macmillan Education.

Cresswell, M. (Ed.). (2000). *Research studies in public examining*. Guildford: Associated Examining Board.

Crofts, J.M., & Caradog Jones, D. (1928). *Secondary school examination statistics.* London: Longmans, Green & Co.

Dearing, R. (1996). *Review of qualifications for 16–19 year olds.* London: School Curriculum and Assessment Authority.

Department for Education and Employment. (1997). *Guaranteeing standards. Consultation paper on the structure of awarding bodies.* London: Department for Education and Employment.

Department of Education and Science. (1978). *School Examinations. Report of the steering committee established to consider proposals for replacing the General Certificate of Education Ordinary-level and Certificate of Secondary Education examinations by a common system of examining (Waddell Report).* London: Her Majesty's Stationery Office.

Department of Education and Science. (1987). *Improving the basis for awarding GCSE grades.* Paper presented at the 1st Annual Conference of the Joint Council for the GCSE. London: Department of Education and Science.

Department of Education and Science/Department of Employment/Welsh Office. (1991). *Education and training for the 21st Century.* London: Her Majesty's Stationery Office

Department of Education and Science/Welsh Office. (1988a). *National curriculum task group on assessment and testing: A report.* London: Department of Education and Science and the Welsh Office.

Department of Education and Science/Welsh Office. (1988b). *Advancing A levels. Report of a committee appointed by the Secretary of State for Education and Science and the Secretary for Wales (Higginson Report).* London: Her Majesty's Stationery Office.

Edgeworth, F.Y. (1888). The statistics of examinations. *Journal of the Royal Statistical Society, 1.1,* quoted in Hartog, Rhodes & Burt (1936).

Elwood, J., & Comber, C. (1996). *Gender differences in examinations at 18+.* London: University of London Institute of Education.

Forrest, G.M., & Shoesmith, D.J. (1985). *A second review of GCE comparability studies.* Manchester: Joint Matriculation Board on behalf of the GCE Examining Boards.

Forrest, G.M., & Vickerman, C. (1982). *Standards in GCE: Subject pairs comparisons, 1972–1980.* Occasional Publication 39. Manchester: Joint Matriculation Board.

Gillan, D. (2003). The northern CSE boards. In Assessment and Qualifications Alliance, *Setting the standard: A century of public examining by AQA and its parent boards* (pp. 95-112). Manchester: Assessment and Qualifications Alliance.

Gipps, C., & Murphy, P. (1994). *A fair test? Assessment, achievement and equity.* Buckingham: Open University Press.

Good, F.J., & Cresswell, M.J. (1988). *Grading the GCSE.* London: Secondary Examinations Council.

Gosden, P. (1983). *The education system since 1944.* Oxford: Martin Robertson.

Hartog, P., Rhodes, E.C., & Burt, C. (1936). *The marks of examiners.* London: Macmillan & Co.

House of Commons, Education and Skills Committee. (2003). *A level standards.* Third report of session 2002–03. HC 153. London: The Stationery Office Limited.

House of Commons, Expenditure Committee. (1977). *Session 1976–1977: Tenth report: Attainments of the school leaver.* London: Her Majesty's Stationery Office.

Joseph, K. (1984). Speech by Sir Keith Joseph, Secretary of State for Education and Science, at the North of England Conference, Sheffield, Friday 6 January, 1984. *SEC annual report 1983–1984.* London: Secondary Examinations Council.

Massey, A.J. (1994). Standards are slippery! *British Journal of Curriculum and Assessment,* 5(1), 37–8.

Matthews, J.C. (1985). *Examinations: A commentary.* London: George Allen & Unwin.

Ministry of Education. (1960). *Secondary school examinations other than the GCE. Report of a committee appointed by the SSEC in July 1958 (Beloe Report).* London: Her Majesty's Stationery Office.

Montgomery, R.J. (1965). *Examinations: An account of their evolution as administrative devices in England.* London: Longmans, Green & Co Ltd.

Newbould, C.A. (1994). *Year on year standards.* Unpublished report, Standing Research Advisory Committee of the GCE Boards.

Northern Examinations and Assessment Board. (1996). *Standards in public examinations, 1975 to 1995: A review of the literature.* Conducted for the School Curriculum and Assessment Authority and the Office for Standards in Education by the Northern Examinations and Assessment Board on behalf of the GCSE and GCE boards. London: School Curriculum and Assessment Authority.

Nuttall, D.L. (1973). *Mode comparability: Comparability of standards as between modes of examining.* Sheffield: The West Yorkshire and Lindsey Regional Examining Board.

Nuttall, D.L. (1993). Presentation at Centre for Policy Studies Conference, 21 September 1993. In R. Murphy & P. Broadfoot (Eds.), (1995), *Effective assessment and the improvement of education: A tribute to Desmond Nuttall* (pp. 236-241). London: Falmer Press.

Office for Standards in Education. (1996a). *A review of vocational GCSE courses.* London: Office for Standards in Education.

Office for Standards in Education. (1996b). *GCE Advanced Supplementary and Advanced level examinations 1996.* London: Office for Standards in Education.

Petch, J.A. (1953). *Fifty years of examining.* London: Harrap.

Roach, J. (1971). *Public examinations in England 1850–1900.* Cambridge: Cambridge University Press.

School Curriculum and Assessment Authority/Office for Standards in Education. (1996). *Standards in public examinations 1975 to 1995: A report on English, mathematics and chemistry examinations over time.* London: School Curriculum and Assessment Authority.

Schools Council. (1971). *A common system of examining at 16+.* Schools Council Examinations Bulletin 23. London: Evans/Methuen.

Secondary School Examinations Council. (1932). *The School Certificate examination. Report of the panel of investigators, appointed by the Secondary School Examinations Council to enquire into the eight approved certificate examinations held in the summer of 1931.* London: His Majesty's Stationery Office.

Secondary School Examinations Council. (1939). *The report of the 1937 H.S.C. investigation. Report on the Northern Universities Joint Matriculation Board.* London: His Majesty's Stationery Office.

Skurnik, L.S. (1974). *Monitoring grade standards in English.* Schools Council Working Paper 49. London: Her Majesty's Stationery Office.

Tattersall, K. (1983). *Differentiated examinations: A strategy for assessment at 16+?* Schools Council Examinations Bulletin 42. London: Methuen Educational.

Whittaker, R.J., & Forrest, G.M. (1983). *Problems of the GCE Advanced level grading scheme.* Manchester: Joint Matriculation Board.

Willmott, A.S. (1977). *CSE and GCE grading standards: The 1973 comparability study.* Schools Council Research Study. London: Macmillan Education.

Willmott, A.S., & Nuttall, D.L. (1975). *The reliability of examinations at 16+.* Schools Council Publications. Basingstoke: Macmillan Education.

Appendix 1 Examining bodies offering public examinations for schools in England[1]

University and GCE Boards 1800s to 1990s

UODLE	University of Oxford Delegacy of Local Examinations	1857–1995	
UCLES	University of Cambridge Local Examinations Syndicate	1858–1995	
OCSEB	Oxford and Cambridge Schools Examination Board	1873–1995	
UBSEC	University of Bristol School Examinations Council	1911–1957	
SUJB	Southern Universities Joint Board (for School Examinations)	1954–1990	successor to UBSEC; merged with UCLES 1990
OCEAC	Oxford and Cambridge Examinations and Assessment Council	1995–1998	UODLE+UCLES+OCSEB
UDMSEB	University of Durham Matriculation and School Examination Board	1858–1964	closed 1964
ULEB	University of London Extension Board	1902–1930	
ULMSEC	University of London Matriculation and School Examinations Council	1930–1951	Different names used by London board[2]
UE&SEC and SED	University of London University Entrance and School Examinations Council and School Examinations Department	1951–1984	
ULSEB	University of London School Examinations Board	1984–1991	
ULEAC	University of London Examinations and Assessment Council	1991–1996	ULSEB+LEAG
UB	University of Birmingham	1900(?)–1916	Joined JMB
JMB	(Northern Universities) Joint Matriculation Board	1903–1992	
NEAB	Northern Examinations and Assessment Board	1992–2000	JMB+NEA
AEB	Associated Examining Board	1953–1994	
AEB/SEG	Associated Examining Board/Southern Examining Group	1994–2000	AEB+SEG

CSE Boards 1960s to 1990s

EMREB	East Midland Regional Examinations Board	1963–1993	
TWMEB	The West Midlands Examination Board	(?)–1998	
EAEB	East Anglian Examination Board	1962–1990	
MREB	Metropolitan Regional Examinations Board	1962–1979(?)	merged into LREB 1979 (?)
MREB	Middlesex Regional Examining Board	1962–1979(?)	
LREB	London Regional Examining Board	1979(?)–1990	MREB+MREB
ALSEB	Associated Lancashire Schools Examining Board	1964–1992	
NREB	North Regional Examinations Board	1964–1992	
NWREB	North West Regional Examinations Board	1964–1992	
TWYLREB	The West Yorkshire and Lindsey Regional Examining Board	1964–1982	merged into YHREB 1982
YREB	Yorkshire Regional Examinations Board	1964–1982	
YHREB	Yorkshire and Humberside Regional Examinations Board	1982–1992	TWYLREB+YREB
SEREB	South East Regional Examinations Board	1965–1985	
SREB	Southern Regional Examinations Board	1965–1985	merged into OSEB 1985
SWEB	South Western Examinations Board	1965–1987	
OSEB	Oxford Schools Examinations Board	1986–1995	UODLE+SREB

GCSE Groups 1980s to 1990s

MEG	Midland Examining Group	1985–1998	UCLES+OCSEB+SUJB+TWMEB+EMREB
LEAG	London and East Anglian Group	1987–1991	ULSEB+EAEB+LREB (aka University of London School Examinations Council)
ULEAC	University of London Examinations and Assessment Council	1991–1996	ULSEB+LEAG
SEG	Southern Examining Group	1987–1994	AEB+SEREB+SWEB+OSEB
AEB/SEG	Associated Examining Board/Southern Examining Group	1994–2000	AEB+SEG
NEA	Northern Examining Association	1985–1992	JMB+ALSEB+NREB+NWREB+YHREB
NEAB	Northern Examinations and Assessment Board	1992–2000	JMB+NEA

Unitary Awarding Bodies 1990s onwards

OCR	Oxford Cambridge and RSA (Examination Board)	1998	OCEAC+MEG+Royal Society of Arts Examinations Board *
Edexcel	Edexcel	1996	ULEAC+Busines and Technology Education Council *
AQA	Assessment and Qualifications Alliance	2000	AEB/SEB+NEAB with City and Guilds of London Institute *

* Unitary awarding bodies had to offer vocational provision as well as school examinations

Blue – OCR predecessor bodies
Red – Edexcel predecessor bodies
Green – AQA predecessor bodies

(?) – denotes uncertainty. Setting up, closing down and merging examining boards was not a clear cut process. Different sources give different dates which may denote first board meeting, gaining official recognition, first examinations, change of name, agreement to merge or close, last examinations, etc. At different times a body might use one name for trading and another for legal purposes, and might trade in its own right and as part of a group. Changes of name and changes of status are not necessarily related. Confederations may represent mergers or agreements to work together with members maintaining legal independence. Boards appear twice if they offered both GCSE and GCE. By 2000 the complex history of school examining boards in England had resulted in three unitary awarding boards which also made vocational provision.

Endnotes

1 This appendix was prepared by Helen Patrick.
2 The University of London Extension Board (1902) marked the start of a closer relationship with schools than had previously been the case for the London Matriculation examinations which had been held since 1836.

Appendix 2 Geographical distribution of the CSE boards

Reproduced from AQA's *Setting the Standard*, 2003 (AQA material is reproduced by permission of the Assessment and Qualifications Alliance.)

Appendix 3 Advisory and regulatory bodies in England

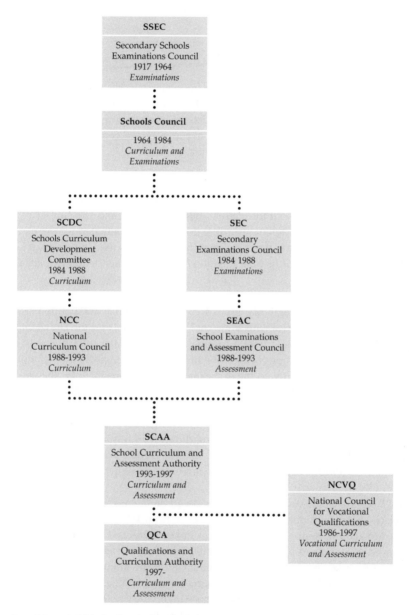

Reproduced from AQA's *Setting the Standard*, 2003 (AQA material is reproduced by permission of the Assessment and Qualifications Alliance.)

COMMENTARY ON CHAPTER 2

Mike Kingdon

The chapter maps the structural changes in the systems of UK public qualifications since the creation of the first public examination – the University of London Matriculation Examination – in 1838. It is also the story of how, over a century, the succession of regulatory bodies has sought to promote and control the delivery of, first, school examinations and then all qualifications.

The chapter identifies how the traditional British concern about the fairness of examinations came to be expressed through the discussion of different forms of comparability. Concerns about the comparability of the 16+ and 18+ subject examinations offered by different awarding bodies have dominated for over a century, but it has not always been so. From the early 1840s the University of London monitored the pass rates for its Matriculation examination, so the initial focus was on comparability over time[1].

The seeds of today's comparability issues were sown in 1857 when London issued new Matriculation syllabuses, with some choices of subjects, and the University of Oxford introduced its Local (school) Examinations. A year later the University of Cambridge Local Examinations began. The first systematic investigation of any aspect of comparability followed the first examination in July 1859[2] for the new London Matriculation syllabuses. For the first time ever, the pass rate for the new examination was lower than previous years. The issue was referred to the University's Committee on Examinations for investigation and systems were put in place to monitor the characteristics of the candidature in future examinations. As the author of the chapter has illustrated, issues about the comparability of the London, Oxford and Cambridge examinations were not long in following.

In the 19th century pass/fail decisions were based on the aggregated raw marks for all subjects that a candidate had taken. However, from 1857 candidates were also expected to achieve minimum performances in key subjects. One consequence was that candidates who had passed overall could be 'referred' – invited to retake – one or more of their key subjects. The later School Certificate model, which required success in prescribed combinations of subjects for an overall award, drew attention to inter-subject comparabilities – especially those involving English Language, where standards were generally perceived to be poor (see Bruce's first law of examining in Bruce, 1969, pp. 3–4). Today, students' overall success in the GCSE and A/AS level subject examinations is once again recognised by the aggregation of results. Grade-based points are used as the basis of school performance tables and university selection systems. Therefore, to paraphrase Robert Wood (1976), 'your French has to

92

equal my chemistry,' and inter-subject comparability is, for many, more important than the inter-awarding body variety.

The author is correct when she identifies the search for comparability – specifically inter-awarding body comparability – as a product of the current UK system and its history. Indeed, all national systems of qualifications face issues of comparability, although the mix of types differs. In the UK case, the reverse is also true. The search for comparability has generated many of our contemporary understandings of the current system, its implementation and structure. The downside of over-emphasising comparability, at the expense of the more general concept of fairness, has been that issues such as validity and special needs have not always received due attention.

In stressing events and structures the chapter can be criticised for obscuring the human achievements that underpin them. It is also the story of how ever-wider access to recognised qualifications has been granted to generations of learners. Further, no history of the structure and regulation of UK qualifications can be complete without reference to the generations of examiners, markers, administrators and later researchers who, through their day-to-day work, created and applied the principles of modern qualifications delivery. Their attempts to make fair and equitable (comparable) decisions as new situations arose generated the practical case law and principles on which our current regulatory codes are based.

My concern is not with the content of the chapter but with what might be inferred from it. Readers may assume that ever-tighter regulation will have produced increasing levels of comparability but this argument has yet to be demonstrated. Similarly, to resolve the issue of comparability by amalgamating all of the awarding bodies into one, would be to destroy other positive features of the current system such as teacher choice and the efficiencies that follow from today's fierce competition between the unitary awarding bodies.

Readers may also assume from the chapter that the three universities were in conflict over standards and methods of examining. Instead the University of London Senate Minutes record the cooperation between the three universities through their membership of the Joint Board for the Promotion of University Teaching[3]. Premises were shared, examination timetables aligned and responses to Ministers coordinated. This cooperation continued throughout the 19th and 20th centuries via meetings of the Secretaries of the School Examination Boards, and constituted a forum for self-regulation.

Finally, what the chapter has not considered is how Cambridge University and London University (later Edexcel) came to predominate among the English school examination awarding bodies in the provision of examination services to countries, institutions and individual students in the Commonwealth and beyond. The school examinations and other qualification systems of almost all Commonwealth countries began when they 'budded' from the English system at some point in the 19th century. In doing so they imported the contemporary comparability issues, ideas about fairness and qualifications management systems that underpinned their selected model. How these issues evolved, as countries developed their qualification systems to meet local needs, is probably a book in itself.

Cambridge and Edexcel continue to provide examination services to the Commonwealth and beyond, especially to smaller countries that do not have sufficient resources to fulfil all assessment functions themselves. These examinations also provide alternatives and supplements to national systems of qualifications for individual students throughout the world.

Endnotes

1 See statistical appendices at the back of the bound copies of the University of London Senate Minutes from 1842 onwards.

2 University of London, Senate Minutes for 1860, *Report of Examiners on the July 1959 Matriculation Examination* – referred to Committee on Examinations for investigation, statistical tables pages 56–58.

3 University of London, Senate Minutes for 1876, *Receipt of letter from the London Society for the Promotion of University Teaching inviting the University to appoint representative to a Joint Board of the Universities of Cambridge, Oxford and London*, Minute 121, page 50, representatives appointed, Minute 122. The Minutes of the Board were received and discussed at meetings of the Senate throughout the 19th century.

References

Bruce, G. (1969). *Secondary school examinations: Facts and commentary*. London: Pergamon Press.

Wood, R. (1976, July 30). Your chemistry equals my French. *The Times Educational Supplement*.

RESPONSE TO COMMENTARY ON CHAPTER 2

Kathleen Tattersall

I am grateful to Mike Kingdon for highlighting events in the story of comparability to which the chapter did not make reference. In particular, his reminder that, over the years, thousands of individuals have been involved in the administration, setting and marking of examinations is welcome. It is unfortunate if the text did not make clear that improvements in the design and comparability of assessments owed everything to individual Secretaries to examining boards, chief examiners and researchers, and I am glad to have the chance to rectify this lack of clarity. However, a single chapter cannot do justice to the history of a topic which lies at the heart of assessment and so, in effect, is the history of the examination system itself; the story demands a book in its own right.

Kingdon is also correct in pointing to the influence of the English examination system on students in the Commonwealth and beyond. However, this dimension falls outside the scope of a chapter whose focus is on the history of comparability in the English system. For the same reason the systems of other countries of the United Kingdom received little mention.

Like Kingdon I believe that factors other than comparability are of importance: fairness, validity, equity and, I would add, the involvement of teachers. As someone who started her career in a CSE board I believe strongly that teachers should play a key role not only as examiners and moderators but as assessors of their own students – a huge challenge to comparability but one worth the effort if assessment is to be fit for purpose and part of the teaching/learning dynamic. A single examining board in the interests of comparability, as argued by some, would do nothing to promote those other key values of the examining system.

The chapter covers the period of ever-increasing regulation in the interests of comparability. However, I would be alarmed if the chapter were to be read as support for a further tightening of the regulation noose. Indeed, I would hope that the juxtaposition of tighter regulation and the 2002 crisis of public confidence in A levels would raise questions about the role and purpose of regulation. From the standpoint of the author – a player in the events of 2002 – it seemed that the regulator was, at least in the first instance, unable to safeguard the system from its critics. What was at stake was public confidence in the first awards of the new A level system. An enquiry by the regulator into the grading of one of the three unitary bodies failed to satisfy the critics. A more wide-ranging enquiry was set up, not under the auspices of the regulator but chaired by an independent senior figure, Sir

Mike Tomlinson, recently retired Head of the Office for Standards in Education (Ofsted). That enquiry, with which both QCA and the awarding bodies cooperated, resulted in a more open and transparent awarding process

Sadly, a debate about regulation, like other points which Kingdon makes, falls outside the remit of this chapter – but I am glad to have the excuse to express a personal view on the issue.

3

AWARDING EXAMINATION GRADES: CURRENT PROCESSES AND THEIR EVOLUTION

Colin Robinson

Abstract

The aim of this chapter is to describe the process by which each awarding body tries to ensure that the grading of candidates is comparable, no matter when, by whom, or on what aspects of the subject the candidate is assessed. These processes have developed over the years, mainly as a result of the experiences of the awarding bodies themselves, but also because of the impact of regulation, which has grown over time. The chapter describes this key activity of the awarding bodies, looking at the personnel involved, the information that is available to them and the decisions they have to make in order to ensure that the results maintain the multifaceted comparability requirements laid upon the awarding bodies. Changes that have been made over the years and the reasons for them are also outlined. The April 2007 edition of the code of practice lays out the comparability requirements quite clearly:

> The awarding body's governing council is responsible for setting in place appropriate procedures to ensure that standards are maintained in each subject examined from year to year (including ensuring that standards between GCE and GCE in applied subjects, as well as between GCSE and GCSE in vocational subjects, are aligned), across different [syllabuses] within a qualification and with other awarding bodies.
>
> QCA (2007)

1 Awarding grades

Necessary conditions for comparability involve choosing appropriate subject matter to be embodied in the syllabus, selecting personnel with appropriate background knowledge and experience, developing question papers that give candidates the opportunity to demonstrate their knowledge, preparing marking schemes that give fair rewards and appointing markers who are reliable. But accurate marking is only part of the process. No matter how well the markers follow the mark scheme, the marks this session will have been obtained in different ways from last session and there remains the issue of how to relate the marks to the grades.

The purpose of grading is to group candidates' results in ways that allow the user to compare performances. It is not essential to have a two-stage process: grades can be awarded directly without the intervention of marks. In higher education, for example, it is common for marks to be awarded that can be directly related to grades, on the basis of judgements of quality. For example, a mark of 70 is a first-class mark. However, when examinations are marked and the marks are then converted into a limited number of grades, it is necessary to consider the relationship between the marks and the grades. Public examinations have very large numbers of students, so marking has to be carried out by large teams of markers. Research has shown that it is easier to train people to mark reliably to a mark scheme than to grade holistically (Black, 1962). In higher education, there are fewer students and often only one or two markers for a class, so standardisation is not as much of a problem.

Marks in GCSEs and A levels are dependent upon the specific questions asked and the marking scheme attached to the question paper. Because the question papers are different on every occasion, the marks cannot retain a common standard. The two-stage process allows real differences between question papers to be taken into account so that the grades are comparable.

The function of the marking process, including standardisation, reviewing and re-marking, is to judge the candidate's work against the marking scheme. Having done that, the assumption is that all candidates on the same mark in a component are equivalent in terms of their attainment (where a component may be one of a series of question papers or coursework that comprise the entire examination assessment). Throughout the marking process, the focus is on ensuring that the rank order of the candidates is as accurate as possible. Given this, the task of 'awarders' (members of the awarding committee) is to determine 'grade boundary' marks (the cut-off points) that indicate the same standards of achievement this year as they did last year. Grade boundary marks are identified separately for each component of an examination. The award of subject grades, for the examination as a whole, requires the identification of subject grade boundaries; although these are aggregated differently if the syllabus is modular, as explained below. Students' subject grades derive from their total subject mark, the aggregation of their component marks, rather than being dependent upon a specific profile of component grades.

2 The awarding committee

With the exception of the reviser and the scrutineer, the people involved in the meeting are those who were responsible for designing the question papers and supervising the marking: the Chair of Examiners is responsible for all syllabuses within a subject area and chairs all the awarding meetings, the Chief Examiner has overall responsibility for the particular syllabus and the Principal Examiners lead on individual components. They are supported by one or more awarding body officers who will be responsible for making sure the procedures are followed and for advising on the statistics. If a single awarding committee cannot deal with all syllabuses in the subject, there will be overlapping membership with other awarding committees, 'to consider the consistency of the recommendations in the light of standards applied in other [syllabuses]' (QCA, 2007, p. 35). Some of the committees, dealing with a large number of syllabuses, can be very big, with as many as twenty awarders, not counting awarding body officers and other participants. The greater the number of specifications in a subject, the bigger the awarding meeting, but the average number of awarders across all subjects at all levels in the major awarding bodies is 8–10 (Baird & Dhillon, 2005).

Awarding meetings occupy most of the time between the end of the marking process and the publication of results, and consume a vast amount of resources. Extrapolating from figures in one awarding body (the Assessment and Qualifications Alliance), Baird & Dhillon (2005) estimated that across the country senior examiners spend a total of more than 3,400 person days each year in awarding meetings at a cost of more than £1.5 million in examiner time alone. In addition to the awarders themselves, each meeting is attended by one or more members of staff from the awarding body and will sometimes include observers from QCA, or from Ofsted, representatives from subject or teaching associations and even members of the press. The judgements are all made by the awarders who will be senior examiners with many years' experience. They are provided with information that helps them to ensure that the awards remain in line with those in other syllabuses and with other awarding bodies. Their job is to weigh all the evidence about the performance of candidates at each judgemental grade and come to a consensus as to the mark on the year's paper that represents the lowest level of achievement worthy of the award of that grade. The outcomes are then recommended to the Accountable Officer of the awarding body, who makes the final decision.

The evidence presented to the awarders is substantial as the following list of minimum requirements from the code of practice (QCA, 2007) indicates:

Qualitative

i. copies of question papers/tasks and final mark schemes

ii. reports from the principal examiner(s)/principal moderator(s) on how the question paper functioned

iii. archive scripts and examples of internally assessed work (including, in appropriate subject areas, photographic or videotaped evidence) at the relevant grade boundaries, together with relevant question papers and mark schemes

iv. samples of current candidates' work (marked scripts and/or internally assessed material) distributed evenly across key boundary ranges for each component, with enough representing each mark to provide a sound basis for judgement so far as the size of entry and nature of work permit. The material should be selected from a sufficient range of centres where work has been marked/moderated by examiners/moderators whose work is known to be reliable

v. any published performance descriptions, grade descriptions and exemplar material, where available

vi. any other supporting material (such as marking guides for components where the evidence is of an ephemeral nature)

Quantitative

vii. technical information – including mark distributions relating to the question papers/tasks and individual questions for the current and previous series, where available

viii. information on candidates' performance in at least two previous equivalent series, where available

ix. details of significant changes in entry patterns and choices of options

x. information on centres' estimated grades for all candidates including:

 – qualification-level estimates for linear (including linear unitised) [syllabuses]

 – unit-level estimates for externally assessed units in all other unitised [syllabuses]

xi. information about the relationship between component/unit-level data and whole-subject performance, where available

Regulatory authority reports

xii. relevant evidence from the regulatory authorities' monitoring and comparability reports.

How do they deal with all this information? In the following section, references to the above extract from the code of practice are shown in italics.

Of course, all examiners will have received *copies of question papers/tasks and final mark schemes* as part of their normal marking duties but the main purpose of them at the award is to help to decide if the paper is more or less difficult compared with previous ones. This can only be done by considering both the questions and the credit given. The awarders will need to take into account *reports from the principal examiners… on how the question paper functioned*. The Chief Examiner and Principal Examiners will have marked candidates' work directly themselves and second-marked samples of marking from those examiners they supervise. This is an essential part of the exercise, giving the senior examiners first-hand experience of the question paper in action.

Before the meeting can consider the grade boundaries for the current series of examinations, the awarders must familiarise themselves with the quality of work that characterises the grade they are looking at. This they will do by checking the standards upon which the grades were awarded previously, by looking at *archive scripts… at the relevant grade boundaries, together with relevant question papers and mark schemes*, typically from the previous year's examination. This evidence will be considered alongside the statistical information such as *mark distributions relating to the question papers and individual questions for the current and previous series*. From these, the awarders will be able to see how the component performed: what range of marks was obtained, how the average mark and spread of marks compared with last year, whether the mark distribution was skewed (with lots of candidates scoring either high or low marks and fewer candidates scoring marks in the middle of the range). The aim is to refresh their understanding of the quality of work that typified the performance of candidates at the lowest level deemed to be worthy of the grade, bearing in mind the questions asked and what the examiners were crediting in the mark scheme. For A level syllabuses, they will also have copies of performance descriptions and exemplification of the standard of work at each of the boundaries scrutinised by awarders, prepared by QCA in the light of the Tomlinson Report (Tomlinson, 2002). For GCSE, they will have the 'mid-range' grade descriptions contained in the syllabus and/or the relevant GCSE subject criteria.

Between examination sessions, a number of investigations take place to identify possible issues. Examination teams within an awarding body may ask for research to be carried out to check on apparent problems of comparability or on the likely effects of any planned changes in the nature of the assessments. Awarding bodies conduct their own internal enquiries on examinations that appear to be out of line with performances in other awarding bodies; the regulatory bodies report on scrutiny exercises that have been carried out during the year, and the awarding bodies jointly may have undertaken comparability studies. Some analyses are conducted routinely, such as OCR's 'unit pairs' analyses, in which the performances of the same candidates are compared across different question papers. The results of all these exercises will be collated and fed into the awarding meeting's deliberations by the awarding body officer. In some cases there may be a specific requirement to ease or tighten standards in a syllabus, in order to bring the results into line with national standards.

Significant changes in entry patterns and choices of options can have a considerable effect on the proportions of candidates getting each grade without reflecting any real change in the standard of the examination. If able candidates (that is, those with higher prior achievements) move to another syllabus in large numbers, leaving the syllabus dominated by lower-attaining candidates, it is to be expected that smaller numbers of candidates will achieve higher grades. There is now a considerable amount of data which can be drawn upon – from earlier national assessments and also from other subjects in the same examination series. The awarding bodies use this information to provide the awarding committee with comparisons of *candidates' performance in at least two previous examination series.*

At A level, one way of doing this is by grouping candidates according to their overall performance across GCSE examinations and then looking at how those groups perform in a particular A level subject across the country as a whole. There is usually a strong correlation between these performances and it is possible, therefore, to use the relationship to predict the expected results of candidates for whom the awarding body has similar prior achievement data. This information can be useful both before and after the examinations. As Eason writes,

> Not only can these methods be used to predict examination results, they can be used *post hoc* to identify whether there are inconsistencies between a particular awarding body's outcomes and the national pattern for a given subject.

> Eason (2004)

In addition the awarding bodies collect information about *centres' estimated grades for all candidates*. These are a useful flag that can alert the awarding body to possible discrepancies in the awards, leading to a review of grade boundaries.

A large proportion of the time at the meeting will be spent looking at the *samples of current candidates' work (marked scripts or internally assessed material)*. On the basis of their experience of previous award decisions and their marking of the current year's scripts, the Principal Examiner and the awarding body officer will have agreed the range of marks within which they expect each judgemental boundary to lie – usually a spread of about six or seven marks – and will have arranged for sufficient scripts (booklets of candidates' work in the examination) to be available in the meeting room so that each awarder will be able to scrutinise scripts at each of the marks.

3   The conduct of the awarding meeting

The format of the meeting follows broadly the same pattern across the awarding bodies (where minor variations exist, this chapter discusses the procedures used by AQA). Figure 1 presents an overview of the process. First, the Chair of Examiners opens the meeting by outlining the task ahead for the committee. The awarding body officer will then present the statistics and point out any implications that the committee needs to consider. Reports from the Principal Examiners for each component are given next, indicating how the paper performed, what questions were found difficult or easy by the candidates, and any issues arising from the marking. Unless they have done so in advance of the meeting, members of the committee will refresh their understanding of the standards by reference to the grade descriptions, the archive scripts and exemplar material.

Armed with the information provided by the awarding body officers and the Principal Examiners, the awarders will then consider the quality of the work in this year's examination scripts. The time available is limited and it is certainly not possible (even if it were desirable) for the awarders to read through every response. The exercise is one of determining whether the script as a whole merits the award of the grade under consideration. Marks and any explanatory comments are shown on the scripts.

Their individual judgements on each script – worthy of the higher grade, not worthy, or unsure – are then tallied for each mark in the range, starting at the highest mark and working down until they come to the point where there is reasonable consensus that all scripts at or above that mark are worthy of the higher grade. This mark is referred to as the Upper Limiting Mark. The committee then works up from the lowest mark until they reach consensus on a mark that is the highest that is not worthy of the grade. The mark above this is referred to as the Lower Limiting Mark.

In the example shown in Figure 2, the awarders agreed that all the scripts they had considered at a mark of 64 were not worthy of the grade and although there were a couple of scripts at 65 that were of an acceptable standard, following discussion it was agreed that by and large scripts with this mark were also below the grade.

Figure 1 Overview of the process followed in an awarding meeting (from AQA, 2005a, p.7)

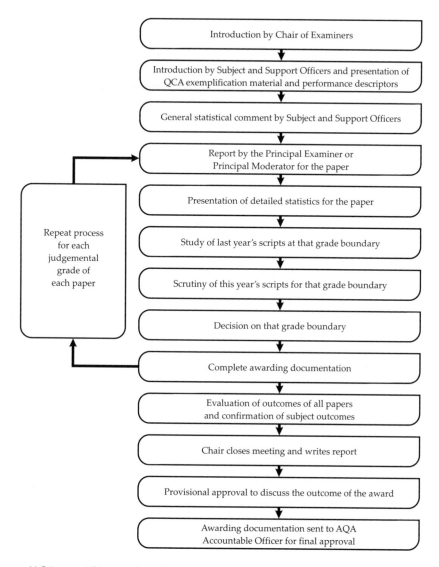

(AQA material is reproduced by permission of the Assessment and Qualifications Alliance)

Working from the top, only two awarders had managed to review scripts with a mark of 70, but they were convinced of their standing. There were a couple of scripts at 69 that were thought to be below standard and only one at 68. The awarders therefore came to the conclusion that the Upper Limiting Mark was 68 and the Lower Limiting Mark was 66.

Figure 2 Example of a tick chart (from AQA, 2005a, p.6)

Statistically Recommended Boundary = 67
Principal Examiner's Recommendation = 67–70

	Mark	Awarder 1	Awarder 2	Awarder 3	Awarder 4
Upper limiting mark: marks of 68 and above are definitely worth the grade	70	✓			✓✓
	69	✓	✗✓✓	✓✓✓	✗✓
	68	✓✓	✓✓	✓✓✓✗	✓✓
	67	✓✓✗✓	✗✓✓	✓✓	✓✗?
Lower limiting mark: marks of 65 and below are definitely not worth the grade	66	✓✓	✓?	✓✓✗	✗✗
	65	✓✗	✗✗	✗	✓✗
	64	✗✗	✗	✗	✗

✓   script 'worthy' of the grade in question

✗   script 'not worthy' of the grade in question

?   awarder unsure of whether the script is worthy of the grade in question

(AQA material is reproduced by permission of the Assessment and Qualifications Alliance)

Having established these limits, the awarders seek to agree a single mark that represents the boundary for the grade, using their collective professional judgement. They also consider statistics – the proportion of candidates that would get the grade if it was awarded on 66 or 67 marks – and they may also consider further scripts. If the marks on individual questions were recorded, the item-level statistics can provide additional pointers.

Only certain grade boundaries are determined through this judgemental process. Typically, these are the A/B, C/D and F/G boundaries (for GCSE), and the A/B and E/U boundaries (at A level).

4   Setting subject boundaries for linear syllabuses

Having set all of the component boundaries, the awarding committee will need to consider the appropriate grade boundaries for the subject as a whole. For linear syllabuses – those, as for most GCSEs, whose examinations are all taken at the end of a course of study – two indicators are calculated: one based upon marks (the addition method), the other on percentages of candidates (the percentile method). As the code of practice explains, the lower indicator is chosen.

The obvious way of doing this is to add together the grade boundary marks for each component: the addition method. So, for example, if the boundaries for the grade are at 37 on one component and 36 on another, the total would be 73 (if they are equally weighted). Yet this can lead to apparent anomalies. As is shown in Figure 3, the addition method – Indicator 1 – would lead to only 1.07% of the candidates being awarded grade A overall, which might seem a bit harsh (1.67% of students were awarded grade A on component 1, 6.39% were awarded grade A on component 2). At the other end of the range, it would lead to 88.89% of candidates being awarded grade F or better, which might, if anything, seem a bit generous (although 91.39% of students were awarded grade F or better on component 2, only 81.94% of students were awarded grade F or better on component 1). Clearly, different proportions of candidates might be thought to deserve the grades for different question papers because the awarders may consider performances on paper 2 to be better than those on paper 1, for example.

Having said that 1.67% deserve a grade A on paper 1 and 6.39% deserve a grade A on paper 2, why is the proportion getting the subject grade less than either of those, at 1.07%, using the addition method? The reason is that it is not *the same* candidates who were thought worthy of a grade A on each question paper. Candidates who scored over 37 on component 1 were likely to score less than 36 on component 2, so scored less than 73 overall. In the early 1990s, the method based on percentages was introduced to combat this effect because of the perceived unfairness to candidates.

Figure 3 Effects of the addition and percentile methods of boundary score aggregation (from AQA, 2005b)

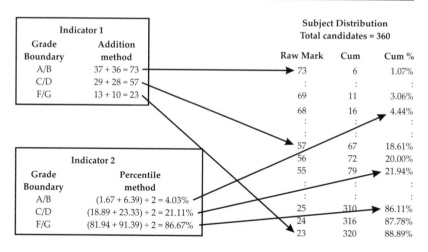

Example: Applying the indicators to two equally weighted components

Component 1					Component 2			
Total candidates = 360					Total candidates = 360			
Grade Boundary	Raw Mark	Cum no. Cands	Cum % Cands		Grade Boundary	Raw Mark	Cum no. Cands	Cum % Cands
A/B	37	6	1.67%		A/B	36	23	6.39%
C/D	29	68	18.89%		C/D	28	84	23.33%
F/G	13	295	81.94%		F/G	10	329	91.39%

Indicator 1			Subject Distribution		
Grade Boundary	Addition method		Total candidates = 360		
			Raw Mark	Cum	Cum %
A/B	37 + 36 = 73		73	6	1.07%
C/D	29 + 28 = 57		:	:	:
F/G	13 + 10 = 23		69	11	3.06%
			68	16	4.44%
			:	:	:
			:	:	:
			57	67	18.61%
Indicator 2			56	72	20.00%
Grade Boundary	Percentile method		55	79	21.94%
A/B	(1.67 + 6.39) ÷ 2 = 4.03%		:	:	:
C/D	(18.89 + 23.33) ÷ 2 = 21.11%		25	310	86.11%
F/G	(81.94 + 91.39) ÷ 2 = 86.67%		24	316	87.78%
			23	320	88.89%

In the percentile method (Indicator 2), the weighted average of percentages of candidates considered to be worthy of the grades is calculated. Going back to the previous example (see Figure 3), the average of 1.67% and 6.39% is 4.03%. There is no subject mark with exactly 4.03% of candidates attaining that mark, so the nearest percentage to 4.03% has to be found. That is 4.44%, on a mark of 68.

The code of practice (QCA, 2007) explains how the indicators are calculated and how to choose which one represents the subject boundary mark.

Indicator 1

  i. The boundary mark for each component is scaled as necessary to reflect the mark allocation for that component as detailed in the [syllabus].

  ii. The resulting scaled component boundary marks are added up and the result is rounded to the nearest whole number (0.5 rounded up).

Indicator 2

  iii. The percentage of candidates at and above the boundary mark on each component is determined.

  iv. A weighted mean of these percentages is calculated, using the weightings of the components as detailed in the [syllabus].

  v. The mark is identified on the distribution of total examination marks at which the cumulative percentage of candidates most closely corresponds to the weighted mean.

Conclusion

  vi. Whenever the two indicators do not coincide, the grade boundary should normally be set at the lower of the two indicator marks, unless, in the awarders' judgement, there is good reason, as a result of a review of the statistical and technical evidence, to choose a higher mark within the range spanned by the indicators.

Only judgementally determined boundaries lead to the calculation of Indicator 1 and Indicator 2. The remaining subject grade boundaries are determined arithmetically; by creating bands of equivalent width (as equivalent as possible) according to procedures specified in the code of practice (QCA, 2007).

5 Setting subject boundaries for modular syllabuses

The introduction of modular syllabuses has led to a completely new approach to the aggregation of component boundary marks. The rationale of modular syllabuses is that candidates are assessed after they have completed each module – more commonly referred to as a 'unit'. In the current GCE A level, there are typically six units to be taken over two years. Three of these (the AS units) are designed to be taken in the first year of the course and can lead to the Advanced Subsidiary award. These AS units also count towards the full A level, when combined with three further units (the A2 units), designed to be taken in the second year. Candidates taking the same unit on different occasions will not have been assessed on exactly the same materials and it would be impossible to determine subject grade boundaries (from component ones) in the same way as for linear syllabuses.

We need to be able to save the details of each candidate's attainment for use when all units have been completed and the overall subject grade needs to be calculated. We could, of course, just 'bank' the grades achieved by the candidate in each unit, and then aggregate unit grades, but that would suffer a number of problems – candidates who gained a very high mark within the grade would be indistinguishable from those who just scraped through and when we aggregated across the units we would end up with a distribution that showed less discrimination between the candidates. What we need is a mechanism that records the candidate's attainment in a form that maintains the fine discrimination of the marks but that also recognises the 'grade-worthiness' of marks in different units.

The mechanism for this is the Uniform Mark Scale (UMS). In the UMS, the scaled marks for each grade are pre-determined and depend only on the weighting given to the unit. Table 1 gives the UMS for units of different weight and shows how they contribute to the overall subject awards. Thus, for an A level which comprises six units, an individual unit might well have a weighting of 16.7%; this would mean that grade boundaries on its raw mark scale would be converted to grade boundaries on the 100-mark UMS.

Table 1 Grade boundaries in terms of uniform marks according to weighting of unit (from AQA, 2006)

Weighting as % of total AS assessment	30%	33.3%	35%	40%	100%	AS subject award	Advanced subject award
Weighting as % of total Advanced assessment	15%	16.7%	17.5%	20%	50%		
Max uniform mark	90	100	105	120	300	300	600
A	72	80	84	96	240	240	480
B	63	70	74	84	210	210	420
C	54	60	63	72	180	180	360
D	45	50	53	60	150	150	300
E	36	40	42	48	120	120	240
(N)	27	30	32	36	90	–	–

The method for linking the unit raw mark grade boundaries to the UMS and the aggregation procedure is outlined in Box 1 (adapted from AQA, 2006).

Despite the reference to marks in its name, the UMS marks are really a form of grade. Just like grades, the UMS marks have a common interpretation irrespective of the

Box 1

This example is based on Curriculum 2000 A levels, which had a total maximum UMS of 600. The table below shows typical grade boundaries for a GCE unit which is marked out of 80 raw marks and has 20% weighting. For this unit, the total maximum UMS is 120 (20% of 600). The second column shows the raw mark boundaries. The grade A boundary is 61 (approximately 76% of the raw mark total). The third column shows the uniform mark boundaries. For a GCE unit with 20% weighting, the maximum uniform mark is 120 and uniform marks in the range 96–120 correspond to grade A. This does not mean that the paper is marked out of 120 or that a candidate has to score 80% of the raw marks (96/120) to obtain grade A on the unit. A candidate who scores 61 (the lowest raw mark for grade A) will receive a uniform mark of 96 (the lowest *uniform* mark for grade A). Similarly, a candidate who scores 43 will receive a uniform mark of 60 and a candidate who scores 49 will receive a uniform mark of 72. A raw mark between 43 and 49 corresponds to a uniform mark between 60 and 72; for example, a raw mark of 46 (exactly half way between 43 and 49) corresponds to a uniform mark of 66. This is illustrated in the figure below.

GCE unit with maximum raw mark of 80 and accounting for 20% of the A level assessment: typical raw mark grade boundaries, together with the uniform mark boundaries

Grade	Lowest raw mark in grade (maximum 80)	Corresponding uniform mark (maximum 120)
A	61	96
B	55	84
C	49	72
D	43	60
E	37	48
(N)	31	36

Conversion to uniform marks (for part of the mark range) for the above data

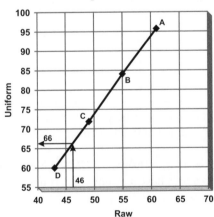

underlying raw marks of individual units. The advantage is that the UMS marks retain much finer distinctions than the grades. Once candidates have taken all of the units, their UMS marks are aggregated and their grade is evident from their final score. As Table 1 shows, a UMS of 480 means that the candidate has attained a grade A at A level.

6 Making the final decision

The balance between the examiners' qualitative assessment of standards and the statistical information is a delicate one. In large-entry subjects it may be argued that the performance of the candidature as a whole is unlikely to change substantially from one year to the next unless there are changes in the entry pattern (for example, more students with high prior attainment scores) or changes within the examination itself (for example, more marks available in a particular component) that would explain the difference. Such changes may be taken into account in a 'statistically recommended boundary' for a judgemental grade, which is based on the quantitative evidence available for the question paper under discussion and calculated as the mark which maintains standards from last year as closely as possible, statistically speaking (AQA, 2005a, p. 9). The statistically recommended boundary takes into account the subject-level standards, not just those at component level, as it would be unwise to wait until the end of the process to find out what the judgements on each component did to the grading of the examination overall. Analyses of the types of candidate entering the examination in each year are carried out prior to the meeting, and if the entry type has changed between years the statistically recommended boundaries can be modified to reflect that fact (Baird, 2000). Within AQA, if the awarding committee wishes to place a subject grade boundary at a mark that departs substantially from the statistically recommended boundary, it is required to document the reasons for its recommendation.

The recommendations of the awarding committee are referred to the Accountable Officer within the awarding body, upon whom the code of practice places responsibility for setting the final grade boundary, 'to ensure that grades awarded represent continuity and parity of standards across years, over time and across [syllabuses]' (QCA, 2007, p. 38). The Accountable Officer is appointed by the awarding body's governing council and 'is accountable directly to its governing council for ensuring the quality and standards of its qualifications' (QCA, 2007, p. 6). For every syllabus the awarding body offers, the Accountable Officer must approve the grade boundaries.

If the Accountable Officer does not believe the grade boundaries recommended by the awarding committee to be appropriate, it is the responsibility of the Accountable Officer to change them. In such a case, the Accountable Officer would discuss changes to the boundaries with the Chair of Examiners. If the changes were outside the range of marks considered at the meeting, it would be necessary to recall the awarding committee. The Accountable Officer, having received recommendations from all of the committees, may make a change to boundaries to bring consistency across the decisions being taken in, for example, new qualifications.

7 Evolution of the awarding process

7.1 School Certificate

The processes of awarding have evolved over the last century, though the basic principle – that of converting the rank order of the marks into a smaller number of grades whose standards are comparable across years and across syllabuses – has remained the same since the first local examinations in 1858. In the words of Circular 849 issued by the Board of Education in July 1914, the standard of a pass in the School Certificate 'will be such as may be expected of pupils of reasonable industry and ordinary intelligence in an efficient Secondary School' (quoted in Board of Education, 1943, p. 27). Subjects were grouped into three sets, (i) English subjects, (ii) Languages and (iii) Science and Mathematics and candidates were 'expected to show a reasonable amount of attainment in each of these groups...' (ibid.).

The introduction of the School Certificate (SC) and Higher School Certificate (HSC) as the first truly national qualifications brought pressure on the examining boards to ensure similar standards, even though the Ministry had no power to enforce agreement and there was much dispute. The HSC was the basis of both the award of State Bursaries and the matriculation requirements for many universities. Any divergence of standards would therefore result in injustice to some candidates. Accordingly the Secretaries of the examining boards met regularly and exchanged views on issues of comparability, agreeing amongst themselves what adjustments needed to be made in order to bring the different boards into line. Nevertheless, the Norwood Committee was concerned that the standards were not necessarily the same: '...even under present conditions two apparently similar certificates mean very different things, and illusory uniformity can be bought too dearly' (ibid.).

7.2 General Certificate of Education

When the General Certificate of Education (GCE) was introduced in 1951, the examining boards had to devise new procedures to ensure that the standards of the old SC and HSC were carried forward into the new Ordinary (O) and Advanced (A) level respectively. The Ministry of Education had laid down, through the Secondary School Examinations Council (SSEC), the basic form of the certificates: both O level and A level were to be pass or fail with no grading.

7.3 Ordinary level

The O level pass would be continuing the standards of the Credit in the School Certificate. This was to compensate for the fact that candidates were no longer required to pass all their subjects before a certificate could be issued. The practicalities of how this was to be achieved were left to the boards and they devised their own processes. UCLES (1950), for example, placed great emphasis on the value of school estimates.

Although prohibited from indicating grades on the formal certificates, from the start some released information about the marks obtained; others developed informal grading schemes that were released to schools and to universities. The approach proposed by UCLES was based upon percentages of the raw marks available, as Table 2 shows. This process would now be deemed unsatisfactory, as it would not maintain standards from year to year. Even if the *same candidates* took two years' examination papers, different proportions of them would be awarded a pass under this system because, as described earlier, a raw mark from one year is not equivalent to a raw mark in another year. That is the whole reason for having an awarding process.

Table 2 Rankings of candidates (from UCLES, 1951)

Pass	Fail
1 – 82%	6 – 40%
2 – 75%	7 – 35%
3 – 64%	8 – 30%
4 – 54%	
5 – 45%	

On the other hand, the Joint Matriculation Board (JMB) approach related grades separately to the proportions of candidates above and below the pass mark (Table 3).

Table 3 JMB grading guidance (from Forrest, 1970)

For candidates to be awarded passing grades	
Grade	Cumulative percentages of candidates
1	9
2	18
3	45
4	63
5	85
6	100
For candidates to be awarded failing grades	
7	30
8	70
9	100

7.4 Advanced level

The change from the Higher School Certificate to the Advanced Level was less of a problem, with the standard for the new examination being that of the pass in a principal subject in the HSC. The rationale for the grouping of subjects in the HSC had been almost exactly the opposite of that of the SC. Whereas in the SC the aim was to ensure that candidates covered a wide range of different subject areas, the aim of the HSC groups was to enforce specialisation. However, it swiftly fell into disuse and awarding bodies found ways around the regulations on grouping.

The relationship of the SSEC to the boards remained advisory throughout its existence, with the result that most changes were instituted by the boards themselves rather than as a response to the SSEC. The only major area over which it held sway was what was published on the actual certificate issued to successful candidates partly because, to add to their credibility, they were counter-signed by an official on behalf of the Ministry of Education. It exercised this oversight with considerable caution, with changes to what was recorded on the certificate happening very slowly.

In the years following its introduction, the A level moved quickly from a pass or fail approach to one in which degrees of achievement were recognised: the distinction grade was re-introduced in 1953, at the same level as the distinction in the HSC. This satisfied the immediate need to distinguish candidates for state scholarships and bursaries, but it was not enough for the selection purposes of the universities. In that same year the JMB proposed that the A level should be reported in terms of grades. It took the best part of a decade before the SSEC put forward guidelines for the grading of the GCE A level (SSEC, 1960), which were adopted by all the boards.

In spring 1960, Professor Oliver, Professor of Education at Manchester and a member of the JMB, gave an address to the Association of Assistant Mistresses in which he argued not only that the GCE was providing insufficient information for university selection but also that 'the harmful effects of a defective examination on the work of the schools and the education of adolescents are positive evils which call for changes in the G.C.E irrespective of its use for selection' (Oliver, 1960, pp. 3–4).

In the same year, the SSEC issued a report that looked at the tensions between the use of the GCE A level as a selection instrument for university entrance and its use as a certification of attainment at the end of the sixth form course (SSEC, 1960). The report concluded that,

> The most promising reform would be the introduction of a system of grading of passes at the Advanced level, with supplementary grading for those in the higher ability ranges, effected by means of a special or 'S' paper available with the advanced level papers. Grading should be recognised by the Minister and the results entered on the candidate's certificate as well as being circulated to universities and other users.
>
> SSEC (1960)

The recommendations for grading the 'basic' A level papers were couched in terms of approximate proportions of the candidature: 10% grade A, 15% grade B, 10% grade C, 15% grade D and 20% grade E, with a further 20% being allowed an O level pass. The unequal divisions (and in particular the narrow grade C band), and the fact that the grades were described in terms of the candidature, was to store up problems for the future.

The report emphasised that these proportions were guidelines and the awarding bodies did not stick rigidly to them; for example, there were, and still are, large differences in grades awarded between subjects. Nevertheless, the overall proportion of A level candidates passing remained around the 70% mark from its inception until well into the 1980s. At the same time, the report called for a greater degree of uniformity:

> the Examining Boards should all agree both on a uniform set of symbols for presenting candidates' results, on both basic and S papers, and, so far as is possible, on similar methods of assessment in arriving at those results, so that universities and other users can feel some confidence that they are comparing like with like.
>
> SSEC (1960)

8 A variety of grading systems

The advent of the Certificate of Secondary Education (CSE) in 1965 was a clear challenge to the status quo. It was from the outset a graded examination: four passing grades with two grades defined by reference to 'the calibre of candidates',

> The definition of standards will therefore be as follows:
>
> In each subject the examination should be so constructed that:
>
> (i) a 16-year-old pupil of average ability who has applied himself to a course of study regarded by teachers of the subject as appropriate to his age, ability and aptitude, may reasonably expect to secure grade 4; and
>
> (ii) a 16-year-old pupil whose ability is such that he may reasonably have secured a pass in the 'O' level of the GCE examination, had he applied himself to a course of study for that examination, may reasonably expect to secure grade 1, having followed a course of study defined in (i) above.
>
> SSEC (1963a)

In addition to the four passing grades a fifth grade was agreed for those who had been correctly entered but whose performance was 'not quite up to the standard of grade 4'. Candidates whose performances were below grade 5 were ungraded – a term that was to be used in preference to 'fail' in the examinations that followed.

The SSEC recognised the problems of comparability between boards, different modes of examination and between the two examination systems, but it stood firm against any heavy involvement.

> The difficulty of this range of problems is increased by the fact that no solution can be regarded as acceptable if it involves detailed intervention by the council in the conduct of the boards' examinations, formalising pressures by the boards on the work of the schools, or alignment of syllabus content and methods of examining as between CSE and GCE examination systems. In short, the job must be done without interfering in any way with the natural development of the work of schools, or the independent development of the two examination systems.
>
> SSEC (1963b)

In terms of ensuring comparability between GCE O level and CSE examinations, the boards faced three major problems. As indicated above, they were precluded from changing their syllabuses to make it possible for candidates to follow a common course leading to both examinations. The new CSE boards were regional and there was no overlap, so a candidate in one area could not take the examinations of a different regional board. Finally, the boards were required to provide three different modes of examining. The balance of these three modes of examining had an important impact on the mechanisms used for awarding grades. The boards were dominated by teachers and a wide variety of different models were adopted. Most boards required that teachers nominated to their subject panels were actively involved in teaching the subject, so they had a vested interest in having an assessment model that was sympathetic to their preferred model of the curriculum. Whalley (1969) outlined the different approaches:

> Some Boards treat the modes as being, in effect, distinct examining systems. In such regions, in Mode 1, the school uses a syllabus constructed by the Subject Panel which also externally examines the candidates. There is an examiner appointed for each subject and he works with the Panel. In Mode 2, the school's syllabus is externally examined, also by the panel and the examiner. Schools using Mode 3 construct their own syllabuses and examine their own candidates. The Board appoints moderators who discuss with the teachers in the schools the Mode 3 syllabuses and methods of examination and, when the examination has been carried out, look at the work of the candidates and their marks so that they can check on standards. There is therefore no link between the modes other than that the same Panel is concerned, in different ways, with all three; the methods of examining might be very different in each case.
>
> Whalley (1969)

Some boards, however, merged the three modes as closely as they could while maintaining their distinctive nature. In one example, teachers marked the examinations of all three modes, using marking schemes supplied by the board for Modes 1 and 2 and one devised by the school (approved by the board) for Mode 3. The teacher then graded the candidates and sent the written work of the lowest candidate in each grade to a member of the Moderation Committee. Schools were grouped into sets of no more than 24 and teachers from those schools attended a Group Moderation meeting to consider the standards represented by these candidates who had been judged to be at the lowest acceptable standard for each grade. After any necessary adjustments had been made to bring centres' assessments into line, the Moderation Committee met to make any final adjustments and award the final grades.

However, it was felt that with a completely new examination it was necessary to have a basis of comparison. The mechanism used was a reference test – a multiple choice test of general scholastic ability, or aptitude. Twenty representative schools from each of the CSE boards and nine from each of the GCE boards were selected and the reference test given to all the examination candidates in early 1965, as Whalley described.

> Also early in the year, the candidates' teachers were asked to forecast their CSE or GCE grades in the six subjects concerned. On the basis of these forecasts and the results of the reference test it was possible to suggest to each of the CSE Boards, before the examination was held, the proportion of candidates who might appropriately obtain Grade 1 in each of the six subjects, and a mean grade for the subject. Tolerance limits were supplied. The

Boards were not obliged to conform to these standards but were expected to justify any significant departure from them.

Whalley (1969)

When the 1965 results were analysed, no major discrepancies were found in the final results across the boards but there was a general tendency to award grade 4 to a higher proportion of candidates than had been predicted by the test scores. In the spirit of leaving the final judgement to the boards, this was accepted by the newly formed Schools Council for Curriculum and Examinations (commonly referred to as the Schools Council), which had taken over the role of the old SSEC. An interesting outcome of the first monitoring experiment was the comparison of standards at grade 1 with those of the GCE O level pass. If anything, it showed that the CSE boards might have been slightly more severe than the GCE boards at this level.

In 1975, the Department of Education and Science finally succumbed to pressure to allow grades on the GCE O level certificate. But notions of the old 'Pass' were not lost, despite an attempt to remove it. The grades ranged from A to E with those failing to reach the standard required for an E being Unclassified. The standard of the pass was set at grade C and it was so heavily entrenched that even in the years immediately prior to the introduction of the GCSE, the certificates still distinguished between the upper grades which were printed as A(a), B(b) and C(c) so that the lower grades D and E could not be altered to look like higher grades. In the awarding committees, C/D remained the main judgemental boundary, though judgement was also used at grade A/B and E/U.

9   The attempt at criterion referencing

In 1983, the government set up a new body, the Secondary Examinations Council (SEC), to replace the old Schools Council, which it considered cumbersome and an obstruction to reform. Whereas the Schools Council had been representative of stakeholders, with its membership drawn from the teaching profession and local education authorities, the SEC was entirely appointed by the Secretary of State. One of its first functions was to advise on the introduction of a new examination at age 16.

Pressure for the end to the dual system of assessment at 16+ (CSE and O level) led to proposals for a single system of examining at 16+. These were originally put forward in 1976 but the government of the time was unwilling to take the step of abolishing the O level. However, in 1984 Sir Keith Joseph, then Secretary of State, having agreed that the GCSE should be introduced with effect from 1988, indicated one of his hopes for the new examination

> We need to define more precisely, for each subject, the skills, competences, understanding and areas of knowledge which a candidate must have covered and the minimum level of attainment he must demonstrate in each of them, if he is to be awarded a particular grade.
>
> Joseph (1984a)

At the time, criterion referenced assessment was regarded as the panacea to all examining ills. James Popham argued strongly that assessment should be against clearly defined objectives that were known to the candidates as well as to the examiners (Popham, 1978). Work had already begun on developments in Scotland for criterion referenced certification (CRC, 1987). The trouble with Popham's proposals, however, was that they primarily referred to multiple choice questions. These were not common in the English system and relating criterion referencing to British examinations was problematic.

The proposed answer was to be 'grade-related criteria'. This was based upon the assumption that, because examiners could recognise in a script the qualities that would lead them to award it a particular grade, they could articulate what those qualities were. Working parties in the main subject areas were set up, comprising experienced examiners, practising teachers, local authority advisers, representatives of the subject associations, higher and further education, and industry. The terms of reference of the working parties were,

> ...having viewed the literature dealing with the construction of grade-related criteria and considered the national criteria:
>
> i. to identify a maximum of six domains of the subject that may be assessed;
>
> ii. to specify the skills and competencies which candidates must demonstrate in order to achieve the grades at present denoted by CSE grade 4 and O level grades C and A and to suggest appropriate techniques of assessment;
>
> iii. to determine the method by which the scores on each individual domain may be aggregated to produce a single overall score preserving a level of criterion-referencing compatible with the requirement that current standards are to be carried forward;
>
> iv. to ensure that the effects of the proposals on the curriculum will be beneficial.
>
> SEC (1984)

In September 1985, the draft grade criteria were published for consultation. Respondents to the consultation were critical of the complexity of the draft grade criteria and the potential damaging impact they would have on the curriculum. In response, the Secondary Examinations Council (SEC) put forward a different approach:

> Rather than defining the criteria from the outset, and then arranging for syllabuses to be produced which incorporated these criteria, it decided to take as its starting point a number of existing approved GCSE syllabuses... and to ask the examiners of these syllabuses to articulate their implicit judgements as to the award of grades: in other words, to develop a performance matrix for each of these syllabuses.
>
> DES (1987)

With hindsight this approach was equally doomed to failure. Even if the working groups had been able to identify the qualities they sought, those reading them would have no choice but to make their own interpretations of the requirements. Nevertheless, awarding on the basis of performance matrices was used in at least one awarding body.

It might be expected that, having failed to devise such criteria for the GCSE, the attempt at criterion referencing would be abandoned. However, the development of the General National Vocational Qualifications (GNVQs), based upon the competence statements designed for NVQ work-based assessments, had similar weaknesses. In this case performance statements were devised to identify what the candidates had to do in order to achieve success in a particular aspect. Indeed, in trying to ensure that there was no ambiguity, hurdles were introduced that made it increasingly difficult for candidates to understand the requirements. Box 2 gives an example of some performance statements for a GNVQ in Business (Edexcel, 2007). Problems of interpretation and hurdles are found: who determines whether the candidate's description of the activity is 'clear'? What happens if the candidate has produced a description of what s/he and the teacher regard as four functional areas of the business, but the moderator decides that there are only three? In these circumstances the result was complete failure for the candidate.

Box 2

Pass To achieve a pass your work must show:
- a clear description of the activity, aims and objectives of your chosen business
- a description of four functional areas of the business, including human resources, explaining fully how each contributes to the business activity and giving examples of job roles associated with each area
- a description of how the equal opportunities of employees are safeguarded by legislation
- an explanation, using examples, of how different functional areas communicate with each other and external contacts
- a comparison of the organisational structure of your chosen business with a contrasting structure and explain the different communication flows
- an appropriate list of the sources of evidence you used in your research
- an oral explanation of how the customer service of your chosen business meets customers' expectations and suggestions of any necessary improvements based on best practice
- you can speak clearly during your presentation, keeping to the subject and using an image to illustrate your main point(s).

Criterion referencing for GCSE and GCE was abandoned but there remain some attempts at representing the sorts of performances that might be expected at different grades. Grade descriptions which originate from QCA subject criteria are presented in all GCSE syllabuses as is illustrated in Box 3, taken from a GCSE in geography (OCR, 2007). These are much more general than anything that could be regarded as 'criteria' but are nevertheless used as a reference point in the awarding meetings.

Box 3

Grade C

Candidates recall accurately information about places, environments and themes, at a range of scales, as required by the specification, and show a broad knowledge of location and geographical terminology.

Candidates understand geographical ideas from the specification content in a variety of physical and human contexts. They understand a range of physical and human processes and their contribution to the development of geographical patterns, the geographical characteristics of particular places and environments, and their interdependence. They understand interrelationships between people and the environment and appreciate that considerations of sustainable development affect the planning and management of environments and resources. They understand the effects of attitudes and values of those involved in geographical issues and in decision-making about the use and management of environments.

Candidates undertake geographical enquiry, identifying questions or issues, suggesting appropriate sequences of investigation, collecting appropriate evidence from a variety of primary and secondary sources, using a range of relevant skills and techniques, reaching plausible conclusions, communicating outcomes, and appreciating some of the limitations of evidence and conclusions.

---

10 Greater transparency

Although the exercise failed to produce the desired shift towards criterion referencing, the GCSE was a much more transparent qualification than had ever been designed before. The GCSE syllabuses had to conform to centrally produced criteria. They had to include defined content areas and to follow agreed assessment approaches. For the first time, syllabuses for 16-year-olds had to be approved by a central government agency.

The introduction of the GCSE was accompanied by an unprecedented (and since unrepeated) programme to ensure that teachers as well as examiners were fully aware of the changes that were being introduced and how the new examination was to be assessed. This was partly because the new examination included a coursework element that was to be compulsory in almost every subject, so teachers had to be brought into the assessment community. However, it was also as part of the belief that teachers needed to be more aware of the requirements so that they were better able to prepare their students.

As was the case with the change from School Certificate to GCE, the standards of the new examination were based on the standards of the old ones. Grades A, B and C were to remain at the standards set by the O level. Grades D, E, F and G transferred the standards of the CSE grades 2–5. In this way, those involved in the transfer could draw upon their experiences of the previous system to ensure reasonable comparability from 1987 to 1988 (the transition year). In addition, national data on the overlapping grades of the GCE O level and the CSE were used to give the new GCSE examining groups indications of the likely patterns of results.

One of the major issues facing the awarding bodies in the change from the dual system to the GCSE was how to cope with the wide range of attainment for which the new examination would cater. The Secretary of State had indicated his desire for more pupils to take the examination than had taken either O level or CSE (combined): 'I conclude that it is a realistic objective to try to bring 80–90% of all pupils *at least* to the level now associated with the CSE grade 4' (Joseph, 1984b).

The solution to this problem varied across the different subjects. Most opted for a system of differentiated papers – one covering the lower grades, and another the higher grades, with an overlap of grades in the middle. One subject, mathematics, held out for a three-tier system with no overlap between the highest and lowest tiers. This was heavily influenced by the report of a committee of inquiry into the teaching of mathematics chaired by Sir Wilfred Cockcroft (1982), who had been appointed Chairman of the Secondary Examinations Council. The report argued that there were aspects of mathematics that were essential in the curriculum of the most able that would be so far beyond the understanding of the least able that they would experience only failure. However the desire for a common pattern across subjects has finally brought mathematics into a two-tier system. A few subjects – mainly those that had traditionally used a more narrative response format – chose a form of differentiation that relied upon identifying different levels of sophistication in the responses of candidates to the same stimulus.

The introduction of tiered papers was the subject of much discussion. Work by Tattersall (1983) and a major research project by Good & Cresswell (1988) both concluded that it was difficult to ensure that standards for the overlapping grades were the same. In the event, the awarding of the first GCSE results was carried out with few problems, despite the changes, though the original plan – to have grades A–C awarded by the O level boards and grades D–G by the CSE boards – was never followed. From the start, awarders from both sides considered all grades. The initial reports by Her Majesty's Inspectorate of Schools (HMI) on the introduction of the GCSE were favourable – particularly in terms of its impact on the curriculum and its motivational value within schools. However, this changed when the focus was turned on the operation of the examination in the boards and HMI started to show concerns about the comparability of systems across the boards.

In 1989, another new examination, the GCE Advanced Supplementary was introduced. Despite pleas by the boards that what was needed was an examination bridging the gap between GCSE and A level, it was decided that the new examination would anticipate a two-year period of study and would be assessed at the same standard as A level but on half the content. Because it was at the same standard and awarded at the same time as the A level, the awarding processes could be integrated. It never achieved the take-up the government had hoped for and was ultimately replaced by the Advanced Subsidiary in 2001.

11 Revised A level grading

The problem with the SSEC (1960) grading recommendations gradually increased with the rapid rise of the numbers of candidates taking A level. In 1969, the JMB put forward proposals for the revision of the A level grading system to alleviate the situation. These resulted in a consultation by the Schools Council in July 1970 on a 20-point grading scale in which the margin of error associated with each point was also specified. However, this was rejected by the Secretary of State in 1972 and the problems continued.

Figure 4 An illustration of the width of A level grade bands for two 1982 JMB examinations

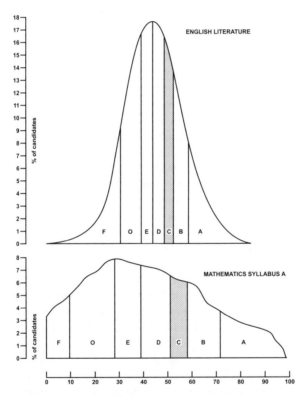

In the late 1970s, increasing concerns were expressed about the inaccuracy of grading at A level. In 1983, the JMB published a pamphlet drawing attention to the narrowness of the mark ranges covering some of the grades. Because the SSEC recommendations for grades were defined in terms of the proportions of candidates, for grades that lay in the middle of the scale, the width could be very narrow indeed; in some cases, the difference between the bottom grade B mark and the top grade D mark – the width of the grade C mark band – was as small as 4% of the mark total (for example, 12 marks out of 300 in an A level geology examination). This is illustrated in Figure 4 (Whittaker & Forrest, 1983, p. 7).

The following year the SEC set up a working party to look into the problems of grading the A level. The working party reported towards the end of 1985, recommending that the basis for grading should be the partitioning of the mark range, rather than the candidature. It recommended two points that should be determined by examiner judgement: the A/B boundary and the E/N boundary. It also recommended a new grade N to indicate those who narrowly missed grade E. This was an opportunity to bring the boards' different practices into line, but the Secretary of State, concerned about a change to the meaning of the high-profile grade A that might be caused by changing board practices, decided that the boards should continue to use their existing methods for determining this grade (even though these methods differed across the boards just as much as any other grade) and that the upper boundary for the new approach should be the B/C borderline, with the grades between this and the E/N boundary determined arithmetically. This approach was introduced in all awarding bodies in 1987 and it was not until the introduction of the first code of practice that the awarding bodies were required to follow the same procedures for all grade boundaries. The present approach is similar, although the modularisation of A level syllabuses (accompanying the introduction of Curriculum 2000) saw the boundaries to be determined by judgement change from A/B, B/C and E/N to A/B and E/U only in 2002.

12   Conclusion

The awarding process is one of weighing the evidence and coming to a judgement on where to locate grade boundaries. It is an essential part of the comparability process: raw marks are too variable to be relied upon.

Although the awarding process relies heavily on awarders' understanding of their subject, it has been shown that even experienced examiners are relatively poor at making judgements about the 'grade worthiness' of a piece of work on one mark compared with another without something other than subject matter understanding to guide them (Baird & Dhillon, 2005). In the past, examiners had somehow, simultaneously, to account for both the quality of the candidature and the difficulty of the paper. This was essentially a circular task, as the examiners had nothing to judge the quality of the candidature by except the performance of the candidates on the paper whose difficulty they did not know. The statistical information now accessible to awarders means that they have much more available to help them in their task. It is still a matter of judgement, balancing the sometimes conflicting information given by the statistics and their own judgement of scripts. However, awarders are now in a position to test their decisions in a number of ways, retaining their professional input, but complementing it with the power of quantitative analysis, to come closer to the goal of comparability that they are seeking.

References

Assessment and Qualifications Alliance. (2005a). *A basic guide to standard setting*. Guildford: Assessment and Qualifications Alliance.

Assessment and Qualifications Alliance. (2005b). *The use of statistics in examinations processing*. Unpublished, Assessment and Qualifications Alliance.

Assessment and Qualifications Alliance. (2006). *Uniform marks in GCE, VCE, GNVQ and modular GCSE examinations* (Version 3.1). Guildford: Assessment and Qualifications Alliance.

Baird, J. (2000). Are examination standards all in the head? Experiments with examiners' judgments of standards in A level examinations. *Research in Education, 64*, 91–100.

Baird, J., & Dhillon, D. (2005). *Qualitative expert judgements on examination standards: Valid, but inexact.* Internal report RPA 05 JB RP 077. Guildford: Assessment and Qualifications Alliance.

Black, E.L. (1962). The marking of G.C.E. scripts. *British Journal of Educational Studies, 11*, 61–71.

Board of Education. (1943). *Curriculum and examinations in secondary schools (Norwood Report).* London: His Majesty's Stationery Office.

Cockcroft, W.H. (1982). *Mathematics counts – Report of a committee of enquiry into the teaching of mathematics under the chairmanship of Dr. W.H. Cockcroft.* London: Her Majesty's Stationery Office.

CRC. (1987). *Criterion-referenced certification project final report.* Glasgow: Jordanhill College of Education.

Department of Education and Science. (1987). *Improving the basis for awarding GCSE grades.* Paper presented at the 1st Annual Conference of the Joint Council for the GCSE. London: Department of Education and Science.

Eason, S. (2004). *Statistical screening procedures to investigate inter-awarding body comparability.* London: Joint Council for Qualifications.

Edexcel. (2007). *Intermediate GNVQ in business (GB206). (Specification).* London: Edexcel.

Forrest, G.M. (1970). *Standards in subjects at the Ordinary level of the GCE.* Occasional Paper 33. Manchester: Joint Matriculation Board.

Good, F.J., & Cresswell, M.J. (1988). *Grading the GCSE.* London: Secondary Examinations Council.

Joseph, K. (1984a). Speech by Sir Keith Joseph, Secretary of State for Education and Science, at the Assistant Masters and Mistresses Association, Bournemouth, Monday 16 April, 1984. *SEC annual report 1983-84.* London: Secondary Examinations Council.

Joseph, K. (1984b). Speech by Sir Keith Joseph, Secretary of State for Education and Science, at the North of England Conference, Sheffield, Friday 6 January, 1984. *SEC annual report 1983–1984.* London: Secondary Examinations Council.

Oliver, R.A.C. (1960). *The effectiveness of G.C.E. Advanced level as a criterion for university selection.* Occasional Paper No. 7. Manchester: Joint Matriculation Board.

Oxford Cambridge and RSA Examinations. (2007). *GCSE geography A (1986). (Specification).* Nottingham: Oxford Cambridge and RSA Examinations.

Popham, W.J. (1978). *Criterion-referenced measurement.* New Jersey: Prentice-Hall Englewood Cliffs.

Qualifications and Curriculum Authority. (2007). *GCSE, GCE, VCE, GNVQ and AEA code of practice.* London: Qualifications and Curriculum Authority.

Secondary Examinations Council. (1984). *The development of grade-related criteria for the General Certificate of Secondary Education – The task of the working parties.* Unpublished, Secondary Examinations Council.

Secondary School Examinations Council. (1960). *The General Certificate of Education and sixth form studies.* Third Report of the Secondary School Examinations Council. London: Her Majesty's Stationery Office.

Secondary School Examinations Council. (1963a). *The Certificate of Secondary Education: Some suggestions for teachers and examiners.* Examinations Bulletin No. 1. London: Her Majesty's Stationery Office.

Secondary School Examinations Council. (1963b). *Scope and standards of the Certificate of Secondary Education.* Seventh Report of the Secondary School Examinations Council. London: Her Majesty's Stationery Office.

Tattersall, K. (1983). *Differentiated examinations: A strategy for assessment at 16+?* Schools Council Examinations Bulletin 42. London: Methuen Educational.

Tomlinson, M. (2002). *Inquiry into A level standards. Final Report.* London: Department for Education and Skills.

University of Cambridge Local Examinations Syndicate. (1950). *Minutes of the awarding committee 12 October 1950 (arrangements for the award of the GCE in 1951).* Cambridge: University of Cambridge Local Examinations Syndicate Archives.

University of Cambridge Local Examinations Syndicate. (1951). *General Certificate of Education: The award and communication of marks.* Cambridge: University of Cambridge Local Examinations Syndicate Archives.

Whalley, G.E. (1969). *The Certificate of Secondary Education.* Institute of Education Paper No. 9. Leeds: University of Leeds.

Whittaker, R.J., & Forrest, G.M. (1983). *Problems of the GCE Advanced level grading scheme.* Manchester: Joint Matriculation Board.

4

ALTERNATIVE CONCEPTIONS
OF COMPARABILITY

Jo-Anne Baird

Abstract

Comparable examinations have to be at the same standard. But what do people mean by 'examination standard' and what kinds of comparability are expected? How is evidence to be gathered about these types of comparability and are all of these approaches valid? This chapter outlines different definitions of examination comparability used in England by academics and the expectations of the media and general public. The purposes to which assessment results are put are discussed, as the alternative conceptions of examination comparability are linked to the uses of the assessment results. Given that there are different approaches, some commentators have proposed that we should select a single definition of examination standards and stick to it, so that the system is clearer and false expectations are not raised about what the examination system can realistically deliver. Whether a particular definition of examination standards can be prioritised above others is considered, as well as the implications of so doing.

1   What does society mean by examination standards?

The word standard is used in a multiplicity of ways, leading to a great deal of confusion. As an example, Aldrich (2000) notes that the Department for Education and Employment White Paper *Excellence in Schools* (1997) has the following sub-heading in one section, 'Raising standards: our top priority'.

Aldrich points out that there is more than one way in which educational standards can be raised. To take a sporting analogy, high-jump standards can be improved by increasing the height of the bar that people have to jump over, or by raising the number of people who can jump over the bar. Educationally, raising standards can mean expecting more of students or expecting more students to be able to demonstrate performance at a given level. Herein lies the root of a problem.

Without being explicit about exactly what is meant by examination standards, many commentators are critical. Whilst some of the definitions of examination standards used are consistent with academic definitions (see later), some are ruled out by assessment specialists as too simplistic or not part of the standard-setting process. Let us take a look at some media attacks on examination standards and consider the definition of standards being used and whether it is encompassed by a definition used in the assessment research literature.

1.1 The curriculum, questions or assessments are too easy

One way in which England's bar has been lowered, some claim, is by making the curriculum too easy. Professor Bernard Lamb, of Imperial College London, has been quoted as stating that the science and mathematics curriculum standards have been lowered so drastically that British students are a year behind foreign students when they start university (see Box 1). The standard-setting process begins with the definition of the curriculum that students will study and this is a matter of national importance.

Box 1

A new science GCSE, for instance, concentrates on topics such as genetically modified food and global warming rather than scientific theory. A level maths has been reformed to allow pupils to cover less challenging topics, while pupils taking a new maths GCSE can get an A grade without answering any of the hardest questions.

Julie Henry, Telegraph Education Correspondent (*Daily Telegraph*, 5 March 2006)

Likewise, there are complaints that some subjects are easier than others (Box 2). This also matters if our systems give equal credit for grades in different subjects, which the Department for Education and Skills (DfES) school performance tables and University and Colleges Admissions Service (UCAS) points systems do. For now, let us take these complaints as qualms about UK students learning the wrong things, although there is clearly another issue here regarding comparability between subjects.

Box 2

The rise in interest in psychology is a consequence of what people are perceiving, that maths and physics are harder and they can get better grades in psychology... It is easy to show that psychology is an easier A level than maths. It is incredibly worrying because maths and modern languages are subjects that the country needs.

John Dunford, General Secretary of the Secondary Heads Association (*Times Educational Supplement*, 14 August, 2003)

When it comes to setting cut scores – the process normally considered to be standard setting – it is too late to influence the curriculum design issues. By that stage, students may have been studying for their examinations for two years. However, involvement of senior examiners in the standard-setting process is a way in which the validity of the content of the examinations can be checked and the curriculum

125

altered for future years if things have gone awry. Likewise, inclusion of expert judgements in comparability studies can be used as a commentary on whether the curriculum is appropriate.

Other, similar, attacks on educational standards relate to the questions themselves. Even if the curriculum is appropriate, questions could be set on the easier aspects. Alternatively, the structure of the qualifications can be questioned, with some claiming that the type of assessment undermines the quality of students' achievements:

- coursework – 'GCSE coursework to be curtailed to stop internet cheats' (Taylor, 2006)

- multiple choice examinations – 'Pick A, B or C for a GCSE' (Mansell, 2006)

- modular examinations – 'Modular exams "damaging degree courses"' (Lightfoot, 2006).

Recently, the examination regulators defended the difficulty of A level questions (Figure 1).

All of the above can be viewed as a tug-of-war with, at one end of the rope, progressive education stakeholders who wish to modernise the curriculum, increasing diversity in the curriculum and widening participation in education. As such, the modernisers are trying to raise standards by increasing the number of people who can jump over the bar. The traditionalists are at the other end of the rope, trying to maintain the highly selective function of the qualifications and keep the bar at the same height or even raise it if too many people are jumping over it. All of this is a question of degree, as the curriculum *must* change to keep up with advances in knowledge. A level computing would not have been a feasible subject 50 years ago when A levels were introduced, but technology is now crucial to development of the economy.

Equally, the examinations fulfil a selective function for higher education and employment. Opinions are bound to differ regarding what should be taught in our education system – should we focus more upon scientific theory or move more towards evaluation of scientific evidence on, for example, genetically modified foods? Should students focus more upon speaking a second language or upon written grammar? Whilst crucially important questions for educational standards, they are beyond the scope of this chapter. Note, however, that when new aspects of the curriculum are introduced, there is less time for treatment of the old curriculum material. If we focus upon the traditional curriculum material then we are almost necessarily going to see a decline in skills in those areas over time because students also have to learn new things. Arguably, the content of the education curriculum receives too little serious attention and debate.

Figure 1 Regulatory body advertisement to congratulate A level students on their results (17 August 2006)

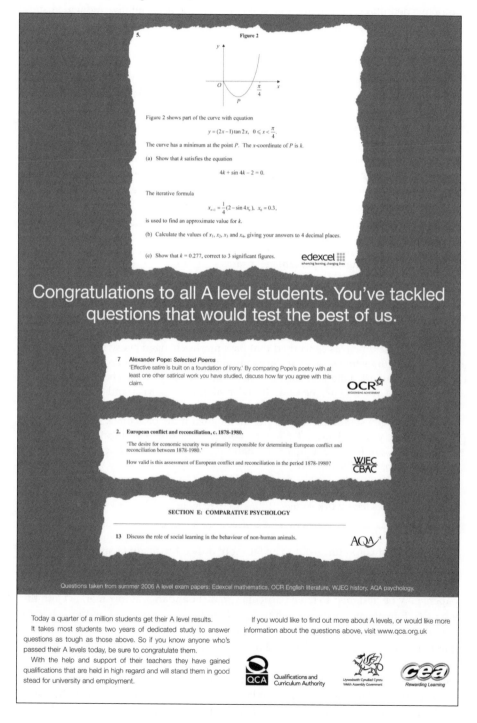

The issues raised by challenges relating to the content of the curriculum and difficulty of the examination questions or assessment styles are subsumed by academic definitions of examination standards relating to qualitative judgements: criterion referencing and weak criterion referencing.

1.2 The pass marks are too low

There is a widespread assumption that grade boundaries are set at fixed proportions of the mark scale year on year, such as a pass being at 50%. The difficulty of the question papers varies from year to year, so to set the grade boundaries at the same mark every year would simply sanction examination difficulty varying between years. As the difficulty varies between years, the grade boundaries must compensate for this, to make it equally difficult between years to be awarded a particular grade. To put it bluntly, grade boundaries mean nothing in themselves. Nevertheless, there are occasional pleas for a simple system based upon fixed percentages of marks, with the proponents arguing that they are easier to interpret (Box 3).

Box 3

Teachers urge return to 'percentage' exams

Teenagers taking A levels and GCSEs should be given percentage marks instead of A, B and C grades, teachers urged today... Former PAT [Professional Association of Teachers] chairman Barry Matthews, who acts as an observer for the Government's exams watchdog, the Qualifications and Curriculum Authority, said he was concerned that pass marks changed every year... 'What I find difficult is that each year the examining boards (exam boards) adjust the actual pass mark. One year the pass mark for an A may be 70. The next year it could come down to 67,' he said. 'If my child got 68 this year and got a B and 68 next year and got an A, I would be concerned. The public would have more faith that exam standards were being maintained if the pass mark stayed the same every year.'... Wesley Paxton, on behalf of the union's education committee, put forward a motion demanding a return to 'numerical marks'... - Delegates passed the motion...

icWales.co.uk (27 July 2005)
http://icwales.icnetwork.co.uk/0100news/0200wales/

When an examination turns out to be far more difficult than anticipated, it would be perverse to penalise students by awarding them lower grades than they would have attained had they sat the examination in any other year. Equally, the examination papers may be designed to have particular grade boundaries at low marks. Until this year, GCSE mathematics examinations had three tiers of assessment, with the highest tier being designed for the most able students. As such, to get a grade C on that question paper, students would score only a few marks on very difficult questions.

Definitions of examination standards relating to pass marks are not addressed by any of the academic definitions in England because we have a system in which the pass marks are adjusted to compensate for changes in demand of the assessments. There is a huge body of research literature on test equating and pre-testing. Creating assessments of equal difficulty year on year is an approach that could be feasible if pre-testing of the questions was conducted, but the high-stakes nature of UK public examinations and the high costs associated with pre-testing have mitigated against this approach. Nonetheless, this leaves the examination system open to attacks that can undermine public confidence if there is a lack of face validity of the boundary marks.

1.3 Too many students are getting the grades

Typically, complaints that too many students are being awarded the grades emphasise the selection purpose of the examinations, and positioning the bar at a particular height, to ensure that only a select few are able to jump over it. This is explicitly not the definition of examination standards in use by the current government (Box 4).

Box 4

We no longer have the quota system of 20 years ago, which condemned 30 per cent of pupils to failure each year, no matter their achievements. Today, hard work merits success, and high quality teaching is enabling every young person to grasp opportunities.

Jim Knight, Schools Standards Minister (17 August 2006)
http://www.dfes.gov.uk/qualifications/news.cfm?page=0&id=105

Box 5

The pass rate has gone up for the 21st year in a row and more pupils are getting A grades than ever before – about 20% of those taking the exams. ...

The former chief inspector of schools Chris Woodhead believes public exams like GCSEs and A levels are getting easier. 'The A level examination is not fulfilling the function that it should be, namely it is not identifying the most gifted students for top universities,' he told the Today programme on BBC Radio Four. 'When you look at the rate of increase and the fact that each year each new generation does do better then I don't think you are a cynic, you are just intelligently sceptical, if you raise questions about the nature of the examination. It can't all be down to better teaching, greater dedication, more intelligent students.'

Angela Harrison (BBC *News Online*, 14 August 2003)
http://news.bbc.co.uk/1/hi/education/3150189.stm

However, rising proportions of students passing the examinations in England has attracted criticism annually. The year 2003 was an interesting year. A level pass rates increased and were subjected to the usual criticisms of dumbing down (Box 5). Also in

2003, the proportion of Scottish students attaining the grades in Higher English reduced. Instead of this being interpreted as a raising of the bar, it was interpreted as a lowering of standards because the education system had failed to produce as many students who were capable of jumping over the bar (Box 6). Thus, viewed from one of these perspectives, there can always be claims that examination standards have gone down. Journalists looking to write about contentious issues can thereby always generate a story about standards in decline: a juicy critique of the government of the day. Whether too many students are being awarded the grades is clearly a legitimate question – the point is that changes in national examination statistics are not a good test if standards can be interpreted as having fallen whether the results go up or down.

Box 6

But there was concern last night when it emerged that a fall in the pass rate for Higher English is even worse than feared, with four out of 10 failing the exam. The true figure is understood to be around 60% this year. That is a further 2% lower than has previously been suggested and represents a 12% fall over the past two years.

Fiona Hyslop, the SNP's shadow education minister... called for smaller class sizes and a greater focus in schools on literacy to drive up standards in English, following allegations that some sitting the exam are 'barely literate'.

Jason Allardyce (*Scotland on Sunday*, 10 August 2003)

Concerns about the proportion of students passing the examinations fall into the statistical camp of assessment literature definitions of examination standards, of which two are considered below: cohort referencing and the 'catch-all' definition.

2   What do assessment specialists mean by examination standards?

Lack of treatment of the assessment field in England as an area where expertise is required, has encouraged the view that assessment users are experts in assessment. Teachers and examiners, for example, are subject matter experts and may or may not be assessment experts, as they may have little training in assessment. Often the training they receive is very focused upon the marking of a particular assessment. In the following paragraphs, the academic educational assessment literature is drawn upon to review the definitions of examination standards from assessment specialists. Let us start with the simplest first.

2.1 Cohort referencing

Under this definition, the same proportion of students are awarded the grades each year. Cresswell (1996) calls this the 'no-nonsense definition'. This is often referred to as 'norm-referencing', but in norm-referencing a population with known characteristics is used to contextualise performance on the current test. For example, in IQ testing a norm-group is used to develop the test such that it has known properties. The Wechsler Adult Intelligence Scale has a mean of 100 and a standard deviation of 15 for all of nine age groups used in the norm-group. Care was also taken to ensure that the norm-group was stratified by sex, ethnic group, geographic area in the US and six occupational categories. When a classroom of students is tested for their IQ, we can compare their results on the same test as individuals, or as a group, with the population-norm because it is exactly the same test that has been used. In examination testing in England, the tests are different each year, for security reasons. There are, of course, other models that could be used: the content of the Wechsler Adult Intelligence Scale test is kept secure. Security matters because it is possible to study for a test in which it is possible to predict the content. Releasing the tests, or at least ensuring that teachers and students are aware of their likely content, is therefore important to educational assessment in England. Norm-referencing gives information that can be used to compare an individual, or group, with a larger population.

Wiliam (1996a) points out that what in England is often called norm-referencing is more correctly called cohort referencing. In cohort referencing, examination standards are cohort specific – they do not tell us how the examination standards compare with last year, between subjects, between different examining boards and so on. This only matters to the extent that the purposes to which examination results are put depends upon being able to draw inferences about these different types of comparability. If examination results were used in a subject-specific manner, with those making inferences from them being knowledgeable about the different syllabuses offered by examining boards and only selecting between students in the same year group, then cohort referencing might well be a suitable system.

Unfortunately, this is not the case in England. Applicants for jobs and university places are drawn from different cohorts, and it would be impossible for employers or admissions tutors to be familiar with the content and demands of the 251 A level and 301 GCSE syllabuses currently on offer. Further, on the assumption that comparability exists between syllabuses, subjects, boards and qualifications, examination results are converted into points which are used in school performance tables and for entrance to universities.

Despite these weaknesses, Goldstein (1986) advocated such a system. So what are its benefits? It is a relatively simple system to deliver and for the public to understand. Moreover, there are those who argue, as this chapter demonstrates, that the present system is not only complex, but fails to deliver the kinds of comparability that it claims to. So why keep up this charade? Why not adopt a simpler system such as cohort referencing with all its known inadequacies?

In theory, this definition could be adopted in England, but in practice, there would be many powerful critics who would not tolerate it. The Working Group on 14–19 Reform (2004) rejected it as an option for standard-setting for the proposed diploma system (para 183):

> However, grading of diplomas should not be norm-referenced over time. If an increasing proportion of young people meet the established criteria for higher grades then the proportion achieving those grades should be allowed to rise.

Teachers and schools would object to the lack of comparability between examining boards, as, under this system, an easier syllabus in one examining board would have the same distribution of examination results as a harder syllabus in another. If the harder syllabus also happened to attract more able candidates, then the disparity between what would have to be achieved to attain the grades would be compounded. Progression to further study or into employment may depend upon the knowledge gained from a course, and if that varies wildly, assumptions about what is learned from a course are not possible. Therefore, lecturers in further education and higher education would have complaints. Evaluation of the education system over time would not be feasible – a fixed proportion of candidates would pass the examinations every year, despite government policies on *Excellence in Schools* (DfEE, 1997), national numeracy and literacy hours (DfES, 2002) or specialist schools (DfES, 2006). Different measures of the impact of government expenditure would be needed. To work the system, cynical students and teachers would select subjects and syllabuses that had a low-ability entry. Thus, dumbing down would be an educational consequence. Simple cohort referencing was used loosely in the early A level and O level examinations, but disenchantment with the lack of information from such a system moved examination boards to change the system (see Chapter 2).

Cohort referencing is the simplest form of statistical approach to the definition of examination standards possible. As no inferences can be drawn from it about candidates' performances in the examinations, very little information is gleaned about examination comparability at all. Nonetheless, it could be argued that this would be a clear approach to the setting of examination standards that has no pretence about delivering more than can be delivered by any system. Educational reform would be difficult under this system, as new qualifications would struggle for recognition. Let us turn next to a more complex statistical definition of examination standards that attempts to address some of the problems of this simplistic method.

2.2 The catch-all definition

Under this definition, we would say that two examinations were of comparable standards if students with the same characteristics were awarded the same grades on average, no matter which examination they entered (Cresswell, 1996). By 'the same characteristics', it is intended that all characteristics that have a legitimate relationship with examination results are controlled for when comparing the outcomes of the examinations. We would take into account how able the students were who entered for each examination, as well as the quality of the teaching, motivation of the students, number of hours spent studying and so on. Chapter 10 discusses studies that have used this definition as the basis of their research into examination comparability. In practice, there are serious problems about measuring *all* relevant factors, but even if we set them aside, there are considerable theoretical difficulties with this approach.s

Put simply, what does it *mean* to be equally prepared for different examinations? I had a brilliant mathematics teacher who was inspirational, but my biology textbook was engagingly modern, well-structured and easy to learn. How do we measure the quality of teaching in mathematics and biology and how do we measure the quality of textbooks? But let us imagine that these problems were solved and we had all of the measures we needed to hand. All that would remain would be to conduct the statistical analysis that controlled for these factors so that we could investigate examination comparability. On constructing this model, if I find that for each hour of studying, candidates do better in mathematics than in physical education, do I conclude that mathematics is too easy? Using this catch-all definition, the answer is yes, as it has to be assumed that the relationship between these controls and the examinations being compared is the same for each examination. As soon as the relationship is allowed to differ, we cannot disentangle the examination difficulty from the supposed control for candidate preparedness. Naturally, life is not like this and these controls do vary between examinations. Girls do better than boys in GCSE chemistry, but worse in GCSE physics. Putting gender into an analysis comparing those examinations would therefore be highly problematical. This argument is more fully explored in Baird & Jones (1998).

Surely, though, there are some more-similar examinations where this definition would be useful? But even this is highly problematical. Examining boards have routinely carried out analyses using rudimentary approaches to this definition to compare different options within examinations – typically coursework with optional written papers (e.g. Massey & Baird, 2001). Having controlled for candidates' performances on the other question papers, candidates who take the coursework route often tend to do better. This could mean that coursework is too easy, but there is more to it than that.

In some examinations, candidates withdraw from the coursework option very late and enter for the optional written examination instead. This pattern, and examiners' experiences of these students, leads us to the question of whether lazy students, who have not completed their coursework, switch to the written paper in some of the qualifications. Completing the coursework may not only involve more effort, but it is possible that students learn more through their experience of that kind of assessment than an examination paper. What the relationship between the control variables and the examination results *should be* is not an empirical or theory-driven question, it is a value judgement.

There are several definitions that can be seen as sub-sets of the catch-all, but of course they are inadequate theoretically precisely because they do not attempt to measure all possible legitimate influences upon the examination results. What all of these approaches have in common is a rationale that attempts to control for the entry characteristics of candidates sitting the examinations. Essentially, the experimental design involves analysing the examination results, having controlled for differences between the candidates taking the two examinations.

Chapter 9 investigates the problems with assuming that a group of candidates should be awarded the same results in two examinations they entered. Another variant is assuming that similar schools ('common centres') should have similar results and the problems with that are outlined by Cresswell (1996). Yet another possibility is using a reference test to control for differences in entry between two examinations, and this is discussed in Chapter 8. Robert Coe expands upon these possible models further in his commentary following this chapter.

A famous example of the inadequacy of a purely statistical definition arose in the introduction of the Curriculum 2000 A level examinations. Outcomes were predicted statistically, on the basis of candidates' prior attainment (mean GCSE scores). An assumption was made, not unreasonably one might think, that the relationship between prior attainment and A level grade would be similar for the new examinations compared with the same subject in the old-style A levels: a value-added definition. Actually, many assumptions have to be borne out for such a projection to be adequate. Equal teaching in both years, equal motivation of students, equivalent quality of textbooks and so on are necessary for this to be a reasonable assumption. In the first year of a new syllabus and examination structure, these assumptions simply do not hold.

The structure of the examinations had changed in the syllabus revision with the introduction of modular examinations (as proposed by Dearing, 1996), the main structural change being that candidates could certificate with an AS examination one year into the course. Students were encouraged to sit four AS level subjects in the first year and focus upon three subjects in their second year. The AS results were aggregated with the second year (A2) results to compose the new A levels. Certainly, the statistical predictions had operated well in the first year, 2001, with senior examiners' qualitative judgements of candidates' performances largely corresponding with the statistical information. Suffice it to say that setting of the AS standards was not generally problematical. When it came to setting the A2 examination standards, the boundary marks that would have been required to produce the statistical predictions were unacceptable to the senior examiners and were, frankly, ludicrous.

To illustrate the problem, in AQA A level French, 76% of students who sat the first AS examinations in 2001 went on to take the first A level examinations in 2002 (Table 1). Results for all AS students in 2001 had been similar to those for all A level students in the previous year, after controlling for prior attainment. Statistical predictions for A level results in 2002 were higher than A level results in 2000 (the last year in which only the old-style A levels were available), as the prior attainment scores (mean GCSE) for the cohort entered for the 2002 examinations were better. To achieve these statistical predictions, the boundary marks would have had to be very low at grade A and very high at grade E. On the oral examination, the difference between the highest and the lowest grade boundaries would have been 8 marks out of a total maximum score of 70. Either the assessments were very poorly designed – and that would have applied across all subjects – or there was something amiss with the assumptions underlying the statistical predictions.

From the actual 2002 A level results (Table 1), it is evident that it was concluded that there was something wrong with the statistical predictions. Investigations showed that there was an enormous disparity between students who dropped a subject at AS

Table 1 AQA French: statistical predictions and actual results

			Grade A	Grade E	Total number of candidates entered
2000	A level	Actual results	23.8%	88.7%	5,321
2001	AS	Actual results – all candidates	25.8%	94.1%	5,100
		Actual results – candidates who went on to study at A level	44.1%	99.8%	3,856
2002	A level	Statistical predictions	24.8%	92.4%	4,019
		Actual results	28.5%	97.2%	3,246

and those who continued to take it to A level. In this case, almost all AS candidates who continued to A2 study passed the AS examination (99.8%) and 44.1% were awarded a grade A at AS level. As a grade A at AS level accumulated enough points for a grade E at A level, 44.1% of A level students had passed the A level examination before they even sat an A2 examination and many more did not need to pass the A2 examinations to pass the A level – they only needed to score a few marks on each question paper (Pinot de Moira, 2002). One interpretation of this information is that the new assessments did not fit the new A level structure and that candidates did not deserve better grades than candidates with the same prior attainment had been awarded in the past. But a value-added definition is a weak version of the catch-all definition and more information was available.

A lower proportion of 18-year-old students had gone on to sit A levels in 2002 than in the previous year (Table 2). The introduction of AS certificates had a dramatic impact upon students' routes through the education system, with those who had been awarded better grades than they expected on the basis of their prior attainment being more likely to continue to the second year of study than those who had been awarded worse grades than they expected. Students were most likely to drop the subject in which they achieved their worst grade (Baird *et al.*, 2003).

Table 2 Proportion of 17-year-olds taking AS examinations and 18-year-olds taking A level examinations in England

	2001	2002
AS	40.0%	48.9%
A level	36.4%	35.7%

Source: calculated from Department for Education and Skills and National Office of Statistics figures

So another interpretation of the statistical information is that the change in examination structure had given students sufficient feedback about their strengths and weaknesses to make better choices about what to continue studying, thereby weeding out students who were not likely to pass the final qualification. Statistically speaking, putting the information we have about students' performances in AS

French into the statistical model would get us closer to the catch-all definition and we would not necessarily expect students' A level results in 2002 to be similar to those in previous years.

But hang on. The statistical value-added model that the predictions were based upon was created from old-style A level results, and the AS was not a feature of the previous A levels, so there was no such possibility. This highlights one of the problems with the catch-all definition: the world changes. If this entails changes in the relationship between the factors that are being used to control for entry between the examinations and the outcomes of those examinations, then the catch-all definition leaves a gap, as it is not possible empirically to know what those new relationships should be. Again, this has to be determined by value judgement.

Choice of factors to put into these statistical models is also a matter of values. If this were left to empiricism, a host of factors are related to examination results that we would think nonsensical to use to predict how students should be awarded grades. For example, anger (Lane et al., 2005), physical attractiveness (Zahr, 1985), comfort of clothing (Bell et al., 2005) and unattractiveness of first name (Erwin, 1999) have all been found to have predictive relationships with academic achievement. Other factors that are more traditionally reported with examination results, such as type of school, ethnic group, age, socioeconomic status and gender may seem more sensible, but we cannot fool ourselves that they are innocuous. Our choice of factors to put into these models represents our values about legitimate relationships with examination results.

By using these factors as controls, we interpret them as legitimate, but an alternative interpretation would be that they are biases in our examination system, and other analyses of the results, by gender or ethnic group for example, do indeed draw these conclusions (e.g. Gillbourn & Youdell, 2000). Now, the assessment specialist cannot control or even very much influence the relationship between these factors and examination results, but which factors are selected matters because students are not randomly allocated to examinations – there is choice. So, if an examination happens to have good results and is sat by a disproportionately higher number of females, then we may conclude that the examination is appropriately graded, but that females do better in examinations than do males. Other researchers may draw the conclusion that the examinations are biased in favour of females. Disentangling the examination standard from the features of the candidates who take the examination is impossible (Baird et al., 2000).

Statistical literature on the best approach to setting up models of data abounds with debate on strategies for selection of factors to include, and criteria for so doing. Raudenbush (1994) argues that researchers should have theoretical reasons for the inclusion or exclusion of variables from models. Fishing expeditions, where researchers include anything that happens to have a significant effect on the model have, he notes, been found to overestimate the values of the coefficients in the models and underestimate the standard errors when cross-validation studies have been conducted. As previously discussed, theoretical reasons for relationships between a disparate range of variables and examination results can be found in the literature.

Disappointingly, theory does not provide the whole answer that we seek, and Raudenbush alludes to this, when he says that there is 'a decision about how to select variables for an analysis' and his paper 'has little to say about this important decision. Rather, the variables are viewed as given and a general approach to their analysis is prescribed.' Choosing the variables for analysis is an experimental design question, involving selecting variables that not only have an empirical relationship with the examination results, but that we consider should be used as controls. After all, this experiment has social justice issues running through the design of it. A different dependent variable may help to illustrate the issues.

Imagine that we wished to use the catch-all definition to investigate fair pay, comparing two occupations: nursing and plumbing. Naturally, we would select control variables that, theoretically speaking, we would expect to have an empirical relationship with pay, such as number of years' experience, amount of time spent training, work-related benefits (e.g. pension, sick leave), ethnic group and gender. All of these variables have significant effects in the model I create. For example, women get lower wages, as do people with a non-white ethnic background. I conclude that, having controlled for these variables, plumbers and nurses are paid equitably. Putting variables in the model for the purposes of exploring empirical relationships is a separate issue from using variables as controls for differences in the types of groups associated with the dependent variable.

Many would object to my model on the grounds that it is not fair that women and ethnic minority groups are paid less, and that this is not an explanation or a good control for differences in pay between nurses and plumbers. Indeed, setting up models like this and interpreting them in this way serves to compound existing inequalities if people accept these discrepancies as empirical and therefore legitimate. This example serves to highlight that the question of what it is legitimate to control for is not an empirical question, it is a value judgement. Value judgements change over time and depend upon individuals' principles – an uncomfortable reality for researchers to accept.

Challenges to the adoption of the catch-all as the sole definition of examination standards arise because no methodology would be able to encompass all possible factors that could be included in a model. Even stronger challenges arise because this definition fails to consider the content of students' performances.

2.3 Criterion referencing

With all of these problems with statistical approaches to the definition of examination standards, the answer to some is obvious – document the criteria that we expect of students' performances and allow subject matter experts to judge the quality of students' work against them. Sir Keith Joseph favoured this system when GCSEs were introduced in the 1980s (see Chapter 2) believing that it would measure 'more absolute standards' (Joseph, 1984). This definition is attractive, as the criteria would be available to educational stakeholders as an illustration and explanation of candidates' grading. Sir Mike Tomlinson's view of examination standards is similar (although he does allow that statistical information is also necessary for setting standards):

> The basis for any system of assessment intended to judge students' achievement using a fixed standard should in principle lie in a comparison of individual students' work against that standard.
>
> Tomlinson (2002, p. 25)

Also underlying this approach is the idea that it should be entirely feasible for examiners, indeed teachers, to make explicit the criteria for attaining particular grades. Teachers must be able to check students' learning by means of some form of assessment and explain why they have failed to make the grade. Students' performances would exemplify these written performance standards at the appropriate grades. Any notion that this is problematical would appear to undermine teachers' expert status, but experts' status in other areas has long been under threat – the literature shows us that doctors are not highly accurate at diagnosis, for example (Dowie & Elstein, 1988). Expert status is now more openly questioned in many areas of life. Like the simple cohort referencing system, this definition seems to have transparency in its favour. Many vocational qualifications have been developed with criterion referencing underpinning them. Wolf (2002) writes of the development of National Vocational Qualifications (NVQs) that the National Council for Vocational Qualifications' theory

> ... was that standards could be so clear and all-inclusive that anyone, in any factory, office or playgroup, would be able to use them to assess and measure performance accurately. As reality stubbornly failed to fall in with NCVQ's vision of perfect clarity, the level of detail required by the Council and the complexity of standards layout increased. It became more and more desirable for industries to acquire... the services of an experienced, all-purpose standards writer from the government's approved list.
>
> Wolf (2002, p. 74)

In practice, delivering a transparent criterion referencing system does not easily translate into the kind of educational standards people expect to ensue. Criterion referenced examinations were introduced in New Zealand in 2004, following a significant teacher training programme to ensure that the standards were widely understood (Gilmore, 2002). The pass rate in the scholarship examinations dropped to half that of the previous year and there was an outcry over the overall pass rate, as well as variability between subjects. Approximately three-quarters of students sitting the Maori and Chinese examinations passed but, at the other end of the spectrum, the pass rate for physical education was 0% (Kingdon, 2005). The New Zealand Qualifications Authority's internal review (Martin, 2005) commented as follows:

> This experience highlighted two problems. These were the level at which the standard was pitched and how realistic that level was. Setting an examination paper requires clarity about what is expected of students at a certain age (or a certain level of learning).

The issue is whether the standards address a certain level that the best students can realistically reach, or whether they are aspirational and aim at a level that the ideal student ought to reach. It is not clear which approach chief examiners and markers put in practice for the 2004 Scholarship, and whether each subject had the same notion of the standard.

Martin (2005, p. 11, paragraph 61)

Curiously, in criterion referencing, students are generally awarded the grade according with their worst performance, as all of the criteria have to be met to be awarded a grade (Forrest & Shoesmith, 1985). Rather than celebrating students' achievements, criterion referencing accredits students at the level of their weakest skill. Attempts to introduce criterion referencing in GCSEs failed because some students who deserved particular grades according with senior examiners' judgements did not meet the criteria (Cresswell, 1996). Compensation for weak performance in one criterion may be made by good performance on another criterion. Wilmut & Rose (1989) give the example of students who were good at seeking out information, but poor at communication and vice versa.

So far, only the problems associated with the criterion referencing system itself have been considered. The pattern of results in New Zealand is not surprising in relation to the educational assessment research literature and there are reasons to question the capacity of any judge to carry out the criterion referenced judgements in a way that is fair to candidates. This is discussed further in relation to the next possible definition of examination standards. For now, suffice it to say that all of the problems applying to human judgements of standards apply to criterion referencing, the main problem being a lack of adaptation of what is required from students depending upon the difficulty of the task being set.

2.4 Weak criterion referencing

Every year, over five hundred committees of eight senior examiners (on average) are convened to make judgements of students' performances on GCSE and A level examinations in England (Baird & Dhillon, 2005). The judgements being made are expected to take into account the difficulty of the examination. If setting examinations of equivalent difficulty was not problematical, these committees would not be required to meet, as the same grade boundary marks could be applied to the examinations every year. Under this definition, students' performances are said to be equivalent if they are of equal merit, in the judgement of senior examiners, after they have taken into account any changes in demand of the assessment. In practice, this is not the only definition of examination standards being adopted by these committees (Baird *et al.*, 2000), but there was a time when statistical information played a much less prominent part in the standard-setting process and it is useful to look at a case from that era, as it illustrates the problems that can arise under this definition. Research evidence on examiner judgements relevant to this definition of examination standards will then be outlined.

A case of weak criterion referencing in practice

In 1991, the Associated Examining Board's (AEB's) A level English examination (syllabus 0652) changed. One of the three question papers was marked out of 80 in

1991, rather than the 100 marks available in the previous year. However, the marking criteria were unchanged and the senior examiners 'could discern no way in which the marking schemes could have adversely or unfairly affected the results' (Day, 1992). The result of the senior examiners' grading judgements was to drastically reduce the proportion of candidates being awarded the top grades, but to increase the proportion of candidates passing (Table 3). So, if the assessment was of equivalent difficulty to the previous year, the candidates or the teaching must have been very different.

There was no evidence from the statistical analysis of the entry for the examination that the explanation was to be found there. The grade boundary marks set were very similar to those set in 1990 (after accounting for changes to the maximum mark) at grades A and B, with large reductions in the outcomes at those grades. If a similar grade boundary mark had been set at grade E, it would have produced 60.1% of candidates passing, but the grade E boundary mark was set at a lower proportion of the maximum mark than in 1990. This demonstrates that using the same boundary marks year on year has unpredictable effects. The scale upon which the boundary marks are being set changes, so it becomes like using a measuring tape made of elastic. The outcomes may or may not be similar to the previous year.

Table 3 AEB A level English (syllabus 0652) results

	Grade A	Grade B	Grade E	Total number of candidates entered
1990	5.7%	15.2%	60.1%	4,401
1991	0.7%	4.8%	71.9%	3,680
1991–1990	–5.0%	–10.4%	+11.8%	–721

Three schools protested to the Independent Appeals Authority for Schools Examinations (IAASE), who instructed the examining board to reconvene the awarding meeting, stating that:

> The Authority was not satisfied with the overridingly judgemental nature of the award and it found that, statistically, the final grades awarded were out of line both with the marks produced by a team of experienced assistant examiners and with the awards in previous years on that syllabus. The Board had not given proper weight to the statistical evidence.
>
> IAASE (1991)

The reconvened meeting included senior examiners from another AEB A level English syllabus (660). The entire panel was given a presentation on the statistical information and then conducted a thorough, independent review of the candidates' work, before producing new grade boundary marks. The new recommendations involved a small reduction in the grade A boundary marks, giving 1.1% of candidates a grade A. None of the upgraded candidates came from the schools who had appealed. The grade B and grade E boundary marks were not revised at all. The examining board documented the rationale for the grade boundary marks, indicating how candidates had performed at each of the key grade boundaries. AEB's procedures in those days gave little authority to the board officers to challenge the grading judged by the senior examiners. The schools took their appeal back to IAASE, and AEB was heavily criticised:

> The Authority, like the School and the LEA, was not satisfied with this response... It did not accept the Board's distinction between 'procedures' and the 'decisions' of its awarders: nothing in the report of the reconvened awarding meeting had altered the Authority finding; the standard of judgement which was applied by the awarders had been inconsistent with the standard applied in all other cases.
>
> IAASE (1991)

This case resulted in a change to AEB's procedures, with statistics being given a more prominent role and awarding committees making recommendations to the chief executive, giving him final authority and accountability for the grading of the examinations. IAASE was clear that statistical information should have played a part in the process, showing that our educational institutions and structures are prepared to point to statistical definitions to challenge examiners' judgements when they believe the outcomes to be unjust. What this case and the New Zealand examination results have in common is the lack of reference to statistical information, and there is systematic research evidence, outlined below, showing that a reliance upon qualitative judgements will produce large swings in examination outcomes.

Research on examiner judgements

Cresswell (1997, 2000) analysed 108 grading decisions made in the 1994 examinations, comparing the boundary marks set by the examiners with those that would have been set to produce statistically equivalent outcomes. With random fluctuations in the sample of students taking examinations in any one year, it might be expected that there would be some changes in outcome and that they would reflect a normal distribution: most changes in outcomes would be small and there would be few extreme changes. Cresswell found exactly the opposite. He found few *small* changes: most were large swings in outcome compared with the previous year. These large swings were not explained by changes in the demographic nature of the candidates entered for the examinations, and they were not part of an ongoing trend.

Fortunately, the matter was not explained simply by the examiners having chosen the same boundary marks every year. There was clear evidence that examiners had responded to changes in difficulty of the examinations, with 77% of the boundary marks moving in the direction predicted by the statistical evidence. In fact, examiners tended to produce boundary marks that went halfway between the previous year's boundary marks and where the statistical information suggested the boundary marks should lie.

Furthermore, there is abundant evidence that examiners are not good at discerning the difficulty of questions (e.g. Impara & Plake, 1998) and question papers. Good & Cresswell (1988) investigated examiners' ability to set grade boundaries on tests that had specifically been designed to be easy, medium and hard and which were sat by the *same* group of candidates. When candidates sat an easy paper, their performances were judged to be worthy of higher grades than when they sat the harder papers. Figure 2 shows the findings for the physics papers, but the same effects were found in French and history. So the reason that there is such variability in outcomes when a weak criterion referencing definition is adopted is that examiners cannot adequately compensate in their judgements of candidates' work for the demands of the question papers.

Figure 2 Grading of physics papers

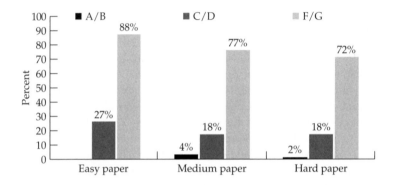

Note: grade A was not available on the easy paper
Source: Good & Cresswell (1988)

For weak criterion referencing to be acceptable, we must be able to trust that the qualitative judgements made by examiners are reliable and fair. We have already seen that they do not adequately compensate for changes in difficulty of the question paper, but there are other reasons to question them. Associated with the weak criterion referencing approach is the idea that examination standards are embodied in examples of students' work, in relation to the question papers. Thus, following Dearing (1996), enormous resources have gone into creating a national archive of question papers and examples of students' performances, so that the standards over the years and in different subjects can be evidenced. Indeed, part of the standard-setting process has long involved reference to candidates' work on the cut score in the previous year.

Baird (2000) investigated whether these exemplars influenced examiners' judgements in A level psychology and English by manipulating the exemplars provided to the examiners in an experiment conducted outside the operational grading process. She found that it made no difference whether examiners were given the correct exemplar for grade E or were deceived by being supplied with an exemplar for grade D. Some of the examiners were given no exemplars at all and they still set standards comparable with the other groups. Therefore, it has to be concluded that examiners are setting standards with reference not to these exemplars that they are being supplied with, but with reference to their own mental models of the standard. There is also evidence that examiners are unduly influenced by the consistency of candidates' performances (Scharaschkin & Baird, 2000). This is an illegitimate effect because candidates are allowed to compensate for weak performances in one area with stronger performances in another in the A level and GCSE examinations. Further, examiners demonstrate a tunnel-vision effect in their judgements, as they make more severe judgements of candidates' work when they judge each question paper independently than when they judge all of their work for A level (Baird & Scharaschkin, 2002).

Weak criterion referencing also relies upon examiners being able to make qualitative distinctions between candidates' work on adjacent marks. Baird & Dhillon (2005) conducted studies with GCSE English and A level physics examiners, asking them to rank-order candidates' work in the seven-mark range in which examiners normally scrutinise candidates' work for a grade boundary decision (see Figure 3). Care had been taken to ensure that the marking of the work included in the study was accurate. Correlations between each examiner's rank-ordering and the marks were low to moderate, and none of the 36 correlations calculated were statistically significant (following correction for multiple testing). None of the examiners rank-ordered candidates' work well for both grade boundaries included in the study. Using a different methodology, Forster (2005) found similar results in business studies, English and geography.

Figure 3 Correlations between examiners' rank-orderings of grade-worthiness and mark

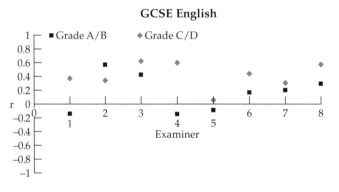

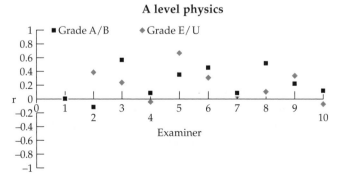

This should not be interpreted as meaning that senior examiners do their job badly. On the contrary, they are selected because they are the best people for the job and show a great deal of diligence in marking and grading candidates' work in the interests of fairness. The task of judging to a precise mark, at the boundary between one grade and the next, is impossible. Candidates can reach that mark through thousands of different routes through the question paper (see Scharaschkin & Baird, 2000). Examiners are expected to be able to make a judgement about the extent to which the performances they see on the question paper are caused by a change in the question paper or in candidate preparedness. Taking these features together, there is no prototypical performance that examiners can look out for – the candidates may have reached their mark by a different, but equally valid, route or the question paper may have enhanced or detracted from their performance.

Nonetheless, if we wish to adopt the weak criterion referencing approach to standards, we would have to accept the inconsistency in results produced (statistically speaking, of course). This would entail not using school performance tables and not using the examination outcomes to measure the health of the education system as a whole. As we have seen in the case of the AEB A level English examination, it is unlikely that education stakeholders in England would be content with the variations in statistical outcomes this definition produces, and would resort to statistical definitions of examination standards to challenge it. This leads us to the next definition of examination standards.

2.5 Conferred power definition

Under this definition, society empowers certain individuals to make judgements regarding where the examination standards lie (Cresswell, 1996; Wiliam, 1996b). The process by which these judgements must be made, the information to be taken into account and the criteria for selection of the individuals to make the judgements are all important for this definition. Once the individuals are appointed, as long as due process is followed, there can be no recourse to appeal against their judgements, which are a speech act (Searle, 1969). Once a speech act has been uttered, it makes no sense to question whether it is true (e.g. 'I pronounce you man and wife' uttered by a priest following a legally conducted marriage ceremony). Under this model, there is no pretence that there is an objective way in which standards can be set – we simply accept the umpire's decision. The 'umpire' could be an examiner, a statistician, an examining board chief executive or anyone who fits the selection criteria defined in the due process. No guarantee about *what* the standard is comes from this definition – it is simply a value judgement that does not necessarily ascribe properties to the objects being judged (Cresswell, 1996).

Baird *et al.* (2000) argued that the due process in the case of examination standards is underspecified because the weight that should be given to different sources of information is not given. (Note that the 'conferred power definition' was termed the 'sociological definition' in Baird *et al.*, 2000.) This leaves the pronouncements about standards open to appeal and standard-setting does not operate as a speech act in practice.

Three significant examination crises have occurred in recent years in the UK:

1. the Scottish Qualifications Authority's (SQA's) problems in releasing examination results on time in 2000

2. Edexcel's problems in delivering examination results in 2001

3. concerns regarding examination standards at A level in the English examining boards, particularly at OCR, in 2002.

In an important paper, McCaig (2003) points out that these crises were linked to government policies and resulted partly from inadequate time for examining boards to deliver the government's objectives: integration of vocational and academic examining boards (applies to all three crises), reduction in the number of examining boards (applies to the 2001 and 2002 crises in particular) and delivery of new qualifications (all three crises). McCaig argues that the government distanced itself from the first two crises, but was not so successful with the third. After all, the then Secretary of State for Education and Skills, Estelle Morris, resigned not long after, stating her lack of capability as one of the reasons.

Throughout what became known as the 2002 examinations fiasco, fascinating statements were made by various parties regarding who had ownership of the standards. Allegations were made that the examination standards had been 'fixed' by examining board chief executives, particularly the OCR chief executive, Ron McLone. The chairman of QCA, William Stubbs, and even Estelle Morris herself were accused of influencing the results. Interference from any of these parties was deemed entirely illegitimate by the media. With the exception of cohort referencing, only the conferred power definition of examination standards could be delivered by chief executives of the examining boards, the chairman of QCA or the Secretary of State for Education and Skills. Sir Mike Tomlinson's review cleared QCA and the Secretary of State of any interference and asked the examining boards to look again at the grading of some of the examinations.

Setting aside the 2002 issues per se, the accountability for examination standards is interesting. If the chief executives of the examining boards cannot adjudicate, who is qualified? Delegation of the standards to the 500 committees is a recipe for chaos, with no co-ordination of the standards, policies and approaches being taken. However, the Accountable Officer at each examining board has a formal role within the QCA's code of practice for examinations. Questioning of their role was a rejection of the notion that there is anything further to examination standards than weak criterion referencing. Arguably, the government should have no role in the setting of examination standards, as it should be for educational assessment experts to decide this for society and it should not be a political matter.

Awarding bodies and QCA accepted that QCA has a role in defining the examination standards (House of Commons Education and Skills Committee, 2003). As mentioned previously, following summer 2002, weak criterion referencing was given more emphasis and Chairs of Examiners were elevated to a new role in the QCA's code of practice – changes to their recommendations could not be made without going through new procedures, which could ultimately result in a public wrangle between the examining board, the Chair of Examiners and the regulator. However, the nature of the accountability of Chairs of Examiners, Accountable Officers, QCA and the DfES and the relations between them have never been specified in a Memorandum of Understanding, as proposed by Tomlinson (2002).

The next section argues that it is not possible to specify the due process completely without making strange decisions in some instances. The conferred power perspective implies a trust in experts that has long since ceased to be a feature of UK society. Accountability is now an integral part of our education system and it would be difficult to envisage a conferred power definition being adopted (Broadfoot, 1996).

3   Construction of an examination comparability preference model

Distinctions can be made between the setting and maintaining of examination standards, as the bar has to be fixed at a particular height in the first year and questions about whether the bar is at the correct height do not necessarily have to be addressed in subsequent years. The previous definitions have been related to the setting of examination standards, although they also apply to the maintenance of examination standards because in practice standard setting and maintenance are similar, with questions about the appropriateness of the bar height being raised fairly regularly and considered to be legitimate. Comparability of examinations can be seen as distinct from standard-setting altogether and comparability issues are often dealt with as part of a research exercise, outside of the standard-setting process. Nonetheless, the definitions of examination standards are integral to examination comparability research and, in practice, comparability issues are part of the considerations during awarding.

Particularly when new examinations are introduced, there is controversy about whether examination standards have been maintained and reference is made to different sources of information supporting different definitions of examination standards. This was evident in the introduction of the Curriculum 2000 examinations, with arguments being made in favour of more reliance upon examiners' judgements. All of the definitions of examination standards outlined are common currency in the debates surrounding the release of examination results. Baird *et al.* (2000) argue that examining boards have to gauge the values that are acceptable to education stakeholders and set standards in that context. After all, these values reflect society's expectations regarding examination standards because of the way in which the results will be used. Standards, they argue, do not exist in any objective sense because the effect of candidate performances and the difficulty of the examination paper cannot be disentangled.

More recently, Newton (2005) argued for a diktat model, in which, for the sake of clarity about educational standards, a single definition is adopted. In particular, Newton argued that a linking construct should be defined whenever standards are set, so that it can be made clear upon what basis the standard is said to be comparable. He does not select a particular definition to favour, but dismisses the approach presented in Baird *et al.* (2000) as unsatisfactory (terming it the 'contest' approach) because it is unclear about what is being maintained. So could we choose to prioritise a particular definition, making clear the construct that is being maintained? Given the discussion surrounding the definitions presented in this chapter, let us consider the implications of the diktat model.

Unfortunately, the situation is not currently even as simple as choosing a particular construct and linking test standards along that construct because examination standards are expected to be maintained in a variety of ways too (Figure 4). Even using a single definition, the evidence regarding comparability for these different things to be compared can be contradictory. For example, the catch-all definition could provide evidence that standards had been maintained between years for a particular syllabus, but that it was no longer comparable with another syllabus in the same subject.

Extending Newton's diktat model, we could also specify not only the definition of examination standards and the construct to be linked, but our priorities for examination comparability; so that it is clear what information should be given preferential treatment. An alternative under the diktat model would be to select only one of the types of possible comparability, most likely between years. Note that this is not the only possibility under the diktat model, as Newton does not specify which construct should be linked, so it is open for use in different systems. Setting up the diktat model with a link between years would explicitly reject any notion that the examination system had any responsibility for comparability of standards between examining boards, between subjects or between qualifications. Therefore, no points systems in which grades are aggregated across qualifications would be fair – undermining the UCAS and school performance table points systems. Given that these represent two important purposes of UK educational examination assessment, it is easier to envisage that we could retain the expectations about what kinds of comparability should be maintained, but prioritise them. An attempt to make one such priority list is given in Figure 4, with items higher up the pyramid being preferred over those lower down. A logical approach like this is consistent with Donald Schön's (1988) 'Technical Rationality' model of decision making, in which rules and preferences can be written in a logical system. Assessment specialists' technical knowledge could be used in this technical-rationality approach to formulate rules for deciding what kind of comparability should be preferred over others.

In general, comparability between years is given supremacy in operational standard setting, as those sitting the examinations and teaching the syllabus are entitled to continuity between years in their expectations about the standards. Otherwise, teaching and learning would be problematical, as the results would give little feedback about expectations of students' performances in the examination. However, the Joint Council for Qualifications has a programme of statistically screening for possible discrepancies between examining boards' standards in the same subject. Where a subject appears to have been out of line with other examining boards, would it make sense to continue to prioritise between-year comparability for that syllabus?

Figure 4 A possible examination comparability preference model

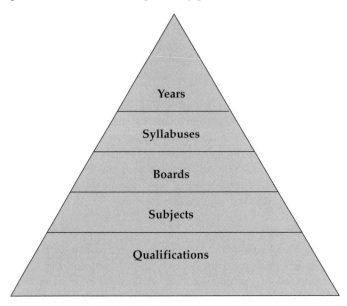

Equally, if two syllabuses in the same subject appeared to have discrepant standards, would it be correct to continue with that situation? Under these circumstances, the order of priority of years, syllabuses and boards may be changed on a rational basis. But this situation could simply be seen as an exception to the general model and logical guidance could be given, such as:

prioritise between year comparability, except

if

specific information is presented showing that between syllabus/board comparability is discrepant,

then

prioritise between syllabus/board comparability.

This would be fine if there were no circumstances under which this would be irrational, but such circumstances do arise in practice. For example, syllabuses have to be classified into subject areas to make comparisons between them. There may be good reasons to question such classifications, as they implicitly set up comparability expectations that may not be legitimate. For example, are philosophy and critical thinking syllabuses in the same subject area? If there is a question mark over any aspect of the comparison, it would make sense to continue to prioritise comparability between years.

Also, if philosophy was too easy compared with critical thinking using a value-added definition of examination standards, but philosophy was much harder than other A level subjects using a common-candidates definition of examination standards, would it be sensible to adjust the standard of the philosophy examination to make it tougher? This is a value judgement, the answer to which will differ between individuals and in different contexts – it can be prescribed, but only if we are willing to accept situations such as philosophy being aligned with critical thinking (statistically speaking), but being made even tougher compared with all other A levels.

Annually, standard-setting examples arise in which different features of examination comparability are given priority:

- GCSE French, German and Spanish have very similar assessment structures and there are expectations *regarding inter-subject commonalities in boundary marks* for certain assessments, even though this may disrupt comparability between years to some extent. Prioritising commonalities in boundary marks between other qualifications would have disastrous effects upon between-year comparability and this would not be given priority elsewhere in the system.

- In the merger between AEB and NEAB, in which AQA was formed, for a number of years priority was given to *between-board comparability* rather than between-year comparability. Attaining similar standards across the new examining board was deemed more important than between year comparability, as the pressure from the government to have fewer examining boards was in part to bring about greater consistency in standards. (In practice no large changes in standards were made in any one year.)

- When the Applied GCEs were introduced in summer 2006, statistical information was used in the standard-setting process that would help to align the standards of the Applied GCEs with their respective academic GCEs. However, it quickly became apparent that the value-added between GCSE and Applied GCE was different from the value-added between GCSE and academic GCE (similar patterns emerged, subject by subject across the examining boards). As the Applied qualifications were designed to be different from traditional GCEs, it would be nonsensical to ignore those differences and expect the same value-added from each type of qualification. In this example, with standards being set for the first time, although a great deal of information was considered from different sources, eventually the decisions reached reflected between-qualification comparability, in terms of the weak criterion referencing approach.

These cases show the kinds of contextual, education stakeholder values that the examining boards and their senior examiners take into account to set the examination standards. To do otherwise, would be to fly in the face of society's expectations of the examination standards. A diktat model is only possible to the extent that it is possible to do this. In practice, under some circumstances, particular standards definitions and types of comparability will come to the fore, but these may change depending upon the context.

Schön (1988) argues that there are features of the real world that make the Technical Rationality model of decision making difficult:

- it is complex, making it difficult to ascertain which features to focus upon

- it is unstable, making it difficult to generate heuristics

- unique instances arise for which the professional has no real reference point

- conflicting values mean that not all constraints can be satisfied (see Table 4).

Major theoretical advantages of the diktat model are its transparency about what standard is being maintained and its scientific, logical approach, but its major drawback is that it would not provide society with the qualifications it currently desires: certain expectations of comparability would be deemed beyond the realms of possibility. Of course, the contest model does not guarantee that these forms of comparability are delivered, but neither does it reject many of them as irrelevant. Even if the diktat model was adopted, it would soon falter, as no attempt would be made to address the concerns of various educational stakeholders. Naturally, education stakeholders adopt different positions regarding examination standards and comparability depending upon their perspectives, and this is not singular even for individuals over time. Examination standards are highly politicised because they are intimately related to beliefs about individuals' and societies' economic prospects (Wolf, 2002; McCaig, 2003).

Nonetheless, some argue that separate credit systems should be set up to deal with linking of examination outcomes in various post hoc ways, such as scaling the examination grades to compensate for differences in difficulty for a university entrance points system. Grading itself should only deal with the originally envisaged linking construct. Australia's university entrance system is based upon students' examination grades, but scaling for differences in difficulty between states' examinations is carried out. Lamprianou discusses this further in his commentary on Chapter 9.

There is no doubt that this is a theoretically attractive way out of the quagmire of comparability as defined in the English examination system, but would the social and political educational structures support such a change? Persuading stakeholders to give up closely valued features of the English grading system would be difficult, even if they are not believed to be well-delivered currently, due to the tensions in definitions of examination standards in use outlined earlier, and because the technicalities of doing something different would be seen as obfuscatory. But this is not an argument for the status quo, it is a statement of the realities that will face any such move. This is not just a technical matter – it is culturally and politically embedded.

Table 4 Features of the real world that make professional, scientific decision making impossible

Feature of real world	Example in the standard-setting task
Complexity	Different forms of comparability. Contradictory evidence regarding different kinds of comparability. Differences between assessment formats. Multiple performance attributes in candidates' work. Changes in the content of assessment.
Instability	Political and educational stakeholder values change. Difficulty of the examinations changes. Statistical relationships between predictor variables and examination outcomes change.
Uniqueness	Candidates respond to assessments in novel ways.
Value conflict	Different definitions of standards. Different perspectives of educational stakeholders.

4 Conclusion

What counts as a definition of examination standards – what do we expect from such a thing? Newton (2005) argues that the important feature of a definition of examination comparability is the construct being used to link the standards. Whilst important, this in itself does not provide the whole definition. Test constructors have in mind a particular construct when they create the tests, but they do not have control over the myriad ways in which society expects comparability to be maintained. These comparability expectations are not inherent to the tests themselves either – they are externally, and often subsequently, imposed requirements. School performance tables were introduced with a credit system expounding comparability between all GCSEs, GNVQs and other qualifications at the same level.

Empirically, it is easy to show the faults in these credit systems, but if they work well enough as a currency system, then pragmatics entail that whatever can be done to root out the worst cases of lack of comparability must be done. So a test may be designed to assess ability in science and two tests can be linked using this construct, but these tests may also be linked with other tests, using different constructs, such as 'general academic ability'. In any case, any particular examination does not assess a single construct and can be linked on more than one theoretical (after all, they are all theoretical) construct. Indeed, different assessments for any particular qualification typically have low correlations, implying that different constructs are being measured.

A definition of examination standards should ideally meet the following criteria (adapted from Fawcett's (2005) criteria for evaluation of theories):

1. It should have a theoretical underpinning, referring explicitly to the educational intentions of standards and comparability. The theory should be consistent, as opposed to predicting more than one outcome for any particular case.

2. The definition should be testable and supported by evidence.

3. As with any good theory, the definition should be parsimonious.

4. The definition should be practically useful in our educational culture. Contributions to academic debate are useful theoretically, but ideally a definition would conform to this criterion.

As the foregoing discussion shows, the author's view is that all of the definitions of examination standards have weaknesses and this is also true in relation to the criteria above. Chapter 11 looks at what developments are needed in this area to strengthen our definitions of examination standards. All of the definitions are open to empirical test, most of them are weak on theoretical underpinnings and there are serious problems with the practicality of some of them in the English educational, cultural context. Moving away from a balance between the weak criterion referencing definition and the statistical, catch-all definition – i.e. away from the contest model – would require a radical shift in England's educational culture.

Expectations about examination standards and comparability exist because of the way examination results are used in society. Prioritising a particular definition would make the examination results less useful, although Newton (2005) argues that assessment specialists have gone too far in trying to achieve the impossible. A single definition would not solve many problems either. Not only are there tensions between different definitions, there are tensions within them, with competing approaches being used to try to measure examination comparability throwing up different results and linking between different kinds of qualifications suggesting different conclusions. Hence, the lively debate in the following chapters and with the respondents.

References

Aldrich, R. (2000). Educational standards in historical perspective. In H. Goldstein & A. Heath (Eds.), *Educational standards* (pp. 39-56). Oxford: Oxford University Press for The British Academy.

Baird, J. (2000). Are examination standards all in the head? Experiments with examiners' judgments of standards in A level examinations. *Research in Education, 64,* 91–100.

Baird, J., Cresswell, M.J., & Newton, P. (2000). Would the *real* gold standard please step forward? *Research Papers in Education, 15,* 213–229.

Baird, J., & Dhillon, D. (2005). *Qualitative expert judgements on examination standards: Valid, but inexact.* Internal report RPA 05 JB RP 077. Guildford: Assessment and Qualifications Alliance.

Baird, J., Ebner, K., & Pinot de Moira, A. (2003, October). *Student choice of study in Curriculum 2000.* Paper presented at the International Association for Educational Assessment Annual Conference, Manchester.

Baird, J., & Jones, B.E. (1998). *Statistical analyses of examination standards: Better measures of the unquantifiable?* Research Report RAC/780. Assessment and Qualifications Alliance.

Baird, J., & Scharaschkin, A. (2002). Is the whole worth more than the sum of the parts? Studies of examiners' grading of individual papers and candidates' whole A-level examination performances. *Educational Studies, 28,* 143–162.

Bell, R., Cardello, A.V., & Schutz, H.G. (2005). Relationship between perceived clothing comfort and exam performance. *Family and Consumer Sciences Research Journal, 33,* 308–320.

Broadfoot, P.M. (1996). *Education, assessment and society: A sociological analysis.* Buckingham: Open University Press.

Cresswell, M.J. (1996). Defining, setting and maintaining standards in curriculum-embedded examinations: Judgemental and statistical approaches. In H. Goldstein & T. Lewis (Eds.), *Assessment: Problems, developments and statistical issues* (pp. 57-84). Chichester: John Wiley and Sons.

Cresswell, M.J. (1997). *Examining judgments: Theory and practice of awarding public examination grades.* Unpublished PhD thesis, University of London Institute of Education.

Cresswell, M.J. (2000). The role of public examinations in defining and monitoring standards. In H. Goldstein & A. Heath (Eds.), *Educational standards* (pp. 69-104). Oxford: Oxford University Press for The British Academy.

Day, J.A. (1992). *652 English literature 1991. Reconvened grade awarding meeting report.* Unpublished internal paper, Associated Examining Board.

Dearing, R. (1996). *Review of qualifications for 16–19 year olds.* London: School Curriculum and Assessment Authority.

Department for Education and Employment. (1997). *Excellence in Schools.* London: Stationery Office.

Department for Education and Skills. (2002). *The national literacy and numeracy strategies. Including all children in the literacy hour and daily mathematics lesson. Management guide.* DfES 0465/2002. London: Department for Education and Skills.

Department for Education and Skills. (2006). *Specialist schools information on the standards site.* Available at http://www.standards.dfes.gov.uk/specialistschools/

Dowie, J., & Elstein, A. (1988). *Professional judgment. A reader in clinical decision making.* Cambridge: Cambridge University Press.

Erwin, P.G. (1999). Attractiveness of first names and academic achievement. *Journal of Psychology: Interdisciplinary and Applied, 133,* 617–620.

Fawcett, J. (2005). Criteria for evaluation of theory. *Nursing Science Quarterly, 18,* 131–135.

Forrest, G.M., & Shoesmith, D.J. (1985). *A second review of GCE comparability studies.* Manchester: Joint Matriculation Board on behalf of the GCE Examining Boards.

Forster, M. (2005). *Can examiners successfully distinguish between scripts that vary by only a small range of marks?* Unpublished internal paper, Oxford Cambridge and RSA

Gillbourn, D., & Youdell, D. (2000). *Rationing education. Policy, practice, reform and equity.* Buckingham: Open University Press.

Gilmore, A. (2002). Large-scale assessment and teachers' capacity: Learning opportunities for teachers in the National Education Monitoring Project in New Zealand. *Assessment in Education, 9,* 343–365.

Goldstein, H. (1986). Models for equating test scores and for studying the comparability of public examinations. In D.T. Nuttall (Ed.), *Assessing educational achievement* (pp. 168-184). London: Falmer.

Good, F.J., & Cresswell, M.J. (1988). Grade awarding judgments in differentiated examinations. *British Educational Research Journal, 14,* 263–281.

House of Commons, Education and Skills Committee. (2003). *A level standards.* Third report of session 2002–03. HC 153. London: The Stationery Office Limited.

Impara, J.C., & Plake, B.S. (1998). Teachers' ability to estimate item difficulty: A test of the assumptions of the Angoff standard setting method. *Journal of Educational Measurement, 35,* 69–81.

Independent Appeals Authority for School Examinations. (1991). *Independent Appeals Authority for School Examinations annual report.* London: Independent Appeals Authority for School Examinations.

Joseph, K. (1984). Speech by Sir Keith Joseph, Secretary of State for Education and Science, at the North of England Conference, Sheffield, Friday 6 January, 1984. *SEC annual report 1983–1984.* London: Secondary Examinations Council.

Kingdon, M.J. (2005). *Tomlinson revisited. A supplement to occasional paper No. 1.* Hellingly, East Sussex: The Examination on Demand Assessment Advisory Group.

Lane, A.M., Whyte, G.P., Terry, P.C., & Nevill, A.M. (2005). Mood, self-set goals and examination performance: The moderating effect of depressed mood. *Personality and Individual Differences, 30*(1), 143–153.

Lightfoot, L. (2006, May 10). Modular exams 'damaging degree courses'. *Daily Telegraph.*

Mansell, W. (2006, June 9). Pick A, B or C for a GCSE. *The Times Educational Supplement,* p. 1.

Martin, D. (2005). *Report on the 2004 scholarship to the Deputy State Services Commissioner by the review team led by Doug Martin.* New Zealand: State Services Commission.

Massey, C., & Baird, J. (2001). *A comparison between practical coursework routes in GCE chemistry (0654).* Internal Report RC/140. Guildford: Assessment and Qualifications Alliance.

McCaig, C. (2003). School exams: Leavers in panic. *Parliamentary Affairs: Special Issue, 56,* 471–489.

Newton, P.E. (2005). Examination standards and the limits of linking. *Assessment in Education, 12,* 105–123.

Pinot de Moira, A. (2002). *Preliminary analysis of the summer 2002 A level results.* Internal paper, RC/188. Guildford: Assessment and Qualifications Alliance.

Raudenbush, S. (1994). Searching for a balance between a priori and post hoc model specification: Is a 'general approach' desirable? *School Effectiveness and School Improvement, 5*(2), 196–198.

Scharaschkin, A., & Baird, J. (2000). The effects of consistency of performance on A level examiners' judgements of standards. *British Educational Research Journal, 26,* 343–357.

Schön, D.A. (1988). From technical rationality to reflection-in-action. In J. Dowie & A. Elstein (Eds.), *Professional judgment: A reader in clinical decision making.* Cambridge: Cambridge University Press.

Searle, J.R. (1969). *Speech acts. An essay in the philosophy of language.* Cambridge: Cambridge University Press.

Taylor, M. (2006, August 1). GCSE coursework to be curtailed to stop internet cheats. *The Guardian.*

Tomlinson, M. (2002). *Inquiry into A level standards. Final Report.* London: Department for Education and Skills.

Wiliam, D. (1996a). Meanings and consequences in standard setting. *Assessment in Education, 3,* 287–307.

Wiliam, D. (1996b). Standards in examinations: A matter of trust? *The Curriculum Journal, 7,* 293–307.

Wilmut, J., & Rose, J. (1989). *The modular TVEI scheme in Somerset: Its concept, delivery and administration.* London: Report to the Training Agency of the Department of Employment.

Wolf, A. (2002). *Does education matter? Myths about education and economic growth.* London: Penguin.

Working Group on 14–19 Reform. (2004). *14–19 curriculum and qualifications reform (Tomlinson Report).* London: Department for Education and Skills.

Zahr, L. (1985). Physical attractiveness and Lebanese children's school performance. *Psychological Reports, 56,* 191–192.

COMMENTARY ON CHAPTER 4

Harvey Goldstein

Jo-Anne Baird quotes me in 1986 as advocating a cohort referenced system. This is correct, and while I would not necessarily advocate this now in its pure form, I do not think it can be so summarily dismissed as in this chapter.

My argument was that the system would be transparent and as such throw the responsibility for interpretation upon the users of examination results, and in particular it would eschew the notion that present procedures can provide objective and fair comparisons. Baird argues that such a system could not be used by government and others to measure trends over time. In fact the present system cannot do that satisfactorily either, despite claims to the contrary (see for example Goldstein, 2000). A system that avoids the ill-informed debates that take place every year when examination results are published is surely to be welcomed. As she points out, specially developed measures would be needed, for example to evaluate policy changes, and the development of these would be welcome.

In fact, something akin to a cohort referencing system applies to university degree classes, where each university decides on its allocation with a minimal attempt to ensure any kind of comparability, even over time within institution. It works, partly, because of the reputation built up over time attached to each institution, of which users are well aware. It is simply not justified to claim that a similar system applied to examinations would lead to dumbing down. Nor do I see why new qualifications would necessarily 'struggle for recognition'. There are all kinds of ways of bringing innovations into the curriculum and examination system.

I can see, however, that for small-entry subjects, initial difficulties could be serious. Thus, if the suggestion were ever acted upon I would suggest that it first is applied on an experimental basis to mass entry subjects such as English and mathematics. Where I do agree strongly with Baird is in her view that such a system would stand little chance of being adopted in the current climate.

Reference

Goldstein, H. (2000). Discussion (of the measurement of standards, by David Bartholomew). In H. Goldstein & A. Heath (Eds.), *Educational standards* (pp. 138-149). Oxford: Oxford University Press for The British Academy.

COMMENTARY ON CHAPTER 4

Robert Coe

In this commentary on Jo-Anne Baird's chapter, I attempt to do three things. Firstly, to try to clarify some fundamental conceptual distinctions in the different meanings of 'comparability'. Secondly, to argue that one particular conception of comparability, construct comparability, is under-recognised in Baird's chapter (and elsewhere), but it provides an important perspective for understanding comparisons of different examinations. Thirdly, to explore the relationships between different views about the interpretation of examination grades or the uses to which they may be put, and the different conceptions we may have of comparability.

Conceptualising 'comparability'

Baird's chapter on comparability points out some of the anomalies that arise from popular understandings of the notion of 'standards' and goes on to describe and evaluate five specific 'definitions of examination standards from assessment specialists'. In doing this she illustrates convincingly the practical problems of each definition. However, she presents no overall conceptual framework for thinking about different meanings of 'comparability', and the reader may be left with some fundamental questions. Are these different definitions merely different operationalisations of the same fundamental conception of what 'comparability' means, or are they conceptually different? Does each definition represent a pure conception, or are some effectively hybridisations arising from the mixing of ideas? In each case, what does 'comparability' actually mean?

Much existing thinking about comparability issues within the UK has focused on the processes by which test scores are translated into an interpretable 'standard' (e.g. Wiliam, 1996a). There seems to be a broad consensus that there are basically two ways one can do this: the standard is either specified in terms of performance criteria, or in terms of statistical norms for some population. The terms *criterion-referenced* and *norm-referenced* are widely used to describe these two approaches, though as Wiliam (1996a) makes clear, the distinction is somewhat problematic in practice: 'a criterion-referenced test is just a well-designed norm-referenced test that has had the luxury of being restricted to a very small domain' (p. 295). A similar idea seems to underlie Jaeger's (1989) use of the terms *test-centred* and *examinee-centred* to distinguish between approaches to setting a standard that consider only features of the test and those that take into account the performance of examinees. The terms *performance comparability* and *statistical comparability* seem to capture this distinction.

In her chapter, Baird appears to adopt this broad dichotomy, describing two of the approaches, *cohort-referencing* and the *catch-all definition*, as coming from 'the statistical camp of assessment literature definitions of examination standards', and two others, *criterion-referencing* and *weak criterion-referencing*, where the standard resides in the observed (and evaluated) test performance, regardless of how many candidates achieved it. It is important to remember that the distinction between these two kinds of comparability can only be maintained at the level of idealisations. A pure *performance comparability* view would require us to judge the standard of a candidate's test performance by considering only the test, the context in which it was taken and the candidate's responses to it, but without any knowledge of how any other candidate had performed on that test – or even on any similar tests. Baird provides comprehensive, well-illustrated and convincing arguments, however, that in practice this cannot be satisfactorily done. On the other hand, a pure *statistical comparability* approach would compare the standards of different examinations using statistical information about how candidates with particular characteristics have performed on them, but without any knowledge of what those candidates were actually required to do. Again, Baird shows that such a method is unlikely to be satisfactory in practice.

Nevertheless, these idealisations are important. If 'comparability' can be understood in theoretically different ways, then terms such as 'standards' or 'difficulty' may also have more than one meaning. Claims such as those by Chris Woodhead that examinations are getting easier (Box 5 in Baird's chapter) may not actually contradict the claims of other studies (McGaw *et al.*, 2004) that they are not. The bases for, and meanings of, these claims are quite different. Characterising this debate as a 'tug of war' between progressives wanting to modernise the curriculum and traditionalists wanting to preserve elitist selection may be reading too much into their differences; they may simply be using the same word to mean two quite different things.

Baird presents a further approach to standard-setting, the *conferred power* definition, which does not fit into either the *performance* or the *statistical* conceptualisation of comparability. This approach sees standards as a pure social convention, defined by the values of a 'community of practice' rather than by any explicit rationale (Wiliam, 1996b). If our goal is to try to understand what is meant by 'comparability', however, then the *conferred power* definition can be dismissed fairly readily, since it offers nothing in the way of a conceptualisation. Of course, it is true that expert judgement and the application of subjective values are required to set standards. It is also true that some degree of trust in the judgements of 'awarders accepted as competent to make such judgements by all interested parties' (Cresswell, 1996, p. 79) must be a requirement of any system. However, this definition tells us nothing about how such trust might be established – or rebuilt if it is lost – or how these awarders come to be 'accepted as competent'. The *conferred power* definition offers no better answer to the question of why one examination is, or is not, comparable to another than 'Because I say so'. Such an answer seems unlikely to convince critics such as Woodhead or Dunford (cited by Baird) that they must simply take it on trust.

The case for 'construct comparability'

How, then, do we operationalise comparability? If the *conferred power* definition of comparability is not really a definition at all, and the *performance* and *statistical* definitions provide useful conceptual idealisations, but have limited practical value, what are we left with? Fortunately, there is an alternative conceptualisation of comparability, *construct comparability*, which is both logically coherent and practically operationalisable.

The concept of *construct comparability* arises from a perspective of trying to understand what it means for two examinations to be compared, rather than trying to define the meaning of a 'standard'. Logically, for a comparison between two things to be meaningful, there must be something they have in common, in terms of which they can be compared. A comparison has no meaning unless it relates to the amount or quality of some construct. In the context of comparing examination standards, it follows that if we can identify some common construct, shared by two or more examinations, then we have a basis for judging whether they are 'comparable'. This idea is developed further in my own chapter on common examinee methods (Chapter 9), where a number of examples of analyses are described whose results can be interpreted in terms of *construct comparability*.

It is possible to see *construct comparability* as subsuming both *performance* and *statistical* conceptions. The whole idea of a criterion-referenced standard arguably depends on identifying a particular level of some construct that can be defined sufficiently precisely. Without some such construct in mind, we cannot say that one criterion would be harder to meet than another. Hence *criterion-referencing* may be seen as a special case of *construct comparability*. It is also arguable that at least some forms of what appear to be *statistical comparability* are actually *construct comparability*. Although it is always possible to make statistical comparisons of the grades achieved in different examinations by 'comparable' candidates, it makes little sense to do so unless some theoretical construct guides the choice of the basis on which candidates are seen as 'comparable'. The mechanism by which a set of starting characteristics can be converted into examination grades in similar ways across different examinations seems to require some common construct to link them if the comparison is to be meaningful. From this, it seems tempting to conclude that, just as 'construct validity is the whole of validity' (Loevinger, 1957, p. 636), perhaps *construct comparability* is the whole of comparability.

Of course, this idea is not new. Wiliam (1996b) actually uses the term 'construct-referenced' assessment to account for the fact that a group of assessors may agree about the standard of a piece of work, even where there are no explicit criteria against which to judge it. They may nevertheless share an understanding of a broad construct which he calls 'levelness' but which might be interpreted as 'English attainment'. An even more explicit presentation of the idea of *construct comparability* can be found in Newton (2005) who discusses how a 'linking construct' can be used to establish the comparability of a group of examinations. This idea is discussed further in Chapter 9 of this volume.

Comparability in relation to interpretation and use of examination grades

From a *construct comparability* perspective, we can compare two or more examinations only if a common construct has been identified. However, just as the same examination may be interpreted in different ways for different purposes, there may be some cases in which more than one possible construct could be used as a basis for comparing the same set of examinations. It follows that there may be more than one view about their comparability: in terms of construct 'A', examination 'X' may be judged 'harder' than 'Y', but in terms of construct 'B' the position would be reversed.

The fact that there are multiple uses for examinations and multiple possible interpretations of their results implies that there may be multiple possible constructs that could be used to define comparability. Realistically, therefore, it is unhelpful to talk about comparability of examinations unless we are clear about the particular purpose for which we want to use and interpret those examinations.

The issue Baird raises about prioritising comparability across years versus comparability across syllabuses, etc., is a secondary one. If we could agree a construct against which to compare, and were in a position to create examinations from scratch, then we could theoretically achieve comparability for all these comparison groups together. In practice, of course, if we found that existing examinations were not comparable in their 'standards', then there would be a tension between achieving comparability within a particular year and across years. This would be a political rather than a technical problem, however.

To the more fundamental theoretical problem of multiple bases for comparability, there are perhaps three possible responses. The first would be to choose one preferred basis for comparability. This is Newton's (2005) *diktat* model, and would amount to privileging one use/interpretation of examination grades, with the corollary that other uses may then not be valid. The second would be to acknowledge that there are a limited number of valid bases for understanding comparability and adopt some kind of optimisation strategy – or 'contest' (Newton, 2005) – among them. One such has been described by Wiliam (1996b) as keeping a number of needles on a dial out of the red zone, so that no valid judgement of comparability would place different examinations too far from being in line. The price to be paid for this approach is that the meaning of 'comparability' becomes blurred in a pragmatic compromise – politically acceptable, but not rationally defensible. Newton (2005) argues that this is too high a price, and hence prefers the *diktat* model. However, it could be argued that the *diktat* model is just a special case of the *contest* model in which one particular interpretation has won the contest.

There may be a third possibility, however. Whatever process is used in the grade-setting process, it should be acknowledged that there is no absolute, universal sense in which different examinations are comparable; comparability is always relative to a particular use or interpretation. Nevertheless, if examinations are to be used for a particular purpose then we can readily convert, or rescale, their results to make them comparable for this purpose. This may therefore be thought of as a *variable conversion* model. Just as there is not a single conversion rate between currencies at any given time (it depends which market you go to), there is no single conversion rate among examination grades. The conversion rate is variable and depends on the particular interpretation of those grades and the linking construct that underlies it. Although the complexity and changeability of meaning of 'comparability' implied in such an approach might make it seem politically unacceptable, the fact that Average Marks Scaling has been used in this way in Australia for many years (see Chapter 9 by Coe) suggests that the political problems may not be insuperable. If that is so, it may be that this approach offers a solution to the problem of comparability that is both socially acceptable and conceptually defensible.

References

Cresswell, M.J. (1996). Defining, setting and maintaining standards in curriculum-embedded examinations: Judgemental and statistical approaches. In H. Goldstein & T. Lewis (Eds.), *Assessment: Problems, developments and statistical issues* (pp. 57-84). Chichester: John Wiley and Sons.

Jaeger, R.M. (1989). Certification of student competence. In R.L. Linn (Ed.), *Educational measurement* (3rd ed.). New York: American Council on Education/Macmillan.

Loevinger, J. (1957). Objective tests as instruments of psychological theory. *Psychological Reports*, 3, 635–694.

McGaw, B., Gipps, C., & Godber, R. (2004). *Examination standards: Report of the independent committee to QCA*. London: Qualifications and Curriculum Authority.

Newton, P.E. (2005). Examination standards and the limits of linking. *Assessment in Education*, 12, 105–123.

Wiliam, D. (1996a). Meanings and consequences in standard setting. *Assessment in Education*, 3, 287–307.

Wiliam, D. (1996b). Standards in examinations: A matter of trust? *The Curriculum Journal*, 7, 293–307.

RESPONSE TO COMMENTARIES ON CHAPTER 4

Jo-Anne Baird

Response to Harvey Goldstein

Goldstein points out that university degree results are interpreted by selectors, employers and other users of the qualifications, who attach value to those results at least partly on the basis of the reputation of the university awarding them. But degree results vary between subjects and institutions, after controlling for prior attainment (Chapman, 1996), raising questions regarding comparability of standards (Chapman, 1997). With such variability, and users of the qualification results having experience of only a few cases from any individual university department, judgements regarding the value of the qualifications are bound to be unreliable and subject to bias. Selection to university should be as free from bias as possible. For these reasons, it is questionable whether higher education is a model for secondary-level standard-setting to follow.

Although I argue that examination standards do not exist except as social constructs (Baird *et al.*, 2000) in this chapter, I do not go as far as Goldstein in support of exploring cohort referencing. Attempts to address discrepancies in comparability are important – I argue that a judicious balance between experts' views of candidates' performances in particular subjects and statistical analyses of the outcomes are necessary parts of the current examination system, unless we are willing to abandon some of our expectations regarding what the system delivers or deliver them by other means.

Response to Robert Coe

Coe argues that one way of meeting certain expectations would be to adopt something akin to the Australian Average Marks Scaling. In some respects, this is an attractive option because it allows the examination results to perform certain functions and converts them into a different currency for use in other functions. Underlying this approach is an assumption that a single construct can be used to link all of the examination results and Coe hints that this may be the case. Ability is the term normally used for such a construct and the consequence of such a system is that subjects or examinations that depart from that construct may not be treated fairly under that system. Who is to say whether this assumption is better than those made in the Universities and Colleges Admissions Service (UCAS) tariff? The UCAS tariff gives points for each grade for a range of qualifications. Some universities use these points for admissions. Assumptions underlying the system include the value of different qualifications and the relationships between the grades. Certainly, there are assumptions underlying both approaches. In the case of the UCAS system, the assumptions are based upon stakeholders' value judgements regarding the worthiness of the qualifications, whereas in the Average Marks Scaling system, they are based upon statistical mechanisms that assume that ability underlies the examination results.

Coe's comments on 'construct comparability' are heavily related to Newton's (2005) argument and his notion of variable conversion follows from my discussion of Newton's argument in the conclusion section of Chapter 4. We are in agreement to the extent that different constructs can be conjured to equate different pairs of tests.

Coe is concerned that no conceptual framework is presented in the chapter and attempts to provide one, with reference to 'norm-referencing' and 'criterion-referencing' distinctions and he also refers to other authors' definitions. Coe has misinterpreted the literature in failing to recognise that the weak criterion referencing (Baird et al., 2000) and conferred power definitions (Cresswell, 1996) were new approaches, adding to the previous and conceptually distinct. Each of the approaches outlined in the chapter has a different stance with regard to what needs to be taken into account and what adjusted for when drawing conclusions about comparability of examination standards (Table 1).

Table 1 Different definitions of examination standards

Statistical approaches	Takes account of ...	Adjusts for ...
Cohort referencing	Students' rank order	Nothing
Catch all	Students' grades	Student, teacher and institutional characteristics
Judgemental approaches		
Criterion referencing	Candidates' performances	Nothing
Weak criterion referencing	Candidates' performances and the assessment itself	Difficulty of assessment
Conferred power	Specified by due process	Specified by due process

Comparability methodologies described in this book may be operationalisations of a specific definition (see Table 1), or they may be applicable to more than one definition. Pollitt et al.'s chapter on examination demands is clearly linked with the weak criterion-referencing approach, but his theoretical analysis goes further, touching upon curriculum issues. Adams' chapter on cross-moderation discusses a technique that could be used in conjunction with any of the judgemental methods and the same is true of the Thurstone-pairs technique, described by Bramley. As Schagen and Hutchinson point out in their chapter on multilevel modelling, statistical techniques in practice have been impoverished attempts to implement the catch-all definition. Included in this are value-added approaches, common centres' analyses, use of reference tests (discussed in Murphy's chapter) and subject-pairs (discussed in Coe's chapter).

Cizek and Bunch (2007) write,

> ... we think it is obvious that any standard-setting procedure necessarily requires participants to bring to bear information about both test content and test takers. It would not be possible for a standard-setting participant to make a judgment about the difficulty of an item or task without relying on his or her knowledge or expectations of the abilities of examinees in the target population. Conversely, it would not be possible for a participant to express judgments about examinees without explicit consideration of the items or tasks presented to the examinees.
>
> Cizek & Bunch (2007, p. 10)

For this reason, operationalisations of standard-setting typically involve use of statistical and judgemental approaches. Attempts to classify them conceptually can quickly become confusing when they are compared with what happens in practice because there are few 'pure' approaches. Techniques for comparing examination standards can often be interpreted according to more than one definition too, as outlined above. Therefore, we cannot simply look at methods or artefacts to tell us which definition is in use – we need practitioners and researchers to be more explicit to be sure what definition they had in mind. For that to happen, assessment organisations would need to make explicit their policy positions in advance.

References

Baird, J., Cresswell, M.J., & Newton, P. (2000). Would the *real* gold standard please step forward? *Research Papers in Education, 15*, 213–229.

Chapman, K. (1996). Entry qualifications, degree results and value added in UK universities. *Oxford Review of Education, 22*, 251–264.

Chapman, K. (1997). Degrees of difference: Variability of degree results in UK universities. *Higher Education, 33*, 137-153.

Cizek, G.J., & Bunch, M.B. (2007). *Standard setting. A guide to establishing and evaluating performance standards on tests.* California: Sage Publications Inc.

Cresswell, M.J. (1996). Defining, setting and maintaining standards in curriculum-embedded examinations: Judgemental and statistical approaches. In H. Goldstein & T. Lewis (Eds.), *Assessment: Problems, developments and statistical issues* (pp. 57-84). Chichester: John Wiley and Sons.

Newton, P.E. (2005). Examination standards and the limits of linking. *Assessment in Education, 12*, 105–123.

5

THE DEMANDS OF EXAMINATION SYLLABUSES AND QUESTION PAPERS

Alastair Pollitt, Ayesha Ahmed and Victoria Crisp

Abstract

Aim

Examiners and many varieties of commentator have long talked about how 'demanding' a particular examination is, or seems to be, but there is not a clear understanding of what 'demands' means nor of how it differs from 'difficulty'. In this chapter we describe the main efforts that have tried to elucidate the concept of demands, and aim to establish a common interpretation, so that it may be more useful in future for the description and evaluation of examination standards.

Definition of comparability

No definition of comparability is necessarily assumed. Sometimes it is apparent that researchers operate with a default assumption that two examinations are expected to show the same level in every aspect of demand, but it would be quite reasonable for one of them to, for example, require a deeper treatment of a smaller range of content than the other; comparability then requires these differences in the demands somehow to balance each other out. It is asking a lot of examiners to guarantee this balance, and a less ambitious approach requires only that the differences are made clear to everyone involved.

Comparability methods

Several methods have been used to look at demands, including: asking informally for impressions of the overall level of demand; asking for ratings of specific demands, or aspects of demand; systematic questionnaires addressing a set of standard demands applicable to many examinations; rating on abstract concepts of demands identified from empirical research. Throughout this work there has been a constant research aspect, as no fully satisfactory system has been developed so far. Theoretical input has come from research in the area, and also from, in particular, taxonomies of cognitive processes, and personal construct psychology.

Strengths and weaknesses

Paying attention to the demands contained within examinations broadens the context of comparability studies, adding a third dimension to comparability. Rather than being just a matter of the ability of the students and the difficulty of the questions, a focus on demands addresses questions about the nature of the construct being assessed: statistical analysis may tell us that two examination grades are equally difficult to achieve, but it cannot tell us if those grades mean the same thing in terms of what the students who get them can do. We are still, however, trying to develop a system to make this kind of comparison secure, and to establish a common set of meanings to the various terms in use to describe demands.

Conclusion

Demands play an important role in examining in that they are the principal means by which examiners try to control the nature of the construct. When they are constructing the papers and the mark schemes in advance of the test, they have an idea of what the students' minds should be expected to do to achieve a particular grade; by manipulating the demands they try to design tasks that are appropriate for this purpose. To the extent that they succeed, appropriate standards are built into the examination in advance. In this chapter we describe three aims for the study of examination demands. We argue that a description of the nature of the demands is worthwhile in itself, that this can provide a basis for comparing different examinations, and that both of these are valuable even if it is not possible to go further and declare that they differ, or do not differ, in overall demand.

1   Introduction – purpose

Each review aims to find out if:
the demand of syllabuses and their assessment instruments (for example question papers, mark schemes) has changed over time
the level of performance required of candidates at key grade boundaries has changed over time.

QCA (2006a)

These two aspects of standards (they are sometimes called examination demand and grade standard) are commonly considered in most modern studies of examination comparability in England. The quotation refers to standards over time, or longitudinal studies of a part of the system, but cross-sectional studies, where two or more contemporary exams are compared, now also normally address both aspects. In this chapter we are concerned with the first of the two – with the meaning of 'demand' and 'demands' and with how comparability studies have tried to assess and evaluate them.

Before exploring how the present systems for judging examination demands have developed it will help if we start by clarifying the different purposes an assessment of demands can serve. Three separate aims can be identified. First, and particularly if the examinations in question have not been studied much, a purely qualitative study may seek a clear description of the various demands each qualification makes on the students who enter for it. This description is worthwhile in its own right, and valuable to the 'users' of the qualifications: teachers – even students – might use it when choosing which exams to enter for, and employers or other selectors might use it to understand what to expect of those who have taken the exams. This might be called Aim 1: *the aim of description*.

Going further, the aim may be to establish whether or not the exams require similar levels of the demands that they share. This aim is central to the public concern with the maintaining of standards over time, as well as to judging the relative appropriateness of different qualifications for given purposes. This aim needs quantification: a suitable set of scale or construct statements needs to be selected and presented as a set of rating scales to appropriate respondents. If the statements are 'simple' they may be presented to teachers and students as well as examiners, but if they are 'distilled' (as in the CRAS – complexity, resources, abstractness and strategy – system that will be discussed below) the necessary exemplification will make it difficult to involve more than just a team of experienced examiners. The resulting data need to be properly analysed. This might be called Aim 2: *the aim of comparison*.

Finally, demands may be assessed as part of a full-scale comparability study, when the aim of the demands part is to make judges aware of differences in demands before they try to compare grade standards in the second part of the comparability study. Since the link between demands and difficulty, or between demands and performance, is far from straightforward it is necessary to ask them to 'use their judgement' in making allowances for differences in demands when they judge the quality of the work in the scripts they see. Whether judges can, in fact, make appropriate allowances for demands is unclear: in a somewhat similar context Good & Cresswell (1988) found systematic bias when examiners were asked to set equivalent performance standards for examination papers that differed only in question difficulty. Nevertheless, this might be called Aim 3: *the aim of compensation*.

In general, the studies described here do not explicitly state which of these aims they followed. It seems that cross-sectional studies usually adopted the most demanding Aim 3, while, as the Qualifications and Curriculum Authority (QCA) quotation above indicates, longitudinal studies usually expect that the levels of demand will not change significantly over time and aim to test this hypothesis – Aim 2 – before looking at the grade standard.

2   Judging demands

2.1 Demands and difficulty

One significant difference between the general concepts of demands and performance standards is the role of judgement. There is no statistical indicator of demands, and no prospect of our developing objective scales for assessing them. Instead we rely on the judgement of experienced professionals. We could ask the judges to look at students' performances on exam papers and let the evidence of how they dealt with the questions inform the judgements of demands, but in practice we usually do not. We choose to separate the concept of demands from that of difficulty as far as is possible, and ask examiners to use their experience of students' performance on other, similar, questions to imagine how demanding a particular paper 'will' be. Thus 'demands' are also distinguished from 'difficulty' in that the former are essentially a concern pre-test while the other is defined and analysed post-test.

That this distinction needs to be made can readily be demonstrated. Consider, for example, two questions from the Third International Mathematics and Science Study (TIMSS):

1 Subtract: 6000
                  −2369

   A. 4369
   B. 3742
   C. 3631
   D. 3531

2 Write a fraction that is larger than $\frac{2}{7}$

Answer: _____

Location of source material: TIMSS (1996a, pp. 105–7). Reproduced with permission from TIMSS Population 2 Item Pool. Copyright (c) 1994 by IEA, The Hague.

On these questions the success rates of Scottish children were 75% and 76% (data from TIMSS, 1996b, p. 58); thus these questions were equally difficult. In England the success rates were 59% and 79%; clearly they were not equally difficult there. Yet the questions were exactly the same in both countries. Whitburn (1999) gives a plausible explanation for the anomalous English success rate in question 1, in terms of differences in the nature and timing of teaching strategies. Thus, the question was the same in both countries, required the same cognitive operations for its solution, and so made the same demands; but because of differences in their classroom experiences up to the date of the test English pupils found it more difficult than Scottish ones. In essence, by 'difficulty' we mean an empirical measure of how successful a group of students were on a question; by 'demands' we mean the (mostly) cognitive mental processes that a typical student is assumed to have to carry out in order to complete the task set by a question.

The distinction becomes difficult to maintain when the demand of mark schemes is considered. Students do not see mark schemes – indeed until about 20 years ago they were kept 'strictly confidential' and not even released to teachers. A student has two kinds of judgement to make with regard to the mark scheme, corresponding to the two meanings of 'quality': what kind of things the examiners are looking for and how good the answer must be to get (say) five marks. If the first of these is problematic the nature of the task is unclear, and this burden of comprehension increases the demands on the student. In the second case, however, there is no extra demand on the student, and it is more appropriate to think of the severity of the mark scheme as an aspect of difficulty rather than demand.

2.2 Simple conceptions of demands

The comments above referred to 'demands' as usually understood in comparability studies. There are, however, several features of an examination that can be easily identified, described, and sometimes quantified, as demands. The most frequently mentioned are listed below.

- The amount of *time* spent in assessment varies considerably between subjects, though it is difficult to say whether more time increases or decreases the overall demand. If twice as much time is given because twice as much work is required then the effect is to increase the overall demand, but if more time is given for the same amount of work overall demand will decrease.

- The amount of *work* to be done in that time may vary. In this respect, a paper with more questions in a given time will be more demanding than a similar one with fewer, but if the nature of the questions varies it is harder to quantify the demand. Also, obviously, a syllabus with more content will be more demanding (other things being equal) than one with less.

- More specifically, the amount of *reading or writing* to be done in a given time may vary.

- In addition, the level of *reading difficulty* in the questions may vary, although this is now closely controlled in certificate examinations.

Taken together, these demands may make different examinations more or less suitable for different candidates. In a recent study of vocational tests, the reviewer concluded:

> [Test A] slightly favours candidates whose reading standard is not high; [test B] favours candidates who are more comfortable with intense reading and thinking; [test C] favours those who do not like to be rushed. Unless the typical candidate can be described in more detail, and unless the candidature is unusually homogeneous, it is impossible to say that any of these tests is more or less demanding overall than the others.
>
> QCA (2006b)

- Examination papers may vary in the amount of *question choice* they allow candidates, but because of the interaction of choice with students' expectations, preparation and syllabus coverage the influence of choice on overall demand is complex.

- Subjects vary in the demand they make on *long-term memory*, and so do their examinations. Within subjects, test format and question type can also affect this demand: for example, 'open book' and 'data-book' formats will reduce memory demand, as will information given in synoptic statements in a question, while an essay format may reduce this memory demand, by allowing students to avoid something they can't remember accurately.

- Differences in the nature of questions may also mean that *working memory* demands will vary. This is closely linked to the issue of 'complexity' to be discussed in section 3.

- More generally, the nature of the *cognitive processes* required varies between questions and examinations. This too will be discussed further in section 3.

- For example, candidates undergoing assessment experience *stress*, which can seriously reduce the capacity of working memory. A commonly accepted distinction from Spielberger (1972) holds that stress may be affective, caused by anxiety about the test or its results – such *trait anxiety* is a relatively stable personality characteristic on which individuals vary considerably – or cognitive, caused by the high demands of the context – the ability to deal with *state anxiety* like this is a component of 'expertise'. Some examinations may be more predictable than others, which tends to reduce stress, to reward conscientiousness rather than quick thinking, and to favour students who have been 'well prepared' by their teachers.

Many other factors can affect exam performance. It's clear that a list like this, of features that might make an exam more or less demanding for some students, is in principle endless. For a study of comparability a decision must be made, perhaps on grounds of their possible impact on validity, on which features should be included.

2.3 Explorations of examination demands

Before 1992, only a few comparability studies attempted to consider the demands that syllabuses placed on students, and they used a variety of ad hoc methods to identify specific demands. A study of English language O level by Massey (1979) 'attempted to discern variations in the style and emphasis of boards' questions, including comparisons of the sorts of tasks faced by candidates and an attempted evaluation of their *inherent difficulty* or *complexity of demand*' (p. 2). Views on whether a paper was relatively demanding, relatively undemanding or average were collected from judges (examiners and non-examiners) by questionnaire. Judgements were made on aspects of reading and writing demand – *summary, comprehension, essay* – and *overall demand*. The author emphasised that this method cannot inform about grading standards directly, as awarding can adjust for differences in demands and that 'the comments will be laced with inferences concerning the face validity of examinations, seen from the user's viewpoint' (p. 3) but he considered the issue of interest because exam questions can vary in their complexity.

In a study of A level economics, Houston (1981) asked participants to rate the demands made on candidates as *excessive, appropriate* or *insufficient* by considering the educational aims and objectives, the range and depth of topics and the range of skills specified. When pressed to comment on relative demands, the judges 'suggested that the nine boards offer examinations which make different demands but not necessarily greater or lesser ones' (p. 9). Evans & Pierce (1982) compared the demands of A level German prose composition and free composition between syllabuses. Their analysis of demands was unstructured and was based on the comments and analyses made by the assessors before scrutiny sessions. The analysis considered the weighting of composition, time allocation, length of response, essay choice, the nature of the essay titles and prose passages and how marks were awarded by the mark scheme. Leigh *et al.* (1983) investigated A level music and asked what each board demanded in terms of content and skills, concluding that there was a close underlying convergence of demands.

In 1985, Pollitt *et al.* reported on a study of the sources of difficulty in five Scottish Ordinary Grade examinations, which sought generalisable factors that might be useful to examiners writing questions for the new Standard Grade examinations soon to be introduced. They identified three categories:

1. *subject/concept difficulty*, which relates to the intrinsic difficulty of the content being assessed and the form in which it appears

2. *process difficulty*, related to the psychological operations required to complete the task

3. *question (stimulus) difficulty*, which relates to the wording and other aspects of how the task is presented.

Today we would consider the first two of these to be aspects of demand. The third is, in a very general sense, part of the reading demand, but in practice there are so many specific possible sources of difficulty or easiness in question presentation that it is very hard to make generalisations that would identify them as discrete demands (Ahmed & Pollitt, 1999).

McLone & Patrick (1990) aimed to compare the demands of the two routes available in double mathematics (mathematics/further mathematics or pure mathematics/applied mathematics). Using a matrix based on Griffiths & McLone (1979) a number of statements were presented to judges for rating on a scale of 0 to 3; for example, *How far does the question define in detail the procedure which the candidate should adopt?* Whole papers were then analysed in a similar way after relevant statements had been defined in discussions. The report discussed difficulties with interpreting the different statements, consistency of judgements, using the whole range of ratings and applying the rating scales. The fundamental problem was to define what exactly constituted demand in mathematics, by identifying factors affecting demands and specifying how these factors affect demand. Previous literature had identified three dimensions of demand in mathematics examinations:

1. *academic demand* (intrinsic difficulty)

2. *contextual demand* (demand of the totality of the context within which students are assessed)

3. *personal demand* (contribution to demand of factors relating to the personal characteristics and responses of students).

They considered that the ways in which these interact make it hard to apply scales of demand with precision, and recognised that the actual demands will vary for different participants with different degrees of preparation or familiarity with the materials. It was also noted that there was a lack of empirical data on how factors affect demands and that personal demand will interact strongly with other aspects of demand in somewhat unpredictable ways. Several factors were listed that might, in addition to these dimensions, make questions more or less demanding. It is clear, in retrospect, that *demand* was equated to *difficulty* in this study; today we would translate the phrase *factors affecting demand* to *demands affecting difficulty*.

In general, it was implicitly assumed in these studies that 'demands' should be the causes of difficulty, and that judgements of demands should predict empirical measures of difficulty. But the third category from Pollitt *et al.* (1985), and both the third dimension and the additional factors from McLone & Patrick (1990), show that the difficulty of a particular question is influenced more by very specific features of presentation, and that these aspects of difficulty will affect different candidates in quite different and unpredictable ways.

2.4 Systematic judgements of demands

In 1992 a series of comparability studies was carried out to prepare for changes in GCSE mathematics, English and science consequent to the introduction of the National Curriculum, 5–16. The participating judges were not experienced GCSE examiners, and hence did not have a clear concept of the nature of A-grade work and could not be asked to judge whether a script was above, below or on the grade boundary. Consequently, after initial familiarisation with syllabus materials, judgements of demands were made for each syllabus against a number of defined dimensions. This served as preparation for the cross-moderation phase in which judges were asked to sort scripts into rank-order on each factor (content, context, etc.) and then into an overall rank-order.

For mathematics and science the rating 'factors' were based on Pollitt *et al.* (1985) and work by the Inter-Group Research Committee on 'setting effective examination papers in the GCSE'. In science ratings were made for 'content', 'context', 'processes/skills' and 'question difficulty' (plus 'experimental and practical skills' when considering coursework), while in mathematics ratings were for 'context', 'process' and 'mathematics'. Some differences in the demands of syllabuses were identified. The English judges used the new national criteria for English and English literature as factors. In general the demands were found to be similar though there were differences on some factors. The summary report states that the ratings could 'offer nothing conclusive about comparability (a demanding paper may be generously marked, a less demanding one more severely marked)' but states that 'it provided the context in which to rate the work of the samples of candidates from different groups' (Jones, 1993). Note that this study did clearly separate the concept of demand and difficulty, since the mark scheme was not assessed for 'demand' (cf. section 2.1). Methodologically, there were some problems, which will be discussed in section 4, but a first phase of comparing demands was thought to be a useful and successful addition to comparability studies (Adams, 1993) and was recommended for future studies. There was, however, a feeling that the results of the review and the cross-moderation should be better related in further work.

The comparability studies of 1993 GCSE exams in history (Stobart *et al.*, 1994) and geography (Ratcliffe, 1994) included a syllabus/paper review stage with examiners being asked to judge syllabus demands against a number of factors based on Pollitt *et al.* (1985). The same method was used for comparability studies in 1994 exams in GCSE mathematics, English and science and A level physics (Alton, 1995; Gray, 1995; Phillips & Adams, 1995; Fowles, 1995). In each study, one examiner from each examining board attended an initial meeting to determine the wording of factor statements to be used and prepare additional guidance on each factor. Every examiner in the study was sent copies of the syllabuses, question papers and mark schemes, and a questionnaire of tables to complete with ratings (1–5) on each factor for each 'foreign' syllabus relative to their own (which they should consider as '3' on each factor). They were encouraged to comment on their ratings, especially at the extremes of a scale.

In general, the factors used were:

- 'content' or 'subject/concept difficulty'

- 'skills and processes'

- 'structure and manageability of the question papers' (question difficulty, language, layout, context, etc.) or 'question difficulty'

- 'practical skills' (in relation to fieldwork) or 'using and applying' (in relation to coursework) – (only used where appropriate).

The range of ratings and mean ratings on each factor were used to compare the demands of syllabuses, and often identified certain specifications as more or less demanding in some ways. Quinlan (1995) used a similar methodology in a study of A level mathematics, but using a list of factors based on McLone & Patrick (1990).

A number of problematic issues were raised, and will be discussed in section 4, but the researchers and the judges were generally satisfied with the methodology (e.g. Stobart *et al.*, 1994; Phillips & Adams, 1995). General satisfaction, however, does not mean that the method was valid and there is a risk that judges may have reported satisfaction just because they were able to carry out the task required of them.

A general caution from several of the study authors warned that the different elements of the studies are not cumulative: 'they provide evidence separately of relative severity or leniency but all three straws pointing in the same direction should not be taken as implying a stronger wind' (Stobart *et al.*, 1994). Differences in demands do not necessarily constitute differences in standards, not least because it does not consider the boundary marks. However, if we were to take on the 'straws in the wind' approach advocated in the 1970s and 1980s (Walker *et al.*, 1987) then consistent outcomes pointing in a particular direction might be taken as more convincing evidence that there is a real difference between specifications, even though they cannot be added up to suggest a larger difference.

In 1996/97 modular and non-modular syllabuses in A level biology, English literature and mathematics were compared. Assessments of demands were made for 'content', 'processes', 'question or stimulus difficulty' and 'modular issues', but the factor statements were finalised by the researchers rather than the judges, and the judges wrote qualitative reports under the four headings instead of making quantitative ratings (D'Arcy, 1997). The judgements were sometimes found to differ because of differing interpretations of the dimensions. Jones (1997) reviewed the methods used and reported several problems mostly centred on the risk of bias arising from judges' familiarity with their own syllabuses or the researchers' summarising of their comments. He concluded that, 'whilst reverting to a tight, quantitative approach was thought not to be desirable, it was considered that more directed guidance, with examples relevant to the syllabuses being reviewed, would enhance this aspect of future studies' (p. 9).

In all these studies, the rating of demands seems to have had two principal purposes: to help ensure that the judges were thoroughly familiar with the materials from all the examination syllabuses before they started the performance judgement task, and to ensure that they could then make appropriate adjustments to their judgements of the quality of performances based on an understanding of any differences in the demands made in each exam. Even when the aim was said to be to 'determine whether or not some of the syllabuses, question papers and mark schemes were perceived as more or less demanding than others' (Stobart *et al.*, 1994) the reason for this was to improve the precision of relative judgements of performance.

In the QCA's Standards Reviews in the late 1990s reviewers were asked to compare sets of examination materials in terms of factors such as: *assessment objectives, rationale, syllabus content, options, scheme of assessment, question papers, tiering,* and *coursework*. In these reviews on behalf of the national regulator, unlike the reports of studies carried out by the examining boards, there does seem to be an assumption that the pattern of demands across alternative syllabuses leading to the same qualification should be comparable – or identical – in its own right.

2.5 Overall demand

Given the complexity of the concept, it is not surprising that very few studies have asked for simple direct ratings of examination demand. When Walker *et al.*, (1987) compared A level chemistry between examining boards and over time they mainly used a variety of statistical methods to compare performance standards but also included a judgemental element mainly looking at demands. Examiners were asked to compare the overall demands of each question paper in the syllabus they were involved with to that of the previous year, and to compare the performance of the candidates with the previous year using a five-point Likert scale running from 'considerably higher' to 'considerably lower'. Teachers were also asked to compare the demands of each question paper in the same way. Whilst the data provided an extra source of information for cross-checking the numeric data, the authors acknowledged the limited value that was added given that the judgements were not made between boards and that most studies only look at the examinations in a single year.

More often judges were, and are still, asked to rate overall demand after rating various specific demands, presumably by imagining the overall demand as some undefined composite of these components. This approach and some problems with it will be discussed later. For the moment it can be noted that the conclusion has generally been that the examinations studied have been identified as similar rather than different in overall level of demand.

2.6 Personal construct psychology

During the 1990s a new approach was introduced to considerations of demands, based on the work of Kelly (1955). Personal construct psychology has been defined as:

> ... an attempt to understand the way in which each of us experiences the world, to understand our 'behaviour' in terms of what it is designed to signify and to explore how we negotiate our realities with others.
>
> Bannister & Fransella (1971, p. 27)

According to Kelly, the reality for each individual person is the universe as they perceive it; reality is subjective rather than objective. As they go through life, they actively build up a system of constructs for making sense of the world that is constantly undergoing modification as they experience new events or different outcomes for familiar events. The ability to construe implies the ability to predict (not necessarily always correctly) future events, and so, perhaps, to control one's fate.

Each individual has their own repertory of constructs, and Kelly's repertory grid analysis is a procedure designed to elicit from an individual how they construe the world. This is the key for our purpose: the repertory of constructs tells us what an individual sees in the world, what is salient, and so offers an insight into what they perceive as demanding in assessment.

Depending on the purpose of the analysis, data may be gathered by eliciting participants' personal constructs or by supplying them with typical constructs to which they are required to respond. The former approach is necessarily used in psychotherapy, where the concern is for the individual client, and often in the early stages of research; while the latter may be used when the individuals are assumed typical of some population, often in later stages of research. Both methods have been used in comparability studies, to explore constructs and to rate examinations against the constructs that have been discovered.

How are constructs elicited? A construct is, says Kelly (1955, pp. 111–112), 'a way in which some things are alike and yet different from others'. As a simple example, he gives the statement 'Mary and Alice are gentle; Jane is not', which would (probably) be interpreted as indicating that gentleness is a construct that the speaker uses to organise experiences of people. 'The minimum context for a construct is three things', he points out: here these are Mary, Alice and Jane. Kelly's main concern was with human personality, and his therapeutic technique involved asking clients to consider the similarities and differences amongst three people who were significant elements in their lives. But it is not always necessary that all three are mentioned explicitly: 'To say that Mary and Alice are "gentle" and not imply that somewhere in the world there is someone who is "not gentle" is illogical. More than that, it is unpsychological.' (p. 112). Since in our context the 'elements' would be examination components not well known to the judges, comparisons of three would be difficult for them to cope with, and we generally depend on the presence of the implied third member in each construct elicitation statement.

After eliciting a set of constructs that members of a group typically use, these are defined as bi-polar constructs, such as 'gentle – not gentle' or 'complex – simple'. They are often then combined into a *repertory grid* for further research use. This is a two-dimensional layout with the construct statements listed in the rows and a set of 'objects' heading each column. Using a four- or five-point scale, participants are asked to rate each 'object' on each construct, simultaneously comparing all of the objects on each construct and all of the constructs as applied to each 'object'.

These techniques were originally used in psychotherapy as a means of understanding and thus helping combat patients' psychiatric disorders. Since the mid-1970s it has been applied throughout the social sciences. The first uses in assessment research were in the field of English as a foreign language; Lee (n.d., about 1990) compared the constructs used by a group of Hong Kong lecturers in evaluating writing, and Pollitt & Murray (1993) combined construct elicitation with Thurstone's paired comparison methodology (see Chapter 7) to explore the criteria used by untrained judges evaluating videotapes of speaking tests.

2.7 Use of construct elicitation and analysis techniques

Construct elicitation methods are generally used to identify factors that may differentiate the exam requirements of different syllabus specifications. The first applications involved the 1998 and 1999 GCSE examinations (Gray, 2000; Adams & Pinot de Moira, 2000; Fearnley, 2000; Pritchard *et al.*, 2000) and were followed by a series of studies on 2001 and 2002 AS, A2 and GCE exams (Arlett, 2002; 2003; Edwards & Adams, 2002; 2003; Greatorex *et al.*, 2002; 2003; Guthrie, 2003).

The method typically involves an initial meeting with one judge from each participating board. They compare examination materials (specifications, question papers and mark schemes) from pairs of syllabuses, and are asked to write down similarities and differences (usually a minimum of three of each per comparison) in the demands placed on candidates taking these examinations. Gray (2000) describes this as enabling examiners to form their own ideas of what constitutes demand as a first step in deriving constructs to define a scale of demands. From this a shared set of constructs is agreed by discussion amongst the participants. In a plenary session the wording of the construct statements is finalised (usually formulated as questions), including a title and labels for the ends of each scale. The statements (their number has varied from 14 to 34 in different studies) are then compiled into a questionnaire, to which a final question is usually added asking for a rating of the 'overall demand' of the examination. There is sometimes further refinement through feedback from the judges involved.

A sample of the construct statements that have been generated in various studies, and the bi-polar scale definitions used in the questionnaires, is given below:

1. How accessible are the language and syntax used in the examination papers? Inaccessible – Accessible.

2. What is the predominant type of questions offered to candidates? Short answer – Essay.

3. Is the time allowed for candidates to answer the examination papers enough for them to complete what they have to do? Too little – Too much.

4. Are the assessment criteria for each board equally demanding at grade A? More demanding – Less demanding.

5. To what extent are the questions understandable? Clear – Obscure.

6. What is the role of resource materials? As a prompt – For manipulation.

7. How demanding is the specification in terms of depth? Very demanding – Not demanding at all.

8. Assess the effect upon candidates of increased structure within papers. More demanding – Less demanding.

9. How helpful are the mark schemes to examiners in ensuring consistency in marking? Very helpful – Not helpful at all.

In most studies the construct statements were presented individually, as shown in Figure 1 (Edwards & Adams, 2002). The implication of this format for analysis will be discussed later.

Figure 1 Example of presentation of construct statement

	How accessible are the language and syntax used in the examination papers?						
	Inaccessible						*Accessible*
	1	2	3	4	5	6	7
AQA							
CCEA							
EDEXCEL							
OCR							
SQA							
WJEC							

These construct statements reflect accurately the statements that the judges made during the elicitation procedure. But they vary in several ways – how explicitly they refer to demands, how directly they affect demands, and whether they will affect all students in the same way. The second question seems merely descriptive, though there may be an implicit assumption that some question types are more demanding than others; the fourth question, as discussed in section 2.1, refers more to estimating the difficulty than the demands. The effect of 'increased structure' has been shown to change the nature of the demand in a question, increasing some components while decreasing others, but it is not easy to predict the overall 'effect' (Pollitt et al., 1998), and this sounds here like a request for judges to guess at the difficulty rather than the demands. The terms that define the poles are not always consistent, as when 'Very' is used opposite 'Not at all'.

It has always been the custom to send the judges involved in a comparability study a set of 'familiarisation materials' for each examination they will be judging, including the syllabus specification, question papers, mark schemes and sometimes other documents. Now, in addition, they are sent the demands questionnaire to complete before they attend the main study meeting. The constructs are presented one at a time, with a row of boxes for the different exams being compared. The instrument is thus uni-dimensional, in that the rating a judge gives to one exam needs to be considered relative to the ratings given to the other exams on that same construct.

The questionnaire is not a repertory grid, even though the constructs in it may have been elicited using Kelly's clinical interview technique. A repertory grid is two-dimensional, with all of the constructs presented simultaneously on a single page, with no gaps between them, so that the judge's response procedure is holistic, with each rating being determined by comparisons *both* with other exams on the same construct *and* with other construct ratings for the same exam. The proper analytic techniques are therefore univariate nominal ones for each construct, rather than the specific multivariate techniques developed for repertory grid research.

Analysis of the ratings has therefore often involved the use of chi-square tests within each construct, to check for significant differences between boards. Some studies have then gone on to cluster the examinations in terms of the pattern of ratings given, using a variety of methods (e.g. Gray, 2000; Edwards & Adams, 2002; Greatorex et al., 2003). Greatorex et al. (2002) also used the number of constructs for which a board was significantly more or less demanding as an indicator of overall differences in demand. Often analyses have also been carried out to check for bias in the ratings.

The studies often found a number of constructs on which there were significant differences in ratings and a smaller number for which there were significant sub-groups of boards that form clusters with similar patterns of demands. However, significant differences have never been found on the final construct statement rating the overall demands, and stable sub-groups have not been identified where the same boards cluster together on different demands. A typical example was the study of 1998 GCSE English exams (Pritchard et al., 2000), which found no significant difference for 24 of the 37 constructs used. For only two of the constructs were the differences considered 'substantial': on the question 'How effectively is cross-referencing (comparison) tested in the written papers?', specifications divided into two sub-groups with mean ratings of 2.7 and 4.6; and on the question 'How explicitly is the required range of writing targeted in the written papers?', specifications fell into three sub-groups with mean ratings ranging from 2.7 to 4.3. There was no significant difference between the boards in the ratings of overall demand. Similar results have occurred in AS chemistry: Greatorex *et al.* (2002) found significant differences between boards in just 7 of the 24 construct questions involving the transparency of mark awarding, concentration on one or more specification areas in questions, depth of subject content, knowledge required in practical work and emphasis on different areas of chemistry. On the basis of the differences on these, the authors suggested that the Assessment and Qualifications Alliance (AQA) and Oxford Cambridge RSA (OCR) exams were a little more demanding than the others, but reminded us that such an inference should be considered with caution.

Using data published in Fearnley (2000), Baird (1999) explored how the ratings of individual construct statements relate to the ratings of overall demand using forward stepwise regression. Six constructs (only four of which would have been expected to have an impact) were found to explain 60% of the variation in overall demand ratings, but the two constructs found by Fearnley (2000) to be rated significantly differently for different syllabuses were not amongst them. It's noticeable that, in general, the constructs for which the level of demands are found to vary do not appear to be the same in different studies, which perhaps means that different demand components are the most important in the different subjects being examined.

In an attempt to make the demand ratings more accurate and so more informative, Edwards & Adams (2003) allowed examiners to revise their original ratings after the cross-moderation exercise if they wished. Six of the eighteen did so for a few constructs, with changes of up to two or three points on the seven-point scale suggesting that their views changed quite considerably after seeing student work. Most of these changes were made with regard to the Scottish Qualifications Authority (SQA) examination, which was less familiar to most of the examiners. The changes affected the analyses for just two construct statements out of the twenty used in this study, indicating clusters amongst the examinations that had not appeared before. At a research seminar in 2003, Greatorex suggested several ways that might improve the syllabus review method including: make scripts available to help raters understand an examination's demands and to help strengthen the link with the judgement of performance standards; interview judges when they are rating the constructs to improve understanding of how they perceive the cognitive demands; reuse existing scales to systematise the method; analyse verbal protocols collected while judges conduct cross-moderation (reported in Jones, 2004). Jones *et al.* (2004) included one script at each of the A and C borderlines in the familiarisation materials, and used construct statements from previous studies. Judges were also invited to describe any differences they saw in demands and asked to relate these to features of the materials where possible.

Some of these proposals cause us concern. In our view, it is not wise to blur the distinction between 'demands' as the generalisable cognitive requirements that question-writing teams intended to be present in the questions, and 'difficulty' as measured empirically after the event. A few scripts are unlikely to provide reliable 'evidence' to show how students were actually affected by the demands (in our research we have always used at least 200 scripts to look at this), and the empirical outcomes from a question are the proper domain of difficulty, measured statistically, not demands.

The QCA's inter-subject comparability studies (reported in general in QCA, forthcoming a, and also in individual reports), also surveyed elicited demands in four sub-categories: Syllabus, Content, Question papers and their associated mark schemes, and Coursework. An Overall demand rating was also asked for. The instrument used (see Appendix B in QCA, 2006a) asks for a rating of every exam being studied on each scale in turn, so focusing the judges on identifying differences between them. Nevertheless, the overall conclusions were that parallel qualifications were usually similar in overall difficulty, even though there might be substantial differences between them on individual aspects of demand. The science report comments:

> It is clear that awarding bodies working with the regulatory bodies can address a number of these issues through specification review, and guidance on question writing and question paper construction. Specification review is likely to be the first step in order to generate new specifications that recognise the above issues and attempt to do something about them.
>
> QCA (forthcoming b)

This conclusion draws attention to the role that demands play before the examination is seen by students. Question writers, and the scrutiny committees that monitor their work, intend to include appropriate levels of the various demands. Even before that, those who write the syllabus specifications, and the regulators who review them, aim to specify appropriate demands into the examination. If we can establish a consistent system for describing the demands of examinations it can only help writers and reviewers in these efforts.

The general report (QCA, forthcoming a) also noted that the 'reviewers are, by definition, subject experts. However, those taking the papers are, to a large degree, novices. It is a commonplace of examination experience that candidates find questions and sometimes whole papers much harder or easier than those setting them had expected.' Following this lead, Wood & Pollitt carried out construct elicitation interviews with A level mathematics students in which they were asked to describe pairs of questions from AS papers similar to the ones they had recently sat. This study confirmed that students can provide coherent data for exploring the demands of the questions they attempt, and showed that there are significant differences between their and the examiners' perceptions of what makes questions demanding (Wood & Pollitt, 2006).

Most of these studies have reported some problems in using techniques based on personal construct theory, and these will be discussed in section 4. Nevertheless, the methodology has generally been thought to be effective and an improvement on earlier methods, offering a more systematic approach to identifying and comparing demands.

3 Scales of cognitive demands

3.1 Hierarchical taxonomies of demands

The previous section dealt with 'demands' in a very general sense, as any and every challenge that students have to face in certificate assessment. In this section we look specifically at the demands that examination questions make on students' cognitive abilities.

Since the introduction of the O level and O grade examinations it has been standard practice to specify the content of papers in terms of cognitive skills or 'assessment objectives' (AOs). These have generally been derived from the taxonomy of cognitive 'objectives' for education of Bloom (1956), except in the cases of languages, art, and so on (Table 1).

Examination syllabuses often simplify this to two or three levels. A current example (from AQA GCSE chemistry 2007/8) is:

AO1 Knowledge and understanding of science and how science works

AO2 Application of skills, knowledge and understanding

AO3 Practical, enquiry and data-handling skills

with each of these expanded with three or four specific objectives. The balance of these AOs in each examination component is specified and, increasingly, is mandated by the regulator.

In almost every comparability study judges have looked for differences between examinations in terms of this *intended* pattern of cognitive demands. The QCA review of GCSE history, for example (QCA, 2001), found differences between boards in the percentages of marks awarded for 'low-level skills', 'source interpretation' and 'recall', although it concluded that there was 'a reasonable degree of comparability' overall. Perhaps because of a tightening of the regulators' requirements there is usually very little variation between examinations, at least within similar subjects.

There are very few studies, and no significant comparability studies, where judges have been asked to classify individual questions in terms of Bloom's taxonomy: in general it is either assumed that the examinations were constructed to fit their specifications, or the awarding bodies are asked to provide evidence that they were. Igoe (1982) provides one example of questions being classified cognitively, from the question papers and mark schemes. Items in biology were classified as requiring: data-deduction (numerical or non-numerical), recall (simple, associative or experimental) and logical, coherent argument. However, Igoe did not attempt to

Table 1 Taxonomy of educational objectives. Adapted from Bloom (1956).

Competence	Skills demonstrated
Knowledge	• observation and recall of information • knowledge of dates, events, places • knowledge of major ideas • mastery of subject matter
Comprehension	• understanding information • grasp meaning • translate knowledge into new context • interpret facts, compare, contrast • order, group, infer causes • predict consequences
Application	• use information • use methods, concepts, theories in new situations • solve problems using required skills or knowledge
Analysis	• seeing patterns • organisation of parts • recognition of hidden meanings • identification of components
Synthesis	• use old ideas to create new ones • generalise from given facts • relate knowledge from several areas • predict, draw conclusions
Evaluation	• compare and discriminate between ideas • assess value of theories, presentations • make choices based on reasoned argument • verify value of evidence • recognise subjectivity

measure or compare how demanding items were in different tests. Anderson & Krathwohl (2001) revised Bloom's taxonomy to bring together the knowledge and cognitive process dimensions by mapping them against each other in a two-dimensional framework. The terms of the cognitive process dimension were presented as verbs instead of nouns (remember, understand, apply, analyse, evaluate, create) displayed against the knowledge dimension (factual knowledge, conceptual knowledge, procedural knowledge, metacognitive knowledge). The revisions aim to provide a more authentic tool for planning curriculum, delivering teaching and classroom assessment by helping teachers plan focused objectives. As far as we are aware the revised Bloom's taxonomy has not been used in relation to external assessment, but it may be worth considering how it might be used in at least a descriptive comparison.

Pollitt *et al.* (1985), investigating sources of difficulty rather than demands, rejected the notion of a hierarchy in favour of a list of more specific cognitive processes that might provide a basis for predicting difficulty. The list included:

- explaining

- generalising from data

- selection of data relevant to a general theme

- identifying a principle from data

- applying a principle to new data

- forming a strategy

- composing an answer

- cumulative difficulty

- need for logical consistency.

Examples of most of these were found in each of the five subjects studied.

McLone & Patrick (1990) noted that skilled examiners are able to recognise 'demand' and generally to agree in estimating the overall level of demand in questions. However, they were much less good at explaining it; they could not analyse a question to describe the cognitive elements and processes that were the source of that difficulty. This should not be seen as a criticism of the judges, since they were mathematicians not psychologists, but if we are to arrive at a proper explanation of the demands and difficulties of exam questions, and so to achieve control of this most central element of examining, we need to start by bringing together the expertise of both the subject specialist and the psychologist to develop models for how students think while answering exam questions.

3.2 Analytic scales of demands

Edwards & Dall'Alba (1981) developed and implemented a 'Scale of Cognitive Demand' to quantify the demands placed on the cognitive abilities of students by secondary science lessons, materials and evaluation programmes in Australia. The conceptualisation of demand was derived from a range of learning and thinking theories, including Bloom (1956); Taba (1962, 1967); Bruner *et al.* (1966); Gagné (1970); de Bono (1976); Ausubel *et al.* (1978); and the work of Piaget as interpreted by Novak (1977). Six levels of demand were defined within each dimension, by a list of phrases and command words that were typically used in science textbooks and examinations, or that could be used to describe the processes students were required to carry out. There were four sub-scales:

1. *Complexity*: the nature of the sequence of operations that constitutes a task, that is, the nature of each component operations and the links between operations.

2. *Openness*: the degree to which a task relies on the generation of ideas.

3. *Implicitness*: the extent to which the learner is required to go beyond the data available to the senses.

4. *Level of Abstraction*: The extent to which a task deals with ideas rather than concrete objects or phenomena.

The six levels of 'Complexity' were defined as:

1   simple operations

2   require a basic comprehension

3   understanding, application or low-level analysis

4   [blank][1]

5   analysis and/or synthesis

6   synthesis or evaluation

showing a close resemblance to Bloom's scale. The other sub-scales were new. The scale has not been used directly in Britain.

In a research study conducted for the QCA into the relationship between the increased use of 'structure' in questions and the demands of exam questions the Edwards & Dall'Alba sub-scales were revised to be appropriate for subjects other than science and to be more suitable for rating the demands of exam questions (Pollitt *et al.*, 1998; Hughes *et al.*, 1998). Using insights derived from Pollitt *et al.* (1985) and research into sources of question difficulty (e.g. Pollitt & Ahmed, 1999; 2000), a new trial version of the scales was prepared. This was then revised in discussion with examiners who used it in A level and GCSE chemistry, history and geography, and A level mathematics, and further refined it after a Kelly construct elicitation and repertory-grid rating exercise. The grids were analysed by factor analysis, and revised further.

The final instrument contained four (or five) scales: complexity, resources, abstractness and strategy, and is generally referred to as the CRAS scales.

1. *Complexity* concerned the number of elements that need to be kept in mind while answering, and related to each other.

2. *Resources* related to the extent to which candidates are given all and only the information they need to complete a task, or are required either to supply it themselves or extract it from a source that also contains irrelevant information.

3. *Abstractness* was essentially the same as in Edwards & Dall'Alba.

4. *Strategy* was to assess how much the student was required to devise their own strategies for completing the task. Experience soon showed that the fourth scale should sometimes be split into separate scales called *Problem Strategy* and *Response Strategy*, since exams might differ in the balance of the demands they make on devising strategies for solving problems and on planning how to communicate the answer once it has been found.

It also proved better to define levels 2 and 4, rather than to try to define them all, as Edwards & Dall'Alba had done, or to follow the other common practice of defining the extremes. In later versions some of the statements have been modified to encourage judges to make more use of the extreme categories, such as changing 'No' in the glosses for levels 2 to 'Few' or 'Little'. A current version of the five scales of demands is given in Table 2.

Table 2 The CRAS scales of demands

	1	2	3	4	5
Complexity The number of components or operations or ideas and the links between them.		Mostly single ideas and simple steps. Little comprehension, except that required for natural language. Few links between operations.		Synthesis or evaluation is required. Need for technical comprehension. Makes links between cognitive operations.	
Resources The use of data and information.		More or less all and only the data/information needed is given.		Student must generate or select the necessary data/information.	
Abstractness The extent to which the student deals with ideas rather than concrete objects or phenomena.		Mostly deals with concrete objects.		Mostly abstract.	
Task strategy The extent to which the student devises (or selects) and maintains a strategy for tackling the question.		Strategy is given. Little need to monitor strategy. Little selection of information required.		Students need to devise their own strategy. Students must monitor the application of their strategy.	
Response strategy The extent to which students have to organise their own response.		Organisation of response hardly required.		Must select answer content from a large pool of possibilities. Must organise how to communicate response.	

The scales have also been reworded for use in different subjects, with further subject-specific definition to interpret each category to suit each of them. In modern foreign languages, for example, it is stressed that 'resources' refers to the amount and kind of language required from the students in relation to the language they are given in the stimulus material, or to the amount of support they are given for the task. It has been suggested that the scale called *resources* might be better labelled *tailoring of resources*.

Because the descriptions used to define the CRAS scales have been distilled from evidence in many subjects and from many studies into a generic form, one particular application to which they lend themselves is studies comparing the demands and grade standards in different subjects. A series of such studies was carried out by the QCA in recent years, comparing geography to history, the three sciences, media studies to English literature and history, and psychology to biology and sociology (QCA, forthcoming a). In some of these studies ratings were made across qualifications at different levels, from GCSE foundation to A2, the scales were reduced to four levels in each qualification and then overlapped to give as many as ten levels overall.

Ratings were made for every question in one examination paper, plus an overall rating, and this was then repeated for every other exam paper. Note that this contrasts with the usual method in the other studies reported here where all of the examinations were rated together on each scale. One assumes that, with this method, the 'overall' rating will be an implicit average of the ratings of every question, but there is no report of how the judges did arrive at it.

As an example of the findings, in the last of the studies the mean overall ratings were as presented in Table 3.

Table 3 Mean overall ratings

	Biology	Psychology	Sociology
AS units	2.6	2.8	3.1
A2 units	2.9	4.4	4.2

The report commented:

> ...it can be seen that there is very little difference between psychology and sociology at either AS or A2. It can also be seen that both were judged as significantly more demanding than biology at A2 and a little more demanding at AS.
>
> QCA (forthcoming a)

A study of grade standards was also carried out, using Thurstone's paired comparison methodology (see Chapter 7), and the report concluded:

> ... the analysis suggested that standards in biology and psychology were very well aligned across the grade range in both the AS and A2 examinations. Given that the initial impulse of the work was the suggestion that students were turning away from science to psychology because it was perceived to be the soft option, the study suggests that this perception has little basis in fact, at least in terms of the demand of the examinations and the grading standards set.
>
> QCA (forthcoming a)

In inter-subject comparability studies it is always going to be difficult to find judges who are capable of rating two or more of the subjects. Having found them, in these studies considerable effort was put into training. An initial briefing preceded the rating; in the fourth study some pilot rating of questions was added to help standardise the ratings. In summary, it seems that the raters did feel confident about their part in the process.

4 Problems in assessing cognitive demands

The reports reviewed in sections 2 and 3 frequently record problems with the assessment of demands. Sometimes these are practical difficulties associated with the particular technique used; others are problems with the principle of the method. Most serious are problems with the conceptualisation of demand, demands and difficulty.

4.1 Practical

Several of these studies noted practical problems that face any attempt to collect ratings of demands. First, these judgements take time, and are therefore an expensive element of a comparability study. The time needed obviously depends to some extent on the number of scales used and the number of times each is applied, and important decisions must be made at the design stage of the study. Attempts to capture the whole of 'overall demand' in a few broad statements means that each statement will be a composite of multiple aspects; whenever these do not correlate highly there will be an averaging effect causing ratings to regress towards the middle category (Fowles, 1995), and real differences between exams may be lost. Time problems are further increased if non-examiners participate (Jones, 1993), since they need more time to familiarise themselves with all of the materials and the assessment procedures before they can judge demands. Yet there are good arguments for using groups other than examiners. Teachers, who prepare students for the examination and are not practised in the arts of question writing, may be in a better position to judge how students will be challenged by a particular feature than examiners who recognise it from past papers. Of course the students themselves are even more likely to understand how demands really operate (Wood & Pollitt, 2006).

The 1–5 numerical scales usually used pose some problems. Phillips & Adams (1995) reported that some raters felt them too limiting; given definitions for '1' or '5' they wanted to expand the scale with '-' and '+' sub-divisions, leading to a 15-point scale. Fearnley (2000) reported difficulties with interpreting qualified descriptors at the ends of scales – how 'few' is 'few' to deserve a '1' rather than a '2'? A similar problem with quantifying features was reported in the 1995 studies: asked to compare 'foreign' exam materials to their own 'home' material that defined the category '3', judges wondered how different the sets needed to be to trigger a rating other than '3'.

4.2 Components

Gray (2000) noted that many of the statements formulated from the comments of judges in initial meetings really expressed simple dimensions of descriptive difference that had little or nothing to do with what most people would consider as demands. In one study as few as 6 out of 14 construct statements seemed to relate to demands. This is a natural outcome of the Kelly elicitation procedure: informants are asked to describe 'similarities and differences' they see, not 'similarities and differences in the demands'. It would be a mistake to ask them to consider whether a difference or similarity concerns 'demands' before they speak, since the method depends on spontaneous verbalisation of thoughts, but there is nothing to stop researchers selectively culling the constructs elicited to leave just those that relate to demands.

Simple rating of overall demand, even if it showed differences, would not be very informative, and almost all studies seek ratings of components, or demands. Several reports (e.g. McLone & Patrick, 1990; Jones, 1993) note a concern that as soon as the general concept of 'overall demand' is analysed into components there is a problem with potential interactions between the components. Judges reported problems in rating specific demands separately where they believed the total demand would be augmented by interaction. A further complication was added when the 'style' of two examinations was deemed different: Jones (1993) and Fowles (1995) both reported that judges found it difficult to make comparative quantitative ratings of demands when this happened. Since these studies concerned GCSE English and A level physics respectively, the notion of 'style' clearly must be considered very broadly.

In many studies it is reported that judges had trouble understanding what statements meant. A simple demand like 'Time available per question' or 'To what extent are the questions understandable?' poses no comprehension problems for judges (however difficult it may be for them to judge it), but the meaning of others, most notably the highly distilled scales of CRAS, may be difficult to master. Greatorex *et al.* (2002) suggest that more discussion between judges is needed to promote a shared understanding of statements like 'How stimulating are the materials?', but Fearnley (1999) argues that even this cannot guarantee consistent interpretations.

4.3 Rating scales

Even if a common meaning could be established for each statement, judges might apply different 'values' to the categories within the scale. Every point in the scale needs to be defined quantitatively to avoid this, and this is generally impossible. Language, like judgement, is inherently comparative and only approximately quantitative, and the problems of trying to pin down relative meanings with words are well known. It is not surprising therefore that Adams & Pinot de Moira (2000) question the reliability and validity of some of the data collected.

A further consequence of the comparative nature of judgement (Laming, 2004) is that a 1–5 scale will always be implicitly normed relative to the context in which it is being used. Judges will always tend to place the '3' category, being the middle one, at the centre of what is expected in a particular context. This raises very difficult problems if qualifications at different levels are being compared: GCSE judges and AS judges may both locate '3' as corresponding to the centre of their particular experience, reinterpreting words like 'usually', 'often' or 'frequent' to match their expectation of the average at that level.

A better approach might be devised for controlling the numbers used in the ratings. One study (QCA, forthcoming b) used discussion to partially standardise the rating given by different judges. The same might be achieved more easily by design. For example, consider the form shown in Figure 1: this is designed so that every rater will use the same scale length to represent the four examinations, but will be free to determine the relative sizes not only of the ratings but also of the gaps between them. The ratings will be fully interval, yet will be reasonably well standardised.

Figure 2 A possible standardised rating scale for comparing four exams

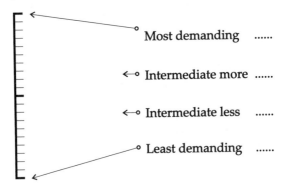

It is tempting to make the statements narrower in order to reduce comprehension problems, but this can cause other problems, from omitting important aspects of demand to increasing the number of scales and the potential for interactions between them. There is a fundamental dilemma that broad general statements of demand are difficult to understand and rate reliably, but narrow specific ones are not generalisable and their ratings are difficult to evaluate.

The consistency both between and within judges also needs consideration. Methods based on Kelly's technique often result in a wide variance between examiners in the ratings applied to a construct for a particular specification, sometimes covering over half of the full range available and even the full range. This suggests that inter-judge consistency is fairly low. However, it is difficult to assess the general level of inter-judge consistency accurately, as data on ratings have often been reported at the level of the sub-group rather than for each board. Intra-judge consistency has also not been established and it is difficult to guess how consistent an individual judge would be with their ratings if they had made them on a different occasion; further, they might be reasonably consistent in terms of the rank-order in which they place examinations in terms of a particular construct, even if they are inconsistent on a particular rating scale. This suggests further caution in interpreting such methods – as well as the need for some formal investigation of raters' test-retest consistency and construct-specific internal consistency.

4.4 Overall demand from components

The desire to be able to declare one exam to be, overall, more or less demanding than another means that judges are usually asked to make an overall rating. Not surprisingly, they sometimes report problems in doing this (e.g. Edwards & Adams, 2002). Aggregating components without explicit rules is bound to be difficult, but it is unlikely that any acceptable set of quantitative rules could be found.

Arrow's paradox sets requirements for a 'fair' system for aggregating simple preferences into a rank-order and shows that it is impossible to devise a scheme that would always meet these requirements (Arrow, 1951; Vassiloglou & French, 1982). 'Simple preferences' are ordinal measurement, and the impossibility can be avoided if interval data are used. If we ask judges to rate demands on fixed scales we can get interval data, encoding the size of differences between two exams rather than just which is the more 'demanding' on each scale, but it would still be very difficult to obtain agreement on a fair weighting to give each demand. In different examinations, and particularly if they are truly different in style, one would expect different relative importance to be attached to any particular demand[2]. As mentioned before, one solution is just to count how often each exam is deemed more or less demanding than the others (Greatorex *et al.*, 2002).

In the inter-subject studies reported in QCA (forthcoming a) and the related specific reports overall ratings were calculated as the arithmetic averages of the four CRAS scales, which were themselves implicit average ratings given after individual questions had been rated. So long as the 'grand overall average' ratings are treated simply as first indications of potential problems there seems no reason to argue for any more complicated approach than this.

4.5 Construct elicitation technique

There is some concern that the basic presumptions of Kelly's method do not apply in these studies (e.g. Fearnley, 2000). The clinical interview was developed by Kelly in the context of psychotherapy as a method for investigating the mind of a patient. The therapist asks the patient to compare two (or three) people with whom they are thoroughly familiar and about whom they have stable perceptions, such as family members and close friends, and to tell instantly ways in which they are similar or different. In comparability studies judges meet materials for the first time when they are asked to judge them, and it is not obvious that the constructs they express when asked to make comparisons would be the same if they were more familiar with them. However, applied research using Kelly's methods generally involves two phases and it is important to keep them separate.

The first phase is elicitation. In it the comparability researcher is interested not in the mind of the judge but in the constructs elicited from him or her; since the judges are experienced examiners (or experienced teachers or experienced students) they will already have developed the constructs that will allow them to make sense of the examination experience, and it is most probable that they will use these same constructs in the elicitation interview. Of course, if a researcher is still concerned about the unfamiliarity of the materials being used, *since this is just the elicitation phase* it would be acceptable to use only materials familiar to the judges.

The second phase is the rating of the material being studied, using the constructs elicited in the first phase. A wide body of research in psychology (e.g. Fransella & Dalton, 2000; Winter & Viney, 2005), sociology (e.g. Dallos, 1994; Butt & Parton, 2005) and education (e.g. Beard, 1978; Beail, 1985; Pope & Denicolo, 2000) supports the view that the constructs elicited in well-designed interviews do prove valid and useful when used by other judges to rate other similar materials or objects. Most of the studies reported in these use 'repertory grid' techniques, in which the rating data are ordered in two dimensions across both the objects being judged and the constructs being used to judge them. As noted earlier, the comparability studies reported in this chapter generally present constructs singly rather than in a grid, but this in no way invalidates the constructs themselves. Indeed, since the studies do not use repertory grid analytic techniques, they do not depend significantly on Kelly's theory for their validity: his elicitation technique is merely a tool to help set up the scales to be used for judgement.

4.6 Quantification

Houston (1981) and Edwards & Adams (2003) both recognise that the result of a demands analysis will be to show that different exams make different demands. It may be possible to go further and say which demands each one requires most of, but it will usually not be possible to aggregate these validly to say that one is more demanding than another. It is perhaps easier to see the strength of this argument when the comparison is between different subjects, but it is equally true within one subject.

Arlett (2003) notes that the construct elicitation technique is designed to discover differences (like the Thurstone quantitative technique described in another chapter) and succeeds in doing so. She and others (e.g. Adams & Pinot de Moira, 2000) add that the method provides no way of quantifying or evaluating the significance of the differences it uncovers. This problem gets to the heart of the conceptual confusions that surround 'demands'. Despite the use of scales and the collection of numerical ratings the method is still fundamentally a qualitative methodology, designed to discover and describe differences in the pattern of demands that different qualifications make. Suitable tests can indicate whether or not the differences observed are statistically significant, but they cannot reliably measure their size or educational significance.

Many of the reported problems are a consequence of an assumption that demands and difficulty should be closely linked. McLone & Patrick (1990) saw the fundamental problem as being to identify what constituted demand in mathematics by identifying factors affecting demand and how these factors affect difficulty; one of their categories, 'academic demand', was glossed as 'intrinsic difficulty'. Jones (1993) reports judges' concerns about questions that appeared more demanding than they actually were, the evidence for the latter coming from the mark schemes and marked scripts, and others wanting to see scripts before rating demands because it was difficult to predict how the wording of questions would affect students' work. Reference has already been made in discussing other reports of the usefulness of seeing performance evidence while rating demands. In all of these cases the problem lies in trying to keep separate the two concepts of 'demands' and 'difficulty', and the next section will address this issue directly.

5 Demands and difficulty

5.1 Discussion of the terms

For a student, the outcome of an examination is the grade they achieve, which depends on the score they make and the grade boundaries that are set, and it is generally assumed that the score depends on two factors – the ability of the student and the difficulty of the questions. (This model is discussed further in Chapter 7.) We would like to ensure that the student's grade is determined solely by his or her ability, so that students with more ability always get higher grades, but this will happen only if we can ensure that all of the students respond predictably to the difficulties in the questions. We need, therefore, to understand and control the sources of difficulty in exam questions.

As described earlier, Pollitt *et al.* (1985) identified three kinds of source, which were called *subject/concept difficulty, process difficulty,* and *question (stimulus) difficulty.* We now consider difficulty resulting from the concepts in a subject as aspects of demand; in the CRAS scheme they are rated under 'abstractness' or 'complexity'. Similarly, difficulty arising from the psychological processes the students are asked to carry out is rated as demand in the scales for 'strategy', 'resource', and 'complexity'. For these categories it is fairly simple: more demand quite directly causes more difficulty, and this can be observed as lower scores from students.

The trouble comes with the third kind of source of difficulty. Experience, supported by research (e.g. Ahmed & Pollitt, 1999; 2007; Crisp & Sweiry, 2006), has shown that the differences in difficulty between individual questions depend at least as much on the presence or absence of various features in the stimulus question, as on the amount of difficulty the examiners intended. Some examples from our research in the University of Cambridge Local Examinations Syndicate will illustrate the problems 'questions' cause for examiners.

Example 1

In a GCSE science paper a complicated context was described, which involved a tower for producing fresh water from sea water while also generating electricity. The first part of the question was:

(a) Air rises inside the tower in a convection current. Explain why convection happens.

Many students tried to explain why the tower caused convection – and usually failed. When this was later discussed with the examiners they explained that this was meant to be an easy 'textbook' question to get the students started; they did not intend the context to get in the way.

Example 2

It's commonly assumed that sub-headings will help students structure their answers. This example comes from a GCSE geography paper:

(ii) Describe Gamble Street before urban renewal using the following headings:

open space _____

_____

factories _____

_____ *(4 marks)*

Performance was disappointing, with students averaging only 33% of the marks. We re-tested the question on a comparable sample without the sub-headings, and – with exactly the same mark scheme – the performance rose to 60%. The students mentioned more of the scoring points listed in the mark scheme when allowed to write more freely.

Example 3

Another GCSE geography question that proved disappointingly difficult, with only 8% success, occurred in a map-reading question:

Using Fig. 1 describe the shape of the valley along this cross-section.

We re-tested this one with the word **shape** printed in bold, and the success rate rose to 37%. The intended task was difficult enough, but the presentation of the question left many students not realising that it was the **shape**, rather than the valley, that they had to describe.

Example 4

The most difficult word in the English language is probably 'not'. This example is from GCSE mathematics:

Alex, Bernice, Christelle, Divya, Elisa and Fernanda play a game.

They all have an equal chance of winning.

(a) What is the probability that Alex does not win?

In our study sample, 84 students gave the correct answer (5/6) but 93 gave the complementary wrong answer (1/6). Was this because they couldn't do the maths, or did it result from a reading failure? How can examiners predict the effect of reading failures of this kind?

Example 5

At A level the problems are sometimes quite different; they may be more subtle but equally dramatic. This example is discussed fully in O'Donovan (2005):

Outline ways in which the Conservative Party has rebuilt itself since 1997. (20 marks)

It is hard to blame the examiners for not predicting that some students would challenge the question (but then again, this is A level politics!) and argue that the party had, in fact, failed to rebuild itself; even harder to blame them for not predicting that at least one student would deny that they had even *tried* to rebuild, citing their choices of William Hague and Iain Duncan Smith as proof. It is not easy for examiners to prepare a mark scheme that correctly anticipates the many ways a student may interpret a question, and so to maintain fairness, without sacrificing reliability.

Many more examples could be given, showing how features of language, of layout or of the visual and other resources given in the question, can cause changes in difficulty (usually increases) that are very hard to predict. Examiners deliberately manipulate the demands that contribute to concept and process difficulty and try not to let the presentation of the questions interfere too much with the operation of these demands. Thus the intended demands, mostly in the first two categories of sources of difficulty, represent the trait that the examiners wish to assess. It helps to distinguish the *task* that the examiners want students to tackle from the *question/stimulus* that they use to present it. The sole purpose of the questions is to present tasks that will make the students' minds engage with the intended demands: validity requires that 'the students' minds are doing the things we want them to show us they can do' (Ahmed & Pollitt, 2007), and the question should not prevent that from happening by misdirecting their attention elsewhere.

The many features that can affect the difficulty of the stimulus question could be considered as part of a broad concept of 'reading difficulty', but this is not helpful when it confuses intended and unintended sources of difficulty. We can find no evidence that judges in comparability studies have noted presentation effects like those in the examples above and allowed for them in rating the reading demand of the papers, and it is not reasonable to expect them to do so when the question writers and scrutineers have failed to do so. It is better if the ratings of demands remain as ratings of *intended* demands, where we include in 'intended' any aspect of demand that the question writers could reasonably be expected to have been aware of. The consequence, however, is that ratings of demands will never accurately predict the empirical measures of difficulty derived from students' marks.

Researchers in America have achieved some success in predicting question difficulty from features of questions that might be considered to be demands, but they have been applied only to very limited test-item types, usually testing some aspect of intelligence and set in multiple-choice format (Bejar et al., 1991; Embretson, 1999). Only rarely did they involve language, as in Stenner et al.'s (1983) study of vocabulary and spelling.

5.2 Definition of the terms

To summarise, we consider demands to be separable, but not wholly discrete skills or skill sets that are presumed to determine the relative difficulty of examination tasks and are intentionally included in examinations. Examiners use these concepts of demands, fairly deliberately, to control both the nature of the construct that the examination measures and the difficulty of the tasks they use to measure it. Overlaid on the demands, however, is the stimulus question, the layout of words and diagrams (usually) that present the task to the students and that may significantly alter the intended difficulty of the task. Over a whole examination paper, where the same general demands are set at similar levels repeatedly it is likely that the effects of presentation will tend to cancel out, leading to reasonable overall success in controlling the difficulty of examination by focusing on demands. Conceptually, examiners are comfortable talking about the demands in their questions; empirically, because of the powerful influence of the question presentation, it is much harder to confirm their influence on difficulty.

Difficulty, on the other hand, is a statistical measure that indicates how likely it is for any given student to score marks, estimated by considering the scores of actual students in an examination. The difficulty measure is therefore a property of a question or test that is defined for a particular group of students (note how 'difficulty' was reported for different student samples in the TIMSS examples described earlier), and it makes sense to talk of the difficulty of a question and of the difficulty of an examination. The term is also often used loosely to talk of the difficulty of a question for a particular student, but this should be understood as a kind of prediction of the outcome that student (given their ability) can expect on that question (given its difficulty) – again see further discussion of this in Chapter 7.

Amongst the principal differences between demands and difficulty are that the former is judged by experienced participants while the latter is calculated from performance data by statisticians. It is quite important that ratings of demands, conceived in this way, should not be contaminated by performance data since these relate to actual rather than intended outcomes. Allowing judges to revise their ratings after seeing scripts, as in Edwards & Adams (2003), will reduce the value of the ratings as indicators of intended demand, and change them into rather unreliable indices of perceived difficulty. While it may be worth asking judges how difficult they think a paper is, this is not the same as asking how demanding it is; the former is a prediction, the latter a judgement. It is different in an award meeting where the grade boundaries are set. There it is essential that examiners combine their perceptions of difficulty from reading completed scripts with the judgements of demands they made earlier in order to select appropriate scores to act as grade boundaries that maintain the established examination standard.

6   Ways forward

One purpose of this book is to guide future debates about issues relating to examination standards, and a good starting point would be to try to make the use of terms more consistent. The last section developed a definition of *demands*, and the technical definition of *difficulty* presented is well established. It is probably also worth trying to define the noun *demand*: in this chapter it has been used in two senses. We prefer to use it to specify one of the component demands in an examination. But it is also commonly used in a global sense, as the aggregate of all the demands of the whole assessment process; we prefer to describe this as the overall demand. Since demands cannot be quantified (or at least not on a common scale) this aggregation is necessarily subjective, and will be specific to an imagined student group. In these two ways, an examination's *overall demand* is a separate concept from its difficulty. In particular, outsiders will be quite unable to judge accurately the standard of examinations merely by looking at the questions. Experienced examiners who are familiar with the kind of students involved find it hard enough to estimate the overall demand, and without access to the mark schemes they cannot predict the overall difficulty; without also knowing the grade boundaries they have no way of judging the examination standard.

Performance is what candidates actually produce in an examination: it is usually their set of written responses to the tasks set, but it may be some other visible or audible product, and may sometimes be unrecorded; the role of examiners (markers) is to quantify the quality of this performance somehow. The relations between *demands*, *difficulty* and *performance* are complex. More difficult tasks will usually lead to poorer performances; more demanding tasks may have a similar effect but equally may lead to better performances by prompting students to respond in a more complex or effective way. For similar reasons, changing the nature of demands in a task may raise or lower the measure of difficulty; in addition, since each demand challenges individual students to different degrees, changing the demands may improve some students' performances while worsening others'.

An analogy from sport may help to clarify the relationships between *demand, demands* and *difficulty*. In any athletics race it could be said that the *demand* against which candidates are being assessed is 'fast running'. A little thought about the various races makes it clear, however, that there is more to running than this: to compare 100-metre and 5000-metre races we need to consider (at least) two *demands* – 'sprint running' and 'endurance running'. Clearly, some runners are better at one of these than the other. In the longer races we might want to consider 'strategy' as another demand, and for the steeplechase races we might need to add 'jumping or hurdling' demands. A comparison of the marathon and the 400-metre hurdles events would involve judging or comparing them against these various *demands* and would show that one is *more demanding* on some demands and *less demanding* on others. As an extension of this analysis, we could consider the *overall demand* of the event to include some assessment of the amount of training, discipline and sacrifice that successful contestants must accept; but this clearly leads into a very subjective realm of judgement. Such considerations are, however, important in deciding who is likely to achieve most in different events.

The *difficulty* of each race could be measured, as some function of the time, or speed, of winners or of average contestants. This would show that, for example, the 200-metre race was more difficult than the 100-metre; where appropriate, as in qualification for Olympic competition, officials would set suitable 'pass marks' for each event to compensate for the differences in difficulty, using empirical data to determine what is appropriate in each case. The *performance* of each contestant is measured as a time (in other athletics events as a distance). In the decathlon competition empirical data are used to establish rules for rescaling performances for aggregation into a composite total, again compensating, normatively, for differences in *difficulty*. None of these measurements or manipulations, however, affect the *demands*.

There are many other words used, more or less loosely, in discussing examinations, such as the adjectives *demanding* and *difficult*, and other pairs like *challenge/challenging* and *toughness/tough* but it is probably overambitious to try to prescribe how they should be used.

7 Conclusion

This review began by considering the purposes that a study of examination demands might serve, and it is worth revisiting the three aims mentioned in the light of the discussions in the chapter. How well have we achieved Aim 1: *the im of description*? Following a suitable elicitation process, a series of rating scales can be presented to appropriate judges to obtain a description of the intended demands in the exam in as much detail as is desired. This has been done quite successfully in many of the studies reviewed. To improve this, consider the value of such a description: its principal use would be in communicating the nature of the qualification amongst all of the people involved in it – examiners, teachers, students, regulators, employers and selectors.

Can we achieve Aim 2: *the aim of comparison*? The descriptions developed for Aim 1 may be written in terms that are quite specific to all of the participants in that qualification, and which may therefore be misunderstood by others not so closely involved. To meet Aim 2 we need more commonality across the descriptions of different qualifications than there has been so far across the comparability studies. This suggests that it would be worth asking all comparability studies to contribute to a common collection of construct statements, and that some suitable body should undertake to develop from them a standard set of demand scales that can be used in future studies. Eventually this set may be complete enough that there will be no need to carry out an elicitation phase in every study, and it will suffice to select from the construct bank all of the scales that might be important in each new case; as we said earlier the set of demands that are intended to operate in an exam constitute an operational definition of the trait the exam is intended to measure. It should then be easy to make three kinds of comparison. Comparison between different subjects will show how each subject differs in its conceptualisation of achievement, and allow consideration of whether these differences are valuable or problematic. Comparison between examinations that appear to offer the same qualification will help regulators and others to judge whether each qualification is indeed fit for the purposes to which its results are put. Finally, if the description of the demands intended in a given exam are published as part of its specification, a requirement that seems very reasonable when they constitute a definition of what it intends to measure, then comparison between the ratings given to the various demands and the specification will be a form of content validation.

When the GCSE system was being planned in England, several groups tried to 'develop a performance matrix which indicates clearly the attributes that examinations will be seeking to assess and how the levels of achievement will be decided' (Bevan, 1988, p. 1). This is close to an explicit specification for the levels of demand deemed appropriate in each of these examinations, and would provide the basis for holding examinations accountable on demands in just the way that they already are on content.

Finally, how realistic is Aim 3: *the aim of compensation*? There is a problem with this aim, which may originate in what is expected of demands. If, as has been argued here, we should think of demands as 'intended demands' rather than as the 'sources of difficulty' then we cannot logically expect the ratings of demands to predict difficulty very accurately, because of the serious interference of question presentation effects. But if we try to improve the link between 'demands' and difficulty by letting evidence from performance (i.e. evidence about difficulty) modify the judges' initial perceptions of the intended demands then any improvement we obtain will be spurious, being brought about by the very property we are supposed to be predicting.

Remembering that the evidence about demands is essentially qualitative, even if it is expressed numerically on a series of scales, it is probably best not to try to imagine how much 'compensation' should be due to some students because their examination has been deemed more demanding in certain ways than another. Demand differences can be used to test the plausibility of the conclusions from performance comparisons, but we are far from understanding the relationships well enough at present to use them to predict quantitatively differences in performance.

Endnotes

1 Edwards and Dall'Alba gave verbal definitions only for some of their six levels, leaving some blank as 'intermediate' between those above and below them.

2 The problem with Arrow's paradox is rooted in his 'Binary Independence' condition, which requires that the group's relative ranking of two alternatives should not be affected by the presence or absence of any other alternatives (it is often called the 'Independence from Irrelevant Alternatives' condition). Saari (2001) shows that this requirement 'emasculates' the most basic of Arrow's conditions, that all of the judges should behave rationally, by turning all ranked data into a disconnected set of binary comparisons. Since Thurstone's method of paired comparison constructs its scale from exactly such a set of data (see Chapter

7) it follows that Thurstone's method cannot be trusted to meet Arrow's BI condition – in fact, the parameterisaton procedure explicitly contradicts it. Therefore, either we must reject Thurstone's method or we must conclude, with Saari, that Arrow's BI condition is unacceptable.

References

Adams, R.M. (1993). *GCSE inter-group cross-moderation studies summer 1992 examination: English, mathematics and science. Report on the experimental methodology used in the studies.* Welsh Joint Education Committee on behalf of the Inter-Group Research Committee for the GCSE.

Adams, R.M., & Pinot de Moira, A. (2000). *A comparability study in GCSE French including parts of the Scottish Standard grade examination. A study based on the summer 1999 examination. Review of question paper demand, cross-moderation study and statistical analysis of results.* Organised by Welsh Joint Education Committee and Assessment and Qualifications Alliance on behalf of the Joint Forum for the GCSE and GCE.

Ahmed, A., & Pollitt, A. (1999, May). *Curriculum demands and question difficulty.* Paper presented at the International Association for Educational Assessment Annual Conference, Bled, Slovenia.

Ahmed, A., & Pollitt, A. (2007). Improving the quality of contextualised questions: An experimental investigation of focus. *Assessment in Education, 14,* 201-232.

Alton, A. (1995). *A comparability study in GCSE science. A study based on the summer 1994 examinations.* Southern Examining Group on behalf of the Inter-Group Research Committee for the GCSE.

Anderson, L.W., & Krathwohl, D.R. (Eds.). (2001). *A taxonomy for learning, teaching and assessing: Revision of Bloom's taxonomy of educational objectives: Complete edition.* New York: Longman.

Arlett, S. (2002). *A comparability study in VCE health and social care, units 1, 2 and 5. A study based on the summer 2001 examination.* Organised by the Assessment and Qualifications Alliance on behalf of the Joint Council for General Qualifications.

Arlett, S. (2003). *A comparability study in VCE health and social care, units 3, 4 and 6. A study based on the summer 2002 examination.* Organised by the Assessment and Qualifications Alliance on behalf of the Joint Council for General Qualifications.

Arrow, K.J. (1951). *Social choice and individual values.* New York: Wiley & Sons.

Ausubel, D.P., Novak, J.D., & Hanesien, H. (1978). *Educational psychology: A cognitive view* (2nd ed.). New York: Holt, Rinehart and Winston.

Baird, J. (1999, November). *Regression analysis of review outcomes.* Paper presented at a seminar held by the Research Committee of the Joint Council for General Qualifications, Manchester. Reported in B.E. Jones (Ed.), (2000), *A review of the methodologies of recent comparability studies*. Report on a seminar for boards' staff hosted by the Assessment and Qualifications Alliance, Manchester.

Bannister, D., & Fransella, F. (1971). *Inquiring man: The psychology of personal constructs.* London: Croom Helm.

Beail, N. (1985). *Repertory grid technique and personal constructs: Applications in clinical and educational settings.* London: Croom Helm.

Beard, R. (1978). Teachers' and pupils' construing of reading. In F. Fransella (Ed.), *Personal construct psychology. Proceedings of the 1977 international conference on personal construct psychology, University of Oxford.* (pp. 69–74). London: Academic Press.

Bejar, I., Chaffin, R., & Embretson, S. (1991). *Cognitive and psychometric analysis of analogical problem solving.* New York: Springer-Verlag.

Bevan, D. (1988). *Report of the MEG performance matrices (science) working group: Interim report.* Cambridge: Midland Examining Group.

Bloom, B.S. (Ed.). (1956). *Taxonomy of educational objectives: The classification of educational goals by a committee of college and university examiners. Handbook I: Cognitive domain.* New York: Longmans, Green.

Bruner, J., Olver, R.R., Greenfield, P.M., Rigney Hornsby, J., Kenny, H.J., Maccoby, M., et al. (1966). *Studies in cognitive growth.* New York: John Wiley.

Butt, T.W., & Parton, N. (2005). Constructivist social work and personal construct theory. *British Journal of Social Work, 35*(6), 793–806.

Crisp, V., & Sweiry, E. (2006). Can a picture ruin a thousand words? The effects of visual resources in exam questions. *Educational Research, 48,* 139–154.

Dallos, R. (1994). *Family belief systems, therapy and change.* Milton Keynes: Open University Press.

D'Arcy, J. (Ed.). (1997). *Comparability studies between modular and non-modular syllabuses in GCE Advanced level biology, English literature and mathematics in the 1996 summer examinations.* Standing Committee on Research on behalf of the Joint Forum for the GCSE and GCE.

de Bono, E. (1976). *Teaching Thinking.* London: Maurice Temple Smith.

Edwards, E., & Adams, R. (2002). *A comparability study in GCE AS geography including parts of the Scottish Higher grade examination. A study based on the summer 2001 examination.* Organised by the Welsh Joint Education Committee on behalf of the Joint

Council for General Qualifications.

Edwards, E., & Adams, R. (2003). *A comparability study in GCE Advanced level geography including the Scottish Advanced Higher grade examination. A study based on the summer 2002 examination.* Organised by the Welsh Joint Education Committee on behalf of the Joint Council for General Qualifications.

Edwards, J., & Dall'Alba, G. (1981). Development of a scale of cognitive demand for analysis of printed secondary science materials. *Research in Science Education, 11,* 158–170.

Embretson, S. (1999). Cognitive psychology applied to testing. In F.T. Durso (Ed.), *Handbook of applied cognition* (pp. 629-660). New York: Wiley.

Evans, B.F., & Pierce, G.E. (1982). *Report of a GCE inter-board study in German at the Advanced level 1980.* Cardiff: Welsh Joint Education Committee.

Fearnley, A. (1999, November). *Kelly's repertory grid and analysis of ratings.* Paper presented at a seminar held by the Research Committee of the Joint Council for General Qualifications, Manchester. Reported in B.E. Jones (Ed.), (2000), *A review of the methodologies of recent comparability studies.* Report on a seminar for boards' staff hosted by the Assessment and Qualifications Alliance, Manchester.

Fearnley, A. (2000). *A comparability study in GCSE mathematics. A study based on the summer 1998 examination.* Organised by the Assessment and Qualifications Alliance (Northern Examinations and Assessment Board) on behalf of the Joint Forum for the GCSE and GCE.

Fowles, D.E. (1995). *A comparability study in Advanced level physics. A study based on the summer 1994 and 1990 examinations.* Northern Examinations and Assessment Board on behalf of the Standing Research Advisory Committee of the GCE boards.

Fransella, F., & Dalton, P. (2000). *Personal construct counselling in action* (2nd ed.). London: Sage Publications.

Gagné, R.M. (1970). *Conditions of learning.* New York: Holt, Rinehart & Winston.

Good, F.J., & Cresswell, M.J. (1988). Grade awarding judgments in differentiated examinations. *British Educational Research Journal, 14,* 263–281

Gray, E. (1995). *A comparability study in GCSE English. A study based on the summer 1994 examinations.* Midland Examining Group on behalf of the Inter-Group Research Committee for the GCSE.

Gray, E. (2000). *A comparability study in GCSE science 1998. A study based on the summer 1998 examination.* Organised by Oxford Cambridge and RSA Examinations (Midland Examining Group) on behalf of the Joint Forum for the GCSE and GCE.

Greatorex, J., Elliott, G., & Bell, J.F. (2002). *A comparability study in GCE AS chemistry: A review of the examination requirements and a report on the cross-moderation exercise. A study based on the summer 2001 examination.* Organised by the Research and Evaluation Division, University of Cambridge Local Examinations Syndicate for Oxford Cambridge and RSA Examinations on behalf of the Joint Council for General Qualifications.

Greatorex, J., Hamnett, L., & Bell, J.F. (2003). *A comparability study in GCE A level chemistry including the Scottish Advanced Higher grade. A review of the examination requirements and a report on the cross-moderation exercise. A study based on the summer 2002 examinations.* Organised by The Research and Evaluation Division, University of Cambridge Local Examinations Syndicate for Oxford Cambridge and RSA Examinations on behalf of the Joint Council for General Qualifications.

Griffiths, H.B., & McLone, R.R. (1979). *Qualities cultivated in mathematics degree examinations.* Southampton: University of Southampton.

Guthrie, K. (2003). *A comparability study in GCE business studies, units 4, 5 and 6, VCE business, units 4, 5 and 6. A review of the examination requirements and a report on the cross-moderation exercise. A study based on the summer 2002 examination.* Organised by Edexcel on behalf of the Joint Council for General Qualifications.

Houston, J.G. (1981). *Report of the inter-board cross-moderation study in economics at Advanced level.* Aldershot: Associated Examining Board.

Hughes, S., Pollitt, A., & Ahmed, A. (1998, August). *The development of a tool for gauging the demands of GCSE and A level exam questions.* Paper presented at the British Educational Research Association Annual Conference, The Queen's University of Belfast.

Igoe, R.A. (1982). *A comparative analysis of the marks awarded in the 1979 Advanced level biology examination of the Joint Matriculation Board and a study of the factors affecting candidates' responses to different types of question.* Unpublished MSc dissertation, University of Warwick.

Jones, B.E. (1993). *GCSE inter-group cross-moderation studies 1992. Summary report on studies undertaken on the summer 1992 examinations in English, mathematics and science.* Inter-Group Research Committee for the GCSE.

Jones, B.E. (Ed.). (1997). *A review and evaluation of the methods used in the 1996 GCSE and GCE comparability studies.* Standing Committee on Research on behalf of the Joint Forum for the GCSE and GCE.

Jones, B.E. (2004). *Report of the JCGQ research seminar on issues related to comparability of standards, 3 December 2003.* Internal Research Paper RC/264. Manchester: Assessment and Qualifications Alliance.

Jones, B., Meadows, M., & Al-Bayatti, M. (2004). *Report of the inter-awarding body comparability study of GCSE religious studies (full course) summer 2003*. Assessment and Qualifications Alliance.

Kelly, G.A. (1955). *The psychology of personal constructs* (Vols. I and II). New York: Norton.

Laming, D. (2004). *Human judgment: The eye of the beholder*. London: Thomson.

Lee, Y.P. (n.d.). *Where markers of essays agree and where they don't – An application of repertory grid analysis*. Unpublished, University of Hong Kong.

Leigh, E.M., Ayling, M., Reeve, R.G., Kingdon, M.J., & Ibbotson, P.M. (1983). *A survey of GCE music A level syllabuses and examinations*. London: University of London, University Entrance and School Examinations Council.

Massey, A.J. (1979). *Comparing standards in English language: A report of the cross-moderation study based on the 1978 Ordinary level examinations of the nine GCE boards*. Bristol: Southern Universities' Joint Board and Test Development and Research Unit.

McLone, R.R., & Patrick, H. (1990). *Standards in Advanced level mathematics. Report of study 1: A study of the demands made by the two approaches to 'double mathematics'*. An investigation conducted by the Standing Research Advisory Committee of the GCE Examining Boards. Cambridge: University of Cambridge Local Examinations Syndicate.

Novak, J.D. (1977). *A Theory of Education*. London: Cornell University Press.

O'Donovan, N. (2005). There are no wrong answers: An investigation into the assessment of candidates' responses to essay-based examinations. *Oxford Review of Education*, *31*, 395–422.

Phillips, E., & Adams, R. (1995). *A comparability study in GCSE mathematics. A study based on the summer 1994 examinations*. Organised by the Welsh Joint Education Committee on behalf of the Inter-Group Research Committee for the GCSE.

Pollitt, A., & Ahmed, A. (1999, May). *A new model of the question answering process*. Paper presented at the International Association for Educational Assessment Conference, Bled, Slovenia.

Pollitt, A., & Ahmed, A. (2000, September). *Comprehension failures in educational assessment*. Paper presented at the European Conference on Educational Research, Edinburgh.

Pollitt, A., Entwistle, N.J., Hutchinson, C.J., & de Luca, C. (1985). *What makes exam questions difficult?* Edinburgh: Scottish Academic Press.

Pollitt, A., Hughes, S., Ahmed, A., Fisher-Hoch, H., & Bramley, T. (1998). *The effects of structure on the demands in GCSE and A level questions.* Report to Qualifications and Curriculum Authority. University of Cambridge Local Examinations Syndicate.

Pollitt, A., & Murray, N.L. (1993). What raters really pay attention to. Language Testing Research Colloquium, Cambridge. Reprinted in M. Milanovic & N. Saville (Eds.), (1996), *Studies in language testing 3: Performance testing, cognition and assessment.* Cambridge: Cambridge University Press.

Pope, M.L., & Denicolo, P. (2000). *Transformative education: Personal construct approaches to practice and research.* Chichester: Whurr/Wiley.

Pritchard, J., Jani, A., & Monani, S. (2000). *A comparability study in GCSE English. Syllabus review and cross-moderation exercise. A study based on the summer 1998 examinations.* Organised by Edexcel on behalf of the Joint Council for General Qualifications.

Qualifications and Curriculum Authority. (2001). *Five year review of standards: GCSE history.* London: Qualifications and Curriculum Authority.

Qualifications and Curriculum Authority. (2006a). *QCA's review of standards: Description of the programme.* London: Qualifications and Curriculum Authority.

Qualifications and Curriculum Authority. (2006b). *Comparability study of assessment practice: Personal licence holder qualifications.* London: Qualifications and Curriculum Authority.

Qualifications and Curriculum Authority. (forthcoming a). *Review of standards between subjects: General report.* London: Qualifications and Curriculum Authority.

Qualifications and Curriculum Authority. (forthcoming b). *Review of standards between subjects: Science report.* London: Qualifications and Curriculum Authority.

Quinlan, M. (1995). *A comparability study in Advanced level mathematics. A study based on the summer 1994 and 1989 examinations.* University of London Examinations and Assessment Council on behalf of the Standing Research Advisory Committee of the GCE Boards.

Ratcliffe, P. (1994). *A comparability study in GCSE geography. A study based on the summer 1993 examinations.* Northern Examinations and Assessment Board on behalf of the Inter-Group Research Committee for the GCSE.

Saari, D.G. (2001). *Decisions and elections: Explaining the unexpected.* Cambridge: Cambridge University Press.

Spielberger, C.D. (1972). *Anxiety: Current trends in theory and research: I.* New York: Academic Press.

Stenner, A.J., Smith, M., & Burdick, D.S. (1983). Toward a theory of construct definition. *Journal of Educational Measurement, 20,* 305–316.

Stobart, G., Elwood, J., Jani, A., & Quinlan, M. (1994). *A comparability study in GCSE history: A study based on the summer 1993 examinations.* University of London Examinations and Assessment Council on behalf of the Inter-Group Research Committee for the GCSE.

Taba, H. (1962). *Curriculum development: Theory and practice.* New York: Harcourt Brace & World.

Taba, H. (1967). *Teacher's handbook for elementary social studies.* Reading, MA: Addison-Wesley.

Third International Mathematics and Science Study. (1996a). *TIMSS mathematics items: Released set for population 2 (seventh and eighth grades).*

Third International Mathematics and Science Study. (1996b). *Mathematics achievement in the middle school years: IEA's third international mathematics and science study (TIMSS).* Chestnut Hill, MA: Center for the Study of Testing, Evaluation and Educational Policy, Boston College.

Vassiloglou, M., & French, S. (1982). Arrow's theorem and examination assessment. *British Journal of Mathematical and Statistical Psychology, 35,* 183–192.

Walker, N.A., Forrest, G.M., & Kingdon, J.M. (1987). *Comparing the boards' examinations: An alternative approach.* Report on the second part [1984–1986] of an exercise conducted by The Standing Research Advisory Committee of the GCE boards involving the examinations in chemistry at Advanced level from 1978 to 1982 and from 1984 to 1986 inclusive.

Whitburn, J. (1999). Why can't the English learn to subtract? In B. Jaworski & D. Phillips (Eds.), *Comparing standards internationally* (pp. 163-182). Oxford: Symposium Books.

Winter, D.A., & Viney, L.L. (2005). *Personal construct psychotherapy: Advances in theory, practice and research.* Chichester: Whurr/Wiley.

Wood, A., & Pollitt, A. (2006, November). *Developing a methodology to enable students to participate in test development.* Paper presented at the Association for Educational Assessment – Europe Annual Conference, Naples, Italy.

COMMENTARY ON CHAPTER 5

Alison Wood

Judgements in formal comparability studies are made by experts: subject specialists, many of whom are senior examiners, with years of experience in question-setting and marking. In their chapter, Pollitt *et al.* refer to a study which took a different approach (Wood & Pollitt, 2006). In this study, A level mathematics (statistics) students made comparative judgements about the overall demand of questions, then went on to identify and describe the factors which they judged to impact on it, that is, they identified the particular demands of the questions.

Pollitt *et al.* acknowledge the general point that students themselves will have a particular perspective on the demands of questions. I suggest that a stronger claim might be made: that students are likely to perceive the demands of particular questions in ways which are inaccessible to experts and, for this reason, we should incorporate their judgements into formal comparability studies. If we want to know what the real demands of questions are, then we need to elicit judgements from those who experience them, that is, the students themselves.

Wood & Pollitt (2006) found that, when describing the demands of questions, although there was much agreement between students and experts, the students identified factors which the experts simply did not recognise. Nathan & Koedinger (2000) reported similar findings from their study of lower-secondary algebra students, so our findings were not unanticipated and the literature on problem-solving suggests that such differences are to be expected. This is because there are important differences between experts and novices in the ways in which they perceive and then engage with problems. Experts and novices represent problems differently (Chi, Feltovich & Glaser, 1981). Novices are far less able to identify and represent problems as being of particular types (Chi, Feltovich & Glaser, 1981; Cummins, 1992; Hinsley, Hayes & Simon, 1978; Mayer, 1982; Riley, Greeno & Heller, 1983; Schoenfeld & Hermann, 1982; Silver, 1981), so are less likely to activate the correct problem-solving schema (Paas, 1992). Experts, on the other hand, activate the appropriate problem-solving schemata very quickly, sometimes as soon as the first phrase of the problem statement is read (Hinsley, Hayes & Simon, 1978). This means that, as soon as an expert begins to read a question, s/he recognises which aspects are relevant, organises those aspects into a coherent model and integrates that model with existing knowledge, in order to solve the problem. Quilici & Mayer (2002) refer to this as structural awareness and it is this structural awareness that makes problem-solving much less demanding, for an expert, than for a novice.

Experts also differ from novices in the ways in which they engage with questions when actually working through the question and generating a response. This is because experts find it easier to recall knowledge during problem-solving, because knowledge in their working memory has strong links to chunks in long-term memory. This facilitates recall, with experts recalling not only more information, but also recalling it in an immediately meaningful way (Larkin, McDermott, Simon & Simon, 1980; Lavigne & Glaser, 2001, in the specific context of statistics). Novices recall information in smaller units and chunk it according to more superficial aspects of the information (Chase & Simon, 1973; Feltovich, 1983). Representing a problem and then engaging with a problem are, therefore, different for experts and novices and so their experience of the demand(s) of the problems will differ. It is for this reason that I am proposing that student judgements be incorporated into comparability studies.

This raises the question of which of the chapters' aims the students might be able to address. Beginning with *the aim of description* – laying bare all of the intended construct-relevant demands which a qualification or an examination paper presents – it seems unlikely that students could describe the *intended* demands of a qualification as a whole, as this ought to be a matter for the curriculum/assessment expert. They did seem, however, to be able to describe the demands of questions, in the sense expressed in Chapter 5: 'the (mostly) cognitive mental processes that a typical student is assumed to have to carry out in order to complete the task set by a question'. They were also able to identify construct-irrelevant sources of difficulty. Wood & Pollitt (2006) found that they could do this consistently, indicating inter-rater reliability and there were some demands/sources of difficulty that were identified only by the students.

Turning to the *aim of comparison* – where judges compare the intended demand profiles between two or more examination papers, highlighting similarities and differences – Wood & Pollitt's (2006) students were able to make comparative judgements about question pairs very easily and give reasons for their comparative judgements, again with evidence of inter-rater reliability. Making judgements at whole-question paper level is a (logical) extension of making judgements about question pairs and a small-scale study, carried out as preliminary work for Wood (2006) suggested that students could compare whole question papers, even between subjects. Again, some of the judgements they made differed from those of experts. If students can provide evidence which cannot be generated by experts, it would seem counter-productive not to include them in comparability studies. At best, with appropriate support, they might well be able to address the aims of *description* and *comparison* in ways which are similar to those of expert judges. At the very least, though, their descriptive and comparative judgements should be made available to experts.

The aim of compensation brings together the notions of construct-relevant demands and construct-irrelevant sources of difficulty. In the formal comparability studies, expert judges make an estimate of the overall demand of an examination paper and then combine that with a further estimate of the difficulty of that particular paper. This judgement is made in the context of the particular sample of students who take that examination. This process gives rise to an estimate of how, on average, those particular students will have experienced that paper. The 'average experienced difficulty' judgement which arises from this process is then used to compare one paper with another.

To address *the aim of compensation*, students would need to be able to make this extremely complex 'average experienced difficulty' judgement. Students would not have the experience to enable them to contextualise their demand judgement, but this judgement, if fed into the deliberations of expert judges, could enable those experts to make their 'average experienced difficulty' judgements more reliably.

Quite clearly, thinking about the use of students in comparability studies is at an early stage and raises many questions. Wood (2006) identifies the range of issues requiring further research, focusing on validity (for example, whether the demands identified by the sample of students really did have an impact on (a) their performance and/or (b) the performance of the whole cohort) and generalisability (for example, whether students from a wider range of ages/levels of ability can make demand judgements). She proposes a programme of work to investigate such issues further.

References

Chase, W.G., & Simon, H.A. (1973). Perception in chess. *Cognitive Psychology, 4*, 55–81.

Chi, M.T.H., Feltovich, P.J., & Glaser, R. (1981). Categorization and representation of physics problems by experts and novices. *Cognitive Science, 5*, 121–152.

Cummins, D.D. (1992). Role of analogical reasoning in the induction of problem solving categories. *Journal of Experimental Psychology: Learning, Memory and Cognition, 18*, 1103–1124.

Feltovich, P.J. (1983). Expertise: Recognising and refining knowledge for use. *Professions Education Researcher Notes, 4*(3), 5–9.

Hinsley, D.A., Hayes, J.R., & Simon, H.A. (1978). From words to equations: Meaning and representation in algebra word problems. In P.A. Carpenter & M.A. Just (Eds.), *Cognitive processes in comprehension*. Hillsdale New Jersey: Erlbaum.

Larkin, J.H., McDermott, J., Simon, D.P., & Simon, H.A. (1980). Expert and novice performance in solving physics problems. *Science, 208*, 1335–1342.

Lavigne, N.C. & Glaser, R. (2001). *Assessing student representations of inferential statistics problems*. CSE Technical Report 553. CRESST/Learning Research and Development Centre, University of Pittsburgh.

Mayer, R.E. (1982). The psychology of mathematical problem solving. In F.K. Lester & J. Garofalo (Eds.), *Mathematical problem solving: Issues in research*. Philadelphia: The Franklin Institute Press.

Nathan, M.J., & Koedinger, K.R. (2000). An investigation of teachers' beliefs of students' algebra development. *Cognition and Instruction, 18*(2), 209–237.

Paas, F. (1992). Training strategies for attaining transfer of problem-solving skills in statistics: A cognitive-load approach. *Journal of Educational Psychology, 84,* 429–434.

Quilici, J.L., & Mayer, R.E. (2002). Teaching students to recognise structural similarities between statistics word problems. *Applied Cognitive Psychology, 16,* 325–342.

Riley, M.S., Greeno, J.G., & Heller, J.I. (1983). Developmenst of children's problem-solving ability in arithmetic. In H.P. Ginsburg (Ed.), *The development of mathematical thinking* (pp. 153–196). San Diego, CA: Academic Press.

Schoenfeld, A.H., & Hermann, D.J. (1982). Problem perception and knowledge structure in expert and novice mathematical problem solvers. *Journal of Experimental Psychology: Learning, Memory and Cognition, 8,* 484–494.

Silver, E.A. (1981). Recall of mathematical problem information: Solving related problems. *Journal for Research in Mathematics Education, 12,* 54–64.

Wood, A. (2006). *What makes GCE A level mathematics questions difficult? The development of the Preferred Alternative Construct Elicitation (PACE) methodology for enabling students to make and give reasons for demand judgements: The findings from a pilot study and an outline programme of work arising from the pilot study.* Unpublished Masters in Research Methods dissertation. University of London Institute of Education.

Wood, A., & Pollitt, A. (2006, November). *Developing a methodology to enable students to participate in test development.* Paper presented at the Association for Educational Assessment – Europe Annual Conference, Naples, Italy.

RESPONSE TO COMMENTARY ON CHAPTER 5

Alastair Pollitt

I fully agree with these comments. Even the best teachers sometimes struggle to see why students find a problem difficult – it is not easy for an expert to 'think like a novice'.

We need not stop with students. There are also good arguments for inviting other groups to take part in certain kinds of comparability study. Suppose, for example, we want to compare the standard of two examinations in Spanish. Who could be better able to judge the communicative quality of students' speech in Spanish as a foreign language than native Spanish speakers, preferably with no knowledge of English and not trained in teaching? If the purpose of language teaching is to enable communication with speakers of that language, then the demands of the exam should be those involved in 'communicating with a native speaker'. The point, once again, is the difference between experts and novices, but in a rather different way this time. We have some evidence (Pollitt & Murray, 1993) that judges with no experience of teaching look for different criteria than trained judges look for, and that they may be quite happy to ignore errors and hesitations (for example) if these do not impede understanding. Teachers may be biased by their professional experience to pay too much attention to the elements that they are used to thinking about explicitly in the teaching context. There may be many other cases, especially in vocational assessment, where this sort of 'consumer comparability' would be worthwhile. If the hairdressers' customers go away equally happy then, by definition, the standards of the hairdressers are equally high.

Reference

Pollitt, A., & Murray, N.L. (1993). What raters really pay attention to. Language Testing Research Colloquium, Cambridge. Reprinted in M. Milanovic & N. Saville (Eds.), (1996), *Studies in language testing 3: Performance testing, cognition and assessment*. Cambridge: Cambridge University Press.

6

CROSS-MODERATION METHODS

Robert Adams

Abstract

Aim

The aim of this chapter is to give an account of cross-moderation methods of studying comparability of examination standards – that is, methods based on the scrutiny and judgement of candidates' examination work – in order to describe how methods have evolved over time and to summarise the current understanding of how the methods work.

Definition of comparability

The methods described in this chapter pursue the weak criterion referencing definition of comparability. The criteria exist in the minds of experienced teachers and examiners, and the methods described here rely on their applying those criteria to specially selected samples of candidates' work, as expressed in examination scripts.

Comparability methods

Cross-moderation methods are then simply systematic ways of looking at candidates' work, that ought to look to be of the same standard.

History of use

Comparability approaches based on looking at candidates' work go right back to the beginnings of collaborative work by the then GCE boards – forerunners of today's awarding bodies – in the 1950s, though the first studies to be published date from the 1960s. Much of this chapter is concerned with tracing the history and evolution of the methods since then.

Strengths and weaknesses

The undoubted strength of cross-moderation methods is that they appear 'sensible', that is to say that a lay person would understand how they address the problem, for example, of comparability between boards. From the practitioner's point of view, the methods also closely mimic parts of the standard-setting and grade-awarding procedures.

The weakness of the method is that the findings can never be unequivocal. The nature of examination standards and of human judgements is so nebulous that little definitive can be said of them.

Conclusion

The evolution of cross-moderation methods set out in this chapter represents a great deal of work by the awarding bodies over the 50-plus years that have seen comparability work undertaken. In that time, the nature of examinations has changed, as has the collective understanding of what examination standards actually might be.

1   Background

One of the features of the education scene in England is that there has always been, since public examinations were introduced in the 19th century to widen opportunity in the professions, more than one institution running and certifying them. The question as to whether different certifying authorities' certificates were 'worth the same' or, equivalently, were 'easier or harder' to get has occupied the minds of users, candidates and those authorities themselves since the very beginning.

That that preoccupation has survived to this day is shown by the existence of this book. There is still public concern that the examinations and certificates offered by the current awarding bodies are equivalent. In some contexts, this equivalence is required of different syllabuses in the same subject offered by different awarding bodies: for instance, it is not unreasonable to expect that a GCSE grade A in English is worth the same, or is of the same standard, regardless of which body awarded it.

Similarly, for university entrance, offers may be made to candidates provided that they get 'BBB' at A level in a stipulated subject and (almost) any other two subjects. It is not unreasonable to expect, therefore, that, in some sense, a grade B in French is worth the same as a grade B in chemistry.

Again, it is commonplace nowadays for certain pundits to assert that the examinations are being devalued by dumbing down, and that grades are easier to get now than once they were. It is countered that what candidates have to do for their grades is changing, but that standards are not. Indeed the awarding bodies' *raison d'être* is to make sure that standards in individual subject examinations are maintained year on year.

Over the years the awarding bodies have taken seriously their collective responsibility to try to establish and to demonstrate that each of these legitimate public concerns is being met. The whole broad question of comparability investigations is the subject of this book, and this chapter addresses a particular technique for monitoring comparability, known as cross-moderation.

A note on the structure of this chapter. It starts with a definition of cross-moderation methods and moves on to speak of the entities that can form the subject of such work. Different approaches under the cross-moderation umbrella are then classified. A major section of the chapter deals with how a cross-moderation study should be designed, followed by a section on techniques of analysing the findings that come from these studies. The problems involved in reconciling the findings from different strands of comparability studies are then described.

1.1 Definitions

The definition of comparability that this technique is predicated on is an extension of the 'weak criterion referencing' definition. If the conditions described in that definition are met, and two awarding bodies' syllabuses are comparable, then the scripts of two candidates who just got a grade A, say, with two different awarding bodies should closely resemble each other in standard. This proposition can be tested (more or less) empirically: if the scripts are found to be ostensibly not of the same quality then one explanation would be that the weak criterion referencing definition of comparability does not hold. Note that this need not be the only explanation of the mismatch, and note that a perfect match of quality does not necessarily mean awarding standards are in line. Important questions lurk under the surface about the relationship of apparently identical exam questions in the contexts of different syllabuses, for example. If one syllabus is a complete sub-set of another, then awkward questions might be raised about what comparability actually means, as well as how it might manifest itself.

The first published review of the then GCE boards' comparability work (Bardell et al., 1978) concluded that 'The boards' current view is that cross-moderation involving the boards' examiners (possibly with outsiders too) is the most fruitful and sensitive of the methods available for the study of comparability' (p. 36). Nearly 30 years on, the awarding bodies might agree or might argue that statistics have become more sensitive, though cross-moderation still has its place. Perhaps a more relaxed view of 'outsiders' in the light of developments in the methods would be taken.

Complete catalogues of the studies undertaken by the boards between 1964 and 1978 can be found in Bardell et al. (1978); a successor, Forrest & Shoesmith (1985) carries the catalogue forward to 1983. Perusal of these two invaluable lists will persuade the reader that cross-moderation methods, as defined below, are indeed at the core of comparability research.

At about the same time as this second catalogue was published, the then Schools Council commissioned a rigorous review of cross-moderation, by Johnson & Cohen (1983), which summarised the history and current understanding of the method, suggested improvements, conducted three studies and undertook analysis of findings using generalisability methods.

The boards' own catalogue was brought up to 2000 by the publication by Cambridge Assessment of the third instalment, Bell & Greatorex (2000).

214

For the purposes of this chapter, the term 'cross-moderation' will be taken to mean any investigative comparability activity that is based on inspection of candidates' examination work. The term may have meaning in other parts of the examinations process, for example, techniques for establishing common assessment standards for schools' coursework; equally, some may quibble that certain script-based activities may not be considered to be cross-moderation, but for this chapter a broad definition will be assumed, so that it will deal with any approach to comparability work that consists of the judgements, by suitably equipped individuals, of the quality of candidates' examination work, scripts, coursework or practical artefacts of one sort or another. Throughout the rest of the chapter, the term 'script' will be used for the sake of conciseness to mean any sort of examination work produced by candidates.

1.2 An outline cross-moderation exercise

The bare definition of the method probably doesn't convey the actuality of what happens. This is covered in some detail in this chapter, but at the outset it might be helpful to present an outline of what all studies have in common.

The definition baldly says that the method depends on judgements of the quality of candidates' examination scripts by people suitably qualified to make such judgements. The vital elements of a study are then:

1. samples of these scripts drawn from those produced by candidates attempting the entities: syllabuses of different awarding bodies, years or subjects

2. scrutineers to do the judging of the quality of the scripts

3. an experimental design to set out which scrutineer looks at which scripts, in what order and for how long

4. attendant staff to make sure that the design is implemented and runs smoothly

5. a systematic means of recording the results of the judgements

6. a means, perhaps simple, of analysing the results

7. a report to communicate any findings of the study.

The detail that fleshes out this bare outline is covered later on in this chapter, but first a description of the evolution of the technique is described.

1.3 Evolution

Reference will be made throughout what follows to a sort of evolution in the methods used in cross-moderation studies over the period in which the awarding bodies have been active in the field. Christie & Forrest (1980) had as part of their intention the design of a comparability study that could be used and reused, transported at will to cover any comparability study. This turned out to be a vain aspiration.

The first cross-moderation study on public record, in Bardell *et al.* (1978), dates from 1964 and concerned two boards' GCE O level examinations in biology, French and Latin. The technique had been tried earlier, and reports can be found included in minutes of Secretaries' (as Chief Executives were then known) meetings. (See Secretaries of the Examining Bodies, 1952, for example.)

Since then, perhaps the main driver of innovation in comparability work has been the fact that findings have never been unequivocal: it has never been possible to say with certainty as a result of a comparability study that 'awarding body X is lenient or severe in its grade standards'. The quest for an experimental protocol that would furnish this sort of evidence has led to the restless urge to innovate that is to be seen down the history of comparability work described in this book.

But that is not the only driver. Repeated mention will be made of the convergence of syllabuses over the years. Plurality has ceased to be celebrated and the trend in England, Wales and Northern Ireland has been toward a centralised, uniform model of the curriculum, culminating in the National Curriculum itself. (Interestingly, though, the trend is being reversed and in the name of providing each child with teaching and learning opportunities that suit him or her as an individual, plurality is being allowed to creep back into schools' provision.)

The first fruits of this convergence were the round of five comparability studies based on the first GCSE examinations in 1988. The number of such studies was determined by the number of GCSE examining boards at that time, four in England with the Welsh and Northern Ireland boards jointly organising a study. All six boards collaborated in producing a coordinated design for the studies and organised the production of the final reports through the newly formed Joint Forum for the GCSE. Typically, the choice of subjects was arbitrary: the core subjects of English, mathematics and physics seemed obvious choices, the reasons for choosing the other two, French and history, are probably lost for ever. Following the next year's GCSE examinations, in 1989, studies were carried out in English literature, CDT Technology, geography, chemistry and music.

For the awarding bodies, and in particular their research staffs, the convergence has had a weighty influence on the design of cross-moderation studies. In effect, one source of variation among syllabuses has been all but removed, and studies can be designed in the knowledge that awarding bodies' syllabuses will not be so different as to defy comparison of their resulting examination scripts.

The flurry of interest in standards over time in 1995 led the awarding bodies to incorporate a longitudinal element into their next series of studies.

The increasing popularity of modular A level syllabuses during the 1990s led to a number of studies comparing their examination outcomes – examination scripts – with non-modular versions. See, for instance, D'Arcy (1997). The introduction of modular syllabuses across all subjects with Curriculum 2000 led to a suite of studies comparing their examination products with non-modular versions; the introduction of GNVQs and latterly vocational A levels led to studies that compared them with suitably cognate 'academic' A levels. See, for instance, SCAA (1995) and Guthrie (2003).

Furthermore the evolution of methods is also susceptible to the influence of individual researchers. Much mention will be made of the revolution that was the introduction of paired comparison methods and the associated Rasch analysis of their results. This was entirely down to the bursting onto the research scene like a bright comet of one individual – Alastair Pollitt – upon his appointment to the research team of one of the awarding bodies.

Thus, the evolution of the design of cross-moderation methods, and indeed comparability studies in general, has been driven by a combination of these factors: the quest for methods that would yield authoritative findings; the response to developments in the curriculum and methods of assessment; and the particular resources and people available to the awarding bodies to design and carry out the work.

A particular difficulty that has beset the designers of cross-moderation studies is that it has always been difficult to evaluate successive designs. It has long been acknowledged that it is almost impossible to be certain that any effect identified in a cross-moderation study is the direct result of different grading standards having been applied, and there could be no other check on the effectiveness of the designs used. Evaluation has been more intuitive: a study was held to be successful if it ran smoothly, the participants thought a good job had been done and the report seemed authoritative. For this reason, it is difficult to present the evolution of the methods – save for the milestone events described above – as being logical and evidence based.

1.4 What is compared?

Over the years, the preoccupation of the GCE and GCSE examining boards and groups (lately awarding bodies)[1] has been the study of the comparability of grades in different syllabuses in the same subject. Until the mid-1980s, there was a robust tradition of diversity, freedom of choice and experimentation in the curriculum and in individual subjects within England and Wales, which meant that there was a rich variety of syllabuses with varying characteristics – different approaches, curriculum projects – to suit all tastes. A disadvantage of this richness was that the assertion that a grade B, say, in A level history represented the same standard of attainment in a host of different and deliberately diverse syllabuses was hard to justify. We shall return to this variety later, but back in the 1970s it was an important driver in the attempt to find ways of demonstrating the comparability of grades in different syllabuses in the same subject, usually across examining boards.

Most examining boards in those days offered two, three or more syllabuses in most subjects, and comparability of grades between syllabuses offered by the same examining board was as legitimate a subject for research as was comparability of grades between examining boards. The great bulk of the bibliography of comparability reports addresses these questions of cross-syllabus comparability.

Latterly (see, for example, Edwards & Adams, 2003) the Scottish Qualifications Authority has, at its own request, been included in certain comparability studies, to test the assertion that Scottish Highers are equivalent to GCE A levels. The Scottish Certificate of Education Examination Board was included in a study in O level French in 1969, though no formal report was produced.

The examining boards themselves have seen the potential for expanding the method beyond the comparability of syllabuses in the same subject and, in the past, attempts have been made to extend the methods to judge grade comparability between subjects. There are no published formal reports of the boards' early attempts at such work, though Wood (2006) has resurrected the idea with some experimental work using students (recent A level candidates) as judges, partly prompted by the wave of confidence inspired by the adoption of paired comparison methods. It appears, though, that the success of the approach might be compromised by the reading demands on these students. We shall be returning to the arrival of paired comparison methods; indeed a whole chapter (Chapter 7) is devoted to them. The early tentative attempts were in subjects that were seen as cognate, where it might reasonably be expected that suitably qualified expert scrutineers could make judgements about the quality of scripts in, say, French and German. These early attempts were not seen as particularly successful, in part because of the unconvincing precept that any human agency is capable of making these highly subjective judgements across syllabuses in different subjects, though UCLES (for instance, see Elliott & Greatorex, 2002) have undertaken some between-subject work in their international examinations.

A question of perennial interest, in the world at large as well as to the awarding bodies, is that of grade comparability over time. It is a commonplace of saloon-bar (if not public-bar) theorising that A level grades are not worth half of what they were 20 years ago. *Prima facie* support for this proposition is that so many more students get them now than did then; indeed the theory has progressed so far out of the saloon bar that it has acquired the importance of its own technical-sounding name: grade inflation. It is not clear, though, whether this phenomenon is simply the greater profusion of grades, or the supposed concomitant erosion of standards. Wherever the truth lies, the awarding bodies have attempted on a few occasions, for example, Quinlan (1995), to harness cross-moderation methods to scripts gathered from different examinations in different years, based on the same syllabuses, or even different successive syllabuses. Bell *et al.* (1998) provide another example.

Prompted by a supposed public unease SCAA (predecessor of QCA) and Ofsted[2] themselves undertook a script-based study to compare standards over time in three subjects at A level and GCSE (SCAA/Ofsted, 1996). The conclusion in all three subjects was that they had all changed, and that whether the changes represented diminution or enhancement of standards was a matter of the values of the observer. Some tentative comments were made about standards, but the tone was cautious.

The present author holds an extreme view that comparability of standards over time, even year on year in principle, is a meaningless idea, given the ineffable web of changing social, cultural and economic influences on the context of the whole idea of education, and in particular, schooling and examination performances. (See Adams, 1994.) At the same time it is recognised – having tried it – that this is a hard line to sell in the saloon bar; it also has to be accepted that many processes – university admissions, for example – have to be predicated on the assumption that standards *are* comparable year on year.

Again, the success of this sort of study over time was regarded as limited and the awarding bodies continued to put their resources into the study of comparability between their syllabuses in the same subject at the same sitting.

Curriculum 2000 saw the incorporation into the mainstream of modular GCE A level schemes as well as the introduction of so-called 'vocational' A levels, which had evolved from GNVQs and relabelled to establish their equivalence to 'academic' A level subjects. This gave at once opportunities for different applications of cross-moderation methods. The studies of 1996 examinations, for example, Gray (1997), concerned comparison of the grade standards of modular and non-modular syllabuses; in 2002, in, for example, Guthrie (2003) the comparison of 'academic' and 'vocational' syllabuses in business studies was incorporated.

Special mention should also be made of various one-off studies that have been based on scrutiny of scripts. GCSE French, for instance, has had, since its inception, a highly particular form of aggregation of the four language elements (reading, writing, speaking and listening), each of which could be offered for examination at a higher or foundation tier[3]. The myriad possibilities of attainment that would lead to a grade C, say, were such that it was impossible to identify a 'just-passing grade C candidate', the type of candidate whose work forms the routine material for cross-moderation studies. Various methods have been devised to deal with such subjects, some of great ingenuity. (See, for instance, Fowles (1989), one of the first series of GCSE studies that had to contend with the points system for aggregation of component results to determine final grades.)

2   Classification of cross-moderation methods

Cross-moderation methods can be characterised and classified in a number of ways, some overlapping, some independent. The following classes can be established by perusal of the historical catalogue of cross-moderation studies.

2.1 Identification, ratification, re-marking or distribution studies

This categorisation expresses the basic design purpose of a cross-moderation study. An *identification* study seeks to identify afresh grade boundaries in a range of candidates' scripts, and then compare those so identified with the actual grade boundaries determined at the operational grade awards conducted by the examining boards. Thus, typically, a carefully selected range of scripts – from the indifferent to the excellent – are set out in a metaphorical or actual row, for each board. Scrutineers move along the row, and scrutinise each script. Periodically they declare that they have come to a grade cut-off. 'Script i is grade G standard; script i + 1 is grade G + 1 standard.' This is repeated over many scrutineers and it is relatively straightforward to compare these decisions, board by board, with the actual grades as determined by the award. An outstanding example was the study conducted on GCSE CDT Technology, where candidates' work under scrutiny included actual artefacts as well as written papers, which were literally laid out in rows in a hotel basement (more accustomed to hosting wedding receptions) in Cambridge. (See Patrick & McLone, 1990.)

This approach could be (and in some cases has been) used by a single board on a single syllabus to check its grading standards with scrutineers other than those responsible for the operational award. According to our definition, this would still be a cross-moderation study. It was also used to powerful effect by Good & Cresswell (1988) to investigate some of the characteristics of awarding in tiered examinations.

A *ratification* study, by contrast, takes scripts deliberately chosen to be near certain grade boundaries – typically A/B and E/U at A level; A/B, C/D and F/G at GCSE – and judges them according to whether scrutineers from other boards agree that they are of a standard typical of that boundary, in their experience. Most studies are of this form. Ratification studies, which once relied on scrutineers' internalised notions of grade standards, have been transformed into studies based on paired comparisons of scripts, which comparisons don't need internalised grade standards in the scrutineers at all, but rely on intuitive 'snap' judgements – barely articulable – of script quality.

Re-mark studies are for the moment obsolete. They are characterised by scrutineers' re-marking of scripts selected to be at important grade boundaries, using other boards' mark schemes so that they can absorb the standards as they mark. An example is to be found in an O level study in three subjects (JMB & London, 1966). See also Christie & Forrest (1980).

In a *distribution* study, the boards supply equal numbers of scripts at each grade and scripts are independently judged, producing a new distribution. Johnson & Cohen (1983) used such an approach in their work for the Schools Council, one of the predecessor bodies of the current QCA.

2.2 The basis of judgement

All cross-moderation methods, according to our definition, depend upon scrutineers judging scripts against some standard. Studies can be categorised according to what those judgements are made against. These can come from a variety of sources.

Defined by the study

In the days when diversity in the classroom and syllabuses was celebrated, part of the business of a practical comparability study was to decide exactly how scripts, or for that matter other material, were to be compared. Thus, the first part of a cross-moderation study would be a sort of committee meeting to establish the criteria or dimensions against or along which judgements were to be made. In one case (UCLES, 1981) this process broke down: the assembled scrutineers were unable to find enough ground in the syllabuses common enough to make judgements of script quality in the time available. Similarly, a 1976 study (Bardell, 1977) reports that not only were independent scrutineers recruited, but they too were unable to agree upon the terms upon which scripts should be judged. Nevertheless, the study went ahead. In other cases, though, the method appears to have functioned adequately. See, for instance, Francis & Lloyd (1979). This report is also instructive in what it reveals about the discretion allowed scrutineers in designing the study as they went along. They had pretty well free rein; nowadays studies are more tightly designed and typically scrutineers are more or less told what to do rather than asked what they think they should do.

Internalised standards

Given the convergence of syllabuses at both 16+, with the advent of GCSE with its normalising national criteria for syllabuses, the National Curriculum, with its even greater control on subject content, and at 18+ with A level common cores and then restrictive subject criteria, the need for an identification of criteria phase has largely passed. Syllabuses are now so similar that the importance of at least one source of variation has been much reduced in comparing syllabuses.

It thus became ever more reasonable to ask experienced senior examiners to look at scripts from other boards' examinations and ask them to make judgements of quality. Typically, an examiner from Board *A* could be shown a script from Board *B* and asked to say whether he or she was not surprised to see this script as representing borderline grade C, say; or, if he or she was surprised, whether it was because the script was too good or too bad for that grade boundary. It transpired that these judgements could be made quite quickly, and so large bodies of data could be assembled in reasonable time.

A phase of syllabus scrutiny was nevertheless retained, partly as a worthwhile experiment in its own right, to judge the relative demands of syllabuses as a separate comparability strand, and partly as an exercise in familiarising scrutineers with the various syllabuses under study. In this context, 'syllabus' is understood to mean question papers and mark schemes, as well as the description of the cognitive content that the examination will address. The studies of GCSE subjects in 1989 dropped this process, reasoning that the syllabuses were so similar, because of the constraints of the National Criteria for GCSE subjects, that a review would be unnecessary. Hindsight suggested, though, that it was still a good idea and most studies since 1989 have included such a review.

Comparison with grade descriptions

One view of the first of these approaches, described earlier, is that the scrutineers begin the study by deriving a set of grade descriptions for the subject in question, and then go on to compare scripts with those descriptions. When the vogue for grade descriptions as part of syllabuses arrived in the 1980s, this had been done for them, and scrutineers were spared the task of deriving them. Some studies made use of them. In particular, when work on grade descriptions for GCE O level subjects started in 1980, a study (Forrest & Williams, 1983) was designed and undertaken particularly to exploit them.

The general consensus, though, about grade descriptions, whether as a basis for comparability work or for awarding of grades, is that they can never be precise enough to describe the differences in scripts that are one mark apart; grade awarding ultimately boiling down to judging such scripts as 'in' or 'out'. Further, the impulse to describe in ever greater detail the characteristics of a typical script at some grade has been found to lead to an atomisation of the subject as expressed through examination papers. Further still, the fact of the matter is that one of the cornerstones of the British public examination system is the principle of compensation: that a candidate can make up for a less than competent performance in one part of an examination by a very good performance elsewhere. Grade descriptions don't sit too comfortably with this principle.

Another difficulty is that if a grade description is meant to be a description of a 'typical, mid-grade C' for example, then in its own terms, it is no use for determining a 'just-grade-C' performance; and if it purports to be a description of a 'just-grade-C' performance then it is inconceivable that it should differ from the description of a 'top-grade-D' performance.

3   The design of cross-moderation studies

3.1 Organisation and location

The emphasis in what follows is on designing a ratification study, since these are by far the most frequent sort of studies organised. The detail will be more or less applicable to other sorts of study, but the principles will be found to be applicable in those sorts of study too.

At the outset, let it be said that a cross-moderation exercise cannot be over designed. The role of scrutineer at a cross-moderation exercise is not one of life's more pleasing byways, and one of the ways in which the organisers can palliate the experience for scrutineers is by making sure that the event runs as smoothly as possible. It may be that an 'objective' scientific experiment is being conducted, but the instruments – that is, the scrutineers – are distinctly human, and will respond to being treated as humanely as possible. Also, of course, good organisation will mean that as much data as possible can be obtained during the study. A strict timetable for the whole exercise should be devised, with clear breaks for refreshment and meals. An example from the study in GCE geography (Edwards & Adams, 2003) is shown in Appendix 1.

To get the necessary amount of data, especially if two, three or even four grade boundaries are to be addressed in a study, it is necessary for it to last for about two days. Any longer than that and scrutineer fatigue would become a serious matter, and it might be doubted whether the quality of judgements could be sustained. For this reason, if for no other, the tendency from the earliest studies has been for cross-moderation exercises to be held in comfortable hotels, so that scrutineers get the feeling of being pampered in exchange for the mind-numbing activity that the exercise requires of them.

Questions about who the scrutineers are, what scripts are available and what is done with them are addressed below, but, in general, it may be said here that scrutineers respond well to knowing exactly where they should be at any particular time, exactly what they should be doing and having arrangements made for them to do it as comfortably as possible. All this needs planning and arranging with the hotel in advance. The hotel also has a part to play in ensuring that refreshments are available at the times set out in the programme for the study, and that, for instance, everyone can be served with lunch in the time available.

Typically, a study will entail scrutineers sitting in small groups to work on scripts; these groups should be located in separate rooms with enough space for comfort. The necessary scripts should be set out in advance of the working session. Some designs require that scripts be passed around the scrutineers and it may be that the organising body will need to have staff on hand for each scrutineer group to assist in the management of scripts.

3.2 What are the entities to be studied?

It may seem an obvious remark, but it should be established unambiguously at the outset of the design of a study exactly what entities – usually syllabuses – are to be the focus of the study. There will then follow an identification of what materials – scripts in our shorthand – will form the raw material of the cross-moderation. This will be an essentially practical decision. Most syllabuses will have a coursework component and if this is to be included in the study, it will be necessary to make sure that enough coursework is available. And, of course, some coursework doesn't come neatly in folders. There may be artefacts of greater (e.g. furniture) or lesser (e.g. Yorkshire puddings) durability, musical compositions, gymnastic or dramatic performances: in each case it will be necessary to decide exactly which components are to be used. Where there is difficulty in finding the complete work of candidates, for example, in studies involving modular syllabuses, it is often necessary to use 'synthetic candidates', with scripts of different individuals chosen at the necessary component or unit grade boundary.

Again, to reduce sources of variation as much as possible, attempts should be made to choose scripts where, when there is a choice among questions, the same questions, or sections or even papers, have been chosen by the selected candidates.

3.3 Who are the scrutineers?

In general, the terms of the experimental design will make clear who is to make up the team of scrutineers. The majority of studies over the years have relied on the experience of awarding bodies' senior examiners in the subject in question. The intention of any study will be to generate as many judgements as possible during the time available, bearing in mind the limits to what can be expected of individual scrutineers. In this case, then, the more senior examiners that can be assembled the better, though for most comparability studies about three suitably experienced (Chief) Examiners from each awarding body seems a reasonable number. The number is also limited by cost, though with the diminution in the number of awarding bodies this pressure has been eased.

For reasons to do with the experimental design, where scrutineers can be thought of as 'representing' their parent awarding body, it seems sensible to recruit the same number from each. There appears to be a 'home-and-away' effect in judging, with scrutineers reacting differently to scripts from their 'own' syllabus as they do to scripts from others'. This is evened out by having the same number of scrutineers from each awarding body. The existence of this effect is well established and has been referred to in, for instance, Forrest & Shoesmith (1985). For this reason, many studies are designed so that no scrutineer ever looks at scripts from his or her own awarding body.

Inevitably, scrutineers may be prevented at the last minute from taking part in a study, or may even have to leave a residential study half way through. Every effort should be made to have reserves available, though it is recognised that this is more easily said than done.

The story of cross-moderation methods has been, as outlined in the section on their evolution, one of experimentation interspersed with refinement. One innovation, perhaps born of a desire to try something different on the part of the collected examining boards' research community, or perhaps in response to pressure from regulators, or perhaps again to add legitimacy to the enterprise, was to replace experienced Chief Examiners, with their internalised standards, by independent subject experts, who could perhaps be relied upon to make judgements based on what they saw in scripts, unsullied by any examination experience. In seeking suitably qualified subject specialists not associated with the examining process, Local Authorities (LAs), schools and universities have been consulted, their ranks being identified as a well-populated source of the necessary experts. Three studies in GCSE subjects (Jones, 1993) tried this approach, though many variants on using independent judges had been tried over the years (Jones & Lotwick, 1979; Massey, 1979; and see previous comment about Bardell, 1977). Experience in the more recent studies was mixed, but in general the studies were not regarded as great successes. For one thing, the judgements seemed very difficult for the experts, who took a very long time over the task, and seemed to want to pore over examination papers and syllabuses, perhaps in a vain attempt to turn themselves into the sort of examination veteran that we were trying to avoid. Often, the criteria upon which the independent judges were to make their judgements were articulated in a preliminary part of the study, but often, too, they were left to the judges themselves.

The introduction of paired comparison methods in cross-moderation studies, which rely upon snap judgements of pairs of scripts, one being identified as 'better' than the other, by as many judges as possible, has raised exciting prospects of using all sorts and conditions of person as a judge. For instance, Wood (2006) piloted the use of students to make judgements about comparability between subjects – recent A level candidates who did the two subjects in question at A level – to judge pairs of scripts, one from each of the subjects. Experimental work is also taking place in using these methods for grade awarding year on year, in which circumstance any number of individuals can be called upon to make the comparative judgements, and can do so in the comfort of their own homes without having to travel to a residential meeting for the purpose. A full discussion of these pair-based methods is the subject of Chapter 7 of this book.

3.4 Which scripts should be used?

The principle of what scripts to look at can be easily expressed. In a ratification study, the most commonly used design to compare standards of two syllabuses at grade C is to assemble the complete examination work of a sample of candidates who just attained grade C in each of the two syllabus' examinations (i.e. attained the minimum aggregate mark for the award of grade C), and then to get scrutineers to make judgements about their quality. If the work of those representing Board A's syllabus is consistently judged to be better than that of those representing Board B, then an effect has been identified. One explanation for this effect may lie in differences in grade standards between the two boards. (A brief discussion of one reason why we can only say 'may' here is given later in the chapter, when a central conundrum regarding standards is described.)

The principle of compensation, referred to above, means that the complete work of candidates attaining the same total mark may, and indeed probably does, look very different in terms of the questions the candidates have attempted and the relative successes and lack of success on those questions. Thus, scripts representing work of any given grade may look very different from each other. Further, where an examination has several components, there will be markedly different profiles of performance across those components by candidates who have the same grade. Further still, candidates may be allowed to choose different components, sections or questions.

Because of concerns expressed by scrutineers taking part in the 1988 GCSE studies, that they found it difficult to judge work with markedly different profiles of performance across components, the custom has evolved of trying to control some of this variation in ostensibly similar grade performances by specifying quite closely the actual marks that components and individual scripts should bear. It seems reasonable to specify that a candidate should have as uneccentric a profile across components as possible: in other words, candidates whose scripts are to be selected for inclusion in a study should have a balanced performance across components. 'Balanced' may be defined in a number of ways: a useful statistical definition is that a candidate's performance is balanced if each component score has the same z-score in the components' mark distributions. For each score in the distribution, the z-score is defined to be the deviation of the score from the mean of the distribution (including the sign, plus or minus) divided by the standard deviation. In most cases this will be equivalent to the scores being the same percentiles of their score distributions. A description of the effects on examiners' judgements of using balanced scripts is found in Scharaschkin & Baird (2000).

There is a difficulty here in that such balanced performances are quite rare: typically, candidates produce lop-sided performances, showing strength in parts of the examination and relative weakness elsewhere, so we are apparently led to consider comparability judged on the basis of abnormal candidates. Nonetheless, it is generally reckoned that this restriction is a price worth paying to remove a source of variation in scripts representing the same awarding body, and to make the scrutineers' task less difficult.

Balance is also a useful way of establishing the equivalence of scripts where an ephemeral or unwieldy component has to be left out of the study. Thus, if a practical artefact is to be ignored, making sure that the components that are to be included in the study are equivalent can be achieved by using a strict definition of balance in those components' scores. The concept of balance can also be used to select scripts where components of different weights have, for logistical reasons, to be left out of consideration in a cross-moderation study.

If possible, the principle of balance should be extended into the individual script itself: it will make comparisons of scripts easier if the performance on individual questions within a script is fairly well balanced too. It is accepted that this is difficult to attain in practice, though extremes are easy to detect. For example, a grade C candidate at GCSE who has one completely correct answer in his or her script, and nothing else, is presumably so atypical in most subjects that comparing the performance with any other is difficult. Scripts with rubric infringements – that is where candidates have not followed the instructions concerning which questions to answer and which may be regarded as quixotic if marked in accordance with the rubric (e.g. marking the first five questions on the script where five were required but where the candidate had attempted six) and hardly representative of attainment at the grade boundary – should be avoided at all costs.

3.5 How many scripts?

All decisions about the scale of a cross-moderation exercise are based upon the fact that scrutineer time is a scarce resource, if only because there is a limit to the amount of judging that the average human mind is capable of doing at one meeting. Thus, the number of judgements that can be expected and the resulting quantity of data that a study will yield are not limitless.

Further, whatever the judgements of scripts are based on, comparisons of pairs of scripts or comparison with a standard, there is virtue in having the same script or scripts judged many times, so that aside from the main analysis of the outcomes, subsidiary analyses can be undertaken to shed light on the consistency of judgements and the idiosyncrasy of judges. Greatorex et al. (2003) give a discussion of this sort of analysis and its consequences.

Also, it is to be recognised that some awarding bodies are smaller, in terms of numbers of candidates, than others, and in all but the core subjects there may be difficulty in finding enough balanced performances to meet the experimental design. There will be other practical considerations to be taken into account when selecting scripts or artefacts: in the case of the latter, organisers of a study may well have access to only a limited amount of work; in the case of scripts, it makes good sense not to choose scripts marked by an examiner who had to be adjusted during the customary post-marking check on the standards of markers, for instance.

To balance these factors, the practice has evolved to its present state of using about five scripts per boundary per syllabus as being representative while allowing repeated judgements to be made, though in the past widely different numbers have been used. It seems to be recognised everywhere that all syllabuses are equally important in comparability terms, and that the total entry for a syllabus has no bearing on its importance: grade standards exist in some absolute sense and not in a sense weighted by entries for different syllabuses.

3.6 Component or complete work?

In so far as grades are *awarded* for subjects and not for components, it is clearly desirable that, if possible, cross-moderation judgements of grade standards are made of the complete work of candidates. Against this ideal are to be set the practical realities of making the judgements, which may have to be based on, say, two examination scripts and a coursework folder. But again, it might be argued that grade awarding decisions are made at the level of examination component, particularly at A level, with its post-Curriculum 2000 unitised schemes. If cross-moderation is to resemble grade awarding, then it is preferable that judgements should be made at component level too. In former times, when candidates sat all the examination components at the same session, it was possible to assemble the complete examination work of candidates for confirmation of grade standards, even if the mechanics of the awarding process were carried out by components. Sometimes, of course, a component such as practical work will have been dropped from the study on pragmatic grounds.

There are logical difficulties in comparing components, especially A level unit tests, which may cover different content; may, in general terms, be of different difficulty or levels of demand; and which may be of different weighting in contributing to the final A level grade. Such considerations should be taken account of in designing the cross-moderation exercise.

3.7 Which grade boundaries?

This again is a balancing act. On the one hand, if fewer boundaries are covered, there will be more judgements and more data about those that are; on the other hand, to set up the study, and assemble the materials and scrutineers gives a rare chance to get information about as many boundaries as possible. In general, each case should be treated on its merits.

At GCSE, the grade boundaries regarded as important are the C/D boundary, which is still held by lay persons to represent a 'pass' performance, the A/B boundary and the F/G boundary. In most GCSE subjects grade C is available on two tiers of the examination, and it may be regarded as of paramount importance that grade C is equivalent on either tier. Grade A, the boundary which is determined by awarders' judgement rather than arithmetically, is also important. Also determined by judgement is grade F, possibly because it was held to correspond to the former CSE grade 4 standard. The F/G boundary is for this reason often included in a comparability study, though experience suggests that the evidence of candidates' attainment at this level is sparse, and judgements of quality are difficult to make.

At GCE A level, only two grade boundaries are currently determined at grade award by judgement – A/B and E/U. The latter still counts as the 'pass–fail' boundary, and as the numbers of grade A awards continue to grow, and universities ask for grade A passes correspondingly more often, comparability of grade A awards is increasingly important. In former times, all grade boundaries – if you go back far enough – were made by judgement, and this is reflected in the boundaries chosen over the years for study.

In unitised schemes for A level subjects, it is virtually impossible, since awarding bodies do not have the warehouse space to keep all scripts indefinitely, to assemble the complete examination work of any candidates, so there is a good reason to carry out cross-moderation exercises at the level of the individual units at any grade boundary. Since the aggregation of six (in a typical A level scheme) bare grade A performances in the units is bound to result in a bare grade A for the subject, this is quite acceptable and does at least mean that the tasks of judgement are manageable: each end-of-unit test generally generating a single examination script. But where units do not correspond particularly between awarding bodies' syllabuses, synthetic candidates could be assembled across the units to provide a sort of whole grade A, for instance, performance.

Compare this with GCSE, where awarding is carried out by component, but where Indicator 2, for which the aggregate grade boundary is arrived at via the average percentages of candidates attaining each component grade boundary, intervenes in the aggregation of components to give subject grade boundaries (see also Chapter 3). It is then by no means the case that a collection of bare grade A component performances will result in a bare grade A in the aggregate mark scale. This raises a whole discussion about where grade standards actually reside: the aggregation of notional component grade boundaries into a grade boundary in the aggregate mark scale will depend in its effect in part on the degree of correlation among the components. So the relationship between component and aggregate grade boundaries is determined in part by the characteristics of the particular candidates taking the examination. This seems somehow to offend natural justice, and the idea that candidates' performances should be judged against standards that are in some sense independent of the actual group of students doing the examination. Put bluntly, it is reasonable to assert that the grade one candidate gets should not depend upon whether or not another person entered for the examination.

A neat way round this problem is to calculate component grade boundaries in such a way as to make sure that they add up to the aggregate boundaries. This can be achieved using equal z-score methods, so that the component grade boundaries thus obtained can be represented as the average performance on the component of candidates who just got a grade C, for example, *for the subject.*

3.8 Randomisation

It is a matter of good experimental practice to randomise or balance every possible feature of the exercise. It is usual to group scrutineers together into two or three groups to address one grade boundary each, perhaps. The allocation of scrutineers to groups and the allocation of scripts to groups should, if necessary, be randomised. For the prevention of any conceivable bias, the order in which scripts are presented should be randomised, and a randomised sequence recorded in advance of the exercise, whether it is pairs of scripts or individual scripts. Where pairs are being judged, it is preferable that a new pair be taken for each comparison, rather than a scrutineer hanging on to one script and changing the second. Appendix 2 shows the randomised sequence of paired comparisons from a recent study, in which the scrutineer doesn't ever look at scripts from his or her own boards' examination.

On a broader front, it is possible to conceive of an incomplete, though balanced, design in which scrutineers only look at some of the other awarding bodies' scripts. (Or, indeed, only some awarding bodies are represented at all.) Received wisdom opposes these refinements, and a discussion of why this should be is to be found in Forrest & Shoesmith (1985, p. 43).

Experience suggests that among scrutineers a group dynamic can arise, with certain individuals competing to do as many judgements as they can. This may be harmless, but it might actually influence the quality of the judging. A way of addressing this question is to stage a completely replicated cross-moderation exercise, with every detail of the design identical, except for a different crew of scrutineers. The extent to which the findings agree would give valuable insight into the merits of the method. Replication would address all sorts of other questions too, including how much confidence we could have in the findings and taking any action as a result.

Such an experiment was conducted in 2004 (Jones & Meadows, 2005), and the results were encouraging, two independent versions of the same study producing similar results. There is scope for more such studies to be undertaken.

The one area where randomisation is not possible, or at least tends not to be practised, is in the selection of the scripts that are going to represent the awarding body at the cross-moderation exercise. If balanced scripts are sought, there may be precious few to choose from, and detailed inspection of scripts chosen to be balanced and unremarkable will mean that they will be far from typical and far from random. It is suggested that, nevertheless, comparability of grade standards can be realistically approached via these non-randomly selected scripts. To deny this – to assert that two awarding bodies may be comparable in the cases of balanced scripts, but not comparable in cases of unbalanced performances – would take some dexterous rhetoric.

Note, though, that the selection of scripts is based on the same premise as awarding: two scripts with the same mark on them are *de facto* equivalent, however unlikely that may seem in particular cases. How often have phrases like 'But this 62 is better than that 63' rung out over awarding meetings? This question, which also has a marked effect on grade awarding, is fully discussed in Cresswell (1996).

3.9 Real scripts or copies?

The orthodoxy of comparability work has always been that it is essential to work with real scripts rather than copies. The step of copying might introduce variation in the scripts that was not there in the originals. Where single scripts were passed around a group of scrutineers, this was no great handicap, but developments in paired comparison methods, that ideally require the same script to be in more than one place at the same time, are tending to make the insistence on original scripts a luxury that cannot be sustained. An associated question is whether the original examiners' marking of scripts should be left visible or whether it should somehow be removed. Whereas it is thought that scrutineers may be influenced by seeing the marks awarded to a script, only a little progress has been made to identify an efficient, cheap and quick way to remove the marking, which is always in red ink, using filtered photocopying to remove the marking.

In particular, the display of scripts on screen, either because they were composed there or because they had been scanned, raises such a host of possibilities that the advantages outweigh the purity of using real scripts. For instance, for paired comparisons, randomised pairs can be set up in advance and images loaded onto disk. These can then be shown on split screens to facilitate comparison. Moreover, the comparisons can be done by judges in the comfort of their own homes; any number of judgements can be collected over a reasonable timescale, and any number of scrutineers can be used.

Parallel developments are taking place in awarding methods, where scales can be aligned from successive years' examinations using paired comparisons of scripts from the two examinations. There are fewer limits to the sort of person who can be asked to judge pairs: the ownership of awarding can be thus extended to all sorts of interested parties. Indeed, ultimately, the marking of scripts could be abolished and awarding carried out simply by paired comparison methods. A full discussion of these exciting possibilities is given in Pollitt & Elliott (2003).

3.10 Timed judgements?

In studies where scrutineers were judging the quality of scripts against their own internalised grade standards it was common to set a time for scrutineers' interactions with individual scripts or sets of scripts. See, for example, Adams, *et al.* (1990). Each group of scrutineers was presided over by a member of the awarding bodies' research staff who timed each judgement and rang a bell after, for example, ten minutes. This was the signal for scrutineers to record their judgement and move on to the next script. After initial scepticism, scrutineers were able to keep pace with this regime.

With the introduction of paired comparisons, it was generally conceded that because of the vagueness of how the judgements were to be made, it was impossible to restrict scrutineers to a fixed time, and they had to be allowed to proceed at their own pace. This in turn meant that detailed schedules of pairs of scripts could not be drawn up in advance, because it could never be assumed that a particular script was available when a scrutineer needed it: it might be in use by someone else.

So randomised sequences of pairs of awarding bodies' scripts were prepared and stewards in the rooms where the groups of scrutineers operated were employed to provide scripts from those available at any one time, according to the sequence. Again, this operation was carefully planned, to the extent that dummy sessions were held to make sure that the logistic processes were feasible.

The liberal possibilities of the open-to-all paired comparison methods make all this concern seem irrelevant, if scrutineers up and down the land can switch on their computers and do a few paired comparisons before dinner each evening, though the pairs would be presented in a carefully designed sequence.

3.11 Feedback

One of the spin-off benefits of residential comparability study sessions is that senior examiners of different awarding bodies' examinations congregate and spend a lot of time looking in detail at others' syllabuses and scripts. They often comment that the opportunities to gather these insights makes the whole experience – even doing the judging – worthwhile. Also, social parts of the programme – breaks and meals – give opportunity for a free exchange of views and ideas. It was suggested earlier that a comfortable hotel should be used, so that scrutineers can feel that they are being pampered.

Another way of giving scrutineers a degree of ownership of the study, so that they have a stake in its success, is to give as much feedback as possible during the event. For instance, partial results can be compiled and presented to scrutineers in a plenary session. Their views on the design and conduct of the study should be sought, perhaps formally by means of a questionnaire, and received attentively.

Sometimes this process has gone as far as to ask scrutineers exactly how they made the judgements that they were called upon to make. Given that no instructions are given on this in detail, and the point is made that the judgements should be snap judgements based on a sort of instinct, this seems a bit illegitimate. For one thing, you may not like what they say: 'I always judge against anyone who can't spell 'receive'; and for another, it may be that respondents will feel obliged to say something, and will dream up some principle just for the sake of having an answer. In no case should these responses be included in the final report of the study or used in the preparation of scrutineers for another study, if it is intended to stick to the original principle that the judging of pairs of scripts should be instinctive.

We have seen, in section 2.2, that in earlier days, agreeing exactly how to judge scripts that arose from what might have been markedly different syllabuses formed a large part of the actual studies. The convergence of syllabuses has made this phase of work unnecessary, and has indeed led to the need for agreeing the basis of judgement to wither and die.

Although the basis of judgement no longer has to be overtly agreed, it is a central feature of cross-moderation work about which little is known. It is debatable whether the question should be followed up at all. Great stress is laid on the fact that the judgements are rapid, instinctive opinions, and it may well be that they are best left at that. On the other hand, it can be argued that the more that is known about the whole process the better it will get.

3.12 Scheduling and character of judgements

The sample cross-moderation study programme displayed as Appendix 1 shows an efficient way of organising scripts and scrutineers. They are divided into three groups and each group addresses one grade boundary. Then all change over and a new grade boundary is addressed by each group. In this way, all scripts are in use at any one time and all scrutineers are occupied all the time.

In former times, judgements of scripts – one at a time – were made against standards that had either been articulated in advance, or against the scrutineers' internalised standards that were identical to those mobilised at grade award meetings. Appendix 3 shows the results of part of such a study, Abbott *et al.* (1989), in GCSE English with the judgement of an individual scrutineer of an individual script being shown as '−', '0' or '+'. It is clear from Appendix 3 that the design of the study meant that no scrutineer looked at scripts from his or her own awarding body.

Parallel to the evolution of cross-moderation methods, and strongly influencing that evolution, has been the convergence of syllabuses. At one time, teachers in the UK enjoyed a great deal of freedom in designing and choosing their syllabuses. The introduction of examinations based on the National Curriculum in 1994, with its centrally determined programmes of study in a range of subjects, forced Key Stage 4 (GCSE) syllabuses into a common, or at least more common, mould. Similar developments in the regulation of GCE syllabuses have had a similar effect on AS and A level syllabuses.

While adherents of plurality might find this regrettable, organisers of comparability studies can be quietly grateful that one source of variation among syllabuses – that of content and treatment – has been largely removed. Similarly, the extent of candidates' freedom to choose among questions has been substantially reduced.

This is not to say that syllabuses are identical, simply a lot more similar than they were in the 1970s. Syllabus variety indeed gives rise to a fundamental question about comparability in general and the judging of scripts in particular.

The point is made by reference to a specific if slightly hypothetical example: suppose two awarding bodies each offer a syllabus in GCSE history. (The details are a little unrealistic to make the point clearly.) Syllabus I is a complete sub-set of Syllabus II, that is, everything that is in Syllabus I is in Syllabus II, but Syllabus II has some material that is all its own.

In one year's examination, an identical question appears on the French Revolution (which is, it goes without saying, part of the common material). Is this question easier, harder or of the same difficulty in the two examinations? Convincing answers can be constructed for all three possibilities.

1. It is harder for Syllabus II candidates, because the candidates must choose from a wider bank of knowledge to answer it for the Syllabus II examination.

2. It is easier for Syllabus II candidates, because having done more history, candidates will be better at the subject, so Syllabus II candidates will benefit from this wider experience.

3. It is of the same difficulty, because a question is a question: if you meet the success criteria then this is absolute and cannot depend on anything else.

(This, incidentally is similar to the question that faced the examining boards in 1986/7 when the first Advanced Supplementary – forerunners of the current Advanced Subsidiary – examinations were introduced. The political stance was that AS examinations were of the same standard as A levels in the subject but had half the volume. The practical question was if an AS examination comprises half the components of its corresponding A level examination, should the same component grade boundaries be used for the two awards? Significantly, the collective wisdom of the boards' research officers couldn't agree on the answer to this. It was referred to their superiors, the then GCE Secretaries, whose collective wisdom also couldn't reach agreement. The issue was settled by the then regulators, who ruled that the same grade boundaries should be used, though on what basis this conclusion was reached is not recorded.)

Here's the same question in another context: in two religious studies syllabuses, one embraces three world religions, the other four. One year, candidates are asked to explore wedding rites in three world religions. Is this easier for the first group or the second? The same convincing answers can be adduced.

1. It must be easier to answer if you've only done three religions, because you won't get the details of any of them confused with the fourth extraneous one.

2. It must be easier if you've done four religions, because you can choose the three you know best, and, moreover, by studying four you'll have greater all-round religious know-how.

3. The question is the same, therefore the answers will be directly comparable.

This matter has a direct bearing on how scripts are to be judged, yet no-one is absolutely clear as to what that bearing may be. And this is on top of the difficulty of comparing the merit of an easy task done well and a more difficult task done moderately.

These cases epitomise this central conundrum about comparability and indeed, for that matter, awarding: the judgement of tasks arising from different contexts. Experience suggests that there is no simple answer, and answers may be different for different subjects and for different candidates. In practice, it has had to be tacitly assumed that the same answer to the same question is of equal worth, whatever the rest of the syllabus or examination may look like.

3.13 Preparatory work

In spite of, or perhaps because of this central conundrum, it is to be regarded as good practice in preparing scrutineers for the cross-moderation study by making sure that they are familiar with the syllabuses and examination materials that they will be scrutinising. In the early years, when the basis upon which comparisons could be made was a serious preliminary, this work arose naturally. In latter years, with the convergence of syllabuses that has already been described, this was formalised into a phase of comparability that was concerned with the judgement of cognitive demand of syllabuses and examination materials. This is covered in detail in Chapter 5 of this book.

There is an optimistic school of thought (see, for example, Gray, 1997) that holds that this preparation is not only worthwhile in its own right, but also prepares scrutineers to 'lay off' their judgements in the light of what they have seen of the relative demands of the syllabuses. Sceptical colleagues find this degree of mental gymnastic nimbleness difficult to imagine. In some ways, the two attitudes are restatements of the two sides of the central conundrum: the importance of context in judging standards.

So the central conundrum remains unresolved. Comparability methods are after all quite approximate and crude, and it is unwise to expect too much of them by way of precise findings.

4 Analysis of findings

Until the paired comparison revolution, the data generated by cross-moderation studies tended to be simple enumerations of a limited number of judgements (see, for example, Kingdon et al. 1984). There was a clear tendency to avoid sophisticated statistical analysis because of the unsophisticated nature of the devices that produced the data, that is, extremely tenuous human judgement.

With the first round of similar-syllabus studies, a simple means of scoring was devised. Scrutineers were all experienced Chief Examiners-and-awarders who were selected because they had the notional grade standards internalised. They were then to mobilise their minds to judge scripts carefully selected to be *just* grade C, say. The question posed over each script was quite simple: are you surprised to see this script here posing as a just grade C script? If you are not surprised record a zero. If you *are* surprised, record a '+' if it's too good to be masquerading as a low grade C; or record a '−' if you think it too poor to be even a low grade C. Analysis of these data was then mainly enumeration. An example of the results of this activity has been shown in Appendix 3.

The principle of the analysis was simple: if the scripts from one awarding body all got a lot of + scores, then it was concluded that there was an effect, one explanation of which could be a difference in the standard of grade C for that awarding body. It's difficult to identify any other possible explanation for such an effect, but all sorts of possibilities could be envisaged concerning the outward aspect of the scripts from different awarding bodies.

Incidentally, part of the design of these studies, carried over into paired comparison ones, is that in recent years' studies, no scrutineer looks at scripts – either singly or for a paired comparison – from the awarding body that he or she 'represents'. There is a 'home and away' effect that runs as a consistent seam through all this work. It was observed in several early studies and is discussed in Forrest & Shoesmith (1985, p. 35). This fact alone might serve to remind practitioners of the tenuous nature of the data that studies yield.

A number of statistical techniques were used to analyse the data arising from these studies. Simple χ^2 tests of the frequencies of judgements were mobilised to detect 'significant' differences among syllabuses; the '+' and '−' judgements were turned into 1 and −1 values and a one-way analysis of variance conducted on the results. Kolmogorov-Smirnoff tests of similarity of distributions were used. All were informally criticised as being too elaborate given the nature of the data, and for requiring assumptions to be made that clearly didn't hold. Adams (1995) did, however, show by simulation that the test statistic arising from the analysis of variance did have the predicted F distribution, which lent some legitimacy to the use of that technique.

An interesting sideline of these studies is to look at how ready scrutineers are to stick their necks out and make '+' or '−' judgements, rather than playing safe and recording '0'. Extremes are to be found in a GCSE science study (Cron & Houston, 1990) where one scrutineer was so certain of his or her fine-tuned sense of standards that he or she was able to give a '+' or '−' to every single script; another was so uncertain that he or she recorded '0' for every script. This generated a brief spurt of interest in the 'width of zero' question, though it is nowhere formally aired. The 1989 study in GCSE English literature (Fearnley, 1990) used a five-point scale for judging script quality but no mention in the report is made explicitly about the 'width of zero'.

An important point might be made here that applies to all statistical analyses of these sorts of data, no matter how simple. Statistical procedures are designed to find effects, and find effects they will. It is as well to bear in mind that in a typical cross-moderation exercise, there are countless effects *not* identified. It is inevitable, though, that those that are will be seized upon and interpreted. If classical significance tests are used, then, at the 5% level of significance, by definition, about 5% of comparisons will yield an effect, *even where none is present*: that is precisely what 5% significance means.

The paired comparison revolution came with a built-in analytical method, and a sophisticated statistical model of the data. The Rasch model could be used to place all scripts on a single scale. The technique was first used in a suite of GCSE studies published in 1997 but based on the 1996 examinations. A useful summary is given in Adams (2000). Chapter 7 deals with this approach fully.

A useful by-product of the Rasch modelling of paired comparisons is that the patterns of judgements of individual scrutineers can be analysed to detect any who might be eccentric, that is, give judgements that seem to conflict with those of the majority of judges more often than mere chance would suggest.

Over the years a number of investigators have tried to examine the stability or replicability of statistical findings of these analyses. For instance (Adams, 1995; 1999) simulated large numbers of data sets to see if statistical predictions and distributions were realised. As suggested above, these analyses partly legitimised the use of analysis of variance techniques in these contexts, and also the use of χ^2 tests of the frequencies of judgements by an awarding body.

In Jones & Meadows (2005), as we have already seen, an attempt was made to replicate a study of GCSE religious studies. Identical scripts were used in an identical programme in the same hotel but using different scrutineers. The results were encouraging in that the main profile of script parameters was roughly reproduced. Certainly, on the basis of that study, it could never be claimed, as some feared, that the outcomes of cross-moderation studies were entirely random!

5   Reconciling different strands

In the previous section, some attention was given to the preparatory work that scrutineers undertook, ostensibly to familiarise themselves with the various syllabuses, question papers and mark schemes whose scripts would eventually be judged. This has become formalised into a separate form of comparability study, described in Chapter 5.

It is tempting to relate the two strands, and to ask if any systematic effect emerges in the grade standards of the awarding bodies corresponding to whether their syllabuses are seen as more or less demanding. This does have some interest, though a neat instance of complete correspondence has never been found. A problem is that awarding intervenes between the demand of the syllabus and the grade standard. Grades can be relatively easy to get in a very hard syllabus, if the grade boundaries are set low enough. Likewise a grade A in a 'less demanding' GCSE syllabus can be made very difficult to attain if the grade boundary is set high enough. That, after all, is what grade awarding is all about.

Two strands that might be thought to show effects, if any, are present in the cross-moderation strand and the statistical strand, that uses multilevel statistical models to account for as much variation between schools and pupils as possible. These models are fully discussed in Chapter 10, which also addresses the question of consistency of findings.

It is disappointing to find that such approaches, asking the same question but approaching it in entirely different ways, tend to yield different if not contradictory conclusions. For instance, in While & Fowles (2000) substantially contradictory results were found by the cross-moderation and statistical modelling strands.

6 Conclusion

The story of cross-moderation comparability work goes right back to the 1950s. This was the beginning of the period when diversity, innovation and experiment were the hallmarks of the UK education systems and the examination bodies that served them. It is to the then GCE examining boards that the credit must go for taking comparability so seriously. It is the present author's contention that few research findings have made the examination administrator's life easier; generally they have made it more difficult. And yet the boards and their successor organisations have continued to spend a lot of money to fund this work: comparability in particular but examinations research in general.

An earlier section has described the evolution of the methods used and the factors that weighed upon them, but now the current state of evolution is that we have arrived at a sophisticated method of carrying out script-based comparability studies, with a correspondingly sophisticated method of analysis.

The vagaries of the notion of standards, though, always leaves a slight doubt over the meaning of any experimental findings. As yet, for instance, there is no answer to the central conundrum posed earlier in this chapter. This explains the reluctance of the awarding bodies to take decisive action based upon the results of comparability studies. The code of practice for examinations (QCA, 2006) stipulates that awarding committees should have any pertinent comparability study reports available, but no advice is adduced concerning how they might be used.

It is unlikely that a definitive answer can ever be found: the arguments are so well trodden, and the ground so often gone over, that if an answer were discoverable, it would have been elicited by now. But nonetheless, promising lines of development are emerging. The paired comparison methods are still in their infancy in the realm of awarding and comparability, and the potential for progress seems to be huge. An exciting aspect of these developments is the fact that it opens the ranks of potential scrutineers to many sorts of interested persons hitherto excluded.

Endnotes

1   The term appropriate for the historical context will be used where it makes sense. Similarly, the word 'syllabus' is used throughout this chapter, despite the recent practice of calling them 'specifications'.

2   The Office for Standards in Education, responsible for inspections of schools and colleges in England.

3   A tier of an examination is a scheme of assessment that is aimed at a range of grades rather than at all grades. Foundation tier GCSE typically gives candidates access to grades C to G; higher tier gives access to A* to E.

References

Abbott, M.K., McLone, R.R., & Patrick, H. (1989). *GCSE inter-group comparability study 1988: English*. Organised by the Midland Examining Group on behalf of the Inter-Group Research Committee for the GCSE and the Joint Council for the GCSE.

Adams, R.M. (1994, April). *Standards over time*. Paper presented at the Standing Research Advisory Committee of the GCE boards symposium on year-on-year standards, Meriden, Warwickshire.

Adams, R.M. (1995, October). *Analysing the results of cross-moderation studies*. Paper presented at a seminar on comparability, held jointly by the Standing Research Advisory Committee of the GCE boards and the Inter-Group Research Committee of the GCSE groups, London.

Adams, R.M. (1999, November). *The Rasch model and paired comparisons data: Some observations*. Paper presented at a seminar held by the Research Committee of the Joint Council for General Qualifications, Manchester. Reported in B.E. Jones (Ed.), (2000), *A review of the methodologies of recent comparability studies*. Report on a seminar for boards' staff hosted by the Assessment and Qualifications Alliance, Manchester.

Adams, R.M. (2000). *Comparability studies in GCSE English, mathematics and science 1998: A summary*. Unpublished report for the Research Committee of the Joint Council for General Qualifications, Cardiff, Welsh Joint Education Committee.

Adams, R.M., Phillips, E.J., & Walker, N.A. (1990). *GCSE inter-group comparability study 1989: Music*. Organised by the Welsh Joint Education Committee and the Northern Ireland Schools Examinations Council on behalf of the Inter-Group Research Committee for the GCSE and the Joint Council for the GCSE.

Bardell, G.S. (1977). *Report of the inter-board cross-moderation study in 1976 Advanced level pure mathematics*. Cardiff: Welsh Joint Education Committee.

Bardell, G.S., Forrest, G.M., & Shoesmith, D.J. (1978). *Comparability in GCE: A review of the boards' studies, 1964–1977*. Manchester: Joint Matriculation Board on behalf of the GCE Examining Boards.

Bell, J.F., Bramley, T., & Raikes, N. (1998). Investigating A level mathematics standards over time. *British Journal of Curriculum and Assessment, 8*(2), 7–11.

Bell, J.F., & Greatorex, J. (2000). *A review of research into levels, profiles and comparability.* London: Qualifications and Curriculum Authority.

Christie, T., & Forrest, G.M. (1980). *Standards at GCE A-level: 1963 and 1973.* Schools Council Research Studies. London: Macmillan Education.

Cresswell, M.J. (1996). Defining, setting and maintaining standards in curriculum-embedded examinations: Judgemental and statistical approaches. In H. Goldstein & T. Lewis (Eds.), *Assessment: Problems, developments and statistical issues* (pp. 57-84). Chichester: John Wiley and Sons.

Cron, N., & Houston, J. (1990). *GCSE inter-group comparability study 1989: Chemistry.* Organised by the Southern Examining Group on behalf of the Inter-Group Research Committee for the GCSE and the Joint Council for the GCSE.

D'Arcy, J. (Ed.). (1997). *Comparability studies between modular and non-modular syllabuses in GCE Advanced level biology, English literature and mathematics in the 1996 summer examinations.* Standing Committee on Research on behalf of the Joint Forum for the GCSE and GCE.

Edwards, E., & Adams, R. (2003). *A comparability study in GCE Advanced level geography including the Scottish Advanced Higher grade examination. A study based on the summer 2002 examination.* Organised by the Welsh Joint Education Committee on behalf of the Joint Council for General Qualifications

Elliott, G., & Greatorex, J. (2002). A fair comparison? The evolution of methods of comparability in national assessment. *Educational Studies, 28,* 253–264.

Fearnley, A.J. (1990). *General Certificate of Secondary Education. A comparability study in English literature. A study based on the work of candidates in the summer 1989 examinations.* Organised by the Northern Examining Association on behalf of the Inter-Group Research Committee for the GCSE and the Joint Council for the GCSE.

Forrest, G.M., & Shoesmith, D.J. (1985). *A second review of GCE comparability studies.* Manchester: Joint Matriculation Board on behalf of the GCE Examining Boards.

Forrest, G.M., & Williams, C.A. (1983). *Report on the inter-board study in physics (Ordinary) 1980.* Manchester: Joint Matriculation Board.

Fowles, D. (1989). *GCSE inter-group comparability study 1988: French.* Organised by the Northern Examining Association on behalf of the Inter-Group Research Committee for the GCSE and the Joint Forum for the GCSE.

Francis, J.C., & Lloyd, J.G. (1979). *Report on the inter-board cross-moderation study in history at Advanced level 1979.* Aldershot: The Associated Examining Board.

Good, F.J., & Cresswell, M.J. (1988). *Grading the GCSE.* London: Secondary Examinations Council.

Gray, E., (1997). *A comparability study in A level biology.* Organised by the Oxford and Cambridge Examinations and Assessment Council on behalf of the Joint Forum for the GCSE and GCE.

Greatorex, J., Hamnett, L., & Bell, J.F. (2003). *A comparability study in GCE A level chemistry including the Scottish Advanced Higher grade. A review of the examination requirements and a report on the cross-moderation exercise. A study based on the summer 2002 examinations.* Organised by The Research and Evaluation Division, University of Cambridge Local Examinations Syndicate for Oxford Cambridge and RSA Examinations on behalf of the Joint Council for General Qualifications.

Guthrie, K. (2003). *A comparability study in GCE business studies, units 4, 5 and 6 VCE business, units 4, 5 and 6. A review of the examination requirements and a report on the cross-moderation exercise. A study based on the summer 2002 examination.* Organised by Edexcel on behalf of the Joint Council for General Qualifications.

Joint Matriculation Board & University of London University Entrance and School Examinations Council. (1966). *O-level Latin, French and biology (1964).* Occasional Publication 24. Manchester: Joint Matriculation Board.

Johnson, S., & Cohen, L. (1983). *Investigating grade comparability through cross-moderation.* London: Schools Council.

Jones, B.E. (1993). *GCSE inter-group cross-moderation studies 1992. Summary report on studies undertaken on the summer 1992 examinations in English, mathematics and science.* Inter-Group Research Committee for the GCSE.

Jones, B.E., & Meadows, M. (2005). *A replicated comparability study in GCSE religious studies.* Manchester: Assessment and Qualifications Alliance.

Jones, M.J., & Lotwick, W.R. (1979). *Report of the inter-board cross-moderation exercise in biology at the Ordinary level, 1978.* Cardiff: Welsh Joint Education Committee.

Kingdon, J.M., Wilmut, J., Davidson, J., & Atkins, S.B. (1984). *Report of the inter-board comparability study of grading standards in Advanced level English.* London: University of London School Examinations Board on behalf of the GCE Examining Boards.

Massey, A.J. (1979). *Comparing standards in English language: A report of the cross-moderation study based on the 1978 Ordinary level examinations of the nine GCE boards.* Bristol: Southern Universities' Joint Board and Test Development and Research Unit.

Patrick, H., & McLone, R.R. (1990). *GCSE inter-group comparability study 1989: CDT Technology*. Organised by the Midland Examining Group on behalf of the Inter-Group Research Committee and the Joint Forum for the GCSE.

Pollitt, A., & Elliott, G. (2003). *Monitoring and investigating comparability: A proper role for human judgement*. Research and Evaluation Division, University of Cambridge Local Examinations Syndicate.

Qualifications and Curriculum Authority. (2006). *GCSE, GCE, GNVQ and AEA code of practice, 2006/7*. London: Qualifications and Curriculum Authority.

Quinlan, M. (1995). *A comparability study in Advanced level mathematics. A study based on the summer 1994 and 1989 examinations*. University of London Examinations and Assessment Council on behalf of the Standing Research Advisory Committee of the GCE Boards.

Scharaschkin, A., & Baird, J. (2000). The effects of consistency of performance on A level examiners' judgements of standards. *British Educational Research Journal, 26*, 343–357.

School Curriculum and Assessment Authority. (1995). *Report of a comparability exercise into GCE and GNVQ business*. London: School Curriculum and Assessment Authority.

School Curriculum and Assessment Authority/Office for Standards in Education. (1996). *Standards in public examinations 1975 to 1995: A report on English, mathematics and chemistry examinations over time*. London: School Curriculum and Assessment Authority.

Secretaries of the Examining Bodies. (1952). *Minutes of a meeting held in Bristol, March 17th and 18th 1952*. Unpublished minutes, in Secretaries of Examining Boards 1948–1960. Cambridge Assessment Archive, PP/TSW 3/5.

University of Cambridge Local Examinations Syndicate. (1981). *Report of an inter-board cross-moderation exercise in geography at Advanced level in 1978*. Cambridge: University of Cambridge Local Examinations Syndicate and Test Development and Research Unit.

While, D., & Fowles, D. (2000). *A comparability study in GCSE mathematics. Statistical analysis of results by board. A study based on the work of candidates in the summer 1998 examinations*. Organised by the Assessment and Qualifications Alliance (Northern Examinations and Assessment Board) on behalf of the Joint Forum for the GCSE and GCE.

Wood, A. (2006). *What makes GCE A level mathematics questions difficult? The development of the preferred alternative construct elicitation (PACE) methodology for enabling students to make and give reasons for demand judgements: The findings from a pilot study and an outline programme of work arising from the pilot study*. Unpublished Masters in Research Methods dissertation. University of London Institute of Education.

Appendix 1 Programme for a cross-moderation residential meeting

Welsh Joint Education Committee, Cyd-Bwyllgor Addysg Cymru

GCE A level geography 2002

Comparability Study, Residential Meeting

Holiday Inn Hotel, Cardiff City Centre, 28–29 November 2002

Programme

Wednesday 27 November (early evening)

Participants arrive, check in to rooms and meet for dinner at 8.00pm

Thursday 28 November

9.00am	Welcome, Introduction and Induction (Brecon Two – Boardroom)
9.45am	First Working Session – Group 1 (9) (A Boundary) – Syndicate One Group 2 (9) (E Boundary) – Rhossili Suite
10.45am	Coffee
11.00am	Second Working Session
12.00 noon	Break
12.15pm	Third Working Session
1.15pm	Lunch
2.15pm	Fourth Working Session
3.15pm	Tea
3.30pm	Fifth Working Session
4.30pm	Break
4.45pm	Sixth Working Session – Group 1 (E Boundary) – Rhossili Suite Group 2 (A Boundary) – Syndicate One
5.45pm	Close of first day
8.00pm	Dinner

Friday 29 November

8.45am	Seventh Working Session – Group 1 (E Boundary) – Rhossili Suite
	Group 2 (A Boundary) – Syndicate One
9.45am	Break
10.00am	Eighth Working Session
11.00am	Coffee
11.15am	Ninth Working Session
12.15pm	Break
12.30pm	Tenth Working Session
1.30pm	Lunch
2.15pm	Plenary Session (Brecon Two – Boardroom)
3.00pm	Departure

Appendix 2 Scrutineer's record card. Showing successive pairs of awarding
bodies' scripts to be compared

A=AQA C=NICCEA E=EDEXCEL O= OCR S=SQA W=WJEC

A/B boundary

Scrutineer W1

No	B1	#	B2	#	No	B1	#	B2	#	No	B1	#	B2	#
121	C		E		161	C		E		201	C		E	
122	A		S		162	A		S		202	A		S	
123	C		O		163	C		O		203	C		O	
124	E		S		164	E		S		204	E		S	
125	A		O		165	A		O		205	A		O	
126	C		S		166	C		S		206	C		S	
127	E		O		167	E		O		207	E		O	
128	A		C		168	A		C		208	A		C	
129	O		S		169	O		S		209	O		S	
130	A		E		170	A		E		210	A		E	
131	C		O		171	C		O		211	C		O	
132	A		E		172	A		E		212	A		E	
133	C		S		173	C		S		213	C		S	
134	E		O		174	E		O		214	E		O	
135	A		S		175	A		S		215	A		S	
136	C		E		176	C		E		216	C		E	
137	A		O		177	A		O		217	A		O	
138	E		S		178	E		S		218	E		S	
139	A		C		179	A		C		219	A		C	
140	O		S		180	O		S		220	O		S	
141	C		E		181	C		E		221	C		E	
142	A		S		182	A		S		222	A		S	
143	C		O		183	C		O		223	C		O	
144	E		S		184	E		S		224	E		S	
145	A		O		185	A		O		225	A		O	
146	C		S		186	C		S		226	C		S	
147	E		O		187	E		O		227	E		O	
148	A		C		188	A		C		228	A		C	
149	O		S		189	O		S		229	O		S	
150	A		E		190	A		E		230	A		E	
151	C		O		191	C		O		231	C		O	
152	A		E		192	A		E		232	A		E	
153	C		S		193	C		S		233	C		S	
154	E		O		194	E		O		234	E		O	
155	A		S		195	A		S		235	A		S	
156	C		E		196	C		E		236	C		E	
157	A		O		197	A		O		237	A		O	
158	E		S		198	E		S		238	E		S	
159	A		C		199	A		C		239	A		C	
160	O		S		200	O		S		240	O		S	

Appendix 3 Results from part of a cross-moderation study in GCSE English

Data matrix for the C/D boundary

4 scrutinising teams (I–IV), 18 scrutineers (a–r), 6 boards and syllabuses (A–F), 20 scripts per syllabus

+ above borderline, 0 on borderline, – below borderline

Team	S	A	B	C	D	E	F
I	g	–0–+0	000–		+0++–	+–0+0	0–0+0
	j	0–+0	++0+	+–0–		0–0–	0000–
	m	0–0+0	0–0++	+–0–	++0+0	+000–	00+–0
	p	0–00–	0+–––	+0000	+00+–	+000–	
	b	0–0–0	++000	++0+0	+0++–	0–0+0	0–0+0
II	e	00–0		+000+	0–00	00–00	00+00
	h	0–0–	–0+0–	0–0–0	–++–	++0++	0–0++
	k	–00–	0+–––	0–0–0		––+––	+–0–
	n	–0–	–00–	++0++	0++00		+–0–
	q	00–0–	–0–0	++00+	0++–0	00–00	
III	c		+–00–	00000	0–0–0	+0000	000–+
	f	–000+		+0+00	000–0	+0000	–000–
	i	000–0			0++–0	––0++	0–––
	l	–00–	+00+	0–0–0		00	–00+–
IV	o	0–0–	0–00	+++00	–000–		0++0
	r	0–0	–0–	00––	–0000	00––	
	a		0–000	0+–00	+00++	000+0	000+0
	d	0+–00		+00–+	0–00+	–000	0++–0

7

PAIRED COMPARISON METHODS

Tom Bramley

Abstract

Aim

The aims of this chapter are:

1. to explain the theoretical basis of the paired comparison method

2. to describe how it has been used in the cross-moderation strand of inter-board comparability studies

3. to discuss its strengths and weaknesses as a judgemental method of assessing comparability.

Definition of comparability

The chapter follows the approach of Hambleton (2001) in distinguishing between content standards and performance standards. Cross-moderation exercises are shown to be comparisons of performance standards between the examining boards. The judges are expected to make judgements about relative performance standards in the context of possible differences in content standards. In this chapter the performance standard is conceived as a point on a psychometric latent trait.

Comparability methods

In a paired comparison task a judge is presented with a pair of objects and asked to state which possesses more of a specified attribute. In the context of this chapter, the objects are examinees' scripts on a specified grade boundary from different examining boards, and the attribute is 'quality of performance'. Repeated comparisons between different pairs of scripts across judges allows the construction of a psychological scale (trait) of 'perceived quality'. Each script's location on this scale depends both on the proportion of times it won and lost its comparisons, and on the scale location of the scripts it was compared with. Differences in the mean location of scripts from the different boards have been taken to imply a lack of comparability – that is, differences in performance standards.

The chapter also describes a modification of the method to use rank-ordering rather than paired comparisons to collect the judgements (Bramley, 2005a). The underlying theory and method of analysis are the same.

History of use

The psychometric theory underlying the paired comparison method was developed by the American psychologist Louis Thurstone, who used it to investigate a wide range of psychological attributes (e.g. 'seriousness of crime'). It was first used in comparability studies to compare some of the (then) new modular A level syllabuses against their linear equivalents (D'Arcy, 1997), and since then has been the favoured method for the cross-moderation strand of inter-board comparability studies, which are the focus of this chapter. It has also been used to investigate comparability of standards over time, and, in its rank-ordering guise, as a technique for standard maintaining – enabling a known cut-score on one test to be mapped to an equivalent cut-score on a new test.

Strengths and weaknesses

The method has several advantages in the cross-moderation context. First, the individual severities of the judges are experimentally removed – that is, it does not matter how good (in absolute terms) they think the scripts they are judging are: all that matters is their relative merit. Second, the analysis model naturally handles missing data because the estimate of the scale separation between any two scripts does not depend on which other scripts they are compared with. This means that data can be missing in a non-random way without affecting the results. Third, fitting an explicit model (the Rasch model) to the data allows investigation of residuals to detect misfitting scripts and judges, and judge bias. Finally, the approach is simple and flexible, allowing the design of the study to be tailored to the needs of the particular situation.

One drawback to using the method in this context is its psychological validity when the objects to be judged are as complex as scripts. In Thurstone's own work the judgements could be made immediately, but here a certain amount of reading time is required. Also, the method assumes that each comparison is independent of the others, but this seems implausible given that judges are likely to remember particular scripts when they encounter them in subsequent comparisons. Unfortunately the paired comparison method is tedious and time-consuming for the judges, a drawback that can be remedied to some extent by using the rank-ordering method.

Conclusion

The paired comparison method of constructing psychological scales based on human judgements is well established in psychometric theory and has many attractive features which have led to its adoption as the preferred method in inter-board comparability studies. Many of the issues arising with the method are due to this particular context for its application. In practice, the most serious problem has not been with the method but with the design of the studies, which have not allowed differences between boards in terms of mean scale location to be related to the raw mark scales of the different examinations. This has made it impossible to assess the importance of any differences discovered (for example in terms of implied changes to grade boundaries). Both the paired comparison method and especially the rank-ordering method could easily address this shortcoming in future studies.

1 Introduction

The method of paired comparisons has been used in the cross-moderation strand of inter-board comparability studies for around a decade. The first studies to use it were reported in D'Arcy (1997). It replaced the cross-moderation techniques of *ratification* (where judges decide whether a script is above, at, or below a particular grade boundary) and *identification* (where judges examine a set of scripts in a range around the presumed boundary and identify the mark that best represents the grade boundary). These techniques, and the studies that used them, have been described in detail in Chapter 6. The cross-moderation strand is the part of a comparability study that requires expert judgements about examinee performance. The use of paired comparisons has not diminished the role of the specification review strand, which requires expert judgements about the level of demand of syllabuses and question papers (see Chapter 5) – this work is as important a pre-requisite for paired comparison judgements as it is for ratification or identification.

Section 2 of this chapter reviews some of the work of the American psychologist L. L. Thurstone (1887–1955), who established and developed the theoretical approach to psychological measurement that underpins the use of paired comparisons and related methods. Section 3 shows how the paired comparison method has been used in practice in comparability research in British examinations. Section 4 describes a rank-ordering method – a recent development based on the same underlying theory and using similar techniques of analysis. Finally, section 5 contains more general discussion about the nature and validity of cross-moderation exercises.

2 Background

The method of paired comparisons is a simple and direct way of collecting judgement data. The judge is presented with two objects (or 'stimuli') and has to decide which object is 'x-er' – in other words which object possesses more of a specified attribute, 'x'. In early psychophysical research 'x' was often a physical attribute such as weight, loudness or brightness. One aim of such research might be to discover or verify a mathematical function linking the perceived magnitude of the objects to their actual measured physical magnitude. A second aim might be to discover the 'limen' – the smallest increment in stimulus magnitude that could be discriminated at an arbitrary level of accuracy.

Two well-known results from this field of research are Fechner's law and Weber's law. Fechner's law states that the perceived magnitude of a stimulus is proportional to the logarithm of its physical magnitude, and Weber's law states that the smallest perceptible difference in stimulus magnitude is proportional to the absolute magnitude. Thurstone liked to quote the psychologist William James's view of psychophysics:

> William James said that psychophysics was the dullest part of psychology. He was right. But if we extend and adapt the psychophysical concepts to the theory of discriminatory and selective judgment, the subject takes a different colour and it is no longer dull.
>
> Thurstone (1945)

One of Thurstone's main achievements was to liberate psychophysical judgements from being restricted to attributes of stimuli that had a measurable physical magnitude and to develop a theory of psychological or 'subjective' measurement for non-physical attributes such as 'seriousness of crimes', 'attitude towards gambling', 'excellence of handwriting' and so on. This theory was first expounded in a series of articles published between 1925 and 1935, and Thurstone was still refining his theory in the years shortly before his death in 1955.

The key elements in Thurstone's theory are the 'discriminal dispersion' and the 'law of comparative judgement'. These are described below.

2.1 The discriminal dispersion

Thurstone assumed that each time a judge encounters a stimulus, it has some kind of psychological impact. He called this impact the 'discriminal process' – a term designed to be as neutral as possible regarding what is actually happening in the judge's mind or brain. He further assumed that the same stimulus is not necessarily associated with the same discriminal process each time the subject encounters it, but that there is a 'discriminal dispersion' or distribution of frequencies with which a given stimulus is associated with a particular discriminal process. The mode of this frequency distribution (the 'modal discriminal process') defines the location of the stimulus on the psychological continuum, and the standard deviation defines an arbitrary unit of measurement. The measurement scale is constructed on the basis that the distribution of discriminal processes is Normal (Gaussian).

Figure 1 Example distributions of discriminal processes for objects A and B

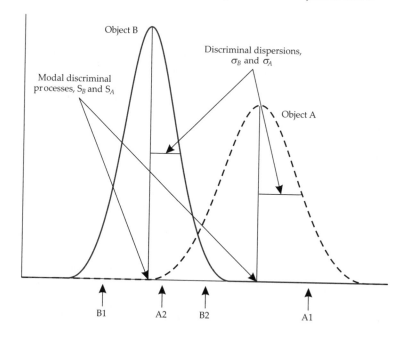

Different stimuli will have different modal discriminal processes on the psychological continuum and the distance between these modes corresponds to the scale separation of the stimuli. Two hypothetical distributions of discriminal processes are shown in Figure 1. The modal discriminal processes for stimuli A and B are located at points S_A and S_B on the psychological scale, with discriminal dispersions σ_A and σ_B respectively. It is crucial to the construction and definition of the psychological continuum that there is overlap between the distributions of discriminal processes along the continuum – in other words that not only can the same stimulus give rise to different discriminal processes, but that the same discriminal process can be evoked by different stimuli.

Thurstone was under no illusions about the nature of the measurement scales his methods produced. He clearly recognised that they existed in their own right in the psychological domain and was at pains to point out that his theory was neutral about whether psychological processes could be related to physiological processes, as the following two extended quotations show.

> The psychological continuum or scale is so constructed or defined that the frequencies of the respective discriminal processes for any given stimulus form a normal distribution on the psychological scale. This involves no assumption of a normal distribution or of anything else. The psychological scale is at best an artificial construct. If it has any physical reality, we certainly have not the remotest idea of what it may be like. We do not assume, therefore, that the distribution of discriminal processes is normal on the scale because that would imply the scale is there already. We define the scale in terms of the frequencies of the discriminal processes for any stimulus. This artificial construct, the psychological scale, is so spaced off that the frequencies of the discriminal processes for any given stimulus form a normal distribution on the scale.
>
> Thurstone (1927b)

> Any perceptual quality which may be allocated to a point on the psychological continuum is not itself a magnitude. It is not divisible into parts. It is not a sum of any mental or physical units. It is not twice, three times, or four times as strong, high, beautiful, or good as some other process on the same continuum. It is not a number. It is not a quantity... With these negations granted, just how do these qualitative entities or processes become a measurable continuum? They acquire conceptual linearity and measurability in the probability with which each one of them may be expected to associate with any prescribed stimulus.
>
> Thurstone (1927c)

Thurstone regarded the concept of the discriminal dispersion as an important theoretical innovation. For example, he used it to show that equally often noticed differences did not necessarily correspond to equal differences on the psychological scale (Thurstone, 1927e); that Fechner's law and Weber's law could be described in the same algebraic framework as his own law of comparative judgement (Thurstone, 1927f); and that it could explain some problems in the prediction of choice, such as voting behaviour (Thurstone, 1945). It is clear that he did not expect the discriminal dispersions of all objects to be the same if the attribute being judged was complex:

> It is probably true that this variability of the discriminal dispersions on the psychological

continuum is of relatively less serious importance in dealing with strictly homogenous stimulus series, but it becomes a serious factor in dealing with less conspicuous attributes or with less homogenous stimulus series such as handwriting specimens, English compositions, sewing samples, oriental rugs.

Thurstone (1927a)

This issue of variability of discriminal dispersions will be considered later.

2.2 The law of comparative judgement

Thurstone linked his psychological theory to experimental data through the law of comparative judgement (Thurstone, 1927b). The discriminal mode and dispersion corresponding to a single stimulus are inaccessible to observation. They can only be estimated when two objects are compared. Thurstone assumed that when two objects are compared with respect to a specified attribute, the object evoking the discriminal process further along the psychological continuum would be judged as possessing more of the attribute. For simplicity assume that the attribute is 'quality of handwriting' and the objects are student essays. For example, in Figure 1, if essay A evoked the discriminal process at A1 and essay B evoked the discriminal process at B1 then essay A would be judged as having better handwriting than essay B. In contrast, if essay A evoked the discriminal process at A2 and essay B evoked the discriminal process at B2 then essay B would be judged as having better handwriting than essay A. It is clear from Figure 1 that the proportion of judgements 'A better than B' is likely to be much higher than the proportion 'B better than A' because the latter can only happen in the small range of overlap between the two distributions of discriminal processes.

The outcome of the paired comparison judgement is therefore related to the distribution of the *difference* between the two distributions of discriminal processes for essay A and essay B. If this difference is positive, we have the judgement 'A beats B', and if it is negative we have the judgement 'B beats A'. The distribution of differences is shown in Figure 2 below.

Figure 2 Distribution of discriminal differences between two objects, A and B

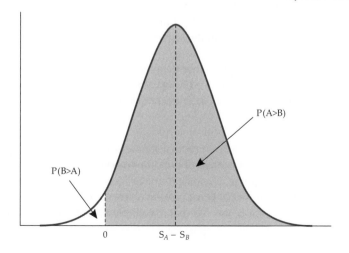

The mean of this distribution is the distance between the two mean discriminal processes – that is, the scale separation between A and B. The standard deviation of this distribution, σ_{AB}, is given by the formula:

$$\sigma_{AB} = \sqrt{\sigma_A^2 + \sigma_B^2 - 2 \cdot r_{AB} \cdot \sigma_A \cdot \sigma_B} \qquad (1)$$

where:

σ_A is the discriminal dispersion for essay A

σ_B is the discriminal dispersion for essay B

r_{AB} is the correlation between the discriminal processes.

The shaded area of Figure 2 to the right of the zero thus corresponds to the proportion of judgements 'A better than B'. This gives the law of comparative judgement:

$$X_{AB} = \frac{S_A - S_B}{\sigma_{AB}} \qquad (2)$$

where X_{AB} is the deviate of the Normal distribution corresponding to the proportion of judgements 'A beats B', and S_A, S_B and σ_{AB} are as defined above.

In words, the scale separation between two objects on the psychological continuum is measured in units of the standard deviation of the difference between the distributions of their discriminal processes.

Equation (2) is the most general form of Thurstone's law of comparative judgement. It applies to repeated comparisons by the same judge of the same pair of objects. However, in order to estimate the unknown quantities in the equation various simplifying assumptions need to be made. Thurstone identified five 'cases' of his law, each requiring more assumptions than the last.

Case 1 merely requires the assumption that the correlation, r, between pairs of discriminal processes is constant for all pairs of objects. Without this assumption no parameters can be estimated because each pair of objects introduces a new 'unknown' into the equation.

Case 2 makes the much bigger assumption that the same equation can be applied to a group situation – in other words instead of the proportion of 'A beats B' coming from replications within the same judge, it comes from replications across judges. Whereas within an individual the discriminal processes are Normally distributed on the psychological scale by definition, this Normal distribution becomes an assumption when applied to the distribution of a single discriminal process in each judge across a group of judges.

Case 3 simplifies by assuming that the correlation term r is zero. Thurstone justified this simplification by identifying two opposing factors at work in a paired comparison – 'mood' and 'simultaneous contrast' – which might cancel each other out. The 'mood' factor would be exemplified by both objects in a pair evoking discriminal processes above the mode when a judge is in a 'generous' mood, and below the mode when the judge is in a 'mean' mood, giving rise to a positive correlation and hence a positive non-zero value for r. 'Simultaneous contrast', on the other hand, occurs when the difference between objects is perceived in an exaggerated way (for example, a tall person might appear taller and a short person appear shorter when they are standing next to each other than when standing on their own). This would give rise to a negative correlation between the discriminal processes, and hence a negative non-zero value for r, counteracting the mood effect. However, Andrich (1978) showed that if a 'judge effect' across judges is parameterised, it is eliminated experimentally in the paired comparison method (see section 3). Hence, for Case 3, the denominator of equation (2) simplifies to:

$$\sigma_{AB} = \sqrt{\sigma_A^2 + \sigma_B^2} \qquad (3)$$

Case 4 simplifies further by assuming that the discriminal dispersions are all fairly similar, which allows the denominator of equation (2) to be simplified to:

$$\sigma_{AB} = \frac{(\sigma_A + \sigma_B)}{\sqrt{2}} \qquad (4)$$

Case 5 makes the greatest simplification by assuming that the discriminal dispersions are all equal, which further simplifies the denominator of equation (2) to:

$$\sigma_{AB} = \sqrt{2} \cdot \sigma \qquad (5)$$

which, if the constant denominator σ_{AB} is treated as the (arbitrary) unit of measurement, means that:

$$X_{AB} = S_A - S_B \qquad (6)$$

In words: the scale separation between two objects is equal to the unit Normal deviate corresponding to the proportion of judgements 'A better than B'. (Note that if this proportion is less than 0.5 the separation will be negative – that is, B will be higher up the scale than A, as we would expect.)

Thurstone seems to have had a rather ambivalent attitude to the Case 5 version of his law, saying 'This is a simple observation equation which may be used for rather coarse scaling' (Thurstone, 1927b), yet it seems to have been the one he used most often in practical applications!

It will perhaps not come as a great surprise to the reader to discover that it is the Case 5 version of Thurstone's law that has usually been used in cross-moderation exercises. The only difference is in the mathematical function linking the observed proportions to the difference in scale values – the more tractable logistic function is used rather than the cumulative Normal.

Equation (2) can be rewritten as:

$$p(A > B) = \frac{1}{\sigma_{AB}\sqrt{2\pi}} \int_0^\infty \exp\left(-\frac{[t - (S_A - S_B)]^2}{2\sigma_{AB}^2}\right) dt \qquad (7)$$

where $p(A{>}B)$ is the probability that object A beats object B in a paired comparison, and t is the scale separation of the discriminal processes evoked by A and B in a single comparison.

The logistic equivalent is:

$$p(A > B) = \frac{\exp[a(S_A - S_B)]}{1 + \exp[a(S_A - S_B)]} \qquad (8)$$

where a is a scaling parameter, which can arbitrarily be set to 1 (just as σ_{AB} is set to 1 in Case 5 of Thurstone's law of comparative judgement).

The logistic distribution is approximately equivalent to the Normal distribution if $\sigma = 1.7/a$, as shown in Figures 3 and 4 below.

Figure 3 Probability density of the logistic and Normal (Gaussian) distributions

—— Logistic
– – Normal ($\sigma = 1.7$)

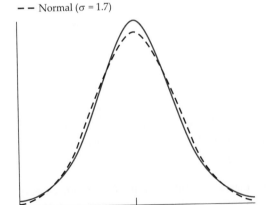

Figure 4 Cumulative probabilities of the logistic and Normal (Gaussian) distributions

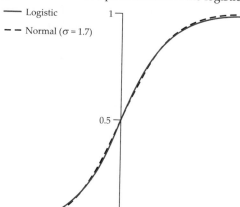

Logistic models are widely used both in general categorical data analysis where equation (8) is known as the Bradley-Terry model (Bradley & Terry, 1952; Agresti, 1990); and specifically in Item Response Theory in the field of educational measurement, where equation (8) has the same form as that of Rasch's (1960) model for dichotomous items. The connections between the Rasch model and Thurstone's Case 5 have been explained in detail by Andrich (1978) and some of these issues will be picked up again later in this chapter.

Rearranging equation (8) into the same form as Thurstone's Case 5 equation (6) gives:

$$\ln\left(\frac{p(A > B)}{1 - p(A > B)}\right) = \ln\left(\frac{p(A > B)}{p(B > A)}\right) = S_A - S_B \qquad (9)$$

Thus, rather than using the unit Normal deviate corresponding to the proportion of times A beats B to estimate the scale separation, this estimate is now based on the log of the ratio of wins to losses, that is, the log of the odds of success. The unit of the scale is known as a *'logit'*, or 'log odds unit'. The logit scale is additive in the sense that the distance between any pair of objects A and B is the sum (difference) between each object and any other object C on the scale:

Log odds (A beats C) = $S_A - S_C$
Log odds (B beats C) = $S_B - S_C$

Subtracting:
Log odds (A beats B) = Log odds (A beats C) − Log odds (B beats C)

$= (S_A - S_C) - (S_B - S_C)$

$= S_A - S_B$

Thus Thurstone's model (in both its Case 5 and Rasch formulation) achieves the goal of sample-free calibration (Wright, 1977) in the sense that the estimate of the distance between A and B does not depend on which other objects they are compared with. The practical importance of this is that it is not necessary to have a completely crossed or balanced design of paired comparisons because the estimation process naturally handles missing data. An object's estimated measure will depend both on the proportion of times it has been the winner in its paired comparisons, but also on the quality (measures) of the objects it has been compared with. The precision (standard error) of the estimate will depend on both the number of comparisons involving the object, and on the information in each comparison – 'off-target' comparisons between objects widely spaced on the scale contribute less information than 'on-target' comparisons. The scale is equal-interval in the sense that a given logit difference between two objects has the same interpretation in terms of the probability of one beating the other in a paired comparison at all points on the scale.

The parameters are usually estimated by an iterative maximum likelihood procedure, which minimises the difference between the observed number of wins and losses and the expected number according to the model. It is worth noting that a measure cannot be estimated for any script that wins (or loses) every comparison it takes part in – we literally have no information about whether this script is just off the scale at the top (or bottom) end, or a long way off. Most software analysis programs will attempt to get round this problem by removing the script from the estimation process, then deriving a value by extrapolating from the measures that could be estimated.

2.3 Summary

In summary, the paired comparison method produces data that, when analysed according to the law of comparative judgement (Case 5), yield a value for each object on an equal-interval scale with an arbitrary origin and unit. The scale is equal-interval in the sense that the same distance between pairs of objects at different parts of the psychological continuum reflects the same probability of one 'beating' the other in a paired comparison. Equation (5) shows that the unit of measurement is the standard deviation of the distribution of discriminal differences, σ_{AB}, or 1.41σ where σ is the presumed constant discriminal dispersion of all the objects.

3 Paired comparisons in UK inter-board comparability studies

In an inter-board comparability study, the objects to be judged are scripts from the syllabuses of different awarding bodies that are intended to be 'comparable'. (Here a 'script' means the work of a candidate on all components contributing to the grading of a particular assessment, unless otherwise stated.) The judges are senior examiners or other experts nominated by the awarding bodies, henceforth called 'boards'. The paired comparison exercise usually takes place at a two-day meeting, where the judges repeatedly compare different pairs of scripts from the same grade boundary and decide which is the better, recording their judgement on a form. The different variables involved in the design and conduct of the exercise are described in some detail in section 3.2. The main advocate of the Thurstone paired comparison method in comparability studies has been Alastair Pollitt, and most of the theoretical arguments and discussions about the application of the method have come from him and his colleagues at Cambridge Assessment[1]; and from Robert Adams and his colleagues at the Welsh Joint Education Committee (WJEC). The following section draws heavily on their work, mostly in the form of papers and presentations for technical seminars organised either by the QCA, or by the Joint Forum. See, for example, Pollitt & Murray (1996); Jones (1997; 1999; 2004); Bramley *et al.* (1998); Adams (1999); Pollitt (1999; 2004); Pollitt & Elliott (2003a; 2003b); Bramley (2005a).

The first part of a comparability study is called the 'specification (formerly syllabus) review'. One purpose of this is to provide a context for the expert judgements that take place in the second part of the study – the 'cross-moderation exercise'. In the specification review the judges consider the assessment-related material from each specification (content of syllabus, assessment structure and objectives, question papers and mark schemes). Various means of collecting, summarising and structuring the outcomes of this review have been tried over the years, for example getting the judges to write short reports, or fill in rating scales and questionnaires, or complete a Kelly repertory grid (see, for example, Elliott & Greatorex, 2002, or Chapter 5 of this book). For the purposes of this chapter, the importance of this part of the comparability study is that it gives the judges the opportunity to form an impression of the demand of the question papers – a factor that is highly relevant to the judgemental task to be carried out in the cross-moderation exercise.

The second part of a comparability study is the cross-moderation exercise where the judges from the different boards make judgements about the relative standards achieved by candidates in different assessments. This chapter concentrates on comparisons across boards within the same subject area in the same year, although the same methods have also been applied to comparisons over time.

The third part of a comparability study is the statistical analysis of grading outcomes. This does not involve expert judges and is the subject of Chapter 10.

3.1 Advantages of using Thurstone pairs methodology in cross-moderation exercises

Judges' internal standards cancel out

The Thurstone method has superseded the method known as 'ratification' or more informally 'home and away' (Elliott & Greatorex, 2002). The ratification method has been described in detail in Chapter 6.

In the ratification method teams of judges from different boards 'fix' their own board's standard in their mind, then make judgements about scripts from their own and other boards as to whether they are above, at or below that standard. The method thus relies on the judges having the same internal standard – or at least assumes the judges within a board will have the same internal standard (see Chapter 6). The main advantage of the Thurstone method is that the judges' internal standards 'cancel out' in the paired comparison judgement. This claim is made in most discussions of the Thurstone method, but rarely spelt out, so for the sake of completeness it is explicated below.

Figure 5 Case 5 scenario for two scripts, A and B

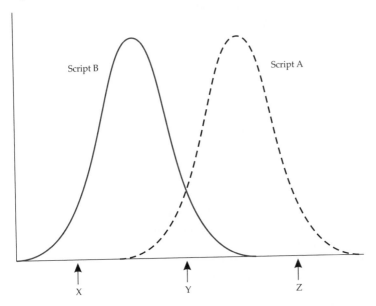

Figure 5 shows a Case 5 scenario, where the probability distributions apply to a group of judges. A and B are two scripts. If a particular judge has an internal standard located at point X on the psychological continuum then in the ratification method they would (probably) judge both A and B as being above the standard. If their internal standard was located at point Y they would (probably) judge script B as being below and script A as being above the standard, and if their internal standard was located at point Z they would (probably) judge both A and B as being below the standard. However, in the paired comparison method, the probability of judging A better than B depends only on the scale locations of A and B for all the judges.

This was shown mathematically by Andrich (1978), who included a parameter for what we might term judge 'severity'. A 'severe' judge is one for whom all scripts 'register' lower than average on the psychological continuum (i.e. they consistently think the quality of the script is lower than the other judges). Conversely a 'lenient' judge is one for whom all scripts register higher than average on the psychological continuum. In this formulation the scale location of the script is the mean of the discriminal processes across judges.

The 'discriminal process' D_{JA} for judge J on script A is:

$$D_{JA} = S_A - F_J + e_{JA} \qquad (10)$$

where S_A is the scale value of script A, F_J is the severity of judge J and e_{JA} is a random error term.

Correspondingly, the discriminal process D_{JB} for judge J on script B is:

$$D_{JB} = S_B - F_J + e_{JB} \tag{11}$$

Section 2 showed that according to Thurstone's model the outcome of the paired comparison judgement for an individual judge depends on the difference on the psychological continuum between D_{JA} and D_{JB}:

$$D_{JA} - D_{JB} = S_A - F_J - e_{JA} - (S_B - F_J - e_{JB}) = S_A - S_B - (e_{JA} - e_{JB}) \tag{12}$$

It can be seen from equation (12) that the judge severity F_J has 'cancelled out'.

It is interesting to note that the judge 'cancels out' *experimentally*, by virtue of the paired comparison design. This was the main point of Andrich's (1978) paper. It is not necessary to use the Rasch model to eliminate the judge *statistically* so in this sense the use of the Rasch model for Thurstone pairs analysis is 'gilding the lily' – more a matter of computational convenience than conceptual purity. However, there are other significant advantages of the Rasch framework in terms of estimation of parameters and analysis of residuals, which will be discussed later in this section. It is also worth noting that it would be possible to analyse data collected by the ratification method using the Rasch partial credit model (Wright & Masters, 1982), and thus obtain estimates of scale values for the scripts that are 'free' from the severities of the judges.

Forced choice removes problem of 'zero width'

The second weakness of the ratification method, as it tended to be used in cross-moderation exercises, was the potential for differences between the judges in how broadly they defined the 'standards equal' category. Since their judgements of 'lower standard', 'same standard' and 'higher standard' tended to be converted to –1, 0 and +1 for statistical analysis, this was referred to as the 'zero width' problem (e.g. Jones, 1997). On more than one occasion, authors have pointed out that a wide enough zero category virtually guarantees that no differences will be found amongst the boards, and some have implied that this might have been intentional (Pollitt & Elliott, 2003a)!

However, the 'zero width' drawback is not really a feature of the ratification method per se, but rather a consequence of giving the judges the option of using a middle category. It could be removed from the ratification method by forcing the judges to decide either 'above' or 'below' for all scripts; likewise the drawback could be introduced to the Thurstone method by allowing ties in paired comparison judgements. However, none of the comparability studies that have used paired comparisons has allowed the judges to make tied judgements. Various practical strategies have been used to stop judges getting 'hung up' over a difficult judgement, such as telling them to toss a coin if they really cannot tell the scripts apart, or to make a note on their recording sheet of any comparisons they were unsure of.

The model handles missing data

As shown in section 2, if the data fit the Case 5 Thurstone model, the estimate of the separation between any two scripts does not depend on which other scripts they are compared with. This means that data can be missing in a non-random way without affecting the results. However, the precision (standard error) of each script's estimate depends largely on how many comparisons it has been involved in, so some effort needs to be made to ensure that each script is compared a similar number of times in total.

Fitting an explicit model gives insight into the data

Using the Rasch approach to analysing Thurstone pairs data means that the outcome of each individual comparison is explicitly modelled. The outcomes of the analysis can be considered in two parts: the 'model' and the 'misfit' (Pollitt & Elliott, 2003b). The 'model' part is the construction of the scale and estimation of the scale values of the scripts, along with the precision of these estimates (the standard errors). It is the features of the 'model' part that have been described in detail above. The 'misfit' part of the analysis investigates the degree to which the observed data fit the expectations of the model. Because the outcome of each individual comparison is explicitly modelled, it is possible to generate a 'residual' at the individual comparison level. This residual is the difference between the observed outcome (1 or 0, corresponding to win or loss) and the expected outcome (calculated from equation (8) using the estimated script parameters). The diagnostic potential of analysing these residuals has been highlighted by Pollitt (1999; 2004) and Pollitt & Elliott (2003a; 2003b). These residuals can be standardised and aggregated in various ways and used to investigate different questions of interest. For example, residuals can be aggregated for each judge to investigate judge misfit. Judges with a high value of misfit have tended to make more 'surprising' judgements than the other judges, that is, they have occasionally (or frequently) rated a low script above a high one on the scale. This can be interpreted as indicating that this judge has a different conception from the other judges about what makes a script better or worse.

Similarly, residuals can be aggregated for each script to indicate the extent to which the judges agreed on its location in the scale. Scripts with a high value of misfit have been involved in more surprising judgements than the other scripts and thus might be investigated to see if they contain anything unusual in terms of candidate performance.

If the surprising outcomes come mainly from paired comparisons involving scripts from the judge's own board then we have some evidence of *bias*. In practice, in most studies judges have not compared scripts from their own board in order to remove the possibility of bias. Other sub-sets of the matrix of residuals (for example male judges judging the work of male candidates) can be aggregated to investigate other forms of bias hypothesised by the analyst.

Finally, at a more mundane level, individual comparisons with a large residual might indicate an error by the judge in recording their judgement on the record sheet, or an error in data entry prior to analysis.

The data collection design is flexible

Since the analysis can cope with non-random missing data (see earlier), the collection of data can be very flexible – tailored to the needs of the particular situation. Because the comparative judgements are all independent, data can be accumulated as needed. The investigator is thus not (in principle) bound by a prior design. At any point more data could be collected and added to the existing data to recover from accidents, to replace an unacceptable judge, to add extra scripts, to resolve conflicts, to investigate possible bias or to deepen the study of any aspect that proves especially interesting. To date, this flexibility has not been fully capitalised on, due to the organisational constraints involved in getting around 20 judges in the same place at the same time. But with the advent of technology for making scanned images of scripts routinely available it is possible to imagine a distributed paired comparison exercise taking place online, with on-the-fly calibration guiding the selection of pairs of scripts to be presented to each judge (Pollitt, 2004).

3.2 Issues in designing paired comparison exercises

Many of the issues that arise and decisions that have to be made in planning and executing a paired comparison exercise are not unique to the Thurstone method, but will be discussed briefly below in terms of the Thurstone/Rasch conceptual framework. Appendix 1 summarises the 'design' features of inter-board comparability studies that have used Thurstone paired comparisons in the cross-moderation strand.

Judge selection

It is obviously important that the judges are appropriately qualified and capable of making the judgements. The validity of the whole exercise depends on the judges sharing, to a certain extent, the same conception of what makes a script better or worse. Whilst the paired comparison method allows for differences in absolute severity between the judges it does require that the underlying latent trait, or psychological continuum, is the same. It is also necessary for validity that the features of the scripts that influence the judges in making their decisions are related in the right way to the intentions of the assessment designers. One operational definition of question validity used in research on question design is:

> A question can only be valid if the students' minds are doing the things we want them to show us they can do.
>
> Ahmed & Pollitt (2001)

Clearly, by extension, the outcome of a judgemental exercise can only be valid if the judges are basing their judgements on the extent to which the students' minds have done the things the examiners wanted them to show us they could do!

There is therefore a limited pool of appropriately qualified expert judges. Those selected are usually senior examiners of the specifications in question from the different boards, who will usually have played a part in the awarding meeting that set the grade boundaries on the examination, and some of whom may have even set the questions. A typical comparability exercise involves around ten to twenty judges, usually two to three from each board. This is in notable contrast to Thurstone's own work where the number of judges was usually over 200! However, the main issue is whether the number of judgements per script is sufficient to allow the scale to be defined with reasonable precision. This is discussed in section 3.3.

Some studies have used 'independent' judges (with no affiliation to a particular board). One potential advantage of this is that it could add credibility to the results in the eyes of the general public (Bardell *et al.*, 1978, cited in Jones, 1999). The Thurstone pairs method is particularly suitable for the inclusion of independent judges because, as mentioned above, they would not need to have internalised a particular boundary standard in order to make their judgements. They would, however, need sufficient expertise to conceptualise the trait being assessed in the same way as the other judges, or their judgements would misfit. Forster & Gray (2000) found that independent judges were no more likely to produce misfitting judgements than board-affiliated judges.

However, Appendix 1 shows that in most of the more recent studies, there have in fact been no independent judges. The usual practice is for judges not to make paired comparison judgements about scripts that have come from their own board. In principle this restriction is probably not necessary, since it would always be possible to investigate the extent of 'home board bias' by analysing residuals (as in Pollitt & Elliott, 2003a). However, given that there is in practice not enough time for each judge to make all possible paired comparisons, it seems sensible to remove the potential for home board bias by design.

Script selection

Assessment or component?
The first choice that needs to be made is whether judgements are going to be made at the level of the whole assessment, or on individual components of the assessment. There are arguments in favour of each. On the one hand, the ultimate aim of the exercise is to confirm (or deny) that the boards' overall standards are in line, which suggests that judgements should focus on the assessment as a whole. Indeed the practice in most inter-board comparability studies has been to make judgements at the level of the overall assessment, as shown in Appendix 1. On the other hand, within each assessment the grade boundaries are set at the individual component level in the awarding meeting. The component grade boundaries are then aggregated to form the boundaries for the assessment as a whole. It is arguable, therefore, that the judges are more experienced at making valid judgements at the level of the component, and that this is where the standards 'really' reside. It has been suggested that future studies could make comparisons at unit level (Jones, 2004), but it seems that this is currently difficult in terms of time and cost.

There may be practical difficulties in bringing together the whole work of a candidate if coursework or oral components were involved in the assessment. It also becomes more difficult to find work exactly at a particular grade boundary as the effective raw mark scale increases (which it does by aggregating to assessment level).

On, or around the boundary?
The next decision to be taken is whether to use scripts exactly on the grade boundary, or covering a range of marks around the grade boundary. The former choice was necessary for the ratification method because that essentially involved asking judges whether work known to be at the boundary from a different board was perceived to be at the standard of boundary level work from their own board. However, it is by no means necessary for the paired comparison method, and it is argued in section 3.4 that there are good reasons for using a range of scripts around the boundary, and even in reconceptualising the comparability task as one of comparing whole mark scales rather than specific points on those scales (the grade boundaries).

Nevertheless, inter-board comparability studies have aimed to use scripts exclusively at the boundary marks. Appendix 1 suggests that the majority of studies have achieved this aim, but in practice it has not always been possible because of the difficulty of locating suitable scripts.

Composite scripts
Once the decision has been taken (as it usually is) to restrict scripts to those at the overall assessment grade boundary then if sufficient scripts cannot be located it is possible to create 'composite' scripts by putting together components from different candidates. These scripts are usually referred to in the reports as coming from 'pseudo-candidates'. Indeed composite scripts are sometimes used anyway in order to create a 'balanced' profile of performance (see below). The impact of composite scripts on the judgement process is not known, although there is some evidence that judges report finding them harder to assess (e.g. Arlett, 2002; Guthrie, 2003).

Balanced performance
It is deemed preferable to use scripts displaying a 'balanced' performance, which is usually taken to mean low variability of individual component totals, or of section or question totals within a component. In other words, an effort is made to avoid scripts that contain a mixture of questions or sections with very high marks along with other questions or sections with very low marks. Of course, there are many more ways to achieve an 'unbalanced' score profile than a balanced one, and the truly 'balanced' candidate is probably very unrepresentative of all the candidates! Scharaschkin & Baird (2000) reported that balanced and unbalanced scripts were judged differently in terms of their grade-worthiness, and that there were differences across subjects in this effect. This has also been reported in some of the inter-board comparability studies (e.g. Gray, 2000).

It is interesting to consider whether the concept of 'balance' could be further extended to include 'misfitting' score profiles (those containing a higher proportion of unexpectedly good answers to difficult questions or unexpectedly poor answers to easy questions). It is quite possible for such a script to appear 'balanced' in the Scharaschkin & Baird sense of containing an even profile of raw marks across questions and sections, and yet it is easy to imagine it causing problems for the judges.

Cleaning of scripts

In some of the earliest studies using Thurstone pairs methodology (these were not inter-board comparability studies) the scripts involved were 'cleaned' of total marks and sometimes also of marker annotations and individual question mark totals (Bramley *et al.*, 1998). This was to avoid the judges basing their judgements on simply adding up the marks. It could be argued that this is only a potential problem if within-assessment comparisons are to be made, and Appendix 1 shows that none of the inter-board studies have involved such comparisons. However, it does seem reasonable to assume that the presence or absence of marks and annotations might have an effect on how the judges make their judgements. None of the inter-board studies has used 'cleaned' scripts, so this is a potential area for future research.

Phrasing of the judgemental task

It is obviously of great importance to know how the judges actually make their judgements! It is equally obviously difficult to determine this. One way is by simply asking them what features of performance influenced them, as done by, for example, Adams & Pinot de Moira (2000), Fearnley (2000) and Edwards & Adams (2002). The problem with this of course, which is not unique to cross-moderation exercises, is that it is merely an instance of the general psychological problem of the validity of introspection or self-report in understanding the true causes of a judge's behaviour.

There is research suggesting that in some conditions self-reported explanations of behaviour are post-hoc justifications aimed at making the behaviour seem rational; and that human judgement in general is subject to many biases and unconscious influences (see, for example, Slovic & Lichtenstein, 1971; Nisbett & Wilson, 1977; Laming, 2004; Leighton, 2004). A preferable method might be to use Kelly's repertory grid technique (see Chapter 5) to discover what the judges perceived to be the salient constructs in the scripts they were comparing, and to relate these to their paired comparison judgements. This Thurstone and Kelly combined approach was used with some success by Pollitt & Murray (1993). A third method (as yet untried in this context) would be to carry out a controlled experiment, systematically varying the features of scripts involved in the comparisons.

In any event, the way the task is explained and phrased to the judges is presumably relevant. It was appreciated early on (Jones, 1997) that the judgements needed to be made quickly in order to complete a reasonable proportion of the possible judgements within the time available. In D'Arcy (1997), in the study comparing linear and modular mathematics A level the judges completed around 26–31% of the total possible comparisons. The judges in the study comparing linear and modular biology A level only managed to complete about 10% (A boundary) and 19% (E boundary) of the possible comparisons (see Appendix 2). Instructions in more recent studies have thus emphasised the need for a quick, or impressionistic judgement. This is more in keeping with the spirit of Thurstone's method but it raises issues about the validity of the task, which will be discussed further in section 3.4. In terms of the judgement itself most studies have tended simply to ask the judges to decide which of the pair of scripts was 'better'. Some studies have used 'higher quality', or 'better in terms of attainment' or 'better in terms of performance'[2].

However, the need for the whole exercise in the first place arises from the fact that the different boards have different specifications and question papers. The judges are really therefore being asked to judge which performance is better, *taking into account any differences in the perceived demands of the questions (and specifications)*. This more complex question is sometimes left implicit, since the cross-moderation exercise follows the specification review, the aim of which is to encourage the panel to focus on similarities and differences in content and demand (amongst other things) in the assessment materials from each board. However, sometimes it has been spelt out more explicitly, as in the quotation below from the instructions to judges in the comparability study on GCE AS chemistry (Greatorex *et al.*, 2002):

> The judgment is an impressionistic 'holistic' judgment as there is insufficient time for more deliberated judgments. In other words do not consider marks awarded, instead quickly read the whole script through, make a mental allowance for differences in specific questions and decide on balance, on the basis of all comparable material which script you feel 'has the edge'.
>
> Greatorex *et al.* (2002)

Allocation of scripts to judges

The general procedure in the inter-board studies has been to avoid within-board comparisons, and to avoid judges making judgements about scripts from their own board. The exceptions have been the comparability studies involving Vocational Certificate of Education (VCE) units (Arlett, 2002, 2003; Guthrie, 2003), where only three boards were involved.

There have been two general procedures for allocating pairs of scripts to judges – the more common one has been to provide the judges with a record sheet showing the entire set of possible comparisons (except for within-board comparisons), ask the judges to cross out the comparisons which they are 'ineligible' to make (i.e. those involving scripts from their own board), then for each new paired judgement to keep one script from the previous comparison and select a new one, never using the same script for more than two successive judgements. The judges are responsible for ensuring that they cover a representative proportion of the set of all possible judgements (i.e. they do not over-represent particular boards or scripts). This method (or variants of it) has broadly been followed in Gray (2000) and others (see Appendix 1). It is a pragmatic solution to the problem of scripts being unavailable if a specific schedule were given to every judge – because judges will inevitably work at different speeds. It is also probably the easiest to organise.

However, it does have the drawback of probably violating one of the assumptions of the Thurstone pairs method – that each paired comparison is independent of the others. If the same script is involved in consecutive pairs of judgements then it is highly likely that features of it will be remembered from one comparison to the next. Of course, this means that the judge will probably not need to read it twice (or at least, spend so much time reading it on the second comparison) so this does seem likely to allow more comparisons to be made in the time available.

The second approach has been to supply the judges with a unique individual schedule of paired comparisons at the level of the board (not individual script within board), ensuring that scripts from the same board are never used in successive comparisons. In some studies the judges have chosen an available script within the set for their assigned board, and in others the administrative staff have handed out specific scripts. This approach (or variants of it) has been followed in Adams & Pinot de Moira (2000) and others (see Appendix 1). This more rigorous approach is probably preferable.

Appendix 2 shows that the judges in studies using this method do seem to have made a lower proportion of the possible comparisons than the judges in studies that used the more pragmatic method, but it is not possible to attribute this entirely to the allocation method – first, because it is not always possible to determine from the reports how much time was available for the comparisons in each study, and second because different subjects produce different quantities of material for the judges to read.

Timings

Most studies have aimed to allow from two-and-a-half to five minutes per judgement. Some have tried to enforce this with a bleeper, set for a longer time interval at the start of the exercise then reducing the time when the judges have become familiar with the task. A comment from the judges, which has been recorded in more than one report, is that they find the bleeper irritating!

There is no particular rationale for this time limit – it has evolved through practice as allowing at least enough time for both scripts to be read through briefly (and thus varies depending on the subjects being compared). As Appendix 2 shows, even with this time restriction, the percentage of possible comparisons which are actually made is often relatively small.

3.3 Analysis of results

There has been some variability in how different authors have chosen to present the results of analysing their paired comparison data. Appendix 3 summarises some of the different features, discussed below.

Frequency table

This is the raw data upon which the analysis is based, and as such can give a very useful summary of both the experimental design (which scripts were compared, and how many times) and of the results (how many times each script won and lost). An example is shown in Table 1. If the design is fully crossed (all possible comparisons made by all the judges) then a simple table of proportion of wins and losses is probably nearly as informative (and easier to communicate!) than the results of the Rasch analysis. Appendix 3 shows that some of the published reports have included such a table – ideally it would always be included.

Script measures

All the reports have included either a table or a plot of script measures, and some have included both. The most common type of plot shows all the scripts on a vertical

Table 1 Example frequency table from a paired comparison exercise (Edwards & Adams, 2002). Entries show the number of times a row script beat a column script.

		AQA 12345	CCEA 12345	EDEXCEL 12345	OCR 12345	SQA 12345	WJEC 12345
AQA	1	00000	14102	10001	10000	10012	22001
	2	00000	01103	01220	00000	10041	00001
	3	00000	00011	02111	00201	01221	20101
	4	00000	02202	11411	01000	01001	10000
	5	00000	20001	00011	00000	00001	10000
CCEA	1	00012	00000	20110	00001	22000	11200
	2	00000	00000	00002	10000	00003	10000
	3	01010	00000	00011	00000	00000	00001
	4	01002	00000	02132	01100	01202	02100
	5	01001	00000	01031	00000	01121	00000
EDEXCEL	1	00011	11210	00000	00100	20121	00010
	2	00010	10010	00000	00010	10001	21001
	3	01110	01210	00000	00010	10011	00000
	4	10001	10102	00000	00000	01101	00000
	5	10210	11010	00000	00000	10001	00001
OCR	1	20001	21110	11312	00000	21010	21102
	2	10111	12122	11211	00000	42140	11003
	3	12102	11101	02111	00000	11200	22120
	4	21113	10101	43003	00000	10111	10021
	5	11112	22302	21010	00000	12130	11021
SQA	1	03001	11220	04112	00000	00000	00201
	2	10312	01021	00222	00111	00000	10010
	3	00002	02110	02020	00000	00000	00120
	4	00111	21001	10210	00000	00000	10001
	5	01120	01101	00000	00010	00100	00002
WJEC	1	00010	11002	01100	00001	20201	00000
	2	14010	31201	21003	10100	10020	00000
	3	12110	21201	40412	10000	12102	00000
	4	22011	12310	12131	01021	00111	00000
	5	21111	21100	01031	00000	01201	00000

scale with each script labelled. This gives a good visual impression of the differences between the scripts. A more detailed plot was chosen by Fearnley (2000) and Arlett (2002, 2003) which spread the scripts out along the horizontal axis and also included 95% upper and lower bounds based on the standard errors of the script estimates. The most recent report (Jones et al., 2004) used a bar chart instead of plotting points, and included a bar for the mean script measure for each board (but did not include standard errors).

None of the reports has yet used what is perhaps the most obvious chart (one used by Thurstone in his paper on the seriousness of different crimes, Thurstone, 1927d) – showing the spread of script measures on a separate vertical column for each board (but not necessarily identifying the individual scripts to avoid cluttering the chart). An example is shown in Figure 6, using data from Arlett's (2003) study at the A boundary in VCE health & social care.

Figure 6 Script measures by board for the 'A' boundary in Arlett (2003)

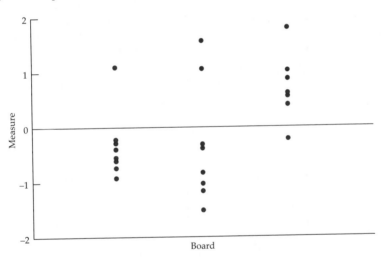

Such a chart allows relatively easy visual comparison of differences within and between boards.

Standard errors and separation reliability

Few of the reports have included the standard errors (SEs) of the script measures, which is a surprising omission, not because these values are of much interest in themselves, but because they allow an assessment of the extent to which the exercise has created a measurement scale. That is, it is useful to report on the extent to which differences between the scripts are due to 'true' differences in scale value, as opposed to measurement error. Several indices have been suggested for this (see, for example, Wright & Stone, 1979; Fisher, 1992), including the separation index, G, and the separation reliability (analogous to Cronbach's Alpha).

These indices are both calculated via the observed standard deviation (SD) of the script measures, and the root mean square error (RMSE) of the script SEs (effectively the 'average' measurement error). First, the 'true' SD of the script measures is calculated from:

$$(\text{True SD})^2 = (\text{Observed SD})^2 - (\text{RMSE})^2 \qquad (13)$$

Then the separation index G is calculated as the ratio of the 'true' spread of the measures to their average error, that is:

$$G = (\text{True SD}) / \text{RMSE} \qquad (14)$$

The separation reliability is defined like reliability coefficients in traditional test theory, as the ratio of true variance to observed variance, that is:

$$\text{Reliability (Alpha)} = (\text{True SD})^2 / (\text{Observed SD})^2 \qquad (15)$$

For example, from the data given in Fearnley (2000) we can calculate for the scale created at the A boundary: G = 4.50, Alpha = 0.95. This shows that only 5% of the variability between the script measures was due to measurement error. These are high values for the separation indices and help justify any later statistical tests. It is important to quote these figures as part of the context for interpreting both tests of fit (the lower the separation indices, the lower the power of tests of fit) and conventional significance tests for differences between board means (which allow for sampling error but not measurement error).

The issue of SEs was raised by Adams (1999) who was concerned by the small number of comparisons for each individual script pairing. He simulated a large number of data sets based on the script measures from the Pritchard et al. (2000) comparability study in GCSE English at the C (higher tier) boundary and obtained empirical estimates of the SEs which were comparable to those reported in Fearnley (2000) and Arlett (2002; 2003). He was also concerned about the implications of measurement error in the script estimates for the validity of the statistical tests of significant differences between board means and his suggested approaches are discussed below under the heading of 'interpreting differences between the boards'. He simulated some data based on random judgements (a 50% probability for each outcome in each paired comparison) but did not calculate the separation indices for this simulated data, which ought to have been close to zero.

Wood (1978) showed that random dichotomous data can fit the Rasch model quite well, which emphasises the need for separation indices to confirm the reliability of the scale, rather than relying on indices of model fit. However, this concern about reliability led to the best designed and most informative of all the inter-board paired comparison studies to date – the exercise on GCSE religious studies reported in Jones et al. (2004). This study was unique in both ensuring that all judges made all 'legitimate' comparisons (i.e. those not involving their own board, or any within-board pairings), but more significantly in that there was a complete replication at each boundary with a different set of judges. The script measure estimates obtained from each replication were plotted against each other showing high correlations (> 0.8) giving an empirical demonstration of the reliability of the scale.

Fit of data to model

Most of the reports have indicated the proportion of misfitting judgements, which has usually been at or below the proportion (5%) that would be expected by chance, using a criterion value of 2 for the absolute value of the standardised residual. None of the reports has presented the usual Rasch fit statistics for the scripts or judges, but several of them have indicated that these statistics were examined. The mathematics study reported in D'Arcy (1997) reanalysed the data without a misfitting judge and noted that it had little effect on the outcome. The studies reported by Arlett (2003) and Guthrie (2003), where judges did make comparisons involving scripts from their own board, did contain 'home board' bias analyses of the kind advocated by Pollitt, but did not find anything significant and did not report any statistical details.

Interpreting differences between the boards

Most reports have presented the mean of the script measures for each board. Some (e.g. D'Arcy, 1997; Jones et al., 2004) also showed what the interpretation of these differences was in terms of the probability of the average script from board X winning a comparison against the average script from board Y. All the studies shown in Appendix 3 have reported the result of some kind of statistical test for differences between the board means. Most often this has been an ANOVA, occasionally repeated t-tests, and once (in Pritchard et al., 2000) a t-test of whether each mean board measure was significantly different from zero (the origin of the scale – set by default to be the mean of all the script measures).

Most authors have (rightly) been extremely cautious in interpreting the results of these statistical tests. For example, Adams & Pinot de Moira (2000) interpreted a significant result as:

> ... unlikely to have arisen by chance; instead it may be concluded there are underlying differences among the syllabuses... An explanation for this may be underlying differences in grading standards among the syllabuses.
>
> Adams & Pinot de Moira (2000)

They were careful to point out that the scale created reflects the judges' preferences and that if they had been influenced in their judgements by extraneous factors such as handwriting then conclusions about differences in grading standard between the boards would not be valid. Many other authors have also been aware of this point and have tried to collect some feedback from the judges about how they made their decisions. See section 5 for further discussion of this issue.

A second reason to be cautious about the results of these tests is that they are essentially treating the scripts as random samples of boundary scripts from each board, and testing the hypothesis that there are no differences in the mean population boundary script judged measures, given the observed differences in the sample means. However, the design of the studies has ensured that the boundary scripts are *not* representative or random samples of all the boundary scripts – they are specifically chosen to have a balanced profile of performance, even to the extent of using composite scripts from pseudo-candidates. They are thus likely to be quite unrepresentative of the typical boundary script.

A final reason to be cautious is that the significance tests treat the script measures as constants – that is, they ignore the measurement error. This issue was first picked up by Adams (1999) who suggested aggregating the data prior to analysis by treating all the scripts from each board as a single script. This obviously would increase the number of comparisons per 'script' and hence the precision of the measure for each board. The resulting comparison between boards would simply be whether their measures were different from each other within the limits of measurement error. This would avoid the problem of testing hypotheses about sampling error mentioned earlier, but would obscure the differences between scripts from the same board (evident in Figure 6 and in all the other reports) and drastically reduce opportunities for investigating misfit.

A second possibility would be to combine the SEs for the individual scripts to obtain a measurement error for the board means. Assuming the errors are independent, the error in the total (sum) of each board's scripts is the square root of the sum of the squared SEs of its individual scripts. The measurement error in the mean, E, is therefore:

$$E = \frac{\sqrt{se_1^2 + \ldots + se_N^2}}{N} \qquad (16)$$

where N is the number of scripts from the particular board.

This could be presented graphically with 95% limits in a high–low chart as shown in Figure 7, where the data are taken from Arlett (2003).

A third possibility, and the most sophisticated statistically, is to analyse the data with a different model than the Rasch model (which can be considered as a special case of a general logistic regression model). John Bell has recommended this approach (in Greatorex *et al.*, 2002), fitting various logistic regression models and arriving at a model that only included parameters for the board, plus those for 'aberrant' scripts with a value very different from the board mean. One advantage of this approach is that it takes into account the SEs associated with estimating the parameters when comparing differences between the boards. A further advantage is that it would be possible to develop models that involve fewer comparisons of a larger number of

Figure 7 Mean script measures by board (data from Figure 6) with 95% measurement error bars

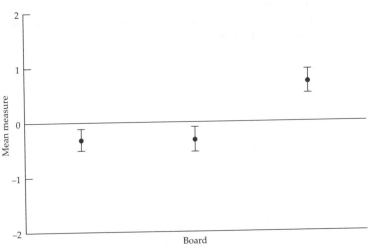

scripts, with explicit modelling of script, judge and board parameters – but at the cost of moving away from the psychological and philosophical underpinnings of the Thurstone and Rasch method. It also increases the difficulty of communicating the results. This approach only appears to have been tried once so far, and there was only space for a brief explanation in the appendix of the report, but it may be an avenue for further investigation.

3.4 Evaluation of the use of paired comparisons in cross-moderation exercises

Psychological validity

The most obvious difference between the paired comparison method as used in cross-moderation exercises compared with those in Thurstone's original work is in the nature of the objects used for comparison. Even though Thurstone moved away from objects with both a physical and a psychological magnitude to objects with a purely psychological (or subjective) magnitude, the judgements could still be made very quickly: for example the judges might be asked to say which of two statements they agreed with more, or which of two handwriting samples they thought was better, or which of two statements reflected a more positive attitude towards religion. The scripts used in cross-moderation exercises, however, are the complete work of a candidate in the assessment and as such could take a long time to read in detail. Allowing five minutes for a paired comparison implies that judges are allowed about two-and-a-half minutes to read each script. This raises the question of whether the judges can apprehend enough of the relevant features of the scripts in such a short time to make a valid comparison between them.

In Thurstone's type of task, the objects could be perceived simultaneously, but in the cross-moderation task the 'discriminal process' of the first script has to be remembered when the second script is compared. Therefore there is an element of recall involved, and it is possible that features of the second script might 'interfere' with the memory of the first script. This raises the question of order effects in paired comparisons, which has not yet been investigated in this context.

Ironically, it is possible that the judges might resort to using an internal standard (this one is a good 'A') when making their judgements – even though one of the main benefits of the method is that in theory it removes the need to do this.

Model assumptions

As described in section 2, Thurstone derived five 'cases' of his law of comparative judgement, each making more assumptions than the last. The Rasch model used to analyse the data is analogous to his Case 5 law, which makes the most assumptions. Of these, the most questionable is the one that the discriminal dispersions of all the objects are equal. Thurstone clearly did not expect this to hold for any but the most simple stimuli. The scripts used in cross-moderation exercises are obviously far more complex than any used by Thurstone, so it seems naïve to expect this assumption to hold here.

Interestingly, inspection of equations (2) and (17) below shows that allowing discriminal dispersions in Thurstone's model to vary would be equivalent to allowing the scaling parameter a (see equation (8)) in the logistic form of the model to vary. This parameter is known as the 'discrimination' parameter in IRT modelling. It is inversely proportional to σ_{AB} in Thurstone's model – that is, the smaller the discriminal dispersions, the greater the discrimination, which makes intuitive sense.

$$X_{AB} = \frac{S_A - S_B}{\sigma_{AB}} \qquad (2)$$

$$\ln\left(\frac{p(A > B)}{p(B > A)}\right) = a_{AB}(S_A - S_B) \qquad (17)$$

The question of whether it is justifiable to use Thurstone's Case 5 law can now be seen to be analogous to the (much debated) question of whether it is justifiable to use a 1-parameter (Rasch) model rather than an IRT model containing more parameters. It is beyond the scope of this chapter to rehearse the arguments in this debate (see, for example, Goldstein, 1979; Divgi, 1986; Andrich, 1989; Wright, 1999). However, there seems to be consensus that the Rasch model is more robust and appropriate with small data sets, such as are produced in a cross-moderation exercise. Furthermore, once the reliability of the constructed scale has been verified with separation indices, and misfitting data removed (if necessary), it is unlikely that using a more complex model would substantively alter the estimated measures of the scripts.

In order to make it possible to estimate the parameters satisfactorily with the relatively small amount of data available it would probably be necessary to reduce the number of parameters estimated in some other way, for example, by representing all the scripts from one board with a single parameter, as in the logistic regression model used in Greatorex *et al.* (2002). Such an approach shifts the philosophy of the exercise from that of Thurstone and Rasch (constructing psychological scales capable of yielding sample-free measurement) to the philosophy of statistical modelling (finding a model that optimises parsimony and variance explained).

However, it should be noted that the issue of discrimination does have an important bearing on the interpretation of results from the Rasch analyses, because each separate analysis creates its own logit scale with the discrimination parameter set to 1. This means that the 'unit' cannot be assumed to have the same meaning across analyses. Again, it is easiest to understand the implication of this by considering Thurstone's formulation (Figure 5). There is the same probability of script A beating script B in a paired comparison if they are a long way apart on the psychological scale, but with large discriminal dispersions, as there is if they are close together on the scale but with small discriminal dispersions. Different analyses define the unit in terms of the discriminal dispersion, but this unit will not have the same substantive meaning if the judges in one analysis are capable of more fine discriminations between the scripts than the judges in another analysis, or if one set of scripts is more conducive to fine discriminations than another (as might be hypothesised to occur between different subjects, for example).

Interpretation of results

Despite the caveats mentioned above, the cross-moderation exercises that have used Thurstone paired comparisons seem to have created valid measurement scales in the sense of being internally consistent (Fearnley, 2000; Arlett, 2002; 2003) and replicable (Jones *et al.*, 2004). This means that (in my opinion) the area where there is most scope for development is in the interpretation of the results, in the sense of what inferences can be drawn from differences in mean script estimates between the boards. In other words, there needs to be some way to determine an effect size, or to translate the differences in perceived quality of boundary scripts (in logits) into differences in grading standards (in marks).

If all the scripts from each board are exactly on the boundary, then the very fact that there is considerable variation in perceived quality within the scripts from each board would seem to provide a context for interpreting differences between the boards. For example, the mean difference between two boards could be expressed as a proportion of the SD of the measures within a board. But this would still only allow conclusions in terms of the psychological scale. What is really needed is a way to relate the psychological scale to the mark scale on which the original grade boundaries were located. This point has been made before (Pollitt 1999; Pollitt & Elliott 2003a).

In order to achieve this, cross-moderation exercises should deliberately aim to use *ranges of scripts* around the boundary. This would have the following advantages:

- it would offer a means of validating the outcomes of the judgemental exercise (by comparing the script measures within each board with their original mark totals)

- it would allow the size of any differences that are found between boards to be quantified (albeit approximately) in terms of the original mark scale, and hence the importance of the difference to be evaluated

- it would reduce (ideally remove entirely) the need to use pseudo-candidates in order to create composite scripts exactly on the boundary mark.

This approach was used in studies comparing standards over time by Bell *et al.* (1998) and Bramley *et al.* (1998), although it was found that the range of marks needed to be quite wide in order to obtain a good relationship between mark and judged measure. Furthermore, on some of the occasions in inter-board studies where non-boundary scripts have been involved they have provided a useful validation of the judgement outcomes (Alton, personal communication; D'Arcy, 1997).

Nearly all the inter-board comparability studies using paired comparisons that have reported the views of the judges have mentioned that they found the task difficult, tedious and repetitive. One could take the view that they are being paid for their discomfort – but it might also be worth considering a method that removes some of the tedium, particularly if it can address some of the problems with the paired comparison method described above. The rank-ordering method described in the next section looks promising.

4   A rank-ordering method for investigating comparability

Given that the nature of the objects being compared (scripts) is such that paired comparisons are unlikely to be independent, and that the scripts take a long time to read, instead of asking judges to make repeated paired comparisons it might be advantageous to ask them to put sets of scripts into rank-order of perceived quality. It is then possible to extract paired comparison data from the rank-ordering in the form of '1 beats 2', '2 beats 3', '1 beats 3', and so on. This strategy was occasionally adopted by Thurstone himself, who wrote:

> The ideal form of the constant method is the method of paired comparison... but is also one of the most laborious experimental methods... Our present problem is to devise a plan whereby simple absolute rank order may be used as the experimental procedure with the advantages of the much more laborious constant method. Given the data for absolute rank order, we shall extract the proportion of judgments 'A is greater than B' for every possible pair of stimuli in the given series. These derived proportions will be used instead of the proportions that are obtained directly in the constant method.
>
> Thurstone (1931)

Rank-ordering has also been suggested by judges who have had to undergo a paired comparison exercise (Edwards & Adams, 2002) and by researchers who have had to organise one (Bramley *et al.*, 1998)!

The application of rank-ordering methodology to the problem of standard maintaining within a subject over time has been described in detail in Bramley (2005a). The method has been used to map cut-scores from the Key Stage 3 English test from one year to another – effectively 'test equating by expert judgement'. The essentials of the method as it has been used to date are summarised very briefly below.

Scripts are selected from the two (or more) tests to be compared, such that the whole effective mark range is covered. Script total marks and question marks (if feasible) are removed from the scripts which are then photocopied as many times as necessary for the study. Packs of scripts are compiled containing scripts from both tests. In studies carried out to date, packs of ten scripts have been used containing five scripts from each test. The scripts within each pack can vary in both the range of marks covered, and in the degree to which the mark ranges from each test overlap or are offset. Each pack contains a unique selection of scripts, but there are many common scripts between the packs allowing the entire set of scripts to be 'linked'. Each judge is given a number of packs covering the whole mark range. Some effort is made to minimise the number of times each judge has to see the same script across packs, but some overlap is inevitable and improves the linking. Judges are asked to rank the scripts in each pack from best to worst, in terms of a holistic judgement of quality. Tied rankings are discouraged. Judges have access to the question papers and mark schemes in order to inform their judgements.

The ranked data are converted to paired comparison data prior to analysis with the Rasch model. The analysis places every single script in the study (i.e. covering the whole mark range of both tests) onto a single scale of perceived quality. Once the usual checks have been made for misfitting judgements, and scripts that have won or lost all their comparisons, the final output of the analysis is a graph that plots the script mark against the script measure for both tests separately, as shown in Figure 8.

The regression lines summarise the relationship between mark and measure and thus allow equivalent marks (in the sense of corresponding to the same perceived measure) on the two tests to be identified. For example, in Figure 8 a mark of 25 on Test A corresponds approximately to a mark of 28 on Test B. If the two tests had come from different boards, and the grade boundary marks were known, it would be possible to determine the boundary marks from board A that were equivalent to the boundary marks from board B, and hence to quantify (in marks) any difference in grading standard.

Figure 8 Example of test equating by expert judgement using the rank-ordering method

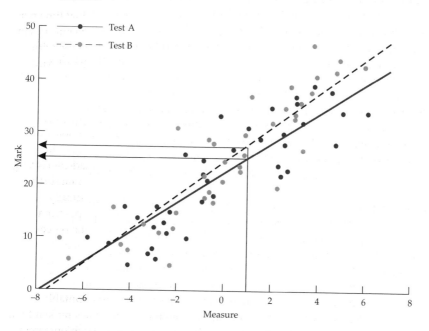

4.1 Evaluation of the potential of the rank-ordering method for cross-moderation exercises

The rank-ordering studies to date (UCLES, 2004; Bramley, 2005a; OCR & UCLES, 2005; Black & Bramley, in press) have just used single components of two assessments. The cross-moderation task involves the whole assessment from several boards. This difference should be borne in mind when considering the rank-ordering method as an alternative to paired comparisons.

Preparation

It is more time-consuming to prepare the materials for a rank-ordering exercise because of the need for cleaning scripts and photocopying them. (It is necessary to remove the marks because, unlike the typical inter-board cross-moderation study, comparisons are made between scripts from the same board and these comparisons should not be influenced by the rank-order according to total mark.) It is also a more complex task to design the allocation of scripts to packs. However, one benefit is increased control for the analyst over all aspects of the linking. Also, since all materials are prepared in advance, and judges work independently, it is possible for the exercise to be carried out postally, reducing the cost. Black & Bramley (in press) found that there was no difference in outcome between a rank-ordering exercise conducted postally and replicated in a face-to-face meeting.

Timing

A rank-ordering of 10 objects yields 45 paired comparisons for analysis[3]. In the studies to date, this has proved feasible in 30–45 minutes, giving a nominal time per comparison of less than a minute, compared to an average of around five minutes in the inter-board studies. There is therefore considerable scope for saving time with this method, even allowing for the fact that the scripts to be ranked in inter-board studies would require more reading time.

Judgemental task

Whilst the task is broadly the same as in a paired comparison exercise (a holistic judgement of overall quality), there is more scope for inter-judge differences in strategy for producing the ranking – for example some judges might read everything through very quickly to create a provisional ranking, then spend more time sorting out their preferred order for adjacent scripts. Others might work methodically through their pack, others might create separate rank orders for the scripts from the same assessment and then try to interleave them. Whether this affects the outcome has not yet been investigated.

Analysis

The requirement for each paired comparison to be independent is indisputably violated by creating the pairs out of a ranking. For example, if script A is ranked first, script B second and script C third then this creates the paired comparison outcomes 'A beats B', 'B beats C' and 'A beats C'. If these three scripts were to be compared in a 'true' paired comparison exercise it would be possible to obtain the inconsistent result 'A beats B', 'B beats C' and 'C beats A'. The ranking therefore constrains the possible set of paired comparison outcomes (Linacre, 2006). The more objects to be ranked, the greater the constraint. The ratio R of possible paired comparison outcomes from a ranking of N objects to the total set of possible outcomes is given in equation (18):

$$R = \frac{N!}{2^{\left(\frac{N(N-1)}{2}\right)}} \qquad (18)$$

However, in practice it is possible that the violations of local independence do not greatly affect the results. Bramley (2005a) showed that effectively the same set of script measures were produced by analysing the rankings with the Rasch partial credit model (PCM) as with the paired comparison model, but the latter appeared to create a more discriminating scale – that is, the separation (reliability) indices were artificially inflated. There is scope for further experimental investigation of the difference between measures created from rankings analysed as paired comparisons and measures created from a genuine paired comparison design.

For example, it may be that if the objects to be ranked are sufficiently far apart on the psychological scale then many of the possible outcomes in the denominator of equation (17) would be so unlikely as to have effectively a zero probability, making the constraint imposed by a ranking in practice much less than it seems in theory. Also, as mentioned in section 3.4, it seems quite plausible that even with a 'genuine' paired comparison design, when the objects being compared are as complex as scripts it is unlikely that each comparison will be truly independent because of memory effects, which might impose a 'virtual' constraint with the same effect as a ranking if the judges either consciously or unconsciously try to be self-consistent as they make their decisions.

Validity

The greatest benefit of using the rank-ordering method is the potential it creates to compare the rank-order of scripts by judged measure to the rank-order by mark – if this relationship is poor it casts doubt on the validity of the exercise. This can be visually assessed by considering the scatter about the regression lines in plots like Figure 8, or by considering indicators of fit such as R^2 or root mean square error (RMSE). Interestingly, the rank-ordering studies carried out to date have often shown that within a judge's pack the correlation between perceived quality and mark for scripts from the same test is often low, in fact sometimes negative – yet when the results are aggregated over the entire mark range for all judges the overall correlation between mark and measure is high (around 0.8 to 0.9).

Once a relationship between mark and measure has been established, it can be summarised by a linear (or non-linear) best-fit line, which effectively allows raw scores on one test to be mapped to the other test via the common construct of perceived quality. If several boards were involved then the actual grade boundary mark for one of them could be mapped to an equivalent boundary mark on the others. This equivalent mark could be compared with the actual boundary mark to find the difference in grading standard (in marks) between the boards, according to the expert judges.

In practice there might be several obstacles to overcome before this method could be used in an inter-board cross-moderation exercise. For example, it might not be feasible to compare the whole mark scale of a complete assessment for several boards in the time available. This could be overcome by using scripts a certain number of marks apart along the mark range, instead of at each mark. Alternatively, separate rank-ordering exercises could be carried out on ranges of marks around the key boundaries of interest.

In summary, the two key benefits of using a rank-ordering method would be to speed up the data collection, making the task less tedious and repetitive for the judges, and to create a way to relate the psychological scale of perceived quality to the raw mark scale, allowing differences between the boards at the grade boundaries to be quantified in terms of raw marks.

5 Discussion

The purpose of inter-board comparability studies is to compare standards across the different awarding bodies. In making this comparison, it is important to distinguish between content standards and performance standards:

> Content standards refer to the curriculum [or syllabus/specification] and what examinees are expected to know and to be able to do... performance standards communicate how well examinees are expected to perform in relation to the content standards.
>
> Hambleton (2001)

The syllabus or specification review strand of a comparability study is an exercise comparing the content standards of the different specifications. From the point of view of teachers and pupils, it is probably true to say that the content standards are most effectively communicated by the question papers and mark schemes for the assessments. The specification review strand thus considers all this material (specifications, question papers and mark schemes) from each board.

It is important to note that judgements about content standards can often depend on values. For example, a mathematics specification including calculus might be seen as having 'higher' content standards than one which did not include calculus but did include matrices, if it were judged that calculus were more intrinsically demanding, or of more fundamental importance to a mathematician. Such a judgement would inevitably have a value-laden subjective element.

Performance standards relate to where the grade boundaries are set on a particular assessment – that is, how many marks are 'good enough' for a script to be worthy of a particular grade. Because question papers inevitably vary in difficulty, despite the best efforts of the paper setters, it is often necessary to set different grade boundaries on different papers to allow for differences in difficulty. The purpose of an awarding meeting is to set the boundaries at points on the raw mark scale that represent an equivalent performance standard to the boundaries set on previous assessments in the same specification. The content standards do not vary from year to year (unless the specification changes). The awarding meeting uses a variety of evidence in order to decide whether to make any adjustments for differences in difficulty. One of these pieces of evidence is expert judgement about the quality of work displayed in scripts on a range of marks around the putative boundary. Once the boundary has been set, scripts on the grade boundary (in conjunction with the question papers and mark schemes) therefore exemplify the performance standard.

In a cross-moderation exercise, boundary scripts from different boards are compared. The exercise is thus comparing the performance standards of the different boards. The extra complication in attempting to accomplish this task in a cross-moderation exercise (compared to in an award meeting) is that not only are the question papers and mark schemes different, the specification is too. Thus the judges are expected to make judgements about relative *performance* standards in a context of possible differences in *content* standards.

I have argued elsewhere (Bramley, 2005b; 2006) that a psychometric approach provides a rational framework for tackling the problem of maintaining performance standards, even if it cannot provide an entirely satisfactory solution. On this approach, the performance standard can be conceived as a location on a latent trait (the psychological continuum representing the construct that the assessment is measuring). Pupils and test questions can also be located on the trait by analysing test performance data (item-level data of pupil marks on individual questions) with a measurement model such as the Rasch model. A question's location on the trait is referred to as its 'difficulty', and a pupil's location as their 'ability'[4]. If there are some common questions in two otherwise different tests that are testing the same construct then it is possible to link scores on one test to scores on the other in terms of both representing the same amount of ability.

The latent trait itself thus embodies the content standards – in the sense that the set of questions spread out across the latent trait would define the construct. Other questions measuring the same construct could also be calibrated on the same scale (provided there was a link via common items or pupils). The level of ability at the performance standard can be interpreted in terms of probability of success on questions at different points on the trait, providing a coherent framework for understanding both content and performance standards.

I would like to suggest that it is *only possible to compare performance standards if the content standards across the boards are similar enough for the different assessments to be considered to be measuring the same construct.* Then we could imagine calibrating the test questions from all the boards onto a single scale. Having done this, we might observe that the average location of the questions from different boards was at different points on the scale – in other words that their tests varied in difficulty. This would mean that a candidate with a given level of ability would get a lower raw score on the assessment from the 'difficult' board than from an 'easier' board. However, this would *not imply anything* about the performance standards of the boards! This important point has been made on several occasions by Robert Adams (e.g. Adams & Pinot de Moira, 2000; Jones, 1999):

> There is no obvious connection between the demand of the papers and grading standards because awarding intervenes. The most demanding papers can yield the most easily attainable grades if grade boundaries are set low enough; similarly higher grades can be difficult to obtain on easier tests if the boundaries are set high enough.
>
> Adams & Pinot de Moira (2000)

The way to use our imaginary calibrated scale to compare the performance standards of the different boards would be to use the measurement model to plot the relationship between raw score and ability on each of the boards' assessments. Then a difference in performance standard would be indicated if the raw score grade boundaries set by the different boards corresponded to different abilities on the overall calibrated scale.

Whilst it is possible to carry out this calibration in the imagination, it is not possible to do it in reality because there are no common questions between the boards' assessments, and no common candidates. Thus the cross-moderation exercise can be conceived as an attempt to achieve this calibration via a link of 'common judges'. What do the judges need to be able to do in order to achieve this? It seems unlikely that their brains are running the kind of iterative maximum likelihood algorithms that the computer would employ if we had a common question or common candidate link! Given a script containing a set of responses to a set of questions with an associated mark scheme, they need to be able to perceive directly the location of the script (i.e. candidate ability) on the latent trait – the *same* latent trait as imagined above. In Thurstone's terms, the script must evoke a 'discriminal process' at the point on the latent trait corresponding to candidate ability. Whilst in Thurstone's type of experiment this was an immediate judgement, in the cross-moderation exercise it seems more plausible that it must be an aggregation of micro-judgements as the judge reads through the pairs of scripts. We expect them to compensate for lower performance when the questions are harder. That is, we want them to be able to compare better performance on easier questions with weaker performance on harder questions. We can imagine this being done by aggregating a series of micro-features from the individual questions and the candidates' responses to them according to the judge's own idiosyncratic weighting system. Studies which have collected feedback from the judges on how they made their decisions have usually found a variety of different features that different judges say that they pick up on – naturally these tend to be very subject-specific.

The purpose of the mark scheme, it might be argued, is to impose a standardised weighting onto specified features of the response in order to allow an explicitly observable numerical aggregation of question marks into a total score. This raw score of course depends on the difficulties of the questions. (Otherwise it would be possible to compare the performance standards of the boards by comparing the raw boundary marks expressed as a percentage of total mark available.) On a Rasch-calibrated latent trait there is a one-to-one (sigmoidal) relationship between raw score and ability for each particular test. In other words, scripts with the same raw score will imply the same ability measure. That is why it is important to check that the measure scale created in the paired comparison exercise corresponds to the (within-board) raw score scale[5]. It is easier to do this with the rank-ordering method than with the paired comparison method, as shown in Figure 8. When all the scripts in a paired comparison exercise are on the boundary mark then all that can be done is to compare the extent to which within-board differences in script measure compare with between-board differences in script measure. There should be no within-board differences for scripts on the same mark.

This verification of a within-board relationship between judged measure and raw mark is necessary to compare performance standards in the current system where grade boundaries are set on the raw mark scale. It is possible to envisage a situation whereby the judges' judgements are held to be *more* valid (i.e. to give a truer estimate of locations on the latent trait) than the locations derived from adding up marks

282

according to the mark scheme. In this utopia cross-moderation exercises (and, indeed, marking!) would become obsolete (Pollitt, 2004).

Adams has expressed doubts that the judges are capable of allowing for differences in demand of question papers when comparing performances:

> It is, after all, the central conundrum of testing educational attainment: the relative merits of easier tasks done well and harder tasks done moderately.
>
> Adams & Pinot de Moira (2000)

Nonetheless, all cross-moderation exercises (regardless of the method they use) do depend on the ability of judges to do this. Experimental work could try to verify whether or not they are capable of it, in situations where it is possible to compare the judged equating of two mark scales with a statistical equating based on common items or persons. Good & Cresswell (1988) found considerable disparity between judgemental and statistical equating in tiered examination papers, but some recent work using the rank-ordering method (Black & Bramley, in preparation) has shown that judges did agree reasonably well with the outcomes of an awarding meeting in aligning the mark scales on two tiers in a GCSE English exam. If they can make this kind of adjustment for difficulty (between two tiers intended to be at a different level of difficulty), then there is some hope that they might be able to allow for the (presumably lesser) differences in difficulty between assessments at the same level from different boards.

6 Conclusion

The paired comparison method of constructing psychological scales based on human judgements is well established in psychometric theory and has many attractive features that have led to its adoption as the preferred method in inter-board comparability studies. Its main theoretical advantages are the experimental elimination of the internal standards of the judges when estimating scale locations, and the fitting of an explicit statistical model that allows investigation of residuals for script and judge misfit, and for various sources of bias. Its main practical advantage is the simplicity and flexibility of the design, which can allow for non-random missing data. Most of the more problematic issues discussed in this chapter arise from its application to the particular context of investigating examination comparability. The fact that scripts are complex objects which take a relatively long time to read, means that the comparison judgement is not based on an immediate impression, in contrast to Thurstone's work. Order effects and memory effects are likely to come into play, making the assumption of independence between judgements, required by the statistical analysis model, seem rather implausible. The paired comparison method is also time consuming and tedious for the judges, a drawback that can be remedied to some extent by using the rank-ordering method to collect the data.

However, the most serious problem in the cross-moderation exercises carried out to date has not been with the method but with the design of the studies, which, by only including scripts on the grade boundaries, have not allowed differences between boards in terms of mean scale location to be related to the raw mark scales of the different examinations. This has made it impossible to assess the importance (for example in terms of implied changes to grade boundaries) of any differences discovered. It has only been possible to draw very tentative conclusions about perceived differences in quality of average borderline scripts, based on significance tests of dubious appropriateness. Both the paired comparison method and especially the rank-ordering method could easily address this shortcoming in future studies, by deliberately involving scripts from a range of marks around each grade boundary.

Further areas for future research are in understanding better the psychological processes involved in the paired comparison judgements, and in discovering the features of the scripts that are most influential in determining the outcome. The validity of the cross-moderation exercise (regardless of which particular method is used) depends on achieving a match between the judges' collective perception of the trait of 'quality of performance', and the trait as intended by the question paper setters and instantiated in the mark scheme. This could be assessed by considering the within-board relationship between mark and trait location, but, again, this would need the design of the studies to be modified to include scripts on a range of marks, rather than on a particular boundary mark.

Finally, the prospect of the availability of high-quality scanned images of scripts will allow researchers to improve the design of studies and reduce logistical problems. It might be possible to carry out the exercise online, involving a larger number of judges and scripts. The data could then be analysed 'on-the-fly', allowing the allocation of pairs of scripts to be targeted so as to achieve the maximum information from each comparison, and for misfitting scripts (and judges) to be removed.

Endnotes

1. Cambridge Assessment is the brand name of the University of Cambridge Local Examinations Syndicate (UCLES), a department of the University of Cambridge. Cambridge Assessment is a not-for-profit organisation.

2. These quotes have come from the actual instruction sheet given to the judge panel, if this was provided in the report. Otherwise, it has been taken from explanatory text within the report. It is possible that the explanatory text does not reflect the literal instruction given to the judges.

3. The number of different paired comparisons in a rank-ordering of N objects is $N(N-1)/2$.

4. Ability here does not imply innateness, or IQ, or potential. It is used in a neutral psychometric sense of location on the trait.

5. Perhaps ideally this should be the ability measure rather than raw score. However, the relationship between raw score and ability is linear over most of the raw score range.

References

Adams, R.M. (1999, November). *The Rasch model and paired comparisons data: Some observations*. Paper presented at a seminar held by the Research Committee of the Joint Council for General Qualifications, Manchester. Reported in B.E. Jones (Ed.), (2000), *A review of the methodologies of recent comparability studies*. Report on a seminar for boards' staff hosted by the Assessment and Qualifications Alliance, Manchester.

Adams, R.M., & Pinot de Moira, A. (2000). *A comparability study in GCSE French including parts of the Scottish Standard grade examination. A study based on the summer 1999 examination. Review of question paper demand, cross-moderation study and statistical analysis of results.* Organised by Welsh Joint Education Committee and Assessment and Qualifications Alliance on behalf of the Joint Forum for the GCSE and GCE.

Agresti, A. (1990). *Categorical data analysis.* New York: Wiley.

Ahmed, A., & Pollitt, A. (2001, September). *Improving the validity of contextualised questions.* Paper presented at the British Educational Research Association Annual Conference, Leeds.

Andrich, D. (1978). Relationships between the Thurstone and Rasch approaches to item scaling. *Applied Psychological Measurement, 2*, 449–460.

Andrich, D. (1989). *Distinctions between assumptions and requirements in measurement in the social sciences.* In J.A. Keats, R. Taft, R.A. Heath & S.H. Lovibond (Eds.), *Mathematical and theoretical systems* (pp. 7–16). North Holland: Elsevier Science.

Arlett, S. (2002). *A comparability study in VCE health and social care, units 1, 2 and 5. A study based on the summer 2001 examination.* Organised by the Assessment and Qualifications Alliance on behalf of the Joint Council for General Qualifications.

Arlett, S. (2003). *A comparability study in VCE health and social care, units 3, 4 and 6. A study based on the summer 2002 examination.* Organised by the Assessment and Qualifications Alliance on behalf of the Joint Council for General Qualifications.

Bardell, G.S., Forrest, G.M., & Shoesmith, D.J. (1978). *Comparability in GCE: A review of the boards' studies, 1964–1977.* Manchester: Joint Matriculation Board on behalf of the GCE Examining Boards.

Bell, J.F., Bramley, T., & Raikes, N. (1998). Investigating A level mathematics standards over time. *British Journal of Curriculum and Assessment, 8*(2), 7–11.

Black, B., & Bramley, T. (in press). Investigating a judgmental rank-ordering method for maintaining standards in UK examinations. *Research Papers in Education.*

Black, B., & Bramley, T. (in preparation). *Using expert judgment to link mark scales on different tiers of a GCSE English examination: A rank ordering method.*

Bradley, R.A., & Terry, M. (1952). The rank analysis of incomplete block designs: I. The method of paired comparisons. *Biometrika, 39*, 324–345.

Bramley, T. (2005a). A rank-ordering method for equating tests by expert judgment. *Journal of Applied Measurement, 6*(2), 202–223.

Bramley, T. (2005b). Accessibility, easiness and standards. *Educational Research, 47*, 251–261.

Bramley, T. (2006, March). *Equating methods used in key stage 3 science and English.* Paper presented at the National Assessment Agency technical seminar, Oxford.

Bramley, T., Bell, J.F., & Pollitt, A. (1998). Assessing changes in standards over time using Thurstone paired comparisons. *Education Research and Perspectives, 25*(2), 1–23.

D'Arcy, J. (Ed.). (1997). *Comparability studies between modular and non-modular syllabuses in GCE Advanced level biology, English literature and mathematics in the 1996 summer examinations.* Standing Committee on Research on behalf of the Joint Forum for the GCSE and GCE.

Divgi, D.R. (1986). Does the Rasch model really work for multiple choice items? Not if you look closely. *Journal of Educational Measurement, 23*, 283–298.

Edwards, E., & Adams, R. (2002). *A comparability study in GCE AS geography including parts of the Scottish Higher grade examination. A study based on the summer 2001 examination.* Organised by the Welsh Joint Education Committee on behalf of the Joint Council for General Qualifications.

Edwards, E., & Adams, R. (2003). *A comparability study in GCE Advanced level geography including the Scottish Advanced Higher grade examination. A study based on the summer 2002 examination.* Organised by the Welsh Joint Education Committee on behalf of the Joint Council for General Qualifications.

Elliott, G., & Greatorex, J. (2002). A fair comparison? The evolution of methods of comparability in national assessment. *Educational Studies, 28*, 253–264.

Fearnley, A. (2000). *A comparability study in GCSE mathematics. A study based on the summer 1998 examination.* Organised by the Assessment and Qualifications Alliance (Northern Examinations and Assessment Board) on behalf of the Joint Forum for the GCSE and GCE.

Fisher, W. (1992). Reliability statistics. *Rasch Measurement Transactions, 6*(3), 238.

Forster, M., & Gray, E. (2000, September). *Impact of independent judges in comparability studies conducted by awarding bodies.* Paper presented at the British Educational Research Association annual conference, University of Cardiff.

Goldstein, H. (1979). Consequences of using the Rasch model for educational assessment. *British Educational Research Journal, 5*, 211–220.

Good, F.J., & Cresswell, M.J. (1988). *Grading the GCSE.* London: Secondary Examinations Council.

Gray, E. (2000). *A comparability study in GCSE science 1998. A study based on the summer 1998 examination*. Organised by Oxford Cambridge and RSA Examinations (Midland Examining Group) on behalf of the Joint Forum for the GCSE and GCE.

Greatorex, J., Elliott, G., & Bell, J.F. (2002). *A comparability study in GCE AS chemistry: A review of the examination requirements and a report on the cross-moderation exercise. A study based on the summer 2001 examination*. Organised by The Research and Evaluation Division, University of Cambridge Local Examinations Syndicate for Oxford Cambridge and RSA Examinations on behalf of the Joint Council for General Qualifications.

Greatorex, J., Hamnett, L., & Bell, J.F. (2003). *A comparability study in GCE A level chemistry including the Scottish Advanced Higher grade. A review of the examination requirements and a report on the cross-moderation exercise. A study based on the summer 2002 examinations*. Organised by The Research and Evaluation Division, University of Cambridge Local Examinations Syndicate for Oxford Cambridge and RSA Examinations on behalf of the Joint Council for General Qualifications.

Guthrie, K. (2003). *A comparability study in GCE business studies, units 4, 5 and 6 VCE business, units 4, 5 and 6. A review of the examination requirements and a report on the cross-moderation exercise. A study based on the summer 2002 examination*. Organised by Edexcel on behalf of the Joint Council for General Qualifications.

Hambleton, R.K. (2001). Setting performance standards on educational assessments and criteria for evaluating the process. In G.J. Cizek (Ed.), *Setting performance standards: Concepts, methods and perspectives*. Mahwah, NJ: Lawrence Erlbaum Associates.

Jones, B.E. (Ed.). (1997). *A review and evaluation of the methods used in the 1996 GCSE and GCE comparability studies*. Standing Committee on Research on behalf of the Joint Forum for the GCSE and GCE.

Jones, B.E. (Ed.). (2000). *A review of the methodologies of recent comparability studies*. Report on a seminar for boards' staff hosted by Assessment and Qualifications Alliance, Manchester.

Jones, B.E. (2004). *Report of the JCGQ research seminar on issues related to comparability of standards, 3 December 2003*. Internal Research Paper RC/264. Manchester: Assessment and Qualifications Alliance.

Jones, B., Meadows, M., & Al-Bayatti, M. (2004). *Report of the inter-awarding body comparability study of GCSE religious studies (full course) summer 2003*. Assessment and Qualifications Alliance.

Laming, D. (2004). *Human judgment: The eye of the beholder*. London: Thomson.

Leighton, J.P. (2004). Avoiding misconception, misuse, and missed opportunities: The collection of verbal reports in educational achievement testing. *Educational Measurement: Issues and Practice, 23*(4), 6–15.

Linacre, J.M. (2006). Rasch analysis of rank-ordered data. *Journal of Applied Measurement*,

7(1), 129–139.

Nisbett, R., & Wilson, T.D. (1977). Telling more than we can know: Verbal reports on mental processes. *Psychological Review, 84*, 231–259.

Oxford Cambridge and RSA Examinations and University of Cambridge Local Examinations Syndicate. (2005). *NAA KS3 English 2005 draft level setting report*. Report to National Assessment Agency.

Pollitt, A. (1999, November). *Thurstone and Rasch – Assumptions in scale construction*. Paper presented at a seminar held by the Research Committee of the Joint Council for General Qualifications, Manchester. Reported in B.E. Jones (Ed.), (2000), *A review of the methodologies of recent comparability studies*. Report on a seminar for boards' staff hosted by the Assessment and Qualifications Alliance, Manchester.

Pollitt, A. (2004, June). *Let's stop marking exams*. Paper presented at the annual conference of the International Association for Educational Assessment, Philadelphia.

Pollitt, A., & Elliott, G. (2003a). *Monitoring and investigating comparability: A proper role for human judgement*. Cambridge: Research and Evaluation Division, University of Cambridge Local Examinations Syndicate.

Pollitt, A., & Elliott, G. (2003b). *Finding a proper role for human judgement in the examination system*. Cambridge: Research and Evaluation Division, University of Cambridge Local Examinations Syndicate.

Pollitt, A., & Murray, N.L. (1993). What raters really pay attention to. Language Testing Research Colloquium, Cambridge. Reprinted in M. Milanovic & N. Saville (Eds.), (1996), *Studies in language testing 3: Performance testing, cognition and assessment*. Cambridge: Cambridge University Press.

Pritchard, J., Jani, A., & Monani, S. (2000). *A comparability study in GCSE English. Syllabus review and cross-moderation exercise. A study based on the summer 1998 examinations*. Organised by Edexcel on behalf of the Joint Council for General Qualifications.

Rasch, G. (1960/1980). *Probabilistic models for some intelligence and attainment tests*. Copenhagen: Danish Institute for Educational Research expanded edition (1980) with foreword and afterword by B.D. Wright. Chicago: The University of Chicago Press.

Scharaschkin, A., & Baird, J. (2000). The effects of consistency of performance on A level examiners' judgements of standards. *British Educational Research Journal, 26*, 343–357.

Slovic, P., & Lichtenstein, S. (1971). Comparison of Bayesian and regression approaches to the study of information processing in judgment. *Organizational Behavior and Human Performance, 6*, 649–744.

Thurstone, L.L. (1927a). Psychophysical analysis. *American Journal of Psychology, 38*, 368–389. Chapter 2 in L.L. Thurstone (1959), *The measurement of values*. Chicago, Illinois: University of Chicago Press.

Thurstone, L.L. (1927b). A law of comparative judgment. *Psychological Review, 34,* 273–286. Chapter 3 in L.L. Thurstone (1959), *The measurement of values.* Chicago, Illinois: University of Chicago Press.

Thurstone, L.L. (1927c). A mental unit of measurement. *Psychological Review, 34,* 415–423. Chapter 4 in L.L. Thurstone (1959), *The measurement of values.* Chicago, Illinois: University of Chicago Press.

Thurstone, L.L. (1927d). The method of paired comparisons for social values. *Journal of Abnormal and Social Psychology, 21,* 384–400. Chapter 7 in L.L. Thurstone (1959), *The measurement of values.* Chicago, Illinois: University of Chicago Press.

Thurstone, L.L. (1927e). Equally often noticed differences. *Journal of Educational Psychology, 18,* 289–293. Chapter 5 in L.L. Thurstone (1959), *The measurement of values.* Chicago, Illinois: University of Chicago Press.

Thurstone, L.L. (1927f). Three psychophysical laws. *Psychological Review, 34,* 424–432. Chapter 6 in L.L. Thurstone (1959), *The measurement of values.* Chicago, Illinois: University of Chicago Press.

Thurstone, L.L. (1931). Rank order as a psychophysical method. *Journal of Experimental Psychology, 14,* 187–201. Chapter 10 in L.L. Thurstone (1959), *The measurement of values.* Chicago, Illinois: University of Chicago Press.

Thurstone, L.L. (1945). The prediction of choice. *Psychometrika, 10,* 237–253. Chapter 13 in L.L. Thurstone (1959), *The measurement of values.* Chicago, Illinois: University of Chicago Press.

Thurstone, L.L. (1959). *The measurement of values.* Chicago, Illinois: University of Chicago Press.

University of Cambridge Local Examinations Syndicate. (2004). *KS3 English 2004 draft level setting report.* Report to Qualifications and Curriculum Authority.

Wood, R. (1978). Fitting the Rasch model: A heady tale. *British Journal of Mathematical and Statistical Psychology, 31,* 27–32.

Wright, B.D. (1977). Solving measurement problems with the Rasch model. *Journal of Educational Measurement, 14,* 97–116.

Wright, B.D. (1999). Fundamental measurement for psychology. In S.E. Embretson & S.L. Hershberger (Eds.), *The new rules of measurement: What every psychologist and educator should know* (pp. 65-104). Mahwah, New Jersey: Lawrence Erlbaum Associates.

Wright, B.D., & Masters, G.N. (1982). *Rating scale analysis.* Chicago: MESA Press.

Wright, B.D., & Stone, M. (1979). *Best test design.* Chicago: MESA Press.

Appendix 1 Design of inter-board comparability studies (part 1 of 2)

Author(s)	D'Arcy	D'Arcy	Adams & Pinot de Moira	Gray	Pritchard, Jani, & Monani	Fearnley	Edwards & Adams
Year published	1997	1997	2000	2000	2000	2000	2002
Year of exam	Summer 1996	Summer 1998	Summer 1999	Summer 1998	Summer 1998	Summer 1998	Summer 2001
Subject	Biology	Mathematics	French	Science	English	Mathematics	Geography
Level	A level (linear v modular)	A level (linear v modular)	GCSE	GCSE	GCSE	GCSE	AS (+ Scottish Higher)
Number of boards	1	4	7	6	6	6	6
Number of components	8 (3L + 5M)	14 (4L + 10M)	3 (Listening, Reading, Writing)	4	3	? - included coursework	3 (2 for SQA)
Number of boundaries	2 (A and E)	2 (A and E)	3 (A & C Higher, C Found.)	3 (A & C Higher, C Found.)	3 (A & C Higher, C Found.)	2 (C Inter. A Higher)	2 (A and E)
Number of judges	12	12	20	18	18	17	17
Any independent judges?	No	No	Yes (6)	Yes (6)	Yes (6)	Yes (5)	No
Number of scripts per board per boundary	A: 10M, 6L E: 6M, 6L	6	5	5	5	5	5
Scripts cleaned of marks?	No?	No?	No?	No?	No?	No?	No?
All scripts exactly on the boundary?	Yes L, No M	No	Yes	Yes	Yes	No?	Yes?
Assessment or component level judgements?	Assessment	Assessment	Component	Assessment	Assessment	Assessment	Assessment
Any composite scripts?	Yes?	Yes (in modular)	No	No?	No	No?	Yes
How were pairs assigned?	?	Planned rotation of scripts	Random scripts from prescribed pairs of boards: never see the same board in consecutive judgements	Random selection by judges, keeping one and swapping the other each time	Random selection by judges, keeping one and swapping the other each time	Random selection by judges, keeping one and swapping the other each time	Random scripts from prescribed pairs of boards: never see the same board in consecutive judgements
Ties allowed?	No	No	No	No	No	No	No
Within board comparisons?	None within scheme	No	No	No	No	No	No
Judge own board's scripts?	Yes?	Yes?	No	No	No	No	No

Abbreviations: L = linear syllabus, M = modular syllabus,
Found = Foundation tier, Inter = Intermediate tier

Appendix 1 Design of inter-board comparability studies (part 2 of 2)

Author(s)	Greatorex, Elliott & Bell	Arlett	Edwards & Adams	Greatorex, Hamnett, & Bell	Arlett	Guthrie	Jones, Meadows & Al-Bayatti
Year published	2002	2002	2003	2003	2003	2003	2004
Year of exam	Summer 2001	Summer 2001	Summer 2002	Summer 2002	Summer 2002	Summer 2002	Summer 2003
Subject	Chemistry	Health and social care	Geography	Chemistry	Health and social care	Business studies (GCE), Business (VCE)	Religious studies
Level	AS (+ Scottish Higher)	VCE	A level (+ Scottish Advanced Higher)	A Level (+ Scottish Advanced Higher)	VCE	A2, VCE	GCSE
Number of boards	6	3	6	6	3	5 (A2), 3 (VCE)	4
Number of components	3 (2 for SQA)	3 (Units 1, 2 & 5)	3	Range from 2 to 6	3 (Units 3, 4 & 6)	3	2
Number of boundaries	2 (A and E)	1 (E)	2 (A and E)	2 (A and E)	2 (A and E)	2 (A and E)	2 (A & C)
Number of judges	16	8	18	17	9	20	11, replication 12
Any independent judges?	No	No	No	No	No	No	No
Number of scripts per board per boundary	5	10	5	5	8	5	5
Scripts cleaned of marks?	No?	No?	No?	No?	No?	No?	No?
All scripts exactly on the boundary?	Yes?	Yes?	No	No?	Yes?	Yes?	No
Assessment or component level judgements?	Assessment	Assessment	Assessment	Assessment	Assessment	Assessment	Assessment
Any composite scripts?	?	Yes	Yes	Yes	Yes	Yes	No
How were pairs assigned?	Random selection by judges, keeping one and swapping the other each time	Random selection by judges, keeping one and swapping the other each time	Random scripts from prescribed pairs of boards: never see the same board in consecutive judgements	Random selection by judges, keeping one and swapping the other each time	Random selection by judges, keeping one and swapping the other each time	Random selection by judges, keeping one and swapping the other each time	Random prescribed order: never see the same script in consecutive judgements
Ties allowed?	No	No	No	No	No	No	No
Within board comparisons?	No	No	No	No	No	Only for GCE v VCE	No
Judge own board's scripts?	No	Yes	No	No	Yes	Yes	No

Appendix 2 Percentage of possible judgements made in inter-board comparability studies

Author(s) of report	Published	Year of exam	Subject	Level	Boundary	Number of comparisons	Number of possible comparisons	%
D'Arcy	1997	Summer 1996	Biology AEB	A level	Ai2	69	720	10%
					Ai1	68	720	9%
					E	81	432	19%
D'Arcy	1997	Summer 1998	Mathematics	A level	A	811	2,592	31%
					E	684	2,592	26%
Adams & Pinot de Moira	2000	Summer 1999	French, Listening	GCSE	C Found.	812	8,400	10%
					C Higher	809	8,400	10%
					A Higher	846	8,400	10%
Adams & Pinot de Moira	2000	Summer 2000	French, Reading	GCSE	C Found.	826	8,400	10%
					C Higher	755	8,400	9%
					A Higher	860	8,400	10%
Adams & Pinot de Moira	2000	Summer 2001	French, Writing	GCSE	C Found.	804	6,000	13%
					C Higher	718	6,000	12%
					A Higher	727	6,000	12%
Gray	2000	Summer 1998	Science	GCSE	C Found.	1,606	5,250	31%
					C Higher	1,675	5,250	32%
					A Higher	1,743	5,250	33%
Pritchard, Jani & Monani	2000	Summer 2001	French, Writing	GCSE	C Found.	804	6,000	13%
					C Higher	964	5,250	18%
					A Higher	907	5,250	17%
Fearnley	2000	Summer 1998	Mathematics	GCSE	C Inter.	2,173	4,875	45%
					A Higher	2,157	4,875	44%
Edwards & Adams	2002	Summer 2001	Geography	AS	A	537	4,250	13%
					E	718	4,250	17%
Greatorex, Elliott & Bell	2002	Summer 2001	Chemistry	AS	A	876	4,000	22%
					E	907	4,000	23%
Arlett	2002	Summer 2001	Health & Social Care	VCE	E	960	1,920	50%
Edwards & Adams	2003	Summer 2002	Geography	A level	A	525	4,500	12%
					E	652	4,500	14%
Greatorex, Hamnett & Bell	2003	Summer 2002	Geography	A level	A	525	4,500	12%
					E	1003	4,250	24%
Arlett	2003	Summer 2002	Health and Social Care	VCE	A	739	1,584	47%-
					E	929	1,584	59%
Guthrie	2003	Summer 2002	Business studies (GCE), Business (VCE)	A2, 1 VCE	G v G:A	536	5,000	11%
					V v V:A	350	1,500	23%
					G v V:A	647	7,500	9%
					G v G:E	565	5,000	11%
					V v V:E	287	1,500	19%
					G v V:E	557	7,500	7%
Jones, Meadows & Al-Bayatti	2004	Summer 2003	Religious Studies 1	GCSE	A	825	825	100%
					C	825	825	100%
Jones, Meadows & Al-Bayatti	2004	Summer 2003	Religious Studies 2	GCSE	A	900	900	100%
					C	900	900	100%

Abbreviations: i1 = Indicator 1, i2 = Indicator 2, Found. = Foundation tier, Inter. = Intermediate tier, G = GCE, V =VCE

Indicator 1 is the term used to refer to the assessment grade boundary derived from weighted aggregation of the component grade boundaries. Indicator 2 refers to the assessment grade boundary derived from weighted averaging of the cumulative percentages of candidates at the component grade boundaries.

Appendix 3 Presentation of paired comparison results in inter-board comparability studies (part 1 of 2)

Author(s)	D'Arcy	D'Arcy	Adams & Pinot de Moira	Gray	Pritchard, Jani, & Monani	Fearnley	Edwards & Adams
Year published	1997	1997	2000	2000	2000	2000	2002
Year of exam	Summer 1996	Summer 1998	Summer 1999	Summer 1998	Summer 1998	Summer 1998	Summer 2001
Subject	Biology	Mathematics	French	Science	English	Mathematics	Geography
Level	A level (linear v modular)	A level (linear v modular)	GCSE	GCSE	GCSE	GCSE	AS
Frequency table	No	No	Yes	No	Yes	No	Yes
Plot of script measures	Yes	Yes	No	Yes	Yes	Yes	No
Table of script measures	No	No	Yes	No	Yes	Yes	Yes
Standard errors	No	No	No	No	No	Yes	No
Scale separation /reliability	No	No	No	No	No	No	No
Script misfit	No	No	No	No	No	Yes (not presented)	No
Judge misfit	No	Yes	No	Yes	Yes	Yes (not presented)	No
% misfitting judgements	No	E 0.7%, A 2.5%	No	FC 2.1%, HC 4.4%, A 2.9%	A 3.1%, HC 4.1%, FC 3.5%	C 3.6%, A 4.5%	No
Size of difference between means	Yes	No?	Yes	No	Yes	Yes	Yes
Sig. of difference between means	Yes	Yes	Yes	Yes	Yes	Yes	Yes
Statistical test	t-test (2 groups)	ANOVA	ANOVA	t-tests	ANOVA + t-test of difference between mean and zero	ANOVA + t-test of difference between mean and zero	ANOVA + t-test of difference between group means

Abbreviations: Sig. = Significance, FC = Foundation tier C boundary, HC = Higher tier C boundary, G = GCE, V = VCE

Appendix 3 Presentation of paired comparison results in inter-board comparability studies (part 2 of 2)

Author(s)	Greatorex, Elliott & Bell	Arlett	Edwards & Adams	Greatorex, Hamnett & Bell	Arlett	Guthrie	Jones, Meadows & Al-Bayatti
Year published	2002	2002	2003	2003	2003	2003	2004
Year of exam	Summer 2001	Summer 2001	Summer 2002	Summer 2002	Summer 2002	Summer 2002	Summer 2003
Subject	Chemistry	Health and Social Care	Geography	Chemistry	Health and Social Care	Business studies (GCE), Business (VCE)	Religious studies
Level	AS	VCE	A level	A level	VCE	A2, VCE	GCSE
Frequency table	No	No	Yes	No	No	No	No
Plot of script measures	Yes	Yes	No	Yes	Yes	Yes	Yes (bar chart)
Table of script measures	Yes	Yes	Yes	Yes	Yes	Yes	No
Standard errors	No*	Yes	No	No	Yes	No	No
Scale separation and reliability	No	No	No	No	No		
Script misfit	No*	Yes (not presented)	No	No	Yes (not presented)	No	No
Judge misfit	No	Yes (not presented)	No	No	Yes (not presented)	No	No
% misfitting judgements	A 5.4%, E 3.2%	E 2.7%	No	A and E 0.009%	A 4.1%, E 3.8%	G v G:A 5.2% G v G:E 4.4% V v V:A 4.6% V v V:E 4.2% G v V:A 4.8% G v V:E 4.8%	No
Size of difference between means	No	No	Yes	Yes	No	Yes	Yes
Sig. of difference between means	Yes	Yes	Yes	Yes	Yes	Yes	Yes
Statistical test	t-tests + logistic regression	ANOVA	ANOVA + t-test of difference between group means	t-tests	ANOVA + post hoc comparison of differences between group means	ANOVA + post hoc comparison of differences between group means	t-tests

* Standard errors and indication of fit were given in the logistic regression output in Greatorex *et al.* (2002).

COMMENTARY ON JUDGEMENTAL METHODS

Sandra Johnson

An alternative to ratification and paired comparisons

The ratification and paired comparison methodologies, described in Chapters 6 and 7 respectively, are at extremes in terms of technical sophistication and complexity. Yet studies that have employed these techniques have shared a common and critical weakness. This is that even where evidence has emerged of relative severity or leniency in boards' grading standards, it has not been possible to indicate by how much and in what direction boundary marks should be moved to bring standards into line (see Edwards & Adams, 1997; Adams & Pinot de Moira, 2000; Pritchard *et al.*, 2000; Greatorex *et al.*, 2002; Guthrie, 2003).

While ratification studies have been able to identify which board(s), if any, could be considered to have the 'right' standard at the boundary under investigation, it has not been possible to quantify the sizes of other boards' deviations from this standard, nor to indicate appropriate remedial action in terms of how boundary marks might need to be adjusted. In paired comparison studies it has not even been possible to identify those boards whose standards could be considered appropriate, given that scrutineers have by design made *relative* judgements about script quality rather than *absolute* judgements about merited grades. Extending paired comparison studies to embrace scripts from a range of marks around boundaries, rather than confining them to scripts at specific boundary points, might improve their ability to quantify the size of difference between different boards' standards. But this will not solve the problem of identifying which board, if any, represents the 'correct' standard (zero points on Rasch scales are not indicators of this), nor how boundary marks for other boards should be moved to rectify deviations from it.

An alternative methodology that potentially solves this problem is a 'distribution study'. Here, boards supply equal numbers of randomly selected scripts at each grade (not exclusively at grade boundaries), and scrutineers independently evaluate and award grades to each script within randomly sorted batches, thus creating new distributions in which new boundary marks emerge. Such studies were piloted more than 25 years ago (Johnson & Cohen, 1983; see also Cohen & Johnson, 1982; Johnson & Cohen, 1984; Johnson, 1989) in a formative evaluation of the cross-moderation methodology as then practised (see Bardell *et al.*, 1978 and Forrest & Shoesmith, 1985, for reviews), and produced promising results. Funded by the Schools Council[1], the research aimed not only to identify weaknesses in the way that cross-moderation techniques had been used in the past – these were well-known already – but also to offer recommendations for design improvement that would render cross-moderation more 'fit for purpose' in the future. A brief reference to this work is included in Chapter 6, but with no discussion of the findings or implications.

Several issues were addressed in the evaluation project, in the form of a number of research questions. Was the assumption underpinning traditional cross-moderation studies tenable, *viz.* that individual examiners could 'carry' and hence 'represent' their boards' grading standards in such contexts? Could scrutineers consistently apply standards – their own or their boards' – when making grading judgements? Could cross-moderation provide clear evidence of differences in boards' grading standards? Where apparent differences in standards emerged, would they necessarily be uniform across the grade range? How much confidence might be attached to scrutineers' perceptions of standards differences – in other words, how technically reliable could cross-moderation outcomes be? How might future cross-moderation studies be better designed to produce more useful outcomes than had been possible in the past?

Three studies were carried out within the formative evaluation, and their results interpreted within the framework of generalizability theory (Cronbach *et al.*, 1972; Cardinet & Tourneur, 1985; Shavelson & Webb, 1991; Brennan, 1992; 2001). Generalizability theory is an extension of classical test theory, and uses variance components derived from ANOVA modelling to estimate measurement reliability. A generalizability study first requires the identification of observable factors that can be assumed or suspected to affect the dependent variable, the dependent variable in this case being scrutineers' grade judgements. An appropriate ANOVA design is then identified with which to investigate factor effects; here a mixed-model factorial design was appropriate, with examiners, nested within examining boards, independently judging scripts nested within board batches, with every examiner judging every script (a 'script' being the total available evidence of a candidate's work – objective test results, responses to structured examination papers, oral test results, etc.). Relative influences on the dependent variable are then quantified in the form of variance components: boards' standards, scripts, interactions between examiners and scripts, etc. The component information is in turn used to calculate 'generalizability coefficients' – ratios of linear combinations of adjusted components that indicate the technical reliability of various pieces of evidence, such as between-board grade differences. Finally, a 'what if?' analysis offers predictions of reliability when features of the current design are changed – such as increasing the number of scripts scrutinised or the number of scrutineers involved.

The studies focused on one or other of three different subjects and levels, *viz.* CSE physics, O level French and A level mathematics, and each involved three senior examiners from each of three participating boards. For each subject, relatively large samples of scripts were randomly selected from across the grade range in each board, using disproportionate stratified sampling to ensure equal numbers of scripts from within each grade: 84 or 98 scripts in total from each board in each subject, comprising 14 scripts from within each of the six or seven grade bands at the relevant examination level. The scripts were randomly distributed into two sets: one set to be evaluated by 'immediate impression' during a 2-day residential meeting, the other for evaluation in a later at-home exercise, in which scrutineers would mark the scripts before awarding grades, using the relevant boards' mark schemes (to see whether a deeper understanding of the qualities being valued in different schemes might produce different grading judgements).

As is current practice, for their information and orientation the scrutineers were sent syllabuses and examination papers for review before they arrived at the residential meeting. During the meeting, scrutineers independently evaluated every script from every board, awarding what they considered to be an appropriate grade. Scrutineers worked through the batches in a given order (their own board last), but no constraint was put on the order in which they judged individual scripts within a batch. To ensure that all scripts were indeed scrutinised by every scrutineer, the scripts, which were original material, were assigned and labelled with unique but arbitrary identifiers, and each individual was given a grade recording sheet, which listed all the scripts within their batches. The same procedure applied to the follow-on at-home exercise, but this time the examiners were provided with the boards' mark schemes and were asked to mark each script with the appropriate mark scheme before making a grade judgement.

Evaluation study findings and implications

One firm finding was that there was no evidence that scrutineers from any one board 'shared' that board's grading standards. In other words, there was as much variation in grading standards among the three scrutineers 'representing' a particular board as there was among the scrutineers in general. No individual examiners, however experienced, could be assumed to have been able to reproduce in these studies the grade distributions originating from their own boards' routine grading exercises. The previous assumption that examiners could singly 'carry' their boards' standards in cross-moderation exercises was shown to be untenable.

Interestingly also, there was no evidence of any 'home board' effect. This is where scrutineers tend to rate scripts from their own board more highly than those from other boards. Presumably the requirement to judge individual scripts within batches rather than batches as entities, as in ratification studies, served to eliminate this possibility. That said, there was evidence in all three studies of a different, less interpretable, scrutineer-by-board interaction. On the evidence of script judgements, different scrutineers tended to judge the different batches, or boards, more or less leniently than others on average. This could be explained by differences in the qualities of subject performance tapped in the different boards' examinations that different scrutineers valued to different extents – differences in personal judging criteria, which the scrutineers were unfortunately not able to articulate. Or it could have reflected prior prejudices on the part of some or all scrutineers about the relative quality of the different boards themselves. If the latter, this would have serious implications for the interpretive value of paired comparison studies, since decisions about relative script quality might to an extent reflect general perceptions about differences between boards; this threat to validity will be exacerbated when ties are not allowed.

There was also evidence, in the form of statistically significant 'interaction' effects between scrutineers and scripts, of a lack of *general* consistency in the grading judgements of individual scrutineers. Such interaction effects will contribute to the phenomenon of 'misfitting judgements' in paired comparison studies, and could in principle threaten the validity of the Rasch model for such comparability exercises.

In two of the subjects, physics and mathematics, clear evidence emerged of overall differences in the boards' grading standards – differences that reached statistical significance at the 1% and 5% levels respectively, with generalizability coefficients of around 0.8 in each subject. Interestingly, while no reliability statistics have been offered in ratification study reports (for example, Edwards & Adams, 1997), generalizability coefficients *could* have been produced for these studies also, since they too have been based on repeated measures designs (a feature that also, moreover, demands F-ratios and not the typically quoted chi-square statistics for significance testing).

In French, no perceived board difference was evident. But the generalizability coefficient was very low, and there was significantly more inter-scrutineer variation here than in the other two subjects, posing a serious challenge for data interpretation. Was there genuinely no difference in board standards in O level French? Or were the scrutineers too variable in their judgements for any difference to emerge? The fact that not all of a candidate's work could be presented for evaluation must be relevant here, oral tests and objective papers being represented by marks only. This issue of missing evidence continues to be a problem today in many subjects.

To the critical question of whether or not cross-moderation studies might be able to provide guidance about how specifically to bring divergent standards together, the answer has to be in the affirmative, provided only that we are prepared to accept that the most valid indicator of 'true' standards lies in the joint judgements of experienced board examiners. By ranking the physics and mathematics scripts in order of original aggregated examination marks, and calculating 'majority votes' on the basis of the nine independent grade judgements provided by the scrutineers, it was possible to see, quite literally, how boundary marks should appropriately have been moved this way or that, and by how much, to achieve standards equivalence. *Every* board would have to have taken action at more than one boundary to achieve parity in standards, and the actions, typically one- or two-mark shifts, would have varied both in direction and magnitude from one boundary to another (see Johnson & Cohen, 1983, Appendices 4 and 6). The weakness in the ratification and paired comparison methods is their inability to provide this kind of information.

Conclusion

Challenges will continue to be faced by those engaging in grade comparability investigations, given the context of diversity that gives rise to the endeavour in the first place. And there will always be doubts about the extent to which the combined judgements of individuals, whether board examiners or others, reflect 'the truth' in terms of a 'national standard'. Despite the difficulties, grade comparability must continue to be investigated.

It is not clear why the formative evaluation findings had so little impact in the UK examining world. In particular it is difficult to understand why ratification studies, with all their demonstrated weaknesses, continued to feature. Could the untimely demise of the Schools Council be a factor? Certainly, the planned continuation of the research was abandoned by default when the Council was closed. Was the relatively unfamiliar methodology not sufficiently well explained in the report for others to adopt? Or was the methodology well understood, but its model assumptions rejected? Was the problem the absence of any user-friendly software with which to carry out generalisability analyses? Or was it simply that the number of examining boards in operation in the mid-1980s, along with the workload that each examiner would be required to accept if all relevant boards were to be involved in any single subject study, precluded any possibility of more widespread application?

The number of examining boards is markedly lower today than it was 25 years ago, the methodology – a special case of multilevel modelling – is more familiar, and G-study software is now readily available.[2] The formative evaluation confirmed the potential of cross-moderation as a fit-for-purpose grade comparability tool. All that remains is for the necessary follow-on research to be carried out to refine the methodology, and for more informative study designs to be adopted in the future.

Endnotes

1   The evaluation report was published just before a government announcement that the Schools Council was soon to be replaced by the School Curriculum and Assessment Authority, another of QCA's predecessors.

2   This has been rectified in the interim with the availability of GENOVA (see Brennan, 2001, Appendix F), and more recently still with the more versatile and more user-friendly EduG (downloadable as freeware from www.irdp.ch/edumetrie/logiciels.htm).

References

Adams, R.M., & Pinot de Moira, A. (2000). *A comparability study in GCSE French including parts of the Scottish Standard grade examination. A study based on the summer 1999 examination. Review of question paper demand, cross-moderation study and statistical analysis of results.* Organised by Welsh Joint Education Committee and Assessment and Qualifications Alliance on behalf of the Joint Forum for the GCSE and GCE.

Bardell, G.S., Forrest, G.M., & Shoesmith, D.J. (1978). *Comparability in GCE: A review of the boards' studies, 1964–1977.* Manchester: Joint Matriculation Board on behalf of the GCE Examining Boards.

Brennan, R.L. (1992). *Elements of generalizability theory* (2nd ed.). Iowa City: ACT Publications. (First Edition: 1983).

Brennan, R.L. (2001). *Generalizability theory.* New York: Springer.

Cardinet, J., & Tourneur, Y. (1985). *Assurer la mesure.* Berne: Peter Lang.

Cohen, L., & Johnson, S. (1982). The generalizability of cross-moderation. *British Educational Research Journal, 8,* 147–158.

Cronbach, L.J., Gleser, G.C., Nanda, H., & Rajaratnam, N. (1972). *The dependability of behavioral measurements: Theory of generalizability for scores and profiles.* New York:Wiley.

Edwards, E., & Adams, R.M. (1997). *A comparability study in Advanced level English literature.* Cardiff: Welsh Joint Education Committee on behalf of the Joint Forum for the GCSE and GCE.

Forrest, G.M., & Shoesmith, D.J. (1985). *A second review of GCE comparability studies.* Manchester: Joint Matriculation Board on behalf of the GCE Examining Boards.

Greatorex, J., Elliott, G., & Bell, J.F. (2002). *A comparability study in GCE AS chemistry: A review of the examination requirements and a report on the cross-moderation exercise. A study based on the summer 2001 examination.* Organised by The Research and Evaluation Division, University of Cambridge Local Examinations Syndicate for Oxford Cambridge and RSA Examinations on behalf of the Joint Council for General Qualifications.

Guthrie, K. (2003). *A comparability study in GCE business studies, units 4, 5 and 6 VCE business, units 4, 5 and 6. A review of the examination requirements and a report on the cross-moderation exercise. A study based on the summer 2002 examination.* Organised by Edexcel on behalf of the Joint Council for General Qualifications.

Johnson, S. (1989). Évaluation de la comparabilité des notations entry jurys d'examens. *Mesure et Évaluation en Éducation, 12,* 5–22.

Johnson, S., & Cohen, L. (1983). *Investigating grade comparability through cross-moderation.* London: Schools Council.

Johnson, S., & Cohen, L. (1984). Cross-moderation: A useful comparative technique? *British Educational Research Journal, 10,* 89–97.

Pritchard, J., Jani, A., & Monani, S. (2000). *A comparability study in GCSE English. Syllabus review and cross-moderation exercise. A study based on the summer 1998 examinations.* Organised by Edexcel on behalf of the Joint Council for General Qualifications.

Shavelson, R.J., & Webb, N.M. (1991). *Generalizability theory: A primer.* Newbury Park: Sage.

8

COMMON TEST METHODS

Roger Murphy

Abstract

Aim

To review the use of common test approaches in comparability research, assessing both the advantages of such an approach and the criticisms that have been levelled against it.

Definitions of comparability

The debate about the usefulness of this method partly hinges on the definition of comparability assumed by those considering its use. The approach fits best with a statistical approach to comparability and least well with a standards referenced approach.

Comparability methods

The common test approach relies upon the examinations being compared having been taken by a sample of students, who have also all taken some other common test. The common test results are used as the basis for comparing the standards of different examinations. This is usually undertaken by plotting regression lines, which attempt to estimate the relationship between common test scores and examination scores.

Strengths and weaknesses

The common test approach is a fairly simple method. It can therefore be easily explained to non-technical individuals who are interested in comparability issues. It is also relatively easy to collect the data needed and draw conclusions. However, it does depend upon the common test having a strong and consistent educational and statistical relationship with the examinations being compared. Critics of the approach point to the fact that common tests rarely have anything like the required relationship with examinations of the type for which comparability studies are required.

Conclusion

The method should only be used in circumstances where the relationship between the common test and the examinations to be compared can be studied closely and critically. Any comparability conclusions drawn from such a study need to be interpreted with caution, taking account of the known levels of uncertainty.

1   Introduction

Already there are some clear themes being built up as we work through the chapters of this volume. Comparability in relation to examination standards can be defined and interpreted in quite a few different ways. No one definition stands apart from the others as the best or most appropriate one. However, when it comes to doing very precise things like designing research studies to investigate comparability questions then it is necessary to work with specific definitions, which can be reflected in the design of such studies. Against that background there has been a sustained and earnest search to develop appropriate methods for researching comparability.

The several different approaches, which have been used over the years, can be delineated fairly clearly and that allows chapters such as this one to review a set of studies that share common features. In this case we will look at comparability research methods that employ a common test approach. As with other methods this general approach can be used in a variety of ways to suit the needs of different situations and it can be seen to have both obvious strengths and weaknesses. Like travellers marooned in a foreign land we cannot afford to dismiss any possible form of transport that comes along, and because this approach, on the face of it, offers some possibilities when it comes to researching difficult comparability questions we will now explore it to see what it has to offer.

In broad terms comparability research methods can be categorised as judgemental and statistical, and this chapter will look at the sub-section of the statistical approaches that are based upon common test approaches. In essence this approach involves addressing comparability questions through evidence gained from situations where the groups of candidates being compared have all also been assessed through a common test. In many situations this will have involved the administration of a common test for research purposes. However in other situations common elements may have been included within otherwise different examinations, or alternatively test scores collected for other purposes may be accessed as the basis for exploring comparability study comparisons

Some of the issues addressed in this chapter will connect with those considered elsewhere in this volume. There are some obvious recurring themes in the chapters, especially those that look at the various statistical approaches. There are for example some close connections between the 'subject pairs' (see Chapter 9) and 'common test' approaches both of which attempt to utilise independent evidence about candidates' ability/achievement levels in order to help investigate the comparability of their results on different examinations. In addition 'multilevel modelling' (see Chapter 10) is a statistical approach, which can be applied to the kind of data generated through several statistical approaches. Also this, like other chapters, will need to continue to refer back to the issues raised in the first four chapters, concerning the general context within which comparability research has emerged, including the attempts that have been made to unpick the variety of ways in which comparability itself can be defined.

My aim in this chapter is to give the reader an insight into the variety of common test approaches that have been used in comparability research, and to explore their advantages and disadvantages. Inevitably this will involve some reference to statistical issues, but I won't be replicating the very detailed statistical discussion to be found for example in Chapter 10. By the end of the chapter we will have looked at the role played by common test approaches over a period of some 40 years. Those who have already read the earlier chapters in this volume will be well prepared for the challenges ahead and will know just what a complicated business it is to tie comparability down in anything other than a very partial way (Nuttall, 1979). The common test approach has at times been seen as controversial, and as such has been both stoutly defended and strongly attacked. As far as is possible I want to look beyond the polarised positions often adopted in such exchanges and help the reader to gain a balanced view of the issues raised. The aim will be to provide a platform of knowledge and understanding through which the strengths and weaknesses of this approach can be assessed.

2   A simple approach to a complex challenge?

Amongst the approaches used to study the comparability of public examinations, the common test (or reference test) approach is undoubtedly one of the simplest. Given a situation in which a comparison needs to be made – say between two groups of students who have taken the same subject exam in different years, or the same subject exam through two different awarding bodies, or different subject exams – the most straightforward version of this method is where both groups of students are given an additional common test for the purposes of researching the comparability of the two exams that are to be compared. In such a situation, the common test results are used to compare the results obtained by the students on the other two examinations.

So, if the overall performance of the two groups of students on the common test is similar and grades obtained by the two groups of students on the two examinations is markedly different, then this is taken as an indication that the two examinations are not comparable in terms of their grading standards. Depending upon the design of the particular comparability study and the nature of the comparisons being made (between years, boards, subjects, etc.) different statistical tests can be applied. These can span comparisons of raw test scores, average scores on each test, least squares regression analysis through to more sophisticated approaches such as multilevel modelling. We will look in more detail at those approaches later in the chapter.

Overall the common test approach is neat and straightforward and fairly easy to explain to users of examination results who may be anxious to know how to compare grades obtained by students in different examinations. It hasn't, however, remained free from controversy, and its relative simplicity has on occasions led some to think that it can be easily misinterpreted as providing very clear answers to what are complex and sometimes highly charged questions about the relative standing of grades obtained from different examinations (Goldstein & Cresswell, 1996; Murphy *et al.*, 1996; Newton, 1997; Baird *et al.*, 2000).

Looking back over more than four decades of comparability research it is fascinating to see the common test approach come in and out of favour on different occasions. The fact that serious doubts have been raised about its suitability in almost every situation where it has been used is not nearly enough to remove it from a comparability scene, where there is no perfect method that can brush aside all others.

Before getting too immersed in the arguments for and against this approach and the added complications of the many different ways in which it can be applied and analysed, I would like to start by presenting a reasonably straightforward explanation of a simple application of this approach.

3   A simple explanation of the common test approach

To illustrate a relatively straightforward use of the common test approach let us take a simple situation in which two different groups of students have entered for two different GCSE mathematics examinations set by two different awarding bodies (A and B) in the same year. As part of an attempt to investigate whether these two examinations have been graded in an equivalent way, an additional common test is given to both groups of students. This specially constructed common test is a test of mathematical ability that is deemed to be appropriate for GCSE mathematics students.

Once the students have taken the common test and it has been marked, there are then two results for each student, their results on the common test and their results on the GCSE mathematics examinations. By comparing the two sets of GCSE and common test results it may be possible to form an impression of how performance in the two GCSE mathematics examinations compares with performance in the common test. If students taking Board A GCSE mathematics obtain higher grades, relative to their common test scores, than those taking Board B, then a case can be made to conclude that the mathematics examination of Board A is easier than that of Board B.

The most common analytical statistical technique used in these situations is linear regression analysis (this is explained more fully in Chapter 10). Using this technique, best fit regression lines can be fitted to the data and plotted to show how in this case the GCSE mathematics grades awarded by Boards A and B relate to the scores obtained by the students on a common test of mathematics ability. Figure 1 shows what the results of such an analysis might look like.

In the majority of similar studies (Bardell et al., 1978) the common test is used to predict examination grades on the basis of fitting best fit linear regression lines to the available data. In order to keep things simple, the two regression lines in this case have been shown as running parallel with each other, indicating that the marks and grades for the two GCSE examinations had similar linear relationships, albeit with Board A appearing to issue higher GCSE mathematics grades relative to those issued by Board B.

In terms of the simple level of analysis, this example illustrates a situation in which the results obtained might be used as the basis for arguing that the standards being used by Boards A and B for issuing GCSE mathematics grades might not be the same. Taken at face value, the analysis reveals that students with the same score on the test of mathematical ability would on average get a higher GCSE mathematics grade with Board A than they would get with Board B.

Figure 1 Regression lines for common test GCSE mathematics comparability study

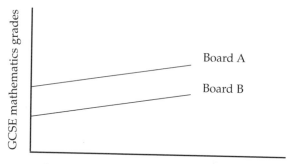

Common test of mathematical ability scores

The type of comparison illustrated in Figure 1 could arise either from studies that compare standards between boards (as shown) or that compare standards across subjects. Studies that compare standards across subjects would be more likely to use a general ability reference test than a subject-specific one, but in other respects the design of the study and the representation of the results would be along exactly the same lines as shown in Figure 1. Studies that use common tests to study possible changes in standards over time require different forms of analysis, which we will discuss later.

Newbould & Massey (1979) provide a fairly comprehensive discussion of the statistical issues that can arise from common tests comparability studies. When the results produce parallel regression lines, such as those shown in Figure 1, then it is possible to test for differences between them using analysis of covariance (Brownlee, 1965). However, as Newbould & Massey point out, examination data rarely behave that consistently and less uniform outcomes are frequently encountered. Figure 2 shows another kind of outcome from this type of study. In this case the regression lines are not parallel and intersect. Such an outcome is far from uncommon and may be taken to reflect the fact that the common test may have different relevance for the candidates in the two groups being compared.

This phenomenon is not just a theoretical possibility, as it has arisen regularly in common test studies which check for parallel regression lines (Meadows, 2003; Stringer, 2005). The consequences of this happening are a quite serious threat to the common test approach and in most cases will be seen to limit the conclusions that can be drawn about the comparability of the tests being compared. In the case

Figure 2 Non-parallel regression lines for common test study

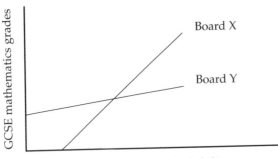

illustrated in Figure 2 the only conclusions that can be drawn are that the study has revealed an inconsistent pattern when it comes to comparing the grading standards applied by Boards X and Y. Board X candidates might be deemed to have been graded more leniently than Board Y candidates on the higher grades, but more severely than Board Y candidates on the lower grades. An alternative conclusion is that the relationship between the common test scores and the examination grades awarded by these two boards is so uneven that it is safer to conclude that the method cannot adequately address the issue of the comparability of the two examinations.

An important lesson here is that anyone conducting a common test comparability study of this type should carry out a precautionary test to see if the regression lines produced are reasonably parallel. In the early days of common test comparability studies this was often overlooked (Willmott, 1980), and that is a serious issue as lack of parallelism poses a serious threat to the validity of any conclusions drawn from a study of this kind.

Newbould & Massey (1979) also point out that it is most common in carrying out such analyses to calculate the regression of the examination grades awarded on the scores on the common test. Such an approach can address the question of whether candidates from different boards, for example, with equivalent scores on the common test receive the same mean grade on the examination. Nevertheless it is also possible to do the analysis the other way around by asking whether candidates from two boards, for example with indistinguishable grades, would receive the same mean score on the common test. In such a case one would be looking at the regression of the monitor on the marks awarded in the two examinations. Figure 3 shows what this type of analysis might look like for a single examination, and if applied to more than one examination it would allow comparisons to be made between, for example, common test scores and the marks and grades awarded by different boards. By plotting similar graphs for the examinations to be compared an overall picture will emerge of the nature of the relationship of each examination with the common test. So, for instance, the borderline scores chosen for grade A in two different examinations might be seen to equate with different scores on the common test. In such a case feedback could be given to those involved stating that grade A in Board

H was shown to be equivalent to a score on the common test that was two marks higher than the grade A of Board G.

Figure 3 Regression of common test on examination marks

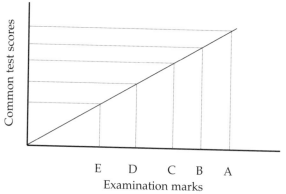

Figure 3 shows a modelling of the relationship between common test scores and examination marks. It also allows estimates to be made of the common test scores equating to each of the minimum examination grade cut-off marks. Newbould & Massey argue that this method leads to a form of feedback that may make more sense to examiners, because the results can be expressed in terms of difference in where grade boundaries have been placed in relation to the total examination marks for a particular examination. In addition they also point out that this approach to analysis typically produces different results from the approach that looks at the regression of the examination results on the common test scores. This represents one more warning that estimates derived from studies of this kind need to be treated with great care and should only be seen as statistical approximations rather than very precise indicators of the relative difficulty of different examinations.

Much of the discussion presented above has assumed straightforward linear relationships between monitor scores and examination results. In reality such relationships are rarely that tidy. Because both examination marks and common test scores are approximations (Murphy, 2004) rather than being highly precise and accurate measures, tolerance limits need to be placed around all such scores. Furthermore, common test comparability studies are frequently conducted on samples that are drawn from larger populations of candidates taking particular examinations, so further account needs to be taken of uncertainty factors associated with drawing conclusions about populations from samples included in research studies.

Figure 4 illustrates this point with findings from Skurnik & Hall (1969), who conducted a common test study of nine 1966 CSE English examinations. Skurnik & Hall, as one part of their study, calculated mean CSE grades and mean scholastic aptitude (CP66) scores for a sample of candidates from each of nine CSE boards. Based upon comparisons between mean CSE English grades and mean common test scores a regression line was plotted as shown in Figure 4. However, as both the regression line and the board points in this figure are estimates based upon data collected from a sample of schools that agreed to participate in the study, they felt that it was necessary to consider the margins of error that were associated with the regression line and the board points in this figure.

Skurnik & Hall treated the board points as fixed and plotted error probability limits on either side of the best fit regression line, taking account of the fact that both the regression line and the board points were only estimates 'based upon a fraction sample of each board's candidates'. The confidence interval shown therefore takes account of the known standard errors both in the regression line and the points that have been plotted to indicate an approximate position for each CSE board based upon its mean grade and mean common test score. These represent a 95% level of confidence (i.e. plus or minus two standard errors), and define a broad band within which nearly all of the nine boards can be seen.

Figure 4 CSE board comparability study results, Boards 1–9, 1966

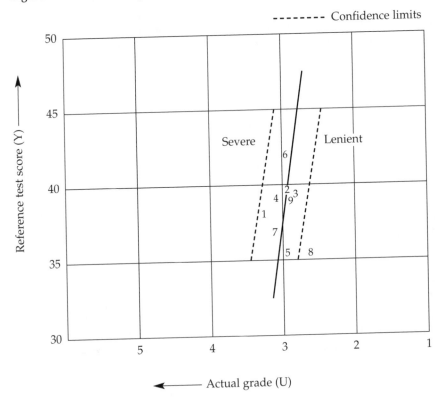

Figure 4 illustrates that with a study of this kind, and with some basic estimation of margins of error, it is not possible to have confidence in the differences in results representing real differences in standards between eight of the nine CSE boards. This is a very graphic representation of the way in which uncertainties concerning the accuracy of common test study results need to be factored into any meaningful interpretation of the results. Without such an appreciation of errors of measurement Figure 4 could have been interpreted quite differently as indicating a good deal of variation say in the grading standards applied by different CSE boards to their English examinations in 1966. Equally one could argue that the error estimates that they have calculated are an underestimate of the real level of uncertainty, given that the common test and exam grades themselves could have been assigned their own 'standard error' estimates, which when combined with the sampling errors could have increased the width of the confidence limits even further.

This single example illustrates a more general point, which we will return to several times. Common test studies of this kind will never give highly accurate outcomes that will allow precise comparisons to be made between boards, subjects and years. Like other statistical approaches to comparability the common test method can provide interesting data, which need to be handled cautiously by those who know both the strengths and weaknesses of the approach. Such an argument needs to be related to wider arguments about the very nature of educational assessments conducted through the UK public examination system, which do not fit the major assumptions of standard psychometric assessments (Gipps, 1994; Broadfoot, 1996; Black, 1998) and which need to be treated accordingly. In the same way that it is foolhardy to expect high levels of precision in the results of such examinations it is even more foolish to expect high levels of precision from research studies that seek to compare different examinations.

Already a section that aimed to present the basic common test approach simply has started to become quite complicated. There is no apology for this because as with all the other statistical and judgemental approaches being discussed in this volume, there are many assumptions being made when one tries to investigate comparability issues through this type of approach. There is as a consequence a good deal more unpicking that we need to do, in later sections, in order to explore the full range of issues involved in evaluating the common test approach.

Before moving on we also need to note at this stage that common test studies that investigate comparability across years generally need to use different forms of analysis. In such studies different groups of students take the common test in different years and their results are analysed year by year using regression analyses to estimate the average examination achievements for students with same scores on the common test. Later in this chapter we will look at an example of such a study, where the results are set out in the form of a graph (Figure 5) showing the grades obtained by students with the same general ability test scores over a period of 16 years. Here the analysis seeks to explore trends over time in the relative performances of students on a common test and A level examinations in a variety of subjects. Even though this approach is somewhat different to the one illustrated through Figures 1–3, the interpretation of the data still tends to depend upon the same issues and assumptions faced in the other studies.

So having started to grapple with the many issues that can influence the interpretation of common test comparability research studies, we will now turn to consider what is probably the most critical issue of all, which is the nature of the relationship between the common test used in any study and the examinations which it is being used to compare.

4 Different ways of incorporating common tests in both operational examinations and research designs

The focus of this volume is upon the use of methods to research the comparability of GCSE and GCE examinations, rather than exploring the ways in which examination boards attempt to ensure the comparability of examination standards through the approaches they use for setting, marking and grading such examinations. In that sense, the major focus of this chapter is upon situations where common tests are given to students as a means of investigating the comparability of examinations. In a limited number of cases common test results have existed for other reasons and have been accessed as the basis upon which to carry out comparability analyses (Massey *et al.*, 2003).

It is, however, also worth noting that some GCSE and GCE examinations have at times had common test elements built into them, usually as a means to help ensure that the examinations lead to comparable grades. In GCSE subjects that use tiered papers, all candidates will normally attempt some common elements of assessment as well as some different elements. The issues arising in tiered GCSE examinations are essentially very similar to those already discussed. A fuller treatment of them can be found in Baird *et al.* (2001). Although the common papers can be used to compare grading standards in optional tiered papers, which are taken by sub-sets of the complete entry, the interpretation of any apparent differences is confused further by the fact that students of different levels of achievement are usually entered for easier or harder optional papers, and in such a situation other possible causal factors can limit the interpretation of apparent differences in the way optional tiered papers are marked and graded. Similarly, multiple choice tests, where used, can be constructed so as to include some common test items as the basis for equating performance from one year to the next. Within National Curriculum testing the 'anchor test' approach is well established and frequently used as one basis for statistical test equating.

Where common test elements are used, whether for researching comparability or for attempting to ensure comparability in live examinations, the same issues arise in terms of the nature of the common test elements and the way in which they relate to the aspects of candidate achievement being assessed through the other elements of the examination. To be useful, common test elements need to relate quite closely to the other assessment elements: otherwise they simply give complementary information about the achievements of the students and have little to offer in relation to predicting candidate performance on the whole examination. Linked to that issue is the requirement for the common tests to be equally fair for all students and not introduce spurious results because they greatly favour some sub-groups over others.

The use of common test approaches is also not restricted to comparability work in the UK. It is an approach that has been used quite widely in Australia, where subject attainment scores are routinely combined as part of university entrance procedures. In Queensland, for example, results from the Australian Scholastic Aptitude Test have been used as part of a procedure for scaling subject marks before combining them to produce tertiary entrance scores. In Sweden, comparability researchers have used the Swedish Scholastic Aptitude Test (SweSAT) within research studying grading standards over time in upper secondary schools (Wikstrom, 2005). Also, in the USA, year to year equating of the highly influential Scholastic Aptitude Test has depended to quite an extent upon the inclusion of a common element of 'anchor items' within successive versions of that national test. In none of these situations has the common test approach been seen as a perfect solution, but in each case it has been regarded as worth employing as one way of trying to get at elusive standard-setting goals.

We should note that statistical models cannot resolve the most fundamental dilemmas at the heart of the debates about the common test approach. The best that statistical treatments of this type can do is to indicate possible interpretations of findings, which need to be hedged with a variety of caveats concerning the need to treat the findings with caution and to remember that there are various interpretations that can be put on apparent discrepancies that may emerge from studies that attempt to investigate comparability questions using general ability measures as their benchmark.

As we shall see in subsequent sections there are fundamental issues that have arisen whenever this approach has been used in the last 40 years.

5 Evaluating the strengths and weaknesses of the common test approach

The previous section has both introduced some of the basic principles of common test comparability research, and inevitably it has also started to open up some of the difficulties that arise when such studies are subjected to rigorous scrutiny. We have also started to see that within what appears at first to be a fairly straightforward approach there are in fact many variations in how such studies can be designed, conducted and analysed. Furthermore, any judgement about the fitness for purpose of such studies of course depends crucially upon the questions that are being addressed by such studies.

As we shall see in a later section the early applications of the common test approach in the UK in the 1960s related to the introduction of the Certificate of Secondary Education (CSE) examinations, and a perceived need for the newly established CSE boards to be given some broad guidance, prior to grade awarding, about the relative 'ability levels' of the candidates entering for their exams (Willmott, 1980). That is a very different context from, for example, more recent standards over time debates, where the common test approach has been used to try to indicate whether GCSE and A level grade awarding standards are being maintained from one year to the next (Tymms *et al.*, 2005).

On the basis that we want to consider a balanced view of both the strengths and weaknesses of the common test approach, let us now summarise some of its advantages. Because of the nature of the challenge faced it is all too easy to dwell too much on the shortcomings and never properly acknowledge the advantages such an approach can have over others.

1. The common test approach to studying comparability is both easy to understand and represents an approach that on the face of it could be expected to yield worthwhile results. In a situation where different groups of students have sat different examinations and obtained different grades, knowing how they have all performed on a common test seems intuitively to be a worthwhile piece of information to be able to acquire.

2. If the common test is a relatively simple test to administer then the additional burden on the students and their schools is not colossal.

3. Common tests can sometimes be already available tests of general ability, so they don't have to be created specially and the same test can if necessary be used time and time again over a number of years. Indeed some common test studies (e.g. Massey *et al.*, 2003) have been able to identify existing test data, held in that case by Local Education Authorities, which could be called up and used without there being any need to retest the students.

4. Common test approaches, especially those based upon the use of general ability tests, can be applied to the more complicated comparability challenges such as changes in standards over long periods of time and the highly contentious area of between-subject comparability.

5. Finally, because all approaches to studying the comparability of examination grading standards have major limitations, the usefulness of the common test approach needs to be assessed in relation to the limitations of the other approaches. Hence it isn't just a matter of whether the common test approach is accurate enough, it is also a matter of whether, even with its shortcomings, it could provide better estimates than other flawed alternatives.

In subsequent sections we will continue to review other strengths and weaknesses of the common test approach. However, it is clear from overviewing the extensive literature that has been devoted to evaluating this method, that there are two key issues which arise most frequently. These relate firstly to the nature and relevance of the common test itself, and secondly to the extent to which a common test, when used, can be seen to offer a comparable challenge to specific sub-groups of students. We will now consider these two key issues in turn. First of all, we will consider the selection of the most appropriate type of common test for use in comparability studies.

Where common tests are employed to study the comparability of subject-based achievement tests such as GCSE and A level examinations, there is a real dilemma over whether to try to include subject content materials that will provide some direct overlap with the content of the examinations to be compared. The counter need is to avoid including specific test items that may bias the common test results towards the content of particular GCSE and A level syllabuses and examinations, and thus unbalance what is supposed to be a fair comparison. Although some early comparability researchers (Wrigley *et al.*, 1967; Newbould & Shoesmith, 1974) did experiment with the creation of subject-based common tests, studies that looked at their performance alongside general ability tests tended to favour the latter rather than the former. It was found to be very hard to avoid syllabus-specific bias with such subject-based common tests. For this reason general ability tests have tended to be used in UK studies of comparability of examination grades since the mid-1970s.

The other factor that tends to favour general ability tests over subject-specific tests is the requirement in common test comparability studies to avoid bias in favour of sub-groups of candidates. Although general ability tests may not be wonderful predictors of subject-specific attainments, they are less likely than subject-specific tests to introduce bias through factors such as their coverage of syllabus areas. Nevertheless, there are other kinds of bias that can arise through using general ability tests as the comparator, and in some comparability studies it has been shown, for example, that they can provide very different predictions concerning the attainment of male and female candidates (Willmott, 1977).

We will look in more detail at some of the specific uses of general ability tests in comparability research studies in later sections. However, it is worth noting at this point that this characteristic of the common test approach is one of the key factors that tends to divide those who favour and those who criticise this type of research. The advocates of the general ability approach often argue that public examinations are in many respects all measures of general academic ability. Even though such examinations are each matched to closely defined subject-based syllabuses and assessment procedures, the highly specific nature of these assessments starts to be diluted as marks are combined from different assessment elements and turned into the grades that are awarded for the overall performance in that examination. They also go on to argue that most users of such examinations results are mostly interested in the way in which they give them a general overview of the students' academic abilities.

On the other hand those whom are less convinced by this approach tend to point to what they see as a serious inconsistency in trying to equate different subject-based examination results on the basis of estimates of the students' general ability. They generally go on to argue that where examinations are attempting to assess highly specific achievements, which reflect more about the quality of the students' learning and motivation in response to specific teaching approaches, it is a complete nonsense to assume that knowledge about their general academic ability will allow judgements to be made about the accuracy of their subject-based examination grades.

This debate about the appropriateness, or otherwise, of the use of general ability tests as the benchmark measure in common test studies is really quite hard to resolve. From a statistical point of view, general ability tests do generally correlate in a positive way with subject-based examination grades. However, such correlations are not terribly high and often fall in the range 0.3 to 0.7, indicating that although there is usually some similarity between general ability test scores and subject-based achievement test results, the relationship is not especially strong, and so it needs to be treated cautiously in the clear knowledge that many other factors are contributing to both sets of scores and the similarities and differences between them.

Even in a study where a general ability common test can be shown to be correlating quite well with the examination results (say of 0.7) there is still potential for plenty of debate about what such a statistical relationship implies. On the one hand, it is possible to argue that because both measures are themselves to some extent unreliable, then the differences between candidates' scores on the two measures can be explained largely in terms of random 'error' factors. On the other hand, it is possible to argue that such differences could reflect highly significant aspects of the subject-based achievements of the candidates, such as teaching, learning and motivation effects, which are highly meaningful and are in great danger of being distorted if any scaling were to be undertaken based upon general ability estimates.

Such a situation can be argued to be just the same as the situation where an examination has separate externally assessed and teacher assessed elements (Cohen & Deale, 1977). Some argue that teacher assessed elements should be scaled to reflect patterns observable in the externally assessed elements (Smith, 1978). Others have argued vehemently that to do such a thing totally undermines the credibility of teacher assessed judgements, which have their own validity and should not be subjected to correction factors that are derived entirely from comparisons being made with very different forms of student assessment (Macintosh, 1986).

Even the application of non-linear (Goldstein & Cresswell, 1996) and multilevel models (see Chapter 10) will not resolve this debate. Even if they provide improvements in the way in which data from common test studies can be analysed, they cannot ultimately resolve the dilemma over how discrepancies between general ability and subject-specific scores are interpreted and treated.

Here it is difficult to see any movement in the state of this debate from the point in time nearly 30 years ago when Bardell, Forrest & Shoesmith (1978) wrote:

> ... to a large extent the... fairness of... [a common test] has to be subjective, since there is no way of distinguishing between biases in the monitor and the very differences in board standards which the exercise sets out to estimate.
>
> Bardell *et al.* (1978, p. 21)

6 An historical perspective on the use of the common test approach (1965 to 1985)

The period from 1965 to 1985 was undoubtedly the era during which the common test approach to comparability in England was most popular. This was also the period when the demand for comparability studies was arguably also at its highest point. There were during that period over 20 separate independent examining boards running CSE, O and A level and other public examinations. This high level of diversity of provision fuelled endless questions about the grades students were obtaining from different boards, subjects and types of examinations (Murphy & Torrance, 1988).

One major strand of comparability work at this time, emanated from the Examination and Test Research Unit (ETRU) at the National Foundation for Educational Research (NFER). That unit was established by the Schools Council to undertake work to support the establishment of the Certificate of Secondary Education (CSE) examinations, which were introduced in 1965. Comparability of assessment standards was the central preoccupation of the ETRU and the common test approach was used extensively by it in a series of investigations over a period of 12 years (Willmott, 1980). Many of the NFER studies used a general ability test as the point of comparison, although there was also some experimentation with subject-based common tests. In contrast, during the same period the GCE examining boards maintained a regular programme of inter-board comparability studies, which utilised a range of comparability research methods. Among the GCE board studies several used a common test approach, but unlike the NFER studies they often used subject attainment tests as the common element, and in quite a number of cases the subject attainment test was included as an integral part of the operational examinations (Bardell *et al.*, 1978).

The very early work by the ETRU in the 1960s involved NFER researchers working closely with the newly established CSE boards to help them to decide how to create appropriate grading standards for the new CSE examination (Willmott, 1980). In fact the very first ETRU comparability study involved the use of a general scholastic aptitude test, which was taken by a sample of CSE candidates sufficiently early in the year, so that the ETRU could compare the common test results with teachers' predicted grades before CSE grades were finalised. On the basis of early analysis letters were sent to the CSE boards 'offering suggestions for standards of grading'. Then later on in the study the CSE grades actually awarded were analysed using the original common test results.

On reviewing the reports of the early ETRU studies in the late 1960s it is clear how there was a recognition of some of the shortcomings of the common test approach. Several attempts were made to improve the appropriateness of the common test and different aptitude tests were tried, sometimes alongside specifically constructed subject-based attainment tests (Wrigley *et al.*, 1967; Skurnik & Connaughton, 1970). In general, any conclusions drawn from these early comparability studies were cautious and were presented alongside warnings about the assumptions upon which they were based. Overall the main aim was to help the CSE boards to establish reasonably comparable grading standards.

Willmott (1980) recalls how the context for comparability research changed in the early 1970s. By this time the relaxed attitude towards such work in the late 1960s had changed to stronger public concerns about the grading standards being employed in CSE, O level and A level examinations. This move towards 'high stake comparability research' threatened the fragile basis upon which common test studies could be regarded as delivering accurate and dependable findings.

> The later studies, however, took place in times of growing public scrutiny of the public examination system and the reference test method of studying comparability simply could not stand up to – and indeed was not designed to stand up to – detailed scrutiny.
>
> Willmott (1980, p. 35)

This dramatic turn in the fortunes of the common test approach to comparability research led to the NFER and the Schools Council abandoning this whole strand of research and resulted in the ETRU being disbanded in 1977.

During this same period the GCE boards continued with a range of inter-board comparability studies utilising a mixture of cross-moderation and common test approaches. Their work differed from that of the NFER group in so far as it utilised a wide range of research approaches (Bardell *et al.*, 1978). Another crucial difference between the GCE board studies and the NFER studies was that the board studies were conducted very much 'in-house' and were to inform those marking and grading the examinations being investigated. In contrast, the NFER studies were more public and led to quite a bit of press speculation about inadequacies in the standards of public examinations. Here we hit the problem of using an approach such as the common test approach to comparability in the knowledge that it has some major limitations that need to be taken into account in assessing any possible conclusions which might emerge from it. The simplicity of the approach can lead to some apparently simple conclusions about the comparability of examination grades – say between two different boards. However, a mass audience is more likely to latch on to the simple conclusions rather than the complicated caveats that might accompany them. It was this issue in particular that led to some fairly acrimonious exchanges between the NFER team and some examining board researchers.

> Dr. Willmott believes that it is better to produce results which may give rise to useful discussions of the assumptions, methodology and indeed the results themselves, than to consider that the problem is too difficult for study… You cannot do as Willmott has done and toss in results on a take-it-or-leave-it basis, much less over-interpret them. It is as if the Wright brothers had said, 'Our aeroplane doesn't fly yet but here is a pair of wings which you can use until it does'.
>
> Wood (1976)

As we have already noted the NFER team soon abandoned the common test approach after this exchange, and the GCE boards themselves started to rely much more on other methods for studying comparability from 1978 onwards (Forrest &

Shoesmith, 1985). It is particularly noticeable in the two published reviews of GCE board comparability work (Bardell *et al.*, 1978; Forrest & Shoesmith, 1985) how the emphasis moved strongly away from common test methods towards cross-moderation studies at this time.

7   The continued use of the common test approach (1986 to 2006)

It seems that claims that the common test approach to comparability of examinations in England died in the 1970s 'have been greatly exaggerated'. Right up until the current time this approach has continued to be used especially by researchers from the Curriculum, Evaluation and Management Centre (CEM), which was located successively at the Universities of Newcastle and Durham. Although this group has been the most prominent user of this approach in recent years, it would be wrong to give the impression that they have been the only users of it. Occasional studies of comparability undertaken by University of Cambridge Local Examinations Syndicate (UCLES) researchers have continued to utilise it in situations where they judge it to have value (e.g. Dexter & Massey, 2000; Massey *et al.*, 2003). In addition others with an interest in debates about possible changes in examination standards over time, such as lecturers in higher education, have from time to time undertaken ad-hoc studies based upon requiring their students to take the same subject-based test over a number of years (Hunt & Lawson, 1996; Tariq, 2002).

Many of the same arguments apply to these studies, and the approaches used are in many respects similar to those used in the 1965–1985 period. Clearly most of the researchers involved are now more aware of the shortcomings of this approach, and their reports frequently contain relevant provisos and references to the limitations of their findings. For example, a study of A level standards by the Curriculum, Evaluation and Management (CEM) Centre, conducted for the GCE boards, acknowledged the following:

> ...no single reference test relates in precisely the same way to all examinations and candidates from one examination may perform better on the reference test than candidates from another examination because working towards the examination is in some way a better preparation for the reference test. As a result scores on the reference test are not comparable for candidates entering the different examinations.
>
> GCE Examining Boards (1994)

In a more recent study Tymms *et al.* (2005) used the common test approach to look at evidence for changes over time during the period of office of the current Labour government. Figure 5 illustrates one aspect of their findings. Using data from their ALIS (A level information system) project they conducted various analyses to compare scores on a Test of Developed Abilities (TDA) with the A level grades obtained by the same students.

Figure 5 Mean UCAS grades achieved by students with a TDA score of 60

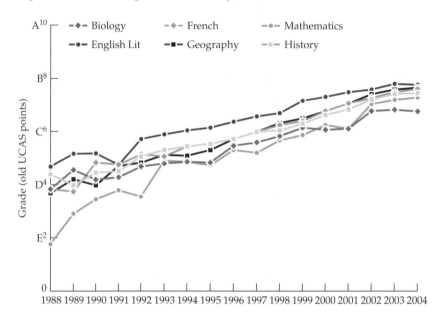

It is clear from Figure 5 that there has been a trend for students with the same score on the Test of Developed Ability (or the International Test of Developed Abilities, which they used before 2000) to achieve better A level results over this time period. Having discussed various possible explanations for this phenomenon, including the fact that it might be the result of better teaching, these authors conclude that:

> It is our view that A levels have generally become more leniently graded through a combination of syllabus change, modularisation and alterations to exam formats. In many ways that has been a good thing. It has allowed increasing numbers of candidates to access education to higher levels. But it has meant that the very top levels of attainment have been removed from A level.
>
> Tymms *et al.* (2005)

As with other common test studies the results from this study are amenable to all sorts of alternative interpretations. The authors themselves acknowledge the fact that causal explanations from the data represented in Figure 5 are far from straightforward. There are numerous possible factors that could have contributed to the trends, including syllabus changes, moves to modular assessments, improvements in teaching and pupil motivation and examination strategies, and indeed a modification of the general ability test itself, mid-way through the period. There is also the problem of their ALIS database containing samples of students who may not be representative, leading to the possibility that the trends reported here may not be reflected in the wider population of A level students.

So once again we have the common test approach yielding findings that on the face of it look straightforward, but that on closer inspection are far from simple to interpret. On what basis should we expect A level grades to mirror students' scores on tests of general ability? How wise is it to discount teaching and learning effects and other factors such as motivation in studies of this kind? Finally, is enough attention being paid to the warnings of earlier researchers in relation to factors such as bias in the common test towards sub-groups of students taking the examinations being compared? There are few satisfactory answers to these questions, and any future use of the common test approach will always have to be seen as potentially defective unless such matters are properly addressed.

8   Towards a better informed use of the common test approach

In this chapter we have reviewed the use of the common test approach to studying the comparability of public examinations in England, Wales and Northern Ireland over a period of more than 40 years. Like other approaches to studying comparability this approach has both strengths and weaknesses.

Looking back over the common test studies that have been conducted during this time period, it is possible to conclude that this method has contributed in significant ways to the highly intractable challenges that comparability research has posed.

Common test studies seem to be most effective when they are conducted in relatively relaxed situations where results can be interpreted carefully and in the full knowledge of the various possible factors that can distort their findings. They can never produce simple answers to complex questions about the comparability of exams. However, they can certainly contribute useful evidence, which can be scrutinised alongside other findings from other methods in an attempt to piece together a case about the comparability of grading standards in alternative examinations.

The key element in the debate about the suitability of this method is undoubtedly the nature of the relationship between the common test and the examinations being compared. If those using the findings have a strong belief that the common test results should provide a firm indication of the results that should be expected from the examinations, then there is a greater likelihood that the results will be seen as significant. The only other challenge to validity then is the second key issue of the extent to which the common test results avoid favouring one sub-set of candidates over another.

There is no such thing as an easy comparability question. Even a question about the relative standing of grades awarded for two parallel forms of the same syllabus can take us into complex discussions about teaching effects. It is, however, possible to identify the most challenging comparability questions, such as the comparability of grades awarded for very different subjects, French and chemistry say, or the comparability of grades awarded for the same subject but 30 years apart. A strength of the common test approach is that it does provide a method for addressing even the most challenging of comparability questions. However, ascribing a sensible level of confidence to the findings of such a study is still a demanding prospect! So we can use common general ability test methods to address both types of challenging comparability question, but the results may not move us very far towards answers in which we can have high levels of confidence.

9   Conclusion

In conclusion, it is possible to state the following as a summary of the key arguments covered in this chapter.

1. Common test methods are worth considering for inclusion in comparability studies, as long as their results can be treated with caution and due attention can be given to the various known threats to the validity of any apparent findings.

2. Those employing this approach must have a degree of confidence in the fact that the common test being used provides a worthwhile prediction of the results expected from the examinations to be compared.

3. Statistical checks need to be applied to the results of common test studies to ensure that the relationship between common test scores and examination results produces reasonably parallel regression lines.

4. Another condition that needs to be met is that the common test does not unduly favour any sub-group of candidates over others in such a way that between-examination comparisons are distorted.

5. In all studies of this kind it is necessary to indicate which definition of comparability is being used. This will help to clarify the relevance, say, of the use of a test of general ability, which may only be regarded as appropriate if comparability is assumed to involve students with the same level of general ability getting the same grades in subject-based public examinations.

6. All reports of future common tests comparability studies should address points 2–5 above, and include an explicit discussion of each issue in order that any users of the findings are fully aware of all major threats to the validity of any conclusions drawn.

A broad conclusion to this review is that things have changed very little since Newbould & Massey (1979) carried out their comprehensive review of this approach from which they concluded that 'Common tests would seem to look more attractive monitors of standards than they really are' (Newbould & Massey, 1979, p. 51).

None of what has happened in the years since that report was written has changed the appropriateness of their overall conclusion that:

> Perhaps the common test, from this particular standpoint, is on balance, harmful, for whilst it is a ready vehicle for emphasising common ground, and hence implying a similarity of examinations, it may tempt people into adopting over-simplistic views of the nature and meaning of the concept of comparability.
>
> Newbould & Massey (1979, p. 51)

Those administering and researching public examinations need to be highly aware of the impact of their actions on public perceptions (Warmington & Murphy, 2004; 2007) and common test approaches to comparability can be seen to be at risk of encouraging oversimplistic views about comparability. Our very sophisticated system of public examinations demands a similarly sophisticated basis for judging the dependability and meaningfulness of candidate results. An approach based upon the common test method isn't likely to ever be described as sophisticated. Comparability studies involve highly complex comparisons between areas of educational achievement, which have little in common with each other. Such comparisons need us to cope with levels of uncertainty found in expert judgements (Murphy, 2004), and an acceptance that many aspects of educational achievement transcend simplistic comparisons on a uni-dimensional scale.

References

Baird, J., Cresswell, M.J., & Newton, P. (2000). Would the *real* gold standard please step forward? *Research Papers in Education, 15*, 213–229.

Baird, J., Fearnley, A., Fowles, D., Jones, B., Morfidi, E., & While, D. (2001). *Tiering in the GCSE.* London: Joint Council for General Qualifications.

Bardell, G.S., Forrest, G.M., & Shoesmith, D.J. (1978). *Comparability in GCE: A review of the boards' studies, 1964–1977.* Manchester: Joint Matriculation Board on behalf of the GCE Examining Boards.

Black, P. (1998). *Testing: Friend or foe? Theory and practice of assessment and testing.* London: Falmer Press.

Broadfoot, P.M. (1996). *Education, assessment and society: A sociological analysis.* Buckingham: Open University Press.

Brownlee, K. (1965). *Statistical theory and methodology in science and engineering.* New York: Wiley.

Cohen, L., & Deale, R.N. (1977). *Assessment by teachers in examinations at 16+.* Schools Council Examinations Bulletin 37. London: Evans/Methuen

Dexter, T., & Massey, A., (2000, July). *Conceptual issues arising from a comparability study relating IGCSE grading standards with those of GCSE via a reference test using a multilevel model.* Paper presented at the 22nd biennial conference of the Society for Multivariate Analysis in the Behavioural Sciences at the London School of Economics, London.

Forrest, G.M., & Shoesmith, D.J. (1985). *A second review of GCE comparability studies.* Manchester: Joint Matriculation Board on behalf of the GCE Examining Boards.

GCE Examining Boards. (1994). *Comparing examination boards and syllabuses at A level:*

Students' grades, attitudes and perceptions of classroom processes. Executive summary of a report commissioned by the GCE Examining Boards. Belfast: Northern Ireland Council for the Curriculum, Examinations and Assessment.

Gipps, C. (1994). *Beyond testing: Towards a theory of educational assessment.* London: Falmer Press.

Goldstein, H., & Cresswell, M.J. (1996). The comparability of different subjects in public examinations: A theoretical and practical critique. *Oxford Review of Education, 22,* 435–441.

Hunt, D.N., & Lawson, D.A. (1996). Trends in mathematical competence of A level students on entry to university. *Teaching Mathematics and its Applications, 15*(4), 167–173.

Macintosh, H. (1986). The sacred cows of coursework. In C. Gipps (Ed.), *The GCSE: An uncommon examination.* Bedford Way Papers 29. London: University of London Institute of Education.

Massey, A., Green, S., Dexter, T., & Hamnett, L. (2003). *Comparability of national tests over time: Key stage test standards between 1996 and 2001.* London: Qualifications and Curriculum Authority.

Meadows, M. (2003). *Comparability of the biology and human biology routes to GCSE biology A 2002.* Unpublished Research Report, Assessment and Qualifications Alliance.

Murphy, R.J.L. (2004). *Grades of uncertainty.* London: Association of Teachers and Lecturers.

Murphy, R.J.L., & Torrance, H. (1988). *The changing face of educational assessment.* Milton Keynes: Open University Press.

Murphy, R.J.L., Wilmut, J., & Wood, R. (1996). Monitoring A level standards: Tests, grades and other approximations. *The Curriculum Journal, 7,* 279–291.

Newbould, C.A., & Massey, A.J. (1979). *Comparability using a common element.* Occasional Publication 7. Cambridge: Test Development and Research Unit.

Newbould, C.A., & Shoesmith, D.J. (1974). *Technical drawing reference test 1973.* Appendix A to the Report on the 16+ Feasibility Study in Technical Drawing by the East Anglian Examination Board and University of Cambridge Local Examinations Syndicate. Cambridge: University of Cambridge Local Examinations Syndicate.

Newton, P.E. (1997). Examining standards over time. *Research Papers in Education, 12,* 227–248.

Nuttall, D.L. (1979). The myth of comparability. *Journal of National Association of Inspectors and Advisors, 11*, 16–18.

Skurnik, L.S., & Connaughton, I.M. (1970). *The 1967 CSE monitoring experiment.* Schools Council Working Paper 30. Evans/Methuen Education.

Skurnik, L.S., & Hall, J. (1969). *The 1966 CSE monitoring experiment.* Schools Council Working Paper 21. London: Her Majesty's Stationery Office.

Smith, G.A. (1978). *JMB Experience of the moderation of internal assessments.* Occasional Publication 38. Manchester: Joint Matriculation Board.

Stringer, N. (2005). *Response to scrutiny report for GCSE PE and PE games.* Unpublished Research Report, Assessment and Qualifications Alliance.

Tariq, V.N. (2002). A decline in numeracy skills among bioscience undergraduates. *Journal of Biological Education, 36*(2), 76–83.

Tymms, P., Coe, R., & Merrell, C. (2005, April). *Standards in English schools: Changes since 1997 and the impact of government policies and initiatives.* A report for *The Sunday Times*, London.

Warmington, P., & Murphy, R. (2004). Could do better? Media depictions of UK assessment results. *Journal of Education Policy, 19*, 285–300.

Warmington, P., & Murphy, R. (2007). Read all about it! UK news media coverage of A level results. *Policy Futures in Education, 5*(1), 70–83.

Wikstrom, C. (2005). Grade stability in a criterion-referenced grading system: The Swedish example. *Assessment in Education, 12*, 25–144.

Willmott, A.S. (1977). *CSE and GCE grading standards: The 1973 comparability study.* Schools Council Research Study. London: Macmillan Education.

Wilmott, A.S. (1980). *Twelve years of examinations research: ETRU 1965–1977.* London: Schools Council.

Wood, R. (1976, July 30). Your chemistry equals my French. *The Times Educational Supplement.*

Wrigley, J., Sparrow, F.H., & Inglis, F.L. (1967). *Standards in CSE and GCE (English and mathematics).* Schools Council Working Paper 9. London: Her Majesty's Stationery Office.

COMMENTARY ON CHAPTER 8

Robert Coe, Peter Tymms and Carol Fitz-Gibbon

In his chapter on common test methods, Roger Murphy presents a critique of the approach. Though he does acknowledge strengths as well as weaknesses of the method, his view seems to be that the latter are more pertinent. Our view is that the weaknesses of this method have been exaggerated and some of its potential strengths overlooked. Furthermore, a few of the criticisms presented in the chapter are simply unjustified. In this commentary we attempt to redress this imbalance and defend the use of common test methods. There are six specific issues on which we comment.

The worst form of comparability research?

Winston Churchill said that 'democracy is the worst form of government, except all those other forms that have been tried from time to time'.[1] As in government, so in comparability research; an approach that is easy to criticise may nevertheless be the best we can do. Like any method applied to the complex business of trying to compare standards across different examinations, common test methods have their limitations. If we use them we must be aware of these limitations, be sensitive to the kinds of assumptions required for their application and be cautious about any claims we make.

But whatever the problems of the common test approach may be, the alternatives to using these methods (including not asking any questions about comparability in the first place) all have their problems too. Murphy seems to acknowledge this, stating that 'all approaches to studying the comparability of grading standards have major limitations', and that 'it is all too easy to dwell on the shortcomings'. However, it is hard to resist the impression that his view of common test methods is, on balance, negative. His position is indicated by describing the approach as 'potentially defective' and confirmed by a concluding quotation that it is, 'on balance, harmful'. What is less clear is whether common test approaches are worse than other statistical methods, whether all statistical approaches, including common tests, are inferior to judgement methods, or even whether all attempts to address the comparability of different examinations by whatever method are 'on balance, harmful'.

In fact, none of these positions is helpful. We cannot talk about the limitations of a method per se, but about the kinds of claims, interpretations and uses it can validly support. On its own a method is neither valid nor invalid; it depends how its results are interpreted. Murphy seems to acknowledge this, accusing common test methods of 'encouraging oversimplistic views' and advising that they are 'worth considering… as long as their results can be treated with caution'. However, he fails to give any examples of uses of the method that he believes to be appropriate.

There are different conceptions of comparability

The issue of the different meanings of the word 'comparability' is treated rather briefly in the chapter, but is a crucial one for understanding the appropriateness of using common test methods. This matter is explored in the commentary on Chapter 4.

Murphy's specification of the requirements for the use of common tests that there should be 'reasonably parallel regression lines' and that the test should not 'unduly favour any sub-group' suggests that he sees their use as limited to comparing standards on examinations that are essentially equivalent forms, measuring the same construct in the same ways. These conditions might be met, for example, in comparing two examinations in the same subject from different boards, but may or may not be true for two examinations in different subjects.

However, other parts of the chapter seem to acknowledge that a common test might also be used within a 'value-added' conception of comparability, as, for example, in the assumptions underpinning conclusion 5. In such a view of comparability, if the common test were a measure of prior attainment or ability, a regression model could be used to estimate the gains made by similar students in different examinations. If students consistently achieve more in one examination from the same starting point, we might conclude, *ceteris paribus*, that it is more leniently graded, i.e. easier. Comparability here is defined in terms of equal gains. This conception of comparability does not depend on parallel lines or subgroup invariance, though it does require us to define what we mean by 'similar students' and to make the additional assumption that other factors (quality of teaching, effort applied, etc.) are either equal or irrelevant. The point here is not that these alternative assumptions are less problematic – they may well not be – but simply that they are different.

Yet another conception of comparability would see the common test as the linking construct in terms of which a set of examinations may be compared. In this case, the requirements are different again. An example of this conception of comparability may be found in the study by Tymms, *et al.* (2005), referred to by Murphy. His suggestion, that factors such as 'syllabus changes, moves to modular assessments, improvements in teaching and pupil motivation and examination strategies' might account for the changes, may have some validity, but does not alter the interpretation in this case. In a 'construct comparability' conception, examinations in different years are compared on the basis of the level of the linking construct, general ability, to which particular grades correspond. Whatever the reason for increasingly higher grades to be awarded to candidates of the same ability – including any of those mentioned above – it remains the case that the award of the same grade denotes progressively lower abilities (as measured by the common test) each year.

Parallelism may not be a requirement

Murphy argues that if the regression lines for two examinations are not reasonably parallel then that 'poses a serious threat to the validity of any conclusions drawn from a study of this kind.' This is because 'the common test may have different relevance for the candidates in the two groups being compared.' In his Figure 2, the gradients of the two regression lines shown are so different as to be a caricature of the kinds of graphs that are routinely found. To suggest that such a finding is 'far from uncommon' is misleading since such an excessive difference would indeed be extremely uncommon.

However, if a common test is interpreted as a linking construct, even such a difference might not matter at all. Consider the hypothetical graph shown in Figure 1.

Figure 1

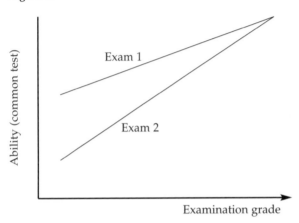

Here the regression lines are clearly not parallel. This kind of situation would arise, for example, if candidates for Exam 1 had a more limited range of ability than those for Exam 2, but the same range of grades was awarded for each. However, whether this means that the common test has 'different relevance' for the two may be questioned; it may simply be a case of some stretching of the scale on which examinations are reported. With a 'linking construct' interpretation of comparability, the question we might ask about the two examinations is: 'What level of ability corresponds to the award of a particular grade in each examination?' The fact that the lines are not parallel is no barrier to asking – or answering – this question. We therefore believe that Murphy's conclusion 3 is unsound.

Statistical significance and the size of the difference

Murphy gives an example from 1969 of a comparison between CSE English examinations from different boards which failed to show a statistically significant difference between them. He goes on to say that such studies 'will never give highly accurate outcomes', and that it is 'foolish to expect high levels of precision from research studies which seek to compare different examinations.'

In fact, of course, given a large enough sample, one can achieve any level of accuracy desired. The fact that a mean-on-mean comparison with n=9 failed to reach the traditional (but quite arbitrary) level of statistical significance (by this method) conceals the fact that there appear to be some very substantial differences between these boards. Interestingly, the converse of this error is made by Newbould & Massey (1979) who apply the common test method to comparisons of different boards. They draw a series of regression lines that to the eye seem very close to parallel, but, because they have a sufficiently large sample, are shown to be statistically 'significantly' different. A clear distinction between statistical and educational significance is important.

How strong a correlation is required?

Murphy suggests that correlations below about 0.7 are too low for the common test method to be valid. It is not clear, however, what the justification is for the choice of this particular value. Correlations of the order of 0.7 are common in value-added analyses, but this does not seem a very good reason for judging them acceptable.

One issue that does not appear to have been considered is the effect of any range restrictions. For example, some of the correlations cited by Coe (1999) do indeed appear quite low. However, if one corrects them for the restricted range of candidates taking these A level examinations, a measured correlation of 0.4 turns out to be equivalent to about 0.7 in the full population, in terms of the strength of the relationship between the two variables.

A second issue relates to the reliability of the examinations – lower reliabilities produce lower correlations and since no tests are perfect all the reported correlations underestimate the underlying relationships.

But neither of these issues helps in answering the question about what is an acceptable correlation. A starting point would have to be a statement as to what type of comparability was being addressed. Then a power calculation could follow which took off from a further statement of the kinds of errors which would be acceptable in any proposed study. To our knowledge this kind of calculation has never been carried out.

Publication is democratic

Murphy makes a number of references in the chapter to the problems of making research on comparability available to a 'mass audience'. He argues that caveats, subtleties and 'our very sophisticated system of public examinations' are hard to convey in public reports, and these studies 'seem to be most effective when they are conducted in relatively relaxed situations', presumably away from the kind of public controversy that often seems to accompany publication of such studies.

We would certainly agree that researchers should make the limitations of their work clear and not oversimplify, giving due attention to threats to validity and alternative explanations. However, it would be wrong to interpret this as meaning that research on comparability should not be made available to a mass audience. The fact that the media may sometimes misrepresent findings is not a reason to confine presentation of them to internal awarding body reports or to seminars attended by only the enlightened few. Such secrecy would be against the academic ideal of open critical debate and the democratic principle of transparency in public institutions. It would also deny those researchers what in our experience have been some of the most valuable insights into these issues that arise from a more public debate.

Endnote

1   Speech in the House of Commons, 11 November 1947.

References

Coe, R. (1999, September). *Changes in examination grades over time: Is the same worth less?* Paper presented at the British Educational Research Association annual conference, Brighton.

Newbould, C.A., & Massey, A.J. (1979). *Comparability using a common element.* Occasional Publication 7. Cambridge. Test Development and Research Unit.

Tymms, P., Coe, R., & Merrell, C. (2005, April). *Standards in English schools: Changes since 1997 and the impact of government policies and initiatives.* A report for *The Sunday Times*, London.

RESPONSE TO COMMENTARY ON CHAPTER 8

Roger Murphy

The commentary on this chapter comes from a group of individuals who are recognisable as enthusiastic users of the common test approach. In my view they have both misrepresented and misunderstood the very serious critique of this method, which I have presented. I did not attempt to compare all comparability approaches, but if I had I certainly would not have agreed with their implied view that the common test approach is 'the best we can do'.

In the commentary I am portrayed as not wanting comparability questions to be addressed (wrong), not wanting research findings to be made publicly available (wrong), and being dogmatic about the statistical properties required of common test studies (again wrong – where for example was I supposed to have said that common test with examination correlations must be higher than 0.7!). My stance in this chapter, and elsewhere, continues to be that assessment data, including statistical assessment research studies, can have serious limitations and that these need to be closely attended to, when drawing conclusions, whether about the findings of comparability research studies or even about the examination results of a single student (Murphy, 2004).

These commentators appear wedded to a view of comparability based entirely upon regarding the 'ability' of students as being the most important deciding factor when it comes to comparing their performance on different examinations. Coe (1999) illustrates this view, when he states that 'it matters less whether the award of each grade represents the same achievement than whether it signifies the same level of general ability in the candidate'. The implication here is that if two examinations give equal grades to students, who demonstrate similar levels of achievement, then those grades should be seen as inappropriate if the levels of general ability of the students getting them are different. Thus one difference between us is that I view public examinations as being measures of educational achievement in relation to highly specific areas of the curriculum, whereas they see such grades as some kind of proxy for students' levels of general ability. This is a very limiting stance to adopt because it does not leave scope for students to achieve more as a result of good teaching or their own hard work – the very essence of what educators are striving for!

For this reason I do continue to stand by the list of issues which I think are essential for future users of the common test approach. Comparability research is about so much more than obsessively checking the general ability levels of students in order to compare examination grades. This commentary depends fundamentally on a 'linking concept', which is in effect no more than the old Spearman/Binet/Burt belief in 'basic intelligence' being the fundamental principle around which all education systems should be arranged. Thankfully educational practices in the 21st century have moved well away from that hugely limiting view of the world, and comparability research has much more to offer than that view has ever provided or ever will provide.

References

Coe, R. (1999, September). *Changes in examination grades over time: Is the same worth less?* Paper presented at the British Educational Research Association annual conference, Brighton.

Murphy, R.J.L. (2004). *Grades of uncertainty*. London: Association of Teachers and Lecturers.

9

COMMON EXAMINEE METHODS

Robert Coe

Abstract

Aim

The chapter aims to provide a full description of the methods that have been used to monitor comparability between different examinations taken concurrently by the same candidate: common examinee methods. Criticisms that have been made of these methods are presented and discussed in relation to different interpretations and conceptions of comparability.

Definition of comparability

Three conceptions of comparability are considered: *performance*, in which comparability is defined in terms of observed phenomena in relation to specific criteria; *statistical*, in which comparability depends on an estimate of the chances of a particular grade being achieved; and *construct*, in which examinations are seen as indicating different levels of a common linking construct.

Comparability methods

A number of methods are described, including simple comparisons of the grades achieved in a pair of examinations (subject pairs analysis); the aggregation of such paired comparisons to compare a larger set of examinations; the Nuttall *et al.* (1974) 'unbiased mean total' method; Kelly's (1976a) method; analysis of variance; average marks scaling; Rasch modelling.

History of use

Most of these methods have been used since the 1970s, though their prominence appears to be less now than in those early days, at least in England.

Strengths and weaknesses

Some of these methods require specific assumptions, such as equal intervals between grades. Other assumptions (for example, that examinations must be uni-dimensional, or that differences in factors such as teaching quality or motivation must be ignored) may depend on how the methods are applied and interpreted. Hence, evaluating the strengths and weaknesses of the methods is complex. Most of the methods considered, however, are capable of valid interpretation under the right conditions.

Conclusion

Common examinee methods should be part of the systematic monitoring of standards across syllabuses, boards and subjects, though, like all comparability methods, they should be used with caution and judgement. However, their main value is probably in informing the interpretation and use of examination results for purposes such as selection.

1 Introduction

Common examinee methods – comparing the achievements of the same examinees in different examinations – have been at the heart of debates about comparability of standards for many years. Some of these methods are quite simple to do and their results may also seem seductively simple to interpret. If common candidates typically and routinely get higher grades in one subject than they do in another, surely this means that the latter is harder?

On further reflection, however, such simplistic interpretations are both unclear and unjustified, at least in a strict sense. A number of writers on this subject have provided strong critiques of such over simplistic interpretations. From these it is clear that there may be many reasons why candidates achieve different grades in different subjects, apart from the obvious one that some are harder. It is also apparent that defining precisely what we mean by 'harder' in this context is very problematic.

Nevertheless, the fact appears to remain that the grades achieved in different subjects by the same candidates are in some cases robustly and substantively different. Unless we can find some convincing explanation for this phenomenon we are left with what appears to be an anomalous and even undesirable situation.

In this chapter I will first outline the general approach of common examinee methods with some specific examples. The different methods that have been used are then presented in detail, followed by an outline of the general criticisms that have been made of them. In trying to evaluate these criticisms it is then necessary to consider a number of different ways in which the concept of 'comparability' might be interpreted, and hence the different ways in which words like 'difficulty' or 'standards' might be understood. I also try to explore their logic and assumptions in relation to specific uses that have been made of their results. A full defence of the methods against these criticisms is then presented.

In trying to structure this chapter it has been impossible to find a way of presenting all the key ideas in logical sequence. In order to discuss any of the strengths and weaknesses of common examinee methods one must first have an understanding of what those methods are. This requires some understanding of the kinds of assumptions that must be made to use them, and hence of their appropriateness. However, one cannot really discuss the critiques of these methods without first making some conceptual clarifications, the justifications for which require an appreciation of some of the confusions that have arisen in using, interpreting and criticising the methods which is hard to do before the methods have been presented in detail. The reader may also find it helpful to refer to the commentary on Chapter 4, in which the different conceptions of 'comparability' are discussed. It is hoped that the resulting structure of the chapter is not too confusing or incoherent.

2 Background to common examinee methods

2.1 Origins of these methods

The use by qualification awarding bodies of statistical comparisons to inform the process of setting and monitoring grade standards has a long history, and common examinee methods were among the first to be used. Certainly as far back as the early 1970s, subject pairs analysis (SPA) was being widely used (Nuttall *et al.*, 1974). Indeed, such methods are still used today, both to set grade standards and to monitor comparability, though the emphasis placed on statistical comparisons across subjects in setting thresholds for the award of particular grades in England, Wales and Northern Ireland may be less (Jones, 2003).

This decline may be traced to the growing emphasis through the 1980s on criterion referencing and the belief that standards could be specified and described in absolute terms without having to depend on comparing performance to statistical norms. Criticisms of common examinee methods began to appear with their earliest uses (Bardell *et al.*, 1978), but a flurry of criticisms of the methods and assumptions of SPA (e.g. Willmott, 1995; Alton and Pearson, 1996; Goldstein and Cresswell, 1996; Newton, 1997) emerged in England in the mid-1990s, perhaps in response to some high profile uses of the method (Fitz-Gibbon & Vincent, 1994; Dearing, 1996).

Many of these critical authors were associated with the examining boards, though some were also users of the method (e.g. Sparkes, 2000). By the end of the 1990s a consensus appeared to emerge among the awarding bodies in England, Wales and Northern Ireland that the problems of these statistical methods for establishing comparability were so great that, as in the subtitle of Newton's (1997) paper, 'statistical techniques do not make the grade'. Instead, the use of examiners' judgements was held to provide a basis for ensuring comparability (Cresswell, 1996).

Although common examinee methods have most often been used in comparing different subjects, they have by no means been limited to this. They have, for example, also been applied to comparisons of different syllabuses in the same subject, or of different examining boards or even of different modules or units within a syllabus (e.g. Bardell *et al.*, 1978; Backhouse, 1978; Forrest & Vickerman, 1982). Nevertheless, most features of the methods can be well illustrated by considering the case of subject comparisons and for the sake of simplicity most of the discussion in this chapter will refer to that case.

2.2 Outline of the general common examinee approach

All the methods described in this chapter broadly share the same underlying logic. They all set out to provide some estimate of the relative 'difficulty' of different subjects or examinations taken at the same time. They all compare the achievement of a given candidate in one examination with that same candidate's performance in one or more other examinations, and then to aggregate such comparisons across all available candidates. All these methods appear to rest on the assumption that if all examinations were equally difficult, other things being equal, one would expect that the grades a candidate is likely to achieve should not depend on which particular examinations they take. Implicit in this must be some rationale for comparing different subjects, though such a rationale often seems implicit rather than explicit. In order to understand what is meant by comparability, we must explicate this notion in rather more detail.

An example: subject pairs analysis

Probably the most widely used common examinee method is SPA. Indeed a number of critics of the general approach have taken this method as a representative example of the whole set of methods. In fact there are a number of different versions of SPA (see below) but it may help to describe the logic of one version to illustrate the general method.

If we pick two subjects to compare we can consider all candidates who have taken both. We then simply calculate the difference between the mean grade achieved by those same candidates in each subject. If they typically achieve better grades in one than the other we may say that the former is 'easier', the latter 'harder' – though precisely what these words mean in this context will be discussed at some length below.

A specific example[1] will illustrate the logic of this method, using data from the National Pupil Database for England. In 2004, 583,300 candidates entered both English and mathematics GCSE examinations. Table 1 shows the percentage of this group that achieved each of the available grades. If we assign each grade the value shown in the table (making the assumption that the intervals between grades are equal, both within and between subjects), we can see that for these candidates the average grade achieved in English was 4.76, compared with 4.46 in mathematics. In other words, the same candidates typically achieved 0.3 of a grade better in their English examination than in their mathematics. As these were the same people in both examinations, we know that characteristics such as their prior attainment, gender, social background and the type of school they attended are matched perfectly, so presumably none of these factors can account for the difference.

Table 1 Percentage achieving each grade

Grade	Value	Percentage achieving that grade in English	Mathematics
U	0	1.7	3.0
G	1	2.4	3.5
F	2	5.7	8.7
E	3	11.0	14.9
D	4	19.3	17.1
C	5	25.5	22.0
B	6	19.2	18.3
A	7	11.5	8.1
A*	8	3.7	4.4

One possible remaining explanation of this difference is that the mathematics examination was more 'severely graded' than the English, and it might be tempting to conclude that this seems the most obvious explanation. However, it might be that the quality of teaching experienced by those candidates in mathematics was not as good as in English; or they might simply have enjoyed English more and so worked harder. Either way, they would have genuinely learned and achieved more and so deserved their better grades. A number of other explanations are possible for this phenomenon and will be discussed below. Moreover, there are some significant conceptual problems with the meaning of terms like 'harder', and several alternative ways of calculating this difference. Hence it would be fair to say the phenomenon is rather more problematic than it first appears.

One specific problem is that even if we believe we can interpret the result as showing that mathematics is harder than English, we have really only shown that this is so for the group of candidates who sat both examinations. In the case of this particular subject pair the problem may not seem too great since 93% of those who entered any GCSE examination took both mathematics and English. For other pairs, however, it seems a good deal more serious. For example, both physics and media studies GCSEs had substantial entries (43,000 and 35,000 candidates respectively), but fewer than 1,300 candidates nationally entered both these subjects. Knowing that for this small proportion, physics was 0.3 of a grade harder than media studies does not seem to tell us much about the relative difficulties for all those who entered (or who might have chosen to enter) each subject.

A further problem is that the relative difficulty of the two subjects calculated in this way varies substantially for different sub-groups. For example, if the comparison between mathematics and English is limited to female candidates who took both subjects, the difference increases to 0.6 of a grade. For males, the difference is only 0.04 of a grade. In other words, for male candidates mathematics and English were about equally difficult, while for females mathematics was substantially harder. When both sexes are combined we get an averaged estimate of the difference in difficulty between the two subjects. It seems counterintuitive that the relative difficulty of two subjects should depend on the population of candidates who happened to take them, rather than being a feature of the examinations themselves. Different estimates of relative difficulty for different sub-groups present a challenge to our understanding of what we mean by 'difficulty', as well as forcing us to consider carefully the sample of candidates on which our estimates are based and to ask of what population it is (or should be) representative. We will return to a discussion of these issues below in the context of criticisms that have been made of the approach.

The appeal of the method

Despite these problems, this kind of approach has a strong appeal. By comparing performance in a particular subject with that same candidate's performance in their other subjects, common examinee methods provide an obvious and superficially compelling control for differences in the general characteristics of individual candidates. Any factor that is a general feature of the individual candidate, such as their prior attainment, gender, social and ethnic background or 'general' ability is automatically matched perfectly. This also applies to any characteristics of the school which the candidate attended, such as its funding status (independent vs. state) or the social, gender and academic mix of its students. Of course, factors that are specific to that candidate in a particular examination, such as motivation or the quality of teaching experienced, are not controlled for.

Common examinee methods generally require no other data to be collected, and no matching with other datasets;[2] hence they may be possible when other methods are not. There is no need to worry about how reliable the measures of any covariates are, since they need not be directly measured. The lack of any reference test (or the use of other covariates) avoids the objection that results of comparisons may be sensitive to the particular kind of test used, or to arbitrary decisions about what variables to include in the model. And of course in practice which variables are included in such models is often not so much a matter of decision as of making the best of what is available.

The best way to illustrate the appeal of the method may be with an example of its application. Analysis conducted by the Advanced Level Information System (Alis, 2004) on A level results over a ten-year period shows that on average, students who take psychology A level achieve 0.9 grades higher in that subject than comparable students who take chemistry.[3] This is a sizeable difference, especially given its consistency over such a long period. One of the main uses of A level grades is as an entrance qualification to higher education. Suppose an admissions tutor in, say, history or economics has to choose between two otherwise equivalent candidates with the same grades, one of whom has taken chemistry, the other psychology. Should the differences in typical performance in these subjects be taken into account?

It seems reasonable to assume that an admissions tutor in an unrelated subject is not particularly interested in the specific skills accredited by these examinations, but interprets them as an indicator of a student's generalisable capacity for learning in other academic contexts. In this case, it might be true that psychology has been better taught than chemistry; candidates in the former might genuinely deserve their better grades. But if so, the higher grades may not reflect a greater capacity for future learning in a different context. Equally, students who chose psychology may have had a special talent or passion for it and so again deserve their higher grades, but again these qualities may not transfer to their future learning in a different context. We can carry on trying to think of reasons why students might have done so much better in one subject than the other, but in all cases the interpretation seems to be the same. Whatever the reasons for better performance, if we want to get a fair indication of a candidate's suitability for a non-overlapping course, those grades in psychology should be reduced by 0.9 to make them comparable with chemistry.

If the logic of this argument is accepted then there is a compelling case for interpreting the statistical differences from common examinee methods as indicating something about the relative value of grades achieved in different subjects. Whether we might want to say that chemistry is 'harder' than psychology is more problematic.

3   Detailed explanation of the different common examinee methods

All common examinee methods estimate some kind of statistical difference between the grades achieved in one subject and the grades achieved by the same candidates in one or more other subject(s). Comparisons may be limited to those achieving a particular grade in one of the subjects, or they may involve some kind of averaging process. There may also be an attempt to quantify the size of the difference. Within these broad similarities, however, there are a large number of different variations of the method.

3.1 Subject pairs analysis and its variants

Pair-wise comparisons of two subjects

The simplest version of all common examinee comparability methods is to consider only those candidates who have taken a particular pair of examinations. For each candidate we could determine whether they have achieved the same grade in each or, if not, in which subject they have done better. Simply counting the proportion of candidates in each category would form the basis of a comparison between the two subjects. An example of this approach can be found in an early report by the UK GCE Examination Boards (1971) which used the fact that in those days candidates might enter more than one board's examination in the same subject.

It may be, however, that, rather than making an overall comparison between subjects, we wish to focus on the performance of candidates who achieved a particular grade in one or other of them. For example, we could consider all candidates who achieved a grade C in Subject 1 and calculate the proportion who achieved the same grade or better in Subject 2, then compare this with the equivalent proportion when the subjects are reversed. This approach is described by Fearnley (1998) as the 'by grade' method used by the Northern Examinations and Assessment Board (NEAB), based on 'conditional cumulative percentages of candidates by grade' (method A, p. 13). This method therefore ignores all candidates who did not achieve a grade C in at least one of the two subjects in order to limit the comparison to this grade.

An intermediate approach, which focuses on a particular grade but slightly less narrowly (Fearnley's method C), is to consider all candidates entering both subjects and calculate the cumulative percentage achieving each grade in each subject. At each grade the percentages can be compared. This method (described by Fearnley, 1998, as 'marginal cumulative percentages of grades') allows a comparison to be made at a particular grade, but includes in the calculation the results of all candidates who achieved at least that grade in either subject.

The methods described so far depend on the ordinal property of grades, but not on any interval property. This, of course, is a strength, since assigning numbers to grades is essentially arbitrary and may misrepresent the relative sizes of the gaps between them (Fowles, 1998). However, a weakness of such ordinal approaches is that they are hard to aggregate. If we are prepared to make a stronger 'interval' assumption about examination grades, then we may be able to make comparisons that can more easily be combined.

One way to do this is to compute an average difference in the grades achieved in the two subjects. These methods may be described as 'interval' approaches since any such average will be sensitive to the sizes of the gaps between grades, not just to their order. The conventional way to do this is to convert examination grades into a numerical scale using consecutive integer values (e.g. at GCSE, U=0, G=1, F=2, ..., B=6, A=7, A*=8). For each candidate who took a particular pair of subjects we can calculate the difference between their grade in Subject 1 and Subject 2. The mean of these differences across all candidates is a measure of the difference in 'difficulty' of the pair, in grade units. This method has been widely used to compute pair-wise comparisons (e.g. Forrest & Smith, 1972; Nuttall *et al.*, 1974, Ch. III). Forrest & Vickerman (1982, p. 9) note that changing the numerical scale to one that reflects the different mark intervals between grade boundaries produces results which are 'almost indistinguishable from those obtained by the simple method', suggesting that the interval assumption is not too problematic for these methods.

It is also possible to limit this average to those candidates who achieved a particular grade in each subject in order to compare the subjects specifically at that grade. This is Fearnley's (1998) method B, 'conditional mean grade by grade'.

A problem with all these variants of SPA, however, is that we can compare only two examinations at a time. One subject can be compared with a second, or indeed with any other in which it has candidates in common, but the result would be a set of pair-wise comparisons between subjects, rather than any kind of overall comparison of a larger set of subjects. Each of these pair-wise comparisons would be limited to the group of candidates who had taken both subjects; for most pairs, this group is unlikely to be representative of all those who take either subject. For example, a comparison between, say, Latin and media studies could be based only on those who had taken both subjects; other than by considering this small and atypical group we would not be able to say anything about the relative 'difficulty' of these two subjects.

A further limitation of such pair-wise comparisons is that some of the pairs of examinations we might want to compare have no candidates in common. For example, in England there is currently a common timetable so that all boards' examinations in the same subject take place at the same time. Comparisons of syllabuses from different boards in the same subject could therefore not be based on candidates who had entered both. Hence the comparison must be more indirect: comparing each syllabus with the same group of other subjects may allow us to compare the two.

Aggregated subject pairs analysis

If we are prepared to adopt one of the 'interval' approaches it is relatively straightforward to calculate the mean grade differences for all possible pairs of subjects and to average the mean differences, for each subject separately. So, for example, we can calculate the average difference in the grades achieved in mathematics and every other subject taken with it. An average of these differences will give an estimate of the overall 'difficulty' of mathematics, compared with all the other subjects taken by candidates who also took mathematics. If we do this for all subjects, we arrive at a list of subjects with an estimate of relative 'difficulty' for each.

This approach is essentially method (iii), described by Alton & Pearson (1996). A full description of the method can also be found in Forrest & Vickerman (1982), along with detailed results from its application. A further example comes from Newbould & Schmidt (1983) who compared the grades achieved by all the candidates who took A level physics with the grades achieved by those same candidates in their other subjects. After doing this for two different syllabuses, physics and Nuffield physics, they concluded that 'the former was too difficult' (p. 20).

This method of averaging the pair-wise comparisons between subjects to get an overall comparison for all subjects is sufficiently different from the simple pair-wise SPA that it seems important to distinguish it. For this reason this approach will be denoted here as 'aggregated subject pairs analysis' (ASPA). Most reported uses of the aggregated approach, however, simply refer to it as subject pairs analysis, so there is plenty of scope for confusion here.

One key difference between SPA and ASPA relates to the problem of representativeness. A criticism that has been made of SPA (mentioned above, but see below for further discussion) is that the group of candidates who enter both subjects in a particular pair may not be representative of those who take either. In ASPA, however, the estimate of the relative 'difficulty' of a subject is based on the relative achievement of all candidates who took that subject with any other subject in the set being compared, so the problem of representativeness appears much less.

A refinement of the basic ASPA method is to use a weighted average in aggregating all the pair-wise differences for a particular subject. Clearly, some of the subject pairs may be expected to have many more candidates than others and it may seem inappropriate for combinations with very few candidates to make the same contribution to the estimate of a subject's difficulty as combinations that are far more popular. Hence each pair's difference is weighted by the number of pairs on which it is based. On the other hand, one could argue that since the analysis is really about subjects, not candidates, each subject should count the same in the calculation. A discussion of this issue can be found in Nuttall *et al.* (1974, p. 48).

An alternative weighting method is to weight each subject pair's difference by the correlation coefficient for the agreement between the grades achieved in the two subjects. In this approach, the estimate of a subject's 'difficulty' would depend more on comparisons with 'similar' subjects than on comparisons with relatively disparate subjects.

Subject triples and other combinations

A logical extension of the idea of comparing two subjects by considering all those who entered both is to do the same for three or more subjects. The analysis of subject triples takes three subjects and the set of candidates who have taken all three. Comparisons can then be made among the three, using any of the methods outlined above for subject pairs. This approach has been used, for example, by Alton & Pearson (1996). The analysis of triples is somewhat more complex than pairs, given the much larger number of possible combinations. Even with large data sets, some triples are likely to have quite small numbers, making them potentially unstable. And the extent to which the group of candidates who have taken a particular triple are representative of those who have taken each of the three subjects is also likely to be less than for pairs. Perhaps for these reasons, this approach does not seem to have been widely used.

Some of the uses of SPA have limited the groups of candidates to be considered in different ways. For example, Newbould & Schmidt (1983), in comparing physics with chemistry using SPA, split the analysis according to what other subjects were taken with the pair (e.g. comparing physics with chemistry for those also taking biology gave quite different results from the comparison for those also taking mathematics with the pair). Massey (1981) did a similar analysis for A level English, comparing English with other subjects for different third-subject combinations. Other studies have used this approach to compare the performance in physics of those who also take mathematics with the performance of those who do not (e.g. Rutter, 1994; Ireson, 1996).

3.2 Subject 'matrix' methods

A number of common examinee methods base their analysis on what may be thought of as a matrix of the results of candidates by examinations. These methods are all quite different, but may be grouped under this heading for convenience. It could also be argued that the ASPA method belongs with this group, though it has been presented above as a continuation of simple SPA.

Use of average performance as a reference

There are a number of different variations on this idea, which uses performance in a set of other subjects as a comparator for the grade achieved in a particular subject. Whereas ASPA estimates the 'difficulty' of a base subject by considering each other subject paired with it in turn, then averaging, by contrast, these approaches conduct some kind of aggregation first, then make the comparison.

One example is presented by the Welsh Joint Education Committee (WJEC, 1973). This analysis was limited to those candidates who had entered precisely eight of the eleven subjects compared. For each subject, a regression line was drawn to show the relationship between the grade in that subject and the grades achieved by that same candidate in all their other subjects. The average grade in the subject was also compared with the average achieved in all the other subjects. This is exactly equivalent to the use of SPA, differing only in the order of aggregation.

A second example is the Nuttall *et al.* (1974) 'UBMT method' (UBMT denotes 'unbiased mean total'). This method is genuinely different from SPA and, unlike the previous one, can be applied to candidates who have taken different numbers of subjects (provided they have taken more than one). As Nuttall *et al.* explain (p. 32): 'For all candidates taking a subject, e.g. chemistry, UBMT is the mean grade of all other subjects attempted for all candidates taking chemistry.' The method consists in first calculating the average grade achieved in chemistry by all candidates taking chemistry and at least one other subject. Then, for the set of all these candidates, the mean grade across all the other subjects they have taken is calculated. Finally, the averaged mean grade achieved in all the other subjects taken by these candidates (i.e. the UBMT) is subtracted from the average chemistry grade to give an index of the 'difficulty' of chemistry. The same process is repeated for the other subjects in the set. The equation for this model is given in the appendix to this chapter.

Kelly's method

One possible objection to the use of the UBMT method described above is that candidates who take a particular 'hard' subject may be likely to combine it with other 'hard' subjects; and, similarly, 'easy' subjects are more likely to be combined – and hence compared – with other 'easy' subjects. This could lead to the extent of the differences between subjects being underestimated.

For example, if a high proportion of those who took chemistry (a relatively 'hard' subject) also took other 'hard' subjects like mathematics and physics, the average grades they achieved in their other subjects might be quite similar to their grades in chemistry. Methods such as UBMT or ASPA (especially the weighted version) would then estimate chemistry to be of only average difficulty. Kelly's (1976a) method essentially uses an iterative procedure to respond to this problem.

The method begins in the same way as the UBMT method, by comparing the grades achieved by candidates in one subject with their average grades in all their other subjects, and so estimating the 'difficulty' of that subject. This is done for each subject under consideration, using the grades achieved by all candidates who have taken it with at least one other in the set. These 'difficulty estimates' are then used to apply a correction factor to the grades achieved in that subject. So, for example, if chemistry is found to be half a grade more 'difficult' than the average, that half grade is added to the achieved grade for all chemistry examinees. The whole process is then repeated using the 'difficulty corrected' grades in each subject instead of the actual achieved grades, to produce a new estimate of the relative 'difficulty' of these subjects with corrected grades. After a small number of iterations, the corrections shrink to zero and so the estimates of 'difficulty' of each subject converge.

Although it may be conceptually helpful to think of this method as iterative, it can be shown that the result is equivalent to solving a set of linear equations (Kelly, 1976a, provides a proof of this, due to Lawley, in an appendix). In practice, solving these equations using a matrix inversion is more efficient than the iterative process for large data sets. The full equations provided by Lawley are presented in the appendix to this chapter.

This method has been used relatively frequently, though perhaps by quite a limited number of researchers. The first reported use was by Kelly (1976a) in Scotland. It has subsequently been used by Fitz-Gibbon & Vincent (1994) and by other researchers at Durham University's Curriculum, Evaluation and Management (CEM) Centre (e.g. Alis, 2004; Yellis, 2006), as well as by Dearing (1996), applied to A level and GCSE data. For a number of years, results from applying this method to Scottish Highers were published annually as 'correction factors' by the Scottish Qualifications Authority (Sparkes, 2000, p. 178). Sparkes (2000) also used this technique in an analysis of Scottish data.

Analysis of variance

This method is described by Nuttall *et al.* (1974) as 'the most versatile and the most likely to yield sensible results with small samples and low numbers of subjects attempted' (p. 50). It essentially applies a two-way analysis of variance with unequal numbers of observations in the cells, equal weights and interaction (Scheffé, 1959). It has also been used by Backhouse (1978) and the calculation is explained in detail by Backhouse (1972, p. 140). Despite the advantages claimed for it, it is acknowledged that it is computationally complex and no reported uses of the method have been found since the 1970s.

The analysis of variance (ANOVA) method seeks to model the performance of a particular candidate in a particular examination as the sum of two factors: the ability of the candidate and the difficulty of the subject. Like Kelly's method, the ANOVA method has the advantage of taking into account simultaneously the abilities of candidates and the difficulties of the subjects they take. However, Kelly (1976a, p. 43) states that the ANOVA method is considerably more complex than other methods whose results are similar. In fact, Kelly's own method is also quite complex, and it is not obvious that there is a lot to choose between them on this score.

Average marks scaling

This method has been used in a number of Australian states for producing aggregated marks from different subjects with different 'difficulties'. Although it does not appear to have been used in the UK, and is therefore strictly speaking outside the scope of this book, average marks scaling (AMS) has qualities that make it conceptually interesting and so worth considering in this context. This method differs from the others described so far in that it aims not just to quantify the different difficulties of different subjects, but to rescale their marks onto a common scale, taking account of the spread of abilities of candidates in that subject.

Average marks scaling can be thought of as a more sophisticated version of methods such as the UBMT, ANOVA or Kelly's method. It has been applied directly to marks rather than grades, as that is how examination results are generally reported in Australia. Average marks scaling corrects both the average mark for a subject and the spread of marks, while preserving the shape of the distribution. Average marks scaling could equally well be applied to grades, provided they were coded on a numerical scale. It would then be essentially similar to Kelly's method, but has the advantage that one does not have to assume that the gaps between grades are the same in different subjects; if grades in one subject are relatively compressed, AMS will stretch them out, as well as moving them up or down. However, part of the 'interval' assumption remains as one must still assume that the gaps between grades within each subject are equal.

Average marks scaling was introduced in Western Australia in 1998, replacing a system in which similar corrections were made on the basis of scores on a reference test, the Australian Scaling Test. It was found that rescaling marks based on the average scores each student had achieved in all their subjects gave results very similar to rescaling based on the reference test, but without the need to sit an additional test (WACC, 1998).

Marks rescaled by AMS have the following properties (Partis, 1997):

- Within a subject, the order of marks and the shape of the distribution are preserved (i.e. a linear transformation is applied to each).

- The mean scaled score in each subject is equal to the mean scaled score across all subjects taken by all the students in that subject.

- The standard deviation of the scaled marks in each subject is equal to the standard deviation of the unscaled standardised marks across all subjects taken by all students in that subject.

The following heuristic account of the process of AMS draws on Partis (1997) and Seneta (1987).

1. Begin with a raw mark, G_{ni}, for each student, n, in each subject, i.

2. In each subject, standardise marks (Z_{ni}) to have mean 0 and standard deviation 1.

3. For each subject, i, calculate for the students who have taken that subject, the standard deviation, R_i, of all their standardized marks (Z_{nj}) in all their subjects. R_i is therefore an index of the relative spread of 'ability' of the students who have taken subject i.

4. For each subject, i, multiply the standardised mark (Z_{ni}) by R_i to get the 'range adjusted' mark U_{ni}. The standard deviations of the U_{ni} in each subject now reflect the amount of variation in ability (as measured by performance in their other subjects) of the students who have taken that subject.

5. For each subject, i, an adjustment, D_i, must be added to these 'range adjusted' marks (U_{ni}) to get the fully scaled marks X_{ni}. In other words, $X_{ni} = U_{ni} + D_i$. The values of the D_is are unknown at this stage.

6. For each subject, *i*, however, D_i will be the mean, for the students who have taken that subject, of all their scaled marks X_{nj} in all their subjects. Hence if there are *n* subjects, we have *n* equations and need to find *n* unknown D_is, so the D_is can be solved uniquely.

Full equations for the solution of this model are given in the appendix to this chapter.

3.3 Latent trait models

An approach that is conceptually quite different from those so far described is to base a comparison among subjects on the idea that they all measure (at least to some extent) a common trait, such as 'general ability'. In fact, references to such an idea can be found in some applications of the methods presented above. For example, in defending her approach against the criticism that different examinations may not all relate to the same kind of ability, Kelly (1976b, p. 26) conducts a factor analysis to show that they broadly do. Only one reported example of an explicitly latent trait model approach has been found, however, by Coe (forthcoming) who applied the Rasch model to GCSE data from England.

Rasch modelling

The Rasch model (Rasch, 1960/1980; Wright & Stone, 1979) provides a method for calibrating ordinal data onto an interval scale. Rasch assumes that the 'difficulty' of items and the 'ability' of persons[4] can be measured on the same scale, and that the probability of a person achieving success on a particular item is entirely determined by the difference between their ability and the difficulty of the item. In the Rasch model, these two are related by the logit function, the difference being equal to the log of the odds, and item difficulties and person abilities are estimated in logit units. Rasch's claim to provide an interval scale rests on the fact that the same difference between item difficulty and person ability anywhere on the scale corresponds to the same probability of success. For any two items of different difficulty, different persons will have different probabilities of success, but the odds ratio[5] for each person will be the same regardless of their ability, provided they fit the model. The equation for this model is given in the appendix.

Rasch analysis uses an iterative procedure to estimate item difficulties and person abilities for a given data set. It allows the fit of the model to be investigated and misfitting items and persons to be identified. It is a requirement of the model that items should be uni-dimensional (i.e. all measuring essentially the same thing) and discriminate appropriately (i.e. more able persons are more likely to be successful). Unlike other latent trait models, the Rasch model further requires that all items discriminate equally, in other words, the relationship between a person's ability relative to an item and their probability of success on it should be the same for all items. For persons, their relative probabilities of success on different items should be in line with those of others in the population.

The process of estimating grade difficulties and person abilities in the Rasch model is iterative. Given some estimate of the abilities of the candidates who have taken a particular subject (based on their overall performance in their other subjects), we can examine the relationship between the probability of a particular grade being achieved and the ability of the candidate. We can use some kind of maximum likelihood procedure to select a value for the difficulty of the grade that best explains this pattern of achievement. Having estimated grade difficulties in this way, we can then refine our estimates of candidates' abilities in an exactly analogous way, selecting a value for each person's ability that best explains their pattern of achievement of grades of known difficulty. The process is then repeated, each time using the latest estimates of difficulty and ability, until estimates converge.

Hence the estimate of the difficulty of a particular grade in a particular subject is based on all the candidates who have taken that subject with at least one other. The grade difficulty depends on the relative probabilities of that grade being achieved by candidates of different ability, as determined by their performance in all their subjects and taking into account the different difficulties of all the grades they have gained.

In this way the Rasch approach is quite similar to the subject 'matrix' methods described above, though it differs in two important respects. The first is that with Rasch it is possible to estimate the difficulties of each grade in each subject independently, using a 'partial credit' model (Masters, 1982). Hence there is no need to make any kind of interval assumption about the scales on which grades are coded; the Rasch model automatically assigns a value to each grade on a scale which may be said to have the 'interval' property, that is, the same interval anywhere on the scale denotes the same difference in the probabilities of being achieved. This is a potentially important advantage since to use methods such as Kelly's or ASPA we must assume not only that the intervals between different grades in the same subject are equal, but also that these intervals are the same across all subjects.[6] Given Coe's (forthcoming) finding that the intervals between grades are far from equal, this may be a significant advantage for the Rasch approach.

The other key difference is that the Rasch model requires the subjects and candidates analysed to fit a particular model. In this context, fitting the model means that it must be possible to assign ability levels to all persons and difficulty levels to all items (i.e. subjects and grades) such that when we consider all candidates of a particular level of ability who have taken a particular subject, the proportion of them who achieved a particular grade should be reasonably close to what is predicted by the model. A key requirement for such fit is that both difficulty of items and ability of persons are uni-dimensional. In other words, there must be essentially just one kind of 'ability' which persons differ in the amount of which they exhibit and which largely accounts for their performance at all grades in all subjects.

If a particular subject, or at least a particular grade in a particular subject, does not fit the model, this will be evident and we can see which grades are not behaving as 'expected'. We can also identify any individuals or groups of candidates who are 'misfits'. The fact that the Rasch model specifically requires a uni-dimensional concept of ability seems to lend its results to interpretation in terms of the general level of ability represented by a particular achievement.

4   Criticisms of common examinee approaches

A number of writers have discussed issues arising from the use of these methods, including Christie & Forrest (1981), Newbould (1982), Forrest & Vickerman (1982), Alton & Pearson (1996), Pollitt (1996), Cresswell (1996), Goldstein & Cresswell (1996), Fitz-Gibbon & Vincent (1997), Newton (1997; 2005) and Jones (2003).

The main criticisms of statistical comparisons may be listed under five headings, and are summarised briefly below. For now, these criticisms are simply stated as they have been presented by their authors. I return to evaluate these criticisms in a later section, having first tried to clarify some of the assumptions required by different interpretations of the methods and the different conceptions of 'comparability' on which they rest.

4.1 Factors other than 'difficulty'

This criticism has already been mentioned above in suggesting that better teaching in English, or higher levels of motivation, might account for candidates' better performance in that subject.

A number of writers point out that examination performance is affected by many factors apart from 'difficulty', so, unless we are prepared to assume (or can show) that these factors are equal or unimportant, we cannot judge 'difficulty' simply by comparing outcomes. Just because common candidates typically get lower grades in one subject than in others it does not necessarily follow that it is more difficult. A number of other factors, including the intrinsic interest of the subject, the quality of teaching experienced, extrinsic motivations such as the need for a particular qualification, the candidates' levels of exam preparation, the amount of curriculum time devoted to it, and so on, could all affect performance, without making that subject more 'difficult' (Alton & Pearson, 1996; Goldstein & Cresswell, 1996; Newton, 1997).

4.2 Multidimensionality

In order to compare standards in different subjects we have to have some basis for comparing them. This amounts to saying that different subjects must all measure the same thing, or at least have some significant trait in common. In other words, that subjects being compared must be uni-dimensional – which of course they are not. It is meaningless to say, for example, that 'art is easier than physics'; they are just different. Goldstein & Cresswell (1996) give an example of a comparison between a spelling test and a degree in English; in theory one could make the two equal in difficulty, at least in a statistical sense, though it would be absurd to say that they were equivalent.

Another subtle variation on this argument is provided by Pollitt (1996). He gives an example of a set of examination results in different subjects where five candidates of equal 'general ability' choose different subjects in which they have different specific aptitudes. When these different aptitudes in different subjects are allowed to interact with different reasons for choosing them, Pollitt shows that the illusion of differential difficulty is created. Some subjects (English and economics in his example) are chosen by those who are best in those subjects, while others (mathematics) are chosen by those who are relatively weak in that subject. The result is that candidates typically do worse in mathematics than in their other subjects and hence mathematics appears 'harder'.

4.3 Unrepresentativeness

The groups of students taking particular combinations of subjects (on whom statistical comparisons are based) are not representative of all those who take (or might take) a particular subject. Again, an example of this has already been mentioned: students who take both physics and media studies are unlikely to be representative of those taking either subject. This point is made by, for example, Goldstein & Cresswell (1996).

Newton (1997) discusses the question of exactly who it is any group of candidates on whom a statistical comparison is made should be representative of. In other words, to what population do we want any claims of comparability to apply? He argues that this should be the whole population of students in the cohort, whether or not they choose actually to take a particular subject. In this case, unless we have truly representative (e.g. random) samples taking every subject, any claims about comparability are very problematic.

4.4 Sub-group differences

If we analyse subject 'difficulties' for different sub-groups (e.g. males and females) we get quite different results. For example, for males, history may appear 'harder' than mathematics, while for females mathematics is the 'harder' (Pollitt, 1996). We might also find that for candidates who take mathematics with it, physics is really no harder than any other subject, whereas for those who take it without mathematics, physics appears substantially more difficult (Rutter, 1994). Hence a judgement about whether one subject is 'harder' than another depends very much on who happened to take those subjects. And if the characteristics of the entry change, so would the supposed 'difficulties' (Alton & Pearson, 1996; Pollitt, 1996; Newton, 1997; Sparkes, 2000). The existence of different relative difficulties for different sub-groups is also a challenge to the assumption of uni-dimensionality.

4.5 Problems of forcing equality

Adjusting the 'difficulties' of different subjects to make them all equivalent would cause problems during any changeover period for users, the public and professional bodies. Some of the currently 'harder' subjects would need to have absurdly high pass rates, while subjects currently graded 'leniently' would have to be failed by most candidates. This situation would be satisfactory for neither group. Requiring grade boundaries to be modified in this way would change the nature of the examining process and could delay the publication of results. There is also the problem that different methods of estimating relative 'difficulties' would give different corrections, and there is no clear consensus about which method is best (Alton & Pearson, 1996; Goldstein & Cresswell, 1996).

5 Clarification of assumptions underlying the methods, and different conceptions of 'comparability'

The criticisms presented above represent a formidable challenge to the validity of common examinee methods. Before we can evaluate these criticisms, however, we must be clear about exactly what assumptions are required by the different methods, and, in particular, by different interpretations of their results. This leads us to an argument that different uses of these methods may rest upon quite different conceptions of what is actually meant by 'comparability', and that some of the criticisms of these methods are based on different conceptions again.

5.1 Assumptions required by the methods

Attempts to clarify the assumptions that underlie the use of common examinee methods seem to have come more often from their critics than their proponents. Some of those who have used these methods have perhaps been less critical of them and less concerned with justifying and validating than with reporting the results (e.g. Fitz-Gibbon & Vincent, 1994). The critics, on the other hand, have often discussed in some detail the validity of the assumptions claimed to underlie the method, for example, the requirement that factors such as motivation in a particular subject, or the quality of teaching experienced, can be treated as equal, or that candidates taking a particular pair of subjects are representative of all those who might take either of them, or that a group of subjects being compared is sufficiently 'uni-dimensional' to justify a basis for comparability (e.g. Forrest & Vickerman, 1982; Newton, 1997).

However, the question of what assumptions are required by a model cannot be answered without considering the interpretations and uses to which any results are put. In fact one could argue that any statistical model, including common examinee methods, can be applied to any data set without strictly speaking having to make any assumptions at all. It is only when one comes to trying to interpret the results that it is really appropriate to talk about validity. An interpretation may be valid or invalid, but a method, without a specific interpretation attached, cannot. In general, the application of any statistical method can be interpreted in a number of ways. One particular interpretation of the results might be valid only if a certain set of assumptions are made, whereas another interpretation could require an entirely different set.

Hence, before we can consider what assumptions are required by these models, we must first be clear what kinds of interpretations might be made of the results. Before we can do this, we must first be clear about the meaning of 'comparability' in this context, or, rather, about the different, but not always well separated, meanings that word can have.

5.2 Conceptions of comparability

I have argued elsewhere in this volume[7] that there are three broad, distinct conceptions of comparability as applied to examination standards. It is important to separate these different meanings of the word 'comparability' as once the distinction is made it becomes clear that much of the discussion of the problems of common examinee methods is actually at cross-purposes. Different arguments (or sometimes different parts of the same argument) have made different interpretations of concepts like 'difficulty' or 'standards', based on different fundamental conceptions of 'comparability'. While it is broadly true that a particular view of the meaning of 'comparability' implies certain interpretations of such concepts, there is not such a simple relationship between these different conceptions and specific methods, such as SPA.

The three conceptions of comparability are *performance* comparability, *statistical* comparability and *construct* comparability. Each of these is briefly outlined below, together with their associated interpretations of terms such as 'difficulty' and 'standards', and examples of applications of common examinee methods that have drawn on each. The extent to which each conception addresses the problem of different relative difficulties for different sub-groups is also discussed, as is the question of which subjects can be compared under each view.

Performance comparability

According to a *performance* view of comparability, the 'standard' of a particular award resides in the levels of skill, knowledge, understanding – or any other qualities – that are required to achieve it. One examination would be seen as more 'difficult' than another if it required skills, knowledge or understanding that were more advanced, in other words if it made a greater demand on the candidate.

This conception often appears to be the default in thinking about comparability, though it is not often explicitly stated. When writers do not explicitly attempt to define concepts such as 'difficulty' or 'standards' it often seems to be implicit that they are thinking in terms of the intellectual demands made by an examination, the skills, knowledge and understanding that must be demonstrated to gain the award of a particular level. However, it is hard to find a clear illustration of this perspective and no doubt many writers who appear to adopt it would object to being so classified.

According to a purely *performance* view of comparability, it should be possible to specify the difficulty of an examination even if no candidate has ever taken it. Perhaps for this reason, the existence of sub-group differences, as illustrated by the example of mathematics and English GCSE, above, has been taken by some critics of common examinee methods as an unequivocal death blow to any hopes of establishing comparability by statistical means (e.g. Newton, 1997). The implicit assumption here may be that all comparability is essentially *performance*. However, other conceptions of comparability may have less difficulty with the problem of sub-group differences.

Another issue that is influenced by our perspective on comparability is which subjects can legitimately be compared. From a *performance* view, only examinations that give rise to the same phenomena can be compared; there must be common skills, knowledge or understandings, defined in terms of common criteria. Discussion of comparability is often presented in terms of identifying 'cognate' subjects; in other words, subjects that are similar in terms of their disciplinary roots, content area or methods. This idea seems to imply a *performance* perspective, since one could only judge the relative demand of tasks that have these kinds of similarities.

Statistical comparability

The second type, *statistical* comparability, holds that two examinations may be seen as comparable if a 'typical' candidate has an equal chance of achieving a particular level in each. Under a *statistical* conception of comparability, the 'standard' depends on its likelihood of being reached, possibly after taking into account other factors. An examination level is 'harder' if it is rarer, or at least estimated to be less likely to be achieved by a 'similar' candidate. Different operationalisations of this general approach include simple norm (cohort) referencing, the use of value-added models (multilevel or otherwise) and, of course, common examinee methods. However, we must be clear that the method itself does not necessarily imply a particular view of comparability; it depends how the results are interpreted.

Examples of *statistical* conceptions of comparability in the use of common examinee methods are perhaps a little easier to find than *performance* ones, though again they are seldom unequivocal. The statement by Nuttall *et al.* (1974) seems to adopt this perspective.

> ... we can see no logical reason why, if a large group of candidates representative of the population took, for example, both English and mathematics, their average grades should not be the same.
>
> Nuttall *et al.* (1974, p. 12)

A similar view can also be found in Fitz-Gibbon & Vincent (1994).

> The term 'difficult' cannot be taken as meaning necessarily or intrinsically difficult. Rather, subjects are said to be either 'difficult' or 'severely graded' if the grades awarded are generally lower than might have been reasonably expected on the basis of adequate statistics.
>
> Fitz-Gibbon & Vincent (1994, p. i)

This definition suggests that there may actually have been no real disagreement between Fitz-Gibbon & Vincent (1994; 1997) and Goldstein & Cresswell (1996); they were simply using the same word to mean two quite different things.

One feature of the *statistical* conception is that it seems to have less difficulty with the problem of sub-group differences. On average, candidates who take both subjects may have a better chance of success in English than they do in mathematics. However, if we know that a candidate is male, for example, our estimate of their relative chances may change. From a *statistical* viewpoint there is no particular reason why an estimate of chances of success should not depend on the characteristics of the candidate as well as on the subjects taken.

While it might be considered a desirable characteristic of different examinations that their relative difficulties should be the same for, say, males and females, it is not a pre-requisite for an understanding of *statistical* comparability between them. Of course, if it turns out that relative difficulties are indeed quite different for different sub-groups, then we can no longer talk about comparability of subjects per se but only of subjects in relation to particular sub-groups.

The *statistical* conception of comparability is the most broad-minded on the question of which subjects can be compared. If comparability is based on the concept of chances of success then there seems to be no reason why any groups of subjects cannot be compared. This conception makes no requirement for different subjects to be related in any way, only that a particular level of achievement should be equally rare in each.

Construct comparability

The third type, *construct* comparability, holds that two examinations may be compared if they have some construct in common. For this version of comparability, the 'standard' of a particular examination performance depends on the level of the linking construct that it signifies. One examination is 'harder' than another if it indicates a higher level of the linking construct.

An example of this kind of comparability can be found in Fitz-Gibbon & Vincent (1997) who talk about the 'common currency' of A level grades. By this they mean that for some purposes, such as when admissions tutors in UK universities make decisions about which applicants to accept, grades in different subjects may be treated as interchangeable.

> What our analyses suggest is that the 'common currency', i.e. that which can be seen as the information contained in any grade about general aptitudes, can be better operationalised by recognising differences between the subjects in 'difficulty'.
>
> Fitz-Gibbon & Vincent (1997, pp. 293–4)

Here the linking construct is 'general aptitudes', though other linking constructs could be imagined. In the context of an admissions tutor using grades in a subject other than their own to infer a candidate's suitability for entry, we might speculate that the construct of interest would be that student's generalisable capacity for learning in another academic context, a construct that is probably reasonably well summarised by the term 'general aptitudes'.

If it is accepted that all the subjects being compared measure (at least to some extent) 'general aptitudes', then we can legitimately compare their outcomes. If we do compare them, then we must interpret these comparisons in terms of our construct of 'general aptitudes'. So in saying that, for example, physics is 'harder' than biology we mean that a particular grade in physics indicates a higher level of 'general aptitudes' than would the same grade in biology.

Another context mentioned by Fitz-Gibbon & Vincent (1997) is the use of examination grades in school performance tables. Here the grades, perhaps after adjustment for the effects of prior attainment or other factors, might be taken as an indication of the effectiveness of the teaching received, so we have an alternative linking construct from the same analysis and with it the possibility of an entirely different interpretation of the differences in 'difficulty' that were found. Indeed, the same study was cited above as exemplifying a *statistical* conception of comparability, so it is clear that the same method can support more than one interpretation.

The problem of sub-group differences is not entirely solved by adopting the *construct* conception of comparability. Some level of uni-dimensionality is required by the assumption of a linking construct and significant variation in relative 'difficulties' for different sub-groups would undermine this. There are a number of possible ways to get around this problem, though none of them is really completely satisfactory.

One approach would be to limit any comparison to groups of subjects in which there were no substantial sub-group differences. For example, we might say that mathematics and English cannot really be compared in relation to a common construct because they are not sufficiently uni-dimensional. We cannot infer levels of 'general aptitudes' from performance in these two subjects since the aptitudes required by each appear to be too specific. On the other hand, despite the differences in the comparison of mathematics and English for different sexes, grades in these two subjects are highly correlated (r = 0.77 in the 2004 data set) so in this particular case we might well conclude that they are sufficiently uni-dimensional for our purposes.

Another approach would be to limit comparisons to particular sub-groups, so we could compare mathematics and English separately for males and females, and accept that 'comparability' will be gender-specific. However, this requires us to invoke gender-specific linking constructs such as 'male general aptitudes' and 'female general aptitudes' – a rather strange idea.

The question of which subjects can be compared is of course related to this issue. If our interpretation of differences between subjects draws on the notion of a linking construct such as 'general aptitudes' to provide a basis for comparability, then comparisons must be limited to subject examinations that broadly measure that trait. Achievements in any subjects being compared would therefore have to correlate reasonably well with each other, so we might adopt a largely empirical criterion to decide whether subjects are comparable or not.

Note that this last criterion is likely to contrast with the idea of 'cognate' subjects since it would be quite possible for examinations even with the same subject title to correlate very poorly. An example of this might be found at GCSE where under the heading of 'science' we would find biology, chemistry and physics, along with combined science, but also vocational science. Variations in the modes of assessment used could make more difference to the correlations among syllabuses than their nominal content.

6   Defence of common examinee methods

Given the number of accounts of uses of the common examinee methods that have been outlined above, and the force of the criticisms that have been made against them, there is surprisingly little in the existing literature by way of systematic defence of these methods. One exception is Fitz-Gibbon & Vincent (1997), who provide a specific reply to the critique of Goldstein & Cresswell (1996). Another is Kelly (1976b) who addresses specific criticisms made of an earlier conference paper she gave. As with the criticisms, however, much of the defence of these methods has been unclear about the exact meanings of terms such as 'difficulty', or, if it has been clear, has not been consistent.

6.1 Evaluation of these criticisms in relation to specific interpretations

I now return to the five broad criticisms of common examinee methods and attempt to evaluate them.

Factors other than difficulty

Viewed from a *performance* perspective, it must be acknowledged that this criticism seems to have some weight. If one interprets the 'difficulty' of an examination as a function of its level of demand in terms of specific criteria, then it is hard to deny that a statistical difference between subjects does not necessarily indicate a difference in 'difficulty'. Given all the other factors that may affect attainment, it seems unsatisfactory either to ignore them, or to assume they will be the same for all subjects. In theory, we could try to measure and take account of them all, but in practice this would also be likely to be somewhat unsatisfactory.

On the other hand, if our conception of comparability is fundamentally *statistical*, then we are likely to interpret the kinds of differences in attainment revealed by common examinee methods as indicating different chances of success in different subjects. From this perspective, it may not matter that the reasons for these differences may vary, since whatever the reasons, the differences remain. This is particularly the case if it is judged to be perfectly acceptable that a typical candidate's chances of success differ in different subjects. However, even if differences are held to be unacceptable on the grounds that one's chances of success should be the same regardless of subject, then one could still attempt to compensate for the 'other factors' so that an individual candidate could make a fair choice between them based on equal expectations.

Similarly, from a *construct* comparability perspective, differences in attainment by equivalent candidates are taken to indicate different conversion rates between a grade in a particular subject and some underlying linking construct such as 'general aptitude'. The example given above, of the admissions tutor judging the suitability of candidates with results in different subjects, illustrates that there may be situations in which any other factor that affects attainment could be seen as wholly irrelevant.

In considering this criticism generally, it is interesting to note that most of the writers who cite the problem of 'other factors' list a number of factors that might in principle affect performance, without actually providing any evidence that these factors do in fact vary by subject. An exception is Newbould (1982) who shows that differences in the apparent severity of grading of different subjects agree reasonably closely with students' expressed preferences for those subjects. In other words, the subjects that appear hardest are also generally the least liked. Newbould speculates that differences in performance levels in different subjects might be accounted for by these differences in preferences. However, liking for a subject is not the same as motivation to work in it and a correlation, no matter how strong, does not necessarily imply that relative attainment is a result of differential preference. It could equally be, for example, that the causal relationship could be the other way: students like most those subjects in which they are doing best.

Multidimensionality

Most critics of statistical approaches to comparability point to the assumption of uni-dimensionality as an untenable requirement. Clearly, examinations in different subjects measure different things; otherwise there would be no point in having different examinations. Hence the basis on which a comparison can be made is problematic. This issue has been discussed briefly above in relation to the restrictions on which subjects can be compared according to the three different conceptions of comparability.

From a *performance* perspective, multidimensionality is a real problem. According to this conception of comparability, we can really only compare two examinations against the same criteria. They may be comparable only to the extent that common phenomena may be observed as the output of both; if there is no such common ground, the question of which is 'harder' is meaningless.

From a *statistical* conception this issue is much less of a problem; indeed we may even deny that any kind of uni-dimensionality is actually a requirement. For example, if we define 'standards' in terms of population norms, there is no requirement that different standards should be measuring the same thing, only that they should be equally rare. Although this kind of cohort referencing is not a feature of common examinee methods, the same logic might be applied to them. For example, the results from Kelly's method could be interpreted as indicating the relative chances of success in different subjects of candidates who are typical of those who actually entered them. An analysis might show, say, that a vocational course in information technology was 'easier' than a traditional examination in Latin. In this context, 'easier' just means that candidates who were similar in terms of their achievement in their other subjects typically achieved better grades in the former; there is no assumption that these two examinations are measuring the same thing.

The position of the *construct* conception of comparability is perhaps somewhere between the other two. If we are to invoke the concept of a linking construct, we must maintain that different subjects, while not perfectly uni-dimensional, are at least sufficiently uni-dimensional to allow meaningful comparison. A pragmatic restriction here would be to accept that making comparisons across all subjects is going too far but that there are groups of 'cognate' subjects, within which a comparison may be valid.

In this context, 'uni-dimensional' may be taken to mean that a large part of the variation in grades in different subjects is shared. Measures such as the correlations between grades in different subjects, loadings on a single factor in a factor analysis, or measures of internal consistency such as Cronbach's Alpha could all provide evidence of this. The Rasch model has a particular requirement for uni-dimensionality, since if this assumption is violated to a large extent the invariance properties of the model (i.e. item-free measurement) are lost. When this happens the results may be misleading or not usable, though in practice some tolerance for deviation from strict uni-dimensionality may be not just necessary, but desirable for valid interpretation of the underlying latent construct (Hambleton, 1989; Linacre, 1998).

The issue of uni-dimensionality is therefore essentially an empirical one; for any set of subjects we can calculate the extent to which they overlap. However, there is no absolute threshold at which a set of subjects is clearly uni-dimensional. Any such threshold would be arbitrary and the question is really one of degree rather than kind. The decision about whether they are uni-dimensional enough must be a matter of judgement.

Having said that, given any reasonable minimum threshold for the amount of overlap that a set of subjects must exhibit in order to be accepted as uni-dimensional, it is beyond question that such a set exists. The higher the correlation we require among different subjects, the smaller the group is likely to be. It is also likely, however, that some subjects could not be included in the group without having to set an unacceptably low threshold. Hence the question is not whether all subjects can be considered uni-dimensional, but which subjects can reasonably be considered sufficiently uni-dimensional. An example of this can be seen in Coe's (forthcoming) application of the Rasch model. He judged that 34 GCSE subjects were sufficiently uni-dimensional to allow them to be compared, but that many others (including General National Vocational Qualifications and some creative GCSE subjects like music and art) had to be excluded in order to meet this requirement.

Unrepresentativeness

This criticism is usually targeted at subject pairs analysis (SPA). For example, Goldstein & Cresswell (1996, p. 438) point out that 'students who happen to take particular pairs (or combinations) of subjects are not typical of either subject'. In fact, many uses of subject pairs (e.g. Nuttall, *et al.* 1974) estimate the severity of a subject's grading by calculating an average of the subject pair differences across all subjects taken with it, so are really ASPA (see above). Hence, the estimate of the severity of, say, chemistry is based on all the students who have taken chemistry and at least one other subject, which in practice is pretty close to being all those who have taken chemistry at all. Moreover, most other common examinee methods, such as that used by Kelly (1976a), or the Rasch model, also base their estimates of a subject's difficulty on all students who have taken it with at least one other. Hence the objection as it is often presented is unfounded.

However, there is a bigger problem here. In certain subjects, the students who typically take them are severely unrepresentative of all those who might potentially take them, and this makes comparisons extremely problematic. In the context of England, for example, examinations in languages such as Urdu or Chinese are taken disproportionately by native speakers of those languages. For a native speaker, a GCSE in Urdu is likely to be easier than the other GCSEs they take and hence they are likely to achieve higher grades on average. This is likely to result in statistical comparisons showing Urdu to be an easy subject (see, for example, Yellis, 2006). This would be no reflection of the difficulty that a non-native speaker would experience to achieve the same.

From a *performance* perspective, this would be a significant problem. However, even the *statistical* conception has something of a problem here, since a person's chances of success would depend significantly on whether they were a native speaker. Hence we would have to add a rider to our interpretation and say that the differences in achievement indicate different chances of success *for students typical of those who typically take the subject*. If a particular student is different in some way from those who typically take that subject, or indeed if they are not known to be the same, then an estimate of their chances of success should be treated with some caution. However, this is not to say that is wholly worthless, since a sensible person will treat most things with some caution anyway.

From a *construct* view the difficulty seems a little less. Although we would admittedly make an incorrect judgement about the 'general aptitude' of an atypical entrant based on their result in that subject, the evidence from that subject is likely to be a small part of the total evidence available. If a judgement is being made about an individual student then it is also possible that their atypicality could be made known.

Sub-group differences

A number of analyses of subject difficulties (e.g. Massey, 1981; Newton, 1997; Sparkes, 2000) have reported that if apparent differences between subjects are found, they vary considerably when the analysis is limited to particular sub-groups. As has already been stated, such variations may be problematic for the *performance* conception of comparability, since 'difficulty' ought to be independent of the particular population of candidates. The issue of sub-group differences presents a particular problem if it is argued that differences in difficulty are inherently undesirable, or that grades should be corrected to eliminate them.

However, from a *statistical* conception, such inconsistencies may be less problematic. Our estimate of a person's chances of success is likely to depend on our knowledge of their characteristics. The factors that have been shown to affect the 'difficulties' of subjects, such as gender, type of school, prior attainment or subject combinations (Newton, 1997; Sparkes, 2000) might all be expected to affect a person's relative chances of success in different subjects. There is no contradiction in saying, for example, that overall, candidates have a better chance of doing well in English than they do in mathematics, but that for boys the reverse is generally true. We can estimate a person's chances of success even if we know nothing about that person, but knowledge of their characteristics will enable us to make a better estimate.

Similarly, within a *construct* perspective, our estimate of a person's 'general aptitude' may also be modified by knowledge of the particular sub-groups to which they belong. It would be possible, for example, initially to estimate a person's aptitude as high, but then to find that they had entered a combination of subjects in which candidates with their characteristics tended to do relatively well, and hence to have to revise our estimate downwards. Hence, provided we remember that statistical differences in performance tell us something about the candidates as well as about the subjects, the problem of sub-group differences may not really be such a problem at all.

One way to interpret these sub-group differences is in terms of bias in the examination process. For example, if history appears harder for males than it does for females, compared to other subjects (as in Pollitt's, 1996, example), this could be seen as indicating that the examination process in history is biased towards females (relative to mathematics). Of course, the 'examination process' here must include, as well as the examination itself and its assessment procedures, the teaching and learning that preceded it. The 'bias' could arise from factors such as differential motivation or effort, better teaching or examination preparation. It could also arise from selection processes or choices about who enters different subjects. In these cases the word 'bias' might not really be appropriate, so it may be important to try to understand the reasons for any differences in relative performance.

Problems of forcing equality

Even if one interpreted performance differences as indicating subject difficulty, it would be perfectly possible to believe that some subjects were harder than others, but that there was no reason to try to change this. Indeed, this appears to be the official stance taken in Western Australia (WACC, 1998). Hence the position that all subjects should be forced to be equivalent is not necessarily implied even by a simplistic interpretation of statistical differences.

However, if one takes the view that standards across subjects should be aligned, then the question remains how this should be done. The rejection of statistical approaches offers no real solution here, since one can no more *judge* the intellectual demand of an assessed attainment than calculate it statistically. Of course it would be possible to align the standards for the population as a whole, but consideration of sub-groups might show substantial misalignment. Sub-groups themselves could then also be aligned, artificially equating the scores of, for example, males and females, though in practice it would be hard to guarantee that all possible sub-groups had been considered. Ensuring that standards are comparable across subjects is far from straightforward (Baird *et al.*, 2000).

Accepting that different subjects may offer different chances of success does also have its problems, but these can be resolved. The main difficulties arise when examination grades are taken as an indication of something other than simply achievement in a particular course of study. For example, if grades are used as a selection tool to indicate a person's general academic ability, or aggregated into league tables to denote the quality of teaching provided in a school, then it matters if some subjects are more severely graded than others. However, if grades are to be used in this way, then it ought to be possible to calculate a fair exchange rate to equate and convert them into some kind of currency fit for these purposes. This in fact is exactly what is done in Western Australia.

Whether we wish to equate standards or merely to calculate an exchange rate between them, however, we are still left with the problem of which method to choose. A number of studies have claimed that this choice makes a substantial difference to the outcome (e.g. Alton and Pearson, 1996). Others, on the other hand, have claimed that there is broad agreement among the different methods (e.g. Nuttall *et al.*, 1974). This debate seems hard to resolve on the basis of existing evidence. And it may be important to distinguish between the amount of disagreement among different methods for estimating subject 'difficulties' and the scale of the differences among subjects, by whatever method.

7 Conclusions: strengths and weaknesses of common examinee methods

7.1 The different methods compared

Whether conclusions from any of these methods are judged to be valid and, if so, conclusions from which of them are judged to be best must depend on the purpose of the comparison. Unless we are clear about why we want to compare different subjects, we cannot really advocate any particular method for doing so. For this reason, it has been important to try to clarify the different bases on which comparisons might be made and how they may be interpreted.

If we adopt a *performance* conception of comparability, then it seems that none of the statistical methods can really do this. The 'difficulty' of a task is so dependent on contextual factors beyond the control of the examination process that it becomes very hard to estimate, either by statistical or judgement methods.

Alternatively, if our perspective is *statistical* then our intention may be simply to compare how likely the same grade is to be achieved. In this case, several of the approaches may be appropriate. Many of the variations of the basic SPA methods, along with Kelly's method or the AMS approaches appear to offer satisfactory solutions to this problem. Of these, AMS is perhaps the best, given its flexibility, sophistication and ease of calculation.

Of course, we must remember that different students with different characteristics will have different probabilities of achieving the same grades, so these likelihoods are not absolute. They are meaningful only when applied to a particular group. Given that a number of different methods appear to be appropriate, it seems important to know how similar their results would be. This does not seem to be clear from our existing knowledge.

This interpretation of differences in grades achieved implied by the *statistical* conception of comparability (that they indicate different chances of success) may be seen to underpin their use in accountability processes such as league tables. Although examinations such as GCSE and A level may never have been intended to be used in this way, such uses are a significant part of their function today. If we take an integrated view of validity (Messick, 1989), then we cannot ignore this issue of consequential validity in considering whether grades are awarded appropriately. If the same grade is more likely to be achieved by a typical candidate in one subject than another, yet both grades are awarded the same value in an accountability process, then it does seem likely that problems will result.

A third rationale for comparison has also been considered: *construct* comparability. Here, in principle, the same grade in different subjects ought to indicate the same level of a common trait, general academic ability. For this interpretation the Rasch model may be the most appropriate, since it explicitly compares different subjects on the basis of a single dimension. The use of ASPA weighted by inter-subject correlations might also address this interpretation. AMS approaches are used for this purpose in Australia, so presumably this and the other approaches that are conceptually similar (subject pairs and Kelly's method) could also be used.

This interpretation of grades in terms of 'general aptitude' is important in practice since it is implied by the use of examination grades for selection into further or higher education – a widespread practice with significant consequences attached to it. If grades are to be used in this way then it is important that the same grade in different subjects should denote the same level of ability. One limitation of the Rasch approach here is that not all subjects can be compared; only those that are sufficiently aligned with the unitary ability construct can be included. However, if examinations depend on substantially different skills it probably is right that they should not be directly compared. Achievements in any examinations that do not fit the uni-dimensional model tell us nothing about that candidate's 'general aptitude' and should not be treated as comparable to those that do fit.

7.2 Directions for further research

A number of areas for further research have been identified already. For example, there is debate about how well the results of different methods agree. More research on this question would be useful to resolve this. Another issue that has not been fully investigated is whether other factors (such as motivation, quality of teaching or preparation, etc.) can really account for the differences we see in attainment. If so, it might be possible to retain the *performance* definition of comparability, but use statistical methods to investigate it.

8 Conclusion

It is clear that no statistical process, however sophisticated, can provide a full and satisfactory answer to the problem of evaluating the comparability of different examinations. There are too many different meanings of the word 'comparability', too many unknown but potentially important confounding factors, and too many different ways in which examinations are used. We must therefore seek to be clearer about our underlying conceptions of comparability and about the specific purposes to which we wish to put examination results. We must also be cautious about the results from any single method, and seek to triangulate the evidence from different approaches involving different assumptions and methods. We must be careful, though, not to combine or make direct comparisons between results that arise from incommensurable conceptions of 'comparability'.

However, from the point of view of monitoring 'standards' in the UK, it does seem clear that there are differences in the grades that typical candidates might expect to achieve in different subjects. It is also clear that the same grade in different subjects can indicate quite different levels of underlying 'aptitude'. Given the ways examination grades are used for purposes such as accountability and selection, these differences give rise to anomalies, the consequences of which can be quite serious. There may be a case, therefore, for the methods that have been outlined in this chapter to play, and be seen to play, a bigger part than they currently do within England in the processes of monitoring and ensuring 'comparability'.

Endnotes

1   This example and the discussion of its interpretation draws on a similar example presented by Newton (1997).

2   Note that most of the early uses of this method were limited to within-board datasets. Later national analyses, such as by Willmott (1995), were possible only because datasets matched across boards started to become available.

3   This result is based on the average differences in the grades achieved during the period 1994–2003, adjusting for the differences in ability of the candidates in different subjects using Kelly's method.

4   The words 'difficulty' and 'ability' are used generally in discussing the Rasch model, even when their normal meanings are considerably stretched. For example, in the context of a Likert scale attitude item one may talk about the 'difficulty' of an item to mean its tendency to be disagreed with (i.e. how 'hard' it is to agree with). The use of these words may initially seem strange to anyone not

familiar with the Rasch model. However, I have adopted this convention, partly in order to comply with standard practice, and partly because although the words 'difficulty' and 'ability' are not quite right for the interpretation intended, I am unable to think of better ones.

5   The odds ratio is the ratio of the odds of the two probabilities. In other words if a person has probabilities p and q of success on two items, the odds are $p/(1-p)$ and $q/(1-q)$ respectively. Hence the odds ratio is $[p/(1-p)]/[q/(1-q)]$. The logit function is:

$$\text{logit}(p) = \ln[\,p\,/\,(1-p)]$$

so the log of the odds ratio is the same as the difference in the two logits, $\text{logit}(p) - \text{logit}(q)$.

6   Of course we do not strictly have to assume that they are equal, but we have to make some assumption about their relative sizes. Note also that the AMS method requires an assumption about grade intervals within subjects, but not between subjects.

7   Commentary on Chapter 4.

References

Advanced Level Information System. (2004). *A level subject difficulties*. The Advanced Level Information System, Curriculum, Evaluation and Management Centre, University of Durham.

Alton, A., & Pearson, S. (1996). *Statistical approaches to inter-subject comparability*. Report for the Joint Forum for the GCSE and GCE.

Backhouse, J.K. (1972). Reliability of GCE examinations: A theoretical and empirical approach. In D.L. Nuttall & A.S. Willmott (Eds.), *British examinations: Techniques of analysis*. Slough: National Foundation for Educational Research.

Backhouse, J.K. (1978). *Comparability of grading standards in science subjects at GCE A level*. Schools Council Examinations Bulletin 39. London: Evans/Methuen.

Baird, J., Cresswell, M.J., & Newton, P. (2000). Would the *real* gold standard please step forward? *Research Papers in Education, 15*, 213–229.

Bardell, G.S., Forrest, G.M., & Shoesmith, D.J. (1978). *Comparability in GCE: A review of the boards' studies, 1964–1977*. Manchester: Joint Matriculation Board on behalf of the GCE Examining Boards.

Christie, T., & Forrest, G.M. (1981). *Defining public examination standards*. Schools Council Research Studies. London: Macmillan Education.

Coe, R. (forthcoming). Comparability of GCSE examinations in different subjects: An application of the Rasch model. *Oxford Review of Education, 34.*

Cresswell, M.J. (1996). Defining, setting and maintaining standards in curriculum-embedded examinations: Judgemental and statistical approaches. In H. Goldstein & T. Lewis (Eds.), *Assessment: Problems, developments and statistical issues* (pp. 57-84). Chichester: John Wiley and Sons.

Dearing, R. (1996). *Review of qualifications for 16–19 year olds.* London: School Curriculum and Assessment Authority.

Fearnley, A.J. (1998). *Update on an investigation of methods of analysis of subject pairs by grade.* Unpublished research paper, Northern Examinations and Assessment Board.

Fitz-Gibbon, C.T., & Vincent, L. (1994). *Candidates' performance in public examinations in mathematics and science.* A report commissioned by the School Curriculum and Assessment Authority from the Curriculum, Evaluation and Management Centre, University of Newcastle-upon-Tyne. London: School Curriculum and Assessment Authority.

Fitz-Gibbon, C.T., & Vincent, L. (1997). Difficulties regarding subject difficulties: Developing reasonable explanations for observable data. *Oxford Review of Education, 23,* 291–298.

Forrest, G.M., & Smith, G.A. (1972). *Standards in subjects at the Ordinary level of the GCE, June 1971.* Occasional Publication 34. Manchester: Joint Matriculation Board.

Forrest, G.M., & Vickerman, C. (1982). *Standards in GCE: Subject pairs comparisons, 1972–1980.* Occasional Publication 39. Manchester: Joint Matriculation Board.

Fowles, D.E. (1998). *The translation of GCE and GCSE grades into numerical values.* Unpublished research paper, Northern Examinations and Assessment Board.

Goldstein, H., & Cresswell, M.J. (1996). The comparability of different subjects in public examinations: A theoretical and practical critique. *Oxford Review of Education, 22,* 435–441.

Hambleton, R.K. (1989). Principles and selected applications of item response theory. In R.L. Linn (Ed.), *Educational Measurement* (3rd ed.). New York: American Council on Education and Macmillan Publishing Company.

Ireson, G. (1996). The effect of studying A level mathematics on the A level physics grade achieved. *School Science Review, 77*(280), 116–119.

Jones, B.E. (2003). *Subject pairs over time: A review of the evidence and the issues.* Unpublished research paper RC/220, Assessment and Qualifications Alliance.

Kelly, A. (1976a). A study of the comparability of external examinations in different subjects. *Research in Education*, *16*, 37–63.

Kelly, A. (1976b). *The comparability of examining standards in Scottish Certificate of Education Ordinary and Higher grade examinations*. Dalkeith: Scottish Certificate of Education Examination Board.

Linacre, J.M. (1998). Detecting multidimensionality: Which residual data-type works best? *Journal of Outcome Measurement*, *2*(3), 266–283.

Massey, A.J. (1981). *Comparing standards between AL English and other subjects*. Test Development and Research Unit, RR 05. Cambridge: Oxford and Cambridge Schools Examination Board.

Masters, G.N. (1982). A Rasch model for partial credit scoring. *Psychometrika*, *47*(2), 149–174.

Messick, S. (1989). Validity. In R.L. Linn (Ed.), *Educational Measurement* (3rd ed.). New York: American Council on Education and Macmillan Publishing Company.

Newbould, C.A. (1982). Subject preferences, sex differences and comparability of standards. *British Educational Research Journal*, *8*, 141–146.

Newbould, C.A., & Schmidt, C.C. (1983). *Comparison of grades in physics with grades in other subjects*. Test Development and Research Unit, RR/83/07. Cambridge: Oxford and Cambridge Schools Examination Board.

Newton, P.E. (1997). Measuring the comparability of standards between subjects: Why our statistical techniques do not make the grade. *British Educational Research Journal*, *23*, 433–449.

Newton, P.E. (2005). Examination standards and the limits of linking. *Assessment in Education*, *12*, 105–123.

Nuttall, D.L., Backhouse, J.K., & Willmott, A.S. (1974). *Comparability of standards between subjects*. Schools Council Examinations Bulletin 29. London: Evans/Methuen.

Partis, M.T. (1997). *Scaling of tertiary entrance marks in Western Australia*. Osbourne Park, Western Australia: Western Australia Curriculum Council.

Pollitt, A. (1996). *The 'difficulty' of A level subjects*. Unpublished research paper, University of Cambridge Local Examinations Syndicate.

Rasch, G. (1960/1980). *Probabilistic models for some intelligence and attainment tests*. Copenhagen: Danish Institute for Educational Research expanded edition (1980) with foreword and afterword by B.D. Wright. Chicago: The University of Chicago Press.

Rutter, P. (1994). The effect of studying A level mathematics on performance in A level physics. *Physics Education*, 29(1), 8–13.

Scheffé, H. (1959). *The analysis of variance*. New York: Wiley.

Seneta, E. (1987). *The University of Sydney scaling system for the New South Wales Higher School Certificate: A manual*. Sydney: Department of Mathematical Statistics, University of Sydney.

Sparkes, B. (2000). Subject comparisons – A Scottish perspective. *Oxford Review of Education, 26*, 175–189.

UK GCE Examination Boards. (1971). *Dual entry in the 1966 GCE examination. A report prepared by the GCE examination boards in the United Kingdom, January 1971*. Cambridge Assessment Archive, PP/TSW3/8.

Welsh Joint Education Committee. (1973). *Standards in subjects at GCE ordinary level, June 1971*. Research Report No. 1. Cardiff: Welsh Joint Education Committee.

Western Australia Curriculum Council. (1998). *Scaling*. Western Australia: Western Australia Curriculum Council.

Willmott, A. (1995). *A national study of subject grading standards at A level, summer 1993*. Report commissioned by the Standing Research Advisory Committee of the GCE boards.

Wright, B.D., & Stone, M. (1979). *Best test design*. Chicago: MESA Press.

Year 11 Information System. (2006). *Relative ratings. Year 11 indicator system*. Durham: Curriculum, Evaluation and Management Centre, University of Durham

Appendix: Equations for the models

General notation used

For simplicity, any subjects taken by only one candidate, or candidates taking only one subject, are excluded from the analysis in all models.

The following symbols and notation have been used across all models.

D_i is the relative difficulty, or grade correction, for subject i

A_n is the ability of candidate n

D_{ig} is the relative difficulty of grade g in subject i

F_{ig} is the incremental difficulty of grade g relative to the overall difficulty, D_i, of the subject i. Hence, $D_{ig} = D_i + F_{ig}$

P_{nig} is the probability that candidate n taking subject i achieves grade g

S_n is the number of subjects taken by candidate n

C_i is the number of candidates taking subject i

N is the total number of examinations taken in all subjects by all candidates (i.e. $N = \sum_i C_i = \sum_n S_n$)

Φ_i is the set of candidates taking subject i

Θ_n is the set of subjects taken by candidate n

G_{ni} is the grade achieved by candidate n in subject i (if taken)

H_{ni} is the mean grade achieved by candidate n in their $S_n - 1$ other subjects, so

$$H_{ni} = \frac{1}{S_n - 1} \left(\left[\sum_{j \in \Theta_n} G_{nj} \right] - G_{ni} \right) \quad \text{(provided subject } i \text{ is taken by candidate } n\text{)}$$

μ_i is the mean grade for all candidates in subject i, so

$$\mu_i = \frac{1}{C_i} \sum_{n \in \Phi_i} G_{ni}$$

σ_i is the standard deviation of grades for all candidates in subject i, so

$$\sigma_i^2 = \frac{1}{C_i} \sum_{n \in \Phi_i} (G_{ni} - \mu_i)^2$$

Unbiased mean total (UBMT) method

The difficulty, D_i, for each subject, i, is defined as the difference between the mean grade achieved in that subject (μ_i) and the mean of all grades achieved in their other subjects by candidates who took subject i. Hence,

$$D_i = \mu_i - \frac{\sum_{n \in \Phi_i} [H_{ni}(S_n - 1)]}{\sum_{n \in \Phi_i} (S_n - 1)}$$

Kelly's method

Grade corrections, D_i, for each subject can be found as the solution to the matrix equation:

$$\mathbf{B} \cdot \mathbf{d} = \mathbf{v}$$

where $\mathbf{B}$ is a symmetric matrix $[b_{ij}]$, $\mathbf{d}$ is a vector of grade corrections for each subject $[D_i]$, and $\mathbf{v} = [v_i]$, such that

$$v_i = \sum_{n \in \Phi_i} (H_{ni} - G_{ni})$$

and

$$b_{ij} = \begin{cases} C_i + \dfrac{C_i^2}{N} & \text{if } i = j \\ \\ \dfrac{C_i C_j}{N} - \displaystyle\sum_{n \in \Phi_i \cap \Phi_j} \dfrac{1}{S_n - 1} & \text{if } i \neq j \end{cases}$$

These equations are taken from Lawley's Appendix to Kelly (1976a).

Analysis of variance (ANOVA)

The grade achieved by candidate n in subject i is modelled as

$$G_{ni} = u + A_n + D_i + e_{ni}$$

where u is 'an average grade for all candidates and subjects' (not necessarily the mean as calculated) and e_{ni} is the residual or error term (Nuttall $et\ al.$, 1974, p. 38).

If the e_{ni}s are further constrained to average 0 for each candidate and for each subject, and the D_is to sum to 0, then all terms are defined uniquely. The solution amounts to the inversion of a $k \times k$ matrix, where k is the number of subjects.

Average marks scaling

If G_{ni} is the unscaled (raw) mark awarded to candidate n in subject i, then the (within-subject) standardised mark, Z_{ni}, is given by

$$Z_{ni} = \frac{G_{ni} - \mu_i}{\sigma_i}$$

The scaled mark, X_{ni}, is given by

$$X_{ni} = R_i Z_{ni} + D_i$$

where R_i is an index of the relative spread of 'ability' of the students who have taken subject i, and D_i is its relative difficulty.

R_i is defined to be the standard deviation of the Z_{nj}s for all the subjects taken by all candidates who took subject i. Hence,

$$R_i^2 = \frac{\sum\limits_{n \in \Phi_i, j \in \Theta_n} Z_{nj}^2}{\sum\limits_{n \in \Phi_i} S_n} - \left(\frac{\sum\limits_{n \in \Phi_i, j \in \Theta_n} Z_{nj}}{\sum\limits_{n \in \Phi_i} S_n} \right)^2$$

And the D_is are then calculated by solving the simultaneous equations:

$$D_i \cdot \sum_{n \in \Phi_i} S_n = \sum_{n \in \Phi_i, j \in \Theta_n} \left(R_j Z_{nj} + D_j \right)$$

(Derived from Partis, 1997)

Rasch

The partial credit model used here is:

$$\ln \left(P_{nig} / P_{ni(g-1)} \right) = A_n - D_i - F_{ig} = A_n - D_{ig}$$

COMMENTARY ON CHAPTER 9

Iasonas Lamprianou

Heated discussions about the comparability of standards between subjects have worried qualification authorities and the public around the world for many years. Coe's well-thought-out chapter about 'common examinee methods' presents various statistical methods that have been used in the past, and discusses three different conceptions of comparability as applied to examination standards. Coe claims that a comparability method may be validated only under the light of a specific conception of comparability and that 'most of the methods considered [in the chapter] are capable of valid interpretations under the right conditions'. Having this in mind, the author concludes that 'there may be a case, therefore, for the methods that have been outlined in this chapter to play, and be seen to play, a bigger part than they currently do within England in the processes of monitoring and ensuring "comparability"'.

However, international experience has shown that it is often difficult to achieve 'the right conditions' in order to make undisputed interpretations of the results of comparability methods. This commentary briefly reviews three international case studies (based on Lamprianou, 2007) to illustrate that the practical application of comparability methods has been marked with severe and continuous doubts and fierce criticisms by local societies. Contrary to Coe's suggestion for a more systematic use of common examinee methods, this commentary draws a line of caution: more explicit uses of such methods in the English context should probably be done with extra care and only after significant consideration and public debate.

The case of Western Australia

In the case of Western Australia, the Average Marks Scaling (AMS) method (a common examinee method discussed by Coe) is used to accommodate for the fact that students are examined on different subjects in order to be awarded an overall University Admission Index. The Technical Committee on Scaling, a committee responsible for the application of the method, has frequently come forward with admittedly compelling evidence about the fairness of the method but it failed to persuade everybody. The governmental agencies have published widely, albeit in vain, trying to explain the scaling process and to persuade parents and students that there are no problems regarding the comparability between subjects (Universities Admissions Centre, 2006).

The Technical Committee on Scaling (2002) urges 'students… not to try to "work the system" – they are likely to get it wrong' because students often try to identify 'easy' subjects (that are said to be scaled down) in order to avoid them. There is a number of 'frequently asked questions' that come up in governmental leaflets and discussions in the media: 'Are there subjects that are always scaled down?', 'Is it true that if I study this course I can't get a high [scaled score]?' etc. During a recent discussion in the

Parliament (House of Representatives, 2006) it was heard that 'We have... had evidence that if you are studying chemistry you are likely to have your marks downgraded as well' and that 'We have certainly had significant evidence that there is deep concern about the UAI formula'. The scaling method has been accused of threatening the students away from specific subjects and the Technical Committee on Scaling (2002) has commented that 'each year brings its own myths and conspiracy theories'.

The case of Cyprus

The very same 'frequently asked questions' are raised by politicians, parents and students in Cyprus, a country with a long tradition of using scaling methods to make the scores of students on different subjects comparable. Chemistry, a subject notorious among parents and students for allegedly 'consistently being scaled down' compared to other subjects has seen its enrolment dropping by 70% from 2001 to 2006. The source of the problem – as has been repeatedly claimed – mainly lies in the ('qualitatively') different groups of students that actually happen to be examined on the same subjects and in their varying motivations.

It would be very difficult for any comparability method to accommodate for such strong sub-group and motivation effects – except perhaps if different scaling is used for different candidates. At the moment, however, the Cyprus Testing Service has problems persuading the public and politicians about the fairness of the existing comparability method (which one MP has recently characterised as 'complicated formulae... that no one will understand'); how might somebody try to convince them that different methods should be used for different groups of students?

The case of Fiji

The third, and last, example of public distrust comes from the Fiji islands where a statistical method is used to scale the marks of the students in different subjects in order to award a single aggregate score. The Ministry of Education has tried hard to convince the public about the fairness of the method, giving examples of its widespread use abroad; alas, with little success. The minutes from a 2004 session of the Parliament read:

> Currently, there is a strong public debate on the scaling of marks and the general feeling is that, it is a bad practice... The session on the scaling of marks by the Ministry of Education's Exam Office was very revealing... It had a formula that made little sense [and] factors no one knew how they were derived.
>
> Parliament of Fiji (2004)

The Fiji Human Rights Commission was reported in the summer of 2006 to be investigating alleged breaches of human rights when students' external examination marks were scaled. According to Radio New Zealand International (2006), 'the *Fiji Times* reports that this follows complaints that the mark scaling system is unfair, non-transparent and violates the Bill of Rights in the Constitution and the Fiji Human Rights Commission Act'.

A pattern of doubts and distrust

There is a pattern in all three case studies above: (a) the comparability methods in use are difficult for the layperson to understand; (b) there are beliefs of allegedly unfair effects on the system; and (c) there is a general feeling of distrust. But is there a relationship between these issues and the conceptions of comparability suggested by Coe and others in this book?

It is difficult to see how students or parents could argue in favour of the 'performance' conception of comparability: being examined on different subjects, e.g. French or chemistry is obviously a non-comparable experience. If we would ever try to publicly support a performance conception of comparability, we would hit problems; people would not understand our complex web of specifications and assumptions about the intellectual demand made by each of the examinations. This might provoke feelings of unfairness, and we would probably spark a new round of doubt and distrust.

Having said this, however, the stakeholders in the three case studies mentioned above (as well as in other places like Tasmania, Singapore, Canada's British Columbia, etc.) seem to compromise with the idea that there must be something common between all subjects – albeit 'practically' different – so that one is justified in aggregating scores on different subjects for practical ranking purposes. It seems that when the public is faced with the need to make direct comparisons between candidates to allocate scarce educational resources, the 'construct' conception is easier to endorse. The problem, though, with the construct conception of comparability is that it is best (though not solely) served by complex statistical techniques like the Rasch model (used by the Tasmanian Qualifications Authority) or the AMS. Complex methods, however, are incomprehensible to the layperson and even rare examples of 'unfair' scaling results are usually put forward by the media to erode public trust in the system. Such models imply that the success rate will not be the same on different subjects, therefore generating allegations of unfairness (tapping into the concept of 'statistical' comparability).

The statistical conception of comparability initially looks deceptively easier to endorse by parents and students. Intuitively the public will question the results when the pass rates on different subjects are widely different; so would keeping the grade distribution similar on each subject solve the problem of perceived unfairness? Such an approach to comparability could probably involve simpler statistics so the first problem (that the layperson does not understand the statistics) could be solved. However, the media would probably fail such an approach on the grounds of first-page 'case study examples', i.e. bright students being awarded very different grades on different subjects depending on their popularity and the competition within them.

Unravelling the Gordian knot of comparability is very difficult. The public seems to have a dual approach: they generally endorse the construct approach for practical purposes, while they hesitate to drop the statistical approach altogether. Drawing on the experience of other countries, England must be very careful before proceeding with further (and probably formal) use of comparability methods. Since pragmatism should prevail when attempting to solve practical educational problems with social consequences, it is important to seek a general consensus from the major stakeholders before taking the next step.

References

House of Representatives. (2006, March 10). Standing committee on agriculture, fisheries and forestry. Armidale: Commonwealth of Australia, House of Representatives.

Lamprianou, I. (2007). *The international perspective of examination comparability methods. Technical report.*

Parliament of Fiji. (2004, July 29). *Parliamentary debates, House of Representatives.* Daily Hansard.

Radio New Zealand International. (2006, August 31). *Fiji human rights commission to investigate exam scaling.*

Technical Committee on Scaling. (2002). *Report of calculation of universities admission index 2001.* Academic Board Report. New South Wales: Committee of Chais, University of New South Wales.

Universities Admissions Centre. (2006). *You and your UAI. A booklet for 2006 New South Wales HSC students.*

COMMENTARY ON CHAPTER 9

Alastair Pollitt

This commentary concerns the causes of apparent differences in the 'difficulty' of different subjects that appear in common examinee analyses. In Chapter 9 Coe refers several times to Pollitt (1996), but each time only to relatively minor points in that paper, whose main purpose was to report a comparison of the results of common examinee analyses in England and Singapore which helps shed light on some factors that contribute to the pattern obtained. Since that paper has not been published, the gist of the report is repeated here.

Our interest was aroused by discussion surroundings Dearing's (1996) review of 16–19 qualifications, in which the results of common examinee analyses seemed to imply that some A level examinations were consistently harder than others. A very similar pattern had been reported for Scottish exams by Kelly (1976), and since then in other 'old Commonwealth' countries.

The Dearing report recommended that England should 'raise the demand of any subjects found to be decidedly below the average'. But the consistency of the pattern argued against that conclusion. How could it be that Scotland and the other countries somehow took their subject standards from England, where the original standards had been set wrongly? Alternatively, how could every one of these independent assessment systems have accidentally made the same pattern of errors as each other? It seemed to me more reasonable to see the consistent patterns as evidence that England (and the others) had got things more or less right than that everyone had got them wrong. But it was possible that the common cultural foundation of the old Commonwealth could be a consistent source of some kind of bias.

A level results data were available from one other country – Singapore – which had not been analysed in this way before, and which was culturally rather different. In just three decades it had risen from third world status to achieve a GNP per head at least as high as its former colonial master; also, in each of 1995, 1999 and 2003 it was the most successful country in the world in the TIMSS 8th grade mathematics studies. The majority of the population are ethnically Chinese, but with a generally high level of English as a second language, and Europeans are a small minority. Singapore is different from old Commonwealth countries in many ways: would these differences lead to a different pattern?

Comparing subject pair analyses

In the early 1990s most of the University of Cambridge Local Examinations Syndicate (UCLES) overseas A level examinations were either identical to the UK ones or constructed in parallel by overlapping teams of examiners. The mathematics exam was identical. The 'Management of Business' exam differed from the UK 'Business Studies' one in that an extra written paper replaced the course work element, but the common papers were used to set the standard. There is no reason why any of these minor differences should interfere with the analysis here, given that the UK pattern of apparent difficulty holds up so consistently across so many different UK syllabuses.

A subject pairs analysis was carried out using mathematics as a reference. Every other subject for which pair information was available from more than 1,000 candidates per year was compared to mathematics. All analyses are based on the averages of three years, 1993–95.

Figure 1 shows the results of the analysis for Singapore plotted against the 'corrections' for England published in Dearing (1996); the scale is grades, so physics seemed to be 1.7 grades 'harder' than mathematics for Singaporean students. As in the Dearing and ALIS studies,[1] physics and general studies appear at the top of the order of 'difficulty', and English at the bottom.

Figure 1 Relative 'difficulties' in Singapore and England

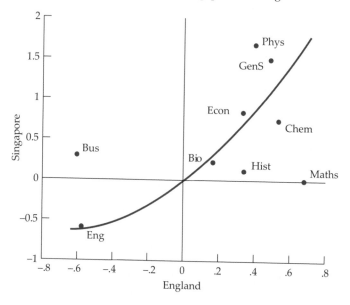

The Singapore differences are clearly larger, the difference between 'hardest' and 'easiest' (physics and English) being 2.28 grades compared to 1.30 in Dearing. And chemistry has moved substantially, becoming 0.85 grades 'easier' than physics (or perhaps physics has become 'harder' by the same amount) while in England they seem equally difficult. Nevertheless, with the help of the quadratic regression line plotted on the figure, the Singapore pattern can be interpreted as similar to that observed in other developed Western nations – supporting the view that there is some overall truth in the relative order.

In order to plot this line, however, it is necessary to omit two subjects that stand out as very different, business and mathematics. In the Western countries mathematics is consistently in the 'most difficult' group, but in Singapore it is 'easier' than anything else except English. In fact it was a concern on the part of their Ministry that mathematics might really be too easy that initiated this study. Of course we might consider it remarkable that English should seem so easy, in a country where it is not the native language of the vast majority of candidates. A special educational effort is certainly, and necessarily, put into English language teaching to compensate for this so that school pupils are able to study through the medium of English. It is likely too, though, that the group who choose to take English literature as an A level subject are rather different from their British counterparts.

Why should mathematics seem to be so easy in Singapore? It is common for British newspapers to report that Eastern children are much better than England's at mathematics – with the implication that they are better at everything else as well. The analysis here seems to agree that, at A level at least, they are superior in mathematics – but only in mathematics, since it seems so much more easier relative to the others than in England.

However, another familiar stereotype is that the 'tiger economies' are very business oriented. It is therefore something of a surprise to see that they find 'Management of Business' so much more 'difficult' than Western candidates do. If *they're good at mathematics* explains its relative 'easiness' how does *they're good at business* fit with its relative 'difficulty'? It is of course quite easy to invent a plausible explanation: suppose that 'business oriented' really means that many of them expect to get jobs in business or set up their own businesses, and they therefore take business as an A level even if they are not particularly good at it – perhaps alongside mathematics which they are good at. Perhaps most of the good mathematics students think that they ought to combine mathematics with something practical, so that they will be able to get – or create – proper jobs. The result would be that most mathematics+business students would be better at mathematics than at business.

Such explanations may or may not be true; we have no way of knowing from the statistics alone. The main conclusion of this analysis has to be that we cannot interpret differences between subject mean grades, whether from subject pair analyses or any other analysis, as evidence of differences in 'difficulty' unless we know who took each subject, and why. The 'appeal of the method', as Coe notes, depends heavily on the presumption that perfectly matching the *general* features of the individual candidates is an adequate basis for comparing the two examinations, but the discussion in the last paragraph shows that the *specific* interactions between student and subject – their interest in it, their motivation to succeed, and their reasons for choosing to study it – are likely to affect their level of success in ways that *general* characteristics cannot predict. A similar argument applies at the level of schools: the method presumes that matching samples in terms of the *general* characteristics of the schools they attend is sufficient to equate the students' expected grades. However, when 85% of England's secondary schools are now 'Specialist schools' (DfES, 2007), with *specific* expertise in just one or two out of ten curricular areas, we can no longer assume that any school will provide the same quality of teaching and preparation in every subject.

Demands and conceptions of comparability

The differences between Coe's three kinds of comparability arise from how they consider *difficulty* and *demands* (see Chapter 5 for an extended discussion of how these two concepts can be distinguished). His 'statistical' comparability is wholly concerned with the difficulty (not the demands) of examinations. Evidence of sub-group differences like those reported here, or of sex differences within England, make this conception of comparability very problematic. The use of terms like 'a "typical" student', and the quotation from Nuttall *et al.* (1974), show that it is fundamentally a norm-referenced approach, and inappropriate for an examination context where the samples taking any two examinations will *never* be representative of the same population. Examination boards routinely use common examinee analyses to monitor standards, but they do not act on first-order differences like those discussed here; instead they look for second-order differences – *changes* in the normal pattern – as indicators that something may have gone wrong on a particular occasion.

'Construct' comparability relates wholly to demands (not to difficulty), since the *linking construct* will in fact be the subset of all the demands in either exam that is common to both of them; this common subset may well be unrepresentative of all the demands in either of them. Thus with this conceptualisation it is quite possible, on a subject pairs basis, for A to be 'harder' than B, for B to be 'harder' than C, and for C to be 'harder' than A, since the linking construct will be different for each comparison. If many examinations are included in the comparison the linking construct, being common to all, must be a very small subset of the demands of some of them, which will seriously undermine the usefulness of the comparisons. Further, it is very important to remember that, as in factor analysis, giving a 'label' to the common subset is far from a trivial exercise, and it is very dangerous – to claim that 'here the linking construct is "general aptitudes"' or 'here... might be... the effectiveness of the teaching received' unless you have compelling empirical evidence to support the label.

Coe's 'performance' comparability involves a mixture of difficulty and demands. The phrase 'would be seen as more "difficult"'... if it made a greater demand on the candidate' shows that examiners who judge comparability with this conception must consider both the demands the examination made and how hard the candidates found it to meet them. The two examinations will not contain the same questions, and the judges must estimate how much 'ability' is needed to produce the observed quality of performance after compensating for their estimates of the levels of demands in the tasks. 'Ability' in this sense is estimated on some scale that the judges have formulated intuitively as the *common* scale for the two (or more) exams. As with 'construct' comparability, this common-scale comparison is then used to infer the standard on the rest of each examination even though the rest of their demands may well be quite different. This is certainly the most complex of the three conceptions: it requires the judges to combine different kinds of evidence in a sophisticated way that cannot easily be modelled statistically or even described theoretically.[2] The real world of examining is complex in just this way, and we should not be surprised that 'construct' comparability 'appears to be the default in thinking about comparability'.

In passing, we explain in Chapter 5 why the view that 'it should be possible to specify the difficulty of an examination even if no candidate has ever taken it' will for ever remain an illusion.

To summarise, we cannot get rid of the sub-group anomalies just by switching to a different conceptualisation of comparability; they are real and problematic. The demands of A level mathematics are the same whether you are a boy from Singapore or a girl from England but, because of a different cultural setting and the expectations and exam preparations that result from it, the difficulty of the exam is quite different for the two groups.

Endnotes

1 The ALIS studies were reported in Dearing (1996).

2 Indeed, Good and Cresswell (1988) provided evidence that even the wisest examiners may be systematically biased in making these judgements.

References

Dearing, R. (1996). *Review of qualifications for 16–19 year olds*. London: School Curriculum and Assessment Authority.

Department for Education and Skills. (2007). *The standards site. Specialist schools: What are specialist schools?* Available at: http://www.standards.dfes.gov.uk/specialistschools/

Good, F.J., & Cresswell, M.J. (1988). Grade awarding judgments in differentiated examinations. *British Educational Research Journal, 14*, 263–281.

Kelly, A. (1976). A study of the comparability of external examinations in different subjects. *Research in Education, 16*, 37–63.

Nuttall, D.L., Backhouse, J.K., & Willmott, A.S. (1974). *Comparability of standards between subjects*. Schools Council Examinations Bulletin 29. London: Evans/Methuen.

Pollitt, A. (1996). *The 'difficulty' of A level subjects*. Unpublished research paper, University of Cambridge Local Examinations Syndicate.

10

MULTILEVEL MODELLING METHODS

Ian Schagen and Dougal Hutchison

Abstract

Aim

The aim of the chapter is to introduce multilevel modelling as a key methodology for the analysis of data in comparability studies and show how it can be applied in different situations and to different data sets.

Definition of comparability

The main definition addressed is that of Cresswell (1996):

> Two examinations have comparable standards if two groups of candidates with the same distributions of ability and prior achievement who attend similar schools with identical entry policies, are taught by equally competent teachers and are equally motivated, receive grades which are identically distributed after studying their respective syllabuses and taking their examinations.

Following the consideration of interaction effects, the chapter suggests limitations with this definition and suggests consideration of a new and more robust definition.

Comparability methods

Although not a comparability method in the same sense as those described in other chapters, multilevel modelling underpins the quantitative approaches discussed elsewhere. It is a statistical modelling tool, derived from multiple regression with the ability to include within-group clustering at a variety of levels in a unified and consistent fashion.

History of use

Since its development in the 1980s, multilevel modelling has been applied in a wide variety of fields, including education, although examination comparability studies have been in some ways a minority application. Over recent years it has tended to replace other less sophisticated analysis methods as the preferred statistical approach. A brief review of studies using multilevel methods is included in the chapter.

Strengths and weaknesses

The main strength of multilevel modelling is its power and flexibility, and ability to model a wide range of scenarios and situations. As with all modelling, the weaknesses lie in the quality of the available data and problems with setting up models correctly to represent the important underlying relationships.

Conclusion

The main conclusions of the chapter are as follows:

- The advantages of multilevel modelling far outweigh any perceived disadvantages for this kind of work.

- Modelling should explore all possible aspects of comparability, including interactions between boards and key measures such as prior attainment.

- Where such interactions are detected, it is not clear that comparability is maintained – a new definition may be needed to encompass this.

1 Introduction

In this chapter we propose to start from the definition of comparability as given by Cresswell (1996). In this he states that 'two examinations have comparable standards if two groups of candidates with the same distributions of ability and prior achievement who attend similar schools with identical entry policies, are taught by equally competent teachers and are equally motivated, receive grades which are identically distributed after studying their respective syllabuses and taking their examinations.' From this starting point, we aim to show how the use of multilevel modelling techniques can help to investigate comparability understood in this way.

Statistical methods for ensuring comparability may appear to be more objective than those that rely solely on expert judgements, and in many ways this is true. However the objectivity is relative, in the sense that all statistical methods rely on a mathematical model of the underlying situation, and the choice of this model will in most cases affect the results produced and the conclusions reached. There is therefore still an important element of judgement involved in the choice of such models, and in this chapter we aim to inform such judgement with an overview of the range of statistical models available, mostly based on multilevel analysis (see Goldstein, 2003).

In any comparability analysis we are asking questions of the kind: 'What are the differences between these boards/subjects/questions/syllabuses in terms of actual results achieved compared with expected results?' It is in the definition of 'expected results' that the statistical model comes in. The complexity of the statistical model required depends on the data that is available and the assumptions we are able to make about the relationships between examination outcomes and other factors about which we have information, and which may affect examination performance.

At the simplest possible level, we could imagine having no other data than the test scores for two groups of candidates, one of which took Test A and the other Test B. With no further information, our model might be that both groups were equivalent simple random samples from the underlying population and then our statistical test of equivalence would be a two-sample t-test[1]. In this case, the 'expected results' for the two groups are assumed identical. This equates to the 'no nonsense' definition set out by Cresswell (1996). Obviously this simple assumption is quite likely to be falsified, leading to a lack of robustness and validity in this minimal form of comparability study.

Moving to a more complex and perhaps more reasonable example, let us assume we still have the two groups doing different examinations, but in this case we have a great deal more background information on the two groups, including a number of measures of prior attainment in earlier tests, background information such as the candidates' sex, ethnicity and social status (perhaps even parental income), as well as data about the institutions in which they are studying.[2] We now have much more scope for computing 'expected results', based on a complex regression model taking account of all these factors. We need to be aware, however, that decisions about which variables to include in a comparability study model are a matter for judgement, not just a technical issue depending only on the information that happens to be available.

Once we have reached agreement on which factors should be controlled for, there are some extra complications we would want to take into account.

- Candidates are grouped into institutions or examination centres – probably there is more similarity in outcomes between candidates in the same centre than between centres. Also, relationships with (for example) prior attainment may vary from centre to centre – the so-called 'random slopes' situation.

- There may be interactions between results for the two different tests and background factors. For example, Test A may produce better results for boys rather than girls relative to Test B, or one test may have a stronger relationship with prior attainment than the other. If this is the case, of course, it raises a number of issues about comparability and whether different 'adjustments' should be made for different groups of candidates to bring the tests into line.

Both the above complications can be taken account of by using a suitably complex model, with a structure that allows explicitly for these inter-relationships. The use of multilevel modelling, with which this chapter is largely concerned, will help us to deal with the first complication above. The second complication can also be dealt with in the setting up of the model by including suitable interaction terms. The identification of such potential relationships and the inclusion of them in the model used are very important elements of any comparability study, and will form a major part of the theme of this chapter. However, modelling does not solve the interaction problem, it merely allows us to quantify it. It could be argued that, by the Cresswell definition, as soon as statistically significant interaction terms are detected then comparability is violated – since we could find a sub-set of candidates with identical characteristics but different results in the two examinations.

Throughout this book there are issues that need to be addressed in the course of any comparability study, and these will not all be rehearsed here. An example, however, is the issue of unmeasured factors that are confounded with the differences we are interested in, the outcomes from the different examinations.

Let us suppose that the Test B syllabus is more attractive to candidates and encourages a more positive motivation and response to the subject, and hence a better set of results. In the model we set up, we cannot control for this and must assume that motivation and response are the same across the two groups. The comparability study will therefore adjust the results of the unmotivated Test A group to be equivalent to those of the motivated Test B group. Is this fair? If we were able to measure motivation and allow for it in the modelling, then Group B would be acknowledged to have achieved comparatively better results than Group A, and as the study has not shown this it has actually failed to achieve true comparability between the *examinations* rather than the syllabuses. For further discussion, see Jones (1997).

It is possible to think of other examples where unmeasured confounding factors or selection effects can lead to misleading results. The only rigorous way in which such confounding effects can be eliminated is through the adoption of a Randomised Control Trial (RCT) approach (see Mosteller & Boruch, 2002; Styles, 2006). In this approach, candidates or centres would be randomly allocated to syllabus A or B and thus would take the equivalent Test A or Test B. Because of the randomisation, confounding factors would be equally likely to apply to either test, and if sufficiently large samples were used it should be possible to carry out a powerful test for the comparability of the two syllabuses. (Note, however, that this would not overcome the difficulty set out in the previous paragraph – differential motivation between syllabuses. This could only be detected by random allocations to examinations as well as syllabuses, with further administrative and practical difficulties.)

A number of practical and ethical objections could be raised to this particular design of comparability study. One is that it would be an administrative and logistical nightmare to assign candidates within the same centre to different syllabuses, and that only randomisation at the centre level would be at all feasible. This modification of the RCT design would work also, but would suffer from the problems of correlations within centres and would thus require a larger sample size to detect a given difference. Although in theory an RCT 'randomises away' all the effects of related variables, and could therefore be analysed by a simple t-test, in practice the use of a multilevel model even in this case would be recommended, for two reasons. One is that it would allow for the effects of measured background factors that were not completely balanced between the two groups. The other is that it would allow for the within-centre clustering mentioned above, if randomisation occurred at the centre level.

Of course, this kind of comparability study never happens, for what may well be good reasons to do with practicality, customer choice and other pragmatic considerations. Without going into the arguments in favour of attempting such a study, for our purposes we shall treat it as an ideal and see to what extent the examples we shall consider in this chapter fall short of this design. In the meantime, let us just list some of the effects that can and cannot be taken into account when modelling administrative data rather than analysing a full RCT.

The following can be included in a suitable model:

- overall effects of measured background factors on performance, plus non-linearities in these effects

- interactions between measured factors in their effect on performance

- clustering of candidates within centres

- random variations between centres in the effects of background factors

- interactions between different examinations and background factors.

The following cannot generally be allowed for in modelling:

- options effects – candidates or centres preferentially choosing different examinations[3]

- other unmeasured factors, especially those that vary systematically across syllabuses

- differences between examinations that mean they are testing different constructs, or mixtures of constructs.

Sophistication of modelling does not guarantee the validity of a comparability study – on the other hand, unsophisticated models may be missing something critical that fatally challenges their validity. In this chapter we shall set out some of the features of complex models and the advantages they can bring, but it will always be important to bear in mind the caveats and health warnings expressed above.

2 Advantages of using multilevel modelling

A widely used technique in statistics and in research with educational applications is regression. This explores how a number of variables, described as explanatory variables, relate to another variable, referred to as a response or outcome variable. Explanatory variables are also sometimes referred to as independent variables or predictor variables, and outcome variables are also referred to as dependent variables. An example would be to predict the score on a later test given knowledge of earlier test scores.

The earliest and probably still the best known type of regression is known as Ordinary Least Squares (OLS) regression. In this the outcome Y is assumed to be some function (often a linear function) of the explanatory variables X, Z; and to take account of the fact that one does not expect such a relation to be exact, an error or residual term e is introduced. To distinguish the cases, each one is numbered, using the suffix i, so that we get Y_i, X_i, Z_i and so on. Then a very simple relationship with one X variable can be written in equation form:

$$Y_i = \beta_0 + \beta_1 X_i + e_i \qquad (1)$$

β_0 is described as the *intercept* and β_1 as the *slope*.

To provide a worked example to illustrate the differences between OLS regression and multilevel modelling and to show the kinds of analyses that are possible, we have constructed simulated data with an assumed underlying structure, as follows:

- Twenty candidates in each of twenty centres have GCSE subject results represented as Uniform Mark Scale[4] (UMS) scores (Y) plus a measure of prior attainment based on Key Stage 3 fine grades[5] in the same subject (X).

- There is a linear relationship between X and Y, plus a random error quantity for each candidate.

- Each centre is classified as either Type A or B; the relationship between X and Y is in general slightly different for the two types of centre.

- In addition, the relationship between X and Y varies from centre to centre.

The explanatory variable is the Key Stage 3 fine grade (X) and the response variable is the UMS score (Y). Equation (1) can have values of its coefficients (β_0 and β_1) estimated by a standard OLS regression package from the simulated data set; in this case the estimates are shown below:

$$Y_i = -106.93(18.44) + 79.82(3.05) * X_i + e_i \qquad (2)$$

This shows that, on average, for an increase of one point in X, there is a corresponding increase of approximately 80 points in Y. The figures in brackets are the standard errors of the coefficients. These indicate the uncertainty in the estimates due to the fact that they are derived from finite data sets. Assuming the error terms in the model are Normally distributed (see later), then from the standard error estimates it is possible to derive 'confidence intervals' for the coefficients, such that there is a specified chance that the true value of each coefficient lies within its given interval. For example, the coefficient of X has a standard error (SE) of 3.05 – to derive the 95% confidence interval for this value we multiply by 1.96 and add and subtract this value from the estimate. This yields an interval from 73.84 to 85.80. The constant term (–106.93) is the intercept, the expected value of Y if X were to have the value zero – in practice, not ever attained but a necessary element of the model.

The e_i error term in this model is assumed to be independent of the response variable and the explanatory variables, and to be normally distributed with mean zero. Explanatory variables do not have to be continuous, so we could include a categorical variable – for example, to compare Type A and B centres by giving Z a value of 0 for Type A and 1 for Type B.

The estimated coefficients corresponding to this extended model are given by

$$Y_i = -106.38(18.66) + 79.83(3.05) * X_i - 1.17(5.88) * Z_i + e_i \qquad (3)$$

The 95% confidence interval for the difference between Type A and B centres (taking account of prior attainment) is –12.69 to 10.35, implying there is no clear evidence from this analysis of a real difference overall between the two centre types.

This kind of model makes a key assumption that the candidates in the analysis are all equally representative of candidates in general, and takes no account of the fact that they are grouped within centres. It is frequently the case, however, that candidates in the same centre are more similar than they are to candidates in other centres.[6] This means that it is not legitimate to use the standard OLS regression, which assumes that all units are independent. We could get biased results, in particular for the standard errors in the coefficients, which could be underestimated by assuming that all the observations were independent.

The OLS model (1) above assumes that there is no additional information obtained by knowing the higher-level unit (centre) from which a lower-level unit (candidate) comes. One possible approach to taking account of this would be to define a set of 'centre effects', one per centre, and include these in the OLS model. This obviously makes the model much more cumbersome, and also assumes that the centre effects are to be treated as *fixed* – in other words, we are interested in these values in their own right, rather than as a general addition to the uncertainty in the modelling. If we turn to the multilevel modelling approach, these centre effects are treated as *random* – we are only interested in their overall effects and the differences they make to the model as a whole. We shall now consider this approach to the analysis of the same data. Model (1) can be extended by including a term to take account of the similarity of items within higher-level units.

$$Y_{ij} = \beta_0 + \beta_1 X_{ij} + u_j + e_{ij}$$
$$u_j \sim N(0, \sigma_u^2), e_{ij} \sim N(0, \sigma^2) \qquad (4)$$

The term u_j ('centre residual') is assumed to include all those unmeasured factors at a centre level that influence results for all candidates at the centre; in general we assume this combined factor is Normally distributed. However, in certain cases such as modelling binary outcomes (see later) a non-linear model may be required, although centre residuals may still be assumed to be Normally distributed in the transformed metric.

Each equation now has two subscripts, i, j, corresponding to candidate and centre. This means that there is a separate regression for each higher-level unit. In this equation, because β_1 has no j subscript, the relationship between Y and X is the same in each centre, and these regressions are all parallel. This is an example of multilevel modelling.

Estimating the same model as in (3) above, but taking account of within-school similarities using multilevel modelling, gives:

$$Y_{ij} = -101.65(18.89) + 79.03(2.81) * X_{ij} - 1.15(12.43) * Z_j + u_j + e_{ij} \tag{5}$$

There are small differences between the coefficients in the two sets of results, but the main difference lies in the standard error of the Z coefficient, which has increased from 5.88 under the OLS estimation to 12.43 under multilevel modelling. This is a fairly common feature of moving from OLS regression to multilevel modelling: standard errors for variables that relate to higher-level units tend to increase, due to the clustering of data within such units. In the above example it makes no difference to the significance of the coefficient, but it is easily possible to find cases in which this difference can affect the conclusions drawn from the analysis.

When setting up our example data we said that the relationship between Y and X was different for the two centre types, and also that it varied from centre to centre. To see how both these effects can be included in the modelling we will discuss interactions and random slopes. We have seen that there is no apparent significant difference between the centre types when we assume the regression lines are parallel; however, to model a non-parallel situation we need to define an interaction term:

$$I_{ij} = Z_j (X_{ij} - 6) \tag{6}$$

For Type A centres, the value above is zero; for Type B it introduces a change in the regression slope against prior attainment. The value 6 is the mean value of X and ensures that the interaction term is zero on average or 'centred'. Including this extra term in the model gives us the following fitted model:

$$Y_{ij} = -25.82(23.85) + 66.31(3.73) * X_{ij} - 0.39(12.18) * Z_j + 27.16(5.45) * I_{ij} + u_j + e_{ij} \tag{7}$$

The coefficient of the interaction term is clearly significant, and this implies that the two centre types do have different regression slopes: 66.31 for Type A and 93.47 for Type B. In order to look in more detail at the above model, we need to consider the so-called 'random part' of the model – the variances and covariances between the various parameters which vary from candidate to candidate and from centre to centre. In the above model there are only two elements to this, and the estimated variances and standard errors are set out below:

Between-candidate variance:	2629.5 (190.8)
Between-centre variance (intercept):	609.7 (234.6)

From the above figures we can surmise that variation between centres accounts for about 19% of the total variance in the outcome, once other factors are allowed for.

To add an extra complexity to the above model, let us assume that the regression slopes vary from centre to centre, as well as between centre types. To model this we assume that the coefficient of X is made of two parts:

$$\beta_j = \beta_1 + u_{1j} \tag{8}$$

where the first term is the overall fixed part of the coefficient and the second, with mean zero, is the part that varies from centre to centre. The centre-level covariance matrix becomes:

$$\begin{bmatrix} Var(u_{0j}) & Covar(u_{0j}, u_{1j}) \\ Covar(u_{0j}, u_{1j}) & Var(u_{1j}) \end{bmatrix}$$

Fitting this model to the data gives us the following:

$$Y_{ij} = -27.95(26.75) + \{66.64(4.68) + u_{1j}\} * X_{ij} - 0.137(12.48) * Z_j + 26.07(6.74) * I_{ij} + u_{0j} + e_{ij} \tag{9}$$

In order to look in more detail at the above model the random parameters are set out below, together with the standard errors of the estimates:

Between-candidate variance:	$Var(e_{ij})$:	2551.9 (189.9)
Between-centre variance (intercept):	$Var(u_{0j})$:	2053.4 (2318.6)
Between-centre variance (slope):	$Var(u_{1j})$:	78.8 (70.8)
Centre covariance (intercept/slope):	$Covar(u_{0j}, u_{1j})$:	−353.3 (395.3)

From the above, it seems that the standard errors in the slope variance and the intercept/slope covariance are both close to the estimated values, implying that neither is statistically significant. To confirm this more rigorously, we should consider the change in the likelihood (represented in MLwiN by the 'deviance') in adding the random slopes. This gives a change of 3.63, compared with a critical chi-squared value (5% significance, two degrees of freedom) equal to 5.99. From this, it seems that this extension to the model does not result in significant random parameters at the centre level – in particular the assumption of random slopes is not supported by the data. It should be noted that this does not mean there are no random slopes, but rather that our data is insufficient to detect them with confidence.

Reverting to model (7) above, Figure 1 shows a graph of expected UMS score (Y) versus prior attainment (X) for each type of centre. It shows the lines based on the model results above, plus the 'actual' relationships on which the original simulated data was based.

Figure 1 Expected outcomes versus prior attainment by centre type (model and actual)

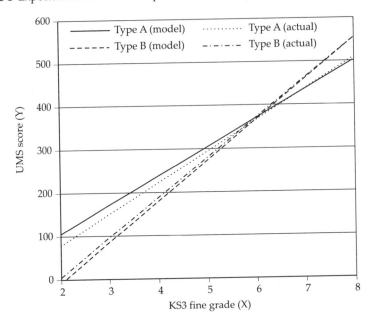

It is clear that we have made a reasonable job of recreating the underlying relationships from a relatively small amount of data. However, normally we do not have the luxury of knowing what these relationships should be, and our model fitting process cannot guarantee that we have uncovered all possible details of the structure of the data. Models of increasing complexity, with additional terms, interactions, and random parameters can be created, and this kind of model fitting relies heavily on the modeller's insights and judgement rather than explicit rules. There is no substitute for experience and a deep understanding of the subject matter when engaged in this kind of activity. In this section we have used simulated data to illustrate some aspects of the different kinds of models that are possible; in later sections we will be using real data to illustrate particular applications in examination comparability studies.

What difference does it make if we do not use multilevel modelling? Some authorities argue that it is not necessary to use multilevel modelling if the within-school clustering is sufficiently small. This can be assessed by comparing the variance at the higher level with that at the lower level; however, in order to assess this it is necessary to run a multilevel model or equivalent. Even where this holds and the differences between intercepts are negligible, there is still the possibility that there will be differences between slopes, so it is advisable at least to investigate the use of multilevel modelling.

Other approaches include, on the one hand, ignoring the level structure and simply attaching all variables, no matter what level they arise from, to the lowest-level unit (in this instance, pupils); or, on the other hand, aggregating lower-level scores, and dealing with aggregates (here, schools). The first of these risks giving a highly exaggerated impression of the effect of higher-level effects. The second is effectively throwing away data, and largely ignores individual-level pupil differences and differences in slopes between higher-level units. Also, using this approach means that the ecological fallacy[7] can give a completely biased and inflated estimate of individual correlations.

Another approach, which goes some way towards a multilevel approach, carries out a series of separate OLS regressions, one for each higher-level unit, and then attempts to model the residuals from each (Burstein, 1980). However, this can give biased estimation and also loses sight of the essential unity of the data. It can also lead to excessive numbers of parameters and loss of parsimony, as well as giving no way to generalise to the population of higher-level units. Multilevel modelling, by treating every effect at the appropriate level, gives unbiased estimates of standard errors, and enables the modelling of between-level interactions. Multilevel modelling, generally, provides a unified treatment for effects at all levels. It is efficient in terms of the number of parameters to be estimated and allows the extension of existing generalised linear model techniques by taking account of hierarchical structures in the data.

The value of using multilevel modelling has been attacked by some writers (for example Fitz-Gibbon & Tymms, 2002; Gorard, 2003a). While in general they appear to accept in principle the benefits that may be adduced by using multilevel analysis, they are unhappy with the widespread use of it on two main grounds: first, that it is complicated to understand the details, thus potentially alienating users and audience; second, while apparently implicitly accepting that multilevel modelling is a technically superior exercise, they argue that it fails to produce any new results, and that the results are closely correlated with those from Ordinary Least Squares. Gorard has a number of other theoretical points and these may be assessed in the debate between Gorard and Fielding & Plewis (Gorard, 2003a, 2003b; Plewis & Fielding, 2003).

The writers of this chapter favour the use of multilevel modelling methods in these applications and more generally. First, we believe that the objections to the difficulty of the technique are overstated, and that it is more important that analyses such as these are carried out to the best of our available techniques – it is more important to be correct than to appear simple. Second, the main difference arising as a result of using multilevel methods is not that new real findings are made that would be otherwise overlooked, but rather that we avoid making findings that are not there. That said, it is often true that the values of fixed effects found in these analyses will be similar to those found using OLS regression, although this is not true in all cases.

3   What can be compared using multilevel modelling?

There are many ways in which multilevel modelling techniques (Goldstein, 2003; Raudenbush & Bryk, 2002) may be used in examination comparability studies. Very simply, their strengths may be summed up as:

- they are a type of regression technique used to compare like with like

- they take account of the structure of the education and examination system, and allow for the fact that candidates within entry centres or teacher groups are likely to be more similar to each other than to the rest of the population as a whole.

We shall describe the statistical basis of a number of applications. Nothing is said here at this stage about the realism or otherwise of any assumptions used. Later, we shall also describe applications to real data, both from our own work and that of other researchers, and comment on some of the features and assumptions. For this section of the description, a simple linear model treating the outcome examination result as a continuous variable is used. Later in this chapter we show how different types of model can give different results.

3.1 Application 1: Comparing different boards for the same subjects

The characteristics of the pupils taking their exams via different boards may well be very different, so a number of proposed factors are included in the analysis. The equation is given by

$$Y_{ijk} = \beta_0 + (\sum_p \beta_p x_{pijk}) + v_k + u_{jk} + (\sum_q \beta_q z_{qijk}) + (\sum_q e_{qijk} z_{qijk}) \qquad (10)$$

where:

Y_{ijk} = the examination outcomes (assumed to be a continuous variable, e.g. UMS score) for candidate i in teaching group j in centre k

β_0 = the intercept (the expected value of Y_{ijk} when all variables are equal to zero)

$\sum_p \beta_p x_{pijk}$ = the sum of the coefficients for the explanatory variables times the value of the variables for candidate i in teaching group j in centre k. Explanatory variables may include prior attainment, sex, age and other relevant background characteristics.

z_{qijk} is an indicator variable for the board q (= 1 if candidate sits board q, = 0 else)

β_q is the coefficient for board q (the amount by which the expected scores for board q differ from β_0, when all variables except board indicators are equal to zero)

v_k = the effect of centre k, assumed Normally distributed with mean zero

u_{jk} = the effect of teaching group j in centre k, assumed Normally distributed with mean zero

e_{qijk} = residual error for candidate i in teaching group j in centre k, at board q, assumed Normally distributed with mean zero and variance σ_q^2. This allows for a different variance for each board.

In setting up such models, there are two kinds of background variables that can be included – those which are assumed to be numerical scales (such as previous test scores), and those which are categorical (such as board taken). To include categorical variables, we produce a set of binary indicators (taking values 0 or 1) to represent each category *except one*. The omitted category is the 'default' or 'base' category against which the others are tested. It is important not to include indicators for all categories, otherwise the model becomes 'over determined' and fails to run.

If the coefficients of the β_q are statistically significant, then the results for the boards are considered as different in overall level.

It is not just the overall levels of attainment that are of interest. The comparative spread of grades within the boards should also be considered. Thus a board could give 'too many' (however defined) grade A passes, but compensate for this by giving give 'too many' (however defined) grade F, so that while the distribution of grades was quite different, the mean levels were the same. This can be investigated by comparing the within-board variances. If there is a statistically significant difference between the estimated values of σ_q^2 for the different boards, that is, for different values of q, then the spread of grades can differ between boards. This is an example of 'complex variance modelling', which will be discussed in more detail later in the chapter (see section 6).

A variation of the above application is comparing 'standard' and alternative syllabuses within boards for the same subject. The approach and equations are the same as those given above, except that the values of q relate to the two syllabuses.

So far this treatment has dealt with the scenario where the groups of candidates taking each type of examination are distinct, and we had to attempt to equate these by taking account of other measured characteristics of the individual. An alternative is where each candidate takes more than one exam, and thus performance may be compared more directly (for example, in a variant of the above, some candidates may be entered for more than one board). This is dealt with next.

3.2 Application 2: Comparing results from different boards for the same subjects taken by the same or overlapping sets of candidates

If some or all of the candidates in the study have taken the two examinations to be compared, then the analysis is essentially multivariate (see Goldstein, 2003, pp. 139ff). In this situation an additional lowest level (board within candidate) may be proposed. If we are dealing with a candidate within centre model, and teaching group is disregarded, then the equation for two boards is given by a three-level model:

$$Y_{ijk} = \beta_{1ijk} board_1 + \beta_{2ijk} board_2$$
$$\beta_{1ijk} = \beta_1 + v_{1k} + u_{1jk} \tag{11}$$
$$\beta_{2ijk} = \beta_2 + v_{2k} + u_{2jk}$$

where:

β_1	= the grand mean for board 1
β_2	= the grand mean for board 2
v_{1k}	= the effect of centre k on board 1
v_{2k}	= the effect of centre k on board 2
u_{1jk}	= the level 2 effect of candidate j in centre k on board 1
u_{2jk}	= the level 2 effect of candidate j in centre k on board 2.

There is no level 1 variation because of the way the problem has been set up (see section 4). Because the exams are being taken by the same candidates, and generally in the same centre, they are assumed to be correlated:

$$\begin{bmatrix} v_{1k} \\ v_{2k} \end{bmatrix} \sim N(0, \Omega_v): \quad \Omega_v = \begin{bmatrix} \sigma_{v1}^2 & \sigma_{v12} \\ \sigma_{v12} & \sigma_{v2}^2 \end{bmatrix}$$
$$\tag{12}$$
$$\begin{bmatrix} u_{1jk} \\ u_{2jk} \end{bmatrix} \sim N(0, \Omega_u): \quad \Omega_u = \begin{bmatrix} \sigma_{u1}^2 & \sigma_{u12} \\ \sigma_{u12} & \sigma_{u2}^2 \end{bmatrix}$$

The covariances indicate a common factor for that board. As such, they are comparable to an overall within- or between-centres variance for that subject, but with fixed board-specific factors taken into account.

If the difference $\beta_1 - \beta_2$ is statistically significant, then the results for the boards are considered as different in overall level. Similarly, the values of the within-board variance may be compared at centre level, or at candidate level; or the sum of the two levels may be compared.

If the assumptions of the model are met, then this is a more powerful model than the two-sample model considered previously. In principle, it is not necessary to include any more home background or prior attainment predictor variables, since all differences between individuals are allowed for in a more powerful fashion than by attempting to measure them. Other variables may be included, if it is considered that the contrasts vary with other factors. On the other hand, variables involved in the pupils' experience of taking exams, such as number of hours studied per week or motivation, could be included if available.

This approach will give an average difference between boards for the pupils involved. For this to be an unbiased estimate of the overall difference between the boards the candidates would have to be a random sample of all candidates. In fact this is unlikely, since candidates taking the same subject twice, with different boards, are likely to be untypical. On a practical level, timetabling issues can prevent candidates taking the same subjects with different boards under live examination conditions. This application relates strongly to Chapter 9, on common examinee methods.

3.3 Application 3: Comparing optional questions within an examination paper

In a sense all questions within an examination paper are optional, to the extent that pupils may choose to do any sub-set of them. In this situation, a possible multilevel modelling approach could be similar to that used for comparing boards. The model could be a three-level one, for example questions within candidates within centres. In this model questions are treated as fixed effects, as we have a separate model parameter that is estimated for each question. However, candidates' responses to these questions form the bottom-most level and include a random element. If there were any further or intermediate levels, for example teaching unit within centre, then a four-level or higher model might be used. This kind of modelling assumes that the omitted questions form a random pattern (see discussion in Yang et al., 2002).

This illustrates the fact that multilevel models can be used in a whole range of applications, provided it is possible to cast the situation into terms that can be analysed in this way. As experience and fluency with manipulating these kinds of model grows, the analyst will be able to see ways in which more complex situations become amenable to analysis in this way. Goldstein (2003) contains a range of different applications of multilevel modelling to social and educational data.

So far we have said nothing about the realism or otherwise of these models and their inherent assumptions. Later in this chapter, we give some examples of the application of these models, both from our own research and those of other workers, and discuss aspects of the modelling assumptions.

4 Examples of modelling different structures

As we start to consider the use of multilevel modelling in comparability studies, we need to model two quite different possible structures in the data, depending on the procedures used in the particular study. There are essentially two data structures that we need to consider:

1. **Separate forms**: Each individual in the study completes just one form of assessment (one board, or syllabus or subject, etc.). Comparability between forms is therefore evaluated through relationships between outcomes and other common background factors. These are exemplified in Application 1 in section 3.

2. **Multiple forms**: Each individual in the study completes more than one of the forms of assessment being compared, and comparability is evaluated in a more 'direct' fashion. These are exemplified in Applications 2 and 3 in section 3.

In this section we will consider how to use multilevel modelling to analyse both structures, with worked examples.

4.1 Example 1: Separate forms

As an example for this we shall take data from the study into alternate forms of the GCSE mathematics examination carried out in 2005 (see Stobart *et al.*, 2005). In this case we shall not consider the alternatives to the existing three-tier structure, but use data supplied by four different examining boards on results in their three-tier version of the examination. In addition to the GCSE results for these candidates, information was available on the centre in which they entered and their Key Stage 3 (KS3) results, in terms of 'fine grades' in all three core subjects.

Results for the three-tier mathematics examination were presented for each candidate in terms of both grade awarded and Uniform Mark Scale (UMS) score. For this example, the UMS scores were harmonised to give 60 points per grade (e.g. grade A = 540 to 600; grade B = 480 to 539; etc.), and these were used as outcomes for the modelling, on the assumption that they could be treated as essentially numerical outcomes rather than categorical.

Table 1 shows the basic statistics for the UMS scores for each board, out of the total of 7,347 cases with complete data.

In the model set up to analyse this data we assume a single outcome (UMS score) but a number of background factors that may affect the outcome. One group relates to prior attainment, and includes the KS3 mathematics fine grade result for each candidate, plus (possibly) their KS3 results in English and science. The assumption here is that, given candidates with equal KS3 results their GCSE outcomes should be, on average, equivalent irrespective of the board taken. In order to test this assumption we need to include in the model indicators related to the board taken.

Table 1 GCSE mathematics UMS scores by board

Board	Mean UMS score	Standard deviation	Number of cases
Board A	389.9	102.4	3147
Board B	337.1	56.5	1330
Board C	378.8	93.3	858
Board D	388.5	99.8	2012
Total	**378.7**	**95.9**	**7347**

With this in mind, the variables included in our Model 1 for this example are:

- **Cons** – a constant term (= 1) whose coefficient represents the intercept on the vertical axis when all factors are set to zero

- **Board B, Board C, Board D** – indicators for three of the boards relative to Board A, the 'default'

- **KS3mfine, KS3efine and KS3sfine** – fine grade measures in maths, English and science.

The outcome for this model was **T3umstot**, the UMS total score for the three-tier examination. Before putting the data into the multilevel modelling, an OLS regression was run using SPSS with the results shown in Table 2.

Table 2 OLS regression coefficients for Example 1 Model 1

	Variables	Estimates from modelling		
Name	Description	Coefficient	SE+	Significant?
T3umstot	*UMS total score*	*Outcome variable*		
Cons	Constant term	–136.90	3.99	*
Board B	Board B indicator (vs. A)	25.72	1.62	*
Board D	Board D indicator (vs. A)	18.53	1.36	*
KS3mfine	KS3 maths fine grade	57.26	0.94	*
KS3efine	KS3 English fine grade	7.65	0.85	*
KS3sfine	KS3 science fine grade	18.85	1.09	*
Board C	Board C indicator (vs. A)			Omitted – not significant

* = significant at 5% level

+ Here and in other tables 'S.E.' is the standard error of the estimate in the preceding column

The results of this modelling imply that there is no statistically significant difference between Boards C and A in terms of results controlling for KS3 attainment, but that both Boards B and D seem to produce higher UMS scores than would have been predicted for Board A. However, the OLS model takes no account of within-centre clustering of candidates and the next step is to turn to multilevel modelling to deal with this. The same basic model was run using MLwiN (Rasbash *et al.*, 2005), and the results are shown in the equations window from that program reproduced as Figure 2, as well as in Table 3.

Figure 2 MLwiN output for Example 1 Model 1

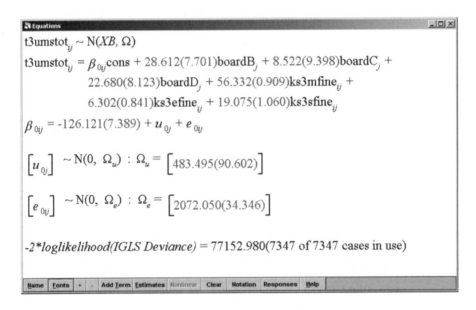

Figure 2 shows the model fitted to the outcome (variable name 't3umstot'), with estimated coefficients and standard errors. The centre- and candidate-level error terms are also included, and the random variance estimates of these are also given. The final line is the 'deviance' (–2*log likelihood) and gives a measure of the extent to which the model explains the data, which can be compared with the same measure for alternative models. These model parameter estimates are replicated in Table 3.

In many ways, the results are very similar to those obtained from the OLS analysis – coefficients are similar in magnitude, and all are clearly significant except for the Board C effect. However, if we look at the coefficient standard errors (in brackets in the MLwiN output) we can see some clear differences. The standard errors for the KS3 fine grades are actually very similar, but for the board variables there are real differences. The standard errors from the multilevel modelling analysis are

Table 3 Multilevel modelling coefficients for Example 1 Model 1

Variables		Estimates from modelling		
Name	Description	Coefficient	SE	Significant?
T3umstot	*UMS total score*	*Outcome variable*		
Cons	Constant term	−126.12	7.39	*
Board B	Board B indicator (vs. A)	28.61	7.70	*
Board C	Board C indicator (vs. A)	8.52	9.40	
Board D	Board D indicator (vs. A)	22.68	8.12	*
KS3mfine	KS3 maths fine grade	56.33	0.91	*
KS3efine	KS3 English fine grade	6.30	0.84	*
KS3sfine	KS3 science fine grade	19.08	1.06	*
Random variances and covariances		**Estimate**	**SE**	**Significant?**
Centre-level random variance		483.50	90.60	*
Candidate-level random variance		2,072.05	34.35	*

* = significant at 5% level

five or six times as large as for the OLS run, due to the fact that these estimates of board effects are seriously influenced by the clustering of candidates within centres, all of which take the same board. In this case the increased standard errors did not affect the significance of the results, but the use of OLS estimates could lead to incorrect conclusions about the standard errors of the between-board differences.

In Model 1 the centre-level variance in UMS scores (483.5) is 19% of the total variance (483.5 + 2072.1), showing that candidates at the same centre are more similar than candidates at different centres. Model 1 also assumes a fixed difference between examining boards, once KS3 attainment is taken into account. However, it may be reasonable to ask if the differences between boards vary for different levels of prior attainment. To answer this, we set up Model 2 in which we include interaction terms between examining boards and KS3 maths fine grade. To simplify the model, we include only maths fine grades – the other two core subjects do have an impact on UMS score, but this is small compared with KS3 maths.

Three interaction terms are included: **Bint, Cint** and **Dint**. In each case the term is equal to the board indicator (0 or 1) times the KS3 maths fine grade minus its mean (6.13). Thus a positive interaction term implies that the relation between outcome and KS3 fine grade is stronger for this board than the default (A), while a negative interaction implies the reverse. Results for Model 2 are shown in Table 4.

Table 4 Multilevel modelling results for Example 1 Model 2

Variables		Estimates from modelling		
Name	Description	Coefficient	SE	Significant?
T3umstot	UMS total score	Outcome variable		
Cons	Constant term	−95.22	7.65	*
Board B	Board B indicator (vs. A)	14.12	7.15	*
Board C	Board C indicator (vs. A)	10.76	8.65	
Board D	Board D indicator (vs. A)	28.91	7.43	*
KS3mfine	KS3 maths fine grade	75.09	0.81	*
Bint	Board B × KS3mfine	−22.30	1.86	*
Cint	Board C × KS3mfine	−7.49	1.73	*
Dint	Board D × KS3mfine	5.70	1.36	*
Random variances and covariances		**Estimate**	**SE**	**Significant?**
Centre-level random variance		400.95	76.51	*
Candidate-level random variance		2,163.94	35.87	*

* = significant at 5% level

The main effects are similar to Model 1, with the Board C indicator non-significant (and Board B only borderline significant at the 5% level). However, all three interactions are statistically significant, including Board C. In two cases (Boards B and C) the interaction is negative; for Board D it is positive. The combined effects of the main effects and interactions from this model are illustrated in Figure 3, which shows a plot of the expected UMS scores for different values of KS3 fine grade for each board.

In this case the centre-level variance is 16% of the total variance, implying that part of the difference between centres can be explained by the examining board interactions.

Figure 3 Expected UMS scores for each board from Example 1 Model 2

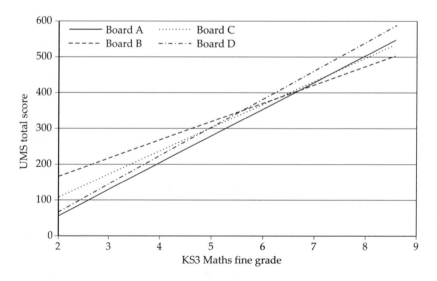

This model could be developed in a number of different ways, but one possible addition is to consider the possibility that the relationship between UMS score and KS3 fine grade may vary from centre to centre, as it appears to vary from board to board. To model this possibility we need to make the coefficients of KS3 maths fine grade random at the centre level. If we do this, we get the fitted Model 3 results as shown in Table 5.

Table 5 Multilevel modelling results for Example 1 Model 3

Variables		Estimates from modelling		
Name	Description	Coefficient	SE	Significant?
T3umstot	*UMS total score*	*Outcome variable*		
Cons	Constant term	–93.57	17.49	*
Board B	Board B indicator (vs. A)	12.72	6.52	
Board C	Board C indicator (vs. A)	11.03	7.89	
Board D	Board D indicator (vs. A)	27.85	6.73	*
KS3mfine	KS3 maths fine grade	74.80	2.53	*
Bint	Board B × KS3mfine	–23.35	3.60	*
Cint	Board C × KS3mfine	–10.05	4.19	*
Dint	Board D × KS3mfine	4.73	3.46	
Variances and covariances		**Estimate**	**SE**	**Significant?**
Centre-level				
Random variance (intercept)		3,487.14	816.97	*
Random variance (KS3mfine)		72.84	18.37	*
Covariance (intercept and KS3mfine)		–481.50	120.34	*
Candidate-level random variance		2,122.87	35.32	*

* = significant at 5% level

Results are similar to Model 2, except that neither Boards B nor C are overall significantly different from A, and although the overall Board D effect remains significant this is not true for the Board D interaction term. The variance at the centre level in the coefficient of KS3 fine grade is estimated as 72.8, equal to a standard deviation of 8.5, whereas the overall average coefficient is 74.8. This implies there is a reasonable amount of variation between centres in the relationship between prior attainment and GCSE results, and not taking this into account can change the conclusions of the comparability study.

So what have we learned from this example comparability study using separate forms? In terms of the differences between examining boards the following was found:

- There are overall differences in the results obtained for certain boards (controlling for KS3 prior attainment) and those for Board A; there is clear evidence of this for Board D and less clear evidence for Board B.

- The relationship between KS3 prior attainment and final outcome also varies between examining boards; Boards B and C have significantly less strong relationships than Board A.

- This relationship also varies between centres, and this variation if not taken into account may affect the conclusions of our comparability study.

These results should be regarded as indicative, based on the final model fitted. Other models, or the inclusion of more background information, may change these conclusions. In terms of what we have learned about the modelling process, we can say the following:

- OLS regression may give similar coefficients to those obtained from multilevel modelling, but is likely to underestimate the standard errors if within-centre clustering is not taken into account. This can affect the conclusions of comparability studies.

- Interactions to study differential effects for different boards relative to prior attainment are an important element of such studies and should be included in the model.

- Random coefficients at the centre level can be fitted in multilevel modelling, and these can be informative and affect the conclusions of the study.

Interaction terms are, of course, not restricted to multilevel modelling and can be fitted in other types of model, including OLS. When such models are used it is important to take account of what they mean in terms of 'comparability'. In essence we are saying that comparability needs to be assessed not just at a single point on the prior attainment scale, but at every point. Two boards may appear comparable on average, but if one produces higher scores for lower-attaining pupils than the other, and vice versa for higher-attaining pupils, then comparability is not achieved.

One option is to use the fitted model to standardise or adjust the results of different boards onto a consistent scale. This would be relatively straightforward when allowing for board effects, but it is not clear to what extent random coefficients for each centre should be allowed for. In the main, the results of such comparability studies are not used to adjust marks or grades retrospectively, but to inform the grade-setting process for the next round.

Other examples of multilevel modelling applied to this 'single forms' scenario can be found in Baird & Jones (1998) and Pinot de Moira (2000; 2002a).

4.2 Example 2: Multiple forms

In the previous example no candidate took more than one examination, and the comparison between boards had to be based indirectly on the relationship with prior attainment. It would seem in principle more powerful to be able to compare boards, or forms of examination, directly by getting candidates to take more than one form so that unmeasured differences between candidates can be controlled for. As ever, there are drawbacks with this approach: candidates may be differentially motivated between forms, or there may be an effect due to the order in which forms are taken or because of a time gap between taking them. In any case, we need to assume that the candidates who take both papers are a representative sample of the appropriate population. However, data from 'multiple forms' trials can be analysed in a powerful way using multilevel modelling, subject to these and other caveats.

As an example for this analysis we shall also take data from the study into alternate forms of the GCSE mathematics examination carried out in 2005 (see Stobart *et al.*, 2005), but in this case we will consider data from candidates who attempted two different alternatives to the three-tier paper, the so-called 'Pilot' and 'Trial' structures. In this case the candidates were all from the same board: 7,146 attempted the Pilot version, 732 the Trial version and 695 did both.

Here we have in some ways a more powerful data set for investigating differences in standards for two or more different forms of a test, because we have data on identical individuals who have attempted more than one form. Perhaps the most straightforward way of comparing standards is to carry out equipercentile equating using the 695 candidates who did both versions (see Stobart *et al.*, 2005) – Figure 4 shows the resulting equating graph. Note that to simplify the equating procedure we have divided the UMS score by ten in both forms.

Figure 4 Equating Pilot and Trial versions using common candidates

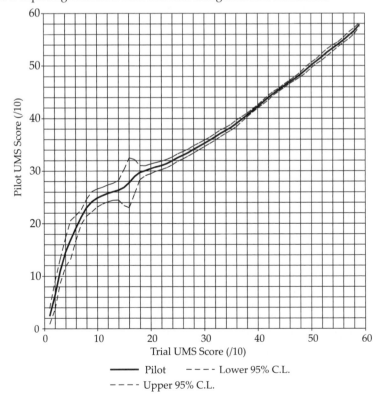

This is quite informative, but the estimated confidence intervals (CI) are based on a relatively simple formula and take no account of clustering within centres. We shall therefore explore this relationship further, taking account of all available data including background information on KS3 fine grades and the centres in which the examinations were taken.

In this case the kind of model we want is multivariate (see Goldstein, 2003, pp. 139ff), because candidates have more than one outcome to be modelled. We therefore introduce a lower level below the candidate for a version indicator (1 = Pilot, 2 = Trial) to enable this to be modelled. In addition we introduce separate indicators (0/1) for both Pilot and Trial, and include both in the model with separate random variances. No constant term is included in this case, as we have separate intercepts for the two forms and a constant would make the model over-determined. Table 6 shows the results for this Model 1 with no background factors.

Table 6 Multilevel modelling results for Example 2 Model 1

Variables		Estimates from modelling		
Name	Description	Coefficient	SE	Significant?
Umstot	*Total UMS score*	*Outcome variable*		
Pilot	Indicator for Pilot version	342.73	6.87	*
Trial	Indicator for Trial version	296.16	8.75	*
Random variances and covariances		**Estimate**	**SE**	**Significant?**
Centre-level				
Pilot variance		2,488.11	500.60	*
Trial variance		2,265.31	717.22	*
Pilot/Trial covariance		2,304.91	554.32	*
Candidate-level				
Pilot variance		10,007.64	170.84	*
Trial variance		20,674.04	848.43	*
Pilot/Trial covariance		11,772.58	369.73	*

* = significant at 5% level

From this it is clear that the two forms have different overall means (342.7 and 296.2) but similar between-centre variances (2,488 and 2,265). The within-centre variances are rather different, with the Trial having over twice the variance between candidates of the Pilot.

Relative relationships with prior attainment were modelled by including KS3 maths fine grade for both forms, plus an interaction term to see if the relationship was different for the Trial (interaction term = 0 for Pilot, and KS3 fine grade minus 5.9 for the Trial)[8]. However, Figure 4 indicates a possible non-linear relationship between Pilot and Trial, so non-linearities in the relationship of each with KS3 fine grade were also included in the model.

The full set of variables included in the model is therefore:

Pilot   Indicator for Pilot version (random at centre level)
Trial   Indicator for Trial version (random at centre level)
KS3mfine   KS3 mathematics fine grade (fixed effect)
Verk3int   Interaction between version and KS3 fine grade. Set to zero for the Pilot, and equal to fine grade value minus 5.9 for the Trial (fixed effect)
KS3msq   Square of KS3 mathematics fine grade (fixed effect)
Verk3sq   Interaction between version and fine grade squared. Set to zero for the Pilot, and equal to (fine grade minus 5.9) squared for the Trial (fixed effect)

Results for this model are shown in Table 7.

Table 7 Multilevel modelling results for Example 2 Model 2

Variables		Estimates from modelling		
Name	Description	Coefficient	SE	Significant?
Umstot	*UMS total score*	*Outcome variable*		
Pilot	Indicator for Pilot version	−181.89	12.81	*
Trial	Indicator for Trial version	−237.25	15.19	*
KS3mfine	KS3 maths fine grade	108.17	4.38	*
Verk3int	Version × KS3mfine	15.38	2.81	*
KS3msq	KS3mfine squared	−2.67	0.37	*
Verk3sq	Version × KS3msq	7.95	2.03	*
Random variances and covariances		**Estimate**	**SE**	**Significant?**
Centre-level				
	Pilot variance	321.72	68.19	*
	Trial variance	633.23	374.56	
	Pilot/Trial covariance	333.89	161.20	*
Candidate-level				
	Pilot variance	2,793.78	47.72	*
	Trial variance	10,435.20	519.60	*
	Pilot/Trial covariance	3,196.03	172.75	*

* = significant at 5% level

In this case the interaction terms are statistically significant, implying the relationship with prior attainment is different for the two forms. The between-centre variance for the Trial is now not significant, but the residual within-centre variance for the Trial is almost four times that for the Pilot. The non-linear terms in KS3 mathematics fine grade are significant, although the form of the non-linearity is different for the two versions. Figure 5 illustrates Model 2 in terms of the expected UMS score for each form as a function of KS3 fine grade.

From the above, there is clearly a mismatch between the two forms for much of the prior attainment range. This is consistent with Figure 4, although taking prior attainment into account clarifies where the main mismatch is. Putting the relationship with KS3 fine grade random at the school level gives Model 3, shown in Table 8.

Figure 5 Expected UMS scores for each form from Example 2 Model 2

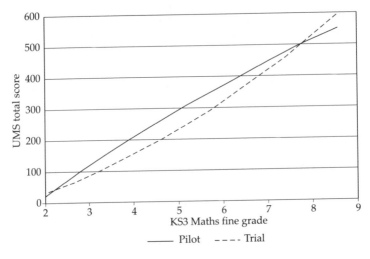

Table 8 Multilevel modelling results for Example 2 Model 3

Variables		Estimates from modelling		
Name	Description	Coefficient	SE	Significant?
Umstot	*Total UMS score*	*Outcome variable*		
Pilot	Indicator for Pilot version	−162.79	15.74	*
Trial	Indicator for Trial version	−212.49	17.69	*
KS3mfine	KS3 maths fine grade	103.19	4.86	*
Verk3int	Version × KS3mfine	16.16	2.81	*
KS3msq	KS3mfine squared	−2.41	0.41	*
Verk3sq	Version × KS3msq	8.00	2.03	*
Random variances and covariances		Estimate	SE	Significant?
Centre-level				
	Pilot variance	3,440.18	823.15	*
	Trial variance	4,530.73	1,377.34	*
	KS3mfine variance	72.88	18.71	*
	Pilot/Trial covariance	3,848.62	1,003.78	*
	Pilot/KS3mfine covariance	−487.56	122.60	*
	Trial/KS3mfine covariance	−562.84	150.95	*
Candidate-level				
	Pilot variance	2,733.72	46.85	*
	Trial variance	10,407.86	519.01	*
	Pilot/Trial covariance	3,149.62	171.17	*

* = significant at 5% level

So what have we learned from this example comparability study using multiple forms?

- There are significant differences between results obtained in the Pilot and Trial forms, in terms of the relationship with prior attainment. For example, a candidate with a KS3 fine grade of 6.0 would be expected to score 371 on the Pilot and 317 on the Trial.

- There are significant non-linearities in the relationship with prior attainment, and these vary between forms.

- Only at the highest and lowest levels of prior attainment are the two forms approximately comparable.

- Variation between candidates, controlling for prior attainment, is much higher for the Trial form than for the Pilot.

- The correlation between Pilot and Trial versions at the centre level is 0.975, implying that centres tend to perform overall equally well or equally poorly on both versions.

- The correlation between Pilot and Trial versions at the candidate level is 0.590, implying that there is a less strong relationship between the two versions for individual candidates.

- As a result of these differences we would be forced to conclude that the two forms were not directly comparable.

In terms of what we have learned about the modelling process, we may say:

- Multivariate models require an extra, lowest level to allow multiple outcomes per candidate.

- Separate indicators for each form can be used, random at all levels above the lowest, and the constant terms should then be omitted.

- Graphs of expected outcome as a function of prior attainment for the different forms may be a powerful way of illustrating the comparability or otherwise of different forms.

In a later section we will return to this data set when we consider complex variance models.

5   Modelling different outcomes

In the previous section we examined different ways of modelling the structure of the data in comparability studies, but throughout we assumed that the outcome of interest could be treated as a continuous numerical variable. However, this is often not legitimate – examination results can be reported as ordered categorical outcomes (grades or levels) or just as a binary outcome (pass or fail). The linear models with

Normally distributed error terms that we have used so far in this chapter are inappropriate for such outcomes, and in this section we will describe suitable models, using initially an example from previous literature in the area.

Probably the earliest attempt to compare examination 'standards' using multilevel modelling and the 'catch all' definition was the work of Baird & Jones (1998). Other more recent studies working in a comparable way include Pinot de Moira (2000, 2002a).

In their paper Baird & Jones (1998) compare three different statistical techniques in the analysis of an inter-board comparability study on 1996 GCSE art and design (Unendorsed) grades, which was undertaken by the boards themselves on behalf of the Joint Forum for the GCSE and GCE (Jones et al., 1997). They concluded that ordered logistic multilevel modelling was the best option, but that it still failed to deal with the fundamental problems. To quote from their report:

> It is argued that ordered logistic multilevel modelling is the most appropriate of the three forms of statistical analysis for comparability studies using examination grade as the outcome variable. Although ordered logistic multilevel modelling is considered an important methodological advance on previous statistical comparability methods, it will not overcome fundamental problems in any statistical analysis of examination standards. It is argued that ultimately examination standards cannot be measured statistically because they are inextricably bound up with the characteristics of the examinations themselves and the characteristics of the students who sit the examinations.
>
> Baird & Jones (1998)

The Baird & Jones (1998) study is now described in some detail to make the method clear and to highlight features of interest. A random sample of approximately 1,500 art and design candidates from each of the four English GCSE examining boards, stratified by centre type, was sent a questionnaire, designed to measure a few of the key variables expected to have a significant relationship with awarded grades. There was an approximately 33% response rate to this questionnaire. The variables used in the analyses included individual responses and responses aggregated to examination centre level. Variables found to have statistically significant effects in the analyses were measures of pupil attitudes, plans, gender and background. It was not possible to obtain a measure of prior attainment for the individual pupils, but an aggregated ability measure from school league-table information was included.

Three different kinds of statistical methodology were used in the analysis of this project. These were:

1. Ordinary Least Squares (OLS) linear regression at candidate level treating the grade outcome as a continuous variable.

2. Linear multilevel modelling treating the grade outcome as a continuous variable.

3. Ordered logistic multilevel modelling considering whether the candidates succeeded at various grades within the examination. Thus a candidate who gains

a B grade will be considered as having also gained a C, D or E grade, but not an A grade. See below for a fuller treatment.

The first two analyses are largely similar to those described previously, so we will not describe these models in detail. The main focus of interest for us is on the third model, the ordered logistic multilevel model.

In an ordered logistic model, examination grades are treated as ordered categories, instead of as numerical values. In this type of analysis, an equation is first found for the probability that a case is above the first (lowest) category. Following this, an equation is found for the probability that the case is above the second lowest category and so on. The response variable in the ordered logistic regression is the cumulative grade (s) for each candidate i in teaching group j in centre k,

$$\log it(\pi_{ijk}^{(s)}) \quad = \quad \beta_0^{(s)} + \sum_{p=1}^{P} \beta_p x_{pijk} + \sum_{q=1}^{Q} \beta_q z_{qijk} + v_k^{(s)} + u_{jk}^{(s)} \qquad (13)$$

where:

$\pi_{ijk}^{(s)}$ = the probability the examination grade is s or better

$\beta_0^{(s)}$ = the intercept for the particular grade s

β_p = the coefficient for the pth explanatory variable

x_{pijk} = the value of the pth explanatory variable for candidate i in teaching group j in centre k for the particular grade s

β_q = the effect of board q

z_{qijk} = an indicator that candidate i in teaching group j in centre k is taking the particular board q

$v_k^{(s)}$ = the effect of centre k for the particular grade s

$u_{jk}^{(s)}$ = the effect of teaching group j in centre k for the particular grade s.

This model investigates the effect of the qth board, assuming this is uniform at all of the categories. If it is suspected that the difference between boards is greater at some categories than others then different values $\beta_q^{(s)}$ can be fitted. For a fuller discussion of multilevel models for discrete outcomes, see Goldstein (2003, pp. 95ff).

Table 9 shows the results from the three types of analyses side by side. Only an extract of the results from these tables is shown here: other aspects of the analysis, not referring directly to the inter-board comparability, are not shown here. Interested readers should consult Baird & Jones (1998). Four boards are compared. As before, in each case, Board 0 is taken as a reference category, and the results for the other boards are expressed in comparison with these.

The first two columns relate to an OLS analysis. The first column shows the value for the difference (Board q vs. Board 0), and the second column shows the standard error for this. An impression of the probability value for these comparisons can be gained by dividing the difference by the corresponding standard error, and comparing the result with the 0.05 level for a two-tailed z-distribution. It can be seen that Board 3 appears to have a lower value than Board 0, while there is no statistically significant difference between Board 0 and the other two boards (Boards 1 and 2). The figures here relate to the contrasts between Board 0 and the other three boards. There are of course other contrasts that could be considered, such as Board 1 vs. Board 2. While this has not been considered specifically it seems quite likely that the contrast between Board 3 and Board 1 would also be statistically significant. This could be easily investigated, if required. Comparisons using this method are likely to give biased estimates of the statistical significance however, since candidates taking their exams within a single centre are likely to be more similar to each other than are candidates chosen completely at random.

This problem can be met by the use of multilevel modelling techniques. The results of this are shown in the third and fourth columns of figures. The standard errors are all substantially larger than those estimated for the OLS analysis, and largely as a result, while Board 0 is the lowest, none of the inter-board differences are statistically significant. In fact, the fitted constants are also different from the results in the OLS analysis.

Table 9 Comparison of different models on inter-board comparability results

Board (vs. Board 0)	OLS results		Multilevel modelling (linear) results		Multilevel modelling ordinal results for Grade A*		Multilevel modelling ordinal results for Grade A	
	Coeff	SE	Coeff	SE	Coeff	SE	Coeff	SE
Board 1	0.03	0.09	−0.16	0.20	−1.87	0.59	−0.81	0.34
Board 2	−0.02	0.08	−0.06	0.19	−0.94	0.38	−0.90	0.30
Board 3	−0.17	0.08	−0.16	0.20	−1.17	0.40	−0.63	0.31

Such results are of general eye-catching interest, but may not be the best way to look at possible differences. Examination results are awarded by grade and it is generally considered that the grade awarded is accurate to plus or minus one grade (Newton, 2005). Consequently, the main focus should be on grade borderlines. If there is a difference between the standards set at just one borderline it is conceivable that this could give a statistically significant overall mean difference. The process of awarding a grade combines two processes: first awarding a mark to a script, and then comparing the mark awarded with the grade boundaries. Only key grades are considered at award meetings – the rest are set arithmetically. If one examining board finds that its grading is out of line with others, then it will be concerned to find out whether this is due to boundary decision-making between grades.

The next analysis reported therefore treats the grade outcome as an ordered categorical variable. Only the results for the A* borderline and the A borderline are shown in this chapter, since the inter-board differences at other grade boundaries were not statistically significant. The last four columns in Table 9 show the results for these. Taking one example for illustration purposes, the fitted constant for Board 1 for grade A* is negative, and more than twice its standard error. This figure relates to the log-odds, ceteribus paribus, of getting this grade from Board 1, compared with those of getting this grade from Board 0. Transforming to a more intuitive metric, this means that the odds of getting a result this good in Board 1 are only 15% of those in Board 0. However, it should be noted that these results are subject to large margins of error, and that analysis of a data set with good measures of prior attainment at the individual candidate level might provide different results.

In this section so far we have reported results based in practice on logistic modelling, where the outcome of interest is a single binary variable (i.e. does the candidate get grade A* or above, or not?). When looking at comparability over several grade boundaries, this approach requires the application of a separate model for each grade. Another approach is to use an ordered categorical multinomial model (see Goldstein, 2003, pp. 101ff). An example is taken from Stobart *et al.* (2005), and considers whether candidates with different levels of KS3 attainment have different probabilities of getting higher grades in the Pilot compared with the Trial version of the examination, or vice versa.

An ordered categorical multinomial model (see Goldstein, 2003, p. 104) was fitted (see also equation (13)), looking at three categories:

1. Trial grade higher than Pilot grade

2. grades the same on two tests

3. Pilot grade higher than Trial grade.

The default category was taken as the first ('Trial>pilot'), and a model with constant parameters for KS3 fine grade was fitted, with two levels – school and candidate. Essentially we are fitting two linked logistic models: one for the grades being the same on the two tests ('Same'), and the other for the Pilot grade being higher than the Trial ('Pilot>trial'), with the same relationship assumed with prior attainment in both cases. The full fitted model is shown in Figure 6. This is an example of a more complex equation window from MLwiN, and one whose features may need more time to understand. Model parameters are also displayed in tabular form in Table 10.

Figure 6 Ordered multinomial multilevel model fitted to Trial and Pilot data

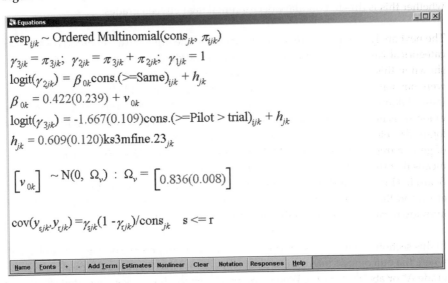

Table 10 Multilevel modelling results for ordered multinomial multilevel model fitted to Trial and Pilot data

Variables		Estimates from modelling		
Name	Description	Coefficient	SE	Significant?
Resp	*Three-category response*	*Outcome variable*		
Cons. (>=Same)	Constant term for contrast between categories 2 and 1	0.4217	0.2388	
Cons. (>=Pilot>trial)	Constant term for contrast between categories 3 and 2	−1.667	0.1092	*
KS3mfine	KS3 maths fine grade (centred on 6.0)	0.6094	0.1196	*
Random variances and covariances		Estimate	SE	Significant?
Centre-level				
	Random variance	0.8357	0.0085	*

Two categories are explicitly featured in the model: 'Pilot>trial' and 'Same'. The modelled probability for the latter includes the former. In both cases there is a relationship with prior attainment ('ks3mfine') which has the same slope (0.609) in the logit metric.[9]

The log-odds for 'Pilot>trial' has a constant estimate of −1.667, whereas for the log-odds of 'Same' or 'Pilot>trial' the constant estimate is 0.422. The coefficient of *ks3mfine* (centred on the value 6.0) is 0.609. Substituting a value of 0.0 for *ks3mfine*, we estimate the two log-odds as −1.667 and 0.422 respectively, with corresponding probabilities of 0.159 and 0.445. By subtraction, we find: P['Pilot>trial'] = 0.159; P['Same'] = 0.445; and P['Trial>pilot'] = 0.396.

In this case there is a clearly significant random variance at the school level, implying that the relationship between Pilot and Trial grades does vary from school to school. Expected results of this model, controlling for KS3 results, are shown in Figure 7.

Figure 7 Probabilities for Pilot and Trial comparison from ordered multinomial model

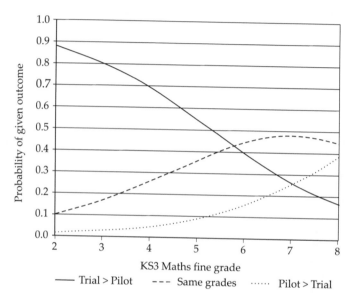

This model illustrates that for candidates with lower prior attainment, the Trial structure seems to be advantageous as they have a higher chance of getting a better grade on this than on the Pilot. As prior attainment increases, the two systems become more balanced and the apparent advantage of the Trial disappears.

This kind of ordered categorical model is very powerful, and in principle should be used more widely. The truth is that our most common examination outcomes (grades or levels) are actually ordinal in nature, although much of the quantitative analysis carried out tends to treat them as if they were numerical interval scales.

6 Complex variance models

In the previous two sections we have dealt in some detail with two important aspects of model selection in comparability studies – modelling the structure of the data and the outcome of interest. It may seem that modelling the variance structure of the data is of less importance, but in certain cases false assumptions about this can lead to incorrect conclusions from the study.

Let us take as an example the data for Model 1 from section 4, with UMS scores from four examining boards. In Figure 8 we plot the standard deviation in the UMS score as a function of the KS3 mathematics level for each board. From this there is some evidence that the standard deviation (and therefore the variance) in UMS score is not constant across the KS3 prior ability range, as has been assumed in all the models to date. It is not clear whether this will affect the conclusions of the modelling, but in a comparability study this should be checked by including this feature of the data in the model.

Figure 8 Standard deviation in UMS score versus KS3 level

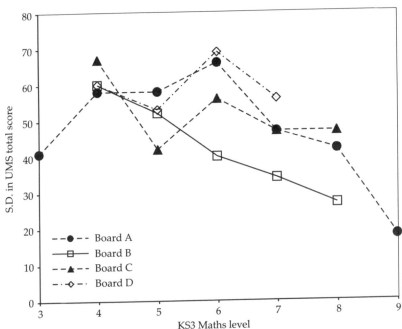

Goldstein (2003, pp. 63ff) shows how this may be done, by suitable modification of our models. By introducing a random coefficient of the relevant background variable at the lowest level of the model, we can generate a quadratic function of this variable as a model for the pupil-level variance.[10] Note that although some of the coefficients of this function may be described as variances in the output from the software, they are not and need not be constrained to be non-negative – the true pupil-level variance is defined by the whole function, not by any of its elements individually. This means that non-negativity constraints on variance parameter estimation in the software used need to be relaxed when complex variances are being fitted.

We will go back to our examples from section 4 to show how these complex variances can be fitted, starting with Model 1. Table 11 shows the results of setting prior attainment (*ks3mfine*) random at the candidate level.

Table 11 Complex variance model fitted to Example 1 data

Variables		Estimates from modelling		
Name	Description	Coefficient	SE	Significant?
T3umstot	*Total UMS score*	*Outcome variable*		
Cons	Constant term	−107.63	17.40	*
Board B	Board B indicator (vs. A)	12.78	6.43	*
Board C	Board C indicator (vs. A)	10.79	7.77	
Board D	Board D indicator (vs. A)	28.18	6.61	*
KS3mfine	KS3 maths fine grade	76.99	2.58	*
Bint	Board B × KS3mfine	−36.08	3.71	*
Cint	Board C × KS3mfine	−11.37	4.23	*
Dint	Board D × KS3mfine	3.01	3.55	
Random variances and covariances		**Estimate**	**SE**	**Significant?**
Centre-level				
Random variance (intercept)		3,555.67	838.27	*
Random variance (KS3mfine)		78.83	19.53	*
Covariance (intercept and KS3mfine)		−506.46	125.75	*
Candidate-level				
Pseudo variance (intercept)		−253.30	690.67	
Pseudo variance (KS3mfine)		−135.66	15.90	*
Pseudo covariance		625.08	106.00	*

* = significant at 5% level

Comparison with Table 5 shows little difference in terms of the main coefficients and the substantive findings of the modelling. The candidate-level variance matrix now shows apparently negative variances, but as mentioned above this is not problematic, as these are not real variances but coefficients in the variance equation:

Pupil-level variance $= -253.30 + 2*625.60*ks3mfine -135.66*ks3mfine^2$ (14)

Figure 9 illustrates the model standard deviations as a function of KS3 fine grade.

A similar complex variance model was fitted to the Example 2 data, by modifying Model 3 (Table 8) to allow *ks3mfine* to be random at the candidate level – results are shown in Table 12.

Again, there is little change in the main coefficients, although this time the diagonal terms of the candidate-level variance matrix are all positive. The effects in terms of standard deviation of outcomes as a function of prior attainment are shown in Figure 10, where the variance models are different for the Pilot and Trial outcomes.

Figure 9 Model candidate-level standard deviation as a function of KS3 level

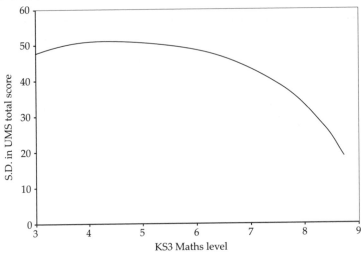

Table 12 Complex variance model fitted to Example 2 data

Variables		Estimates from modelling		
Name	**Description**	**Coefficient**	**SE**	**Significant?**
Umstot	*Total UMS score*	*Outcome variable*		
Pilot	Indicator for Pilot version	−174.66	16.79	*
Trial	Indicator for Trial version	−224.98	18.73	*
KS3mfine	KS3 maths fine grade	107.60	5.05	*
Verk3int	Version × KS3mfine	15.71	2.77	*
KS3msq	KS3mfine squared	−2.82	0.41	*
Verk3sq	Version × KS3msq	8.86	1.93	*
Random variances and covariances		**Estimate**	**SE**	**Significant?**
Centre-level				
	Pilot variance	3,561.67	868.31	*
	Trial variance	4,696.08	1,473.47	*
	KS3mfine variance	79.00	20.17	*
	Pilot/trial covariance	3,976.98	1,061.92	*
	Pilot/KS3mfine covariance	−516.00	130.78	*
	Trial/KS3mfine covariance	−592.32	161.35	*
Candidate-level				
	Pilot (pseudo) variance	10,299.57	1,015.93	*
	Trial (pseudo) variance	10,208.55	1,601.44	*
	KS3mfine (pseudo) covariance	86.87	24.47	*
	Pilot/trial (pseudo) covariance	6,758.68	1,136.35	*
	Pilot/KS3mfine (pseudo) covariance	−907.79	159.03	*
	Trial/Ks3mfine (pseudo) covariance	−240.69	170.78	*

* = significant at 5% level

Figure 10 Model 2 standard deviations as function of KS3 level (modelled)

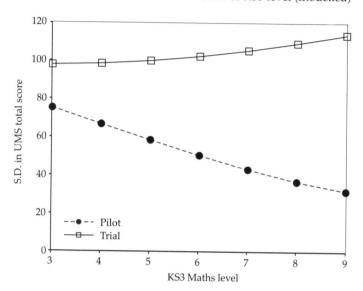

The assumption of constant variance is one which is frequently made when modelling comparability study data, but it should always be critically evaluated, either by exploratory data analysis and/or by allowing for non-constant variance in the modelling. If this is not done, there is the potential for misleading results to be obtained and for the findings of the model study to be challenged.

7 Review of existing studies

In this section we will pause in our development of multilevel techniques in order to summarise and review existing comparability studies that have used this approach in order to address Cresswell's (1996) 'catch-all' definition, described in the introduction. This is a pretty ambitious definition, but there have been a number of studies that have at least tried to model its requirements statistically, though Baird & Jones (1998) admit that 'research can only approximate the "catch-all" definition, as the researcher does not have access to measurements of all of the factors which influence examination performance'. Problems and issues are discussed in detail in Baird & Jones (1998) so they will be touched on only briefly here, using their terminology. First, there is the problem of measurement, one aspect of which is the assumption that the relation between the ability measure and the examination outcome is the same for each syllabus or board. Second, there is the problem of interactions of independent variables with syllabus or board, when, for example, girls do better in one examination than boys, but not in another. The third problem touched on is that of extrication: it could arise if one syllabus or board were more attractive than another, and increased the motivation of the pupils involved, so that difficulty and motivation were confounded.

A number of studies have been conducted using multilevel modelling by or on behalf of the examining boards or the QCA. They are too numerous to mention individually in the relatively short space of this chapter, but a selection showing the techniques involved is now considered. The studies we cover here include Baird & Jones (1998), Pinot de Moira (2000; 2002a; 2003), Jones et al. (1997), Tymms & Vincent (1995), Bell & Dexter (2000). We compare how effective these are likely to be in operationalising the Cresswell definition. Two main aspects are considered: first the techniques employed, and second the predictor variables used.

7.1 Techniques used

In reviewing this type of work we consider that it is especially important to bear in mind the practical applications as well as any theoretical considerations, and a comment on how boards arrive at final grades is relevant. Each examination for each board is scored to give a total number of marks (although there are some recent developments in the use of IRT methods). Each board then organises meetings to convert these marks into grades, which are the major currency in the public examination world. These meetings determine the boundary point in terms of score for major cut-points: for example, F/G, C/D and A/B for GCSE. An interpolation procedure is then used in determining the grades between these boundaries.

Baird & Jones (1998), as described earlier (Table 9), compared three techniques in their investigation: Ordinary Least Squares at candidate level, treating the (ordinal) grade outcome as a continuous variable; a multilevel model also treating grades as continuous; and a multilevel ordinal multinomial model. In the two multilevel analyses, candidates were nested within teacher groups, which were nested within centres. Baird & Jones did not investigate the possibility of doing a series of dichotomous outcome logistic investigations, stating only that 'Ordered logistic modelling is the most appropriate method for the analysis of examination grades' (p. 15). Bell & Dexter (2000), however, also compared a series of binary ordered logistic models.

Probably the main objection to multilevel modelling (MLM) on the part of critics is that it is more complex to execute and understand than OLS. It is generally considered that where OLS and MLM results differ, the latter are to be preferred. In their example, Baird & Jones showed that the continuous multilevel model was preferable to the OLS model since OLS found a difference in level between boards, but no difference in spread, while linear MLM found the opposite – no difference in levels, but differences in spread. Since, as noted earlier, the main focus of examination results, both in reporting and in 'fixing' any apparent problems lies in the actual grades awarded, it makes good sense to concentrate on grades and use an ordinal model. This model focused the locus of the differences to one particular boundary, that between A and A* for one board. This seems to show that ordinal regression is superior to continuous variable regression in this instance.

Another possibility is that, instead of carrying out a single ordinal variable regression including all of the levels, one carries out a series of binary logistic analyses, concentrating on each of the relevant boundaries in turn. Bell & Dexter (2000) considered that this approach was preferable because 'the results are much simpler and more interpretable for less experienced users'. In general, a principle in statistics is to borrow strength from adjacent observations to supplement sparser data. It should be noted that that using a single ordered model rather than a set of binary splits means that we have a single random effect for each centre rather than a series of unrelated ones from each binary analysis that may not even be mutually consistent. However, in this example, where a substantial amount of data is available and we are not certain that mechanisms will be the same from one boundary to another, we agree that it can make more sense to carry out the analyses as parallel but separate exercises.

Comparative analyses assume that the 'same' process is taking place for all examination entrants. In practice, however, some cases appear to be outliers from the rest. In some instances the data are obviously errors, for example mis-transcriptions, but in other situations they may arise because they represent a different population or process. Errors and missing data may be corrected if it is obvious what the correct value should be. Otherwise the missing or erroneous data may be imputed, or the whole case excluded. Either of these procedures has to be carried out with care. Alternatively, it may be that such apparently anomalous outliers do not represent a problem with the recording of the data, but are indicative of the existence of a separate population. Bell *et al.* (2004) quote an example where apparently anomalous data arose as a result of 'mature' entrants. They found that it was possible to extend the model to take account of these, but the resulting model proved to be relatively complex. They found that simpler models arose by analysing the two populations separately.

7.2 Predictor variables included

This section has benefited from the theoretical papers of Bell & Dexter (2000) and Pinot de Moira (2002b). If the average performance on an examination for one board is higher than that on another, it is not necessarily the case that the first examination is 'easier'. The first possible explanation is that one group of pupils is simply better on that topic on the day, and that tested on another occasion, or in different circumstances, this difference might disappear.

Another alternative explanation is that the two groups of pupils taking the exams are different in some important relevant way. One can take account of this by carrying out some kind of regression, as described in this chapter, and including some measure of ability. The boards have carried out or commissioned a number of studies and we now describe the type of data used in a representative selection of these.

Bell & Dexter (2000) distinguish between prior, concurrent and subsequent attainment (though somewhat confusingly they refer to them all as 'outcomes'). They state that 'the word outcomes has been deliberately chosen so that it covers the results of a wide range of measures including tests of aptitude, achievement, subsequent job performance'. According to Bell & Dexter (2000), prior attainment could include Key Stage 3 scores for GCSE, or GCSE score for A level, while a concurrent measure could be a test to measure 'general ability', 'aptitude', or 'calibre', or a subject-based reference test, or a common element included as part of all examinations. Bell & Dexter also include subsequent attainment, but this may be thought to measure the rather different characteristics of usefulness and relevance.

Most studies aiming to use a measure of ability have used a measure of prior ability, though Dexter & Massey (2000) and While & Fowles (2000) have used some kind of concurrent measure of attainment. Each of these studies raised some questions[11]. While & Fowles used a common element of a mathematics tests. This was, however, a coursework aspect for all but one of the boards involved. This is unfortunate, in that it seems likely that coursework may be a less 'pure' measure of attainment, since there is the possibility of parental input to any such work. Further, even if it is accepted that this is not a problem, or at least that it is a comparable problem for all, the fact that one of the boards did not treat it as coursework means that this common element is not comparable for this board. Finally, and to an outsider really rather surprisingly, given that this was planned to be a comparability exercise, while four of the boards agreed a common grading, the remainder were unable to concur. Dexter & Massey used a calibration test containing verbal, spatial and numerical reasoning in a study comparing GCSE and IGCSE (International GCSE) results for a number of subjects. Newbould & Massey (1979, cited in Dexter & Massey, 2000) discuss whether to use a general or a subject-based calibration test, and advocate the former since the latter is more likely to be differentially biased against some of the syllabuses being compared.

The value of using a measure of attainment as a term in the regression is dependent on the degree of relationship between that measure and the outcome. A test of academic attainment or 'general ability' may well do a good job in allowing for prior differences for exams in (for example) English or mathematics, but is likely to be of less value for art or physical education. In the extreme, if there is no relation between the test and the outcome, the attempted adjustment will be ineffectual. Dexter & Massey suggest that this may be less of a problem than might first be imagined, since correlations between their general ability test and outcomes in the six 'most popular' examination subjects range between 0.56 and 0.74: even art and design grades correlated 0.53 with the calibration test, though it should be noted that this means that less than 30% of the variance in the examination grade is accounted for by the calibration test.

A further complication potentially arises if there is an interaction between examination type and ability. In this situation the difference between examinations will vary over the ability scale. A single 'difference' factor may be produced by producing an average of the differences, but it may be preferable to show the entire picture in graphical form (see, for example, Figure 3 in this chapter).

Additional complications arise if one tries to allow for other possible background factors. For example, if girls do better at GCSE on one topic than boys after allowing for KS3 attainment, and there are more girls on one examination than on another, what exactly are we doing if we allow for this statistically? It may be appropriate to reweight the sample so that equal proportions of boys and girls are present in the weighted sample, or include a gender term in the model, which has a comparable effect. There is a danger that doing so will disguise an important phenomenon, namely that boys who have done as well as girls up to Key Stage 3, are now finding themselves less successful. Is the examination biased against them, or is the curriculum in schools failing to hold their attention, or is there some other reason? Similar considerations apply also to such factors as ethnic background or type of centre attended (independent school, type of state school, etc.). It is important to bear in mind that simply because these techniques are statistical, this does not mean that they are all value-neutral.

Table 13 shows in tabular form the extent to which a range of 'typical' studies were able to meet the conditions of the Cresswell definition in terms of allowing for relevant background characteristics.

Most of the studies have some kind of individual-level measure of ability or attainment, though not all of these even have this: for example Jones et al. (1997) and Pinot de Moira (2000) have some correlates of attainment, such as reported age planning to leave school, and Baird & Jones (1998) have prior attainment measures aggregated to centre level only. It is very likely that the predictive ability of the different measures of prior attainment used in these studies will vary, especially between subjects (see Pinot de Moira, 2002a; Dexter & Massey, 2000). None of the studies appears to have any information on school entry policy (except for While & Fowles, who considered tiered entry), or the competence of their teachers.

A few of the studies make an effort to obtain some measure of motivation, though this can prove problematic. While & Fowles (2000) described some of the difficulties in attempting to produce a good measure of attitudes. Such information did not already exist, and they were forced to ask the examination centres to distribute questionnaires to candidates taking exams. In their own words, 'a high proportion of centres failed to distribute (the questionnaire), and some of the candidates who did return it gave some questionable responses, thus calling into question the reliability of the questionnaire data'.

Table 13 Comparability studies and the Cresswell definition

Subject	Level and date	Outcome scale	Ability measure	Motiv-ation	Other pupil variables	Refer-ences*	Notes
English	GCSE 1998	Dichotomous	Some correlates	Some	Some	(1)	
English	GCSE 1998	Dichotomous	KS3 English		Some	(1)	
English	GCSE 1998	Grades as continuous	KS3 total			(2)	
Business	A/Voc A 2002	Dichotomous	Mean GCSE		Male/female	(3), (4)	Also 2001
Chemistry	A level 2002	Dichotomous	Mean GCSE		Male/female	(3), (4)	Also 2001
Geography	A level 2002	Dichotomous	Mean GCSE		Male/female	(3), (4)	Also 2001
Health Care	AVCE 2002	Dichotomous	Mean GCSE		Male/female	(3), (4)	Also 2001
12 subjects	A level 1993	Grades as continuous	Mean GCSE 'ability'		Male/female	(5)	12 studies
Art	GCSE 1996	Grades as continuous	Some correlates	Yes	Male/female, FSM, homework	(6)	
Maths	GCSE 1998	Dichotomous	Common test element	Yes	Male/female, homework	(7)	Considered tiering; problems with response rates
French	GCSE 2004	Dichotomous	KS3		Male/female	(8)	Convergence problems
9 subjects	GCSE	Grades as continuous	Anchor test		Male/female, language	(9)	
Art & Design	GCSE 1998	Continuous and ordinal	Aggregated measures	Some	Male/female, FSM, homework	(10)	

Key to pupil variable abbreviations:
Male/female   Male/female differences
FSM   Eligibility for free school meals

*Key to references:
(1)   Pinot de Moira (2000)   (6)   Jones, Baird and Arlett (1997)
(2)   Bell and Dexter (2000)   (7)   While and Fowles (2000)
(3)   Pinot de Moira (2003)   (8)   Al-Bayatti (2005)
(4)   Pinot de Moira (2002a)   (9)   Dexter and Massey (2000)
(5)   Tymms and Vincent (1995)   (10)   Baird and Jones (1998)

It is clear from Table 13 that none of these studies comes near meeting the criteria for properly assessing comparability under the Cresswell definition. Certainly sophisticated models are being employed to carry out the analyses, but this is going to be of little practical value if the underlying data is weak. If this area of application is to continue, then the work so far should be used as a jumping-off point for devising more rigorous investigations. It may be that some aspects of the factors to be allowed for are less critical, but it will be important for credibility to provide a valid justification for not including these.

All the above studies were selected because of their use of multilevel techniques, but it can be seen that this approach to modelling is not a sufficient condition for a fully effective comparability study. It could be argued that it is a necessary condition, but the study as a whole needs to be carefully designed in order to meet the challenge set by the Cresswell definition of comparability.

8   Practicalities

In this section we shall deal with:

1. software packages

2. acquiring suitable data

3. pitfalls and problems.

8.1 Software packages

When running multilevel modelling it will normally be necessary to acquire a specialist software package that is capable of dealing with all the necessary complexities of the modelling. Some general-purpose packages (e.g. SPSS, SAS, S+ and STATA) are now starting to include multilevel modelling modules, and new software is continually appearing in this area. For example, the WinBUGS software (Bayesian inference Using Gibbs Sampling) provides flexible software for the Bayesian analysis of complex statistical models using Markov chain Monte Carlo (MCMC) methods[12]. There are two specialist packages that have been widely used over a long period: MLwiN and HLM.

MLwiN was developed by the Centre for Multilevel Modelling at the Institute of Education, University of London[13] (see Rasbash et al., 2002; 2004). It provides data-entry and manipulation facilities, a graphical interface, a range of options for estimation, a facility for displaying models in terms of equations and fitted parameters (see screen shots within this chapter) and a command interface that replicates the structure of the earlier DOS-based version, MLn. The latest version, MLwiN 2.0, has a number of additional features including the ability to fit more complex models, such as ordered and unordered multinomial models. The program can fit up to five levels of hierarchy, and the size of data set that can be handled appears to be limited only by the capacity of the machine on which it is run. The authors have run four-level models with up to two million cases successfully in MLwiN.

HLM[14] (see Raudenbush et al., 2001) is probably more used in North America than in the UK, but is also a powerful multilevel modelling package with a range of facilities including data input, graphical displays, and logistic and multinomial modelling capabilities. The development of the program started as a two-level concept, although it now supports three levels. The main conceptual difference between the two packages is that, whereas MLwiN requires the model to be specified as a single entity encompassing all levels, HLM allows the user to specify the models for different levels separately. In some ways this can aid accessibility to the user and the ease with which results, including complex interactions, can be described to a non-technical audience. It is probably the case, however, that in the UK MLwiN is better understood and there is a greater community of support than for HLM. Another new package, which supports multilevel modelling in addition to a range of other modelling options is Mplus (see http://www.statmodel.com).

8.2 Acquiring suitable data

No comparability study is possible without suitable data, and for multilevel modelling to be used successfully this data needs to be comprehensive, accurate, representative and to contain all relevant variables, including the information needed to define the levels in the data (such as centre identifiers). Good data on background factors that are likely to be strongly related to outcomes (e.g. prior attainment) is essential, in order to ensure that we are comparing 'like with like'.

From the above remarks about packages, it would seem that in most cases software packages are able to cope with all available cases, so there is no merit in sampling cases for modelling – the whole dataset can be included in the analysis. However, when planning data collection it may be necessary to give consideration to sampling issues. Power calculations to determine suitable sample sizes to detect specified differences are important, but should take account of the clustering of candidates within centres and hence the design effect. Estimates of the effects of such clustering from previous studies may help to inform such calculations.

It is likely that the sampling will be done at the centre level, in which case it is important that the centres chosen are sampled randomly, probably using a stratified sampling technique that ensures they are representative in terms of important centre characteristics. If all candidates, or a fixed proportion per centre, are selected then the resulting sample will be self-weighting at the candidate level. However, if a fixed number per centre are selected, candidates in larger centres will be under-represented and consideration may need to be given to sampling with probability proportional to size to compensate for this. If there is strong clustering within centres (i.e. the centre-level variance is statistically significant compared with the candidate-level variance) then it becomes more important to get a reasonable number and spread of centres, rather than a large number of candidates per centre.

8.3 Pitfalls and problems

From all the above, some of the pitfalls and problems that may be encountered are fairly clear. These include:

- inadequate or insufficient data, or data that is biased in some way

- failure to collect suitable information, such as measures of prior attainment

- analysis that is superficial, or does not adequately model the structure of the data

- software failures, including failure to converge

- misinterpretation of the results of the modelling.

All these and other problems are controllable, but need appropriate planning, time and assistance when required. In our experience the best guard against most of these is collegiality – a community of practice that has a wide range of experience and expertise in these areas and can work as part of a team to ensure that problems do not arise or can be dealt with effectively when they do.

9 Conclusions

In this chapter we have tried to show many of the options that are available when analysing comparability study data using multilevel modelling. The challenge for the researcher is to select the appropriate model to fit the structure of the study and the type of outcome that is being modelled. Wrong choices can give misleading results, and we would strongly advise the use of variant approaches to the same data in order to obtain some idea of the sensitivity of the main results to the modelling assumptions being made.

There are big issues, discussed elsewhere in this book, which also impinge on the task of analysing comparability study data. One of the big issues is the purpose of the study. The vast majority of studies are carried out after the event, when candidates have been awarded results and the main rationale for the study is to show that results from different boards or whatever are in fact comparable. In this case, the main outcome must be to test the null hypothesis: 'Results from different boards are comparable'; if this is rejected there is no immediate action that can be taken, except to use the results to inform standard setting for the next cohort. Information on the exact degree and type of lack of comparability will be interesting, and perhaps useful for the future, but cannot directly affect outcomes.

An alternative scenario is one in which the results of a study are used to rescale results onto a common and consistent metric, for example to provide measures of school performance. Something like this happens in setting standards for National Curriculum tests, where pre-test data on the new test is used to compare with the results on the previous test and the outcomes of this analysis inform the setting of levels on the new test. In this kind of scenario the important question is not whether there is comparability, but the exact nature of the relationships determined from the model and the degree of confidence in those relationships. Details of the exact models fitted become much more important in this case, as does the need for some kind of 'sensitivity analysis'. However, even the most careful modelling requires to be interpreted in the light of the purposes of the study, the provenance of the data and the unmeasured influences that may be operating. Analysing data of this kind is partly an art as well as a science, and no single model is likely to give us the full picture.

At this stage it is probably worth returning to the original Cresswell definition of comparability that we began with – how have our discussions in this chapter influenced our approach to this? It has to be said that the use of sophisticated modelling techniques on examining data has revealed some potential inadequacies in this supposed 'catch-all' definition. This has mainly been shown by the existence of interactions between examining boards and measures of prior attainment in some examples. It is arguable that, under Cresswell's definition, it might be possible to find two samples of pupils for which the examinations are comparable despite the significant interactions. However, at the same time it would be possible to selectively enter pupils for different boards in order to enhance their outcomes. So, are the examining boards comparable or not? We would argue that such interactions are *prima facie* evidence for lack of comparability, and a new definition is required that rules them out. We would suggest something along the lines of:

> Two examinations have comparable standards, if for all potential groups of candidates, it is not possible to selectively enter individuals for one examination or another, based on measured background information, in such a way as to improve significantly their outcomes.

Finally, what can we say about the advantages of using multilevel modelling in this kind of work? It is clear to us that the advantages of using this methodology in comparability studies far outweigh any perceived disadvantages. These advantages include:

- a unified system that encompasses other models (e.g. OLS) while allowing for hierarchical clustering

- powerful and integrated software that can fit a range of models

- the ability to allow for complicating factors, including interactions, random coefficients and complex variances, in a coherent and efficient way

- efficiency of estimation, with fewer parameters required than in alternative approaches.

Overall it is true that multilevel modelling is a powerful tool for the analysis of comparability study data, and without it the work in this area would be seriously hampered.

Endnotes

1   In principle, assuming the normality of the outcome distributions – however, the Central Limit Theorem should ensure this is a valid test for most distributions with reasonable sample sizes.

2 The so-called 'delta method' (see Eason, 1995) is an early example of a crude adjustment procedure designed to detect such relationships.

3 Although in some circumstances it may be possible to model options effects and include these in a comparability study.

4 Uniform Mark Scale (UMS) scores are based on the grade awarded and the total mark received in the examination, in such a way that the grade boundaries are defined consistently at the same UMS value. See Chapter 3 for a discussion of UMS.

5 Key Stage 3 'fine grades' are derived from scores obtained from the examinations taken, mapped on to the National Curriculum levels awarded and put on a scale such that one level = 6 points.

6 It can be argued that this within-centre or within-school homogeneity effect is a consequence of selection effects, teaching, social ordering, etc. Although it is not inevitable with educational data sets, it is sufficiently common that it should be taken into account when setting up models in this field.

7 When a correlation between two quantities is estimated using aggregated data, such as school-level mean scores, this can give a completely different result from estimating the same quantity on individuals, such as pupils. If the 'aggregated' correlation is taken as an indicator of the individual correlation, then this is described as the ecological fallacy (Robinson, 1950).

8 5.9 is the mean value of prior attainment – it is subtracted in the interaction in order to ensure it is centred about zero.

9 The logit metric allows us to model probabilities with linear functions, using the transformation $logit(x) = ln(x/(1-x))$ where $0 < x < 1$.

10 For full technical details, refer to Goldstein (2003).

11 See Chapter 9 for a fuller discussion of prior and concurrent measures.

12 See http://www.mrc-bsu.cam.ac.uk/bugs/

13 Note that the Centre for Modelling is now located at Bristol University. See http://www.cmm.bristol.ac.uk/, which also contains a review of relevant software.

14 See http://www.ssicentral.com/hlm/index.html

References

Al-Bayatti, M. (2005). *A comparability study in GCSE French. A statistical analysis of results by awarding body.* A study based on the summer 2004 examinations. London: Qualifications and Curriculum Authority.

Baird, J., & Jones, B.E. (1998). *Statistical analyses of examination standards: Better measures of the unquantifiable?* Research Report RAC/780. Assessment and Qualifications Alliance.

Bell, J.F., & Dexter, T. (2000, October). *Using multilevel models to assess the comparability of examinations.* Paper presented at the Fifth International Conference on Social Science Methodology of the Research Committee on Logic and Methodology (RC33) of the International Sociological Association, Cologne.

Bell, J.F., Vidal Rodeiro, C.L., & Malacova, E. (2004, August). *The use of multilevel logistic regression to investigate the comparability of French GCSE.* Paper presented at the Sixth International Conference on Social Science Methodology, Amsterdam.

Burstein, L. (1980). The analysis of multilevel data in education research and evaluation. *Review of Research in Education, 8,* 158–193.

Cresswell, M.J. (1996). Defining, setting and maintaining standards in curriculum-embedded examinations: Judgemental and statistical approaches. In H. Goldstein & T. Lewis (Eds.), *Assessment: Problems, developments and statistical issues* (pp. 57-84). Chichester: John Wiley and Sons.

Dexter, T., & Massey, A. (2000, July). *Conceptual issues arising from a comparability study relating IGCSE grading standards with those of GCSE via a reference test using a multilevel model.* Paper presented at the 22nd Biennial Conference of the Society for Multivariate Analysis in the Behavioural Sciences at the London School of Economics, London.

Eason, S. (1995). *A review of the delta analysis method for comparing subject grade distributions across examining boards.* Research Report RAC/667. Guildford: Associated Examining Board.

Fitz-Gibbon, C.T., & Tymms, P. (2002). Technical and ethical issues in indicator systems: Doing things right and doing wrong things. *Education Policy Analysis Archives, 10*(6).

Goldstein, H. (2003). *Multilevel statistical models* (3rd ed.). London: Arnold.

Gorard, S. (2003a). What is multi-level modelling for? *British Journal of Educational Studies, 51,* 46–63.

Gorard, S. (2003b). In defence of a middle way: A reply to Plewis and Fielding. *British*

Journal of Educational Studies, 51, 420–426.

Jones, B.E. (1997). Comparing examination standards: Is a purely statistical approach adequate? *Assessment in Education*, 4, 249–263.

Jones, B., Baird, J., & Arlett, S. (1997). *A comparability study in GCSE art and design unendorsed. A study based on the summer 1996 examinations.* Organised by the Northern Examinations and Assessment Board on behalf of the Joint Forum for the GCSE and GCE.

Mosteller, F., & Boruch, R. (2002). *Evidence matters: Randomized trials in education research.* Washington DC: Brookings Institute.

Newton, P.E. (2005). The public understanding of measurement inaccuracy. *British Educational Research Journal*, 31, 419–442.

Pinot de Moira, A. (2000). *A comparability study in GCSE English: Statistical analysis of results by board.* A study based on the summer 1998 examination and organised by the Assessment and Qualifications Alliance (Southern Examining Group) on behalf of the Joint Forum for the GCSE and GCE.

Pinot de Moira, A. (2002a). *An inter-awarding body comparability study: The statistical analysis of results by awarding body for AS GCE and VCE business, AS GCE chemistry, AS GCE geography and AS VCE health and social care.* A study based on the summer 2001 examination and organised by the Assessment and Qualifications Alliance on behalf of the Joint Council for General Qualifications.

Pinot de Moira, A. (2002b). *Statistical robustness in comparability studies.* Unpublished report, Assessment and Qualifications Alliance.

Pinot de Moira, A. (2003). *An inter-awarding body comparability study: The statistical analysis of results by awarding body for GCE A level and AVCE business, GCE A level chemistry, GCE A level geography and AVCE health and social care.* A study based on the summer 2002 examination and organised by the Assessment and Qualifications Alliance on behalf of the Joint Council for General Qualifications.

Plewis, I., & Fielding, A. (2003). What is multi level modelling for? A critical response to Gorard (2003). *British Journal of Educational Studies*, 51, 408–419.

Rasbash, J., Browne, W., Goldstein, H., Yang, M., Plewis, I., Healy, M., *et al.* (2002). *A user's guide to MLwiN. Version 2.1d* edition. London: University of London Institute of Education.

Rasbash, J., Steele, F., Browne, W., & Prosser, R. (2004). *A user's guide to MLwiN. Version 2.0 edition.* London: University of London Institute of Education.

Raudenbush, S., & Bryk, A. (2002). *Hierarchical linear models. Applications and data analysis methods* (2nd ed.). Thousand Oaks, California: Sage Publications.

Raudenbush, S., Bryk, A., Cheong, Y., & Congdon, R. (2001). *HLM 5: Hierarchical linear and nonlinear modeling*. Lincolnwood, Illinois: Scientific Software International, Inc.

Robinson, W. (1950). Ecological correlations and the behaviour of individuals. *American Sociological Review*, *15*, 351–357.

Stobart, G., Bibby, T., & Goldstein, H., with Schagen, I., & Treadaway, M. (2005). *Moving to two-tier GCSE examinations: An independent evaluation of the 2005 GCSE pilot and trial*. London: Qualifications and Curriculum Authority.

Styles, B. (2006). Educational research v. scientific research. *Research Intelligence, 95,* 7–9.

Tymms, P., & Vincent, L. (1995). *Comparing examination boards and syllabuses at A-level: Students' grades, attitudes and perceptions of classroom processes*. Curriculum, Evaluation and Management Centre, University of Newcastle-upon-Tyne. Technical report commissioned by the GCE Examining Boards. Belfast: Northern Ireland Council for the Curriculum, Examinations and Assessment.

While, D., & Fowles, D. (2000). *A comparability study in GCSE mathematics. Statistical analysis of results by board. A study based on the work of candidates in the summer 1998 examinations*. Organised by the Assessment and Qualifications Alliance (Northern Examinations and Assessment Board) on behalf of the Joint Forum for the GCSE and GCE.

Yang, M., Goldstein, H., Browne, W., & Woodhouse, G. (2002). Multivariate multilevel analyses of examination results. *Journal of the Royal Statistical Society A, 165*(1), 137–153.

COMMENTARY ON CHAPTER 10

Anne Pinot de Moira

Ian Schagen and Dougal Hutchison open their chapter by correctly warning against the assumption that statistical modelling provides objectivity. They describe model-fitting as an art rather than a science where 'there is no substitute for experience and a deep understanding of the subject matter'. While this is indisputably true, the element of subjectivity in any statistical analysis extends beyond the choice of model, the formulation of dependent variable, the decision to include given independent variables and the sampling of data. Even for a technically sound model, the findings are only valid to the extent they are interpreted legitimately.

In the literature a naïve faith in statistical significance testing is blamed for creating the illusion of much sought-after objectivity in research work (Schmidt, 1996). The system where a null hypothesis is defined and then rejected whenever the probability of being wrong in that decision is less than some critical value is appealing in the sense that it is rule-based. In his paper of 1951, Yates lamented the emphasis placed upon tests of significance suggesting they are often regarded as the 'ultimate objective'. As Tukey (1991) observed, however, a null hypothesis is always false at some level of decimal places; adding an element of futility to such an objective. Cohen (1990) made the same argument more forcefully:

> If [the null hypothesis] is false, even to a tiny degree, it must be the case that a large enough sample will produce a significant result and lead to its rejection. So if the null hypothesis is always false, what is the big deal about rejecting it?

The abundance of candidate-level data for national examinations in England brings Cohen's observations into sharp focus when considering the interpretation of comparability. Carver (1978) writes that 'statistical significance ordinarily depends on how many subjects are used in the research'. The larger the sample size, the smaller the difference between effects which will be detected as statistically significant. In the context of national examinations, where data are plentiful, it seems sensible that the modelling and comparison of standards should not rely solely on statistical significance testing. It has long been argued that the magnitude of the difference between effects, or effect size, is of much greater practical significance (Cohen, 1988; Kirk, 1996).

Consider a study of GCSE English which used a sample of data to compare the grading standards applied between awarding bodies (Pinot de Moira, 2000). A logistic multilevel model was fitted to data to determine the probability of exceeding the foundation tier grade C threshold dependent upon awarding body of entry. There were 6,651 candidates nested within 111 centres. The resultant model suggested no overall statistically significant difference in grading dependent upon awarding body (Table 1).

Of real interest to the educational practitioner, however, should be the magnitude of the difference in grading standards between awarding bodies.

Table 1 Estimates for the two-level logistic model describing the log odds of a GCSE English candidate exceeding the foundation tier grade C threshold

		β	se	p	Joint χ^2	p
Fixed Effects	Constant	1.245	0.287	0.000		
	English Key Stage 3 result	1.008	0.062	0.000		
	Mean mathematics & science Key Stage 3 result	0.188	0.069	0.007		
	Mean GCSE result	1.296	0.061	0.000		
	Female	0.668	0.084	0.000		
	Awarding Body 2	−0.914	0.348	0.009	8.821	0.066
	Awarding Body 3	−0.558	0.344	0.105		
	Awarding Body 4	−0.783	0.322	0.015		
	Awarding Body 5	−0.433	0.345	0.210		
Random Effects Centre level		0.658	0.119	0.000		

(Awarding body 1 is set as the base category.)

In their introduction to multilevel modelling, Snijders and Bosker (1999) describe effect size as an approximate relationship between the standard error of an effect, the power of the test and the significance level (Equation 1).

$$\text{Effect Size } (\gamma) \quad \approx \quad (z_{1-\alpha} + z_{1-\beta}) \times se\ (\gamma) \qquad\qquad (1)$$

Where $z_{1-\alpha}$ is a z score associated with the significance level of α and $z_{1-\beta}$, is the z score associated with a given power $1-\beta$[1]. The z scores are derived from the standard normal distribution. For the purposes of inter-awarding comparability, let us define:

$$\text{Effect Size } (\gamma) \quad = \quad \gamma_A - \gamma_B$$

Where γ_A is the parameter estimate for awarding body A which is greater than γ_B the parameter estimate for awarding body B.

In the current context, therefore, effect size is described as the difference between two awarding bodies in the log odds of exceeding a given grade threshold. Using the model displayed in Table 1 for illustration, the standard error associated with the awarding body effects can be estimated as approximately 0.4. From Equation 1 the effect size which would be detected at a significance level $\alpha = 0.05$ and power $1-\beta = 0.8$ would be approximately 0.996. Such a statistic has little useful meaning but, because the model is logistic, the effect size can be transformed to be expressed in terms of a probability. Expressed as a difference in the probability of exceeding a grade threshold, effect size becomes a statistic with practical utility.

Effect Size (γ) $= \gamma_A - \gamma_B$

$$= \ln\left(\frac{p+\delta}{1-(p+\delta)}\right) - \ln\left(\frac{p}{1-p}\right)$$

Where   p   is the probability of exceeding a given grade threshold

             δ is the difference in probability of exceeding a given grade threshold between awarding bodies B and A

         se (γ) is now defined as an approximation of the standard error associated with the awarding body parameter estimates

The minimum difference between awarding bodies that would be detected as statistically significant is estimated thus,

$$\delta \approx \frac{p - p^2 - e^m + p^2 e^m}{p - 1 - p e^m}$$

Where   m $= (z_{1-\alpha} + z_{1-\beta}) \times se\,(\gamma)$

For the GCSE English multilevel model (Table 1), the minimum detectable difference between awarding bodies would be described by the solid curved line in Figure 1. Figure 1 also describes the relationship between δ and p for other values of se (γ) where $\alpha=0.05$ and $1-\beta=0.8$.

Figure 1 The relationship between δ and p for a logistic model with varying values of se(γ) where the significance level a=0.05 and power 1–β=0.8

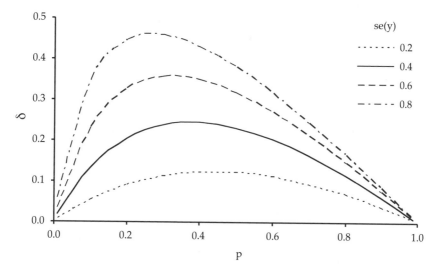

Among the candidates included in the multilevel model just over 20% were awarded a grade C. An initial estimate of the probability of exceeding the grade C threshold would therefore be 0.2 with the minimum statistically detectable difference between awarding bodies also being 0.2 (see Figure 1). While the statistical significance tests flagged no overall differences between the awarding bodies (Table 1), the subsequent analysis of effect size suggests that differences of up to 20% in the award of grade C between award bodies would be regarded as statistically non-significant. However, a difference of such magnitude would clearly be unacceptable, not least because the specifications and the awarding processes would lack face validity and, therefore, lose credibility in the eyes of the public.

The process of evaluating effect size allows a translation of the statistical outcomes from a complex model into terms to which those involved in standard-setting can relate. Even though an effect size expressed as a probability provides more information about comparability than an unqualified statistical test, standards in national examinations are set by determining boundary marks for each of the contributing components. An effective assessment of comparability between awarding bodies would require reference to the mark scale in order to fulfil a remit of advising awarding committees of any necessary remedial action.

The extent to which comparability between national examinations can be expected is, however, limited by the fact that most are marked on a discrete ordinal scale and marking is completed before determination of grade boundaries. It would therefore be unrealistic to expect that grading standards could be *exactly* the same between awarding bodies (an interesting observation when considered alongside Tukey's (1991) assertion that a null hypothesis is always false at some level of decimal places). With a large enough sample and small enough mark range, it is possible to conceive of a situation where a one-mark increase in the positioning of a grade boundary applied by an awarding body could mean that the grading standards of that awarding body changed from statistically significantly lenient to statistically significantly severe. Delap (1992) discussed this matter in the context of grade award meetings and the maintenance of year-on-year grading standards.

Empirically, it is possible to explore the statistical sensitivity of grading standards to a mark scale which is discrete. Returning to the GCSE English data, the grade C boundary for Awarding Body 5 was determined as 105 in the award meeting. Figure 2 illustrates the effect that repositioning this boundary would have had on the joint statistical test applied to assess comparability of the GCSE English specifications. Given a naïve assumption that comparability is assured if the p-value is more than 0.05, a grade boundary placed in the range 105–108 would lead to the conclusion that grading standards are aligned. These 'satisfactory' extremes of grade C boundary would award between 31.3% and 25.8% of candidates a grade C.

Rather than accepting that grading standards are aligned with grade boundaries in the range 105–108, a judgement is required as to whether the extremes exceeding the grade threshold are defensible. When setting grade boundaries to maintain year-on-year comparability some awarding bodies have derived acceptable deviances, in percentage terms, between years. All other things being equal, for large-entry subjects, the percentage of candidates exceeding a given grade threshold is not expected to vary from the previous year by more than 2%. Further work would be needed to establish whether the use of such acceptable deviances could be extended to between-

Figure 2 Test of the null hypothesis that there is no difference between the grading standards applied by awarding bodies dependent upon the grade C subject boundary mark applied to the awarding body specification

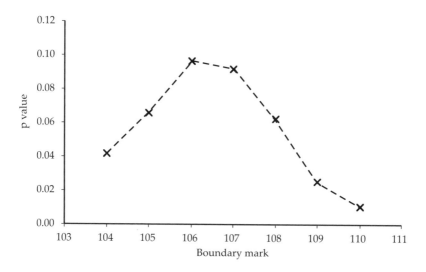

awarding body comparability. However, it is contextual information of this nature which should be fed into the design and interpretation of a model of comparability. Indeed a retrospective look at effect size might never be needed were an educational researcher more often afforded the luxury of a controlled experiment where data could be sampled to target a particular hypothesis and power calculations could be performed in advance of any analysis. Instead, inter-awarding body comparability studies are largely based on opportunity samples with missing data and self-selected entry patterns. It is essential, therefore, that the limitations of any data are explored both before and after analysis and that, to be of practical value, model outcomes are related to the measurement scale where remedial action can be effected.

As Ian Schagen and Dougal Hutchison correctly conclude 'the challenge for the researcher is to select the appropriate model to fit the structure of the study and the type of outcome that is being modelled'. Implicit within this challenge must be the understanding that outcome should be presented in terms that are relevant to the target audience (Schagen, 2004). Consequently, when discussing the findings from an ordered categorical multilevel model (Table 5), for example, the authors helpfully transform their findings to an 'intuitive metric'.

When considering comparability in the national examinations of England, the researcher must go beyond presenting the headline news, which in itself might be misleading, to suggest to awarding committees appropriate remedial action. Furthermore, it should be recognised that the cocktail of large datasets and small mark ranges, available for national comparability studies, makes blind acceptance of statistical hypothesis testing a risky business. The researcher would do well to heed the advice given by Reese (2004):

> Calculating statistical significance is a tool, a step in the process of analysis. The interpretation of a result requires the researcher's knowledge, in particular to put new data into the context of previous scientific knowledge.

The modelling techniques presented in Chapter 10, and indeed throughout the rest of the book, provide powerful instruments with which to describe data but, without valid interpretation and contextualisation, the statistics produced are utterly redundant in a practical sense.

Endnote

1   The significance level of a statistical test is the probability (α) of wrongly rejecting the null hypothesis if it is actually true (Type I error). The power of a statistical test is the probability ($1-\beta$) that it will correctly reject the null hypothesis if it is actually false.

References

Carver, P.C. (1978). The case against statistical significance testing. *Harvard Educational Review, 48*(3), 378–399.

Cohen, J. (1988). *Statistical power analysis for the behavioural sciences* (2nd ed.). Hillsdale, New Jersey: Lawrence Erlbaum Associates.

Cohen, J. (1990). Things I have learned (so far). *American Psychologist, 45*(12), 1304–1312.

Delap, M.R. (1992). *Statistical information at awarding meetings: The discrete nature of mark distributions*. Research Report RAC/585. Guildford: Associated Examining Board.

Kirk, R.E. (1996). Practical significance: A concept whose time has come. *Educational and Psychological Measurement, 58*(5), 746–759.

Pinot de Moira, A. (2000). *A comparability study in GCSE English: Statistical analysis of results by board*. A study based on the summer 1998 examination and organised by the Assessment and Qualifications Alliance (Southern Examining Group) on behalf of the Joint Forum for the GCSE and GCE.

Reese, R.A. (2004). Does significance matter? *Significance, 1*(1), 39–40.

Schagen, I. (2004). Presenting the results of complex models – Normalised coefficients, star wars plots and other ideas. In I. Schagen & K. Elliot (Eds.), *But what does it mean? The use of effect sizes in educational research* (pp. 25–41). Slough: National Foundation for Educational Research.

Schmidt, F.L. (1996). Statistical significance testing and cumulative knowledge in psychology: Implications for training of researchers. *Psychological Methods, 1*(2), 115–129.

Snijders, T., & Bosker, R. (1999). *Multilevel analysis: An introduction to basic and advanced multilevel modelling*. London: Sage Publications.

Tukey, J.W. (1991). The philosophy of multiple comparisons. *Statistical Science, 6*(1), 100–116.

Yates, F. (1951). The influence of statistical methods for research workers on the development of the science of statistics. *Journal of the American Statistical Association, 46*(253), 19–34.

COMMENTARY ON CHAPTER 10

Peter Tymms

There can be no doubt that Hierarchical Linear Models (aka multilevel models, MLMs) represent a major advance and that they have solved some key statistical problems through the use of clever algorithms and modern computing power. They have provided useful new perspectives and they rightly continue to be at the forefront of some aspects of educational research. But they have not been accepted without question; see, for example, Fitz-Gibbon (1997); De Leeuw and Kreft (1995); Gorard (2003a; 2003b; 2004; 2007). There have also been staunch defences; see, for example, Plewis and Fielding (2003). Space does not permit a full discussion but five broad issues are set out below to indicate some key points.

When should multilevel models be used?

A number of researchers have carried out studies in which they have analysed data using traditional methods only to find that in order to get published they have been required to use multilevel models. When doing as they were told and getting their papers published, they discovered that the newly analysed results hardly differed from the original.

Schagen and Hutchison state that because Ordinary Least Squares (OLS) approaches assume that the units are independent the OLS results will give 'biased estimates of the statistical significance'. This must be true, but that is not the point. The question is 'how big is the bias?' This was extensively investigated as part of The Value Added National Project (see, for example, Trower & Vincent, 1995) and the findings summarised in Fitz-Gibbon (1997). Not only were the regression coefficients identical to all intents and purposes but the OLS and MLM 'school effects' were found to correlate around 0.99 with one another. This held when the analyses involved both linear or curvilinear relationships and single or multiple predictors. But, it is argued, a primary advantage of MLMs is that the errors are better estimated than in OLS regression. Again this must be true but how big is the difference? Tymms (in Fitz-Gibbon, 1997, p. 110) found 'little difference' between the errors on the coefficients in OLS regressions and MLMs. He also found almost identical estimates of errors on the residuals from the two procedures. This was not the case in the example shown by Schagen and Hutchison. Under what circumstances are important differences found?

Given a choice between a simple approach and a more complex analysis it could be argued that one should always go for an MLM since, as Schagen and Hutchison note, that is the standard against which other analyses will be judged. But there is the matter of communication. They state 'we believe that the objections to the difficulty of the technique are overstated'. Have they successfully explained variance at the second level to a politician or a journalist?

434

They also write 'it is more important to be correct than to appear simple'. But the issue may not be a choice between such stark alternatives and it seems reasonable to ask what amount of clustering ensures that traditional approaches are misleading. Clearly the lower the intra-class correlation the less the importance of explicitly modelling the clustering; the key question is about the degree to which the results of analyses might mislead. Indeed, Kennedy and Mandeville (2000) state 'the question of when to use multilevel modelling is an important one.'

Complexity

Can a model be too complex? Assuming that we do have situations where the clustering is large enough to mean that it makes sense to use MLMs, the models themselves can become exceedingly complex. There can be several levels with cross-classification, interactions, and any or all variables used at the lower levels can reappear at a higher level in some aggregate form. Such models can become extremely difficult to construct, understand and interpret. But is it possible for a model to become too complex? The well-respected statistician Steve Raudenbush (1994) advises on the need for 'parsimonious pre-specified models'. He does this because of the 'precariousness of knowledge based on exploratory analyses using trimmed models and retrospective explanation'. Not only are MLMs statements of a theoretical position but they also tend to be isolated and self-referential. This leads to the question 'when does the model become so complex it becomes impossible to gainsay?' This asks about the falsifiability of the chosen model which is in some senses a theory. In the same way that Popper (1963) writes about the falsifiability of scientific theories, we should ask about the falsifiability of multilevel models.

Terminology

Within the reports of MLMs the writing often involves words as such as 'effects', 'explanation' and 'impact'. Schagen and Hutchison use the phrases, 'the model explains the data', 'Board C effect' and 'do have an impact on'. These are misleading terminologies as they all imply causal relationship. Occasionally, very occasionally, MLMs are used to analyse the data from randomised control trials (see, for example, Tymms and Merrell, 2006), but most commonly MLMs deal with passive observational data. As Kennedy and Mandeville (2000) note 'for purposes of drawing inferences about school effects students would be randomly assigned to schools and schools would be randomly assigned to process conditions'. Naturally, the sophisticated users of MLMs are aware of the issue but they do little to discourage the use of the established terminology.

How can the causally-laden words often used in statistics be discouraged?

Errors on predictors

In OLS regression and in MLMs, except where dummy variables are used, there are errors on the predictors, and yet the errors are assumed to be non-existent. This can lead to problems. If, for example, attainment were modelled using socio-economic status as a predictor at the pupil level and at another level, perhaps the board level, using the average socio-economic status, then it is quite likely that a significant compositional effect would be found. But that compositional effect would inevitably appear because of the error of measurement in the predictor. Indeed the extent to which the predictor is measured with error can be used to indicate the extent to which a compositional effect will appear. This phantom effect is a consequence of one of the assumptions of multilevel models. The difficulty was established before the advent of MLMs (Hauser, 1970) but has been demonstrated more recently using MLwiN (Harker and Tymms, 2004).

Bias from shrinkage

When constructing MLMs there is a danger that unstable relationships can appear at the second, or higher, levels because very small units can produce wild results. To get round this the results at the higher levels are shrunk in proportion to the reliability of their measurement. This produces more stable models; however, the shrinking introduces bias. A very small unit with a genuinely high or low value is artificially shrunk towards the mean, hiding its true colours. Comparability studies will not usually need to worry about this issue but it could arise if small samples are being analysed or when the standards adopted for a less popular syllabus from one awarding body are being assessed.

References

De Leeuw, J., & Kreft, I.G.G. (1995). Questioning multilevel models. In I.G.G. Kreft (Ed.), Hierarchical linear models: Problems and prospects [Special issue]. *Journal of Educational and Behavioral Statistics, 20*(2), 171-189.

Fitz-Gibbon, C.T. (1997). *The value added national project final report – Feasibility studies for a national system of value-added indicators.* London: School Curriculum and Assessment Authority.

Gorard, S. (2003a). What is multi-level modelling for? *British Journal of Educational Studies, 51,* 46-63.

Gorard, S. (2003b). In defence of a middle way: A reply to Plewis and Fielding. *British Journal of Educational Studies, 51,* 420-426.

Gorard, S. (2004). Comments on modelling segregation. *Oxford Review of Education, 30,* 435-440.

Gorard, S. (2007). The dubious benefits of multi-level modelling. *International Journal of Research and Method in Education, 30*(2), 221-236.

Harker, R., & Tymms, P. (2004). The effects of student composition on school outcomes. *School Effectiveness and School Improvement, 15*(2), 177-199.

Hauser, R.M. (1970). Context and consex: A cautionary tale. *American Journal of Sociology, 75,* 645-664.

Kennedy, E., & Mandeville, G. (2000). Some methodological issues in school effectiveness research. In C. Teddlie & D. Reynolds (Eds.), *The international handbook of school effectiveness research* (pp.189-205). London: Falmer Press.

Plewis, I., & Fielding, A. (2003). What is multi level modelling for? A critical response to Gorard (2003). *British Journal of Educational Studies, 51,* 408-419.

Popper, K.R. (1963). *Conjectures and refutations: The growth of scientific knowledge.* London: Routledge & Kegan Paul.

Raudenbush, S. (1994). Searching for a balance between a priori and post hoc model specification: Is a 'general approach' desirable? *School Effectiveness and School Improvement, 5*(2), 196-198.

Trower, P., & Vincent, L. (1995). *The value added national project technical report.* London: School Curriculum and Assessment Agency.

Tymms, P., & Merrell, C. (2006). The impact of screening and advice on inattentive, hyperactive and impulsive children. *European Journal of Special Needs Education, 21*(3), 321-337.

RESPONSE TO COMMENTARIES ON CHAPTER 10

Ian Schagen and Dougal Hutchison

Response to Anne Pinot de Moira

To a large extent we agree with the comments about statistical significance. It is not enough for something to be statistically significant – the size of the effect is important. See, for example, Schagen and Elliot (2004) for a discussion of effect sizes in educational research. However, effect sizes and significance tests are not mutually incompatible: the latter attempts to answer the question 'is there evidence for a difference due to something other than chance?' while the former addresses the question: 'how big is the difference and does it matter?' Both are important in comparability studies, and can be addressed through multilevel analysis.

The comment about using 'statistically significant' rather than just 'significant' is probably good practice. However it can turn out very cumbersome, and it is often more elegant to say, for example, 'significantly different' than 'statistically significantly different'. Given that our chapter is very technical, we feel that it is reasonable to assume that readers will not confuse the technical use of the word with the common English usage.

We agree with the final comment about the need for valid interpretation and contextualisation, alongside powerful and appropriate modelling tools and high quality data.

Response to Peter Tymms

Peter Tymms takes a more general overview of the value and application of multilevel modelling, and queries some of our justifications for advocating its use in the comparison of examining boards. Most of his comments are unexceptionable but some criticisms are more general in their focus than the current application. In many ways we are inclined to feel that the confrontation between Ordinary Least Squares (OLS) or logistic regression on the one hand and multilevel modelling (MLM) is more apparent than real. In fact, it is possible to consider OLS to be a special case of MLM, with zero variance at higher levels, in much the same way as a strictly hierarchical model could be considered a special case of a model with nested and crossed variance components. Each has its place, and can provide valuable information, and one has to balance statistical soundness, ease of use, and computing feasibility.

A cautious statistician would usually want to test the hypothesis that higher level variances were zero before proceeding further, which would mean running the MLM anyway – and then why not proceed in this way, especially if the hypothesis is rejected? Tymms' convention that MLM is significantly more complex to run than OLS is not really true with modern software. MLM is certainly more powerful and can fit more complex models in situations where they are needed.

It is generally accepted that the fixed coefficients in a variance component model will be close to those in an OLS model, though they will not generally be completely the same. However one finds that the standard errors of fixed coefficients in MLM, especially those of variables at higher levels, will typically be larger, and in some cases substantially larger, than those of OLS models, and thus coefficients are less likely to be statistically significant. In a sense in this situation therefore it is less a question of MLM finding new effects, but rather of MLM not finding effects that are not there.

Modelling is never an exact science, but a balancing act between parsimony and fitting the data well. The chapter is not intended to present a precise recipe for carrying out comparability studies, but to show what models are possible and the consequences of omitting certain elements from the model, for example higher level variances or random slopes. Communicating the results of any sort of model may well be a challenge, but key elements should not be omitted because of this. Simple formulations can often be found to explain, for example, higher level variances: for example, '84% of the variation in the results was between pupils in the same schools, and 16% due to differences between schools'.

As Tymms points out, at some value of intra-class correlation the OLS and MLM models are likely to give very similar results. What this value is will vary from case to case. Even if we knew this critical value, we would then need to run an analysis to determine the intra-class correlation for our data before deciding to opt for OLS or MLM. Busy statisticians such as ourselves prefer to eliminate this extra work and go into MLM which will estimate all the required parameters and give the same results as OLS if the intra-class correlation is effectively zero.

To a large extent, choice between examining boards at the level of individual subjects is a school-level decision. In this connection Anne Pinot de Moira's illustration of an inter-board comparison in her comment on our paper is highly relevant. One's first reaction is that a sample of over 6,000 is going to be big enough to identify any phenomenon that is actually of any real world importance. However, since the board decision is more nearly a school-level one than an individual one, it turns out that using MLM probably makes a substantial difference. She has very kindly agreed to re-run the analyses from her commentary, using a non-hierarchical model, and the relevant part of the results is shown in Table 1.

Table 1 Non-hierarchical modelling of data from commentary by Pinot de Moira

Exam board effects	MLM Analysis			OLS Analysis		
	β	Se	χ^2	β	Se	χ^2
Awarding Body 2	−0.914	0.348		−0.558	0.136	
Awarding Body 3	−0.558	0.344	8.821	−0.304	0.132	35.427
Awarding Body 4	−0.783	0.322	(P=0.066)	−0.558	0.120	(P=0.000)
Awarding Body 5	−0.433	0.345		−0.147	0.125	

Columns 2 and 3 correspond to the results in the table in her commentary, run using MLM, and 5 and 6 are the corresponding results using a non-hierarchical model. It can be seen that there are some differences in the β coefficients for the awarding bodies between the two analyses. More important in this context however is the difference in size of the standard errors of these coefficients, which are very much larger in the MLM than in the OLS analysis. The results in the OLS analysis are thus highly significant statistically, while those in the more appropriate MLM are not.

Our exposition of the benefits of MLM did not confine itself to simple fixed inter-board differences. An important aspect of inter-board differences lies in the fact that they vary between subgroups, between schools and over ability ranges, and this formed an important part of the examining boards' contention that there was no 'quick fix' of apparent differences between subjects (see Newton, 1997, for a discussion of this point). We believe that MLM is the appropriate statistical technique for addressing questions of this type.

Tymms also mentions that there is little difference between the estimated standard errors for school residuals using OLS and MLM, which may or may not be true, but does not appear relevant to our exposition. He also comments that apparent aggregated school-level effects may be due to a biasing effect of measurement error. This is certainly true (see Hutchison, 2007, for an extensive exposition) but again is not particularly relevant. Finally he refers to the discussion on whether shrunken residuals should be used for second or higher level units (for example, in these applications, schools or examination centres) – again, an interesting point for discussion, but not relevant here. These last three points indeed appear to have strayed in from some other paper.

Finally we confess that in writing the chapter we did on occasions use terminology which could be interpreted causally, and this is something which ideally should be avoided. It is not always possible to find circumlocutions which avoid this without becoming clunky and interrupting the flow of an argument, but this is clearly an area where we need to improve our language and the way we use it.

References

Hutchison, D. (2007). When is a compositional effect not a compositional effect? *Quality and Quantity, 41*, 219–232.

Newton, P.E. (1997). Measuring the comparability of standards between subjects: Why our statistical techniques do not make the grade. *British Educational Research Journal, 23*, 433–449.

Schagen, I., & Elliot, K., (Eds.). (2004). *But what does it mean? The use of effect sizes in educational research*. Slough: National Foundation for Educational Research.

GENERAL COMMENTARY

Tim Oates

This book in general, but Tattersall's and Baird's chapters in particular, engages with vital issues of the way in which avowed concerns regarding comparability are located in economic, political, social and scientific development. Their analysis usefully draws our attention to the fact that there are different forms of comparability – at the very least between-board comparability, between-year and between-subject – and this variation combines with different conceptions of 'standard' as well as different conceptions of the purposes of assessment, of public examinations and of education. The potential and real complexity which emerges from this requires us to explain what it is that gives rise to preoccupations with certain forms of comparability at certain times. Shifting focus is demonstrated clearly through the last three decades, which have seen Carol Fitz-Gibbon's work on the possible movement of achievement standards in science A levels relative to other subjects (Fitz-Gibbon, 1991); concerns regarding the extent to which different A levels prepare learners for university-level education (for example, Beckett, 2006); the imperative for 'taking forward the standard' during times of system transition (exemplified in 2002 by the problems experienced with the wholesale Curriculum 2000 A level reforms); and the introduction of performance tables as a public policy tool for school accountability.

The latter is a perfect illustration of how shifts in 'comparability concerns' can be driven by things other than concerns within the assessment community to improve the technical performance of instruments and systems. The 'league tables' have at their heart embedded assumptions about the equal value of different qualifications in counting towards a school's overall performance table score. Classes of qualification tend to attract an identical score (all GCSEs get the same number of points); scores in different years are considered comparable and vital to judging a school's trajectory over time and its changing position relative to other schools. Between-subject comparability is presupposed in the model of performance tables which we have today, yet such comparability remains a contested and problematic issue. What's more, the performance tables increasingly have been expanded to include a very wide range of diverse qualifications – with contrasting origins, purposes, design models, assessment and grading systems. This has given rise to some significant anomalies and accompanying controversies about 'easier' routes (by schools) to high performance table scores (Revell, 2001) – with all the implications of 'falsely elevated position'. The peculiar, embedded assumptions regarding comparability within performance tables matter, since the performance tables are such a prominent mechanism, and carry real purchase on schools' reputations. For some, comparability may seem to be a desirable technical objective in its own right; others see it as a prerequisite of assessments which provide the foundation for much broader policy instruments.

The specific and peculiar factors which drive societal preoccupation with certain forms of comparability are capable of being examined and subjected to critique. This in turn gives rise to a key question – who should do this analysis and what approaches are most appropriate for it to be done with precision? Kathleen Tattersall's chapter gives one of the most comprehensive overviews of the development of public examinations which has been seen in recent years. Jo-Anne Baird's chapter highlights the issues of comparability which were at the heart of policy management of the complex system transition during the 2000 reforms of A levels. But this does give rise to an issue of method. Many of the key debates and decisions regarding comparability are embedded in 'grey' policy papers and in undocumented exchanges between policy-makers, officials and ministers. Baird connects conceptions of comparability with some of the seismic events in qualifications awarding in the UK, using these to illustrate the sociologically and politically embedded nature of these conceptions. Incisive analyses of these events are vital elements in the explanation not only of the implications of using different concepts of comparability, but also to the way in which the conceptions are themselves constituted. Who said what and who did what, and when, become important to scientific understanding of the conceptions of comparability. This invokes a requirement for formal historical, social and political analysis – with all the attendant requirements for sound investigative method. Currently, it is largely left to assessment specialists to produce accounts of events in their world. In one sense, they are the right people; they understand measurement theory and are immersed in the operation of systems. But things in the world of assessment are connected to, and determined by, social, economic and other drivers. To strengthen understanding and critique, the assessment community needs to encourage historians and sociologists to join in with the task of understanding movements and developments in assessment in general, and comparability in particular.

In trying recently to encourage leading sociologists and economists to present a challenging critique of assessment, I became aware that they felt an acute lack of confidence in being able to talk with any authority about assessment. There is no such reluctance on their part to engage with issues such as access to education, inequalities, etc. But assessment appears to be too technical, too specialist, for them to bring their own science to bear on it. This only leads to a diminution of our understanding of the historical, social and political location of assessment. Many have pointed to the complexity of adequate explanation in education and training, highlighting the need for multidisciplinary analysis in order to generate adequate understanding – for example, of incentives for participation (such as the ESRC Centre on Skills, Knowledge and Organisational Performance – SKOPE)[1], or of patterns of inequality (such as the ESRC Centre for Longitudinal Studies)[2]. This book is more than 'a start' on comparability, but elements of it suggest that a wider community of analysts needs to be created to fully reveal the mechanisms at work. It could be argued that this deeper understanding and transparency is essential for creation of effective public policy.

Of immense import, Baird's and Newton's analysis suggests that adoption of an operational definition of comparability is not determined by the selection of an approach which rises to the surface as a result of superior technical characteristics. Rather, approaches are adopted as a result of compromise, or deliberate choice, over purpose. So getting the historical detail right about who said and did what, when, is indeed crucial. Who decides on purpose, who asserts the choice of approach, who determines the mechanisms by which the results are asserted on learners and society, all count. Public accountability is not simple, it is a complex, fraught and mediated business.

The power relations around selection of purpose are thus crucial. Baird helpfully asks questions such as whose views have predominated in current arrangements, and why? What are the dominant social views of which form(s) of comparability are of most significance for society and the economy? These are empirical questions, almost certainly best explored by specialists in social systems. Beyond these questions of fact, whose voice(s) should determine revised arrangements? It should be remembered that the education and training system in England is diverse in form, function and content. GCSE and GCE as classes of qualification may dominate public discourse, but among these categories there is a wide variety of modes of assessment, and different balances of different modes. Beyond and within schooling, vocational and occupational qualifications possess very different models of assessment. The conceptions and apparatus of comparability vary here to a greater extent than in GCSE and GCE – to the extent that comparability is a grossly under-developed area in some compartments of the system. These system discrepancies are illuminating – why is comparability less of a (social and political) issue in some parts of the education and training system, and is this lack of prominence tenable; does it constitute an implicit neglect of the interests of certain learners/candidates? Or does this lack of concern hint at an over-developed sense of concern for certain types of comparability in assessment within mainstream education?

Endnotes

1   SKOPE homepage: http://www.skope.ox.ac.uk/ (accessed 13 October 2007).

2   CLS homepage: http://www.cls.ioe.ac.uk/ (accessed 13 October July 2007).

References

Beckett, F. (2006, August 29). 'Website says no'. *The Guardian.*

Fitz-Gibbon, C.T. (1991). A levels: Corrective comparisons. *Managing Schools Today*, 2, 44–45.

Revell, P. (2001, August 21). Couldn't do better. *The Guardian.*

COMMENTARY ON STATISTICAL ISSUES ARISING FROM CHAPTERS

Harvey Goldstein

Several contributors have emphasised that statistical techniques can at best provide evidence to assist comparability judgements, but cannot themselves define comparability in the absence of experienced interpretation. To quote Murphy 'Statistical methods cannot resolve the most fundamental dilemmas... The best that statistical treatments of this type can do is to indicate possible interpretations'. Even so, there remain considerable problems with the statistical methods currently in use. In addition to specific comments on individual chapters in this note I want to draw from the different chapters to highlight the generic issues and suggest possible directions for future exploration.

A key issue addressed by several authors, especially Murphy, is that of 'interactions', for example in the case of a reference test, different 'slopes' for different sub-groups such as males and females. In one sense identification of these (and they do exist in at least some cases) implies that comparability cannot be achieved, yet on the other hand it is possible to argue that while there is no single common adjustment, differential adjustments, for example separately for males and females, are possible. The problem is that this will raise equity issues. To avoid this, what is effectively done in practice is to ignore any such differences and fit a single adjustment model. This has the effect of averaging over all the actual differences in the data, which may be justifiable but needs to be explicitly stated. If we do model differential relationships then this can lead to improved understandings about how candidates respond, and the exploration of such models should be encouraged.

A similar issue arises when basic item response models (IRMs) such as Rasch are used, as advocated by Bramley and Coe. A problem with simplistic models of this kind is that they ignore not only group interactions but, in the case of Rasch, also differential discriminations. Thus, for example, in equation (17) in Bramley's chapter, if the discriminations denoted by α_{AB} are not equal then the assumed properties of the Rasch model do not hold and interpretations based on the model are not justified. Thus, for example, the probability of one object exceeding another will depend on which two are being compared, and so one cannot claim that the method is 'sample free'. Moreover, the fact that there is 'consensus' on the use of the model is not the same as the existence of good evidence for its use. A further problem is that conformity to the model often results in 'discrepant' data being discarded – thus helping to confirm the model. Of course, if the data are manipulated so that judges and objects that do not conform to the assumptions of a simple model are removed, then Bramley is likely to be correct. That, however, is bad science; it prioritises making the data conform to a particular statistical model rather than trying to understand how the data are actually structured and fitting models that attempt to describe such structures. If there are good, large-scale, studies that have explored this issue it is a pity that they are not discussed. If there are no such reliable studies then we need to be very cautious about interpreting results.

This point is relevant to the Bramley's discussion of 'misfit'. Essentially what happens with the Rasch models is that a model is fitted to the data and various diagnostics used to determine whether it is indeed a good description of the data structure. This approach is the one typically used in this kind of item response modelling work, but at best it will only indicate where a model may be inadequate – it does not itself constitute a proper exploration of alternative models, which is a crucial issue. To do this, as I have suggested, requires the setting up of a statistical model that explicitly incorporates parameters for the effects being sought, for example examiner interactions, and then making inferences based on their estimated values. One of the problems, of course, is that to properly explore models that allow different discriminations, interactions etc., requires very large samples that typically may not be available. Nevertheless, I would suggest that it is the responsibility of those who promote and use any particular technique to justify its assumptions and compare its performance against reasonable alternatives.

A further issue arises with item response model-fitting, namely that of multi-dimensionality. Coe discusses this in the context of large common factors implying a single underlying dimension. Without getting into a general debate about dimensionality, it does seem important that whenever a model is fitted, the existence of more than one dimension is studied, in particular after adjusting for social and other background factors. There are other concerns when using very simplistic models such as Rasch. Thus Bramley's equations (10)–(12) are valid only if one assumes no interactions, for example between judges and boards. It is possible to elaborate these models to study such possibilities directly, yet this seldom seems to be done, and it is worth pointing out that studies of item 'misfit' are technically very poor substitutes.

Those who would use the results of statistical models need to be careful. Certainly, as Schagen and Hutchison point out, all the techniques used, whether based upon item response models or more traditional regression procedures, should have a multilevel component, and software for fitting such models is available. In addition, such models should routinely incorporate interactions as well as adjustments for background factors in order properly to inform any subsequent adjustments. One of the uses of multilevel modelling not covered by Schagen and Hutchison is their extension to handle general item response models, of which the Rasch model is just the simplest version. These models are in fact just factor analysis models with a binary (correct/incorrect) response and can readily be extended to explore more than one factor and to handle multilevel structures where, for example, there can be factors (dimensions) at the level of the school as well as at the level of the pupil. A discussion of such models with educational examples is given by Goldstein *et al.* (forthcoming). It should also be noted that the most efficient modelling procedures for fitting IRMs use a random effects formulation that not only allows the generalisation to multilevel structures but also avoids the need to discard instances where all the responses are the same (see Bramley's chapter, section 3). This would in fact seem to be an obvious development from the current use of 'fixed effect' models.

There are several further directions that multilevel modelling could follow. An important one, mentioned by Schagen and Hutchison, is the use of random coefficient models, where the relationship between an examination mark or grade and another variable is allowed to vary across centres such as schools. As already mentioned in the case of interactions, the existence of such differential effects can impose important questions of interpretation. For example, we may not only find that the relationship with a common test varies from boys to girls, but also from school to school. We may also discover, say in the context of a common examinee analysis, that the relationship between a pair of marks varies from school to school; differential entry policies or other unobserved factors may be responsible. The existence of such variation will again raise difficult questions about interpretation and use, but it should not be ignored. More advanced versions of the basic multilevel model (see, for example, Goldstein, 2003) allow us to take account of data cross-classifications such as when pupils move from the Key Stage 4 period to a post-16 school or college, and we can apply multiple membership models such as when, during the course of a Key Stage period, pupils move across schools.

In short, multilevel models can and should introduce more complexity than is typically assumed in current procedures. If there is to be any really useful development of statistical methods for monitoring comparability in the near future, the adoption of these techniques is both desirable and necessary.

References

Goldstein, H. (2003). *Multilevel statistical models,* (3rd ed.). London: Arnold.

Goldstein, H., Bonnet, G., & Rocher, T. (forthcoming). A study of procedures for the analysis of PISA reading data. *Journal of Educational and Behavioral Statistics.*

RESPONSE TO COMMENTARY ON STATISTICAL ISSUES

Tom Bramley

In those of his comments which related to my chapter Harvey Goldstein focused on the perceived inadequacies of the Rasch model for analysing the kind of data collected in a paired comparison study. Within the chapter I showed the connection between the Rasch model and Thurstone's Case 5 specialisation, and between the discrimination parameter in a 2-parameter IRT model and Thurstone's 'discriminal dispersion'. I indicated one alternative possibility for analysis (logistic regression), and Goldstein has suggested some more (multi-dimensional and/or multilevel models).

However, I feel that to concentrate on improving the statistical models would be a misdirection of effort. The current constraints on cross-moderation studies in terms of available scripts, numbers of judges and time, mean that the data sets are not large enough to support more complex modelling, as Goldstein acknowledges. The real issue is to produce an outcome which is interpretable in terms of the performance standards (grade boundaries) in the different boards.

To do this I have argued that it is necessary to relate the latent trait implicit in the judges' ordering of scripts to the latent trait implicit in the raw mark totals created by applying the mark schemes. Understanding the meaning of these latent traits is therefore very important. This is what is so striking about Thurstone's work – his attempts to get to grips with the underlying philosophy of 'subjective measurement' and his concern to relate it to psychological processes. This concern is not always apparent in the writings of some of those who spurn 'simplistic' measurement models.

If researchers in this field are not to be haunted by Gene Glass's well-known quote about the language of performance standards (but which could be applied much more widely) – that it is '… pseudoquantification, a meaningless application of numbers to a question not prepared for quantitative analysis' (Glass, 1978) – then we need to take the issue of measurement seriously, as Thurstone and Rasch did. The Rasch model can be seen as specifying requirements which the data must meet to yield additive, linear measures. Assessing whether the data do indeed meet such requirements is not 'bad science', nor is trying to understand the causes of any specific, localised, misfit to such a model.

It is interesting to note that psychometricians generally have been accused of 'bad science' in their refusal to consider the hypothesis that the latent variables in their statistical models might not possess the structure necessary to support quantification (Michell, 2000). Michell would see this issue as logically prior to any fitting of a simple *or* complex statistical model. In my view we need to draw on, and integrate, developments in cognitive psychology, measurement theory and statistical modelling. Progress in the latter has resulted in a 'psychometric embarrassment of riches' (Borsboom, 2006) in the variety and complexity of models available, but this has yet to be well integrated with the first two. In the context of cross-moderation exercises, I therefore feel that our efforts are better devoted to understanding the psychological processes underlying the experts' judgements, discovering the features of candidates' performances which influence them, and knowing exactly what we mean when we say one script is 'better' than another.

References

Borsboom, D. (2006). The attack of the psychometricians. *Psychometrika*, 71(3), 425–440.

Glass, G.V. (1978). Standards and criteria. *Journal of Educational Measurement*, 15, 237–261.

Michell, J. (2000). Normal science, pathological science and psychometrics. *Theory and Psychology*, 10, 639–667.

RESPONSE TO COMMENTARY ON STATISTICAL ISSUES

Robert Coe

Harvey Goldstein claims that the use of the Rasch model is 'simplistic', fails to take account of a number of commonly found characteristics of the data such as multi-dimensionality, differential discrimination and different relationships for different sub-groups, and so constitutes 'bad science'. He suggests that a solution to all these problems is available in the form of multilevel modelling.

These criticisms confuse modelling, which, as Goldstein says, aims 'to determine whether [a model] is indeed a good description of the data structure', with measurement, which is the aim of the Rasch model. The requirements of the Rasch model are precisely those of adequate measurement; if data do not fit the model, one cannot simply change the model.

The issue of multi-dimensionality is particularly interesting, and Goldstein is right that it is 'important that whenever a model is fitted the existence of more than one dimension is studied', though a statistically purist view of uni-dimensionality could prevent any measurement ever being allowed. We must remember that any valid measure of anything that is worth measuring will always contain more than a single pure dimension. The crucial question is not whether we can find more than one dimension in a measure – we almost always can – but whether its interpretation in terms of a single construct is defensible and useful. Andrich (2006) refers to the 'fractal' nature of measurement, in which the same construct can be seen as both uni-dimensional and multi-dimensional, depending on how it is viewed. For example, it may be appropriate to view a set of GCSE examinations as measuring a common construct, 'general academic attainment', while simultaneously acknowledging that a particular subject, such as mathematics, measures something interpretable uniquely as attainment in 'mathematics'. This too may be subdivided into components, and for some purposes the construct 'mathematics' may be too broad. We might, for example, wish to talk about performance specifically in 'algebra', though for other purposes we might want to subdivide further and talk about understanding of 'simultaneous equations'. The fact that our original construct can be subdivided so many times does not necessarily make it inappropriate to view it as a single 'uni-dimensional' construct.

This apparent paradox seems counter-intuitive and this may account for some of the resistance to the use of statistical methods to establish comparability across different examination subjects. It seems obvious that examinations in different subjects measure quite different things, so the basis for comparison must be problematic (e.g.

Goldstein and Cresswell, 1996). In fact, in the application of the Rasch model referred to in my chapter (Coe, forthcoming), the latent trait measured by the 34 GCSE subjects in the analysis proved to be impressively uni-dimensional, with a person-reliability (internal consistency) estimate of 0.94 and 83% of the item variance explained by the latent trait in Principal Components Analysis, and the eigenvalue of the biggest residual contrast being just 1.9. This suggests that despite the perspectives of the examiners, teachers and candidates in GCSE examinations in different subjects that they are measuring very different things, the empirical data seem to tell a rather different story; examinations in many different subjects are remarkably consistently measuring the same thing.

References

Andrich, D. (2006, April). *On characterising the roughness of an educational measurement.* Paper presented at the 13th International Objective Measurement Workshop, Graduate School of Education, University of California, Berkeley.

Coe, R. (forthcoming). Comparability of GCSE examinations in different subjects: an application of the Rasch model. *Oxford Review of Education, 34.*

Goldstein, H., & Cresswell, M.J. (1996). The comparability of different subjects in public examinations: a theoretical and practical critique. *Oxford Review of Education, 22,* 435 441

COMPARABILITY MONITORING:
PROGRESS REPORT

Paul E. Newton[1]

Abstract

This conclusion presents a synthesis of the major themes that have emerged throughout the book. Some tentative answers are offered to the questions that motivated the review and some of the underlying tensions that make research in this field so challenging are revisited. The conclusion ends by considering prospects for the future of comparability monitoring in England.

1 Tentative answers

A number of guiding questions were identified at the beginning of the book. Given the complexity of the issues, and the controversies that still persist, it would be impossible to provide a definitive answer to each one. However, not to provide any answers would be unnecessarily precious since there are conclusions that can reasonably be drawn, albeit somewhat tentatively. Where possible, the conclusions drawn from this review will be contrasted with those drawn during the first and second reviews of comparability monitoring research (Bardell *et al.*, 1978; Forrest & Shoesmith, 1985).

1.1 To what extent have the trends in different techniques reflected real methodological progress?

Comparability monitoring has been a prominent feature of examinations research in England for more than 50 years. During this period there has been a substantial expansion in the number of students entered for formal examinations, to a point where almost all students are now examined for the GCSE and more than a third of the cohort is examined at A level. This period has also witnessed a substantial increase in regulation, driven particularly by a concern to ensure comparability. This has been associated with a reduction in the number of examining boards and examination syllabuses, the introduction of common subject cores, criteria and grade descriptions, and the requirement to adhere to codes of practice for processing examinations. Where, once, the examining boards were largely self-regulating, this is now formally the responsibility of an independent regulator. This, in turn, has had implications for the conduct of comparability monitoring research, much more of which is now being initiated and funded by the regulator.

The past half century has not only seen change in the examinations context, it has also seen change in the context of research. Processing national examinations necessarily involves the collation of vast quantities of results data. Mechanisms for dealing with such data have changed beyond recognition, making it possible to store, manipulate and analyse full cohort results easily, rapidly and cheaply. Statistical techniques have improved radically too, enabling data to be investigated using far more sophisticated analytical models; and the software for running these analyses has not only improved, but has become far more widely available (see also Bell & Greatorex, 2000).

Within this context of change, numerous techniques for monitoring comparability have been developed. The history of judgemental techniques – which rely upon the inspection of performances from different examinations – has witnessed, most notably, the development of ratification, identification and paired comparison methods. Similarly, the history of statistical techniques – which involve comparing results from different examinations whilst controlling for cohort characteristics – has seen the development of common test methods, common examinee methods and multilevel modelling methods.

As new methods have been developed, they have sometimes simply displaced previous ones. Thus, in recent years, the paired comparison approach has displaced ratification and identification methods. Other times, the new methods have merely followed in the wake of previous ones, rather than displaced them. For example, despite a flurry of research in the 1960s and 1970s, which relied upon common test methods, enthusiasm fell substantially during the 1980s, to the extent that their use had largely been discontinued by the mid 1980s (Forrest & Shoesmith, 1985). However, a new wave of enthusiasm for purely statistical methods began in the early 1990s with the application of far more sophisticated statistical modelling (e.g. Tymms & Fitz-Gibbon, 1991). This movement gained momentum during the late 1990s, to the point where multilevel modelling methods are now routinely deployed. Finally, on occasion, newly developed techniques have just failed to gain widespread support, as happened with the distribution method. This raises an important question: to what extent have these trends reflected genuine methodological progress?

Progress in the development of judgemental methods

Judgemental methods have been used since the earliest days of comparability monitoring and their use has continued to the present day. Indeed, judgemental methods have been the mainstay of comparability monitoring research throughout.

From the late 1960s to the 1980s, the choice of judgemental method basically came down to a decision between ratification (where examiners are asked to ratify, or to repudiate, decisions on grade boundary marks) and identification (where examiners are asked to identify grade boundary marks anew). In both of the two major reviews of comparability monitoring efforts the substantial majority of studies involved ratification. Yet, even the second review was undecided on which alternative was preferable, commenting that: 'Identification gives results with less confidence, but repudiation makes it difficult for boards to take corrective action.' (Forrest & Shoesmith, 1985, p. 43). Both of the techniques were recognised to have numerous weaknesses.

The paired comparison technique was introduced with the intention of remedying certain key limitations of earlier methods; most notably, by controlling for severity of individual examiner judgement. Usefully, it also enabled subtle statistical analyses of judgements, providing important insights into the validity of the procedure. It has proved to be fairly simple and flexible, although it does have a tendency to be tedious and time consuming for judges. On balance, it seems fair to conclude that the introduction of paired comparison represented a genuine methodological advance from earlier cross-moderation methods.

The major issue concerning the use of judgemental methods – which still remains unclear despite decades of reliance upon them – is just how accurate judges can be expected to be. As noted in the report of a major investigation into the comparability of standards over time, approaches like ratification and identification assume that senior examiners are able 'to spot a borderline script at twenty paces' (Christie & Forrest, 1980, p. 21) despite those performances being responses to entirely different tasks. Yet it is a commonplace finding of examinations research that quality of performance is highly task-sensitive (e.g. Cresswell & Houston, 1991). How well even senior examiners are able mentally to control for task complexity – and thereby to identify the true levels of attainment that reside beneath qualitatively different performances across examinations – is questionable.[2] There is a body of research from England which suggests (at best) that they may be unable to do so very precisely and (at worst) that their judgements may be susceptible to substantial systematic error (e.g. Good & Cresswell, 1988; Cresswell, 2000; Baird & Dhillon, 2005). Indeed, there is research from further afield which suggests that judges are poor at identifying differential task difficulty, per se, let alone controlling for it (e.g. Impara & Plake, 1988).

Although paired comparison methods do not require judgements of absolute grade-worthiness – merely of relative worth – they still require senior examiners to adjust their perceptions of task performance, to control for differential task difficulty across examinations, and thereby to spot the true levels of attainment that reside beneath qualitatively different performances. And appearances can be deceptive. An examination paper which looks fairly straightforward to a senior examiner may not have been experienced in that way by students. If the senior examiner fails to take this into account when comparing performances between examinations then the judgement of comparability may prove to be inaccurate. Incidentally, even consistency of judgement, both within and between judges, may provide spurious reassurance, since consistency is no guarantee of accuracy. The appearance of comparability may be similarly deceptive to all involved.

These general limitations of judgemental methods affect even the most straightforward of comparability contexts: when comparing different versions of the same examination (e.g. from one year to the next). When entirely different examinations are under comparison – which is typically the case during monitoring exercises – there is the additional complication of judges having to identify a construct, or trait, which is common to both. If senior examiners find themselves simply unable to identify a common basis for comparison (whether directly within paired comparison or indirectly within ratification and identification) then they will be unable to make any sense of the task with which they are faced. This has proved problematic when comparing standards across decades (e.g. Christie and Forrest, 1980; see also Patrick, 1996) and poses a substantial challenge for the comparison of standards across subjects.

An interesting story remains untold as to exactly why distribution studies were never pursued. The work of Johnson & Cohen (1983) was given short shrift in the second review of comparability studies, which acknowledged that the boards were aware of the problems with identification and ratification, but which concluded that: 'Despite their optimism, Johnson and Cohen were no more successful in solving these sorts of problems than the boards have been.' (Forrest & Shoesmith, 1985, p. 45). Unfortunately, the review gave little indication of exactly why the boards were dissatisfied with the new approach. Until this debate is revisited it will be impossible to determine whether distribution methods represent a real methodological advance over identification or ratification methods, or whether they might even challenge the current supremacy of paired comparison methods.

Progress in the development of statistical methods

Statistical methods for monitoring comparability have also been in existence for a long time, but their use has been limited. During the 1960s and 1970s, with the introduction of a new examination for school leavers around the middle of the ability range (the Certificate of Secondary Education), and with standards to be linked across a large number of new examining boards, the use of common test methods seemed to offer a promising pragmatic solution. From the outset, the inherent weakness of this approach was acknowledged by most researchers: the common test would inevitably measure a somewhat different construct from that assessed by the examinations under comparison; and the more similar it was to any one of those examinations, the more biased it would be in favour of the students who sat it (Newbould & Massey, 1979).

The use of statistical methods is generally assumed to be premised upon a principle of control: differences in average examination results which remain, once the characteristics of respective examination cohorts have been controlled for, are attributed to differences in grading standards between those examinations. From this perspective, the cohort characteristics that need to be controlled for are those related to attainment in the examinations under comparison. So, for example, the use of an aptitude test for monitoring comparability would control for the impact of aptitude upon attainment. The fundamental limitation of the common test method is that it only controls for the impact of factors measured by the test.[3] This is a problem since attainment is affected by a wide range of factors – such as amount of time spent studying, quality of teaching, quality of educational resources, etc. – and, unless all of these factors are effectively controlled for, statistical analyses may generate misleading conclusions.

To draw valid conclusions from statistical methods, where variables remain uncontrolled, it must be assumed that those uncontrolled variables would not have impacted differentially upon attainment in the examinations under comparison. Unfortunately, this assumption can often be problematic. It is not uncommon for examination cohorts to be clustered according to variables which might be expected genuinely to impact upon attainment. One example might be the impact of a national teaching strategy upon the quality of teaching from one year to the next – students who had received better teaching would, in this instance, be clustered in the second cohort. Another example might be the impact of differential motivation; where, for example, students who studied for certain examinations tended to study harder than those who studied for others. Indeed, differences are sometimes designed into examination syllabuses specifically to impact differentially upon attainment, for example, with the intention of making students more motivated (e.g. Jones, 1997).

From the perspective of statistical control, it seems fair to conclude that common examinee methods represent a significant methodological advance over common test methods, since more of the factors which impact on attainment will be controlled for (given that the analyses are limited to a single group of students, all of whom take both examinations). Some of the earliest implementations of common examinee methods involved the use of all candidates who entered for the same examination with different boards. Indeed, Forrest & Shoesmith (1985, p. 9) suggested that this was, in a sense, the paradigm for all comparability studies. It does, however, suffer from the limitation that those students who voluntarily enter for both examinations are unlikely to be representative. If so, then conclusions from results may, once more, prove to be misleading.

Despite this reservation, it is tempting to assume that common examinee methods must be the ultimate in statistical control: surely, if analyses are restricted to a single group of students, then all relevant causal factors must be controlled for? This is incorrect, though, as becomes especially apparent when common examinee methods are used for monitoring comparability between subjects. In this context it seems fairly obvious that students may (both individually and on average) study harder for certain subjects than for others, or be taught better (both individually and on average) in certain subjects than in others.

From the perspective of statistical control, multiple regression methods – and multilevel modelling techniques in particular – seem to offer the potential for the ultimate comparability study. As long as a variable can be measured, either directly or by proxy, it can be fed into a sophisticated multilevel model which is specifically designed to accommodate the kind of cohort clustering that is common in the world of examinations research. In theory, then, the use of these techniques represents a genuine methodological advance over both common test and common examinee methods. Indeed, in a sense, the more sophisticated statistical techniques can be understood potentially to subsume the other methods.

In practice, though, the potential of sophisticated statistical modelling – and multilevel modelling in particular – is unlikely ever to be fully realised for a range of reasons, of which the following three are particularly significant (see also Chapter 10 of this book; Baird & Jones, 1998).

First, unmeasured factors. If there is even one critical factor missing from a multilevel model, then conclusions may be misleading. For example, it would be quite possible for students to be clustered within examinations according to the quality of teaching experienced. This might occur if, for example, an unusual, although rewarding examination syllabus was chosen far more frequently by enthusiastic teachers. Assuming that teaching quality had a substantial impact on student attainment, but that no measure (or proxy measure) of teaching quality was provided, the conclusions from a monitoring exercise based upon multilevel modelling would be misleading. Multilevel models offer the potential to control for factors that other statistical methods simply cannot control for. However, if the more sophisticated techniques do not actually include measures of these factors then, in practice, they may not represent much of an advance over the less sophisticated ones.

Second, poorly measured factors. This is essentially just an extension of the first point. If a factor is measured, but badly, then it will not be possible to take proper account of it within a monitoring exercise based upon multilevel modelling.

Third, and more subtly, a limited theory of causation. The standard use of multilevel modelling for monitoring comparability seems to be premised upon the following theory of attainment in the examined syllabuses: amount A of factor F will, on average, have impact I upon results in both examinations. According to this theory, it is possible to derive estimates such as the following: if a student studies for ten hours then this will have an impact of 0.045 of a grade on her examination outcome, regardless of whether this is an examination for syllabus x1 (a well-conceived syllabus whose structure facilitates learning of subject x) or for syllabus x2 (a poorly conceived syllabus whose structure hinders learning of subject x). The precise size of this impact is estimated from the modelling of live data, i.e. by modelling the impact of study time upon examination results while all other factors are held constant, at this point in the analysis treating grades from syllabuses x1 and x2 equivalently.

Unfortunately, even if all relevant factors were measured accurately and included in the model, the underlying theory of attainment would compromise the modelling if it turned out not to be true. That is, if it were not actually true that a specific amount of a certain factor had the same impact upon attainment across the examined syllabuses, then the modelling would be undermined. For example, it might be true that ten hours of study following syllabus x1 caused twice the impact upon attainment of ten hours of study following syllabus x2. Yet, this would not be reflected in the modelling, being premised upon a theory of equivalent impact from equivalent input. In theory, the use of interaction terms could enable the investigation of differential impacts for equivalent inputs. However, in practice, it is not clear how the computations could disentangle differences in impact upon attainment across syllabuses from differences in the grading standards of their respective examinations.

The same might be true for other factors which might very well be clustered by examination syllabus. For example, even if a plausible measure of teaching quality could be developed, it might not be true that equivalent teaching quality would have an equivalent impact upon attainment across examined syllabuses. One might simply be harder to teach than another, thereby requiring higher teaching quality for the same attainment gain.

Conceptualising comparability

To achieve substantial methodological progress – indeed, to be able to conclude that substantial methodological progress has been made – it is often important to grapple with the theoretical underpinnings of a field. In the field of comparability monitoring research, there is a requirement to identify with precision what we mean by terms such as demand, difficulty, quality, standards, comparability and so on. It is very easy to use words like these quite loosely or heuristically. But there comes a time when precision is necessary.

Unfortunately, the past half century or so has seen little in the way of focused theoretical analysis. With the exception of some notable contributions (e.g. Christie & Forrest, 1981; Cresswell, 1996; Baird *et al.*, 2000; Goldstein & Heath, 2000; Pollitt, this book) few researchers have tackled the major questions of meaning and purpose head-on. While progress has undoubtedly been made with conceptualising comparability, there is clearly still a long way to go. Indeed, as suggested in the commentary by Oates, fully to understand the construct of comparability we need to interrogate it from a wide range of perspectives; not just theoretical, but historical, sociological, political and so on.

1.2 To what extent can each of the methods be improved and is there scope for developing entirely new approaches?

Contributors to this book were invited to consider the scope for improvements to be made to the techniques under review, and numerous avenues for investigation have been suggested. With paired comparison methods, for instance, the obvious next step will be to use scripts from various points along the mark scale of each examination (rather than simply from grade boundary marks) to quantify any degree of difference in grading standards observed. It will be important also to continue to investigate the strengths and weaknesses of the rank-ordering method, since this offers economies of time, making the task less tedious for judges.

With multilevel models, it will be important to continue to develop measures of critical control variables. It will also be important to investigate the strengths and weaknesses of different approaches to modelling, and the inclusion or otherwise of interaction terms.

There is also a case for revisiting certain of the methods which have been identified as particularly significant, but which have seen limited development. The common examinee approach may be a case in point; particularly, its use in monitoring comparability between the same examinations offered by different examining boards (see also Bell & Greatorex, 2000). The use of this method seems far from unreasonable nowadays, with common subject cores, criteria and grade descriptions which apply to all syllabuses in a subject area. Moreover, by setting up an experimental design in advance of the examination period, it would be possible to engineer far more representative samples than were possible in the original studies of the 1960s. Obviously, there would be an expectation that students would perform better in the examination whose syllabus they actually studied (although, if they did not, then this might raise very significant questions concerning comparability). Yet relative patterns of achievement across the examinations might still provide useful insights into comparability.

It is probably fair to conclude that – given more than 50 years of research using these techniques – there has been insufficient research into their validity and reliability. Such studies are not straightforward to conduct and are less straightforward to interpret, but they are crucial in establishing the defensibility of comparability monitoring exercises. This kind of evaluative research is far from absent in the literature; in fact, it has often been an implicit feature of reports on specific investigations. The introduction of new methods into the field carries a particular obligation to demonstrate reliability and validity, so it is reassuring to see that researchers are taking this responsibility seriously (e.g. Jones & Meadows, 2005; Black & Bramley, in preparation; Black & Bramley, in press). More could be done to extend this body of work; for example, by replicating judgemental exercises using multiple groups of judges, or by answering the same comparability questions using different multilevel models or software packages, or by investigating the stability of multilevel model parameters and variance components using (randomly and non-randomly) split samples, and so on.

Further investigations into the judgement of senior examiners in monitoring exercises would be worthwhile. For example, through robust experimental pre-testing, it would be possible to engineer pairs of parallel examinations to be substantially more or less difficult than each other. These non-equivalent examinations could then be administered to students, and scripts at various mark points selected for scrutiny. If the test construction and linking was done with sufficient care – such that we could be fairly confident in the degree of non-equivalence of the examinations – we would be able to explore the degree of sensitivity of judges to these differences.

1.3 Are certain techniques to be preferred over others?

As noted earlier, there seem to be reasonable grounds to prefer paired comparison methods over identification and ratification techniques. And there seem to be reasonable grounds to prefer multilevel modelling to common test and common examinee methods (particularly if the former is understood to subsume the latter, as noted earlier). But ought we to prefer judgemental methods to statistical ones, or vice versa? Here, the answer is not at all clear. The reports of the first and second reviews of comparability monitoring research concluded as follows:

> cross-moderation involving the boards' examiners (possibly with outsiders too) is the most fruitful and sensitive of the methods available for the study of comparability.
>
> Bardell *et al.* (1978, p. 36)

the boards believe that cross-moderation is probably the best methodology to pursue at the present time.

Forrest & Shoesmith (1985, p. 45)

Until recently, neither the boards nor the regulator would have placed a great deal of stock in statistical methods for monitoring comparability, given that even the best of the methods left certain key variables uncontrolled. Nowadays, with the widespread adoption of multilevel modelling, there is a renewed interest in purely statistical approaches. Multilevel modelling methods are not without their weaknesses, but clearly nor are any of the judgemental methods.

It is interesting to speculate upon why judgemental techniques have been so influential in the history of comparability monitoring, while statistical techniques have been far more frequently and resolutely dismissed, particularly by the examining boards. Perhaps it is because simple statistical techniques are so easy to criticise from first principles, given their inability to control for all relevant factors (while the limitations of judgement are far less easy to identify and to characterise). Or perhaps society is simply more willing to trust the judgement of senior examiners (over professional statisticians) in this context?

The primary argument in favour of judgemental methods was expressed in the first review as follows:

> Perhaps one of the greatest advantages enjoyed by cross-moderation over other comparability methodologies is that it comes closest to a simulation of the normal task of an examining board in its moderation and awarding procedures. It relies on the actual examination scripts rather than, for example, the results of general ability or specially constructed subject tests. It also invariably utilises the very examiners who are responsible within the boards for the syllabuses, examination papers and forms of assessment.

Bardell et al. (1978, p. 30)

On the other hand, precisely the opposite argument could be made: that methods for monitoring comparability ought not to mirror methods used for achieving it. If there are biases of judgement which might compromise decisions during awarding meetings, then similar ones are likely to bias monitoring exercises, and to similar effect. Perhaps alternative insights into comparability are best provided by using alternative methods? The first review went on to propose that:

> In addition, cross-moderation has the marked advantage that of all the formal methodologies available for studying comparability it alone depends on human judgment which can allow for variation in intention between examinations; objective monitoring techniques are invariably insensitive to such variations.

Bardell et al. (1978, p. 30)

Precisely what 'variation in intention' means is somewhat unclear, but probably refers to differences in demands between examinations. Importantly, though, the assertion that human judgement 'can' allow for this kind of variation remains debateable to the present day. Even the first review acknowledged that human judgement is highly subjective, which can lead to findings that may not be very reliable.

Given the potential of sophisticated regression models to control for far more of the critical variables, it is not so easy to dismiss the use of purely statistical techniques such as multilevel modelling. On the other hand, given that even these methods are far from infallible, it is not clear that there is a great deal of evidence to opt for them over, say, paired comparison methods. Having said that, given the kind of experiments suggested in the last paragraph of the previous sections, it should be possible to pit multilevel model against paired comparison directly (at least, under certain conceptions of comparability, a point that will become clearer shortly).

1.4 To what extent are the techniques ultimately based upon the same problematic assumptions?

Given the analysis of the preceding sections, the following broad conclusions might be drawn:

1. Judgemental techniques are based on the assumption that senior examiners are able to adjust their perceptions of task performance, to control for differential task difficulty across examinations, and thereby to spot the true levels of attainment that reside beneath qualitatively different performances.

2. Statistical techniques are based on the assumption that it is possible effectively to control for the various factors that lead to attainment in examined syllabuses, and thereby to interpret differences in results between examination cohorts (which remain once relevant factors have been controlled for) in terms of differential grading standards.

In this sense, it is true to say that all statistical methods share a basic common underlying assumption and that all judgemental methods also share a basic common underlying assumption. Whether these underlying assumptions are problematic, though, is a slightly different matter. As far as judgemental techniques are concerned, the assumption might be more problematic for identification and ratification than for paired comparison (since the latter only requires relative judgements of worth). However, it is fair to conclude that the assumption is problematic for all judgemental techniques. As far as statistical techniques are concerned, the assumption might be more problematic for common test methods than for common examinee or multilevel modelling methods (since the latter can control for more factors). However, once again, it is fair to conclude that the assumption is problematic for all statistical techniques. There are no perfect methods for monitoring comparability.

2 Underlying tensions

An evaluation of techniques for monitoring the comparability of examination standards would be complicated enough if the concept of comparability itself were not contested. Unfortunately, it is contested, and this makes evaluation more complicated still. The following section summarises the challenge of alternative conceptions – which has been considered from a variety of different perspectives by Baird, Coe, Murphy, Newton, Bramley and other contributors to this book – and explores the implications of alternative conceptions for the conduct of comparability monitoring exercises. It proposes that the primary reason for differences of opinion between stakeholders is their different perceptions about how examination results are, or ought to be, used. Since different inferences are drawn from results when they are used for different purposes, different users and stakeholders will prioritise different conceptions of comparability.

2.1 Alternative conceptions of comparability

The relationship between uses of examination results and conceptions of examination comparability can be illustrated using the following three assessment purposes (from Newton, 2007):

1. qualification – individual results are used to judge whether a person is sufficiently qualified for a job, course of instruction or role in life, i.e. whether or not they are equipped to succeed in it

2. selection – individual results are used to predict which applicants – all of whom might, in principle, be sufficiently qualified – will be most successful in a job or course of instruction

3. programme evaluation – aggregated results are used to evaluate the success of educational programmes or initiatives, nationally or locally.

In each case, the critical issue is the inference that is drawn from examination results to support the particular purpose. All sorts of inferences are possible, but some are more legitimate than others. Given the uses identified above, the following inferences might be drawn:

1. a qualification inference – a student with a grade C in GCSE ICT has the essential knowledge, skills and understanding that will enable him or her to operate confidently, effectively and independently in life and at work

2. a selection inference – a student with an A level grade profile of B (English), B (media studies), B (biology) will be more successful in an undergraduate psychology course than a student with a profile of C (French), C (economics), C (chemistry)

3. a programme evaluation inference – a cohort with an average point score of 6.5 for GCSE physics (treatment 1) will, on average, have attained a superior level of knowledge, skill and understanding of physics than a cohort with an average point score of 5.8 (treatment 2).

Each of these different uses might encourage a slightly different perspective on comparability. The qualification inference seems to take examination results as indicators of sufficient competence to function effectively as citizens; in this example, competence in ICT. For the qualification inference to be valid, equivalent grades from different ICT examinations must represent the same capacity to overcome the ICT challenges of everyday life and work. We might call this a 'contextualised' attainment-based conception of comparability: it is grounded in the attainment of a specific body of knowledge, skill and understanding, but seen in the context of how this attainment is likely to be deployed (such that the degree of proficiency required for the award of a particular grade would need to increase over time as the technological demands of everyday life and work increased).

By contrast, the selection inference seems to take examination results as indicators of potential, or aptitude, for success in any of a range of higher education courses; in this example, psychology. For the selection inference to be valid, equivalent grades from different examinations must represent the same level of general ability. We might call this an aptitude-based conception: it is not grounded in the attainment of a specific body of knowledge, skill and understanding, but in the general ability of students awarded each grade.

Finally, the programme evaluation inference seems to take examination results straightforwardly as indicators of attainment; in this example, attainment in physics. For the programme evaluation inference to be valid, equivalent grades from different examinations must represent the same level of attainment in physics. We might call this a 'straightforward' attainment-based conception of comparability: it is grounded in the attainment of a specific body of knowledge, skill and understanding, and is blind to any contextual factors (such that the degree of proficiency required for the award of a particular grade would need to remain constant across examinations, period).

These are just three possible uses of results alongside three possible inferences from results to support those uses. None of these uses, nor inferences, is necessarily the correct one. Indeed, the point of the example is simply to illustrate that – just as it is possible to identify different uses of results – so is it possible to identify different conceptions of comparability. Other uses or inferences might encourage entirely new conceptions.

The problem generated by alternative conceptions of comparability is that they cannot all be operationalised simultaneously. Consider, for example, the maintenance of standards across a ten year period of time during which teaching quality improved substantially (due to the impact of national teaching initiatives) and during which the ICT challenges of everyday life and work increased substantially (due to the progressive creep of technology into new aspects of life). How ought standards in GCSE ICT to be maintained over time? From the perspective of a straightforward attainment-based conception: a demonstration of the same knowledge, skill and understanding, from one decade to the next, ought to be rewarded with the same grade, regardless of educational or societal change. Conversely, from the perspective of an aptitude-based conception: the increase in knowledge, skill and understanding attributable to improvement in teaching quality ought not to be reflected in grades (where the increase in attainment is not associated with an increase in aptitude), so – to maintain standards under this conception – students would need to demonstrate higher levels of knowledge, skill and understanding over time for the award of the same grade. Similarly, from the perspective of a contextualised attainment-based conception: as the demands of everyday life increase, so too should the requirement to demonstrate higher levels of knowledge, skill and understanding for the award of the same grade. This fundamental tension plays out in a range of arenas; most notably, during grade awarding, when debating the appropriate uses of results and when monitoring comparability.

Grade awarding

The procedure by which grade boundaries are set for GCSE and A level examinations prioritises the maintenance of standards from one year to the next, in the same (and similar) syllabus(es), within respective examining boards. There is often at least some evidence on broader concerns, such as comparability with parallel syllabuses from other boards. However, as the most recent code of practice makes clear: 'The prime objectives are the maintenance of grade standards over time and across different specifications within a qualification type.' (QCA, 2007, 6.2).

On the one hand, the code of practice is relatively silent concerning the specific conception of comparability which ought to be adopted during awarding meetings. On the other – given that the mechanism for deriving grade boundary recommendations involves human judgement of performances from successive examinations – this might be taken to imply, or at least to default to, a straightforward attainment-based conception.

The main problem with defaulting to this conception is that it leaves the very idea of comparability between subjects quite ambiguous. Indeed, the most recent code of practice says virtually nothing on the matter; nor does it require that any action be taken to ensure it. Instead, the view of the regulator is that a general sense of comparability between subjects is engineered at a much earlier stage, through the specification of subject criteria. This involves the identification of subject content of an appropriate level and the development of appropriately pitched grade descriptions. This is a far looser understanding of comparability between subjects than some would recommend (see Dearing, 1996, for instance).

In fact, the relative silence of the code of practice could be read to leave open the possibility of embracing different definitions in different circumstances, or of acknowledging multiple definitions simultaneously through a process of compromise (see also Baird et al., 2000; Baird, this book; Newton, 2005a).

Debating the appropriate uses of results

To some, even among the assessment profession, there seems to be only one possible conception of comparability: the straightforward attainment-based one (see the response from Murphy to Coe et al., in this book). Others, though, are more liberal in their views and accept the potential validity of multiple definitions (see the chapter and commentary by Coe, for instance, as well as the chapter by Baird). In fact, a wide range of alternative conceptions have found expression in the various contributions to this book. None of these can necessarily be elevated as the correct one, nor even as the preferred one.

Although accepting that a straightforward attainment-based conception might be appropriate for grade awarding meetings, Coe suggested that grades might be recalibrated *post hoc* for use in performance tables, or even for selection purposes. As demonstrated by Lamprianou, though, this kind of technical solution can flounder in the face of public confusion and mistrust. This raises a stark challenge. In many countries which share a similar examination system to England there is an undercurrent of suspicion that standards are not comparable between subjects. However, when technical 'solutions' are implemented in response to such concerns, the outcomes may still fail the test of public confidence. Even though recalibration may seem attractive (to some) from a technical perspective – as an attempt to operationalise multiple conceptions of comparability in response to multiple uses of results – the ultimate proof of the pudding is in the eating. And the 'apples and pears' of between-subject comparability often prove unpalatable howsoever they are prepared!

Monitoring comparability

The implications of alternative conceptions of comparability for monitoring exercises are complicated, as the controversies identified in various chapters have indicated. In exactly the same way as for grade awarding meetings, comparability monitoring exercises have tended to be unclear concerning the conception of comparability operationalised. However, since most of the studies have investigated comparability between parallel examinations offered by different boards, and since most have relied upon the judgement of senior examiners, they have probably also tended to default to a straightforward attainment-based conception.

This has not always been true though, and investigations into the comparability of standards over long periods of time have explicitly thrown up questions concerning the appropriateness of alternative conceptions (e.g. Christie & Forrest, 1980; 1981). There is an interesting point to be made here. When monitoring between-board comparability, differences between their respective syllabuses and between the social and educational contexts of their delivery, are often small enough not to have to call into question the appropriateness of a straightforward attainment-based conception of comparability. However, when those differences exceed a certain threshold, this conception is thrown into relief and the monitoring exercise itself may founder. For example, one examiner, during the Christie and Forrest (1980) investigation into standards in chemistry between 1963 and 1973 described the monitoring exercise as: 'A puzzling task, and not very satisfying.' More generally, the researchers concluded:

> What has been established is that 1973 examiners are much more favourably impressed by the efforts of 1963 candidates than were the 1963 examiners. But these efforts are in the context of 1963 Chemistry and it a moot point as to whether the 1973 examiners were able to adjust their mental set to take account of the intervening change in what constitutes an education in Chemistry. Is it not more probable that the 1973 examiners saw these performances in a more favourable light because, in the context of a different approach to

the teaching of Chemistry, work of this type will be produced by fewer candidates? The pass marks offered by groups 3 and 4 suggest that this is a highly plausible explanation of the pattern of results.

Christie & Forrest (1980, pp. 59–60)

Technically speaking, a straightforward attainment-based conception of comparability is only entirely valid when the examinations under comparison correspond to exactly the same syllabus. This is often the case during awarding meetings. For comparability monitoring exercises, though, this is almost never true. Almost all require some kind of 'mental set' adjustment for differences in syllabus content, and sometimes also for educational and social context.

This is, perhaps, the central conundrum for comparability monitoring: the conception of comparability that is typically assumed to underpin the *maintenance* of examination standards – the straightforward attainment-based conception – may appear manifestly inappropriate for the contexts in which the maintenance of examination standards is typically *monitored*. Yet, to adopt an alternative conception purely for the purposes of a monitoring exercise would seem faintly odd; akin to moving the goal-posts. In this sense, Murphy is surely correct to argue that only a straightforward attainment-based conception of comparability is defensible.

Yet Coe is surely also correct to argue the opposite: multiple conceptions of comparability are required for multiple uses of results. For Coe, comparability needs to be monitored from a range of alternative perspectives, which correspond to the range of different conceptions of comparability. This is not a matter of using multiple methods to achieve a triangulation of findings. On the contrary, it might involve acknowledging that even a single set of results, from a single method, may have more than one valid interpretation, depending upon the conception of comparability in mind.

This brings us back to the earlier discussion of progress in methods for monitoring comparability, where it was argued that common examinee and multilevel modelling methods represent a substantial advance over common test methods since they control for a greater number of the factors that impact upon attainment. It should now be evident that this is only necessarily true in relation to a straightforward attainment-based conception of comparability. In fact, if an aptitude-based conception of comparability were to be adopted for monitoring purposes, then a robust test of general ability would be the appropriate tool for the job. This would be true regardless of the (potentially different) relationships between the reference test and the examinations under comparison. Likewise, a complex multilevel model which measured many background variables would be an inappropriate tool for monitoring comparability under an aptitude-based conception. And it is hard to see how any judgemental approach could have much legitimacy; unless, that is, we are prepared to accept that judges may be able accurately to spot true levels of aptitude (that reside beneath true levels of attainment) that reside beneath qualitatively different performances.

Which is the correct conception to use when monitoring comparability? Given that results are used for many different purposes, any attempt to rule certain conceptions in or out would inevitably prove to be controversial. Typically, though, certain conceptions will often be ruled in or out, albeit implicitly, by the choice of method and the style of interpretation. Transparency could be improved, in these circumstances, by making the reasoning explicit. More generally, consideration ought to be given to the range of alternative conceptions, each time a comparability monitoring exercise is undertaken, even if certain conceptions are subsequently rejected. These deliberations ought also to be included in the report of any exercise.

2.2 Additional issues

Before considering the future of comparability monitoring it is worth underlining a number of the key challenges that investigators face when conducting comparability monitoring research.

Interpreting results

As explained above, we are not yet in a position to defend the claim that either judgemental or statistical approaches are superior and should be favoured. Until there is a weight of evidence which clearly favours one technique or class of techniques over another, the questions of which and how many methods to employ will always arise. Given the inevitable limitations of both statistical and judgemental methods, it might seem sensible, wherever feasible, to conduct both. There is an important rider, though: certain techniques might be more or less appropriate for investigating different conceptions of comparability. This possibility needs to be confronted explicitly at the outset of any investigation.

This highlights a two-dimensional challenge to the correct interpretation of findings from comparability monitoring studies:

1. Different conclusions might be drawn from the findings of different methods (within a single conception).

2. Different conclusions might be drawn from the findings of a single method (between different conceptions).

Separating these dimensions of interpretation can be awkward, but is necessary all the same, to interpret findings appropriately. Within a single conception, we might hope that conclusions from all methods employed would point in a single direction (were it not for the inevitability of error). Where findings do converge, this fosters some confidence in the defensibility of conclusions. Where findings diverge, this might recommend returning a verdict of unproven.

Between conceptions, the patterns of similarity and difference do not have the same significance. Here, we would not necessarily expect findings to converge. Indeed, we might expect them to diverge. Standards might well be aligned under a straightforward attainment-based interpretation, but not aligned under an aptitude-based interpretation.

Acting on results

Even within a single conception, a convergence of findings can prove problematic to act upon. If, for example, an apparent discontinuity over time was revealed for one examining board, then bringing it back into line might simultaneously threaten comparability of standards between boards. This suggests that some consideration would need to be given to prioritising comparability in different planes. It might, for example, be considered appropriate to tolerate an apparent discontinuity of standards over time, within a board, if there was no evidence of discontinuity of standards between boards for the current examinations. However, if a discontinuity of standards were detected between boards – and between-board comparability were to be prioritised – then this would recommend remedial action. This action would be taken in the subsequent examination session or perhaps, for a large discontinuity, over a number of subsequent sessions. Inevitably, though, this would introduce a discontinuity of standards within the board in question which might, at the very least, present a public relations challenge.

Where only a single method has been used the problems of acting upon results are more stark still. Although there is little in the way of systematic research exploring the accuracy of monitoring methods, there is a general feeling that none can be assumed to be very accurate (see, for example, the contributions from Adams, Murphy and Pinot de Moira). Moreover, despite more than 50 years of research in the field, we have still not entirely cracked the problem of quantifying apparent differences in standards.

Finally, even if findings from multiple studies could be interpreted as strong evidence of a difference in grading standards between boards, and even if the size of that difference could be quantified, there is still a challenge in acting upon those results. This is how to decide which of the divergent examining boards, if any, could be said to represent the 'correct' standard.

Communicating results

In the Foreword to the first major review of comparability monitoring studies, the convenor of the GCE Board Secretaries wrote:

> In presenting this booklet to the public, and inviting applications for the full reports, where available, for those who wish to probe deeper, we in the GCE boards have found ourselves in a dilemma. If we merely state that comparability exercises are regularly conducted and do not show our hand, we appear to have something to hide. If we try to explain them, their complexities and limitations invite misunderstanding and misrepresentation. On balance, the preferable alternative seemed to be to 'publish and be damned'. We have, and probably shall be.
>
> Bardell *et al*. (1978, p. 6)

This concern resonates to the present day (see Newton, 2005b; 2005c). Yet, despite a fear that outcomes may be misunderstood and misrepresented, examining boards, advisory councils and regulators have regularly published the outcomes of comparability monitoring research for the best part of 40 years now. Although this does result in the occasional public damning, the system is surely better for this level of openness.

As was clear from Baird's chapter, though, not only do different stakeholders hold different conceptions of comparability, some hold technically indefensible views; sometimes very adamantly, passionately and loudly (albeit, perhaps, with entirely noble intent). In this context, it is crucial for the results of comparability monitoring exercises to be presented in a careful and considered manner. The findings must be explained as straightforwardly as possible – particular care must be taken with findings from sophisticated statistical analyses such as multilevel models – and any limitations and caveats must be made explicit and highlighted.

3 Future challenges

The nature of public examining in England has remained fairly constant over the past 50 years or so. There have been some major innovations – such as the introduction of differentiated assessment at GCSE and the modularisation of A level – but within most of the traditional subject areas the kind of examinations sat and the methods of marking and grading have remained fairly similar. Times change, though, and an emerging agenda of issues may change the face of examining in England. What implications might these changes hold for the monitoring of examination standards? Here are a few preliminary thoughts.

3.1 E-assessment

E-assessment is becoming a reality of large-scale educational assessment internationally. Although examinations in England are still largely paper-based, procedures for data capture and script marking are increasingly becoming automated. Although e-assessment offers the potential for radically rethinking the nature of examining, it also makes certain traditional approaches seem more attractive than they otherwise might have. This is certainly true with respect to selected-response tests. Although these have always had the advantages of speed, automation of marking and data collection, and reliability, their delivery via electronic media now offers further benefits in terms of the potential for the calibration (and continuous re-calibration) of items within item banks and the potential for adaptive testing. These advantages may even prove to be possible with constructed-response tests.

Although reaping the full potential of e-assessment presents many a technical challenge, if these kinds of examination were to come to predominate in England, the implications for both grade awarding and comparability monitoring would be radical. The likelihood is that procedures would become more experimentally and statistically driven. They would likely become more automated and more detached from human interrogation. Although this might have many benefits, there are inherent dangers here. The conceptual tensions and challenges would not go away, but they might well become substantially obscured.

Even if the nature of public examining were not to change radically in the short- to medium-term, there are ways in which e-assessment can support conventional approaches. For example, presenting performance evidence on-line can overcome cost constraints, allowing the involvement of many more experienced examiners in judging standards. This is likely to improve the reliability of comparability monitoring. The challenge to overcome is how to present large quantities of performance evidence – via the Internet – in a manner which is conducive to the kind of judgements required within comparability monitoring exercises.

3.2 Unitisation

In the past, even though grade boundary decisions were made on a component-by-component basis, the derivation of subject grade boundary marks represented the ultimate goal. This process was independent of the derivation of component grade boundaries: it was based upon information from component-level decisions, but was not entirely driven by it. Examiners within awarding meetings were able to see work from all components (although this did not necessarily involve coursework for practical reasons) and they were able to trade-off decisions on component standards when reaching recommendations on the subject standard. Only subject grades were officially reported to students. In short, from an historical perspective, standards were understood to reside firmly at the subject level. This is still largely true for GCSE examinations.

Nowadays, following the modularisation of A level, this is no longer necessarily true. Standards are judged at the unit level, against unit level script archives, and subject grade boundaries, based upon scaled uniform marks, are pre-set. Results are officially reported at the unit level. At least in practice, if not in theory, A level standards now increasingly reside at the unit level.

If standards within modularised qualifications are increasingly perceived to reside at the unit level then this has obvious implications for comparability monitoring studies. These would need to be focused at the unit level, with implications drawn at the subject level only where appropriate (subject-level conclusions are unclear when students within the 'same cohort' will have taken different combinations of units).

3.3 Selection tests

There has been increasing debate in England over the use of selection tests, particularly for entrance to higher education (e.g. Admissions to Higher Education Steering Group, 2004). To date, the concern has largely been restricted to elite departments within elite universities, whose selectors are forced to make decisions between students whose A level grade profiles are insufficiently distinct (due to ceiling effects). However, if the move toward the use of selection tests increased, this would have implications for the uses of A level results, and consequential implications for monitoring comparability.

Certainly, if selection tests were routinely used in addition to A level results, this might take away some of the pressure to ensure precise comparability between examinations in different subject areas. Instead, the selection tests would bear the brunt of the burden of indicating aptitude. Of course, the pressure would not be eliminated entirely, as long as results were still aggregated across subject profiles for inclusion in local, regional and national performance tables.

3.4 Functional skills

Functional skills qualifications are presently being developed in the areas of English, mathematics and ICT. Passing a functional skills examination is intended to certify that students have the essential knowledge, skills and understanding that will enable them to operate confidently, effectively and independently in life and at work. As explained earlier, this means that they are intended to fulfil a 'qualification' function: students who pass are deemed minimally qualified for the challenges that life will present in the domains of English, mathematics and ICT.

As noted earlier, this implies a contextualised attainment-based conception of comparability, which is not defined purely in terms of what a student knows and can do. Instead, it ought to be defined in terms of whether what a student knows and can do equips her sufficiently for the challenges of life. If, for example, the challenges of life were to increase, correspondingly more should be expected of students who pass. The difference between this and a straightforward attainment-based conception is subtle, but crucial; especially when considering comparability over extended periods of time.

3.5 Diplomas

One of the most radical changes on the horizon is the introduction of new Diplomas. These will be portmanteau qualifications – comprising combinations of separate qualifications – and will be offered initially in one of five vocationally-oriented lines of learning: society, health and development; engineering; creative and media; construction and the built environment; and information technology. Each Diploma will comprise functional skills qualifications, a qualification covering principal learning in the sector, a project-based qualification and additional qualifications of the student's choice.

The challenges involved in introducing these new diplomas are not dissimilar to those associated with the introduction of the Certificate of Secondary Education in the 1960s. Whereas standards in the CSE were monitored using reference tests (e.g. Skurnik & Hall, 1969; Willmott, 1977) it seems likely that multilevel models would be the preferred statistical tool for the Diplomas. However, this might depend on what conception of comparability was being aspired to. Across such diverse qualifications, perhaps an aptitude-based conception might be deemed defensible, after all? There is a debate to be had here – potentially a heated one, if previous experience is to be a guide.

Conceivably, though, new methods for monitoring comparability might be developed, better to represent alternative conceptions. For instance, it might be worth revisiting the 'fitness-for-purpose' method developed in the mid-1990s by Coles and

Matthews (1998). This method explored comparability between qualitatively different types of qualification (general versus vocational science qualifications), seeking views of expert groups (employers and academic selectors of science students) on the suitability of those qualifications as preparation for the 'next step' in the students' careers. This logic resonates with the contextualised attainment-based conception of comparability noted earlier: comparability concerns whether the level of knowledge, skill and understanding that constitutes the passing standard for each Diploma equally equips learners for progression in their respective fields.

3.6 Provision and regulation

Over the decades, there have been repeated calls for a reduction in the number of examining boards, to reduce the threat of different standards between them. There is some logic in this sentiment, since the more boards offer the same examination the more likelihood that differences in standards will exist. On the other hand, even with a single examining board, and a single examination for each subject, the challenges of comparability would still persist (particularly over time and between subjects). In addition to offering schools some choice over syllabuses, the diversity of boards is beneficial from the perspective of innovation, not simply in terms of delivering and processing examinations but also in terms of the development of techniques for monitoring comparability.

A key issue for coming years will be where the locus of responsibility for monitoring comparability ought to lie. In recent years, although the examining boards have continued to conduct comparability monitoring research, the regulator has increasingly initiated and funded similar work (sometimes contracting specialist researchers from the examining boards to conduct this research on its behalf). Whether this trend will, or ought to, continue is a moot point. Is there a particular role for the regulator in initiating and funding comparability research (as opposed to validity and reliability research) given that this often requires the co-ordination of efforts across examining boards (which would not necessarily be true in relation to reliability or validity)?

3.7 Internationalisation

Finally, the internationalisation of the qualifications market may need to be recognised more explicitly than it has been in the past. Comparability monitoring work has, almost exclusively to date, been concerned with comparability between examinations offered by the English examining boards; especially, within A level and within GCSE. However, with increasing population mobility, qualifications need to have a currency that can cross national borders. A case could be made for extending comparability monitoring work accordingly.

4   In conclusion

> There is no scientific way to determine in retrospect whether standards have been maintained.
>
> Baker *et al.* (2002)

This book has reviewed the development and evolution of the science of comparability monitoring in England. Is it a story of success or of failure? On the one hand, despite more than 50 years of monitoring, there is still no consensus on exactly what comparability might mean when two examinations are designed to different content and statistical frameworks. Even within the assessment profession, there are some who would not accept the legitimacy of certain forms of comparability – such as between subjects or over extended periods of time – while there are others who believe that these forms ought to be prioritised. What hope, then, for a science of comparability monitoring?

On the other hand, we have made substantial progress in the specification of alternative conceptions of comparability and in the development of techniques for monitoring comparability. It may still not be possible to derive definitive conclusions from the application of any particular method, given any particular conception, but that does not mean that findings from comparability monitoring work are either indefensible or not useful. Far from it. Monitoring exercises have the potential to provide valuable insights and a legitimate basis for action in an inherently pragmatic world.

The research described in this book shows how – with appropriate caution and with due reflection on meaning – systematic, *post hoc*, investigations can be designed and undertaken, with the potential to offer persuasive findings concerning the comparability of examination standards. We have developed substantially better methods than existed 50 years ago and are becoming progressively better at interpreting their findings. There is certainly much work still to be done, but substantial progress has been achieved so far.

Endnotes

1. This concluding chapter was prepared by the Lead Editor, with support and guidance from the other members of the Editorial Board, and with advice from a number of chapter authors.

2. This statement is premised upon the assumption that comparability, like assessment more generally, relates ultimately to the quality of the student that produces a piece of work, not to the quality of the work, per se (certificates are awarded to students, not to their work). In this particular case, the quality of the student is being defined in terms of an underlying level of attainment.

3. There is one special case in which controlling for a single factor might be considered sufficient: when the construct measured by all examinations under comparison is identical with the construct measured by the common test. This amounts to controlling for attainment directly, rather than controlling for the many factors that underlie attainment.

References

Admissions to Higher Education Steering Group. (2004). *Fair admissions to higher education: Recommendations for good practice*. Nottingham: Department for Education and Skills.

Baird, J., Cresswell, M.J., & Newton, P. (2000). Would the *real* gold standard please step forward? *Research Papers in Education, 15,* 213-229.

Baird, J., & Dhillon, D. (2005). *Qualitative expert judgements on examination standards: Valid, but inexact.* Internal Report RPA 05 JB RP 077. Guildford: Assessment and Qualifications Alliance.

Baird, J., & Jones, B.E. (1998). *Statistical analyses of examination standards: Better measures of the unquantifiable?* Research Report RAC/780. Assessment and Qualifications Alliance.

Baker, E., Sutherland, S., & McGaw, B. (2002). *Maintaining GCE A level standards: The findings of an independent panel of experts.* London: Qualifications and Curriculum Authority.

Bardell, G.S., Forrest, G.M., & Shoesmith, D.J. (1978). *Comparability in GCE: A review of the boards' studies, 1964-1977.* Manchester: Joint Matriculation Board on behalf of the GCE Examining Boards.

Bell, J.F., & Greatorex, J. (2000). *A review of research into levels, profiles and comparability.* London: Qualifications and Curriculum Authority.

Black, B., & Bramley, T. (in press). Investigating a judgmental rank-ordering method for maintaining standards in UK examinations. *Research Papers in Education.*

Black, B., & Bramley, T. (in preparation). *Using expert judgment to link mark scales on different tiers of a GCSE English examination: A rank ordering method.*

Christie, T., & Forrest, G.M. (1980). *Standards at GCE A Level: 1963 and 1973.* Schools Council Research Studies. London: Macmillan Education.

Christie, T., & Forrest, G.M. (1981). *Defining public examination standards.* Schools Council Research Studies. London: Macmillan Education.

Coles, M., & Matthews, A. (1998). *Comparing qualifications – Fitness for purpose. Methodology paper.* London: Qualifications and Curriculum Authority.

Cresswell, M.J. (1996). Defining, setting and maintain ing standards in curriculum-embedded examinations: Judgemental and statistical approaches. In H. Goldstein & T. Lewis (Eds.), *Assessment: Problems, developments and statistical issues* (pp. 57-84). Chichester: JohnWiley and Sons.

Cresswell, M.J. (2000). The role of public examinations in defining and monitoring standards. In H. Goldstein & A. Heath (Eds.), *Educational Standards* (pp. 69-104). Oxford: Oxford University Press for The British Academy.

Cresswell, M.J., & Houston, J.G. (1991). Assessment of the National Curriculum -

Some fundamental considerations. *Educational Review, 43*(1), 63–78.

Dearing, R. (1996). *Review of qualifications for 16-19 year olds*. London: School Curriculum and Assessment Authority.

Forrest, G.M., & Shoesmith, D.J. (1985). *A second review of GCE comparability studies*. Manchester: Joint Matriculation Board on behalf of the GCE Examining Boards.

Goldstein, H., & Heath, A. (Eds.). (2000). *Educational standards*. Oxford: Oxford University Press for The British Academy.

Good, F.J., & Cresswell, M.J., (1988). Grade awarding judgments in differentiated examinations. *British Educational Research Journal, 14*, 263-281.

Impara, J.C., & Plake, B.S. (1998). Teachers' ability to estimate item difficulty: A test of the assumptions of the Angoff standard setting method. *Journal of Educational Measurement, 35*, 69-81.

Johnson, S., & Cohen, L. (1983). *Investigating grade comparability through cross-moderation*. London: Schools Council.

Jones, B.E. (1997). Comparing examination standards: Is a purely statistical approach adequate? *Assessment in Education, 4*, 249-263.

Jones, B.E., & Meadows, M. (2005). *A replicated comparability study in GCSE religious studies*. Manchester: Assessment and Qualifications Alliance.

Newbould, C.A., & Massey, A.J. (1979). *Comparability using a common element*. Occasional Publication 7. Cambridge: Test Development and Research Unit.

Newton, P.E. (2005a). Examination standards and the limits of linking. *Assessment in Education, 12*, 105-123.

Newton, P.E. (2005b). Threats to the professional understanding of assessment error. *Journal of Education Policy, 20*, 457-483.

Newton, P.E. (2005c). The public understanding of measurement inaccuracy. *British Educational Research Journal, 31*, 419-442.

Newton, P.E. (2007). Clarifying the purposes of educational assessment. *Assessment in Education, 14*, 149-170.

Patrick, H. (1996, September). *Comparing public examination standards over time*. Paper presented at the British Educational Research Association annual conference, Lancaster University.

Qualifications and Curriculum Authority. (2007). *GCSE, GCE, VCE, GNVQ and AEA code of practice*. London: Qualifications and Curriculum Authority.

Skurnik, L.S. & Hall, J. (1969). *The 1966 CSE monitoring experiment.* Schools Council Working Paper 21. London: Her Majesty's Stationery Office.

Tymms, P.B., & Fitz-Gibbon, C.T. (1991). A comparison of examination boards: A levels. *Oxford Review of Education, 17,* 17-32.

Willmott, A.S. (1977). *CSE and GCE grading standards: The 1973 comparability study.* Schools Council Research Study. London: Macmillan Education.

BIOGRAPHIES OF THE CONTRIBUTORS

Robert Adams joined the Associated Examining Board (later to become part of the Assessment and Qualifications Alliance) in 1977 as Statistics Officer, having been since 1969 a lecturer and senior lecturer in Probability and Statistics at Thames Polytechnic. At the AEB he was inducted into some of the mysteries of public examinations by, principally, Dr Jim Houston. Having received this rigorous initiation, he went overseas to assist in the setting up of a diagnostic examination system in Mauritius. Reluctantly returning to Britain in 1984, he worked briefly in the Somerset Technical and Vocational Education Initiative project, liaising with AEB over the design and assessment of a modular curriculum. This gave place in 1985 to the position of Head of Research at the Welsh Joint Education Committee, the schools examination board for Wales. Robert occupied this position for twenty years until 2005 when he got itchy feet and left Wales for brief sojourns with nferNelson, the assessment publishers, and latterly the AQA, from where he retired in August 2007. He now lives in Cardiff.

Dr Ayesha Ahmed has a degree in Psychology and Philosophy from the University of Warwick and a PhD in Cognitive Development from the University of Sussex. She held a research post at the University of Cambridge Local Examinations Syndicate from 1997 to 2006. In 2007 she set up Cambridge Exam Research with Alastair Pollitt, to provide research and training services in educational assessment.

Her particular interests are in the cognitive psychology of assessment, and how this can be used to improve exam validity. She has focused on the effects of context on question answering, the effects of question structure on demands, the development of an interactive formative assessment tool and the development of a theoretical model of the psychological processes involved in answering exam questions.

Dr Jo-Anne Baird works at the University of Bristol's Graduate School of Education, where she teaches assessment, management and research methods. She is an Executive Editor of the journal *Assessment in Education: Principles, Policy and Practice*. Previously, Jo-Anne was Head of Research at the Assessment and Qualifications Alliance, where she managed the research programme and was responsible for the standard setting systems for public examinations. Her first degree was in psychology, from Strathclyde University and her PhD from Reading University was on human reasoning. Over the years, Jo-Anne has taught psychology from A level to Masters level.

Her research interests include examination standards, e-assessment and human judgment in assessment. She is a member of the Professional Affairs Board of the Association for Educational Assessment – Europe and the Independent Reviewer for the standard setting process for England's national Key Stage tests.

Tom Bramley is the Assistant Director of Cambridge Assessment's Research Division. He has a degree in Experimental Psychology from Oxford University and an MSc in Operational Research from Lancaster University. He has been at Cambridge Assessment for twelve years and during that time has worked on a wide range of projects, including: studying the factors affecting question difficulty and the psychological processes used by pupils in answering test questions; the initial pilot of the test for medical and veterinary applicants to Cambridge University (now the BMAT); item analysis, test equating and standard setting for the national tests at Key Stage 3 in Science and English; simulating different kinds of marker aberrancy in order to evaluate statistical marker monitoring models.

His main areas of expertise are Rasch measurement, and the psychometric issues surrounding test development and standard setting. He has developed a new method of judgmental test equating based on rank-ordering.

Dr Robert Coe is Reader in Education and Director of Secondary Projects in the Curriculum, Evaluation and Management (CEM) Centre, Durham University. He has overall responsibility for the CEM Centre's work with secondary schools and colleges, including the ALIS, Yellis and MidYIS projects, which support thousands of schools in monitoring their own performance.

Before embarking on an academic career, Robert was a teacher of mathematics, with experience in a range of secondary schools and colleges. He left teaching in 1995 to study full-time for a PhD at Durham University, and then stayed on as a Research Associate and Lecturer.

His research interests are wide-ranging and include evaluation methodology; Evidence-Based Education and the involvement of practitioners in research; school effectiveness and improvement, including the methodology of school effectiveness research; the use and effects of feedback, especially in performance monitoring information systems and the statistical comparability of examinations in different subjects and over time.

Victoria Crisp has a degree in Psychology from the University of Birmingham and a Masters degree in Education from the Open University. She has worked as a researcher at Cambridge Assessment from 2000 to date. Areas of research have included: issues in question difficulty and examination validity; investigating the potential for new marking methods to reduce restrictions on the way questions are written and hence improve validity; investigating how answer spaces in examinations affect student responses; developing and evaluating a prototype online formative assessment in pedagogical psychology; investigating the judgement processes underpinning A level marking decisions. She has also been involved in providing training for examiners on issues in question writing.

Victoria is currently undertaking part-time doctoral research with the University of London Institute of Education alongside full-time work. The research aims to investigate the cognitive judgement processes involved when teachers mark their students' work in the context of GCSE coursework assessment.

Professor Carol Fitz-Gibbon started a research career after 10 years teaching physics and mathematics in both privileged and inner-city schools in the UK and the US, and after taking time out for children. Whilst working on a masters' degree at The University of California, Los Angeles, she obtained a grant from the US Office of Education to study the identification of mentally gifted, inner-city students. She obtained a grant on the design of compensatory education and co-authored a best-selling series of textbooks on *Evaluation* (Sage, 1977), re-published in a second edition in 1987. Her book *Monitoring education: indicators, quality and effectiveness* (Cassell, 1996) was awarded 'best book by an established author' by the Standing Conference on Studies in Education.

She has long advocated the use of cross-age tutoring, particularly to benefit the tutor. Returning to the UK in 1978, she continued work on cross-age tutoring (with a Social Science Research Council award), published an early article on meta-analysis, and developed the project that came to be called ALIS, the A-level Information System. This formed a model for the subsequent growth of the Curriculum, Evaluation and Management (CEM) Centre into the largest educational research group in a UK university, with over 60 staff on site and working with thousands of schools that voluntarily join projects (illustrated on the website). The limitations of indicator systems have always been stressed and the need for experimentation as a guide to practice is encouraged by biennial conferences on Evidence-Based Policies and Indicator Systems.

She objected, on scientific grounds, to the inspection system designed by the Office for Standards in Education (Ofsted) and subsequently established the Office for Standards in Inspection (Ofstin), to challenge the use of unvalidated methods.

Professor Harvey Goldstein was Professor of Statistical Methods at the Institute of Education, University of London, from 1977 to 2005, and is presently Professor of Social Statistics at the University of Bristol. He is a chartered statistician, has been editor of the Royal Statistical Society's Journal, *Series A*, a member of the Society's Council and was awarded the Society's Guy medal in silver in 1998. He was elected a member of the International Statistical Institute in 1987, and a fellow of the British Academy in 1996. He was awarded an honorary doctorate by the Open University in 2002.

There are four main foci of his research interests. The first is the use of statistical modelling techniques in the construction and analysis of educational tests. The implications of adopting such models have been explored in a series of papers since 1977. In a number of papers he has also explored the ideas of criterion referenced assessment, comparability of assessments and the interaction of assessment modes and the purposes of assessment. The second interest lies in the area of 'educational (school) effectiveness'. He is involved in a number of longitudinal studies of 'value added indicators' for comparing institutions and the use of such indicators for school improvement purposes. The third interest is in studies of the effects of class size on student achievement and other outcomes. He has been particularly concerned with issues surrounding the kinds of inferences which can be drawn from observational studies as opposed to randomised controlled trials. The fourth, and most important, research interest is in the methodology of multilevel modelling. He has had research funding for this since 1986 and has supervised the production (with Jon Rasbash) of a widely used software package (MLwiN) and made a number of theoretical developments. The major text on multilevel modelling is his book *Multilevel Statistical Models* (London: Edward Arnold, 2003).

Dr Dougal Hutchison is Chief Statistician at the National Foundation for Educational Research, where his work focuses on measurement error, randomised control trials, international comparisons, multilevel modelling, item response theory, and methodological development generally.

During his career, he has worked as a volunteer teacher in Africa, a university lecturer, a civil servant, and as a statistical researcher in a range of academic research organisations. He has a particular interest in the process of mathematisation, and the interface between statistical techniques and the world out there, and has published, inter alia, theoretical papers on the conceptualisation of measurement error and biasing effects of measurement error, as well as practical papers on value added, international comparisons, and computer marking of essays. This is his first excursion into the analysis of public examinations, though, with Ian Schagen, he has jointly edited a book on the reliability of National Curriculum assessment.

Sandra Johnson graduated in mathematics from the University of Manchester, where she also took an MSc in Mathematical Statistics. Short periods in marketing research and secondary mathematics teaching preceded educational research in the Universities of Manchester and Leeds. In Manchester she worked on two Schools Council projects, investigating, respectively, examination reliability (a first encounter with generalizability (G-) theory) and reading development. The move to Leeds was to join the Assessment of Performance Unit Science Monitoring team, where, as Deputy Technical Director, she promoted domain sampling and generalizability theory as the measurement methodology of choice. It was during this time that she worked as consultant on another Schools Council project, using G-theory to evaluate the cross-moderation methodology in grade comparability investigation. A move to Switzerland in the late 1980s saw a switch to statistics teaching within international management programmes, and research collaborations in vocational and distance education. It was from here that she gained an MA in distance education from the University of London. Since the late 1990s she has been working from France as an independent consultant, principally for Scotland's national assessment programmes, and distance teaching for the University of London (online MA).

Dr Mike Kingdon, during 13+ years as a science teacher, taught in a grammar, a secondary modern and a comprehensive school, the last two as head of science. He gained a BA in Maths and Education and his MEd in Maths and Science Education. He began his career in educational research with a science curriculum review for Hertfordshire. During this work he noted consistent space/time patterns in schools' curriculum choices that became the inspiration for his PhD.

He joined the University of London School Examinations Board (ULSEB) as 16+ research officer in 1979, became acting Head of Research a year later and was confirmed in post soon afterwards. His work for ULSEB, and its successors, ranged across 16+ and 18+ examinations, university and professional qualifications and Commonwealth examination systems. As Director of the assessment consultancy arm of the University of London Examinations and Assessment Council and then as General Manager for Edexcel, he managed National Curriculum assessment projects at KS1 to KS3, the KS2/3 national data collection project. Since leaving the latter he has worked as an assessment consultant to UK and overseas regulators, professional institutes and awarding bodies. He is currently Principal Assessment Consultant to the Entity Group.

Mike's specialisms include the mathematical modelling of educational and supporting infrastructure systems using stochastic, spatial and business process models. He holds an MBA degree and is both a chartered mathematician and a chartered scientist. He is also a lifelong student of the history of education.

Dr Iasonas (Jason) Lamprianou is a Research Fellow at the University of Manchester and an Examination Officer at the Cyprus Testing Service. He has obtained an MEd in Assessment and Evaluation and a PhD in Educational Measurement.

Jason has participated in research projects involving educational assessment and measurement, test equating, item banking, computerized adaptive testing, etc. In recent years Jason has offered his services to many organizations, like the Qualifications and Curriculum Authority (UK), the National Assessment Agency (UK), the Assessment and Qualifications Alliance (UK), the University of Manchester (UK), the University of Malta, the Agha Khan University in Pakistan, the Cyprus Testing Service etc. Jason is also a Consultant to commercial products like the 'MaLT: Mathematics for Assessment, Learning and Teaching' software provided by Hodder Education.

His publications are of quantitative nature, usually involving item response theory, and have been published in diverse journals such as the *Journal of Educational Measurement*, the *Journal of Applied Measurement*, the *International Journal of Testing*, the *Australian Journal of Educational and Developmental Psychology*, *Australian Educational and Developmental Psychologist*, *Physical Education and Sport Pedagogy*, etc.

Professor Roger Murphy is Professor of Education and Director of the Centre for Developing and Evaluating Lifelong Learning (CDELL) in the School of Education at the University of Nottingham. He is a past-President of the British Educational Research Association, and he has for much of the last 30 years been actively involved in research related to educational assessment and examinations. In a career which started in the research unit of a UK awarding body, and which has involved substantial periods in higher education, he has led a large number of major investigations relating to the design, conduct and impact of educational assessments.

A defining theme throughout his research has been the impact of assessment and examinations on the educational experiences of students. This interest has been pursued in highly different contexts within schools, colleges, universities, work-based and informal learning. The work has also involved collaborations and consultancies in countries throughout the world. From this work many ideas for innovations in educational assessment have emerged and Roger has been the author of a number of influential reports. He has also written a large number of academic books and journal articles including *The Changing Face of Educational Assessment* (Open University Press, 1987), *The Impact of Graded Tests* (Falmer Press,1988), *Effective Assessment and the Improvement of Education* (Falmer Press,1995), and *Grades of Uncertainty* (Association of Teachers and Lecturers, 2004).

Dr Paul Newton is Head of Assessment Research in the Regulation and Standards division of England's Qualifications and Curriculum Authority, where his work focuses on issues related to the design and evaluation of large-scale educational assessment systems (including GCSEs, A levels, National Curriculum tests, diplomas, etc.).

Paul originally trained as a developmental psychologist and has held education research posts within academic, local authority and charitable organisations; but he has spent most of his professional life conducting research for assessment agencies. Paul is a Visiting Fellow of the University of London Institute of Education and a member of the Assessment Reform Group. He serves on the Editorial Board of *Assessment in Education: Principles, Policy and Practice*.

Paul has a particular interest in the relationship between assessment theory, policy and practice. He has published papers on a range of assessment topics, including: comparability theory; marking reliability; the defensibility of England's National Curriculum assessment system; systems for appealing against results; assessment purposes; and the public understanding of measurement inaccuracy.

Tim Oates is Group Director of Assessment Research and Development at Cambridge Assessment, leading a 40+ research group which focuses on national and international research on assessment and measurement. He started his career as a Research Officer at the University of Surrey. He moved to the FE Staff College in 1987 where he helped run the Work-Based Learning project. London University's Institute of Education then appointed him as National Council for Vocational Qualifications Research Fellow. In 1993 he joined one of the QCA's predecessor bodies, the National Council for Vocational Qualifications (NCVQ), as Head of General National Vocational Qualifications Research and Development. Promotion to Director of Research followed two years later and, on the merger of the School Curriculum and Assessment Authority and NCVQ to form QCA, he was appointed Head of Research, a position he held from 1997 to 2006 - at which point he moved from QCA to join Cambridge Assessment. He has a first from the University of Sussex in Philosophy with Literature and an MA in Philosophy from the same institution. He was a member of the 2004 Research Assessment Exercise (RAE) panel for education, was co-author with Mike Coles of the new pan-European Qualifications Framework, and has advised a number of governments and agencies on qualifications strategy.

His research background/interests include: vocational and professional learning (pedagogy; assessment; concepts of competence; generic/key skills; analysis of participation, including international comparisons); policy studies (research-policy relation; management of change; transnational comparisons); development of qualifications and national qualification frameworks; evaluation and research methods; impact of social background on attainment and life chances.

Dr Helen Patrick graduated in history from the University of Aberdeen, where she also took her MEd. She trained as a teacher at Aberdeen College of Education. After teaching at Bankhead Academy, she became a researcher at the University of Leicester School of Education, where she gained her doctorate. Her work at Leicester included projects on initial teacher education, staff in university departments of education, teacher supply, small primary schools and the teaching of history. In 1987 she took a research post at the University of Cambridge Local Examinations Syndicate (UCLES, now Cambridge Assessment), where she was involved in a range of research, evaluation and monitoring studies in the field of public examinations. She was seconded to the research team at the Qualifications and Curriculum Authority in 2001-2002, to work on developing a code of practice for National Curriculum assessment and on projects evaluating new technologies in assessment. She returned to Cambridge as a Senior Research Consultant, investigating standard setting issues and developing assessment training resources. She is now combining early retirement with consultancy. Her specific interests are comparability, particularly standards over time, and standard setting.

Anne Pinot de Moira joined the Assessment and Qualifications Alliance (AQA) as a Senior Research Officer in June 1996 following a number of jobs in the social statistics field. At AQA her work has been varied and has included comparability studies, investigation of theoretical and operational aspects of assessment, policy advice and general research. She is a Chartered Statistician, having graduated firstly from Plymouth Polytechnic with a degree in Mathematics and Statistics and subsequently from Southampton University with a Masters in Medical Statistics.

Alastair Pollitt graduated from the University of Aberdeen with degrees in Chemistry, Education and Psychology. He learned test development and analysis in the Godfrey Thomson Unit for Educational Research in the University of Edinburgh, where he became Assistant Director in charge of assessment research and test development. He developed many tests for commercial publication, and led government-funded projects in item banking, researching question difficulty and the national monitoring of standards in English.

In 1990 he moved to the Research Centre for English and Applied Linguistics in the University of Cambridge, in order to pursue interests in language testing and psycholinguists. After four years there he was appointed Director of Research in the University of Cambridge Local Examinations Syndicate (UCLES, now Cambridge Assessment). In 1995 he restarted research into the causes of question difficulty, constructing with Ayesha Ahmed a theoretical model of the psychological processes involved.

He left UCLES in 2004 to work as an independent consultant and set up Cambridge Exam Research with Ayesha Ahmed in 2007. He is a member of the Professional Affairs Board and Professional Development Committee of the Association for Educational Assessment – Europe.

Colin Robinson graduated in Old, Middle and Modern English from the National University in Ireland and went on to obtain the Higher Diploma in Education at the University of Dublin (Trinity College) specialising in teaching English and mathematics to children with special needs. After teaching at Archway School, Stroud in Gloucestershire, he joined the staff of the National Foundation for Educational Research, initially developing test materials for the LEAs' and Schools' Item Bank and later advising on test development and use as Deputy Head of Test and Research Services.

He joined the newly formed Secondary Examinations Council in 1983 as Principal Professional Officer with responsibility for research and in this capacity oversaw a variety of research including work on the development of grade criteria and the revision of the A level grading scheme. As Head of the Evaluation and Monitoring Unit of the School Curriculum and Assessment Authority he was responsible for the evaluation of assessment models for the National Curriculum, the establishment of the School Coordinating Unit and the management of National Evaluations. In the Qualifications and Curriculum Authority he supervised the National Value Added Project and the Monitoring National Curriculum and Assessment Project. He has been an active member of the International Association for Educational Assessment, the Association of Commonwealth Examinations and Accrediting Bodies and the British Educational Research Association, serving as Honorary Secretary and Treasurer from 1993 to 2002, for which he was awarded Honorary Life Membership. He retired from QCA at the end of 2006 and is now an independent consultant with QCA, the Department for Children, Families and Schools and Cambridge International Examinations amongst his clients.

Dr Ian Schagen is Head of Statistics at the National Foundation for Educational Research with previous experience in industry and as a university lecturer. He is a Chartered Statistician and a member of the editorial board of *Educational Research*, and is currently a member of the Research Committee of the Assessment and Qualifications Alliance examination board. Ian has published a book, *Statistics for School Managers* (Courseware Publications, 2000), aimed at helping school staff to make use of statistical information, as well as being joint editor of a book on the use of effect sizes in educational research, *But What Does It Mean?* (NFER, 2004).

Recently Ian has been involved with advising the Department for Education and Skills (DfES) on methodology for analysing the National Pupil Database (NPD); in particular, as a member of the Value Added Methodology Advisory Group. He has also recently acted as external consultant to the DfES on their review of data systems underpinning their Public Service Agreement targets. He was Project Director for the analysis of combined NPD/ILR data for the Learning and Skills Development Agency, looking at the impact of local patterns of post-16 provision on participation, retention and attainment, and has recently directed a project for the Learning and Skills Council to evaluate the robustness of their value-added models.

Kathleen Tattersall, a graduate of Manchester University, began her career as a teacher, working in both primary and secondary schools before joining a Certificate of Secondary Education board, the Associated Lancashire Schools Examining Board (ALSEB), in 1972. Just prior to becoming its Chief Executive in 1982, Kathleen was seconded by ALSEB to the Schools Council to conduct research into differentiated examinations – a freedom which she later claimed she paid for dearly by being responsible for running organisations and assuring standards rather than indulging in research. Until her retirement in 2003 she was Chief Executive of four other boards, the North West Regional Examinations Board, the Joint Matriculation Board, the Northern Examinations and Assessment Board and the Assessment and Qualifications Alliance. Between 1982 and 2003 she also chaired various national bodies of examination boards. She was also a member of the initial School Examinations and Assessment Council.

At the time of her retirement Kathleen was a member of the Tomlinson 14-19 Working Party and played an active role in its Assessment Group. She is currently a member of the Board of Manchester University and chairs the University's Audit Committee. Kathleen is the first Chair of the Institute of Educational Assessors, which was launched in May 2006 and granted a Royal Charter in July 2007. Kathleen was awarded an OBE in 2003 for services to education and assessment.

Professor Peter Tymms is Director of the Curriculum, Evaluation and Management (CEM) Centre at Durham University and, as Director, he is responsible for projects monitoring the progress and attitudes of a million pupils across the UK and beyond each year. The CEM Centre is the largest educational research group in a UK university with a staff of 70. His main research interests include monitoring, assessment and research methodology. Work in these and related areas have produced more than a hundred publications. He devised the PIPS project, which is designed to monitor the affective and cognitive progress of children through primary schools starting with a computer adaptive on-entry baseline assessment, which is used in thousands of schools.

He started work as a teacher in Central Africa with a degree in natural sciences, and after teaching posts in England at a secondary modern school, a comprehensive school and a tertiary college he moved to an academic career and was the first Research Associate to work on the A Level Information System (ALIS) the first of the CEM Centre's monitoring projects.

Alison Wood is Deputy Head of Standards in Assessment at the National Assessment Agency, the organisation which is responsible for National Curriculum assessment and aspects of general qualifications in England.

Her work focuses on methods of setting, maintaining and monitoring standards in National Curriculum assessment and her particular area of interest is in developing approaches which can be used when curriculum and assessment arrangements change. Her more general interests lie in qualitative methods of test validation, exploring issues around novice/expert judgement and developing methodologies to enable students to contribute to test development and evaluation.

Alison's first degree was in philosophy and she has worked on assessing high-level constructs, such as reasoning and problem-solving skills. She trained as a teacher and taught in sixth form colleges and schools. She retains a strong interest in pedagogy, working with classroom teachers to develop approaches to formative assessment.

SUBJECT INDEX

AUTHOR INDEX